CONCORD HARVEST

PUBLICATIONS OF THE CONCORD SCHOOL OF

PHILOSOPHY AND LITERATURE

WITH NOTES ON ITS SUCCESSORS AND

OTHER RESOURCES FOR RESEARCH IN EMERSON,

THOREAU, ALCOTT AND THE LATER

TRANSCENDENTALISTS

Edited by

KENNETH WALTER CAMERON

VOLUME

II

TRANSCENDENTAL BOOKS—DRAWER 1080—HARTFORD 06101

TABLE OF CONTENTS

THE CONCORD SUMMER SCHOOL OF PHILOSOPHY.

THE CONCORD SUMMER SCHOOL will open for a fifth term on Wednesday, July 18, 1883, at 9, A. M., and will continue four weeks. The lectures in each week will be ten; they will be given morning and evening, except Saturdays, on the secular days (in the morning at 9 o'clock, and in the evening at 7.30) at the *Hillside Chapel*, near the Orchard House.

The terms will be $4 for each full week; for the course, $15. Board may be obtained in the village at from $7 to $12 a week, — so that students may estimate their *necessary* expenses for the whole term at $45. Single tickets, at 50 cents each, will be issued for the convenience of visitors, and these may be bought at the shop of H. L. Whitcomb, in Concord, after July 10, 1883. Any to whom this circular is sent can now engage course tickets by making application, and sending $5 as a guaranty. For those who make this deposit, tickets will be reserved till the tenth day of July, 1883, and can then be obtained by payment of the balance due. They entitle the holder to reserved seats.

All students should be registered on or before July 10, 1883, at the office of the Secretary, in Concord. No preliminary examinations are required, and no limitation of age, sex, or residence in Concord will be prescribed; but it is recommended that persons under eighteen years should not present themselves as students, and that those who take all the courses should reside in the town during the term. The Concord Public Library of 17,500 volumes, will be open every day for the use of residents. Students coming and going daily during the term, may reach Concord from Boston by the Fitchburg Railroad, or the Middlesex Central;* from Lowell, Andover, etc., by the Lowell and Framingham Railroad; from Southern Middlesex and Worcester Counties by the same road. The Orchard House stands on the Lexington road, east of Concord village, adjoining the Wayside estate, formerly the residence of Mr. Hawthorne. For fuller information concerning the town and the school, we would refer applicants and visitors to the "Concord Guide Book" of Mr. George B. Bartlett.

Lodgings with board may be obtained at the following houses in Concord village:

Mrs. O'BRIEN, Monument Square.	Mrs. KENT, Main Street.
Mrs. CUTTER, Sudbury Street.	Mrs. GOODNOW, Main Street.
Mrs. B. F. WHEELER, Belknap Street.	Mrs. N. DERBY, Walden Street.

Mrs. HOW, Hubbard Street.

Lodgings without board can be obtained in the neighborhood of each of the above-named houses. Students and visitors will make their own arrangements without consulting the undersigned.

A. BRONSON ALCOTT, *Dean.*
S. H. EMERY, JR., *Director.*
F. B. SANBORN, *Secretary.*

CONCORD, August 2, 1883.

*Express train from Boston leaves Fitchburg Depot at 8 A. M., and arrives at Concord in time for the morning session. On Thursdays, train for Boston by Fitchburg R. R. leaves Concord at 9.40 P. M.; and on Wednesdays, train for Boston by Middlesex Central leaves at 9.38 P. M., giving opportunity to attend the evening session and return to Boston after the lecture.

PROGRAMME OF LECTURES.

JULY, 1883.
18th,   9   A. M.   Prof. Harris.
         7.30 P. M.   Prof. James.
19th,   9   A. M.   Dr. Kedney.
         7.30 P. M.   Prof. Howison.
20th,   9   A. M.   Prof. James.
         7.30 P. M.   Prof. Harris.
23d,   9.   A. M.   Prof. James.
         7.30 P. M.   Prof. Howison.
24th,   9   A. M.   Dr. Kedney.
         7.30 P. M.   Mr. Sanborn.
25th,   9   A. M.   Prof. Harris.
         7.30 P. M.   Mr. Snider.
26th,   9   A. M.   Dr. Bartol.
         7.30 P. M.   Prof. Howison.
27th,   9   A. M.   Prof. Harris.
         7.30 P. M.   Mr. Blake.
30th,   9   A. M.   Mr. Wasson.
         7.30 P. M.   Prof. Howison.
31st,   9   A. M.   Mr. Hawthorne.
         7.30 P. M.   Mr. Snider.

AUGUST, 1883.
1st,   9   A. M.   Prof. Harris.
         7.30 P. M.   Mr. Mead.
2d,   9   A. M.   Mr. Sanborn.
         7.30 P. M.   Mr. Snider.
3d,   9   A. M.   Mr. Sanborn.
         7.30 P. M.   Prof. Harris.
6th,   9   A. M.   Mr. Albee.
         7.30 P. M.   Prof. Harris.
7th,   9   A. M.   Mrs. Cheney.
         7.30 P. M.   Mr. Albee.
8th,   9   A. M.   Prof. Harris.
         7.30 P. M.   Mr. Snider.
9th,   9   A. M.   Mrs. Howe.
         7.30 P. M.   Mr. Block.
10th,   9   A. M.   Miss Peabody.
         7.30 P. M.   Mr. Sanborn.

Slight changes in the above Programme may hereafter be made, and other names may be added to the list of lecturers.

LECTURERS AND SUBJECTS.

MR. A. BRONSON ALCOTT, Dean of the Faculty, is not expected to deliver the Salutatory or to converse on special subjects, but it is hoped he can be present.

DR. JONES will not lecture this year.

___

The Courses will be as follows:

PROF. W. T. HARRIS. Four Lectures on *Man's Immortality in the Light of Philosophy and Religion;* and Four Lectures constituting a *Course of Elementary Lessons in Philosophy.* The latter will be

1. JULY 18th, 9 A. M. *Space and Time Considered; Basis of Kantian Philosophy, Ground of certainty deeper than Scepticism or Agnosticism.*

2. JULY 20th, 7.30 P. M. *Causality and Self-cause; Force Transient and Persistent; Self-existent Energy underlying all change.*

3. AUGUST 1st, 9 A. M. *Fate and Freedom; Individuality; Distinction of Reality and Potentiality from True Actuality, of Phenomenon from Substance.*

4. AUGUST 3d, 7.30 P. M. *Laws of Thought, the Principles of Identity, Contradiction and Excluded Middle; Categories of Being, Essence, Cause and Personality.*

Prof. Harris's special subjects will be:

1. JULY 25th. *The Absolute a personal Reason. Discussion of Plato's insight (Tenth Book of the Laws) and Aristotle's (the eighth book of his Physics and the eleventh book of his Metaphysics).*

2. JULY 27th. *Triune Nature of God.—St. Augustine, St. Thomas Aquinas, St. Anselm,—Justice and Grace in the Divine Nature.*

3. AUG. 6th. *The World as Revelation of the Divine First Cause,—Nature and Man: the doctrine of Evolution; the Orders of Being as Progressive Revelation of the Divine.*

4. AUG. 8th. *Immortality of the individual man in the light of Psychology,—in the light of the Christian Religion; the Vocation of Man in the Future Life.*

GEORGE H. HOWISON, LL. D. Four Lectures on *Hume and Kant and the Merits of the Issue between them.*

Prof. Howison's subjects will be:

1. *Hume's Aim and Method; the Problem, as handed over to Kant.*

2. *Kant's Mode of Dealing with this Problem.*

3. *The Strength and Weakness of Kant's Methods and Results.*

4. *The Same Subject, concluded; The Outlook from Kant.*

PROF. WILLIAM JAMES, of Harvard University. Three Lectures on *Psychology.*

MR. DENTON J. SNIDER. Four Lectures on *Homer and the Greek Religion.*

1. *Literary Bibles—Homer.*

2. *The Iliad.*

3. *The Odyssey.*

4. *The Gods.*

REV. R. A. HOLLAND, S. T. D., will not lecture this year. In place of his lectures, as advertised, PROF. HARRIS will give four Lectures on *Elementary Insights in Philosophy.*

REV. J. S. KEDNEY, D. D. Two Lectures on *Art Appreciation and the Higher Criticism.*

MR. F. B. SANBORN. Four Lectures on *The History of Philosophy in America.*

1. *The Puritanic Philosophy:*
        Jonathan Edwards.

2. *The Philanthropic Philosophy:*
        Benjamin Franklin.

3. *The Negation of Philosophy.*

4. *The Ideal and Vital Philosophy:*
        R. W. Emerson.

MR. JOHN ALBEE. Two Lectures. *The Norman Influences in English Language and Literature.*

REV. DR. BARTOL. A Lecture on *Optimism and Pessimism,—a Personal Equation.*

MISS E. P. PEABODY. A Lecture on *Milton's Paradise Lost.*

MRS. E. D. CHENEY. A Lecture. *A Study of Nirvana.*

MR. EDWIN D. MEAD. A Lecture. *Carlyle and Emerson.*

MRS. J. W. HOWE. A Conversation. MARGARET FULLER.

MR. JULIAN HAWTHORNE. A Lecture on *Novels.*

MR. DAVID A. WASSON. A Lecture. *Herbert Spencer's Causal Law of Evolution.*

MR. LEWIS J. BLOCK. A Lecture on *Platonism and its Relation to Modern Thought.*

Readings from the Thoreau Manuscripts will occupy one evening, as usual.

1879—1884.

THE CONCORD SUMMER SCHOOL OF PHILOSOPHY.

THE CONCORD SUMMER SCHOOL will open for a sixth term on Wednesday, July 23, 1884, at 9, A. M.. and will continue two weeks. The lectures will be morning and evening, except Saturday evenings, on the six secular days (in the morning at 9 o'clock, and in the evening at 7.30) at the *Hillside Chapel*, near the Orchard House.

The terms will be $7 for the course. Single tickets, at 50 cents each, may be bought at the shop of H. L. Whitcomb, in Concord, after July 10, 1884, in packages of *twelve* for $5, and of *six* for $2.50.

Students may reach Concord from Boston by the Fitchburg Railroad, or the Middlesex Central; from Lowell, Andover, etc., by the Lowell and Framingham Railroad; from Southern Middlesex and Worcester Counties by the same road. The Orchard House stands on the Lexington road, east of Concord village, adjoining the Wayside estate, formerly the residence of Mr. Hawthorne. For information concerning the town and the school, we would refer applicants and visitors to the "Concord Guide Book" of Mr. George B. Bartlett, published by D. Lothrop & Co., Boston, and containing an account of the origin of the School.

Lodgings, with board, may be obtained at the following houses in Concord village.

Miss E. BARRETT, Monument Street.	Mrs. KENT, Main Street.
Mrs. O'BRIEN, Monument Square.	Mrs. GOODNOW, Main Street.
Mrs. CUTTER, Sudbury Street.	Mrs. N. DERBY, Walden Street.
Mrs. HOW, Hubbard Street.	Mrs. B. F. WHEELER, Belknap Street.

Lodgings without board can be obtained in the neighborhood of each of the above-named houses. Students and visitors will make their own arrangements without consulting the undersigned.

A. BRONSON ALCOTT, *Dean*.

S. H. EMERY, JR., *Director*.

F. B. SANBORN, *Secretary*.

CONCORD, June 30, 1884.

The Faculty of the Concord School have decided on the arrangements for the summer of 1884 as follows: (1). Six or seven days devoted to a discussion of *Emerson's Genius and Character;* beginning July 23, 1884, and including the subjects and writers named below.   (2.) Two days devoted to a discussion on *Immortality*, with essays by Dr. Peabody, Dr. Holland, Dr. Harris, and Mr. John Fiske, the latter taking for his subject *The Origin and Destiny of Man.*

(I). The Genius and Character of Emerson. To be considered July 23–30, 1884, under the following heads:

1. *Emerson's View of Nature*, by W. T. Harris, LL. D., of Concord.
2. *Emerson's Religion*, by Rev. C. A. Bartol, D. D., of Boston.
3. *Emerson's Ethics*, by Mr. Edwin D. Mead, of Boston.
4. *Emerson's Manners and Relation to Society*, by Mrs. Julia Ward Howe, of Boston.
5. *Emerson as seen from India*, by Protap Chunder Mozoomdar, of Calcutta.
6. *Emerson as an American*, Mr. Julian Hawthorne, of New York.
7. *Emerson in the Pulpit*, by Miss E. P. Peabody, of Boston.
8. *A French View of Emerson*, by M. René de Poyen Belleisle, of Paris.
9. *Emerson in Boston*, by Mrs. E. D. Cheney, of Boston.

10. *Emerson as an Essayist*, by Mr. John Albee, of Newcastle, N. H.
11. *Emerson and Thoreau.*
12. *Emerson's View of Nationality*, by Rev. G. W. Cooke, of Dedham.
13. *Emerson Among the Poets*, by Mr. F. B. Sanborn, of Concord.
14. *Emerson's Relation to Goethe and Carlyle*, by W. T. Harris, LL. D., of Concord.
15. *The Genius of Emerson*, by Mr. W. E. Channing, of Concord.

(II). The question of *Immortality* will be opened July 31, 1884, by Rev. A. P. Peabody, D. D., of Cambridge, who will be followed by Mr. John Fiske, of Cambridge; Rev. R. A. Holland, D. D., of New Orleans; Dr. Harris, of Concord, and others; the discussion closing on the 1st of August.

In the absence of Mr. Snider, Prof. Harris will take his place. and Mr. Blake may take the place of Mr. Whitman.

PROGRAMME OF LECTURES.

July, 1884.

23d,	9	A. M.	Opening Exercises.
			A Sonnet by Miss Emma Lazarus.
			Readings from the Diary of Mr. Alcott.
	7.30	P. M.	Mr. Hawthorne.
24th,	9	A. M.	Dr. Bartol.
	7.30	P. M.	Prof. Harris.
th,	9	A. M.	Mr. Albee.
	7.30	P. M.	Mr. Mead.
26th,	9	A. M.	Mrs. Howe.
28th,	9	A. M.	{ Mrs. Cheney. Miss Peabody.
	7.30	P. M.	Mr. Sanborn.

July, 1884.

29th,	9	A. M.	{ Prof. Harris. Mr. Mozoomdar.
	7.30	P. M.	M. de Poyen Belleisle.
30th,	9	A. M.	{ Mr. Channing. Mr. Whitman.
	7.30	P. M.	Mr. Cooke.
31st,	9	A. M.	Dr. Peabody.
	7.30	P. M.	Mr. Fiske.

August, 1884.

1st,	9	A. M.	Dr. Holland.
	7.30	P. M.	Prof. Harris.

1879—1884.

THE CONCORD SUMMER SCHOOL OF PHILOSOPHY.

THE CONCORD SUMMER SCHOOL will open for a sixth term on Wednesday, July 23, 1884, at 9, A. M., and will continue two weeks. The lectures will be morning and evening, except Saturday evenings, on the six secular days (in the morning at 9 o'clock, and in the evening at 7.30) at the *Hillside Chapel*, near the *Orchard House.*

The terms will be $7 for the course. Single tickets, at 50 cents each, may be bought at the shop of H. L. Whitcomb, in Concord, after July 10, 1884, in packages of *twelve* for $5, and of *six* for $2.50.

Students may reach Concord from Boston by the Fitchburg Railroad, or the Middlesex Central; from Lowell, Andover, etc., by the Lowell and Framingham Railroad; from Southern Middlesex and Worcester Counties by the same road. The Orchard House stands on the Lexington road, east of Concord village, adjoining the Wayside estate, formerly the residence of Mr. Hawthorne. For information concerning the town and the school, we would refer applicants and visitors to the "Concord Guide Book" of Mr. George B. Bartlett, published by D. Lothrop & Co., Boston, and containing an account of the origin of the School.

Lodgings, with board, may be obtained at the following houses in Concord village.

Miss E. BARRETT, Monument Street.	Mrs. KENT, Main Street.
Mrs. O'BRIEN, Monument Square.	Mrs. GOODNOW, Main Street.
Mrs. CUTTER, Sudbury Street.	Mrs. N. DERBY, Walden Street.
Mrs. HOW, Hubbard Street.	Mrs. B. F. WHEELER, Belknap Street.

Lodgings without board can be obtained in the neighborhood of each of the above-named houses. Students and visitors will make their own arrangements without consulting the undersigned.

A. BRONSON ALCOTT, *Dean.*

S. H. EMERY, JR., *Director.*

F. B. SANBORN, *Secretary.*

CONCORD, July 22, 1884.

The Faculty of the Concord School have decided on the arrangements for the summer of 1884 as follows : (1). Six or seven days devoted to a discussion of *Emerson's Genius and Character;* beginning July 23, 1884, and including the subjects and writers named below. (2.) Three days devoted to a discussion on *Immortality*, with essays by Dr. PEABODY, Dr. HOLLAND, Prof. DAVIDSON, Dr. HARRIS, and Mr. JOHN FISKE, the latter taking for his subject *The Origin and Destiny of Man.*

(I). THE GENIUS AND CHARACTER OF EMERSON. To be considered July 23-30, 1884, under the following heads :

1. *Emerson's View of Nature,* by W. T. HARRIS, LL. D., of Concord.
2. *Emerson's Religion,* by Rev. C. A. BARTOL, D. D., of Boston.
3. *Emerson's Ethics,* by Mr. EDWIN D. MEAD, of Boston.
4. *Emerson's Manners and Relation to Society,* by Mrs. JULIA WARD HOWE, of Boston.
5. *Emerson as seen from India,* by PROTAP CHUNDER MOZOOMDAR, of Calcutta.
6. *Emerson as an American,* Mr. JULIAN HAWTHORNE, of New York.
7. *Emerson in the Pulpit,* by Miss E. P. PEABODY, of Boston.
8. *A French View of Emerson,* by M. RENÉ DE POYEN BELLEISLE, of Paris.
9. *Emerson in Boston,* by Mrs. E. D. CHENEY, of Boston.

10. *Emerson as an Essayist,* by Mr. JOHN ALBEE, of Newcastle, N. H.
11. *Emerson and Thoreau.*
12. *Emerson's View of Nationality,* by Rev. G. W. COOKE, of Dedham.
13. *Emerson Among the Poets,* by Mr. F. B. SANBORN, of Concord.
14. *Emerson's Relation to Goethe and Carlyle,* by W. T. HARRIS, LL. D., of Concord.
15. *The Genius of Emerson,* by Mr. W. E. CHANNING, of Concord.

(II). The question of *Immortality* will be opened July 31, 1884, by Rev. A. P. PEABODY, D. D., of Cambridge, who will be followed by Mr. JOHN FISKE, of Cambridge; Rev. R. A. HOLLAND, D. D., of New Orleans; Dr. HARRIS, of Concord, and others; the discussion closing on the 2d of August.

In the absence of Mr. SNIDER, Prof. HARRIS will take his place.

PROGRAMME OF LECTURES.

JULY, 1884.

23d,	9	A. M.	Opening Exercises.
			A Sonnet by Miss Emma Lazarus.
			Readings from the Diary of Mr. Alcott.
	7.30	P. M.	Mr. Hawthorne.
24th,	9	A. M.	Dr. Bartol.
	7.30	P. M.	Prof. Harris.
25th,	9	A. M.	Mr. Albee.
	7.30	P. M.	Mr. Mead.
26th,	9	A. M.	Mrs. Howe.
28th,	9	A. M.	{ Mrs. Cheney. Miss Peabody.
	7.30	P. M.	Mr. Sanborn.

JULY, 1884.

29th,	9	A. M.	{ Prof. Harris. Mr. Mozoomdar.
	7.30	P. M.	M. de Poyen Belleisle.
30th,	9	A. M.	{ Mr. Channing. Mr. Whitman.
	7.30	P. M.	Mr. Cooke.
31st,	9	A. M.	Dr. Peabody.
	7.30	P. M.	Mr. Fiske.

AUGUST, 1884.

1st,	9	A. M.	Dr. Holland.
	7.30	P. M.	Prof. Davidson.
2d,	9	A. M.	Prof. Harris.

THE CONCORD SCHOOL OF PHILOSOPHY.

THE CONCORD SUMMER SCHOOL will open for a seventh term on Thursday, July 16, 1885, at 7.30 P.M., and may continue three weeks. The lectures in each week will be eleven; they will be given morning and evening, except Saturday evenings, on the six secular days (in the morning at 9.30 o'clock, and in the evening at 7.30) at the *Hillside Chapel*, near the Orchard House.

The terms will be $5 for each full week; for all the lectures, $10. Single tickets, at 50 cents each, may be bought at the shop of H. L. Whitcomb, in Concord, after July 10, in packages of *ten* for $4.50, and of *three* $1.40. Any one to whom this circular is sent can now engage course tickets by making application, and sending $5 as a guaranty. For those who make this deposit, tickets will be reserved till the tenth day of July, and can then be obtained by payment of the balance due. They entitle the holder to reserved seats. Students coming and going daily during the term, may reach Concord from Boston by the Fitchburg Railroad, or the Middlesex Central; from Lowell, Andover, etc., by the Lowell and Framingham Railroad; from Southern Middlesex and Worcester Counties by the same road. The Orchard House stands on the Lexington road, east of Concord village, adjoining the Wayside estate, formerly the residence of Mr. Hawthorne. For fuller information concerning the town and the school, we would refer applicants and visitors to the "Concord Guide Book" of Mr. George B. Bartlett.*

Lodgings with board may be obtained at the following houses in Concord village:

Miss E. BARRETT, Monument Street.   Mrs. KENT, Main Street.
Mrs. O'BRIEN, Monument Square.   Mrs. GOODNOW, Main Street.
Mrs. CUTTER, Sudbury Street.   Mrs. HOW, Hubbard Street.
Mrs. B. F. WHEELER, Belknap Street.

Lodgings without board can be obtained in the neighborhood of each of the above-named houses. Students and visitors will make their own arrangements without consulting the undersigned

A. BRONSON ALCOTT, *Dean.*
S. H. EMERY, JR., *Director.*
F. B. SANBORN, *Secretary.*

CONCORD, June 30, 1885.

* Published by D. Lothrop & Co., Boston, and containing an account of the origin of the School.

PROGRAMME OF LECTURES.

JULY, 1885.

16th,	7.30 P. M.	Mr. Albee.
17th,	9.30 A. M.	Mrs. Cheney.
	7.30 P. M.	Mr. Snider.
18th,	9.30 A. M.	Dr. Bartol.
20th,	9.30 A. M.	Prof. Harris.
	7.30 P. M.	Mr. Sanborn.
21st,	9.30 A. M.	Mrs. Sherman.
	7.30 P. M.	Prof. White.
22d,	9.30 A. M.	Mr. Emery.
	7.30 P. M.	Mr. Snider.
23d,	9.30 A. M.	Prof. Hewett.
	7.30 P. M.	Prof. Harris.
24th,	9.30 A. M.	Mr. Blake.
	7.30 P. M.	Dr. Soldan.
25th,	9.30 A. M.	Mrs. Howe.
27th,	9.30 A. M.	Mr. Partridge.
	7.30 P. M.	Prof. Harris.
28th,	9.30 A. M.	Mr. Snider.
	7.30 P. M.	Mr. Davidson.
29th,	9.30 A. M.	Mr. Ernst.
	7.30 P. M.	Mr. Fiske.
30th,	9.30 A. M.	Dr. Abbott.
	7.30 P. M.	Prof. Harris.
31st,	9.30 A. M.	Dr. Peabody.

LECTURES AND SUBJECTS, 1885.

THE GENERAL SUBJECTS FOR THIS YEAR WILL BE

I. Goethe's Genius and Work.

II. Is Pantheism the Legitimate outcome of Modern Science?

I. GOETHE'S GENIUS AND WORK.

Under this head will come lectures on

1. *Goethe's Self-Culture;* by Mr. JOHN ALBEE.
2. *Goethe and Religion;* by Rev. Dr. R. A. HOLLAND.
3. *Goethe's Relation to Kant and Spinoza in Philosophy;* by Dr. F. L. SOLDAN.
4. *Goethe's Faust;* by Prof. HARRIS.
5. *Goethe's Youth;* by Prof. H. S. WHITE, of Cornell University.
6. *The "Ewig-Weibliche";* by Mrs. E. D. CHENEY.
7. *Goethe's Faust;* by Mr. D. J. SNIDER.
8. *Goethe's Relation to English Literature;* by Mr. F. B. SANBORN.
9. A Lecture by Mr. JULIAN HAWTHORNE.
10. *The Novellettes in "Wilhelm Meister;"* by Prof. HARRIS.
11. *"Wilhelm Meister" as a Whole;* by Mr. D. J. SNIDER.
12. *Goethe and Schiller;* by Rev. Dr. BARTOL.
13. *The Women of Goethe;* by Mrs. JULIA WARD HOWE.
14. *The Elective Affinities;* by Mr. S. H. EMERY, Jr.
15. *Goethe's Titanism;* by Prof. THOMAS DAVIDSON.
16. *Goethe at Weimar;* by Prof. HEWETT, of Cornell University.
17. *Child-Life as portrayed in Goethe's Works;* by Mrs. CAROLINE K. SHERMAN, of Chicago.
18. *Goethe as Playwright;* by Mr. WILLIAM O. PARTRIDGE.
19. *The Style of Goethe;* by Mr. C. W. ERNST.

II. A SYMPOSIUM: IS PANTHEISM THE LEGITIMATE OUTCOME OF MODERN SCIENCE?

Papers by Rev. Dr. PEABODY, Mr. JOHN FISKE, Prof. HARRIS, Dr. G. H. HOWISON, and Dr. F. E. ABBOTT.

Readings from Thoreau; by Mr. H. G. O. BLAKE; and *Readings from Mr. Alcott's Diaries* will also be given.

Slight changes in the above Programme may hereafter be made, and other names may be added to the list of lecturers.

THE CONCORD SCHOOL OF PHILOSOPHY

THE CONCORD SUMMER SCHOOL will open for a seventh term on Thursday, July 16, 1885, at 7.30 P.M., and may continue three weeks. The lectures in each week will be eleven; they will be given morning and evening, except Saturday evenings, on the six secular days (in the morning at 9.30 o'clock, and in the evening at 7.30) at the *Hillside Chapel*, near the Orchard House.

The terms will be $5 for each full week; for all the lectures, $10. Single tickets, at 50 cents each, may be bought at the shop of H. L. Whitcomb, in Concord, after July 10, in packages of *ten* for $4.50, and of *three* $1.40. Any one to whom this circular is sent can now engage course tickets by making application, and sending $5 as a guaranty. For those who make this deposit, tickets will be reserved till the tenth day of July, and can then be obtained by payment of the balance due. They entitle the holder to reserved seats. Students coming and going daily during the term, may reach Concord from Boston by the Fitchburg Railroad, or the Middlesex Central; from Lowell, Andover, etc., by the Lowell and Framingham Railroad; from Southern Middlesex and Worcester Counties by the same road. The Orchard House stands on the Lexington road, east of Concord village, adjoining the Wayside estate, formerly the residence of Mr. Hawthorne. For fuller information concerning the town and the school, we would refer applicants and visitors to the "Concord Guide Book" of Mr. George B. Bartlett.*

Lodgings with board may be obtained at the following houses in Concord village:

Miss E. BARRETT, Monument Street.   Mrs. KENT, Main Street.
Mrs. O'BRIEN, Monument Square.   Mrs. GOODNOW, Main Street.
Mrs. CUTTER, Sudbury Street.   Mrs. HOW, Hubbard Street.
Mrs. B. F. WHEELER, Belknap Street.

Lodgings without board can be obtained in the neighborhood of each of the above-named houses. Students and visitors will make their own arrangements without consulting the undersigned.

A. BRONSON ALCOTT, *Dean.*
S. H. EMERY, JR., *Director.*
F. B. SANBORN, *Secretary.*

CONCORD, July 23, 1885.

* Published by D. Lothrop & Co., Boston, and containing an account of the origin of the School.

PROGRAMME OF LECTURES.

JULY, 1885.

16th,	7 30 P. M.	Mr. Albee.
17th,	9.30 A. M.	Mrs. Cheney.
	7.30 P. M.	Mr. Snider.
18th,	9.30 A. M.	Dr. Bartol and Dr. Hedge.
20th,	9.30 A. M.	Prof. Harris.
	7.30 P. M.	Mr. Sanborn.
21st,	9.30 A. M.	Mrs. Sherman.
	7.30 P. M.	Prof. White.
22d,	9.30 A. M.	Mr. Emery.
	7.30 P. M.	Mr. Snider.
23d,	9.30 A. M.	Prof. Hewett.
	7.30 P. M.	Prof. Harris.
24th,	9.30 A. M.	Mr. Blake.
	7.30 P. M.	Dr. Soldan.
25th,	9.30 A. M.	Mr. Davidson.
27th,	9.30 A. M.	Mr. Partridge.
	7.30 P. M.	Prof. Harris.
28th,	9.30 A. M.	Mr. Snider.
	7.30 P. M.	Mrs. Howe.
29th,	9.30 A. M.	Mr. Ernst.
	7.30 P. M.	Mr. Fiske.
30th,	9.30 A. M.	Dr. Abbott.
	7.30 P. M.	Prof. Harris.
31st,	9.30 A. M.	Dr. Peabody.

LECTURES AND SUBJECTS, 1885.

THE GENERAL SUBJECTS FOR THIS YEAR WILL BE

I. Goethe's Genius and Work.

II. Is Pantheism the Legitimate outcome of Modern Science?

I. GOETHE'S GENIUS AND WORK.

Under this head will come lectures on

1. *Goethe's Self-Culture;* by Mr. JOHN ALBEE.
2. *Goethe and his " Mährchen;"* by Rev. Dr. F. H. HEDGE.
3. *Goethe's Relation to Kant and Spinoza in Philosophy;* by Dr. F. L. SOLDAN.
4. *Goethe's Faust;* by Prof. HARRIS.
5. *Goethe's Youth;* by Prof. H. S. WHITE, of Cornell University.
6. *The " Ewig-Weibliche";* by Mrs. E. D. CHENEY.
7. *Goethe's Faust;* by Mr. D. J. SNIDER.
8. *Goethe's Relation to English Literature;* by Mr. F. B. SANBORN.
9. *A Lecture by Mr. JULIAN HAWTHORNE.*
10. *The Novellettes in " Wilhelm Meister;"* by Prof. HARRIS.
11. *" Wilhelm Meister" as a Whole;* by Mr. D. J. SNIDER.
12. *Goethe and Schiller;* by Rev. Dr. BARTOL.
13. *The Women of Goethe;* by Mrs. JULIA WARD HOWE.
14. *The Elective Affinities;* by Mr. S. H. EMERY, Jr.
15. *Goethe's Titanism;* by Prof. THOMAS DAVIDSON.
16. *Goethe at Weimar;* by Prof. HEWETT, of Cornell University.
17. *Child-Life as portrayed in Goethe's Works;* by Mrs. CAROLINE K. SHERMAN, of Chicago.
18. *Goethe as Playwright;* by Mr. WILLIAM O. PARTRIDGE.
19. *The Style of Goethe;* by Mr. C. W. ERNST.

II. A SYMPOSIUM: IS PANTHEISM THE LEGITIMATE OUTCOME OF MODERN SCIENCE?

(*Beginning July 29.*)

Papers by Rev. Dr. PEABODY, Mr. JOHN FISKE, Prof. HARRIS, Dr. G. H. HOWISON, and Dr. F. E. ABBOTT.

Readings from Thoreau; by Mr. H. G. O. BLAKE; and *Readings from Mr. Alcott's Diaries* may also be given.

THE CONCORD SCHOOL OF PHILOSOPHY

The Concord Summer School will open for a seventh term on Thursday, July 16, 1885, at 7.30 P.M., and may continue three weeks. The lectures in each week will be eleven; they will be given morning and evening, except Saturday evenings, on the six secular days (in the morning at 9.30 o'clock, and in the evening at 7.30) at the *Hillside Chapel*, near the Orchard House.

The terms will be $5 for each full week; for all the lectures, $10. Single tickets, at 50 cents each, may be bought at the shop of H. L. Whitcomb, in Concord, after July 10, in packages of *ten* for $4.50, and of *three* $1.40. Any one to whom this circular is sent can now engage course tickets by making application, and sending $5 as a guaranty. For those who make this deposit, tickets will be reserved till the tenth day of July, and can then be obtained by payment of the balance due. They entitle the holder to reserved seats. Students coming and going daily during the term, may reach Concord from Boston by the Fitchburg Railroad, or the Middlesex Central; from Lowell, Andover, etc., by the Lowell and Framingham Railroad; from Southern Middlesex and Worcester Counties by the same road. The Orchard House stands on the Lexington road, east of Concord village, adjoining the Wayside estate, formerly the residence of Mr. Hawthorne. For fuller information concerning the town and the school, we would refer applicants and visitors to the "Concord Guide Book" of Mr. George B. Bartlett.*

Lodgings with board may be obtained at the following houses in Concord village:

Miss E. Barrett, Monument Street.

Mrs. O'Brien, Monument Square.

Mrs. Cutter, Sudbury Street.

Mrs. Kent, Main Street.

Mrs. Goodnow, Main Street.

Mrs. How, Hubbard Street.

Mrs. B. F. Wheeler, Belknap Street.

Lodgings without board can be obtained in the neighborhood of each of the above-named houses. Students and visitors will make their own arrangements without consulting the undersigned.

A. BRONSON ALCOTT, *Dean.*

S. H. EMERY, Jr., *Director.*

F. B. SANBORN, *Secretary.*

Concord, July 28, 1885.

* Published by D. Lothrop & Co., Boston, and containing an account of the origin of the School.

PROGRAMME OF LECTURES.

July, 1885.

16th, 7.30 P. M. Mr. Albee.

17th, 9.30 A. M. Mrs. Cheney.
      7.30 P. M. Mr. Snider.

18th, 9.30 A. M. Dr. Bartol and Dr. Hedge.

20th, 9.30 A. M. Prof. Harris.
      7.30 P. M. Mr. Sanborn.

21st, 9.30 A. M. Mrs. Sherman.
      7.30 P. M. Prof. White.

22d, 9.30 A. M. Mr. Emery.
     7.30 P. M. Mr. Snider.

23d, 9.30 A. M. Prof. Hewett.
     7.80 P. M. Prof. Harris.

24th, 9.30 A. M. Mr. Blake.
      7.30 P. M. Dr. Soldan.

25th, 9.30 A. M. Mr. Davidson.

27th, 9.30 A. M. Mr. Partridge.
      7.30 P. M. Prof. Harris.

28th, 9.30 A. M. Mr. Snider.
      7.30 P. M. A Conversation.

29th, 9.30 A. M. Mr. Ernst.
      7.30 P. M. Mr. Fiske.

30th, 9.30 A. M. Dr. Abbott.
      7.30 P. M. Prof. Harris.

31st, 9.30 A. M. Dr. Peabody.

Aug.

1st, 9.30 A. M. Mrs. Howe.

LECTURES AND SUBJECTS, 1885.

The General Subjects for this Year will be

I. Goethe's Genius and Work.

II. Is Pantheism the Legitimate outcome of Modern Science?

I. Goethe's Genius and Work.

Under this head will come lectures on

1. *Goethe's Self-Culture;* by Mr. John Alber.
2. *Goethe and his "Mährchen;"* by Rev. Dr. F. H. Hedge.
3. *Goethe's Relation to Kant and Spinoza in Philosophy;* by Dr. F. L. Soldan.
4. *Goethe's Faust;* by Prof. Harris.
5. *Goethe's Youth;* by Prof. H. S. White, of Cornell University.
6. *The "Ewig-Weibliche";* by Mrs. E. D. Cheney.
7. *Goethe's Faust;* by Mr. D. J. Snider.
8. *Goethe's Relation to English Literature;* by Mr. F. B. Sanborn.
9. A Conversation on *Goethe as a Man of Science.*
10. *The Novellettes in "Wilhelm Meister;"* by Prof. Harris.
11. *"Wilhelm Meister" as a Whole;* by Mr. D. J. Snider.
12. *Goethe and Schiller;* by Rev. Dr. Bartol.
13. *The Women of Goethe;* by Mrs. Julia Ward Howe.
14. *The Elective Affinities;* by Mr. S. H. Emery, Jr.
15. *Goethe's Titanism;* by Prof. Thomas Davidson.
16. *Goethe at Weimar;* hy Prof. Hewett, of Cornell University.
17. *Child-Life as portrayed in Goethe's Works;* by Mrs. Caroline K. Sherman, of Chicago.
18. *Goethe as Playwright;* by Mr. William O. Partridge.
19. *The Style of Goethe;* by Mr. C. W. Ernst.

II. A Symposium: Is Pantheism the Legitimate Outcome of Modern Science?
(*Beginning July 29.*)

Papers by Rev. Dr. Peabody, Mr. John Fiske, Prof. Harris, Dr. G. H. Howison, and Dr. F. E. Abbott.

Readings from Thoreau; by Mr. H. G. O. Blake will also be given.

THE CONCORD SCHOOL OF PHILOSOPHY.

THE CONCORD SUMMER SCHOOL will open its eighth term on Wednesday, July 14, 1886, at 9.30 P. M., and will continue two weeks. The lectures in each week will be eleven; they will be given morning and evening, except Saturday evenings, on the six secular days (in the morning at 9.30 o'clock, and in the evening at 7.30) at the *Hillside Chapel*, near the Orchard House.

The terms will be $5 for each full week; for all the lectures, $10. Single tickets at 50 cents each, may be bought at the shop of H. L. Whitcomb, in Concord, after July 10, in packages of *ten* for $4.50, and of *three* $1.40. Any one to whom this circular is sent can now engage course tickets by making application, and sending $5 as a guaranty. For those who make this deposit, tickets will be reserved till the tenth day of July, and can then be obtained by payment of the balance due. They entitle the holder to reserved seats. Students coming and going daily during the term, may reach Concord from Boston by the Fitchburg Railroad, or the Middlesex Central; from Lowell, Andover, etc., by the Lowell and Framingham Railroad; from Southern Middlesex and Worcester Counties by the same road. The Orchard House stands on the Lexington road, east of Concord village, adjoining the Wayside estate, formerly the residence of Mr. Hawthorne. For fuller information concerning the town and the school we would refer applicants and visitors to the "Concord Guide Book" of Mr. George B. Bartlett.*

Lodgings with board may be obtained at the following houses in Concord village:

Miss E. BARRETT, Monument Street.
Mrs. O'BRIEN, Monument Square.
Mrs. CUTTER, Sudbury Street.
Mrs. B. F. WHEELER, Belknap Street.

Mrs. KENT, Main Street.
Mrs. GOODNOW, Main Street.
Mrs. HOW, Hubbard Street.

Lodgings without board can be obtained in the neighborhood of each of the above-named houses. Students and visitors will make their own arrangements without consulting the undersigned.

A. BRONSON ALCOTT, *Dean.*
S. H. EMERY, JR., *Director.*
F. B. SANBORN, *Secretary.*

CONCORD, June 15, 1886.

* Published by D. Lothrop & Co., Boston, and containing an account of the origin of the School.

LECTURES AT THE EIGHTH SESSION
OF THE
CONCORD SCHOOL OF PHILOSOPHY,
JULY 14—31, 1886.

I. DANTE AND HIS DIVINE COMEDY.

JULY, 1886.

14th, 9.30 A. M.—*The Philosophic Structure of the Divine Comedy:*
By Prof. W. T. HARRIS, of Concord.

14th, 7.30 P. M.—*Dante and Michael Angelo:*
By Mrs. E. D. CHENEY, of Boston.

15th, 9.30 A. M.—*Dante's Minor Poetry:*
By Mr. JOHN ALBEE, of New Castle, N. H.

15th, 7.30 P. M.—*Dante as a Poet of the People:*
By Prof. VINCENZO BOTTA, of New York.

16th, 9.30 A. M.—*The Spiritual Sense of the Divina Commedia:*
By the REVEREND BROTHER AZARIAS, President of Rock Hill College, Md.

16th, 7.30 P. M.—*The German Commentaries on Dante :*
By F. LOUIS SOLDAN, LL.D., of St. Louis, Mo.

17th, 9.30 A. M.—*Dante's Tropes :*
By Rev. Dr. C. A. BARTOL, of Boston.

19th, 9.30 A. M.—*Dante's Teachers.*
By Prof. THOMAS DAVIDSON, of Orange, N. J.

19th, 7.30 P. M.—*Dante's Mythology :*
By Prof. W. T. HARRIS.

20th, 9.30 A. M.—*Canto XXII of the Purgatorio,* Translated by Dr. PARSONS, of Boston :—
Dante's Italy :
By Mr. LUIGI MONTI, of New York.

20th, 7.30 P. M.—*Dante and Beatrice :*
By Mrs. JULIA WARD HOWE, of Boston.

21st, 9.30 A. M.—*Dante's Paradiso :*
By Rev. R. A. HOLLAND, S. T. D., of New Orleans, La.

21st, 7.30 P. M.—*Dante and Virgil :*
By F. B. SANBORN, of Concord.

II. PLATO'S PHILOSOPHY.

JULY, 1886.
22nd, 9.30 A. M.—*The Parmenides :*
By S. H. EMERY, Jr., Esq., of Concord.

22nd, 7.30 P. M.—*Aristotle's Debt to Plato :*
By Prof. THOMAS DAVIDSON.

23rd, 9.30 A. M.—*Plato and Modern Thought :*
By Prof. G. H. HOWISON, of the University of California.

23rd, 7.30 P. M.—*Plato's Dialectic and Doctrine of Ideas :*
By Prof. W. T. HARRIS.

24th, 9.30 A. M.—*The Life and Times of Plato :*
By Rev. A. P. PEABODY, D.D., of Cambridge.

25th, 9.30 A. M.—*The Platonic Idea and Vital Organization :*
By EDMUND MONTGOMERY, Ph. D., of Hempstead, Texas.

26th, 7.30 P. M. — *The Dramatic Element in Plato :*
By Mr. JOHN ALBEE, of New Castle, N. H.

27th, 9.30 A. M.— *Woman in Plato's Republic :*
By Mrs. JULIA WARD HOWE.

27th, 7.30 P. M.—*Plato and Socrates :*
By F. B. SANBORN, of Concord.

28th, 9.30 A. M.—*Plato, Buddha, Swedenborg and Fichte, concerning an Immortal Self :*
By Rev. W. R. ALGER, of Boston.

28th, 7.30 P.M.—*Plato and the Sophists :*
By Prof. C. C. SHACKFORD, of Cornell University.

29th, 9.30 A.M.—*The Irony of Plato :*
By Prof. THOMAS DAVIDSON.

29th, 7.30 P. M.—*Plato and Christianity :*
By Rev. F. H. HEDGE, D.D., of Cambridge, Mass.

Ticknor & Co., Boston, publish two volumes of Lectures given at the Concord School, viz. : *The Genius and Character of Emerson;* pp. 469, price $2 ; *The Life and Genius of Goethe;* pp. 479, price $2. The two volumes are sold for $3.50.

It is proposed to publish in December, 1886, *Dante, the World-Poet,* uniform with the above volumes; and perhaps, also, a volume on *Plato's Philosophy.*

THE CONCORD SCHOOL OF PHILOSOPHY.

THE CONCORD SUMMER SCHOOL will open its eighth term on Wednesday, July 14, 1886, at 9.30 P. M., and will continue two weeks. The lectures in each week will be eleven; they will be given morning and evening, except Saturday evenings, on the six secular days (in the morning at 9.30 o'clock, and in the evening at 7.30) at the *Hillside Chapel*, near the Orchard House.

The terms will be $5 for each full week; for all the lectures, $10. Single tickets at 50 cents each, may be bought at the shop of H. L. Whitcomb, in Concord, after July 10, in packages of *ten* for $4.50, and of *three* $1.40. Any one to whom this circular is sent can now engage course tickets by making application, and sending $5 as a guaranty. For those who make this deposit, tickets will be reserved till the tenth day of July, and can then be obtained by payment of the balance due. They entitle the holder to reserved seats. Visitors coming and going daily during the term, may reach Concord from Boston by the Fitchburg Railroad, or the Middlesex Central; from Lowell, Andover, etc., by the Lowell and Framingham Railroad; from Southern Middlesex and Worcester Counties by the same road. The Orchard House stands on the Lexington road, east of Concord village, adjoining the Wayside estate, formerly the residence of Mr. Hawthorne. For fuller information concerning the town and the school we would refer applicants and visitors to the "Concord Guide Book" of Mr. George B. Bartlett.*

Lodgings with board may be obtained at the following houses in Concord village:

Miss E. BARRETT, Monument Street.	Mrs. KENT, Main Street.
Mrs. O'BRIEN, Monument Square.	Mrs. GOODNOW, Main Street.
Mrs. CUTTER, Sudbury Street.	Mrs. HOW, Hubbard Street.

Mrs. B. F. WHEELER, Belknap Street.

Lodgings without board can be obtained in the neighborhood of each of the above-named houses. Visitors will make their own arrangements without consulting the undersigned.

A. BRONSON ALCOTT, *Dean.*
S. H. EMERY, JR., *Director.*
F. B. SANBORN, *Secretary.*

CONCORD, July 1, 1886.

* Published by D. Lothrop & Co., Boston, and containing an account of the origin of the School.

LECTURES AT THE EIGHTH SESSION

OF THE

CONCORD SCHOOL OF PHILOSOPHY,

JULY 14—31, 1886.

I. DANTE AND HIS DIVINE COMEDY.

JULY, 1886.

14th, 9.30 A. M.—*The Philosophic Structure of the Divine Comedy:*
By Prof. W. T. HARRIS, of Concord.

14th, 7.30 P. M.—*Dante and Michael Angelo:*
By Mrs. E. D. CHENEY, of Boston.

15th, 9.30 A. M.—*The Spiritual Sense of the Divina Commedia:*
By the REVEREND BROTHER AZARIAS, President of Rock Hill College, Md.

15th, 7.30 P. M.—*Dante's Inferno.*
A Conversation, conducted by Prof. W. T. HARRIS, of Concord.

16th, 9.30 A. M.—*Dante's Convito.*
A Conversation, conducted by Prof. THOMAS DAVIDSON.

16th, 7.30 P. M.—*Dante's Purgatorio.*

    A Conversation.

17th, 9.30 A. M.—*Dante's Tropes :*

        By Rev. Dr. C. A. BARTOL, of Boston.

19th, 9.30 A. M.—*Dante's Teachers.*

    By Prof. THOMAS DAVIDSON, of Orange, N. J.

19th, 7.30 P. M.—*Dante's Mythology :*

        By Prof. W. T. HARRIS.

20th, 9.30 A. M.—*Canto XXII of the Purgatorio,*
Translated by Dr. PARSONS, of Boston :—
De Monarchia.

    A Conversation.

20th, 7.30 P. M.—*Dante and Beatrice :*

        By Mrs. JULIA WARD HOWE, of Boston.

21st, 9.30 A. M.—*Dante's Paradiso :*

        By Rev. R. A. HOLLAND, S. T. D., of New
Orleans, La.

21st, 7.30 P. M.—*Dante and Virgil :*

        By F. B. SANBORN, of Concord.

II. PLATO'S PHILOSOPHY.

JULY, 1886.

22nd, 9.30 A. M.—*The Parmenides :*

        By S. H. EMERY, Jr., Esq., of Concord.

22nd, 7.30 P. M.—*Aristotle's Debt to Plato :*

        By Prof. THOMAS DAVIDSON.

23rd, 9.30 A. M.—*Plato and Modern Thought :*

23rd, 7.30 P. M.—*Plato's Dialectic and Doctrine
of Ideas :*

        By Prof. W. T. HARRIS.

24th, 9.30 A. M.—*The Life and Times of Plato :*
By Rev. A. P. PEABODY, D.D., of Cambridge.

26th, 9.30 A. M.—*The Platonic Idea and Vital
Organization :*

By EDMUND MONTGOMERY, Ph. D., of Hempstead,
Texas.

26th, 7.30 P. M. — *The Dramatic Element in
Plato :*

By Rev. JOSEPH H. ALLEN, of Cambridge, Mass.

27th, 9.30 A. M.— *Woman in Plato's Republic :*

        By MRS. JULIA WARD HOWE.

27th, 7.30 P. M.—*Plato and Socrates :*

        By F. B. SANBORN, of Concord.

28th, 9.30 A. M.—*Plato, Buddha, Swedenborg
and Fichte, concerning an Immortal Self :*

        By REV. W. R. ALGER, of Boston.

28th, 7.30 P. M.—*Plato and the Sophists :*

    By Prof. C. C. SHACKFORD, of Cornell University.

29th, 9.30 A. M.—*The Irony of Plato :*

        By Prof. THOMAS DAVIDSON.

    Ticknor & Co., Boston, publish two volumes of Lectures given at the Concord School, viz. : *The Genius and Character of Emerson;* pp. 469, price $2 ; *The Life and Genius of Goethe;* pp. 479, price $2. The two volumes are sold for $3.50.

    It is proposed to publish in December, 1886, *Dante, the World-Poet,* uniform with the above volumes ; and perhaps, also, a volume on *Plato's Philosophy.*

THE CONCORD SCHOOL OF PHILOSOPHY.

The Concord Summer School will open its eighth term on Wednesday, July 14, 1886, at 9.30 P. M., and will continue two weeks. The lectures in each week will be eleven; they will be given morning and evening, except Saturday evenings, on the six secular days (in the morning at 9.30 o'clock, and in the evening at 7.30) at the *Hillside Chapel*, near the Orchard House.

The terms will be $5 for each full week; for all the lectures, $10. Single tickets at 50 cents each, may be bought at the shop of H. L. Whitcomb, in Concord, after July 10, in packages of *ten* for $4.50, and of *three* $1.40. Any one to whom this circular is sent can now engage course tickets by making application, and sending $5 as a guaranty. For those who make this deposit, tickets will be reserved till the tenth day of July, and can then be obtained by payment of the balance due. They entitle the holder to reserved seats. Visitors coming and going daily during the term, may reach Concord from Boston by the Fitchburg Railroad, or the Middlesex Central; from Lowell, Andover, etc., by the Lowell and Framingham Railroad; from Southern Middlesex and Worcester Counties by the same road. The Orchard House stands on the Lexington road, east of Concord village, adjoining the Wayside estate, formerly the residence of Mr. Hawthorne. For fuller information concerning the town and the school we would refer applicants and visitors to the "Concord Guide Book" of Mr. George B. Bartlett.*

Lodgings with board may be obtained at the following houses in Concord village:

Miss E. Barrett, Monument Street.	Mrs. Kent, Main Street.
Mrs. O'Brien, Monument Square.	Mrs. Goodnow, Main Street.
Mrs. Cutter, Sudbury Street.	Mrs. How, Hubbard Street.

Mrs. B. F. Wheeler, Belknap Street.

Lodgings without board can be obtained in the neighborhood of each of the above-named houses. Visitors will make their own arrangements without consulting the undersigned.

A. BRONSON ALCOTT, *Dedn.*
S. H. EMERY, Jr., *Director.*
F. B. SANBORN, *Secretary.*

Concord, July 16, 1886.

* Published by D. Lothrop & Co., Boston, and containing an account of the origin of the School.

LECTURES AT THE EIGHTH SESSION

OF THE

CONCORD SCHOOL OF PHILOSOPHY,

JULY 14—31, 1886.

I. DANTE AND HIS DIVINE COMEDY.

July, 1886.

14th, 9.30 A. M.—*The Philosophic Structure of the Divine Comedy:*
    By Prof. W. T. Harris, of Concord.

14th, 7.30 P. M.—*Dante and Michael Angelo:*
    By Mrs. E. D. Cheney, of Boston.

15th, 9.30 A. M.—*The Spiritual Sense of the Divina Commedia:*
By the Reverend Brother Azarias, President of Rock Hill College, Md.

15th, 7.30 P. M.—*Dante's Inferno.*
    A Conversation, conducted by Prof. W. T. Harris, of Concord.

16th, 9.30 A. M.—*The First Canto of the Paradiso.*
    A Conversation, conducted by Prof. Thomas Davidson.

16th, 7.30 P. M.—*Dante's Purgatorio.*

A Conversation.

17th, 9.30 A. M.—*Dante's Tropes:*
By Rev. Dr. C. A. BARTOL, of Boston.

19th, 9.30 A. M.—*Dante's Teachers.*
By Prof. THOMAS DAVIDSON, of Orange, N. J.

19th, 7.30 P. M.—*Dante's Mythology:*
By Prof. W. T. HARRIS.

20th, 9.30 A. M.—*Canto XXII of the Purgatorio,*
Translated by Dr. PARSONS, of Boston :—
Dante's Convito.
A Conversation, conducted by Prof. THOMAS DAVIDSON.

20th, 7.30 P. M.—*Dante and Beatrice :*
By Mrs. JULIA WARD HOWE, of Boston.

21st, 9.30 A. M.—*Dante's Paradiso :*
By Rev. R. A. HOLLAND, S. T. D., of New Orleans, La.

21st, 7.30 P. M.—*Dante and Virgil :*
By F. B. SANBORN, of Concord.

II. PLATO'S PHILOSOPHY.

JULY, 1886.

22nd, 9.30 A. M.—*The Parmenides :*
By S. H. EMERY, Jr., Esq., of Concord.

22nd, 7.30 P. M.—*Aristotle's Debt to Plato :*
By Prof. THOMAS DAVIDSON.

23rd, 9.30 A.M.—*Plato and Modern Thought :*

mead

23rd, 7.30 P.M.—*Plato's Dialectic and Doctrine of Ideas :*
By Prof. W. T. HARRIS.

24th, 9.30 A.M.—*The Life and Times of Plato :*
By Rev. A. P. PEABODY, D.D., of Cambridge.

26th, 9.30 A. M.—*The Platonic Idea and Vital Organization :*
By EDMUND MONTGOMERY, Ph. D., of Hempstead, **Texas.**

26th, 7.30 P. M. — *The Dramatic Element in Plato :*

By Rev. JOSEPH H. ALLEN, of Cambridge, Mass.

27th, 9.30 A. M.— *Woman in Plato's Republic:*
By Mrs. JULIA WARD HOWE.

27th, 7.30 P. M.—*Plato and Socrates :*
By F. B. SANBORN, of Concord.

28th, 9.30 A. M.—*Plato, Buddha, Swedenborg and Fichte, concerning an Immortal Self :*
By REV. W. R. ALGER, of Boston.

28th, 7.30 P.M.—*Plato and the Sophists :*
By Prof. C. C. SHACKFORD, of Cornell University.

29th, 9.30 A.M.—*The Irony of Plato :*
By Prof. THOMAS DAVIDSON.

Ticknor & Co., Boston, publish two volumes of Lectures given at the Concord School, viz. : *The Genius and Character of Emerson;* pp. 469, price $2; *The Life and Genius of Goethe;* pp. 479, price $2. The two volumes are sold for $3.50.

It is proposed to publish in December, 1886, *Dante, the World-Poet,* uniform with the above volumes; and perhaps, also, a volume on *Plato's Philosophy.*

THE CONCORD SCHOOL OF PHILOSOPHY.

THE CONCORD SUMMER SCHOOL will open its eighth term on Wednesday, July 14, 1886, at 9.30 P. M., and will continue two weeks. The lectures in each week will be eleven; they will be given morning and evening, except Saturday evenings, on the six secular days (in the morning at 9.30 o'clock, and in the evening at 7.30) at the *Hillside Chapel*, near the Orchard House.

The terms will be $5 for each full week; for all the lectures, $10. Single tickets at 50 cents each, may be bought at the shop of H. L. Whitcomb, in Concord, after July 10, in packages of *ten* for $4.50, and of *three* $1.40. Any one to whom this circular is sent can now engage course tickets by making application, and sending $5 as a guaranty. For those who make this deposit, tickets will be reserved till the tenth day of July, and can then be obtained by payment of the balance due. They entitle the holder to reserved seats. Visitors coming and going daily during the term, may reach Concord from Boston by the Fitchburg Railroad, or the Middlesex Central; from Lowell, Andover, etc., by the Lowell and Framingham Railroad; from Southern Middlesex and Worcester Counties by the same road. The Orchard House stands on the Lexington road, east of Concord village, adjoining the Wayside estate, formerly the residence of Mr. Hawthorne. For fuller information concerning the town and the school we would refer applicants and visitors to the "Concord Guide Book" of Mr. George B. Bartlett.*

Lodgings with board may be obtained at the following houses in Concord village:

Miss E. BARRETT, Monument Street.	Mrs. KENT, Main Street.
Mrs. O'BRIEN, Monument Square.	Mrs. GOODNOW, Main Street.
Mrs. CUTTER, Sudbury Street.	Mrs. HOW, Hubbard Street.

Mrs. B. F. WHEELER, Belknap Street.

Lodgings without board can be obtained in the neighborhood of each of the above-named houses. Visitors will make their own arrangements without consulting the undersigned.

A. BRONSON ALCOTT, *Dean.*
S. H. EMERY, JR., *Director.*
F. B. SANBORN, *Secretary.*

CONCORD, July 22, 1886.

* Published by D. Lothrop & Co., Boston, and containing an account of the origin of the School.

LECTURES AT THE EIGHTH SESSION

OF THE

CONCORD SCHOOL OF PHILOSOPHY,

JULY 14—31, 1886.

I. DANTE AND HIS DIVINE COMEDY.

JULY, 1886.

14th, 9.30 A. M.—*The Philosophic Structure of the Divine Comedy:*
By Prof. W. T. HARRIS, of Concord.

14th, 7.30 P. M.—*Dante and Michael Angelo:*
By Mrs. E. D. CHENEY, of Boston.

15th, 9.30 A. M.—*The Spiritual Sense of the Divina Commedia:*
By the REVEREND BROTHER AZARIAS, President of Rock Hill College, Md.

15th, 7.30 P. M.—*Dante's Inferno.*
A Conversation, conducted by Prof. W. T. HARRIS, of Concord.

16th, 9.30 A. M.—*The First Canto of the Paradiso.*
A Conversation, conducted by Prof. THOMAS DAVIDSON.

16th, 7.30 P. M.—*Dante's Purgatorio.*

A Conversation.

17th, 9.30 A. M.—*Dante's Tropes:*
> By Rev. Dr. C. A. Bartol, of Boston.

19th, 9.30 A. M.—*Dante's Teachers.*
By Prof. Thomas Davidson, of Orange. N. J.

19th, 7.30 P. M.—*Dante's Mythology:*
> By Prof. W. T. Harris.

20th, 9.30 A. M.—*Canto XXII of the Purgatorio.*
Translated by Dr. Parsons, of Boston :—
Dante's Convito.
A Conversation, conducted by Prof. Thomas Davidson.

20th, 7.30 P. M.—*Dante and Beatrice:*
> By Mrs. Julia Ward Howe, of Boston.

21st, 9.30 A.M.—*Dante's Paradiso:*
> By Rev. R. A. Holland, S. T. D., of New Orleans, La.

21st, 7.30 P. M.—*Dante and Virgil:*
> By F. B. Sanborn, of Concord.

II. PLATO'S PHILOSOPHY.

July. 1886.

22nd, 9.30 A. M.—*The Parmenides:*
> By S. H. Emery, Jr., Esq., of Concord.

22nd, 7.30 P. M.—*The Irony of Plato:*
> By Prof. Thomas Davidson.

23rd, 9.30 A.M.—*Dante's Significance in History and Politics:*
> By Edwin D. Mead, of Boston.

23rd, 7.30 P M.—*Plato's Dialectic and Doctrine of Ideas:*
> By Prof. W. T. Harris.

24th, 9.30 A.M.—*The Life and Times of Plato:*
By Rev. A. P. Peabody, D.D., of Cambridge.

26th, 9.30 A. M.—*The Platonic Idea and Vital Organization:*
By Edmund Montgomery, Ph. D., of Hempstead, Texas.

26th, 7.30 P. M. — *The Dramatic Element in Plato:*

By Rev. Joseph H. Allen, of Cambridge, Mass.

27th, 9 30 A. M.—*Aristotle's Debt to Plato:*
> By Prof. Thomas Davidson.

27th, 7.30 P. M.—*Plato and Socrates:*
> By F. B. Sanborn, of Concord.

28th, 9.30 A. M.—*Plato, Buddha, Swedenborg and Fichte, concerning an Immortal Self:*
> By Rev. W. R. Alger, of Boston.

28th, 7.30 P.M.—*Plato and the Sophists:*
> By Prof. C. C. Shackford, of Cornell University.

29th, 9.30 A.M. — *Woman in Plato's Republic:*
> By Mrs. Julia Ward Howe.

Ticknor & Co., Boston, publish two volumes of Lectures given at the Concord School, viz.: *The Genius and Character of Emerson;* pp. 469, price $2; *The Life and Genius of Goethe;* pp. 479, price $2. The two volumes are sold for $3.50.

It is proposed to publish in December, 1886, *Dante, the World-Poet,* uniform with the above volumes; and perhaps, also, a volume on *Plato's Philosophy.*

LECTURES AT THE EIGHTH SESSION

OF THE

CONCORD SCHOOL OF PHILOSOPHY,

JULY 14—29, 1886.

I. DANTE AND HIS DIVINE COMEDY.

JULY, 1886.

14th, 9.30 A. M.—*The Philosophic Structure of the Divine Comedy:*
By Prof. W. T. HARRIS, of Concord.

14th, 7.30 P. M.—*Dante and Michael Angelo:*
By Mrs. E. D. CHENEY, of Boston.

15th, 9.30 A. M.—*The Spiritual Sense of the Divina Commedia:*
By the REVEREND BROTHER AZARIAS, President of Rock Hill College, Md.

15th, 7.30 P. M.—*Dante's Inferno.*
A Conversation, conducted by Prof. W. T. HARRIS, of Concord.

16th, 9.30 A. M.—*The First Canto of the Paradiso.*
A Conversation, conducted by Prof. THOMAS DAVIDSON.

16th, 7.30 P. M.—*Dante's Purgatorio.*
A Conversation, conducted by Prof. W. T. HARRIS.

17th, 9.30 A. M.—*Dante's Tropes:*
By Rev. Dr. C. A. BARTOL, of Boston.

19th, 9.30 A. M.—*Dante's Teachers.*
By Prof. THOMAS DAVIDSON, of Orange, N. J.

19th, 7.30 P. M.—*Dante's Mythology:*
By Prof. W. T. HARRIS.

20th, 9.30 A. M.—*Canto XXII of the Purgatorio,*
Translated by Dr. PARSONS, of Boston:—
Dante's Convito.
A Conversation, conducted by Prof. THOMAS DAVIDSON.

20th, 7.30 P. M.—*Dante and Beatrice:*
By Mrs. JULIA WARD HOWE, of Boston.

21st, 9.30 A.M.—*Dante's Mythology* (concluded):
By Prof. W. T. HARRIS.

21st, 7.30 P. M.—*Dante and Virgil:*
By F. B. SANBORN, of Concord.

II. PLATO'S PHILOSOPHY.

JULY, 1886.

22nd, 9.30 A. M.—*The Parmenides:*
By S. H. EMERY, Jr., Esq., of Concord.

22nd, 7.30 P. M.—*The Irony of Plato:*
By Prof. THOMAS DAVIDSON.

23rd, 9.30 A.M.—*Dante's Significance in History and Politics:*
By EDWIN D. MEAD, of Boston.

23rd, 7.30 P M.—*Plato's Dialectic and Doctrine of Ideas:*
By Prof. W. T. HARRIS.

24th, 9.30 A.M.—*The Life and Times of Plato:*
By Rev. A. P. PEABODY, D.D., of Cambridge.

26th, 9.30 A. M.—*The Platonic Ideas and Vital Organization:*
By EDMUND MONTGOMERY, Ph. D., of Hempstead, Texas; (read by Prof. DAVIDSON.)

26th, 7.30 P. M. — *The Dramatic Element in Plato:*
By Rev. JOSEPH H. ALLEN, of Cambridge. Mass.

27th, 9.30 A. M.—*Aristotle's Debt to Plato:*
By Prof. THOMAS DAVIDSON.

27th, 7.30 P. M.—*Plato and Socrates:*
By F. B. SANBORN, of Concord.

28th, 9.30 A. M.—*Plato, Buddha, Swedenborg and Fichte, concerning an Immortal Self:*
By REV. W. R. ALGER, of Boston.

28th, 7.30 P.M.—*Plato and the Sophists:*
By Prof. C. C. SHACKFORD, of Cornell University.

29th, 9.30 A.M.—*Woman in Plato's Republic:*
By MRS. JULIA WARD HOWE.

The topics for 1887 will be *Aristotle* and *Bacon*, with a glance at Shakespeare. There may be a Symposium concerning *Ontology.*

Ticknor & Co., Boston, publish two volumes of Lectures given at the Concord School, viz.: *The Genius and Character of Emerson;* pp. 469, price $2; *The Life and Genius of Goethe;* pp. 479, price $2. The two volumes are sold for $3.50.

It is proposed to publish in December, 1886, *Dante, the World-Poet,* uniform with the above volumes; and perhaps, also, in 1887, a volume on *Plato's Philosophy.*

EXTRACT

FROM A

LETTER CONCERNING THE NEW LIFE.

The way to begin the *New Life*, I believe, is to try to try to forget oneself, one's sorrows, one's annoyances; to count oneself happy, if he can have the approval of a good conscience and the sense of having furthered the good. The *New Life*, as I conceive it, is a new attitude of the intelligence, the feelings, the will—a desire to lay aside all prejudice and to know the absolute truth, a wide, sweet sympathy, recoiling at no sin, no suffering, no hardness of heart, but only at selfishness and meanness and lying, a firm resolution to do the best, as far as that is known, in the spirit of love. Such a life, *I know*, is worth living. It is a life in which all wounds soon heal, and all scars are but brands of victory—legal tender for future blessedness.

But the *New Life* is, in its outward form, more than this. It is an association for the *cultivation* of true insight, boundless sympathy and devoted helpfulness. It is the absence of these that makes the Old Life so blind, so dreary and lonely, so unblest. Every human being ought to be a providence to every other, ready, as far as his powers go, to solve every dark problem, sympathize with every joy and every sorrow, however deep and agonizing, and satisfy every need. We are still living in wilful ignorance of our own nature and in barbarous isolation with respect to each other. We wither in silent pain, because we have not confidence in each other. In our agony we invent a God to do for us what we are too miserable and selfish to do for each other. We are so sluggish that we try to make a virtue of faith, instead of laboring earnestly to find out and communicate the truth. We are so selfish that we allow our neighbor to suffer, when we have the means to help him. We are so low spiritually that we doubt the infinite possibilities of being, and sink down into a contented or discontented materialism. We do not rise to a firm and abiding sense of our own dignity and infinite worth. All this, I hope, will be altered in the *New Life*, whether I

[The following "Extract" was apparently distributed to members of the Concord School of Philosophy by Professor Thomas Davidson (1840-1900), who, in London in 1883, "founded the Fellowship of the New Life, of which the Fabian Society was an offshoot. Later he established a branch of the Fellowship in New York...." His lectures in various summer schools were attempts to forward or organize the spiritual life "on the basis of philosophic insight rather than dogma." Students of the Concord School should read the inspiring sketch of his career in D A B, V, 95-97.]

succeed in doing anything to further it or not. I have only a clear insight as to what is necessary and a desire to do the best I can. I see that, if ever life is to be again wholesome and inspiring, we must have a new social order and a new education: an order in which each shall feel the burdens of all, and all of each; an education which shall aim at producing perfect characters, rich in insight, in love, in energy, scorning selfishness, impurity and wrong.

I see no way in which these things can be reached but through a strong, combined effort on the part of those that firmly and earnestly believe in them, through a society, realizing in itself, and in the relations between its members, that ideal which it recognizes as the highest. Such a society cannot be formed in a day, nor by any general vote or resolution. It must be done slowly and quietly, through the gradual formation of a nucleus of earnest men and women, resolved to live a noble life and to make the redemption of humanity from ignorance, selfishness and vice the end of all their efforts, and ready to search out and communicate the means whereby this may be done. In the great work, we need association, with division of labor. There must be some to discover principles, others to apply them; some to teach, others to labor with their hands. What we can do at present is to keep these ends steadily in view and try to make them clear to others; to interest other people in them and to form little societies for the study of the highest things, for religious sympathy, for mutual aid. All this we can do now—to-day—before to-morrow.

And what if it be true that all great attainment calls for suffering, that such is the law of our being? Shall we slink back and tremble, and drug ourselves, like craven cowards? Never! The pure metal rings when it is struck, and the true soul finds itself and its own nobility often only in the throbs of pain and utter self-sacrifice. One true act of will makes us feel our immortality: alas! that we so seldom perform an act of will. In the face of an act of real will, heredity counts as nothing. What makes heredity tell is our own cowardice and sluggishness in not forcing children to conquer it, and also in not conquering it in ourselves. Heredity, like corruption, acts only when the soul is gone. It is utterly debasing to be bullied by heredity. The belief in its power "shuts the eyes and folds the hands," and delivers the soul in chains to the demon of unreality. The reason why people doubt about

the freedom of the will is because they never exercise it, but are always following some feeling or instinct, some private taste or affection. How *should* such persons know that the will is free? Our time is dying of sentimentality—some of it refined enough, to be sure, but still sentimentality—which destroys the will.

We are on our way to all that heart ever wished or head conceived. But the greater Gods have no sympathy with anything but heroism. When we will not be heroic, they sternly fling us back to suffer, saying to us: Learn to will! The kiss of Valkyre which opens the gates of Valhalla, is sealed only upon lips made holy by heroism even unto death.

The hosts of Ahura-Mazda are still fighting, and woe to us if we do not join them! It is the custom among the wise men of the world to laugh at all great heroism—all thirst for self-sacrifice; but we can afford to let them laugh. Somewhere in the shadow there are spectators who laugh at them, and will laugh when these have lost the will to laugh. The sons of Ahura-Mazda laugh forever, and there is no uneasiness in their laughter. Their laugh is the beauty of the universe.

But this will, perhaps, weary you and seem mere poetry to you. Poetry it is; but, as Aristotle said long ago, "Poetry is more earnest and more philosophical than history." The true poetry of the world is the history of its spiritual life, and is as much truer than what is *called* history as spirit is truer than outward seeming. When shall we learn this?

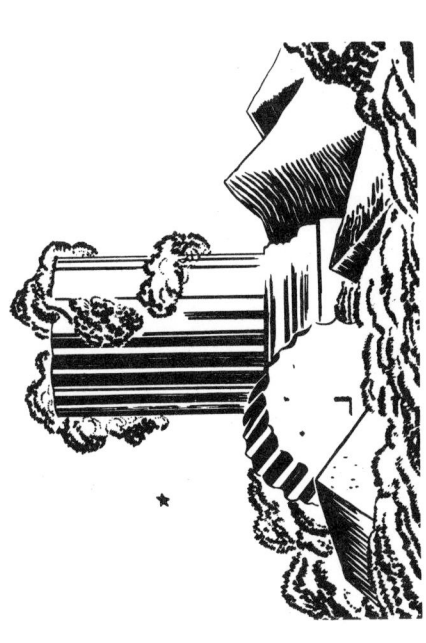

PRINTED FOR THE USE OF

THE CONCORD SCHOOL

OF

PHILOSOPHY.

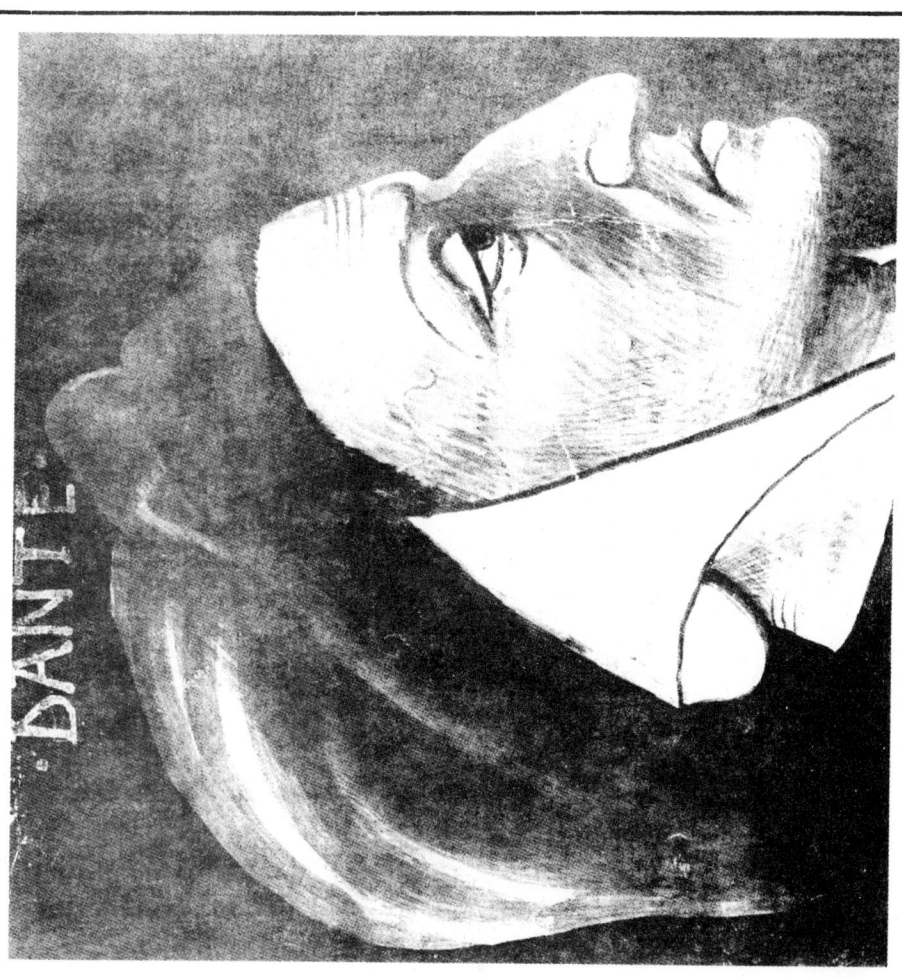

DANTE.

DEVELOPMENT OF CHRISTIANITY

AMONG THE

CULTIVATED CLASS OF ROMANS,

AS IMAGINED BY DANTE, IN THE INSTANCE OF

THE POET STATIUS,

IN THE TWENTY-SECOND CANTO OF THE

PURGATORIO,

INTERPRETED BY MR. PARSONS,

AND PRINTED FOR

THE CONCORD SCHOOL OF PHILOSOPHY.

PURGATORIO.

CANTO TWENTY-SECOND.

BEHIND us now that Angel had been left
To the Sixth Cornice who the passage shows,
Of one more scar my forehead having reft,
And to his 'Blessed they'—pronounced of those
Whose longing is to righteousness—all they
With voice responsive had subjoined—'who thirst':
And nothing further, ending so their lay.

Then I, more light of limb than ever erst
At other openings, easily passed above
Following those rapid spirits with pace the same:
And Virgil thus began discourse:

VIRGIL. "The love
Which goodness kindleth wakes an answering flame,
Always, if love some token truly tell.
Hence from that hour when Juvenal came down
Into the realm of Limbo where we dwell,
And in his fondness told me of thine own,

7

'Curst love of gold! to what excess of wrong
Driv'st thou not mortals?'—I, from side to side
Rolling those weights, had joined the terrible tilt.
Then I perceived the hands could spread too wide
Their spendthrift wings, and bitterly that guilt
Did I repent, and minor sins beside.
How many with clipped locks again shall rise,
Because of ignorance, which for wanton waste
Living or dying, penitence denies!
Learn this: the fault by which one sin is faced
In direct opposition, *with* that sin
Dries its green here, in withering penance placed.
With those that avarice mourn if I have been
Put in purgation, me thereto did bring
Its counter-vice that I offended in."

VIRGIL.

"Now when of that fell contest thou didst sing
Which the twin-troubles of Jocasta tried,
From what thou say'st where Clio touched thy string,
(The singer of bucolic songs replied)
Thee to belief not yet it seems had won
The Faith without which no good deeds avail:
If this be so, what candles or what sun
Dispelled thy night and made thee trim thy sail
That in the Fisher's wake thy bark might run?"

6

My love for thee no kindness could excel
That e'er was felt for one to sight unknown;
So shall I find these stairs a short ascent.
But say, forgiving me in friendly part,
Too large a rein if confidence have lent,
And speak unto me like the friend thou art;
How in thy breast could avarice find a place,
'Mid all the varied wisdom that was thine,
Of so much diligence the crowning grace?"
These words did Statius at the first incline
Slightly to smile; then thus with graver face:

STATIUS.

"Thine every word I take as love's dear sign.
In truth appearances oft do afford
False matter for conjecture, when, without
Regard to causes hidden or ignored,
Blind reason wanders from the truth in doubt.
Thy question certifies to me that thou,
Judging perchance from that round where I lay,
Think'st that on earth my sin was avarice. Now
Be thou corrected: Know I went astray
Far from that vice; its opposite excess
Yea for a thousand moons have purged away.
And had I not from spending turned to spare,
When I heard thee exclaiming in thy song
At human nature, almost in despair,

STATIUS.

And Statius answered: "Thou didst lead me first
Up to Parnassus; then my way didst light
To God, while in its grots I slaked my thirst.
Thou wast like one that walking in the night
Himself in darkness, beareth in his hand
A lamp to make their way behind him bright.

"When thou didst utter: 'Now begins a grand
New order of the ages! reappears
Justice on earth and unto man is given
The peace of Saturn, the primeval years!
Now a new progeny descends from heaven!'
Thou who to poesy—thou led'st me to Christ.
But let some colouring my theme enliven,
Lest my light drawing may not have sufficed;
That thou mayst see more than my sketch hath shown.
Already pregnant was the whole world then
With seeds of the true faith so largely sown
By heaven's eternal messengers to men;
And thy rapt word, which I have touched upon
Seemed from those preachers' lips to sound anew.
Hence I to visit them an usage formed,
And in my thought their sanctity so grew,
That when Domitian's persecution stormed,
Their griefs with pity did mine eyes bedew;

Oft did I help them while on earth I dwelt,
And their chaste customs did mine own so chide
That high disdain for other sects I felt;
And ere in song I led the Greeks beside
Those Theban streams I had in baptism knelt,
But long my Christian creed through fear did hide,
And paganism in outward action showed.
This lukewarmness hath kept me pacing more
Than my fourth century the circling road
Of the fourth terrace. Thee then I implore,
(While in ascending there is time to spare)
Thou who didst lift the veil mine eyes before,
That kept such blessings from me! Tell me where
Cæcilius dwells? Terence our ancient friend?
Plautus and Varro, are they damned down there?
Tell, if thou knowest, and in what ward penned?"

VIRGIL.

"These, with myself and Persius," Virgil said,
And many more, are with that Greek confined,
Whom above all the fostering Muses fed,
In the first circle of Hell's dungeon blind.
Oft in discourse we mention of the steep
Mount where our nurses evermore abide.
With us Euripides, Anacreon keep,
Simonides, Agatho, many a Greek beside,

10

Whose brows won laurels they did justly reap.
There many of thy people may be seen,
Argía, Deíphile, Antígone,

Ismène, mournful with her wonted mien;
The maid who showed Langia's fount, and she
Who 'called Tiresias father; Thetis there,
There with her sisters Deidamia glides.'

Both poets now were silent, and the pair
Free from the passage and its flinty sides,
Again stopped—round them eagerly to stare:
And now the first four handmaids of the day
Being left, the fifth, beside the chariot's beam,
Lifted its bright horn up the flaming way;
When my Guide: 'Tow'rds the cornice's extreme
We should, I think, bring the right shoulder near,
'Rounding the mountain as we wont to do.'
Thus usance was our sole instructor here;
And we went forward, the less doubting too
For the assenting of that worthy seer.

While they advanced, I listening paced alone,
And from their lofty language drew what force
Of intellect my poesy hath shown.
But soon made break in our serene discourse
A tree that in the middle way did rise.

II

With apples grateful both to smell and sight.
And as a fir diminisheth in size,
Bough after bough, even as it grows in height,
So this tree tapered down in adverse wise;
(I think, lest any one to climb it dream.)
And upon that side where our way was closed,
Fell from the lofty rock a limpid stream,
And o'er the leaves above its dews diffused.

Nigh to the tree then the two poets came,
And through the leaves a voice fell that of yore
Sounded: '*Of this fruit ye shall never eat.*'
Then added: 'Mary had in thought far more
To make the marriage honored and complete*
Than her own lips—that now for you implore:'
The women of old Rome could satisfy
Their taste with water; Daniel, too, controlled
Desire of meat, and wisdom gained thereby.
The primal age was beautiful as gold;
Hunger found acorns flavorous, and thirst
Nectar in every rivulet that rolled.
Honey and locusts were the food that nursed
The Baptist in the desert where he dwelt;
Hence is he glorious! and so near The First,
As through the Gospel is distinctly felt.

*At Cana of Galilee where she said,
"They have no wine."

1

Concord Summer School of Philosophy.

CONCORD SUMMER SCHOOL OF PHILOSOPHY.

HINTS TO STUDENTS FOR THE COURSE OF 1887.

It has seemed to the Faculty of the Concord School that the usefulness of the institution might be increased, if those who attend its sessions were to come prepared by previous reading to take part in the discussions. At the close of last session, therefore, it was resolved to prepare and circulate, at an early date, a programme of the lectures for the coming year, as far as it could be made out, and, along therewith, a list of books likely to be of value to intending students. At the same time, a committee was appointed to give direction and aid to such students as might choose to apply for the same.

COURSES OF LECTURES IN 1887.

The main subject of the lectures in 1887 will be ARISTOTLE *and his Philosophy, in its Relation to Modern Thought.* There will be three courses, — two general, and one special. The first, which will be given in the mornings of the session, will deal with Aristotle's philosophic system as a whole, endeavoring to give a complete and, as far as possible, an exhaustive, account of it, its origin and influence, and to determine the points of identity and difference between it and the thought of recent times, since Bacon, Descartes, and Locke. The other general course, which will be given in the evening, will treat, among other themes, of Aristotle's art doctrines, and particularly of his dramatic theory, comparing it with modern theories, and also comparing the Greek with the modern drama, especially with Shakespeare. The special course, or "Symposium," will be devoted to Ontology, and will endeavor to determine whether, and how far, such a science is possible, and how its possibility or impossibility must affect science, ethics, art, and religion. In this

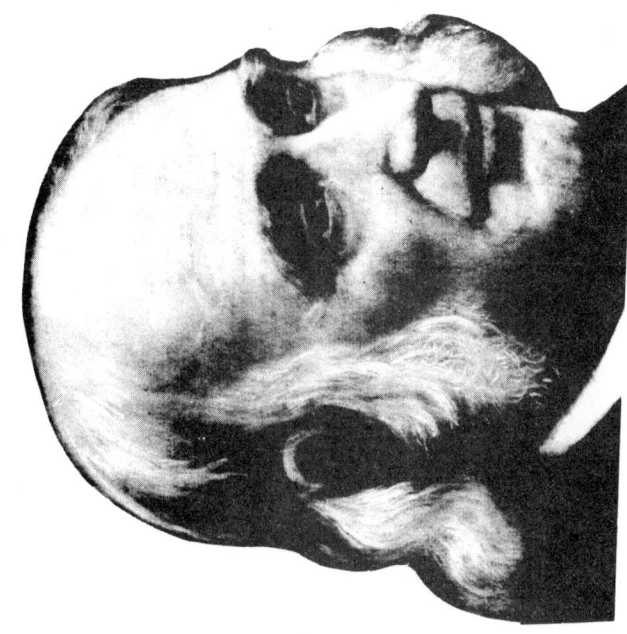

Concord Summer School of Philosophy.

course, also, the thought of Aristotle will be compared with that of our own time.

Aristotle's philosophy presents to us the ripest and most comprehensive thought of the ancient world. No other philosophy, at least in the Western world, ever exerted an influence so profound, extensive, and enduring. To the ancients, Aristotle was "Nature's private secretary;" to the Middle Ages, after 1150, he was simply "The Philosopher," or "The Master of those that know;" and, though, for a brief period, his sun was eclipsed by reactionary influences, philosophers of nearly all modern schools, as well as scientists and poets, have vied with each other in doing him honor. Among these may be named Leibniz, Lessing, Göthe, Hegel, Cuvier, Bain. A comprehensive knowledge of Aristotle's system can hardly fail to be productive of two advantages to the student. *First*, it must add greatly to his knowledge of philosophy; *second*, it must place him in a position to appreciate the character, the limitations, and the exaggerations of our current systems. Indeed, its many-sidedness is the best possible corrective for the one-sided thought of to-day. It is scientific without materialism, and spiritual without mysticism. While this is true with respect to Aristotle's system as a whole, it is especially true of those parts which treat of First Principles, Theory of Cognition, and Art.

The following is a provisional programme of all the courses. Any changes that may hereafter be rendered necessary will be in the direction of the list of "General Topics" appended to the programme adopted.

LECTURES AT THE CONCORD SCHOOL, 1887.

There will be two courses, morning and evening, beginning at 9.30 A. M., on Wednesday, July 13, 1887, — the topics being as follows:—

I. Twelve Morning Lectures on Aristotle.

Aristotle's Doctrine of Reason.
Aristotle's Theory of Sense-Perception, in the light of Recent Psychology.
Aristotle's Logical Treatises.

Concord Summer School of Philosophy.

Aristotle's Theory of the Syllogism, compared with that of Hegel.
Aristotle and the Scholastic Philosophy.
The Ethics of Aristotle.
Aristotle's History of Animals.
Bacon and Aristotle.
The Political Philosophy of Aristotle.
Social Science in Plato and Aristotle.
Aristotle and the Christian Church.
The Protestant Reaction against Aristotle.

II. Ten Evening Lectures on Dramatic Poetry.

The Poetics of Aristotle, in its Application to the Drama.
The Tragic Element in the Greek Drama and in the Norse Edda.
Shakespeare's Poetica.
The Divine Nemesis in Æschylus and Shakespeare.
The Collision of Individuals with Institutions in the Greek, and the English, Drama.
Women in Greek Tragedy and in the Elizabethan Drama.
Acting of Plays in Ancient and Modern Theatres.
Marlowe and his Successors.
Ford and Massinger.
Browning's Dramatic Genius.

III. Four brief Papers on Ontology, in two or three sessions.

———

GENERAL TOPICS FOR ADVANCED STUDENTS.

1. Aristotle's Life and Times. Condition of Science, Education, Morals, Religion, and Art.
2. Aristotle's Teachers. His Studies and his Relations to previous Thinkers, Greek and foreign (Hindu).
3. Aristotle's Writings, their Nature, their History, and their Influence in Ancient Times.
4. Aristotle in the Mediæval World, — among Jews, Syrians, Arabs, and Schoolmen. Reaction against Aristotle; its Causes.
5. Aristotle's conception of Science, its Divisions and Limits, compared with the conceptions of Positivists, — Comte, Spencer, etc.
6. Aristotle's Scientific Method compared with those of Bacon, Descartes, and Hegel.

Concord Summer School of Philosophy.

7. Aristotle's Logic compared with the Logics of Hegel and Mill.
8. Aristotle's Psychology compared with that of the modern English School, as to Method and Results.
9. Aristotle's Ethics compared with the more important Systems of Modern Times,—those of Kant, Rosmini, etc.
10. Aristotle's Theory of the State (particularly in relation to the Individual), compared with Modern Views on the same subject.
11. Aristotle's Views on Education and on the State's Relation to it, compared with Modern Views on the same subject.
12. Aristotle's Views on Profit and Interest, compared with Modern Views.
13. Aristotle as a Natural Scientist,—Astronomer, Physiologist, Zoölogist, etc.,—and his effect upon the progress of Modern Science.

ARISTOTLE'S ÆSTHETICS.

1. Aristotle's Doctrine of the nature of the Art-Activity, and its relation to the other powers of the Mind, compared with modern notions.
2. Aristotle's Doctrine of the purpose of Art, and particularly of the Drama (κάθαρσις, purification), compared with modern notions (Lessing, Göthe, etc.).
3. The Greek and English Dramas, their Origin (social and religious conditions), Form, and Function. Character and Plot.
4. Tragic Guilt in the Greek Tragedians, in Shakespeare, and in Göthe.
5. Orestes and Hamlet.
6. The three Iphigenias (of Euripides, Racine, Göthe).
7. Medea and Brunhild. (The Ancient and the Modern Woman in Art.)

THEORY OF COGNITION AND ONTOLOGY.

1. Aristotle's Theory of Cognition, compared with those of Locke, Berkeley, and Kant.
2. The relation between Theory of Cognition and Ontology. How Modern Phenomenalism and Associational Psychology make Ontology impossible.
3. Aristotle's Doctrine of Form and Matter, and its relation to Modern Thought, especially to Atomism.
4. Aristotle's Doctrine of Potence and Act, and its relation to the modern doctrines of the Thing-in-itself and the Unknowable.
5. On Being, and its various significations. Its relation to Intellect.
6. Aristotle's Doctrine of Causes, compared with modern doctrines.

Concord Summer School of Philosophy.

Suggestions to those beginning the study of Aristotle.

I. THE METAPHYSICS.

1. Study Aristotle's definitions and descriptions of real being (οὐσία, variously translated "essence," "substance," "true nature," "entity," "being," "real substance," "subsistence," "essential nature," etc.). See Book VI. ch. 3, where its definitions are inventoried; as (a) Formal Cause (τὸ τί ἦν εἶναι, i. e. the totality of distinctions that belong to the nature of the thing); (b) the Universal (τὸ καθόλου); (c) the Generic (τὸ γένος); and (d) the Subject or Thing-in-Itself (τὸ ὑποκείμενον). (See Book IV. chapter 28; Book VII. chap. 1.) Compare these definitions with the definition given in Book III. of The Physics, chapter 5 of The Categories, and note the discrimination given in the latter between first and second "real beings."

2. Study in like manner the definitions and descriptions of Formal Cause (τὸ εἶδος or τὸ τί ἦν εἶναι), noting its inclusion or exclusion of the other causes; namely (a) Efficient Cause of Motion (τὸ ὅθεν ἡ ἀρχὴ τῆς κινήσεως), or (b) Final Cause or Purpose (τὸ οὗ ἕνεκεν). (Book I. ch. 3; Book VI. chs. 7 and 17.) Does the Formal Cause always denote energy?

3. Note that definition (ὁρισμός) is the principle (λόγος) of the Formal Cause, and inquire whether εἶδος and ἐνέργεια are identical (Book VII. ch. 2), and whether energy is also Final Cause or Purpose (τὸ οὗ ἕνεκεν). (See Book VIII. ch. 5.)

4. Note the agreement and difference of the Material Cause (ἡ ὕλη), the Subject (τὸ ὑποκείμενον), and Potentiality (δύναμις, translated also "capacity," "potence," etc.). Consider in connection with these the doctrine that Form and Energy are necessary to give any reality to these categories.

5. Read Books X. and XI. together as the Theology of Aristotle. Noting the three kinds of change (Book X. ch. 11),—(a) from Subject to Subject, (b) Generation, and (c) Corruption, compare this with the statement that motion affects only two categories,—quantity and quality (Book X. ch. 12). Note also that movement and change are here discriminated, change

Concord Summer School of Philosophy.

having four species; but that there are no universal causes in nature (Book XI. ch.5); that all causes are in energies which are real beings (οὐσίαι), and that "energies" precede all movements. Compare with *De Anima*, Book I., ch. 3.

6. Consider the doctrine that all motion originates in an unmoved first principle which is of necessity eternal (Book XI. ch. 6); that the unmoved eternal energy which is presupposed by every movement or change in the world, is pure self-knowing (τὸ θεωρεῖν), (a living personal divine reason). (Book XI. ch. 7.) (This seventh chapter, the most wonderful chapter in Greek philosophy.)

7. The earth and the stars receive their movement from the divine energy (Book XI. ch. 8).

8. Study together Books IX., XII., and XIII., as directed against Pythagoras and Plato,—a refutation of the principle of contrariety or polarity as world-principle, and the discussion of what constitutes real independent existence (οὐσία), energy (Is energy the unity of formal, efficient, and final causes?) being requisite to true individuality. Does contrariety always presuppose energy as its ground? (Book XIII., and *Physics*, Book I. ch. 4.)

9. The true first principle, the Good (τὸ ἀγαθόν) (Book XIII. ch. 5). Is "the Good" understood to mean that which helps others and affirms the being and individuality of others,—i. e. is it "altruism"? How is the doctrine that all evil arises from matter (ὕλη), and is good *in potentia*, to be understood?

10. Use Book IV. as a glossary, always comparing definitions given there with those given elsewhere.

II. THE LOGICAL TREATISES.

1. Note the ten Categories and their definitions, especially the definitions of οὐσία and its two kinds, and of κίνησις with its six species (*The Categories*, chs. 4, 5, and 14).

2. Note the doctrine regarding universals (τὰ καθόλου) and singulars (τὰ καθ' ἕκαστον) (*Interpretation*, ch. 7); also of necessary judgments as referring to persistent energies (ch. 9).

3. In the *Prior Analytics*, learn carefully the doctrine of the three figures and fourteen valid modes of the syllogism.

Concord Summer School of Philosophy.

4. Inquire into the practical use of these figures in cognition. (a) Do we not always use the second figure in recognizing the object of sense-perception as belonging to classes already known by us? (b) Do we not use the first figure after the second figure? Having recognized the class to which the object belongs, do we draw out by inference the store of experience already preserved in our knowledge of the class? (c) Finally, inquire as to the use of the third figure in the identification of causal activities in nature,—of two predicates to an object, whether one may be identified as cause and the other as effect,—and whether this figure is the logical instrument of discovery? (*Prior Anal.* Book I. chs. 1–7.) Consider whether the invalid modes of the second and third figures are not by far the most useful in obtaining knowledge.

5. In the *Posterior Analytics* (Book I. ch. 24), note the hint as to the relation of the Universal to the causal principle, and of particular knowledge to general knowledge.

6. The definition of Science (Book I. chs. 27, 28, 29, 30), and the asserted impossibility of reaching science through the senses.

7. The four things investigated by science: (a) that a thing is (τὸ ὅτι); (b) why it is (τὸ διότι); (c) if it is (εἰ ἔστι); and (d) what it is (τί ἐστι). (*Posterior Analytics*, Book II. ch. 1.)

8. How definition differs from demonstration (*Posterior Analytics*, Book II. ch. 3), and that the middle term expresses the definition (*ibid.* ch. 4). On the whole subject of definition, see chapter 13 (*ibid.*); and how the Universal arises in the mind, chapter 19 (ch. 15, Tauchnitz ed.).

9. Study the distinction between universal and dialectic syllogisms (*Topica*, Book I. ch. 1), and inquire whether and how probabilities can be elevated into certainties.

10. Note the important logical principles in Book I. chs. 6, 7, 8, and 9, regarding the subversion or overthrow of definition; the predication of the identical; the reference of all questions to definition, genus, property, and accident; and the limitation of definition to the genera of the ten categories.

11. Induction in chapter 12 of Book I. defined as a progression from singulars to universals; and its difference from the syllogism.

III. The Psychology. *De Anima.*

1. Note that motion (κίνησις) includes locomotion (φορά), alteration or change (ἀλλοίωσις), decay (φθίσις), and increase or growth (αὔξησις); and, since these all involve potentiality not realized, while the soul is pure energy without potentiality, the soul is not any kind of motion or change (Book I. ch. 3).

2. Note the relations of the categories ἐνέργεια, ἐντελέχεια (first and second grades of the latter), and δύναμις as used in Book II. ch. 1, in defining the soul. Does "independent individuality" express ἐντελέχεια? Compare science (ἐπιστήμη) with immediate insight (τὸ θεωρεῖν) (Book II. ch. 1). Does Aristotle's definition (Book II. ch. Γ) make the body and soul inseparable?

3. Consider (Book II. ch. 2) the assertion that the soul is *form* rather than *matter*, and that True Being (οὐσία) is form (εἶδος), because matter (ὕλη) is only the *potentiality* (δύναμις), while form is the *entelechy.*

4. Distinguish the three stages of psychic existence: (*a*) nutritive (τὸ θρεπτικόν), (*b*) sensitive (τὸ αἰσθητικόν), and (*c*) rational (διανοητικόν) (Book II. ch. 2), noting especially what is said in regard to the sensitive, namely, that it receives the *form* only but does not receive the *matter* of the perceived object into itself, — and inquiring whether this doctrine does not make even sense-perception a self-activity or energy. Remember in this connection the function of the second figure of the syllogism, already adverted to above, namely, that it is by the recognition of the class (a universal) as identical with what is already known, that any sense-perception at all takes place.

5. Most important is the further doctrine that objects require a rational nature in order to be known at all (Book III. ch. 4). The act of recognition through the second figure just alluded to could not take place unless the objects possessed predicates identical with *a priori* categories of ·the mind.

6. The doctrine of the reason (νοῦς) (Book III. chs. 4, 5, 6). Reason is twofold: active (τὸ ποιοῦν) (Book III. ch. 5, sect. 2) and passive (παθητικός) (Book III. ch. 5, sect. 2). The active

as creator of all things (τῷ πάντα ποιεῖν) because the perceptibility of objects proves their origin from a rational creator or creative cause (τὸ αἴτιον καὶ ποιητικόν).

The passive reason has the power to become all things (τῷ πάντα γίνεσθαι), that is to say, to assume objectivity in all cases of sense-perception, or to be used in all examples of the second figure.

7. But the active reason is separable from the body, and immortal and eternal (Book III. ch. 5), and is always active, though we are unconscious of its unbroken continuity in action, because it is not affected by objects (ἀπαθές), while the memory, sense-perception, and imagination, which make up the νοῦς παθητικός, are perishable. (Why? Because we continually proceed from ἐπιστήμη to θεωρεῖν, that is to say, from the consideration of particular facts up to the familiar knowledge of causes and principles, which we know apart from the examples that illustrate them. The knowledge which by memory has to hold fast its illustrative facts does not yet see the principle clearly, and its knowledge is perishable, — not hereafter, but here. Such knowledge as is held in the memory is essentially perishable, though it will long outlast this earthly life.) This active reason is the *entelechy* of human beings — their true individuality — and not a mere incarnation of a general World-Soul, because it is required in each case to make the act of cognition possible, even in the lowest sense-perception (καὶ ἄνευ τούτου οὐθὲν νοεῖ) (Book III. ch. 5, at end). The active reason is the principle of individuation; therefore, our conscious ego. For the fact that we attain to insight (θεωρεῖν) proves this. Our ability to think pure·form as found in the categories, which are universals and devoid of matter derived from experience, and are without images from time and space, is an exercise of our true individuality (ἐντελέχεια), the active reason.

IV. The Ethics.—(Nicomachean.)

1. Note, in connection with themes already mentioned, the discussion of true science (Book VI. ch. 6).

The reason (νοῦς) as the source of principles (ἀρχαί) (Book

VI. ch. 3), and the distinction of the understanding ($\delta\iota\acute{a}\nu o\iota a$) from the reason ($\nu o\hat{\upsilon}\varsigma$).

2. Reason the principle of individuation (that which makes us persons) (Book X.); and the source of the highest happiness of man as well as of the gods is $\theta\epsilon\omega\rho\acute{\iota}a$.

3. For the ethical content of the work study chiefly Book III., which sets forth the doctrine of deliberate choice ($\pi\rho oa\acute{\iota}\rho\epsilon\sigma\iota\varsigma$), and Book II. for the doctrine of the Mean ($\mu\epsilon\sigma\acute{o}\tau\eta\varsigma$).

V. THE PHYSICS.

1. Subjects treated elsewhere, especially in Books X. and XI. of the *Metaphysics*, are to be studied also in the *Physics* on account of the explicitness of treatment here. The four causes (Book II. ch. 3; see *Metaphysics*, Book I., and *De Anima*, Book II. ch. 1). A thorough discussion of movement ($\kappa\acute{\iota}\nu\eta\sigma\iota\varsigma$) and of its relation to potentiality ($\delta\acute{\upsilon}\nu a\mu\iota\varsigma$) is given in the Third Book, together with a polemic against the *infinite* ($\tau\grave{o}\ \ddot{a}\pi\epsilon\iota\rho o\nu$) in the sense of the *indefinite*. In Book IV. ch. 12, note the important observation that all that has potentiality belongs to time.

2. Motion from its own nature is derivative, and always presupposes an origin beyond itself, and a first mover, that is itself unmoved (Book VII. ch. 1, and Book VIII. chs. 3, 4, 5, 6). Motion must not be predicated of thoughts, of ideas, or of eternal things, but only of objects of sense-perception (Book VII. ch. 3). Eternal motion is circular motion (Book VIII. chs. 1, 2, 8, 9, 10).

3. Note especially what is said of Time in Book IV. (chapters 10 to 14).

VI. THE POETICS.

1. All poetry Imitation (chapters 1, 2, 3). Inquire into the meaning of $\mu\acute{\iota}\mu\eta\sigma\iota\varsigma$ (ch. 5) and $\mu\iota\mu\epsilon\hat{\iota}\sigma\theta a\iota$, as used by Plato (see *Laws*, Z 812 c; *Republic*, Book III. 394 b; *Sophist*, 265 A), and in this work of Aristotle's. Does it mean impersonations only; or does it hint of the deeper activity of man,—of his symbol-making capacity, a mythopoeic faculty, and thus the fundamental art-faculty?

2. Study chapter 6 on the parts of tragedy, and the famous definition of it which states its object to be the purification of man ($\kappa\acute{a}\theta a\rho\sigma\iota\varsigma$) from like passions to those represented, by pity and fear. Note that this *katharsis* takes place through the vicarious nature of human experience, or the power of learning through the spectacle of another's experience. (See *Politics*, Book VIII. ch. 7.)

3. A dramatic whole and tragic action (ch. 7). The requirements of the plot and the unity of the drama (ch. 8). Parts of a tragedy (ch. 12), and the essentials of a tragic plot (chs. 13 and 14). The significance of $\tau\grave{o}\ \phi o\beta\epsilon\rho\acute{o}\nu$ and $\tau\grave{o}\ \grave{\epsilon}\lambda\epsilon\epsilon\iota\nu\acute{o}\nu$.

4. Poetry more philosophical and worthy of attention than history (ch. 9). Trace out the comparison,—history treating of $\tau\grave{a}\ \kappa a\theta'\ \ddot{\epsilon}\kappa a\sigma\tau o\nu$, and poetry of $\tau\grave{a}\ \kappa a\theta\acute{o}\lambda o\upsilon$.

5. Note that deliberate choice ($\pi\rho oa\acute{\iota}\rho\epsilon\sigma\iota\varsigma$) (see *Nicomachean Ethics*, Book III.) is essential to the characters portrayed in tragedy. Their disposition and behavior, their manner of life ($\tau\grave{o}\ \mathring{\eta}\theta o\varsigma$), their ethical character, should be based on free-will, or else they cannot be made responsible for their fate. (ch. 15.)

6. Note the four kinds of tragedy (ch. 18); the description of epic poetry; and the distinction between epopee and tragedy.

VII. PARTS OF ANIMALS.

1. The best statements on the method of natural science, its subject and form, are to be found in the treatise on the *Parts of Animals* ($\pi\epsilon\rho\grave{\iota}\ \zeta\acute{\omega}\omega\nu\ \mu o\rho\acute{\iota}\omega\nu$) (Book I. ch. 1). Investigation should look especially to the form, but the soul is something higher than the form. The universal before the particular, and the cause before the effect, should be studied in order to find true science (Book I. ch. 5).

2. The principle of division and classification is discussed in chapter 2, and the defects of dichotomy and the principle of contrariety, or polarity, as a basis of classification are exposed — "there can be no genera in the negative." The true basis should be sought in the idea of genus and species (looking at the productive causes of variety). The advantages of this

method over that which proceeds from the individuals. (The whole of the first book, but especially chapters 1, 2, and 5.)

3. Nothing in nature so insignificant as to be unworthy of attention (ἐν πᾶσι γὰρ τοῖς φυσικοῖς ἔνεστί τι θαυμαστόν) (Book I. ch. 5).

VIII. DE COELO.

1. In the work on the heavens (περὶ οὐρανοῦ), note the quantitative aspect as the essence of body (Book I. ch. 1); circular movement as the true and highest form of motion. (Since movement is always impelled by an outside mover, it must be essentially of a relative character; and motion with constant relation to a fixed point must be circular.) (Book I. ch. 1, and Book II. chs. 3, 4, 5.) (The most important thoughts on this subject are to be found in the *Metaphysics* (Book XI. ch. 8).)

2. Note what is said about death as appertaining to all that existence which has been generated, or caused through another (Book I. ch. 12).

3. Of great interest is the reference (*De Coelo*, Book II. ch. 14) to proofs of the earth's rotundity and its size,—its shadow on the moon; the method of measuring a degree on the meridian by the altitude of given stars; and the circumference of the earth estimated at over 40,000 miles (400,000 stadia = 45,200 miles): nevertheless Aristotle regards the earth as one of the smallest of the heavenly bodies.

4. In the treatise on Meteorology (Book I.) there is a discussion of the relation of terrestrial movements to celestial.

IX. POLITICS.

1. In Aristotle's *Politics* note in Book IV. (chs. 14, 15, 16; or 12, 13, 14, Tauchnitz ed.) the three departments necessary to a State: (*a*) the Deliberative Assembly (ἐκκλησία or τὸ βουλευόμενον περὶ κοινῶν); (*b*) the Executive Officers of the state (αἱ ἀρχαί); (*c*) the Judiciary (τὸ δικάζον).

2. Do we see in these departments Aristotle's notion of the three essential logical categories which constitute the fundamental form (εἶδος or τὸ τί ἦν εἶναι) of the intellect,—to wit, (*a*) the Universal (τὸ καθόλου), or the legislative department that an-

nounces the general laws; (*b*) the Particular (τὸ μέρει), the law-applying power or the judiciary; (*c*) the Singular or Individual (τὸ καθ' ἕκαστον), the executive which sums up the personal might of the state in the form of the individual officer?

3. Note, however, that the ἐκκλησία, besides its proper legislative duties of making laws, declaring war, concluding treaties, also exercised, according to Aristotle, judicial functions, inasmuch as it pronounced death-sentences, banishments, confiscations, and impeachments. The executive department (αἱ ἀρχαί) also has legislative functions (Book IV. ch. 12), (βουλεύεσθαί τε περὶ τινῶν), and judicial functions (κρῖναι), as well as purely executive ones, though the latter are regarded by Aristotle as peculiarly its province (ἐπιτάξαι καὶ μάλιστα τοῦτο). (The necessity of the complete separation and independence of these departments has been realized only in modern times.)

14   Concord Summer School of Philosophy.

BIBLIOGRAPHY.

In the preparation of the following list of books, no attempt has been made to give an exhaustive Bibliography. The purpose has been to name some of the more serviceable works, and, among these, those most easily obtained. It is unfortunate that English literature is poor in works on Aristotle. This must be the excuse for the naming of books in other languages.

In preparing for the above courses, the student must first acquire a general notion of Aristotle and his system. To this end he may consult —

*GRANT (Sir Alexander), Aristotle (Edinburgh, Blackwood, 1877, 12mo).

LEWES (Geo. H.), Aristotle. A Chapter from the History of Science (London, Smith, 1864, 8vo. A superficial work).

GROTE (George), Aristotle (London, Murray, 1872, 2 vols. 8vo. Contains a good Life of Aristotle).

BIESE (Franz), Die Philosophie des Aristoteles in ihrem inneren Zusammenhang, etc. (Berlin, Reimer, 1835, 2 vols. 8vo. Written from an Hegelian standpoint).

*ROSMINI (Antonio), Aristotele Esposto ed Esaminato (Turin, Società Editrice, 1858, 8vo. Written in an adverse spirit, but very able).

. Along with these books may be read the chapters on Aristotle in the best histories of philosophy, * Hegel's, * Schwegler's, *Erdmann's, Zeller's (Greek Phil.), and *Ueberweg's. Of Schwegler's history there are two translations, one by Dr. Hutchison Stirling, and one by Dr. Julius H. Seelye. *Zeller's History of Greek Philosophy (translation by Sarah F. Alleyne, O. J. Reichel, Alfred Goodwin, and Evelyn Abbott, London, 1876 to 1886, 12mo, 6 vols. so far) contains the best existing summary of Aristotle's Philosophy. The translation of *Ueberweg's Manual, by Prof. Geo. S. Morris (New York, Scribner, 1872-4, 2 vols. large 8vo), is a work which no student of philosophy can afford to be without. It contains a good Aristotelian Bibliography.

On the works of Aristotle, and their history in ancient times, may be read —

ROSE (Valentin), De Aristotelis Librorum Ordine et Auctoritate (Berlin, Reimer, 1854, 8vo), and Aristoteles Pseudepigraphus (Leipzig, Teubner, 1863, 8vo).

*HEITZ (Emil), Die verlornen Schriften des Aristoteles (Leipzig, Teubner, 1865, 8vo).

*STAHR (Adolf), Aristotelia (Halle, Waisenhaus, 1830-2, 2 vols. 8vo. Contains an excellent life of Aristotle, and the history of his writings in the ancient world).

*BERNAYS (Jacob), Die Dialoge des Aristoteles in ihrem Verhältnis zu seinen übrigen Werken (Berlin, Hertz, 1863, 4to, pp. 178).

On the history and influence of Aristotle's works in the Middle Ages may be read —

*JOURDAIN (Am.), Recherches Critiques sur l'Age et l'Origine des Traductions latines d'Aristote et sur les Commentaires grecs ou arabes employés par les Docteurs scolastiques, Paris, 1819 and 1843, 8vo (Ger. Trans. by Stahr, Halle, 1831).

HAURÉAU (Barth.), De la Philosophie Scolastique (Paris, 1872, 2 vols. 8vo).

PRANTL (Carl), Geschichte der Logik im Abendlande (Leipzig, Hirzel, 1855 sqq., 4 vols. 8vo).

*SCHNEID (Math.), Aristoteles in der Scholastik (Eichstät, Hugendubel, 1875, 8vo).

Concord Summer School of Philosophy.   15

TALAMO (Salvatore), L'Aristotelismo della Scolastica nella Storia della Filosofia (Naples, Fibreno, 1863, 8vo. There is a later edition).

The student, after having acquainted himself with the general outline of Aristotle's system, should turn to his works and read the chief of them. Of the extant works of Aristotle there are two complete editions readily accessible, viz: —

Aristoteles Græce. Ex Recognitione IMMAN. BEKKERI (Berlin, Reimer, 1831-70, 5 vols. 4to. Known as the Berlin edition. Vols. I and II contain the Greek text; Vol. III, a Latin translation; Vol. IV, Scholia; Vol. V, the Scholia of Syrianus, the Fragments of Aristotle's lost works, and an extensive and most valuable Index Aristotelicus).

Aristotelis Opera Omnia Græce et Latine, cum Indice Nominum et Rerum absolutissimo (Paris, Didot, 6 vols. 4to. This is known as the Paris edition. The very exhaustive Index is in Latin, and the references are to the Latin translation).

There is no complete English translation of Aristotle's Works, that by Thomas Taylor having no claim to rank as such. There are, however, translations of many of the works which intending students will find it useful to read. These are the best editions and most accessible translations of these.

(1) The Logic, (2) The Physics, (3) The De Cœlo, (4) The Meteorologica, (5) The Psychology (De Anima), (6) The History of Animals, (7) The Metaphysics, (8) The Ethics (Nicomachean), (9) The Politics, (10) The Poetics. The following are the best editions and most accessible translations of these.

(1) The LOGIC. By Theodor Waitz, Greek Scholia and Latin notes (Leipzig, Hahn, 1844, 2 vols. 8vo). Translation by O. F. Owen (Bohn's Classical Library, 2 vols. 12mo. Has notes and analysis, and contains the very important Introduction of Porphyry).

(2) The PHYSICS. *By Carl Prantl, Greek text with German translation (Leipzig, Wilhelm Engelmann, 1854, 12mo), and by J. B. St. Hilaire, Greek text with French translation (Paris, Durand, 1862, 8vo).

(3) The DE CŒLO and GENESIS AND CORRUPTION. By Carl Prantl, Greek and German (Leipzig, W. Engelmann, 1857, 12mo); and by J. B. St. Hilaire, Greek and French (Paris, Durand, 1866, 8vo).

(4) The METEOROLOGICS. By J. L. Ideler, Greek and Latin, with commentary (Leipzig, Vogel, 1834-6, 2 vols. large 8vo), and by J. B. St. Hilaire, Greek and French (Paris, Durand, 1867, 8vo).

(5) The PSYCHOLOGY. By F. Adolf Trendelenburg, text with Latin notes, very valuable, (Jena, Walz, 1833, 8vo; new edition by Belger); by Adolf Torstrik, text and Latin notes (Berlin, Weidmann, 1862, 8vo), and by * Edwin Wallace, text, English translation, introduction, and notes (New York, Macmillan, 1881, 8vo). There is a French translation by J. R. St. Hilaire (Paris, Durand, 1846, 8vo). There are several German translations, that in Von Kirchmann's Philosophische Bibliothek being the most accessible. C. Collier's Eng. Trans. (London, Macmillan, 1855) is poor.

(6) The HISTORY OF ANIMALS (Thierkunde). By *Dr. H. Aubert and Dr. Fr. Wimmer, text, German translation, and notes (Leipzig, Engelmann, 1868, 2 vols. 8vo. A most valuable work). English Translation by Richard Cresswell (Bohn's Classical Library).

(7) The METAPHYSICS. By *Albert Schwegler, text, German translation and notes (Tübingen, Fues, 1847-8, 4 vols. 8vo.), and by *Hermann Bonitz, text and Latin notes (Bonn, Marcus, 1848, 8vo). There is an English translation by John H. McMahon in Bohn's Classical Library; but it is not of a high order.

16   Concord Summer School of Philosophy.

(8) The ETHICS. By K. L. Michelet, text and Latin notes (Berlin, Schleisinger, 1848, 2 vols. 8vo.); by Hermann Rassow (Weimar, 1862–68). There is a German translation by Adolf Stahr (Stuttgart, Krais & Hoffmann, 1863, 16mo); a French translation by J. B. St. Hilaire (Paris, Durand, 1856); an *English translation, with notes and essays, by Sir Alexander Grant (London, Longmans, Green & Co., 1866, 2 vols. 8vo.), and another by F. W. Browne in Bohn's Classical Library. There are several others, in German and English, the best of which is that by F. H. Peters (London, Kegan Paul & Co., 1881).

(9) The POLITICS. By Fr. Susemihl. Two editions; one with text and Wilhelm von Moerbeke's barbarous Latin translation (Leipzig, Teubner, 1872, 8vo), *another with introduction, German translation, and notes (Leipzig, Engelmann, 1879, 2 vols. 12mo). There is a French translation by J. B. St. Hilaire (Paris, Durand, 1848, 8vo.), an *English translation with notes, by Prof. B. Jowett (Oxford, Clarendon Press, 1885, 2 vols. 8vo.), and another (including the *Economics*) by E. Walford, in Bohn's Classical Library.

(10) The POETICS. By Joh. Vahlen, text and notes (Berlin, Vahlen, 1874, 8vo. Best text); by Fried. Ueberweg, with text, German translation, and notes (Berlin, Heiman, 1869–70, 12mo. The translation and notes belong to Von Kirchmann's *Philosophische Bibliothek*); by *Fr. Susemihl, text, German translation, and notes (Leipzig, Engelmann, 1865, 12mo.) and by Moriz Schmidt, text and German translation (Jena, Dufft, 1875, 8vo). There is *an excellent German version by Adolf Stahr (Stuttgart, Krais & Hoffmann, 1860, 16mo). There is a French translation by J. B. St. Hilaire (Paris, Durand, 1858, 8vo), and another, facing the text, in M. E. Egger's *Essai sur l'Histoire de la Critique chez les Grecs* (Paris, Durand, 1849, 8vo). There is an English translation by Thomas Twining (London, Hansard, 1812, 2 vols. 8vo.), and another (with the *Rhetoric*), in Bohn's Classical Library. There is no good English translation. Compare James Harris, *Three Treatises. The First concerning Art. The Second concerning Music, Painting, and Poetry. The Third concerning Happiness*, in *Works*, London, 1841. The first and second treatises give the substance of Aristotle's *Poetics*, and the third gives the chief thought of his *Ethics*.

In reading these works of Aristotle, the student will often need external help. In addition to those already named, the following works, selected from an almost infinite number, are especially recommended.

I. For the General Course.

*WALLACE (Edwin), *Outlines of the Philosophy of Aristotle*, Oxford and London, James Parker & Co., 1880. This small book contains an admirable statement, in brief form, of the chief doctrines of Aristotle, and appends the classic passages from the original on which this statement is based.

HARRIS (James), *Hermes, or a Philosophical Inquiry concerning Universal Grammar*, in *Works*, Vincent, London, 1841. Book III. contains a good presentation of Aristotelianism.

*EUCKEN (Rudolf), *Die Methode der Aristotelischen Forschung in ihrem Zusammenhang mit den philosophischen Grundprincipien des Aristoteles dargestellt* (Berlin, Weidmann, 1872, 8vo).

TRENDELENBURG (F. A.), *Elementa Logices Aristotelee* (Berlin, Bethge, 1868, 12mo. *Erläuterungen* in German, 1861): *Geschichte der Kategorienlehre* (Berlin, Bethge, 1846, 8vo).

Concord Summer School of Philosophy.   17

EBERHARD (Eugen), *Die Aristotelische Definition der Seele und ihr Werth für die Gegenwart* (Berlin, Adolf, 1868, 8vo). P.

SCHELL (Hermann), *Die Einheit des Seelenlebens, aus den Principien der Aristotelischen Philosophie entwickelt* (Freiburg im Breisgau, Scheuble, 1873, 8vo).

*BRENTANO (Franz), *Die Psychologie des Aristoteles, insbesondere seine Lehre vom Noûs Poïŋtikós* (Mayence, Kirchheim, 1867, 8vo).

WALTER (Julius), *Die Lehre von der praktischen Vernunft in der Griechischen Philosophie* (Jena, Mauke, 1874, 8vo).

*TEICHMÜLLER (Gustav), *Die praktische Vernunft bei Aristoteles* (Vol. III. of *Neue Studien zur Geschichte der Begriffe*, Gotha, Perthes, 1879, 8vo).

HENKEL (Hermann), *Studien zur Geschichte der Griechischen Lehre vom Staat* (Leipzig, Teubner, 1872, 8vo).

VAN DER REST (E.), *Platon et Aristote. Essai sur les Commencements de la Science politique* (Brussels, Mayolez, 1876, 8vo).

*ONCKEN (Wilhelm), *Die Staatslehre des Aristoteles in historisch-politischen Umrissen. Ein Beitrag zur Geschichte der hellenischen Staatsidee und zur Einführung in die Aristotelische Politik* (Leipzig, Engelmann, 1870–5, 2 vols. 8vo).

*KAPP (Alexander), *Aristoteles' Staats-paedagogik als Erziehungslehre für den Staat und die Einzelnen. Aus den Quellen dargestellt.* (Hamm, Schulz, 1887, 8vo).

AQUINAS (Thomas), *De Vitio Usura*, in *Summa Theologica*, Pt. II, Div. I, quest. LXXVIII.

CUNNINGHAM (W.), *The Growth of English Industry and Commerce.* (Cambridge, University Press, 1886. Book 11, Ch. 8, Sec. 36. The Immorality of Usury.)

LORSCHEID (J.), *Aristoteles' Einfluss auf die Entwickelung der Chemie* (Münster, Coppenrath, 1872, 8vo). P.

QUAIN (Richard), *On some Defects in General Education* (London, Macmillan, 1870, 12mo).

BONITZ (F.), *Ueber die Kategorien des Aristoteles. Aus dem Maihefte des Jahrganges 1853 der Sitzungsberichte der philos.-histor. Classe der Kais. Akademie der Wissenschaften, besonders abgedruckt.*

HEYDER (Carl L. W.), *Kritische Darstellung und Vergleichung der Methoden Aristotelischer und Hegelischer Dialektik. Erste Abtheilung: Die Methodologie der früheren griechischen Systeme* (Erlangen, 1845).

*EUCKEN (Rudolf), *Ueber die Bedeutung der Aristotelischen Philosophie für die Gegenwart* (Berlin, Weidmann, 1872, 8vo). P.

II. For the Course on Aesthetics.

*TEICHMÜLLER (Gustav), *Aristoteles' Philosophie der Kunst* (Halle, Barthel, 1869, 12mo). *Die Kunstlehre des Aristoteles* (Jena, Dufft, 1876, 8vo). Contains a Bibliography of the famous Katharsis-controversy.

REINKENS (J. H.), *Aristoteles über Kunst, besonders über Tragödie* (Vienna, Braumüller, 1870, 8vo).

*BERNAYS (Jacob), *Grundzüge der verlornen Abhandlung des Aristoteles über Wirkung der Tragödie* (Breslau, Trewendt, 1857, 4to. It was this essay that started the Katharsis-controversy). P.

STAHR (Adolf), *Aristoteles und die Wirkung der Tragödie* (Berlin, Guttentag, 1869, 8vo). P.

GOTSCHLICH (Emil), *Lessing's Aristotelische Studien und der Einfluss derselben auf seine Werke* (Berlin, Vahlen, 1876, 8vo). P.

Concord Summer School of Philosophy. 19

ENCOMIA.

Aristotle, Nature's private secretary, dipping his pen in intellect. — *Eusebius, Suidas.*

Aristotle, in my opinion, stands almost alone in philosophy. — *Cicero.*

Wherever the divine Wisdom of Aristotle has opened its mouth, the wisdom of others, it seems to me, is to be disregarded. — *Dante.*

I could soon get over Aristotle's *prestige*, if I could only get over his reasons. — *Lessing.*

If, now in my quiet days, I had youthful faculties at my command, I should devote myself to Greek, in spite of all the difficulties I know : Nature and Aristotle should be my sole study. It is beyond all conception what, that man espied, saw, beheld, remarked, observed. To be sure he was sometimes hasty in his explanations ; but are we not so, even to the present day ? — *Göthe* (at 78).

If the proper earnestness prevailed in philosophy, nothing would be more worthy of establishing than a foundation for a special lectureship on Aristotle ; for he is, of all the ancients, the most worthy of study. — *Hegel.*

Aristotle was one of the richest and most comprehensive geniuses that ever appeared — a man beside whom no age has an equal to place. — *Hegel.*

Physical philosophy occupies itself with the general qualities of matter. It is an abstraction from the dynamic manifestations of the different kinds of matter ; and even where its foundations were first laid, in the eight books of Aristotle's *Physical Lectures,* all the phenomena of nature are represented as the motive vital activity of a universal world-force. — *Alexander von Humboldt.*

It was characteristic of this extraordinary genius to work at both ends of the scientific process. He was alike a devotee to facts and a master of the highest abstractions. — *Alexander Bain.*

Aristotle is the *Father of the Inductive Method,* and he is so for two reasons. First, he theoretically recognized its essential principles with a clearness, and exhibited them with a conviction, which strike the modern man with amazement, and then he made the first comprehensive attempt to apply them to all the science of the Greeks. — *Wilhelm Oncken.*

18   Concord Summer School of Philosophy.

*GOEBEL (Julius), *Ueber tragische Schuld und Sühne. Ein Beitrag zur Geschichte der Æsthetik des Dramas* (Berlin, Duncker, 1882, 12mo). P.

*HARTUNG (J. A.), *Lehren der Alten über die Dichtkunst durch Zusammenstellung mit denen der besten Neueren erklärt* (Hamburg and Gotha, Perthes, 1845, 12mo).

*MAYER (Philipp), *Die Iphigenien des Euripides, Racine und Göthe in Studien zu Homer, Sophokles, Euripides, Racine und Göthe* (Gera and Leipzig, Kanitz, 1874, 8vo).

ABEKEN (Guil.), *De Μιμήσεως apud Platonem et Aristotelem Notione* (Göttingen, Dieterich, 1836, 8vo). P.

III. For the Course on Theory of Cognition and Ontology.

*BRENTANO (Franz), *Von der mannigfachen Bedeutung des Seienden nach Aristoteles* (Freiburg im Breisgau, Herder, 1862, 8vo).

*KAMPE (Ferdinand), *Die Erkenntniss-theorie des Aristoteles* (Leipzig, Fues, 1870, 8vo).

*HERTLING (Geo. Freiherr von), *Materie und Form und die Definition der Seele bei Aristoteles* (Bonn, Weber, 1871, 8vo).

*EVERETT (Charles Carroll), *A System of Logic,* Boston, W. V. Spencer, 1869. In the second book there is a noteworthy attempt to show the uses of the different figures of the syllogism in obtaining and expressing our knowledge.

SIEBECK (H.), *Geschichte der Psychologie. Part I. Die Psychologie vor Aristoteles* (Gotha, 1880).

FREUDENTHAL (I.), *Ueber den Begriff des Wortes φαντασία bei Aristoteles* (Göttingen, 1883).

BAEUMKER (C.), *Des Aristoteles Lehre von den äusern und innern Sinnesvermögen* (Leipzig, 1877).

ROSENKRANZ (W.), *Die Platonische Ideenlehre und ihre Bekämpfung durch Aristoteles* (Mainz, 1869).

*RAVAISSON (Felix), *Essai sur la Métaphysique d'Aristote* (Paris, 1846, 8vo).

GÖRZ (L. F.), *Der Aristotelische Gottesbegriff, mit Beziehung auf die christliche Gottesidee* (Leipzig, Matthes, 1870, 8vo). P.

SCHNEIDER (Leonhard), *Die Unsterblichkeitslehre des Aristoteles* (Passau, Waldauer, 1867, 8vo). P.

SCHLOTTMANN (Konstantin), *Das Vergängliche und Unvergängliche in der menschlichen Seele nach Aristoteles* (Halle, Waisenhaus, 1873, 8vo). P.

SCHLÜTER (C. B.), *Aristoteles' Metaphysik eine Tochter der Sankya-Lehre des Kapila* (Münster, Russell, 1874, 8vo). P.

In addition to works on Aristotle, the student will find it useful to consult such books as will give him a general notion of the history of Philosophy and Dramatic Art since the time of Bacon. It is, of course, not supposed that any one will read more than a few of the works named above. A long list has been given, in order that those wishing to undertake special studies may know where to look for information. The works best adapted for the ordinary student are marked with an *. All pamphlets are marked with P.

The chairman of the committee appointed to correspond with students desiring further information is Mr. Thomas Davidson, Orange, New Jersey, who will answer all letters containing stamps for reply. Programmes announcing the name of lecturer and the date of lecture will be sent as usual to members of the School and others.

Concord, Mass., November, 1886.

THE CONCORD SCHOOL OF PHILOSOPHY.

THE CONCORD SUMMER SCHOOL will open its ninth term on Wednesday, July 13, 1887, at 9.30 A. M. and will continue above two weeks. The lectures in each week will be eleven; they will be given morning and evening, except Saturday evening, on the six secular days (in the morning at 9.30 o'clock, and in the evening at 7.30) at the *Hillside Chapel*, near the Orchard House.

The terms will be $5 for each full week; for all the lectures, $10. Single tickets at 50 cents each, may be bought at the shop of H. L. Whitcomb, in Concord, after July 10, in packages of *ten* for $4.50, and of *three* $1.40. Any one to whom this circular is sent can now engage course tickets by making application, and sending $5 as a guaranty. For those who make this deposit, tickets will be reserved till the tenth day of July, and can then be obtained by payment of the balance due. They entitle the holder to reserved seats. Visitors coming and going daily during the term, may reach Concord from Boston by the Fitchburg Railroad, or the Middlesex Central; from Lowell, Andover, etc., by the Lowell and Framingham Railroads; from Southern Middlesex and Worcester Counties by the same road. The Orchard House stands on the Lexington Road, east of Concord village, adjoining the Wayside estate, formerly the residence of Mr. Hawthorne. For fuller information concerning the town and the school we would refer applicants and visitors to the "Concord Guide Book" of Mr. George B. Bartlett.*

Lodgings with board may be obtained at the following houses in Concord village:

Miss E. BARRETT, Monument Street.

Mrs. O'BRIEN, Monument Square,

Mrs. B. F. WHEELER, Belknap Street.

Mrs. KENT, Main Street,

Mrs. GOODNOW, Main Street,

Mrs. HOW, Hubbard Street,

Lodgings without board can be obtained in the neighborhood of each of the above-named houses. Visitors will make their own arrangements without consulting the undersigned.

A. BRONSON ALCOTT, *Dean.*

S. H. EMERY, JR., *Director.*

F. B. SANBORN, *Secretary.*

CONCORD, April 4, 1887.

---

* Published by D. Lothrop & Co., Boston, and containing an account of the origin of the School.

LECTURES AT THE NINTH SESSION

OF THE

CONCORD SCHOOL OF PHILOSOPHY.

JULY 13–31, 1887.

There will be two courses, morning and evening, beginning at 9.30 A. M., on Wednesday, July 13, 1887,—the topics as follows, and the names of lecturers to be supplied or changed hereafter:

TWELVE MORNING LECTURES ON ARISTOTLE.

Aristotle's Doctrine of Reason.
By Prof. W. T. HARRIS, of Concord, Mass.

Aristotle's Theory of Sense-Perception in the light of Recent Psychology.

Aristotle's Theory of the Syllogism, compared with that of Hegel.
By Prof. W. T. HARRIS, of Concord, Mass.

Aristotle and the Scholastic Philosophy.
By Prof. THOMAS DAVIDSON, of Orange, N. J.

The Ethics of Aristotle.
By Rev. Dr. A. P. PEABODY, of Harvard University.

Aristotle's Physiological Doctrines.
By FILLMORE MOORE, M. D., of New York.

Bacon and Aristotle.
By

The Political Philosophy of Aristotle.
By Mr. S. H. EMERY, JR., of Concord, Mass.

Social Science in Plato and Aristotle.
By Mr. F. B. SANBORN, of Concord, Mass.

Aristotle and the Christian Church.
By BROTHER AZARIAS, of Rock Hill College, Md.

The Protestant Reaction against Aristotle.

TEN EVENING LECTURES ON DRAMATIC POETRY.

The Poetics of Aristotle in its Application to the Drama.
By Prof. THOMAS DAVIDSON, of Orange, N. J.

The Dramatic Element in the Greek Drama and the Norse Edda.
By Prof. W. T. HARRIS, of Concord, Mass.

Shakespeare's Poetics.
By Rev. Dr. C. A. BARTOL, of Boston.

The Divine Nemesis in Æschylus and Shakespeare.
By Prof. C. C. SHACKFORD, of Brookline, Mass.

The Collision of Individuals with Institutions in the Greek and the English Drama.
By Dr. JULIUS GOEBEL, of Baltimore.

Aorstophanes and the Elizabethan Drama.
By Mrs. JULIA WARD HOWE, of Boston.

The Acting of Plays in the Ancient and Modern Theatres.

Marlowe and his Successors.
By Mr. F. B. SANBORN, of Concord, Mass.

Ford and Massinger.
By Mrs. E. D. CHENEY, of Boston.

Browning's Dramatic Genius.
By Rev. GEORGE WILLIS COOKE, of Dedham, Mass.

Four brief Papers on ONTOLOGY, in two or three sessions, will follow the above courses.

sagittarius   *virgo*   *pisces*   *gemini*

THE CONCORD SCHOOL OF PHILOSOPHY.

THE CONCORD SUMMER SCHOOL will open its ninth term on Wednesday, July 13, 1887, at 9.30 A. M. and will continue above two weeks. The lectures in each week will be eleven; they will be given morning and evening, except Saturday evening, on the six secular days (in the morning at 9.30 o'clock, and in the evening at 7.30) at the *Hillside Chapel*, near the Orchard House.

The terms will be $5 for each full week; for all the lectures, $10. Single tickets at 50 cents each, may be bought at the shop of H. L. Whitcomb, in Concord, after July 10, in packages of *ten* for $4.50, and of *three* $1.40. Any one to whom this circular is sent can now engage course tickets by making application, and sending $5 as a guaranty. For those who make this deposit, tickets will be reserved till the tenth day of July, and can then be obtained by payment of the balance due. They entitle the holder to reserved seats. Visitors coming and going daily during the term, may reach Concord from Boston by the Fitchburg Railroad, or the Middlesex Central; from Lowell, Andover, etc., by the Lowell and Framingham Railroads; from Southern Middlesex and Worcester Counties by the same road. The Orchard House stands on the Lexington Road, east of Concord village, adjoining the Wayside estate, formerly the residence of Mr. Hawthorne. For fuller information concerning the town and the school we would refer applicants and visitors to the "Concord Guide Book" of Mr. George B. Bartlett.*

Lodgings with board may be obtained at the following houses in Concord village:

Miss E. BARRETT, Monument Street.   Mrs. KENT, Main Street,
Mrs. O'BRIEN, Monument Square,   Mrs. GOODNOW, Main Street,
Mrs. B. F. WHEELER, Belknap Street.   Mrs. HOW, Hubbard Street,

Lodgings without board can be obtained in the neighborhood of each of the above-named houses. Visitors will make their own arrangements without consulting the undersigned.

A. BRONSON ALCOTT, *Dean.*
S. H. EMERY, JR., *Director.*
F. B. SANBORN, *Secretary.*

CONCORD, April 30, 1887.

* Published by D. Lothrop & Co., Boston, and containing an account of the origin of the School.

LECTURES AT THE NINTH SESSION

OF THE

CONCORD SCHOOL OF PHILOSOPHY.

JULY 13-31, 1887.

There will be two courses, morning and evening, beginning at 9.30 A. M., on Wednesday, July 13, 1887,—the topics as follows, and the names of lecturers to be supplied or changed hereafter:

TWELVE MORNING LECTURES ON ARISTOTLE.

Aristotle's Doctrine of Reason.
By Prof. W T. HARRIS, of Concord, Mass.

Aristotle's Theory of Sense-Perception in the light of Recent Psychology.
By Prof. LUIGI FERRI, University of Rome, Italy.

Bacon and Aristotle.
By Dr. EDMUND MONTGOMERY, of Texas.

Aristotle and the Scholastic Philosophy.
By Prof. THOMAS DAVIDSON, of Orange, N. J.

The Ethics of Aristotle.
By Rev. Dr. A. P. PEABODY, of Harvard University.

Theory of the Infinite,—Aristotle and Kant
By Prof. H. N. GARDINER, of Smith College.

Aristotle's Physiological Doctrines.
By FILLMORE MOORE, M. D., of New York.

Aristotle's Theory of the Syllogism, compared with that of Hegel.
By Prof. W. T. HARRIS, of Concord, Mass.

The Political Philosophy of Aristotle.
By Mr. S. H. EMERY, JR., of Concord, Mass.

Social Science in Plato and Aristotle.
By Mr. F. B. SANBORN, of Concord, Mass.

Aristotle and the Christian Church.
By BROTHER AZARIAS, of Rock Hill College, Md.

Aristotle on Education.
By F. L. SOLDAN, LL. D., of St. Louis.

TEN EVENING LECTURES ON DRAMATIC POETRY.

The Poetics of Aristotle in its Application to the Drama.
By Prof. THOMAS DAVIDSON, of Orange, N. J.

The Dramatic Element in the Greek Drama and the Norse Edda.
By Prof. W. T. HARRIS, of Concord, Mass.

Shakespeare's Poetics.
By Rev. Dr. C. A. BARTOL, of Boston.

The Divine Nemesis in Æschylus and Shakespeare.
By Prof. C. C. SHACKFORD, of Brookline, Mass.

The Collision of Individuals with Institutions in the Greek and the English Drama.
By Mr. EDWIN D. MEAD, of Boston.

Aristophanes and the Elizabethan Drama.
By Mrs. JULIA WARD HOWE, of Boston.

By Dr. JULIUS GOEBEL, of Baltimore.

Marlowe and his Successors.
By Mr. F. B. SANBORN, of Concord, Mass.

Ford and Massinger.
By Mrs. E. D. CHENEY, of Boston.

Browning's Dramatic Genius.
By Rev. GEORGE WILLIS COOKE, of Dedham, Mass.

Four brief Papers on ONTOLOGY, in two or three sessions, will follow the above courses.

THE CONCORD SCHOOL OF PHILOSOPHY.

THE CONCORD SUMMER SCHOOL will open its ninth term on Wednesday, July 13, 1887, at 9.30 A. M. and will continue above two weeks. The lectures in each week will be eleven; they will be given morning and evening, except Saturday evening, on the six secular days (in the morning at 9.30 o'clock, and in the evening at 7.30) at the *Hillside Chapel*, near the Orchard House.

The terms will be $5 for each full week; for all the lectures, $10. Single tickets at 50 cents each, may be bought at the shop of H. L. Whitcomb, in Concord, after July 10, in packages of *ten* for $4.50, and of *three* $1.40. Any one to whom this circular is sent can now engage course tickets by making application, and sending $5 as a guaranty. For those who make this deposit, tickets will be reserved till the tenth day of July, and can then be obtained by payment of the balance due. They entitle the holder to reserved seats. Visitors coming and going daily during the term, may reach Concord from Boston by the Fitchburg Railroad, or the Middlesex Central; from Lowell, Andover, etc., by the Lowell and Framingham Railroads; from Southern Middlesex and Worcester Counties by the same road. The Orchard House stands on the Lexington Road, east of Concord village; adjoining the Wayside estate, formerly the residence of Mr. Hawthorne. For fuller information concerning the town and the school we would refer applicants and visitors to the "Concord Guide Book" of Mr. George B. Bartlett.*

Lodgings with board may be obtained at the following houses in Concord village:

Miss E. BARRETT, Monument Street.	Mrs. KENT, Main Street,
Mrs. O'BRIEN, Monument Square,	Mrs. GOODNOW, Main Street,
Mrs. B. F. WHEELER, Belknap Street.	Mrs. How, Hubbard Street,

Lodgings without board can be obtained in the neighborhood of each of the above-named houses. Visitors will make their own arrangements without consulting the undersigned.

A. BRONSON ALCOTT, *Dean.*
S. H. EMERY, JR., *Director.*
F. B. SANBORN, *Secretary.*

CONCORD, June 10, 1887.

* Published by D. Lothrop & Co., Boston, and containing an account of the origin of the School.

LECTURES AT THE NINTH SESSION

OF THE

CONCORD SCHOOL OF PHILOSOPHY.

JULY 13-30, 1887.

There will be two courses, morning and evening, beginning at 9.30 A. M., on Wednesday, July 13. 1887,—the topics as follows, and the names of lecturers subject to change hereafter:

TWELVE MORNING LECTURES ON ARISTOTLE.

Aristotle's Doctrine of Reason.
    By Prof. W. T. HARRIS, of Concord, Mass.

Aristotle's Theory of Causation.
    By Dr. EDMUND MONTGOMERY, of Texas. .

Aristotle and the Scholastic Philosophy.
    By Prof. THOMAS DAVIDSON, of Orange, N. J.

The Ethics of Aristotle.
By Rev. Dr. A P. PEABODY, of Harvard University.

Theory of the Infinite,—Aristotle and Kant.
    By Prof. H. N. GARDINER, of Smith College.

Aristotle and the Christian Church,
    By BROTHER AZARIAS, of Rock Hill College, Md.

Aristotle's Physiological Doctrines.
    By FILLMORE MOORE, M. D., of New York.

Aristotle's Theory of the Syllogism, compared with that of Hegel.
    By Prof. W. T. HARRIS, of Concord, Mass.

Aristotle's Politics, and Montesquieu's Esprit des Lois.
    By Prof. LUIGI FERRI, University of Rome, Italy.

Social Science in Plato and Aristotle.
    By Mr. F. B. SANBORN, of Concord, Mass.

Aristotle on Education.
    By F. L. SOLDAN, LL. D., of St. Louis.

Friendship in Aristotle's Ethics.
    By Mrs. ELLEN C. MITCHELL, of Denver, Colorado.

TEN EVENING LECTURES ON DRAMATIC POETRY.

The Poetics of Aristotle in its Application to the Drama.
    By Prof. THOMAS DAVIDSON, of Orange, N. J.

The Dramatic Element in the Greek Drama and the Norse Edda.
        By Prof. W. T. HARRIS, of Concord, Mass.

Shakespeare's Poetics.
        By Rev. Dr. C. A. BARTOL, of Boston.

The Divine Nemesis in the Greek Drama and in Shakespeare.
    By Prof. C. C. SHACKFORD, of Brookline, Mass.

The Collision of Individuals with Institutions in the Greek and the English Drama.
    By Mr. EDWIN D. MEAD, of Boston.

Aristophanes and the Elizabethan Drama.
    By Mrs. JULIA WARD HOWE, of Boston.

Marlowe and his Successors.
    By Mr. F. B. SANBORN, of Concord, Mass.

Ford and Massinger.
    By Mrs. E. D. CHENEY, of Boston.

Schiller's Relation to Aristotle.
    By Dr. JULIUS GOEBEL, of Baltimore.

Browning's Dramatic Genius.
    By Rev. GEORGE WILLIS COOKE, of Dedham, Mass.

Four brief Papers on ONTOLOGY, in two or three sessions, will follow the above courses.

One of these will be given by Prof. DAVIDSON, another by Dr. MONTGOMERY, a third by Prof. HARRIS, and the fourth by some lecturer still to be announced.

THE DATES OF THE LECTURES WILL BE AS FOLLOWS:

July 13, 9.30 A. M.   Prof. HARRIS.
      7.30 P. M.   Prof. DAVIDSON.
July 14, A. M.   Dr. MONTGOMERY.
      P. M.   Prof. SHACKFORD.
July 15, A. M.   Prof. DAVIDSON.
      P. M.   Mr. SANBORN.
July 16, A. M.   Rev. Dr. PEABODY.
July 18, A. M.   Prof. GARDINER.
      P. M.   Prof. HARRIS.
July 19, A. M.   Brother AZARIAS.
      P. M.   Mrs. HOWE.
July 20, A. M.   Prof. HARRIS.
      P. M.   Mr. E. D. MEAD.
July 21, A. M.   Dr. MOORE.
      P. M.   Mrs. CHENEY.

July 22, A. M.   Prof. FERRI.
      P. M.   Dr. GOEBEL.
July 23, A. M.   Dr. BARTOL.
July 25, A. M.   Mr. SANBORN.
      P. M.   Mr. G. W. COOKE.
July 26, A. M.   Mrs. E. C. MITCHELL.
      P. M.   Prof. DAVIDSON.
July 27, A. M.   Dr. SOLDAN.
      P. M.   Dr. MONTGOMERY.
July 28, A. M.   Prof. HARRIS.
      P. M.   Mr. JOHN FISKE.

These dates are subject to change, but only in one or two instances. Additional **Lectures may** be given on the 29th and 30th of July. With the exception of July 23d and 28th, **the Morning** Lectures will all relate to Aristotle. The morning hour in all cases is 9.30, and **the evening** hour **7.30.**

JUNE 10. 1887.

Central part of Concord village—from J. W. Barber, Massachusetts Historical Collections, *1841*

LECTURES AT THE NINTH SESSION

OF THE

CONCORD SCHOOL OF PHILOSOPHY.

JULY 13-30, 1887.

, There will be two courses, morning and evening, beginning at 9.30 A. M., on Wednesday, July 13, 1887,—the topics as follows, and the names of lecturers subject to change hereafter:

TWELVE MORNING LECTURES ON ARISTOTLE.

Aristotle's Doctrine of Reason.
> By Prof. W. T. HARRIS, of Concord, Mass.

Aristotle's Theory of Causation.
> By Dr. EDMUND MONTGOMERY, of Texas.

Aristotle and the Scholastic Philosophy.
> By Prof. THOMAS DAVIDSON, of Orange, N. J.

The Ethics of Aristotle.
By Rev. Dr. A. P. PEABODY, of Harvard University.

Theory of the Infinite,—Aristotle and Kant.
> By Prof. H. N. GARDINER, of Smith College.

Aristotle and the Christian Church.
> By BROTHER AZARIAS, of Rock Hill College, Md.*

Aristotle's Physiological Doctrines.
> By FILLMORE MOORE, M. D., of New York.

Aristotle's Theory of the Syllogism, compared with that of Hegel.
> By Prof. W. T. HARRIS, of Concord, Mass.

Aristotle's Politics, and Montesquieu's Esprit des Lois.
> By Prof. LUIGI FERRI, University of Rome, Italy.

Social Science in Plato and Aristotle.
> By Mr. F. B. SANBORN, of Concord, Mass.

Aristotle on Education.
> By F. L. SOLDAN, LL. D., of St. Louis.

Friendship in Aristotle's Ethics.
> By Mrs. ELLEN M. MITCHELL, of Denver, Colorado.

TEN EVENING LECTURES ON DRAMATIC POETRY.

The Poetics of Aristotle in its Application to the Drama.
> By Prof. THOMAS DAVIDSON, of Orange, N. J.

The Dramatic Element in the Greek Drama and the Norse Edda.
> By Prof. W. T. HARRIS, of Concord, Mass.

Shakespeare's Poetics.
> By Rev. Dr. C. A. BARTOL, of Boston.

The Divine Nemesis in the Greek Drama and in Shakespeare.
> By Prof. C. C. SHACKFORD, of Brookline, Mass.

The Collision of Individuals with Institutions in the Greek and the English Drama.
By Mr. EDWIN D. MEAD, of Boston.

Aristophanes and the Elizabethan Drama.
> By Mrs. JULIA WARD HOWE, of Boston.

Marlowe and his Successors.
> By Mr. F. B. SANBORN, of Concord, Mass.

Ford and Massinger.
> By Mrs. E. D. CHENEY, of Boston.

Schiller's Relation to Aristotle.†
> By Dr. JULIUS GOEBEL, of Baltimore.

Browning's Dramatic Genius.
> By Rev. GEORGE WILLIS COOKE, of Dedham, Mass.

Four brief Papers on ONTOLOGY, in two or three sessions, will follow the above courses.

One of these will be given by Prof. DAVIDSON, another by Dr. MONTGOMERY, a third by Prof. HARRIS, and the fourth by some lecturer still to be announced.

* Should BROTHER AZARIAS not return from Europe in time, a lecture on *Aristotle's Theory of Substance,* will be substituted for this.
† *A Reading from Shakespeare,* by Mr. W. O. PARTRIDGE, may take the place of this.

THE DATES OF THE LECTURES WILL BE AS FOLLOWS:

July 13, 9.30 A. M.   Prof. HARRIS.
   7.30 P. M.   Prof. DAVIDSON.
July 14, A. M.   Dr. MONTGOMERY.
   P. M.   Prof. SHACKFORD.
July 15, A. M.   Prof. DAVIDSON.
   P. M.   Mr. SANBORN.
July 16, A. M.   Rev. Dr. PEABODY.
July 18, A. M.   Prof. GARDINER.
   P. M.   Prof. HARRIS.
July 19, A. M.   Brother AZARIAS.
   P. M.   Mrs. HOWE.
July 20, A. M.   Prof. HARRIS.
   P. M.   Mr. E. D. MEAD.
July 21, A. M.   Dr. MOORE.
   P. M.   Mrs. CHENEY.

July 22, A. M.   Prof. FERRI.
   P. M.   Dr. GOEBEL.
July 23, A. M.   Dr. BARTOL.
July 25, A. M.   Mr. SANBORN.
   P. M.   Mr. G. W. COOKE.
July 26, A. M.   Mrs. E. M. MITCHELL.
   P. M.   Prof. DAVIDSON.
July 27, A. M.   Dr. SOLDAN.
   P. M.   Dr. MONTGOMERY.
July 28, A. M.   Prof. HARRIS.
   P. M.   Mr. JOHN FISKE.

These dates are subject to change, but only in one or two instances.   Additional Lectures may be given on the 29th and 30th of July.   With the exception of July 23d and 28th, the Morning Lectures will all relate to Aristotle.   The morning hour in all cases is 9.30, and the evening hour 7.30.

JULY 13, 1887.

"The Rocket" built by George Stephenson
of Scotland, about 1825.

LECTURES AT THE NINTH SESSION

OF THE

CONCORD SCHOOL OF PHILOSOPHY.

JULY 13–30, 1887.

There will be two courses, morning and evening, beginning at 9.30 A. M., on **Wednesday,** July 13, 1887,—the topics as follows, and the names of lecturers subject to change hereafter:

TWELVE MORNING LECTURES ON ARISTOTLE.

Aristotle's Doctrine of Reason.
By Prof. W. T. HARRIS, of Concord, Mass.

Aristotle's Theory of Causation.
By Dr. EDMUND MONTGOMERY, of Texas.

Aristotle and the Scholastic Philosophy.
By Prof. THOMAS DAVIDSON, of Orange, N. J.

The Ethics of Aristotle.
By Rev. Dr. A. P. PEABODY, of Harvard University.

Theory of the Infinite,—Aristotle and Kant.
By Prof. H. N. GARDINER, of Smith College.

Aristotle and the Christian Church.
By BROTHER AZARIAS, of Rock Hill College, Md.

Aristotle's Physiological Doctrines.
By FILLMORE MOORE, M. D., of New York.

Aristotle's Theory of the Syllogism, compared with that of Hegel.
By Prof. W. T. HARRIS, of Concord, Mass.

Aristotle's Politics, and Montesquieu's Esprit des Lois.
By Prof. LUIGI FERRI, University of Rome, Italy.

Social Science in Plato and Aristotle.
By Mr. F. B. SANBORN, of Concord, Mass.

Aristotle on Education.
By F. L. SOLDAN, LL. D., of St. Louis.

Friendship in Aristotle's Ethics.
By Mrs. ELLEN M. MITCHELL, of Denver, Colorado.

TEN EVENING LECTURES ON DRAMATIC POETRY.

The Poetics of Aristotle in its Application to the Drama.
By Prof. THOMAS DAVIDSON, of Orange, N. J.

The Dramatic Element in the Greek Drama and the Norse Edda.
By Prof. W. T. HARRIS, of Concord, Mass.

Shakespeare's Poetics.
By Rev. Dr. C. A. BARTOL, of Boston.

The Divine Nemesis in the Greek Drama and in Shakespeare.
By Prof. C. C. SHACKFORD, of Brookline, Mass.

The Collision of Individuals with Institutions in the Greek and the English Drama.
By Mr. EDWIN D. MEAD, of Boston.

Aristophanes and the Elizabethan Drama.
By Mrs. JULIA WARD HOWE, of Boston.

Marlowe and his Successors.
By Mr. F. B. SANBORN, of Concord, Mass.

Ford and Massinger.
By Mrs. E. D. CHENEY, of Boston.

Schiller's Relation to Aristotle.†
By Dr. JULIUS GOEBEL, of Baltimore.

Browning's Dramatic Genius.
By Rev. GEORGE WILLIS COOKE, of Dedham, Mass.

Four brief Papers on ONTOLOGY, in two or three sessions, will follow the above courses.
One of these will be given by Prof. DAVIDSON, another by Mr. ROBERT NIX, a third by Prof. HARRIS, and the fourth by some lecturer still to be announced.

† *A Reading from Shakespeare,* by Mr. W. O. PARTRIDGE, may take the place of this.

LATEST PROGRAMME.

THE DATES OF THE LECTURES WILL BE AS FOLLOWS:

July 13, 9.30 A. M.	Prof. HARRIS.
7.30 P. M.	Prof. DAVIDSON.
July 14, A. M.	Dr. MONTGOMERY
P. M.	Prof. SHACKFORD.
July 15, A. M.	Prof. DAVIDSON.
P. M.	Mr. SANBORN.
July 16, A. M.	Rev. Dr. PEABODY.
July 18, A. M.	Prof. GARDINER.
P. M.	Prof. HARRIS.
July 19, A. M.	Brother AZARIAS.
P. M.	
July 20, A. M.	Prof. FERRI.
P. M.	Mr. E. D. MEAD.
July 21, A. M.	Dr. MOORE.
P. M.	Mrs. CHENEY.

July 22, A. M.	Prof. HARRIS.
P. M.	Dr. SOLDAN.
July 23, A. M.	Dr. BARTOL.
July 25, A. M.	Mr. SANBORN.
P. M.	Mr. G. W. COOKE.
July 26, A. M.	Mrs. E. M. MITCHELL.
P. M.	Prof. DAVIDSON.
July 27, A. M.	Mrs. HOWE.
P. M.	Dr. GOEBEL.
July 28, A. M.	Prof. HARRIS.
P. M.	Mr. JOHN FISKE

These dates are subject to change, but only in one or two instances. Additional Lectures may be given on the 29th and 30th of July. With the exception of July 23d and 28th, the Morning Lectures will all relate to Aristotle. The morning hour in all cases is 9.30, and the evening hour 7.30.

Trains for Boston, on the Fitchburg Railroad, will leave Concord at 9.30 P. M. on every week day evening but Wednesday and Saturday, and on those evenings at 9.52 P. M.

JULY 16, 1887.

ALCOTT MEMORIAL SERVICE

AT THE

Concord School of Philosophy,

SATURDAY, JUNE 16, 1888.

———————

A Special Session of the SCHOOL OF PHILOSOPHY will be held at the Hillside Chapel in Concord, Saturday, June 16, commencing at 10 A. M.   The public are invited.

The order of services will be as follows:

MORNING SESSION.

10   A. M.   Prayer by Rev. J. S. BUSH, of Concord.

10.15 A. M.   *Biographical Address* by F. B. SANBORN, of Concord.

11 A. M. to 1 P. M.   Remarks and Reminiscences by

Rev. Dr. BARTOL, of Boston.

Mrs. E. D. CHENEY, of Boston,

GEORGE B. BARTLETT, of Concord,

Rev. G. REYNOLDS, of Concord,

Rev. Dr. F. H. HEDGE, of Cambridge,

B. MARSTON WATSON, of Plymouth,

W. L. GARRISON, of Boston,

JOHN ALBEE, of New Castle, N. H.,

and others.

AFTERNOON SESSION.

2.30 P. M.   The *Philosophy of Mr. Alcott*, by WILLIAM T. HARRIS, of Concord,

3.30 to 5 P. M.   Remarks or Letters by

Rev. R. A. HOLLAND, S. T. D., of St. Louis,

Prof. THOMAS DAVIDSON, of New York,

DANIEL RICKETSON, of New Bedford,

and others.

There will be no other Session of the Concord School of Philosophy the present Summer.

W. T. HARRIS,

S. H. EMERY, JR.,

F. B. SANBORN, *Secretary.*

Concord, June 2, 1888.

[A BACKWARD GLANCE]

BELFORD'S MONTHLY

—— Sara A. Underwood

Vol. X   APRIL, 1892   No. 5

Pp. 675-688

SKETCHES OF CONCORD PHILOSOPHERS

The Summer School of Philosophy at Concord, Mass., was founded in 1879. It was the realized dream of Amos Bronson Alcott, the dream born of his Socratic studies and transcendental ideals. It was a unique experiment, which drew toward it original thinkers of strangely varying characteristics as students and teachers.

The Hillside Chapel — The Orchard House.

It is to recall, ere the memory of the school fades from public recollection, the strong individualities of which it was the exponent that this article is written. A word should first be said of that brilliant coterie of men and women of genius whose homes or haunts had been in Concord for longer or shorter periods ere the founding of the school, thereby making that quiet New England village the most fitting place in which to attempt Mr. Alcott's ideal experiment.

The first session was held in the library of the Orchard House, that house sacred to the memories of the "Little Men" and "Little Women" of Louisa Alcott's family; her father, the Dean of the faculty of the school, was, thanks to Louisa's generosity, at that time free from those carking cares of poverty entailed upon the family in early years through his unworldliness. Though past his most vigorous intellectual period, he was fully alive to the importance of the new movement and filled with buoyant hopes as to its outcome. He is well described at this period in Sherwood Bonner's audacious poem, "The Radical Club."

"Then uprose a kindred spirit, almost ready to inherit
   The rare and radiant Aïdea that he begged us to adore;
His smile was beaming brightly, and his soft hair floated whitely
   Round a face as fair and slightly as a pious priest's of yore."

"The Mystic" was the name given him by O. B. Frothingham in his "History of Transcendentalism," and that Alcott himself thought the name not ill-bestowed was illustrated by an incident occurring at one of the morning sessions of the school, when Dr. H. K. Jones, of Jacksonville, Ill., had ventured mildly to dissent from some point in Darwin's theory of evolution, to which dissent Prof. Wm. T. Harris as mildly took exception. "Dean" Alcott, vaguely fearing something was wrong, rose to deprecate any misunderstanding between the speakers, whereupon Doctor Jones, looking surprised, exclaimed, "I don't know what you mean, Mr. Alcott." "Nor I," echoed Professor Harris. Then the philosopher smiled, as he subsided into his seat, and said, cheerfully, "Well, I don't think I know what I meant myself"—adding, as a laugh rippled over the audience, "I am a Mystic, you know." Whereat the merriment became general.

His was a genial, childlike, friendly personality, whose soul went out in kindliness toward every sympathetic face he looked into. The writer remembers with pleasure with what a beaming smile, cordial tone and friendly look he turned toward her (till then a perfect stranger to him), as she stood one of a group gathered around him on the greensward in front of the chapel after the morning's lecture, saying, as he held out his hand, "Good-morning, my friend; I can't just recall your name, but recognize your face as some one I ought to know."

Emerson, whose well-won fame will ever make Concord a literary Mecca, attended a few of the earlier sessions of the

worked youth while her father was sowing his "Transcendental Wild Oats," rarely attended the school.

Frank B. Sanborn, the able secretary and one of the most active promoters of the school, was then, and is to-day, a resident of Concord, whose literary and reform record gives added luster to the famous town. He has been before the public in various capacities for many years. He gave many lectures on varied subjects before the school during the years of its existence. In addition to his excellent work as the biographer of Thoreau and John Brown, the liberator, he is a most successful journalist, and was for years one of the prominent officers and workers on the Massachusetts State Board of Charities, while his contributions to the literature of social science have been very valuable.

An interesting personality is that of Elizabeth P. Peabody, one of the originators of the Concord School of Philosophy. She gave several lectures before it, was one of the most faithful attendants during its continuance, and was closely identified with Concord's notables. She was sister-in-law to Horace Mann, the great educator, and to Nathaniel Hawthorne, the novelist, the aunt of Julian Hawthorne and his sister, Rose Hawthorne Lathrop. She was at eighteen the pupil in Greek of Emerson, then but a year her senior, whose lifelong intimate friend she remained. She was the coadjutor, when young, of Alcott in his famous school; the companion of Margaret Fuller, whose renowned "Conversations" were first held in Miss Peabody's rooms in Boston; the teacher of Louisa Alcott's girlhood; one of the select coterie whose work it was to fan the flame of early transcendentalism, until it became the sacred altar from whence was lit torches of spiritual enlightenment, which still burn glowingly in what is best of our modern literature. In this high-thinking circle she was brought into intimate relationship with such minds as Theodore Parker, Doctor Hedge, George Ripley, G. W. Curtis and the whole vanguard of idealism. She has ever been a leader in educational reform, was the first to adopt Froebel's ideas, and is well named "Mother of the Kindergarten" by reason of the brave work she did in introducing the kindergarten system in America. By tongue, pen, financial aid and personal labor she has done a great work in rousing public sympathy in behalf of the Indians, and helping them by education to help themselves. Indeed there is no good cause in which this noble woman has not taken a most active interest—anti-slavery, woman's suffrage, temperance—everything that is worthy and

school. The first year he read before it his essay on "Memory"—his own already beginning to fail him; and the second year, assisted by his daughter Ellen, he read his lecture on "Aristocracy." But he was already at "the beginning of the end," with his thoughts largely indrawn into that unseen spiritual world, whither he soon after betook himself. On the occasional times when he sat on the platform of the "chapel," it was mainly as a lay figure for the inspiration of those present, but it was a pathetic figure to those who had known and loved him at his prime, spite of the seraphic smile upon the serene face.

Thoreau, that true son of nature, had passed away before the school opened—but had he lived

Ralph Waldo Emerson.

his distaste for society would probably have kept him away from the Hill-side gatherings. Hawthorne, too, was gone; resting quietly a little beyond, in the "Sleepy Hollow" cemetery; yet the "Old Manse" still spoke eloquently of him—and his son Julian was of those who gave earnest tribute to Emerson's memory at the school in 1884. So, also, many others who had helped make Concord famous in the past had already vanished into the beyond. Such strong personalities as quaint Ezra Ripley, "the parish minister and county Nestor;" Margaret Fuller, who F. B. Sanborn says resided there "at intervals coming and going in her sibylline way," and William S. Robinson, the "Warrington" of the political press, born in Concord, as Thoreau was. But the shades of these seemed to linger about their olden haunts, to awaken sympathetic response in the hearts of thousands of casual visitors to the Summer School. Frank B. Sanborn, Elizabeth Peabody, Judge and Senator Hoar, F. M. Holland and the recluse poet, Ellery Channing, still lived there, as did Louisa Alcott—who having had her fill of philosophy in her hard-

Brook Farm, Emerson and Margaret Fuller, were still sufficiently vigorous, in spite of their weight of years, to contribute, by their presence and lectures, to the philosophic symposium of the Concord Summer School. These were Rev. Cyrus Bartol, Rev. Wm. Henry Channing, Rev. F. H. Hedge and Rev. James Freeman Clarke.

Rev. W. H. Channing, the nephew of William Ellery Channing, the great Unitarian leader, was, from the beginning of her literary career, the close friend of Margaret Fuller, and he, with Hedge and Emerson, wrote and edited the first memoirs of that remarkable woman. His last years were passed in England, where his daughter became the wife of the poet Sir Edwin Arnold. He was a contributor to the leading English and American reviews, and was the author of an excellent memoir of his distinguished uncle, William Ellery Channing. His death occurred before the Concord School was discontinued.

Rev. James Freeman Clarke was a life-long friend of Margaret Fuller, a contributor to the Transcendentalist magazine, *The Dial*, and a preacher and writer of acknowledged power and ability. His most notable work is entitled "Ten Great Religions." He survived the collapse of the Concord School but a year or so.

Rev. Frederick Henry Hedge, D. D., has also joined "the great majority" since the close of the Concord School. He was born in 1805, studied at Harvard and German universities, and became a Unitarian clergyman whose intellectual power was widely acknowledged. He frequently contributed strong philosophical papers to leading magazines. His preaching, writings and influence were always in the direction of progressive thought.

Rev. Cyrus Augustus Bartol, born in 1813, and drawn into the Transcendental ring about the time of the formation of the club, of which "A. B. Alcott was the suggestor, was, Colonel Higginson says, to this club "the flame of aspiration." Doctor Bartol has been for many years a favorite magazine writer, and is the author of a number of works of which "The Rising Faith," is perhaps the most popular.

Col. Thomas Wentworth Higginson, preacher, poet, story-teller, essayist, historian, reform leader, soldier and statesman, was most appropriately one of the lecturers of the earlier sessions of the Concord Summer School. In appearance he is

of good report. Only a year younger than Emerson, she is still living, as these lines are penned, at her home in Jamaica Plains, Mass., though she is no longer able to attend the public meetings, where for so many years the little lady with round, benevolent face, smiling eyes, serene, placid air, with the lovely "white curls bobbing quaintly from the head-dress that she wore," was once so familiar a figure to Bostonians.

David A. Wasson was another of the lecturers who had made Concord for awhile his home, and there in the beautiful cemetery all that is mortal of him

A. Bronson Alcott.

lies buried. It was John Wiess, Colonel Higginson and D. A. Wasson who were characterized by O. B. Frothingham as the last valiant defenders of Transcendentalism. Mr. Wasson was a native of New England, and educated for the ministry, but he became too doubtful of Christian dogmas to remain long in an orthodox pulpit, and preached for awhile to the more liberal congregations. His essays and poems won a place in the leading magazines by reason of their fine style, broad thought and higher spirituality. His poem entitled "All's Well," has a more than national popularity. He was for a long time an invalid, and it was a brave, strong, sweet nature which, while denied all that ambition craved, and racked with pain, could write and feel such thoughts as these :

"Ask, and receive —'tis sweetly said,
Yet what to plead for I know not,
For Wish is worsted. Hope o'ersped,
And aye to thanks returns my thought.
If I would pray,
I've nought to say
But this, that God may be God still,
For him to live,
Is still to give,
And sweeter than my wish, his Will."

A few years previous to his death he partially recovered health and strength, and it was during this time that he gave his Concord School lectures—ten the first year, two the second, and one on "Herbert Spencer's Causation" the fifth year.

Four Unitarian clergymen, of the era of Transcendentalism,

her own sex. Her Concord lectures were mainly on art and literature.

Julia Ward Howe was also one of the leading spirits of the Summer School of Philosophy, but her work and history are too widely known to be dwelt upon in this connection. Her lovely daughters were frequent visitors at this school, sometimes participating in the discussions, especially the beautiful Julia Romana Anagnos, whose literary work seemed to promise so much ere she was too soon called to higher spheres. She had a voice of singular sweetness, a tender, womanly face with a charming smile, a complexion combined of the rose and lily, with laughing eyes of brown.

Though the idea of the School of Philosophy originated with New England thinkers and was carried out on New England soil, yet a large share of its students and teachers were from the West. This fact rather surprised the "cultured" ones of Boston and Concord, who had no idea of the great interest taken in abstruse met-

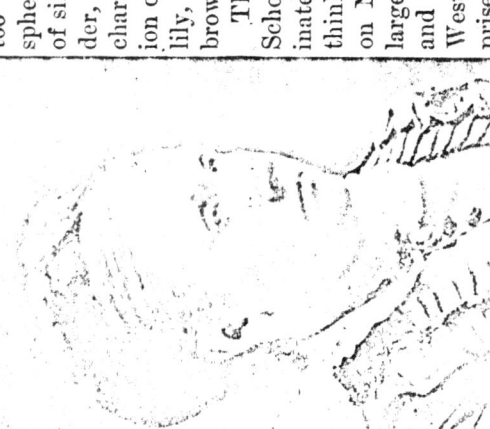

Julia Ward Howe.

aphysical philosophy by the denizens of "the wild and woolly West." It is related in Louisa Alcott's biography that when one of the literary ladies of the East, thinking to give information to a quiet-looking Western woman, whom she met at Concord, advised her patronizingly to look into Plato a little—his works were very suggestive to thinkers, etc.—she was somewhat taken aback when the Illinois visitor heartily agreed with her, saying, "Oh, yes, we have been reading Plato in the original in our philosophical class in Jacksonville the past three winters."

Mrs. E. D. Cheney, in a letter written from Concord to the *Free Religious Index*, of Boston, the first year of the school, says: "The West has responded nobly, and sent us admirable representatives of the fresh thought and life of that region. It

not inaptly described by the author of the poem "The Radical Club," as

"A Colonel cold and smiling with a stately air beguiling,
Who punctuates his periods on Newport's sounding shore."

But the "coldness" is most assuredly only in appearance, since all will acknowledge that it must have taken considerable warmth of heart and strong conviction of soul to impel a man of family, of rare intellectual culture, refined, esthetic taste and scholarly proclivities to publicly advocate, in its most ridiculed stage, the political enfranchisement of woman; the slave's right to liberty at a time when to do so meant social ostracism; unhesitatingly

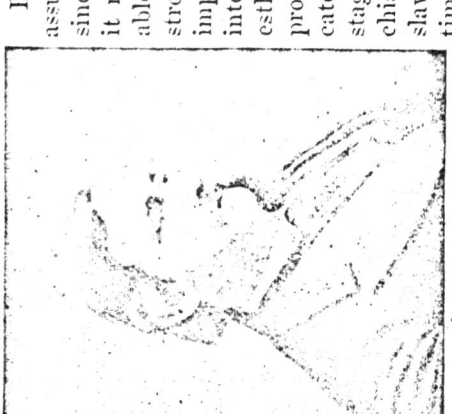

Col. T. W. Higginson.

to leave the pulpit to become the colonel of a colored regiment, and, though an avowed advocate of peace, to shed his blood in defense of the principles held dearest of all things.

Colonel Higginson is not only a poet, but he has lived lyrics. No stories written by him equal his own life's romance. Most of the reforms he urged when in their infancy, he has lived to see adopted. He has not only written history, but he has helped to make it; and with all this he is still a man of the world, who adorns society, and is one of the most charming after-dinner speakers and toast-masters.

Mrs. Ednah D. Cheney properly belongs to the group of Transcendentalists who took part in the Concord School. When a girl she was an attendant on Margaret Fuller's "Conversations," and was one of the few women identified with the "Free Religious" movement. She has been for many years a contributor to the liberal press and is the author of a number of works, among them a "Short History of Art, Life of Louisa Alcott," and a biography of Christian Daniel Ranch, a Berlin sculptor. Her name is associated with many educational, charitable and reform movements, especially those in behalf of

is an astonishment to many, who think of all beyond the Alleghanies as a region devoted to material speculation and party politics, to see the ripe scholarship and philosophic thought which come from her schools." Of one of these Western thinkers who took a leading part in the school from the beginning, she writes: "Doctor Jones is spoken of as the most thorough Platonist in the country, and interprets Plato's most difficult work with great vigor and clearness. The West, too, has furnished others who have added much to the 'Conversations.'" This gentleman is well known throughout the country for his enthusiastic study of Plato, and he has been the means of leading many who would not otherwise have become interested in philosophy to study for themselves the leading thinkers of all ages, in the classes which he organized and has led for so many years at his Jacksonville home.

Dr. William T. Harris, our present Commissioner of Education, is another Western man whose name is strongly identified with Concord and its Summer School. Though born and educated in New England, he gained his reputation as a scholarly thinker partly through his fine educational work in the schools of St. Louis, Mo., where he was for some time Superintendent of the Public Schools, and where in 1867 he established his *Journal of Speculative Philosophy*, which is the only journal of its kind in the English language. During several seasons of the Summer School, Professor Harris with his family occupied the old Alcott homestead, on the grounds on which the Chapel is built.

Prof. Thomas Davidson, a constant attendant and lecturer, though a Scotchman by birth and education, a graduate of Aberdeen University, can well be counted as a Western man, having long been identified with the educational interests of St. Louis. His travels in Europe and his familiarity with Italian and Grecian language and literature make him an excellent tutor in the lessons to be learned from Plato, Aristotle, Dante and the more modern philosophers. Since the close of the Concord School he has started a Summer School of his own in the Adirondacks, where he has bought a tract of land, on which he has built cottages where the Summer Students can board in country style and "loaf and refresh their souls," dividing their time between study of abstruse speculative philosophy, academic interchange of thought, and loitering through lovely woodlands, hunting, fishing or other primitive amusements.

Prof. Denton J. Snider is another Western scholar who has helped the attendants of the 'Concord School to some clear champagne—like draughts of the "Pierian Spring." He is especially interested in the works of Shakespeare and Goethe, and by his bright, earnest manner makes an excellent interpreter of the deeper thought of those two masters. He is well known as a poet, essayist and lecturer in the West.

One lecture of the earlier Concord courses, entitled "Platonism in Its Relation to Modern Thought," was given by Louis J. Block, of Chicago, who is recognized in that city as one of the most thorough students of Plato and an authority on Dantean puzzles. He is a poet, critic and essayist. His volume of "Dramatic Sketcher and Poems" has received high praise from acknowledged authorities in literature.

Though women formed the larger part of the audiences all through the Concord discourses, and many took part in the discussion of the papers presented, yet only five women were among the lecturers during all the years. These were Elizabeth Peabody, Julia Ward Howe, Mrs. Cheney, Mrs. Hathaway and Mrs. Sherman—the two last named being Western women.

Mrs. Amalia J. Hathaway was the wife of the poet, Benjamin Hathaway. As a friend of Doctor Cocker she became early in her career intensely interested in speculative philosophy. A frequent visitor to Chicago from her farm home in Michigan, she joined the Philosophical Society of this city, and for five successive seasons her name was on its programme of lecturers. Her papers were on such subjects as "Mental Automatism," "Immanuel Kant," "The Hegelian Philosophy," "Schopenhauer," and "Pessimism From the Standpoint of Hegelianism." She gave one lecture at Concord in the summer of 1881, which made a decided sensation among the scholars then assembled. The Springfield (Mass.) *Republican*, in a notice of her death, which occurred in December of that same year, said of her: "Mrs. Hathaway was probably by far the best grounded in philosophy among American women. She was an authority on Kant and Hegel. Her paper on Schopenhauer was one of the most notable read before the Concord School of Philosophy last summer and occasioned one remark at the time—that she was the only woman there who thought level with the men—with such men as Doctor Harris, even." To those who enjoyed her personal acquaintance the charm of her learning was enhanced by her thorough womanliness and modesty of manner.

Mrs. Caroline K. Sherman, who gave a lecture in the Goethe course at Concord in 1885, is well and favorably known in the most cultured literary circles of Chicago. She was one of the early members of the Chicago Athena Club, devoted to the study of Herbert Spencer and like philosophical works. She is an honored member of the Chicago Women's Club, which owes to her its department committee of Philosophy and Science. She has given careful study to the works of Plato, Dante, Goethe, Hegel, and kindred thinkers. She has been for years a leader of classes in these studies, given frequent lectures in the same lines, and is President of the Chicago Dante Club and chairman of the Woman's branch of the Department of Philosophy and Science of the World's Fair Congress Auxiliary.

During the whole period of its existence, the Concord School and its philosophers were targets for all the cheap wit of the newspaper humorists. The style and subjects of the different speakers were satirized caricatured, or parodied in paragraph or verse. Once in awhile these hits were really brightly amusing, as when the deeply philosophical paper of Dr. Edmund Montgomery, of Hempstead, Texas, entitled "Plato and Vital Organization," was read before the school, the rhyming wit of the Boston *Record* got off of the following:

Dr. Edmund Montgomery.

OUT-PLATOING THE PLATOISTS.

A Texan has floored the Concord crowd.
Sing hi! and sing ho! for the great Southwest.
He sent 'em a paper to read aloud,
And 'twas done up in style by one of their best.

The Texan he loaded his biggest gun
With all the wise words he ever had seen,
And he fired at long range with death grim fun,
And slew all the sages with his machine.

He muddled the muddlers with brain-cracking lore;
He went in so deep that his followers were drowned,

But he swam out himself to the telluric shore,
And crowed in his glee o'er the earthlings around.

Envoy.

Oh, Plato, dear Plato, come back from the past,
And we'll forgive all that you e'er did to vex us,
If you'll only arrange for a colony vast
And whisk these philosophers all off to Texas.

Another paper represents a later lecturer, the well-known William R. Alger, the essayist and brilliant prose poet, as following in the wake of Doctor Montgomery in the use of those philosophical terms so puzzling to the popular mind, and says: "The Rev. W. R. Alger, of Boston, came up to Concord this morning, with each barrel of his gatling gun of philosophy loaded to the muzzle with equal parts of 'Plato, Buddha, Swedenborg and Fichte, concerning an Immortal Self,' with the hopper in first-class order, with the crank well greased, and in fact with every part so regulated as to do the deadliest execution. It would seem as if he had read the *Record* story of how the wild Texan cowboy philosopher, Doctor Montgomery, 'obfusticated' the philosophers and philosopheresses the other day, and, filled with envy at the tale, had come to Concord thoroughly determined to out-Montgomery Montgomery or die in the attempt."

The cream of these joking allusions to Doctor Montgomery as a "wild Texan cowboy philosopher," can only be enjoyed by those who have had the pleasure of the personal acquaintance of this scholarly, cultured, high-bred gentleman. Dr. Edmund Montgomery, though born in Scotland, of distinguished Scottish lineage, passed his childhood in Paris, and was educated in the best German universities, where he had the advantage of attending the lectures of the leaders in science and philosophy. From his earliest years he had a passion for scientific research and speculative philosophy, and years before coming to America he was a valued contributor to English scientific journals. As his health had been undermined by the vicissitudes of his profession, he bought the Liendo plantation, in Hempstead, Texas, when he came to America, in 1871, partly from motives of health, but mainly to gain quiet and time for his philosophic studies and scientific experiments. Classic in feature, courtly in manner, distinguished in bearing, such is the "Texan cowboy" of the Concord School. He is among those chosen to represent his State at the World's Fair.

Among the most philosophical thinkers heard at Concord, was Rowland G. Hazard, of Rhode Island, since deceased. He was,

339

versity, and Elisha Mulford, author of "The Republic of God" and other striking theological works.

When we take mental stock of this array of intellectual force brought into harmonious activity through the medium of the Concord Summer School of Philosophy, it will be easily perceived that the thought emanating from such a body of men and women could not fail to prove a strong factor in the awakening and uplifting of thinkers everywhere into a stronger and purer intellectual and spiritual atmosphere.

We may call Alcott and the others who made the Concord School a possibility dreamers and students of the impracticable, if we choose, but in the rounded vision which takes in the whole needs and purposes of life, its spiritual cravings as well as its sense longings, it must seem no small thing in this materialistic age, in this swirling rush and roar of commercial greed and mechanical activities, to have called together for a number of years the thinkers and ethical teachers for a few quiet country weeks to compare notes, arouse the intellect, take stock of knowledge in store, and reach daringly forward in search of the unknown. The Concord School is dead, men say, but before it died it accomplished its work — it sowed seeds of culture, of love of knowledge, of desire for virtue, of aspiration for all things good and beautiful; and all over the country to-day circles gather here and there, small though they may be, and pursue the lines of inquiry and of higher thought awakened by the Concord School and its philosophers; for among the attendants at that school were many of strong intellects and highly spiritualized natures, who, absorbing all the varied intellectual and spiritual food set before them in this feast of reason, have since grown strong in power and purpose, and have become awakeners and teachers in their turn.

Chicago.   SARA A. UNDERWOOD.

strange to say, a wealthy manufacturer who was deeply interested in philosophical problems, and held somewhat original views. He was well known as the author of several metaphysical books, among them a work examining Doctor Edwards' theory of the will, wherein he attempted, with considerable skill, to reconcile the doctrine of philosophical necessity with moral freedom. He was recognized by John Stuart Mill and others as a deep thinker and a good logician. His lectures at Concord were on such subjects as "Man as a Creative Power," "Utility of Metaphysical Pursuits," etc.

John Fiske, who has made so indelible an impression on American literature by his splendid work in philosophy and history, was also one of the high intellects which the Concord School called to its aid in discussing the knotty problems of existence. One of his lectures given at the school in discussion of the question "Is Pantheism the Legitimate Outcome of Modern Science?" is embodied in his published work entitled "The Idea of God," and another volume, "The Destiny of Man," is a lecture given there on immortality.

Prof. William James, of Harvard, son of the Swedenborgian philosopher, Henry James, Sr., and brother of the renowned Anglo-American novelist, Henry James, Jr., himself a distinguished specialist in psychology, whose work has been recently so specially helpful

John Fiske.

in psychical research, was another distinguished Concord philosopher who tried there to help unriddle the problem of the universe.

Many widely differing thinkers were invited to voice their philosophic conclusions on congenial subjects on the simply arranged platform of the orchard chapel. We recall among these such as that eminent educator and orthodox authority on ethics and philosophy, Rev. Noah Porter, President of Yale College; Rev. Dr. McCosh, the acute metaphysician of the Scotch school and for so long the head of Princeton Uni-

THE FIRST DERIVATIVE SUMMER SCHOOL—AT ST. CLOUD (NOW A PART OF WEST ORANGE, NEW JERSEY)—JUNE 20 THROUGH JULY 18, 1887—PRECEDED THE CLOSING OF THE CONCORD
— EXPERIMENT ———

Professor Thomas Davidson, formerly of Orange, N.J., was apparently the guiding spirit in the attempt to create a summer session south of New England in New Jersey. ("St. Cloud," a small farming community, for a number of years had its name survive in the St. Cloud Mushroom Farm, located at the intersection of what are now Mt. Pleasant and Mt. Prospect Avenues. A restaurant stands at that crossroads today.) No printed program seems to be extant, but the elaborate one issued for the Farmington Summer School of Philosophy, printed on the following pages, implies a rich one.   The West Orange newspapers, published but once a week, could obviously devote no space to the daily sessions. The Orange Journal ignored the school completely. The Orange Chronicle of Saturday, July 9, 1887 (XIX, no. 962, page 3) made the following comment at its conclusion:

SUMMER SCHOOL OF PHILOSOPHY.

The St. Cloud Summer School of Philosophy, which opened its session on June 20th and closed last evening, was a genuine success. The audience filled the place of meeting twice daily and listened with unabated interest. The morning hours of the course were given to "Practical Philosophy" and those of the Eevening [sic] to "sthetic". The former opened with a paper by Professor Thomas Davidson on "Greek Education up to Aristotle's Time." Fourteen lectures were given on various phases of Aristotle's thought. The evenings were devoted chiefly to eight lectures on Greek art, profusely illustrated by the stereoptican, while the opening six were given to the Greek drama, AEschylus, etc. The speakers, in addition to Professor Davidson, were Mr. Edward D. Mead, of Boston, the well known lecturer, Dr. Filmore Moore and Mrs. Helen Campbell, and the entire course was so arranged as to give a very complete introduction to Greek thought in its highest aspects. Apart from to-day as such thought may seem, the student soon discovers that the best we own begins with the ancients, and that nothing more vital is spoken or thought to-day. At seventy-eight Goethe one day expressed the wish for longer life that he might devote it to the increasing study of Aristotle, and though to a busy generation this may seem impossible, at least, all who have had the good fortune to hear the present course, understand better the source of his enthusiasm. The attendance has numbered interested students from St. Louis, from the South and from New England, and the request is urgent for a repetition of the work another year. Professor Davidson is not only one of the best Greek scholars in the country, but an equal authority on art and archaeology, having lived in Greece, and assisted Dr. Schliemann in some of his researches, and he adds to rare knowledge the power to impart it in the most thorough and delightful manner, with an enthusiasm that never flags and a patience that never wearies in answering all questions. The mountain, well known and loved by a few, has been at its best, not even a few days of excessive heat being sufficient to mar the enjoyment, and it is hoped that the present session is the foundation of more extended work to come.

THE THOMAS DAVIDSON SCHOOL OF PHILOSOPHY IN FARMINGTON, CONNECTICUT, JUNE 18—JULY 6, 1888——ALSO CALLED "SUMMER SCHOOL FOR THE CULTURAL SCIENCES"[1]

In Mrs. Jesse Moore's diary,[2] the Farmington Village Library preserves a few references to the 1888 summer session and to those of the following two (?) years, but no printed circulars or newspaper clippings survive. (Apparently the press of Hartford, Bristol and New Britain gave the school no publicity. Farmington had no paper of its own.) If the Davidson experiment continued in Connecticut beyond 1888, we cannot speak with certainty about its programs except to say with Mrs. Moore that they were "the peak of Farmington intellectual life." When it broke up, some of its leaders formed a summer school in the countryside at Greenacre, Maine. Davidson, for another, selected a farm near Keene, N.Y. The Farmington meetings "were held either in the (then) Methodist Church, near where the library now stands, or in the (then) Chapel, now moved, and the Grange Hall." Among the surviving notations is the following: "The building in which the school was held now is the Recreation Center for the young people. It has at times been chapel, school, Grange Hall, club house for the Italian people and had a variety of other uses.... It has been moved to make way for a new parish house and for this [village] library at a later date. It now stands back from the church at the top of Church St." As might be expected, townsmen contemporary with the school considered the visitors a "group of queer people, with funny ideas, who dressed in an odd manner."[3]

---

1 See "Thomas Davidson," <u>D A B</u>, V, 95-97.
2 Dr. Fillmore Moore, prominent on the program for 1888, seems to have been brother-in-law to Mrs. Jesse Moore, the diarist.
3 The above quotations are taken from a number of anonymous observations sent to me on July 25, 1967, in a letter from Miss Jane Hayward, Reference Librarian in the Village Library, to whom I am grateful for this courtesy.

EMERSON HOUSE — Built in 1828. Owned by Ralph Waldo Emerson
from 1835 to 1882

FARMINGTON

Lectures on Philosophy and Art.

Last year, by way of experiment and with very limited accommodation, a course of lectures, intended as preparatory and supplementary to those of the Concord Summer School, was given at St. Cloud, N. J. The experiment having been beyond all expectation successful, the organizers have resolved to give a similar course this year. As the Concord School, however, has no session this summer, these lectures will be entirely independent, and, with a view to insure sufficient accommodation for all comers, they will be given at Farmington, Conn. There will in all be thirty lectures, two a day, (morning and evening), from June 18th to July 6th. There will be a free discussion after each lecture.

There will be two courses of lectures, one mainly theoretical and historical, the other mainly practical. In the former an attempt will be made to trace the COURSE OF EUROPEAN THOUGHT WITH REGARD TO THE HIGHEST THINGS, FROM THE EPOCH OF THE GREAT REVIVAL OF PHILOSOPHY IN THE THIRTEENTH CENTURY TO THE PRESENT, and to do so, as far as possible, through the great works of poetic art. By this method, it is hoped a human interest will be imparted to philosophic study, and an insight gained into the meaning of true poetry. In the latter will be considered the PRIME CONDITIONS OF HUMAN WELL BEING—WEALTH, HEALTH AND VIRTUE—AND THE MODES OF REACHING THEM. Every effort has been made to give unity to this course.

FARMINGTON.

Farmington is a quaint, old, shady New England town, standing on the western slope of a considerable eminence, overlooking the Farmington and Pequabuck rivers, and affording beautiful and extensive views in many directions. It is on the New Haven and Northampton R. R., about 30 miles from New Haven, 46 from Northampton, and 10 from Hartford. The town is about two miles from the station. The rugged hills and broad valleys about Farmington afford excellent opportunities for pleasant walks, rides, and drives, while the rivers are very convenient for bathing and boating. The climate is salubrious, the heat moderate, and the region almost free from mosquitoes. Board can be obtained in the town at the rate of $10 a week, and, by special arrangements with private families, even at less. The quaint old Inn, which is excellently kept, affords accommodation for a considerable number of persons. Those desiring to secure good rooms for the season of the lectures, are requested to apply to Mrs. Rutherford, Elm Tree Inn, Farmington, Conn.

MORNING COURSE.

(9.30.)

THE LECTURES OF THIS COURSE WITH THE EXCEPTION OF THE 8TH AND 10TH WILL BE GIVEN BY MR. THOMAS DAVIDSON.

June 18.—I. Introductory. The present Status of Thought, and the need for a comprehensive Philosophy, based on Science, to give unity and aim to Life. Followed by a discourse by Thomas Sterry Hunt, L.L. D., on The Present Aspect of Chemical Theories.

A.—*Mediæval Catholic Thought as Embodied in Dante.*

June 19.—II. The Revival of Thought in Europe in the Thirteenth Century. Aristotle in the Schools.

June 20.—III. Dante's Ideology and Logic. (Theory of Cognition.)
June 21.—IV. Dante's Theology and Cosmology. CREATION.
June 22.—V. Dante's Psychology. Origin, Nature and Aim of the Soul.
June 25.—VI. Dante's Ethics and Ethical Sanctions. AUTHORITY.

B.—*The Pagan Renaissance as Summed up in Goethe's Faust.*

June 26.—VII. The Revolt against Scholasticism, (1) in Religion, (2) in Science FREEDOM and EVOLUTION.

June 27.—VIII. The Modern Spirit of Revolt. Marlowe's Mephistophilis and Goethe's Mephistopheles. By RICHARD HOVEY, Washington, D. C.

June 28.—IX. *Natur und Geist* (Nature and Spirit), their Meaning and Relation as set forth in *Faust.*

June 29.—X. Goethe's Ethics and Pedagogics. By WM. T. HARRIS, LL. D., Concord, Mass.

C.—*Modern Catholic Thought as Represented by Rosmini.*

July 2.—XI. Rosmini's Place in Modern Thought. Scholasticism in the Light of Kantian Criticism.

July 3.—XII. Rosmini's Doctrine of Being—Ideal, Real, Moral.
July 4.—XIII. Rosmini's Psychology and Pedagogics.

D.—*Modern Thought, as Exhibited in Tennyson's In Memoriam.*

July 5.—XIV. The Relation of Religion to Science.
July 6.—XV. Feeling as the Ground of Faith.

Although the above seems the most natural order of presentation, it may in a few cases have to be altered to suit the convenience of lecturers. There is reason to hope, however, that no great changes will be needed.

The fee for the whole thirty lectures will be $12; for either the morning or the evening course, separately, $6; single lectures, 50c. Tickets may be obtained after June 1st from Dr. Fillmore Moore, Farmington, Conn.

On some of the afternoons and on Saturdays there will be special entertainments. Mr. Richard Hovey will give readings from Dante, Goethe and Tennyson, and Mr. Frederic Clark and Mrs. Anna Steiniger-Clark will give classic concerts, &c. For these special arrangements will be necessary.

If there be sufficient demand for it, the course of lectures on Greek Sculpture (illustrated with the stereopticon), given at St. Cloud last summer, will be repeated on two afternoons a week. For these a special charge of $2 will be made, except from those persons who attended them last summer.

Persons wishing to attend the lectures will do well to read beforehand:

1. Dante's *Divine Comedy, Feast* (Convivio) and *New Life.*
2. Goethe's *Faust* and *Wilhelm Meister.*
3. Rosmini's *Philosophical System*, (translated by Thomas Davidson; Ginn & Co., Boston), and *The Ruling Principle of Method Applied to Education*, (translated by Mrs. William Grey; D. C. Heath & Co., Boston.)
4. Tennyson's *In Memoriam.*
5. Dr. C. M. Woodward's *The Manual Training School.* (D. C. Heath & Co., Boston.)
6. The works of the different lecturers in the Evening Course.
   Questions relating to the lectures may be addressed to Thomas Davidson, Farmington, Conn.

EVENING COURSE.

(7.30.)

A.—*Wealth, the Material Element in Human Well-Being.*

June 18.—I. The Social Basis of Economic Science. By GEORGE GUNTON. Author of "Wealth and Progress."

June 19.—II. The Relations of the Economic Condition of the Laboring Class to the Prosperity of the Community. By the same.

June 20.—III. The Social Aspect of the Labor Question. The Duty of the State. By the same.

June 21.—IV. The Moral Bearings of Economics. By GARRITT DROPPERS, M. A.

B.—*Health, the Internal Harmony of the Human Powers.*

June 22.—V. The Unity of the Human Being and its Relation to Health. By FILLMORE MOORE, M. D.

June 25.—VI. The Vegetable or Nutritive in Man. Food, &c. By the same.

June 26.—VII. The Animal or Sensitive in Man. By M. L. HOLBROOK, M. D., Editor of the *Herald of Health.*

June 27.—VIII. The Human and Divine in Man. By FILLMORE MOORE, M. D.

C.—*Virtue, the Path of Spiritual Progress.*

June 28.—IX. The Idea of God in Ethics. By J. H. HYSLOP, Ph. D.

June 29.—X. The Groundwork of Ethics. By EDMUND MONTGOMERY, M. D., Hempstead, Texas.

July 2.—XI. The Moral and Intellectual Results of Manual Training. By NICHOLAS MURRAY BUTLER, Ph. D., President of the Industrial Education Association of New York.

July 3.—XII. Education, Intellectual, Emotional and Manual, in Piano-playing By FREDERIC CLARK, Cambridge, Mass.

July 4.—XIII. The Ethics of Self-Sacrifice. By JANET E. RUUTZ-REES, Author "Holbein," "The Sin of Ill Health," &c.

July 5.—XIV. The Intellectual Element in Ethics. By EDWARD M. GALLAUDET, Ph. D., LL. D., President of the National Deaf-Mute College, Washington, D. C.

July 6.—XV. Moral Law from the Standpoint of Evolution. By RAYMOND S. PERRIN, New York, Author of "The Religion of Science."

A DIRECT OR INDIRECT STIMULUS AND RESOURCE FOR SCHOOLS OF PHI-
LOSOPHY AND LECTURE COURSES DURING THIS PERIOD OF CON-
CORD EXPERIMENTING WAS THE FREE RELIGIOUS ASSO-
CIATION OF AMERICA, DESCRIBED IN THE FOL-
LOWING PAGES.

[A glance at the names of those who supported the Free Religious Association and at the titles of lectures given in courses sponsored by it and by derivative groups like the Radical Club will make clear its pertinence to the present volume. Cooke's article appeared in the New England Magazine, n.s. XXVIII, no. 4 (June, 1903), pp. 484–499.]

Photo by
Alfred W. Hosmer

EMERSON'S STUDY AT CONCORD, SHOWING HIS FAVORITE TABLE, CHAIR, AND THE INKSTAND
INTO WHICH HE DIPPED HIS INSPIRED PEN

The Free Religious Association

By George Willis Cooke

THE Free Religious Association was the result of the teachings of Emerson, Parker, and those who agreed with them. It was a protest against the conservatism of the majority of the Unitarian body, who complained of the persecution they had received from the orthodox Congregationalists, but in their turn were not liberal enough to refrain from the same cruel wrong. The causes that led to the organization of this association date back to the beginnings of the transcendental movement, to the criticism of Emerson for his Divinity School address, to the withdrawal of sympathy from Parker because of his South Boston sermon, to the resolution and address of the American Unitarian Association that declared war against the teachings of the more radical persons connected with that body. Not a little of intolerance was shown towards those who thought with Parker, and they were disfellowshipped in fact if not in name. The more conservative men would not exchange pulpits with those who were more outspoken and rationalistic, a thing that Unitarians had complained of bitterly in their relations with those from whom they had come out. In fact, the old theological venom was there still, even if the name liberal had been assumed.

It was at the close of the Civil War that the struggle between the two wings of the Unitarian body, begun as the result of transcendentalism, came to a direct issue. In the spring of 1865 a convention of Unitarians was called to meet in New York, the first delegate gathering of that body. The war was closing, enthusiasm was high, Dr. Henry W. Bellows of New York had shown himself a great leader as the president of the Sanitary Commission, a missionary fund of $100,000 had been secured, and the Unitarian body looked forward to a wide-reaching influence throughout the country. It was proposed to organize a National Conference, and to make Unitarianism a strong and aggressive force. A large number of able leaders appeared in the convention, including such men as John A. Andrew, governor of Massachusetts; Bryant, Curtis, Palfrey, Hoar, Dewey, Bellows, Clarke, Hale and many others.

When the convention came to organize itself permanently it showed two antagonistic tendencies. One of these looked to a broad and inclusive movement, that should gather to itself all the liberal churches and persons of the country, that should have no creed, but should undertake a great humanitarian work that would be thoroughly American in spirit. In some degree this demand found expression, and an effort was made to draw together all the progressive religious bodies and movements in the country. Opposed to this tendency was one that called

for a distinctly Unitarian organization, that should affirm itself Christian, and that should have a creed if possible. The more conservative element won the day, the Unitarian name was adopted, the Lordship of Christ was affirmed; but it was not possible to secure a formal creed.

In 1866 the Unitarian National Conference met in Syracuse, and the struggle was there renewed between the conservatives and radicals. The more liberal ministers and delegates declared that "the only reconciliation of the duties of collective Christian activity and individual freedom of thought lies in an efficient organization for practical Christian work, based rather on unity of spirit than on uniformity of belief." The conservative party, however, had grown more positively Unitarian in its position, and no reconciliation was possible, though the attempt was renewed for several years.

When it was found that nothing could be accomplished in the way of making Unitarianism broad and inclusive in an organized religious body, the younger and more radical men determined to organize a new association. Those who had been affected by transcendentalism, and those who had come into the spirit of the newer scientific methods that had grown out of the teachings of Darwin and his coworkers, were drawn nearer each other as the result of the opposition they had been compelled to encounter. The purpose which drew these persons together was stated by Rev. William J. Potter, the first secretary of the Free Religious Association, in the account he gave of its formation in the first book of its records. "The

cause," he therein wrote of the formation of the new association, "is to be found in the various progressive and converging religious tendencies of the time, away from the conflicting authorities of specific religious systems and from the bonds of creeds and churches, to a union as broad as humanity itself, on the ground of common aspirations to know the truth and common efforts to live pure and beneficent lives. It is these tendencies that brought the Free Religious Association. Still, those who first moved for an organization were a few radical Unitarians, who, having failed in an attempt, first at New York in 1865, and again at Syracuse in 1866, to strike from the constitution of the National Conference every implication of a creed and make it a platform for what is called, in a general way, Christian work, believed that the time had come for some new association, which should be inclusive of the free religious thought of the time, and do a work in behalf of spiritual unity and human brotherhood which could not be done by any of the religious denominations. Upon several of the younger men who attended the Syracuse convention this conviction seems to have been separately and forcibly impressed before they reached their homes, and they inwardly resolved to do whatever was in their power to carry this conviction into action."

Indeed, some conference on the subject was had on the train from Syracuse to Boston, and the result was two meetings held in the house of Dr. Cyrus A. Bartol, pastor of the West Church in Boston, who resided at 17 Chestnut Street. Dr. Bartol was not in favor of a new organization, for he

WM. HENRY CHANNING

DAVID A. WASSON

JOHN WEISS

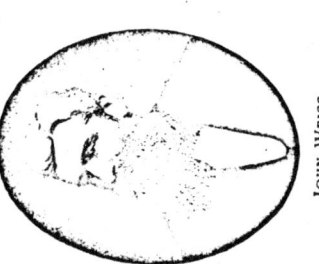

THOMAS W. HIGGINSON

EDNAH D. CHENEY

LUCRETIA MOTT

SAMUEL LONGFELLOW

JOHN S. DWIGHT

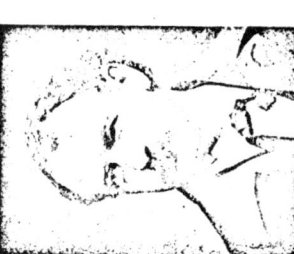

S. H. MORSE

CHRISTOPHER P. CRANCH

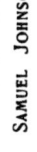

SAMUEL JOHNSON

was of those who preferred to make a strong effort to liberalize the Unitarian body; but he sympathized warmly with the younger men in their efforts to protest against the want of genuine tolerance that had been manifested. At the first of the informal meetings in the house of Dr. Bartol nine persons were present, all of them having a more or less definite connection with Unitarianism. With one or two exceptions the same persons met at the second conference; and two others were present. At these preliminary conferences the feeling was about equally divided for and against a new organization, though all were agreed as to the importance of protesting against the platform of the National Unitarian Conference and on the desirableness of the objects that were to be sought in the proposed new association. But to a portion of those present it seemed that these objects could be accomplished better by individual activity, and thereby the traditional dangers of organization in religion be escaped.

To the insistent efforts of three young ministers was due the organization of the Free Religious Association. These were Francis E. Abbot, of Dover, New Hampshire; William J. Potter, of New Bedford, Massachusetts; and Edward C. Towne, of Medford, Massachusetts. They met at Towne's house to consider the situation. As they were parting in the morning, after a night of consultation, Abbot said to his friends, "Let us three pledge ourselves to each other never to rest until our new association for freedom in religion is formed!" They solemnly and with deep feeling clasped hands over it. After long correspondence and anxious consultation, these three met at the Parker House in Boston and spent a whole day alone together in deliberating over a constitution. Potter wrote out the result, and it was submitted and accepted without change.

In the meantime it had been decided to call a larger conference, to meet at the house of Dr. Bartol, February 5, 1866. This call was signed by O. B. Frothingham, minister of an independent church in New York, formerly a Unitarian: John Weiss, minister of the Unitarian church in Watertown; and Towne, Abbot and Potter. The purpose was set forth in these words: "Since all prevailing denominational religious organizations set limits, more or less strict, to religious inquiry and fellowship, and since the recent attempts to organize even the most liberal denomination of Christians, as shown in the National Conference of Unitarian Churches, have fallen into the same error, and so have failed to satisfy the demands of the liberal faith, it is believed that the time has come to form a new association in spiritual bonds, on the basis of free thought, for the purpose of bringing

like-minded men together, of gathering to a head powers that are working too aimlessly in the same general direction, and of diffusing rational truths by rational methods. The desire is to make a fellowship, not a party; to promote the scientific study of religious truth, not to defend the legacy of theological tradition; to keep open the lines of spiritual freedom, not to close the lines of speculative belief."

In the record book already mentioned, Mr. Potter made the following statement in regard to the character and results of this meeting: "It was a notable gathering that was the result of this invitation. Not nearly all the Unitarian ministers addressed responded in person; but, aside from Unitarians, there were representatives present of liberal Universalism, of progressive Quakerism, of Theodore Parker's society, as well as persons who could not be classified by any theological or denominational name. The discussion was earnest and able. There were some speeches made that will never be forgotten by those who heard them. Women participated in this meeting. A plan of association had been carefully prepared by Messrs. Abbot, Towne and Potter (the three members of the smaller conferences who had most urged organization), and this made the nucleus of the discussion. There was the same division of judgment as appeared in the smaller conferences, and it was especially urged by a number of Unitarian ministers that they would serve liberty better by remaining in the Unitarian organizations and endeavoring to broaden them. To this argument it was replied that the new association did not necessitate nor contemplate a secession from Unitarianism nor any other churches, but provided for a fellowship of liberal minds of various sects for doing a work no one of them was doing. It was finally agreed by a nearly unanimous vote to appoint a committee to call a public meeting at which the same questions which had been presented at the conference should be considered." The call for a public meeting to assemble in Horticultural Hall, Boston, May 30, 1867, was signed by Ralph Waldo Emerson, John Weiss, Robert Dale Owen, William H. Furness, Lucretia Mott, Henry Blanchard, Thomas Wentworth Higginson, David A. Wasson, Isaac M. Wise, Oliver Johnson, Francis E. Abbot and Max Lilienthal.

At the public meeting the hall was crowded to its utmost capacity, and the greatest interest was manifested in the proceedings. The Free Religious Association was organized in the afternoon, the forenoon having been devoted to addresses by O. B. Frothingham, Rev. Henry Blanchard, Lucretia Mott, Robert Dale Owen, Rev. John Weiss, Oliver Johnson, Francis E. Abbot, and David A. Wasson, "its objects being", according to the constitution then adopted, "to promote the interests of pure religion, to encourage the scientific study of theology, and to increase fellowship in the spirit." In 1874 this wording was changed, and the objects were then defined to be "to promote the practical interests of pure religion, to increase fellowship in the spirit, and to encourage the scientific study of man's religious nature and history." It was declared that "membership in this association shall leave each individual responsible for his own opinions alone, and affect in no degree his relations to other associations." This was added to, in 1874, by the statement that "nothing in the name or constitution of the Association shall ever be construed as limiting membership by any test of speculative opinion or belief,—or as defining the position of the Association, collectively considered, with reference to any such opinion or belief,—or as interfering, in any other way, with that absolute freedom of thought and expression which is the natural right of every rational being."

FRANK B. SANBORN

WILLIAM J. POTTER

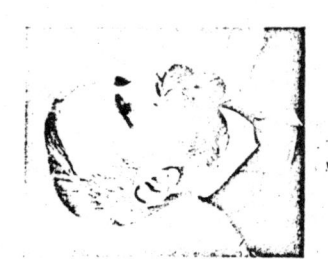

FRANCIS E. ABBOT

The officers elected were Octavius B. Frothingham as president; and Robert Dale Owen, Thomas Wentworth Higginson and Caroline M. Severance, as vice-presidents. William J. Potter was made the secretary, with Rowland Connor, a Universalist pastor in Boston, as his assistant. The directors included Isaac M. Wise, the leader of the progressive Jews of this country; Frank B. Sanborn, the well known editor and philanthropist; and Ednah D. Cheney, lecturer and reformer. The most notable event of the afternoon sessions, however, as of the whole meeting, was the address by R. W. Emerson. He was in fullest sympathy with the purposes of the Association. Most of the younger men and women taking part in this new movement had been largely influenced by his teachings. Although he was not active in bringing about the new organization, as such efforts were not in the line of his genius, he furnished to a large degree the motive and the ideal that brought it into existence. His definition of the purposes of the movement could not be more concisely or comprehensively stated: "I think the necessity very great, and it has prompted an equal magnanimity,

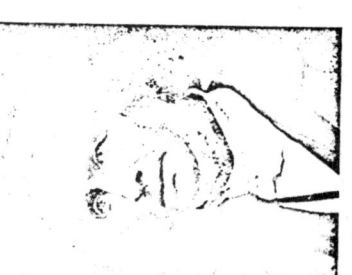

CYRUS A. BARTOL

that invites all classes, all religious men, whatever their connections, whatever their specialties, in whatever relation they stand to the Christian Church, to unite in a movement of benefit to men, under the sanction of religion. We are all very sensible,—it is forced on us every day,—of the feeling that churches are outgrown; that the creeds are outgrown; that a technical theology no longer suits us. It is not the ill-will of the people—no, indeed, but the incapacity for confining themselves there. The church is not large enough for the man; it cannot inspire the enthusiasm which is the parent of everything good in history, which makes the romance of history. For that enthusiasm you must have something greater than yourself, and not less. . . .

"As soon as every man is apprised of the Divine Presence in his own mind,—is apprised that the perfect law of duty corresponds with the laws of chemistry, of vegetation, of astronomy, as face to face in a glass; that the basis of duty, the order of society, the power of character, the wealth of culture, the perfection of taste, all draw their essence from this moral sentiment, then we have a religion that exalts, that commands all the social and all the private action."

At the second annual meeting of the Association Emerson again spoke, and his words are of special interest because he gave a definite statement of his own religious position and faith:

"I think we have disputed long enough. I think we may now relinquish our theological controversies to communities more idle and ignorant than we. I am glad that a more realistic church is coming to be the tendency of society, and that we are likely one day to forget our obstinate polemics in the ambition to excel each other in good works. I have no wish to proselyte any reluctant mind, nor, I think, have I any curiosity or impulse to intrude on those whose ways of thinking differ from mine. But I am ready to give, as often before, the first simple foundation of my belief, that the Author of Nature

has not left himself without a witness in any sane mind; that the moral sentiment speaks to every man the law after which the universe was made; that we find parity, identity of design, through Nature, and benefit to be the uniform aim; that there is a force always at work to make the best better and the worst good. . . .

"I am glad to hear each sect complain that they do not now hold the opinions they are charged with. The earth moves, and the mind opens. I am glad to believe society contains a class of humble souls who enjoy the luxury of a religion that does not degrade; who think it the highest worship to expect of Heaven the most and the best; who do not wonder that there was a Christ, but that there were not a thousand; who have conceived an infinite hope for mankind; who believe that the history of Jesus is the history of every man, written large."

While the free religious movement began as a protest against the narrowness and conservatism of the Unitarian body, and has in some degree always retained that characteristic, it had from the beginning a definite motive and purpose. Its most definitive idea was from the first that of what Colonel T. W. Higginson called "the sympathy of religions", or that essentially all religions are of the same origin and nature. It was therefore maintained that Christianity, instead of being, as Theodore Parker declared, the absolute religion, is but one of the phases of universal religion, and that, in the words of William J. Potter, it is "provisional, preparatory, educational." Another leading idea was that of perfect individual freedom, and the largest assertion of individuality. It was maintained by Francis E. Abbot that "the spiritual ideal of Free Religion is to develop the individuality of the soul in the highest, fullest and most independent

manner possible." It was his conviction that the attitude of Christianity is that of the suppression of self and the imitation of Christ, while he maintained that the spiritual ideal of Free Religion "is the development of self, and the harmonious education of all its powers to the highest possible degree." It will be seen by such parts of the constitution of the Association as have been given above that every effort was made to put no limits upon personal freedom; and that the Association not only did not have a creed, but that it would not define its own position in such a manner as to put the slightest check upon individual opinion. The free religious movement was, in a word, the culmination of transcendentalism, and its acceptance of intuition and self-reliance. It discarded institutional and historical religion, and accepted that of individual spiritual insight and the rational activity of the personal mind. As a result, those transcendentalists, like Hedge and Clarke, who had been influenced by the idea of the historical and racial development of religion, took no part in the free religious movement nor opposed it. While William Henry Channing often spoke at the meetings of the Association, and found himself at many points in agreement with the free religionists, he was not of that school because he fully recognized the social nature of religion, and that there may be a revelation to a race or a nation as much as to an individual.

One of the aims with which the Free Religious Association began was to provide a platform on which the members of all the Christian denominations, and representatives of all the

religions, might meet for the comparison of opinions, and for the furtherance of those interests they have in common. At the time when it began it was very difficult or impossible to bring about such a result. At the first annual meeting, in May, 1868, an attempt was made to secure as many representatives of the various religious bodies as possible, with the result that Rev. Charles F. Malcolm, Baptist; Rev. John P. Hubbard, Episcopalian; Rev. Jesse H. Jones, Congregationalist; Rev. Olympia Brown (Willis), Universalist; Dr. Morris Ellinger, Hebrew; Rev. James Freeman Clarke and Rev. Robert Collyer, Unitarians; Rev. John Weiss, Radical; and Professor William Denton, Spiritualist, gave addresses. It soon became impossible to obtain the aid of representatives of any of the evangelical denominations; but representatives of the Friends, Universalists, Unitarians, Hebrews, Spiritualists, and other radical bodies, frequently took part in the proceedings. In later years many representatives of the Oriental religions realized in the Parliament of Religions in Chicago, the Liberal Congress, and other organizations and movements. While it failed in its own effort, the idea it put forward at a time too early for general acceptance, has not failed of realization, and on a scale of accomplishment far beyond its own resources.

The Association never has had a large following, and it has not organ-

ized a definite movement. Its meetings in Boston for many years were largely attended, and many persons in that city, as well as elsewhere, were in sympathy with its position. Its chief influence has been exercised through the men and women connected with it, and who have spoken from time to time on its platform or held a place among its officers. Such names as Emerson, Alcott, T. W. Higginson, Gerrit Smith, Lydia Maria Child, Lucretia Mott, George W. Curtis, James Parton, John Fiske, Edward L. Youmans, Aaron M. Powell and Elizabeth Cady Stanton, indicate the intellectual quality of the Association and the nature of its influence. That it has deeply appealed to such persons indicates that it met a real need of the time. The same tendency is seen in the succession of men who have held its chief official position, for here may be named Octavius B. Frothingham, an accomplished orator and preacher; Professor Felix Adler, the able originator and leader of the Societies for Ethical Culture; Rev. William J. Potter, a man of saintly temper and a preacher of rare gifts of persuasion; Col. Thomas Wentworth Higginson, widely known as a reformer and littérateur; Dr. Lewis G. Janes, a scholar of ability to originate and guide the Cambridge Conferences; and Mr. Edwin D. Mead, reformer, editor and director of the Old South historical work.

The Free Religious Association has not confined itself to its annual meetings in Boston nor neglected the attempt to extend its ideas and to definitely organize them. One of its first effors was that of a systematic course of lectures given each winter in some

leading hall in Boston. In this work it followed and took the place of the Parker Fraternity, which began about 1858 as a parish society connected with Theodore Parker's Music Hall congregation. In that year Parker gave before it his lectures on Franklin, Washington and Adams, afterward published in his "Historic Americans." As Parker and the other radicals could not be heard in the Boston lecture courses, the Fraternity afforded them an opportunity to utter their word on the burning questions of the day. After Parker's death this society took an active part in the management of the affairs of the Music Hall congregation; and for several years it provided lectures that were progressive. Soon after the organization of the Free Religious Association it took the place of the Fraternity, and gave for a number of winters courses of lectures expository of its position, either in Horticultural Hall or in Music Hall. In 1869 its course was as follows: John Weiss, "Religion Man's Reconciliation with God"; Mrs. Julia Ward Howe, "Of Religion"; David A. Wasson, "Political Protestantism"; William J. Potter, "Prayer"; Francis E. Abbot, "Free Religion and Christianity"; Thomas W. Higginson, "Immortality"; Mrs. Ednah D. Cheney, "Work and its Relations"; Josiah P. Quincy, "The State as an Educator"; O. B. Frothingham, "Supply and Demand in Religious Matters"; Samuel Johnson, "The Piety of Pantheism"; Mrs. Julia Ward Howe, "The Religion of America"; R. W. Emerson, "Natural Religion"; Wendell Phillips, "Christianity a Battle not a Dream." In 1870 the course was opened by John Weiss on "False and True Sen-

timent for Nature"; and he was followed by O. B. Frothingham, on "The Revealed and the Hidden God"; T. W. Higginson, "The Sympathy of Religions"; Samuel Longfellow, "Theism"; Mrs. Howe, "The Ethics of Culture"; Francis E. Abbot, "Jesus and Socrates in the History of Religion"; John S. Dwight, "Music"; W. J. Potter, "The Agency of Law and of Persons in Human History"; Mrs. Cheney, "The Function of Art in Life"; D. A. Wasson, "Jesus, Christianity and Modern Radicalism"; W. H. Channing, "The Church of Universal Unity"; Wendell Phillips, "Christianity." In 1870-1871 the course broadened out as to lecturers and also as to subjects, and became of a more popular character. The programme was as follows: Thomas Hughes, "John to Jonathan"; W. Phillips, "The Political Situation"; George W. Curtis, "Charles Dickens"; Robert Collyer, "Robert Burns"; Emerson, "Immortality"; Frothingham, "The Beliefs of Unbelievers"; Anne E. Dickinson, "Men's Rights"; Mary Grew, "Essential Christianity"; Weiss, "The American Opportunity"; Higginson, "Religion of the Heart"; Abbot, "The Civil War in Free Religion"; Potter, "Immortality and Science"; Wasson, "The Complaint of Labor"; John Fiske, "Auguste Comte and the Positive Polity"; Emerson, "The Rule of Life." For a number of years these lectures were largely attended, and they were widely reported. They were not continued because other courses took their place and because the interest in lectures began to wane about 1880.

The literary output of the Free Religious movement has been consider-

able, and its influence may be found in the published works of Emerson, Alcott, Higginson, Mrs. Howe, Weiss, Wasson, Johnson and many others. A notable series of pamphlets was issued by the Association from 1875 to 1877. The first of these was an address by James Parton on the "Taxation of Church Property." It was followed by John Weiss on "The Bible and Science"; T. W. Higginson, "The Sympathy of Religions"; Theodore Parker, a hitherto unpublished lecture on "Transcendentalism"; a discussion of the school question by Bishop McQuaid and Francis E. Abbot; and a discussion of the Sunday question by Minot J. Savage, William C. Gannett, Charles K. Whipple and Charles E. Pratt. These pamphlets were widely circulated and exerted a considerable influence. A large number of similar tracts were published by *The Index*, and were extensively distributed. In 1875 the Association secured the publication of a volume entitled "Freedom and Fellowship in Religion", which included an introductory interpretation of its position by Frothingham, and addresses that had been given before it by Wasson, Samuel Longfellow, Johnson, Weiss, Potter, Abbot, Frothingham, Chadwick, Higginson and Mrs. Cheney. Other volumes of notable importance published by it or by its leaders include one on Jesus by Samuel Johnson, Frothingham's "Religion of Humanity", and Weiss's "American Religion." The "Fifty Affirmations" of Francis Abbot attracted widespread interest and discussion. Higginson's "Sympathy of Religions" has kept its hold upon the public mind more permanently than any other publication connected with

the history of the Association, and its central idea has been more widely accepted. Emerson's addresses on "Immortality" and "Natural Religion" hold a prominent place in the body of his public teaching, and they embody the best of his later affirmations.

The interests of Free Religion were ably represented in the pages of *The Radical*, a monthly magazine of about one hundred pages, which was begun in Boston in September, 1865, with Sydney H. Morse as editor. He was assisted in the third, fourth and fifth volumes by Joseph B. Marvin. Its publication was continued through ten volumes, and came to an end in 1873. Morse was for a brief period a Unitarian minister, and after the discontinuance of *The Radical* he gained some distinction as a sculptor with his busts of Channing, Emerson, Lincoln, Whitman and others. Among the contributors were nearly all the persons whose names have been mentioned as connected with the work of the Free Religious Association, and several others added to its value. It was ably conducted, in a broad and inclusive spirit, and it represented the best purposes of the later transcendentalism. Morse was a zealous transcendentalist, a poet of no mean ability, and a prose writer of skill and incisiveness. He contributed to the magazine two novels that attracted attention and that deserve republication in more permanent form. *The Radical* had but a limited circulation, and Morse struggled with poverty in order to maintain it. A weekly journal called *The Index* was begun in Toledo in 1870, with Francis E. Abbot as editor. The next year it became in a measure the organ of the Association,

and in 1873 it was removed to Boston. In 1880 the paper came under the control of the Association, and so continued until its demise in 1886. This journal was ably edited by Abbot, Potter and W. H. Underwood; and its pages are filled with the indications of the intellectual ability of those connected with the Association.

As the Free Religious Association was organized to secure intellectual and religious freedom, and in order to maintain an organization without sectarian interests or implications, it has never been able to widely propagate its spirit or to establish its ideas in an aggressive movement. It has repeatedly attempted to undertake practical work of one kind or another, but never with any considerable degree of success. In 1870 it held conventions in Cincinnati, Indianapolis and Toledo, with the purpose of extending its ideas. In 1873 similar conventions were held in Philadelphia and Brooklyn; in 1882 at Syracuse and Chicago; in 1883 at New Haven and Albany; in 1884 at Providence and New Bedford. In Providence a local society, with regular Sunday meetings and a settled speaker, was maintained for a number of years; and it is possible similar organizations may have existed elsewhere. In connection with *The Index*, from about 1873 to 1880, Mr. Abbot established local organizations under the name of the Liberal League, which came to number about four hundred; but these soon proved ineffective, and ceased to exist.

From the beginning of its existence the Association attempted to organize an intellectual propaganda, that should be at once religious and based on perfect individual freedom. All attempts

of this kind, however, were met by objections on the part of a considerable number of its own members. The same difficulty appeared when philanthropic and reformatory work along social and moral lines was proposed. Nearly all the reforms of the day, including those the most radical, socialism being one of them, have been frequently in evidence on its platform, and have met with a hearty approval. In 1879 an urgent move was made to undertake practical work, and in 1881 a definite plan was outlined for this purpose. An agent was secured in the person of the secretary, meetings were held in several cities, state organizations were proposed, and an effective movement was desired by many. A radical division of opinion made success impossible, and in 1884 this attempt was abandoned. The president, Professor Felix Adler, withdrew from any active connection with the Association because it was not willing to push forward the work begun. In 1894, in connection with the organization of the Liberal Congress, another attempt was made to undertake aggressive work; but it was voted down at once and decisively.

The Association has not been without accomplished results, however, in the way of important reforms. It did something to remove the religious conditions qualifying the rights of witnesses in courts. It undertook to secure better Sunday legislation, and to open libraries, art galleries, etc., on Sunday. To this end it proposed, early in its career, to open a reading-room in Boston; but before it could accomplish that result the Boston Public Library and the Boston Art Museum were opened on Sundays. In

the same way it found its efforts for intellectual freedom met by the Unitarian Conference, which, in 1894, discarded the creed it had established in 1866, and took a basis essentially the same as that of the Association. This result was secured by the persistent and conciliatory efforts of Minot J. Savage, for many years minister of the Church of the Unity in Boston, and a devoted worker in the Association. The new constitution of the Unitarian Conference was more liberal and modern than that proposed by Mr. Abbot in 1866. From that time the work of the Association was necessarily subordinate in its nature, in so far as any practical effort is concerned. What it had attempted to accomplish in 1867 was largely brought about by the progressive spirit of the time, and by the new attitude of all the churches with reference to intellectual freedom, the higher criticism, and philanthropic labors in all reformatory directions. It may be justly assumed that in this country the Association pioneered the way for the intellectual advance in religion that has been made in the last forty years. In view of these facts it was eminently appropriate that the Free Religious Association should take the lead in commemorating the centennial of Emerson's birthday, and that it should organize for that purpose the Emerson Memorial School. In this act of large-minded recognition of its greatest leader it has shown that it yet has work to accomplish, and that it can undertake it in the true spirit of intellectual freedom.

A most interesting movement connected with the early history of the Free Religious Association must not be omitted from this recital of its ac-

tivities. The Chestnut Street or Radical Club was a direct outgrowth of the effort to organize the Association. After the large meeting held in the house of Dr. Bartol, in February, 1867, there was organized a club for the free discussion of subjects of interest to free thinkers. The prime mover in this attempt seems to have been Edward C. Towne, at that time minister of the Unitarian Church in Medford. Rev. John T. Sargent, whose home was at 13 Chestnut Street, Boston, invited the club to meet in his house. Mr. Sargent was a Unitarian minister who had charge of one of the churches to the poor, and who lost his place because he fraternized with Theodore Parker. He was too progressive to continue in a pulpit, but gave his aid to such reforms as were near his heart. His large house afforded room for the meetings of the club, which sometimes met in the house of Dr. Bartol, only a few doors away.

The first meeting of the Radical Club was held in the house of Mr. Sargent, in May, 1867. The essayist was Emerson, whose subject was religion. The substance of this essay has appeared in his published works, especially in the address given at the second meeting of the Free Religious Association. One passage may bear repetition. "It is safe to say," he declared, "that no one holds the Christian traditions as they were uniformly held in the last generation. We rest on the moral nature, and the whole world shortly must. The church, you tell us, is an institution of God. But are not wit, and wise men, and good judgment whether a thing be so or no also institutions of God, and older than the other? The commanding fact which the true soul never does *not* see is the sufficiency of the moral sentiment. You can never come to any peace or power until you put your whole reliance on the moral constitution of man, and not at all in any history." The discussion at this meeting was opened by Mr. Sargent, and he was followed by Mrs. Howe, Higginson, Weiss, Phillips, Elizabeth P. Peabody, Potter, Bartol and others. The meeting was one of great interest, and the discussion was vital, incisive and stimulating. In June the speaker was Samuel Longfellow, and his subject was "The Mode of Worship." In the autumn Bartol spoke on "The Idea of God", Alcott on "The Ministry Demanded by the Time", Weiss on "The True Scientific Method in Theology", Wasson on "The Epic Theory of Human Life", Frothingham on "The Historical Position of Jesus", and Potter on "Pre-existence."

The same persons appeared before the club as were connected with the Free Religious Association, either as essayists or as joining in the discussions. Weiss spoke on "Woman", "Music", "Heart in Religion", "Constancy to an Ideal Fatality." Wasson discussed "Democracy", "Thou Shalt", and other important subjects. Higginson read an essay on Sappho. Mrs. Howe discussed "Limitations", "Doubt and Belief", "Representation, and How to Secure it." Among the other essayists were Henry James, senior, Professor Charles Carroll Everett, Christopher P. Cranch, William C. Gannett, William J. Linton, Frank B. Sanborn, Frederic H. Hedge and others. The essays were of a high order and the discussions brilliant. Especially were they incisive on the occasions when Wendell Phillips was the speaker. He was a champion of Christianity of the older type, defending Calvinism, and maintaining that the ideals of the church were essential. As many of the members of the club were radical in their ideas, and some of them positively opposed to Christianity, these occasions were of an exciting nature. William Henry Channing was also disposed to defend the Christian position, as was Mrs. Howe. In regard to this subject, Mrs. Howe says in her "Reminiscences": "I did indeed hear at these meetings much that pained and even irritated me. The disposition to seek outside the limits of Christianity for all that is noble and inspiring in religious culture, and to recognize especially within 'these limits the superstition and intolerance which have been the bane of all religions—this disposition, which was frequently manifested both in the essays presented and in their discussion, offended not only my affections, but also my sense of justice." Doubtless this was due to a reaction against the same attitude taken by many Christians towards the other religions of the world, and their blindness in failing to see good except within Christian limits or even within the limits of their own special party. "While I cannot avoid recognizing the anti-Christian twist which mostly prevailed in the Radical Club," Mrs. Howe continues, "I am far from wishing to convey the impression that those of us who were otherwise affected were not allowed the opportunity of expressing our own individual opinions. The presence at the meetings of such men as James Freeman Clarke, Dr. Hedge, William Henry Channing and Wendell Phillips was a sufficient earnest of the catholicity of intention which prevailed in the government of the club."

During the early years of its existence, transcendentalism was much in evidence in the Radical Club. Not many of its essayists had been connected with the Transcendental Club,—though these included Emerson, Alcott, Bartol, Hedge, Cranch, Clarke,—but the spirit of it was present. Gradually the change to a scientific interest came about, and in its later years the club was dominated largely by the scientific spirit. Among the later essayists were Benjamin Peirce, N. S. Shaler, J. W. Powell, T. S. Hunt, Alpheus Hyatt, George Howison, John Fiske and O. W. Holmes. More and more the attitude of science came into prominence, and the idealistic philosophy disappeared. This change also took place in the management of the Free Religious Association, and led it away from the discussion of theological problems to those of practical ethics and social reform. A notable occasion in the history of the club was that on which Dr. O. W. Holmes discussed the teachings of Jonathan Edwards, and applied to them the tests of modern science. This was in the spring of 1880. The essay was bold, radical, brilliant and entertaining. It was discussed by Professor Peirce and Dr. Bowditch, who spoke in sympathy with the essayist. With them agreed, for the most part, Bartol, Wasson and Clarke. Exceptions were taken by Wendell Phillips, who thought the essayist had not stated the whole truth or done justice to Edwards.

The Radical Club was managed in

a most informal manner, the conventionalities of such gatherings being dispensed with. Mr. Sargent usually presided in a quiet and gentle manner, though he said but little. By his side sat his wife, who had a gift for the management of such meetings, and who gave to the club a social interest and charm that added much to its attractiveness. The parlors in which the club met would hold about one hundred persons, and were usually full, with the overflow placed in the hall and other available places. Mrs. Howe says she was grieved at not being invited to the first meetings of the club, such was their promise and their attractiveness; but she took part in the first formal meeting. She says the club was "a high congress of souls, in which many noble thoughts were uttered. Nobler than any special view or presentation was the general sense of the dignity of human character and of its affinity with things divine, which always gave the master tone to the discussion."

The club met at 10 A. M. on the third Monday of each month, except in the summer. At 10.30 the essay began, and it was followed immediately by the discussion, which lasted until one or two o'clock. A half hour was usually given to social intercourse, and then the members withdrew. Very soon after the club began it attracted attention and was widely reported in the newspapers. For several years Mrs. Louisa Chandler Moulton regularly reported its meetings in the New York *Tribune* with grace and wit. In 1868 she wrote of the meetings of the club: "Thus far the conversations have not been less interesting than the essays, marked by great freedom and

a degree of inspiration very rare in conferences of any kind. To many the club is divinity-school, church and communion, so instructive are the thoughts, so spiritual and sincere are the confessions, and so refreshing the fellowship of these hours of free religious conference. The high priests of new faith, the devotees of the free spirit, the ardent organizers of free religion, the zealous doers of every good work, gather here, full of intense interest, as in days of freshest enthusiasm disciples gathered in upper chambers to make ready for the descent of New Jerusalem out of heaven. Here are mystics who have watched with the Aurora of new revelation; here are prophets to whom, as of old, truth is a burden from the Holy Ghost; here are patient watchers under the cross of life, whose large hope of redemption is a pillar of heaven's presence in the utter darkness of a troubled world; here are workers in the wide field of universal charity, who have, in their single lives, with solid labor of pure love, laid more wall of the city of God than a whole age of sect and dogma might construct. The rare thoughtfulness, the deep human tenderness, the profound earnestness of these reunions are something remarkable."

Not all of the meetings of the Radical Club were devoted to the discussion of problems in theology and science. There were receptions to Emerson, a morning when original poems were read, and a day when Tyndall was the speaker. There came to the meetings such men as Charles Sumner, Dom Pedro of Brazil, Athanese Coquerel from Paris, and Lord Amberley from England. Indeed, one

of the attractions of the club was its social charm, exhibited in a fine spirit of intellectual equality. The ready repartee of the host and his thoroughly democratic spirit doubtless helped to make the meetings successful. The presence of both men and women, and the placing them on a plane of intellectual equality, had its important influence. Mr. Emerson soon withdrew from the club because its meetings were everywhere reported in the newspapers, but doubtless to many persons this was an added stimulus in giving zest and piquancy to their remarks. Certainly the club could have suffered nothing in taking into its fellowship by means of the public journals a wide-reaching company of readers in America and Europe.

The Free Religious Association, the Horticultural Hall Lectures, and the Radical Club were but parts of the same whole. The leaders were the same, and the same men and women belonged to them. They mark a brilliant epoch in the intellectual history of New England, and none can be named that is greater. They came at the culmination of the transcendental movement, and they furnished the medium of its transference to the new scientific interest that signalized the later years of the nineteenth century. That Free Religion seemed to go into eclipse in the process of its transfer of the intellectual movement there can be no doubt, and the seeming was reality.

The reaction against the scientific spirit was other than transcendentalism, though taking many of its features. It also took on an excess, a credulity, an emphasis on the occult, that the older phase of religious awakening did not show. The tendency of science was to forbid enthusiasm, and this is widely shown in the indifference that has invaded all churches. If that indifference to theological speculation made it impossible for the Free Religious Association to realize what its founders aimed at, it has so invaded the churches as to make it undesirable to undertake that work of reformation. But science has by no means come to the end of its influence upon religion, and any day we may look for a reaction in its favor, that will establish rational convictions in the guidance of all religious bodies. That such a change is certain to come about when ritualism and the occult have had their day, is all that the founders of the Association desired. With that result they can rest content, for their part in this renaissance of right-mindedness is not inconsiderable. Having no desire to found a sect, but to make all sectarianism unacceptable, they have secured all they had any right to expect in the hour when they began their labors. The future historian of religion in this country will testify to the importance of that which they accomplished.

Dinner

at the Centenary of

Ralph Waldo Emerson

By the Social Circle in Concord

"Rhodora! if the sages ask thee why
This charm is wasted on the earth and sky,
Tell them, dear, that if eyes were made for seeing, .
Then Beauty is its own excuse for being."

May twenty-fifth Nineteen hundred and three

" Much the best society I have ever known is a club in Concord called the Social Circle, consisting always of twenty-five of our citizens; doctor, lawyer, farmer, trader, miller, mechanic, etc., solidest of men, who yield the solidest of gossip. Harvard University is a wafer compared to the solid land which my friends represent."— *Emerson to a friend in 1844, Dec. 17.*

MENU

Little Necks

Radishes   Olives

Cream of Lettuce
Toaststicks

Turbans of Halibut   Lobster Sauce
Sliced Cucumbers

Fillet of Beef
Potato Croquettes   Green Peas
Asparagus, Hollandaise

Lettuce and Tomato Salad Mayonnaise

Frozen Pudding   Strawberries

Ice Cream and Water Ices
`Assorted Cake

Toasted Crackers
Roquefort Cheese   Cream Cheese

Coffee

"By the rude bridge that arched the flood,
  Their flag to April's breeze unfurled,
Here once the embattled farmers stood,
  And fired the shot heard round the world.

"The foe long since in silence slept;
  Alike the conquerer silent sleeps:
And Time the ruined bridge has swept
  Down the dark stream which seaward creeps.

"On this green bank, by this soft stream,
  We set today a votive stone;
That memory may their deed redeem,
  When, like our sires, our sons are gone.

"Spirit, that made those heroes dare
  To die, and leave their children free,
Bid Time and Nature gently spare
  The shaft we raise to them and thee."

To be sung by those present to the tune of "Old Hundred."

THE NEW ENGLAND MAGAZINE

NEW SERIES MAY, 1903 VOL. XXVIII No. 3

Pp. 255–264

The Emerson Centennial

By George Willis Cooke

A SPONTANEOUS and enthusiastic movement to honor Emerson during this hundredth year since his birth justifies itself, and needs no elaborate interpretation. It is a manifestation of what many persons have felt for him and his teachings, whether they fully agree with his philosophy, his religion and his ethical principles, or whether they are inclined to reject these to a greater or lesser extent. It is the man they honor, and his noble life. They see in him a man of genius, a poet of high lyrical gifts, and a writer of pronounced individuality and consummate skill.

Emerson has commended himself to many persons because he interpreted the democratic spirit as it applies to the daily conduct and the relations of men to each other. In him the spirit of democracy was incarnated; and he represented its love of liberty, its demand for personal freedom, its recognition of the interests of others, and its desire that all mankind should be uplifted and ennobled. He was the friend of the Indian and the negro, the defender of woman, the interpreter of the common people. We may be inclined to qualify his doctrine of individualism here and there, but he largely qualified it himself with his profound regard for the rights of all. He was not an individualist for himself or his class, but that even the lowest man might have the opportunity to express himself and to secure the fullest measure of self-activity. He was no aristocrat that trusts in culture or hereditary descent, but he loved the people and believed in them. According to his view the vision of God may come to any man who desires it, and the deepest intuitions are for any who make room for them in the deeps of the soul. This doctrine made him the great democrat he was, and taught him that all men are kin and have need of each other.

Many will find in Emerson the greatest of modern ethical teachers, and a man of the largest gift as an inspirer of conduct. There is something manly, heroic, courageous in his teaching that will deeply appeal to many men and women. No other ethical writer is his equal as an inspirer of moral purpose or as a quickener of manliness. He calls men to activity, to heroic effort in behalf of duty, reason and justice. No one who has found his way into the full intent of Emerson's teaching can love compromise, ease or moral acquiescence. He demands that the world shall be made right, and that it is the duty of every individual to take up that task in his own person. It is this heroic and courageous quality in Emerson that causes him to appeal most vigorously to youth. He gives them ideals, he inspires them with noble purposes and he has the heroic temper they need in a teacher.

To an increasing number of persons Emerson is a prophet of the new faith in which they find life and joy. He is, in fact, a great religious teacher, not of the conventional type, and not of the religion of form and ritual. His is a religion of the inward life, of direct intuition of spiritual realities, and of individual faith. He is preached in all churches, but many who have found truth in him will not belong to any company of worshippers. He comes especially to the lonely, the struggling, and those who have painfully found their way to individual liberty. For such as these he has a courageous and strenuous word, one that fits well into their need. He has helped many everywhere to find in religion something real, vital and natural; something that is in harmony with the facts of life and the daily experiences of men. Whatever the limitations of his teaching, it gives faith, cheer and earnestness to those who accept it. Its critics may call it rationalism, naturalism, or by whatever other name, yet they fail to find the real meaning of it as it appeals to those who have found truth and hope in it. Its value is in its personal quality, its direct confidence in the truth, its immediate appeal to reason and intuition. It is the word of one who knows that of which he affirms, and who accepts nothing merely on the testimony of other men or of established institutions. It is this simplicity, this trust in the soul itself, this confidence in God, that makes the religion of Emerson one that many gladly accept.

It is the qualities already named that give force and meaning to Emerson's work as poet, essayist and critic. Many who will not care for his religion or his democracy will recognize in him a great author, one of the greatest of the men who have made of literature a means for the interpretation of life. Must we not place Emerson in the company of the greatest of the modern lyrical poets? His poetry is personal and therefore lyrical; and yet it is philosophical, scientific and intuitive at one and the same time. If it is not easy to understand, this is not because of its essential obscurity, but because it interprets the deepest human problems in a distinctly individual manner. The meaning of life and nature Emerson has sung into his verses, and they interpret these as they show themselves to a growing company of thoughtful men and women. Rugged and obscure as is the form of Emerson's poetry, the sentiment and the thought of it are ever beautiful and impressive.

It is as the interpreter of life that

tions of him. He will be judged from all points of view, and estimated as to his worth for every type of mind.

Probably the most notable event in connection with this centennial year will be the publication of a new, annotated and extended edition of Emerson's complete works. This edition, which is to be called the Centenary Edition, will be edited by Mr. Edward Waldo Emerson, the poet's son, who has proven himself a most competent person for such a task. He is to write

since he began to write. They are what have drawn him to many as a friend and daily companion. It is

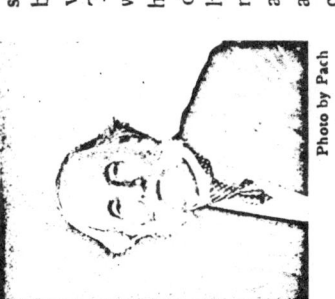

Photo by Pach

T. W. HIGGINSON

THE OLD CHURCH

FIRST PARISH CHURCH, CONCORD

AS REBUILT AFTER THE FIRE

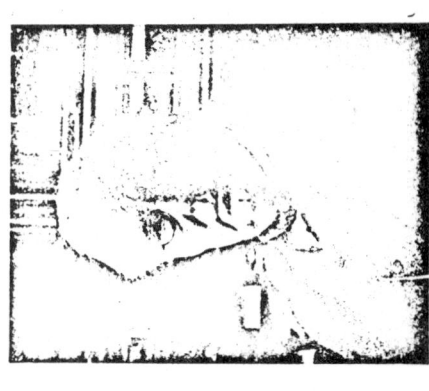

GEORGE FRISBIE HOAR

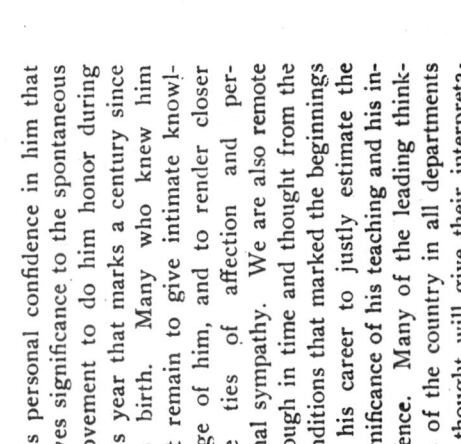

EMERSON'S HOUSE AT CONCORD

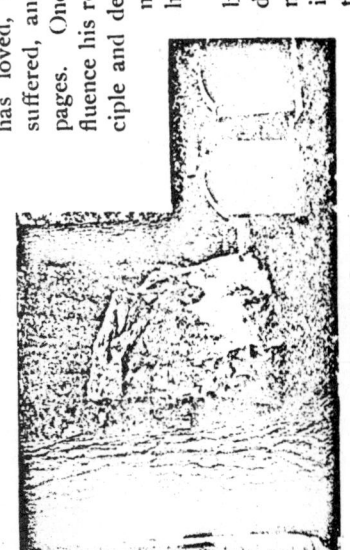

EMERSON'S GRAVE

Emerson will come to the majority of his readers. His essays are not only epigrammatic, brilliant, original, inspiring; but they are brimful of thought, suggestion, incentive, provocation. He is one of the most friendly and personal of authors, and no other is more certain to become "the guide, philosopher and friend" of his reader. For counsel, for admonition, for correction and for brotherly encouragement, Emerson is unsurpassed as a writer. He is thoroughly modern, a man of this generation, one who lives in the open, one who lives wholly in the real world. To him belongs the best that culture has to give, but he is human in all that he writes. He has loved, been tempted, struggled, suffered, and all this appears in his pages. Once within Emerson's influence his reader is thereafter his disciple and devoted follower. He may not be called master, but he is trusted and loved.

Such qualities as have been named have endeared Emerson to his many readers, and have increased the number of them with each decade this personal confidence in him that gives significance to the spontaneous movement to do him honor during this year that marks a century since his birth. Many who knew him yet remain to give intimate knowledge of him, and to render closer the ties of affection and personal sympathy. We are also remote enough in time and thought from the conditions that marked the beginnings of his career to justly estimate the significance of his teaching and his influence. Many of the leading thinkers of the country in all departments of thought will give their interpreta-

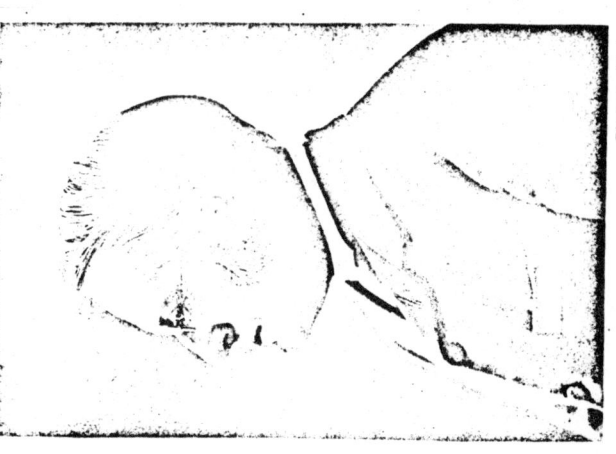

Photo by Pach

Charles W. Eliot

an introduction to this edition, which will give a brief but fresh and authoritative account of Emerson's life and work. He will also furnish notes to each volume, explaining the circumstances attending the delivery of the most famous of the lectures, and describe the impression made by the essays on their first publication. He will also furnish such notes as will make the meanings of the poems better understood, often using the corresponding passages in the essays for this purpose. One, and perhaps two, additional volumes of hitherto unpublished materials will be added, and this announcement gives great importance to this new edition. It has for

several years been known that a number of essays would probably be given to the public sooner or later, and the definite promise of them this year will be most welcome to all readers of Emerson.

Definite announcement has been made of several celebrations to be held in

sessions a day from July 13 to July 31, a morning session in the First Parish Church, Concord, and an evening session in one of the churches in Boston. These churches were intimately associated with Emerson's life, that in Boston being the one of which he was for about three years the minister, and that in Concord being closely connected with his religious life from boyhood to old age. The Free Religious Association selected Edwin D. Mead, George Willis Cooke and John C. Haynes as a committee to have charge of this school, with the first named as chairman. The committee added to their number Frank

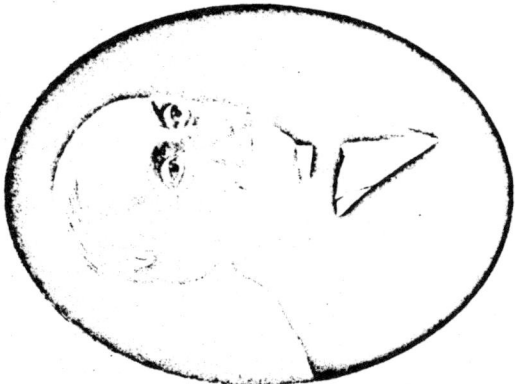

Photo by Notman

Edward Everett Hale

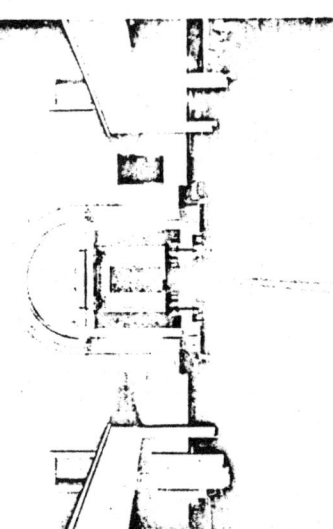

Photo by Pach

Charles Eliot Norton

May. One of the most interesting of these is to be in Concord, for, so many years the home of Emerson. This is to be held in the First Parish Church on May 25, and addresses are to be made

by Hon. George Frisbie Hoar, Col. Thomas Wentworth Higginson, Professor William James and Professor Charles Eliot Norton. A similar meeting is to be held in Symphony Hall, Boston, on the evening of May 24. At this meeting, Dr. Edward Everett Hale will act as chaplain, the Handel and Haydn Society will furnish the music, an address will be given by President Charles W. Eliot of Harvard University, and a poem will be read by Professor George E. Woodberry of Columbia University. Meetings of the same kind are to be held in New York, Washington and many other cities.

The Free Religious Association, of which Emerson was one of the founders, will devote its annual meeting in May mainly to the consideration of Emerson's religious teachings. This association has organized the Emerson Memorial School, which will hold two

Interior First Parish Church, Concord

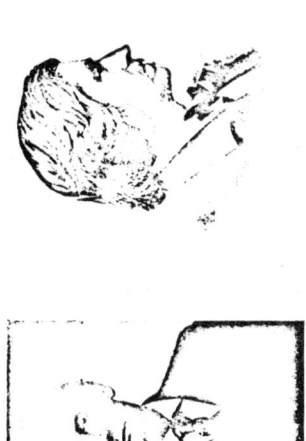

DAVID G. HASKINS, JR.

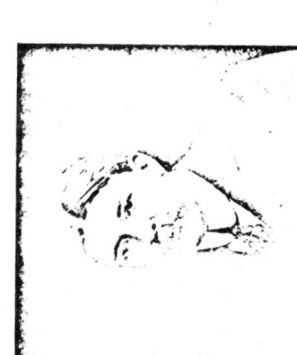

FRANK B. SANBORN

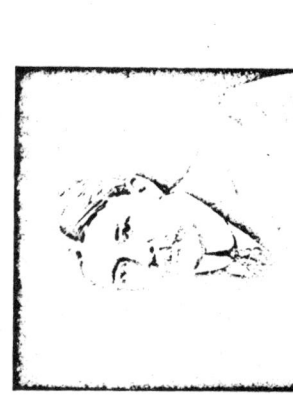

MOORFIELD STOREY

Photo by Dadmun

SYMPHONY HALL, BOSTON

GEORGE E. WOODBERRY

F. Trueblood, "Emerson and the Inner Light"; Henry D. Lloyd, "Emerson's Wit and Humor"; Rev. John W. Chadwick, "The Simpler Emerson"; George Willis Cooke, "Emerson and the Transcendental Movement"; William R. Thayer, "Emerson's Gospel of Individualism"; Rabbi Charles Fleischer, "Emerson, the Seer of Democracy"; Rev. Charles F. Jefferson, "Emerson and Carlyle"; Percival Chubb, "Emerson's Spiritual Leadership in England"; Professor Kuno Francke, "Emerson's Debt to Ger-

Also special Sunday services, with sermons or addresses by eminent lovers of Emerson, will be held both in Boston and Concord.

Every effort is being made to insure the success of the Memorial School. As it will follow immediately after the session of the National Educational Association, to be held in Boston during the first week in July, it is confidently expected that a very large number of persons will avail themselves of the opportunity to attend the lectures. Ample accommodations can

many, and Germany's Debt to Emerson"; Rev. R. Heber Newton, "Emerson, the Man"; Professor Charles F. Richardson, "Emerson's Place in American Literature." Among others who have promised to give addresses are Mrs. Julia Ward Howe, Francis Ellingwood Abbot, Professor Nathaniel Schmidt, Joel Benton and Mrs. Anna Garlin Spencer.

In addition to the regular lectures there will be two afternoons, one at Concord and one in Boston, devoted to "Memories of Emerson," to which many of the men and women who knew the great thinker will contribute

be found in Boston, Cambridge, Concord, Waltham, Bedford, Lexington and the neighboring towns. It will be possible to visit all the sites made memorable by Emerson's presence, including Concord, Brook Farm, the School of Philosophy, the church of which he was the minister in Boston, the Follen Church in Lexington, in which he did his last regular preaching, and many other places connected with his name and fame. Those desirous of obtaining the programme of the Memorial School and such accompanying information as will be helpful to those coming from a

B. Sanborn to represent the old Concord School of Philosophy, Moorfield Storey to represent the Saturday Club, William R. Thayer to represent the Harvard sentiment and David Greene Haskins, Jr., who is the secretary of the committee. A guarantee fund sufficient to secure the financial success of the school has already been provided.

The following is a partial list of the lecturers and their subjects: President T. G. Schurman on "The Philosophy of Emerson"; Frank B. Sanborn, "Emerson and the Concord School of Philosophy"; Rev. Samuel M. Crothers, "Emerson's Poetry"; William M. Salter, "Emerson's Aim and Method in Social Reform"; Charles Malloy, "The Sphinx"; Rev. Samuel

A. Eliot, "Emerson and Harvard"; Rev. Charles F. Dole, "Emerson the Puritan"; William Lloyd Garrison, "Emerson and the Anti-slavery Struggle"; Moorfield Storey, "Emerson and the Civil War"; Rev. Benjamin

Harris, Edwin D. Mead, Mrs. Howe, Miss Elizabeth P. Peabody, Frank B. Sanborn, George Willis Cooke and Dr. Cyrus A. Bartol. These lectures were published in a volume and bear noble testimony to the influence of Emerson.

The two decades that have passed away since Emerson's death have clarified our judgment of him, and have given him a more assured and a loftier place than he occupied when he departed from us. There is no indication that he is losing his hold upon us or that his fame will wane at any time in the future. What remoter generations will say of him we cannot foresee, but that he will be outgrown or suffer neglect we cannot think. He is one of the perennial men, not because of his absolute greatness, but because of his humanity, his ethical quality, his spiritual insight, and his sanity of mind. He had certain affinities with the transcendental movement and was an idealist; but he was not essentially of any school or committed to its methods. Tyndall was drawn to him as well as Carlyle, and Farrar has praised him as enthusiastically as Burroughs. Science had as deep a meaning to him as metaphysics, and he was as much a reformer as a littérateur. Such was the breadth and compass of his mind he was of no party nor sect, but belonged to mankind. His common sense was of near kin to his intuitive power, and his gift was not less as an ethical teacher than as a seer. Such being the man, his fame grows, and is ever more firmly established. In him we see the truest American, the man most worthy to teach and to inspire us.

DRAWN BY Scott Stanton
FOR THE CONGREGATIONALIST.

Edward Everett Hale

---

distance, can do so by addressing the secretary of the committee, David Greene Haskins, Jr., 5 Tremont Street, Boston, Mass.

The Memorial School will be in a real sense a revival of the Concord School of Philosophy, in which Emerson was deeply interested, of which he talked and for which he planned many years before it came into existence. He often attended its sessions, and one of the last occasions on which he read one of his lectures was in the Concord Town Hall before the School. In 1882 one day was devoted to commemorative addresses, Emerson having only recently died. Among the speakers were Dr. Bartol, Joel Benton, Mrs. Julia Ward Howe, Dr. William T. Harris, John Albee, Dr. Alexander Wilder and Mrs. Ednah D. Cheney, with poems by Mr. Alcott and Mrs. Martha Perry Lowe. In 1884 nearly the whole session was given up to lectures on Emerson's Genius and Character, among the speakers being Dr.

EDWIN D. MEAD

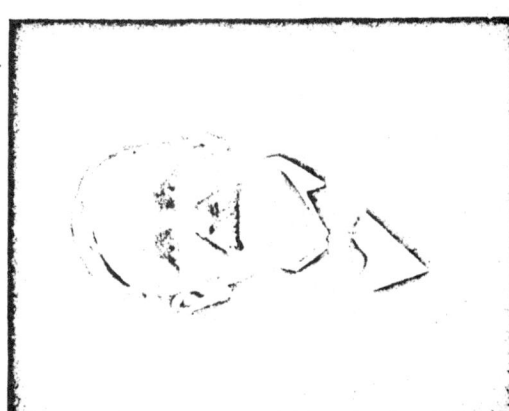

GEORGE WILLIS COOKE

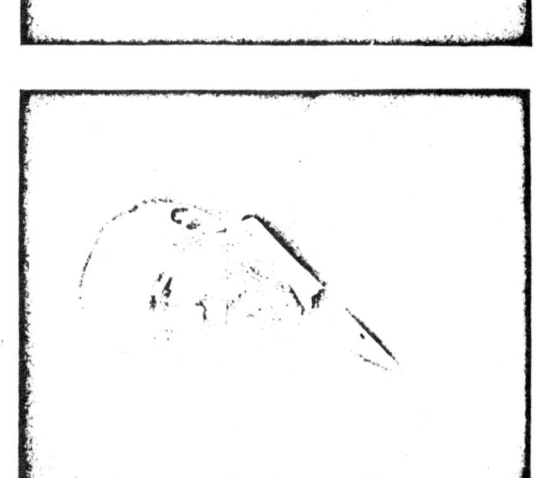

JOHN C. HAYNES

LECTURES AT THE EMERSON MEMORIAL SCHOOL IN CONCORD AND BOSTON DURING JULY, 1903, UNDER THE AUSPICES OF THE FREE RELIGIOUS ASSOCIATION OF AMERICA

The Emerson Centennial at Concord.

The detailed program of the Memorial School to be held at Concord and Boston this summer, under the auspices of the Free Religious Association of America, of which Emerson was one of the founders and vice-presidents, is as follows:

The school will open on Monday, July 13, and continue three weeks. There will be thirty lectures, covering the various aspects of Emerson's life and work. The morning lectures will be given in Concord at 10 o'clock in the Town Hall, where Emerson himself lectured so many times; and the evening lectures in Boston at 7.45 o'clock in Huntington Hall, Massachusetts Institute of Technology. Two afternoons will be devoted to Memories of Emerson, by men and women who were personal friends of the great thinker; and there will be throughout the period of the school special Sunday services, with sermons or addresses by eminent lovers of Emerson.

The time for the commemoration has been fixed so as best to accommodate the great number of teachers and students from all parts of the country who will come to Boston early in July to attend the convention of the National Educational Association.

Address, for any required information, the Secretary of the Committee, David Greene Haskins, Jr., 5 Tremont Street, Boston, Mass., of whom tickets may be ordered by mail; price for both series, $5, or, for one only, $3, or, for single lectures, 35 cents.

MORNING LECTURES IN CONCORD
July.

13. Rev. Charles Gordon Ames, "The Sources of Emerson."
14. Rev. Charles F. Dole, "Emerson the Puritan."
15. Joel Benton, "Emerson with Nature."
16. Mrs. Anna Garlin Spencer, "The American Woman's Debt to Emerson."
17. Prof. Kuno Francke, "Emerson's Debt to Germany and Germany's Debt to Emerson."
20. Edwin D. Mead, "Emerson's Message in Education."
21. Rev. Charles E. Jefferson, "Emerson and Carlyle."
22. Dr. Edward W. Emerson, "The Religion of Emerson."
23. Prof. Charles F. Richardson, "Emerson's Place in American Literature."
24. Percival Chubb, "Emerson's Spiritual Leadership in England."
27. Prof. Nathaniel Schmidt, "Emerson and Oriental Thought."
28. Charles Malloy, "The Sphinx."
29. Rev. John W. Chadwick, "The Simpler Emerson."
30. Moorfield Storey, "Emerson and the Civil War."
31. Mrs. Julia Ward Howe, "A Century from the Birth of Emerson."

EVENING LECTURES IN BOSTON

13. Pres. Jacob Gould Schurman, "The Philosophy of Emerson."
14. Rev. Samuel M. Crothers, "The Poetry of Emerson."
15. Frank B. Sanborn, "Emerson and the Concord School of Philosophy."
16. George Willis Cooke, "Emerson and the Transcendental Movement."
17. Rev. Samuel A. Eliot, "Emerson and Harvard."
20. William R. Thayer, "Emerson's Gospel of Individualism."
21. Dr. Francis E. Abbot, "Emerson the Anti-imperialist or Prophet of the Natural Rights of Man."
22. Rev. R. Heber Newton, "Emerson the Man."
23. Henry D. Lloyd, "Emerson's Wit and Humor."
24. William M. Salter, "Emerson's Aim and Method in Social Reform."
27. Rabbi Charles Fleischer, "Emerson, the Seer of Democracy."
28. Rev. Benjamin F. Trueblood, "Emerson and the Inner Light."
29. William Lloyd Garrison, "Emerson and the Anti-Slavery Movement."
30. Prof. A. E. Dolbear, "Emerson's Thought in Relation to Modern Science."
31. Rev. Edward Everett Hale, "Emerson's Gospel for his Own Time and for Ours."

A man is relieved and gay when he has put his heart into his work, and done his best; but what he has said or done otherwise, shall give him no peace.

R. W. EMERSON.

THE EMERSON CENTENNIAL

Memorial School at Concord and Boston
July 13-31, 1903

The Free Religious Association of America, of which Emerson was one of the founders and vice-presidents, in response to a general demand from students throughout the country for a broad consideration, in this centennial year, of Emerson's life and influence, has perfected plans for an Emerson Memorial School, in July. To secure the broadest possible spirit in the planning of the program for this important commemoration, the committee appointed by the Association has been enlarged by the addition of scholars representing the old Concord tradition, the Harvard sentiment, and the Saturday Club, with which Emerson was so long and so fondly associated,—the committee consisting of Edwin D. Mead, George Willis Cooke, John C. Haynes, Frank B. Sanborn, William R. Thayer, Moorfield Storey, and David Greene Haskins, Jr.

The school will open on Monday, July 13, and continue three weeks. There will be thirty lectures, covering the various aspects of Emerson's life and work. The morning lectures will be given in Concord, and the evening lectures in Boston. Two afternoons will be devoted to Memories of Emerson, by men and women who were personal friends of the great thinker; and there will be throughout the period of the school special Sunday services, with sermons or addresses by eminent lovers of Emerson.

The time for the commemoration has been fixed so as best to accommodate the great number of teachers and students from all parts of the country who will come to Boston early in

MORNING LECTURES IN CONCORD.

July 13. Rev. Charles Gordon Ames, "The Sources of Emerson."
" 14. Rev. Charles F. Dole, "Emerson the Puritan."
" 15. Joel Benton, "Emerson with Nature."
" 16. Mrs. Anna Garlin Spencer, "The American Woman's Debt to Emerson."
" 17. Prof. Kuno Francke, "Emerson's Debt to Germany and Germany's Debt to Emerson."
" 20. Edwin D. Mead, "Emerson's Message in Education."
" 21. Rev. Charles E. Jefferson, "Emerson and Carlyle."
" 22. Dr. Edward W. Emerson, "The Religion of Emerson."
" 23. Prof. Charles F. Richardson, "Emerson's Place in American Literature."
" 24. Percival Chubb, "Emerson's Spiritual Leadership in England."
" 27. Prof. Nathaniel Schmidt, "Emerson and Oriental Thought."
" 28. Charles Malloy, "The Sphinx."
" 29. Rev. John W. Chadwick, "The Simpler Emerson."
" 30. Moorfield Storey, "Emerson and the Civil War."
" 31. Mrs. Julia Ward Howe, "A Century from the Birth of Emerson."

EVENING LECTURES IN BOSTON.

July 13. Pres. Jacob Gould Schurman, "The Philosophy of Emerson."
" 14. Rev. Samuel M. Crothers, "The Poetry of Emerson."
" 15. Frank B. Sanborn, "Emerson and the Concord School of Philosophy."
" 16. George Willis Cooke, "Emerson and the Transcendental Movement."
" 17. Rev. Samuel A. Eliot, "Emerson and Harvard."
" 20. William R. Thayer, "Emerson's Gospel of Individualism."
" 21. Dr. Francis E. Abbot, "Emerson the Anti-imperialist or Prophet of the Natural Rights of Man."
" 22. Rev. R. Heber Newton, "Emerson the Man."
" 23. Henry D. Lloyd, "Emerson's Wit and Humor."
" 24. William M. Salter, "Emerson's Aim and Method in Social Reform."
" 27. Rabbi Charles Fleischer, "Emerson, the Seer of Democracy."
" 28. Rev. Benjamin F. Trueblood, "Emerson and the Inner Light."
" 29. William Lloyd Garrison, "Emerson and the Anti-Slavery Movement."
" 30. Prof. A. E. Dolbear, "Emerson's Thought in Relation to Modern Science."
" 31. Rev. Edward Everett Hale, "Emerson's Gospel for his Own Time and for Ours."

July to attend the convention of the National Educational Association. It is felt that hundreds of these, who will spend the summer in New England, will welcome the opportunity of attending this inspiring summer school; and its opening will therefore immediately follow the Educational Association's convention. The division of the sessions between Concord and Boston will also, it is felt, be pleasing to these visiting scholars, while at the same time a convenience to the large local public.

The quick and easy railroad and trolley connections will enable visitors to take lodgings in Lexington, Bedford or Cambridge, as well as in Concord or Boston. The frequent trains, early and late, between Concord and Boston will make headquarters in either place, or in the pleasant places between, entirely convenient for those attending the full course. Those desiring lodgings and board in or near Concord may address the Emerson School Committee, Concord, Mass.

The lectures in Concord will be given in the Town Hall, where Emerson in his lifetime lectured a hundred times, at ten o'clock. The lectures in Boston will be given in Huntington Hall, at the Massachusetts Institute of Technology, at quarter of eight o'clock. The morning lectures will be followed by discussion.

The price of tickets for the season, covering both the Concord and Boston lectures, will be $5. Tickets will be sold for the morning and evening courses separately, for $3; and also for single lectures, 35 cents. The tickets are sold in Boston at the Old Corner Bookstore, corner of School and Washington Streets, the Congregational Bookstore, 14 Beacon Street, and the Unitarian Rooms, 25 Beacon Street; and in Concord at H. L. Whitcomb's bookstore and Richardson's drugstore.

Address for any required information the Secretary of the Committee, David Greene Haskins, Jr., 5 Tremont Street, Boston, Mass., of whom tickets may be ordered by mail.

The following are typical of the press reports covering lectures delivered at the Emerson Memorial School of Concord and Boston in July, 1903. (Many of the speakers were formerly connected with the Concord School of Philosophy.)

SESSION OF:	PRINCIPAL LECTURERS AND TOPICS:
I. July 17	Prof. Kuno Francke on "Emerson's Debt to Germany and Germany's Debt to Emerson" Herbert Gleason on "Thoreau"
II. July 21	Dr. Francis Ellingwood Abbot on "Emerson the Anti-imperialist"
III. July 22	Edward Waldo Emerson on "The Religion of Emerson"
IV. July 27	Prof. Nathaniel Schmidt on "Emerson and Oriental Thought"
V. July 28-29	Benjamin F. Trueblood on "Emerson and the Inner Light" John White Chadwick on "The Simpler Emerson"
VI. July 29-30	William Lloyd Garrison on "Emerson and the Anti-Slavery Movement Moorfield Storey on "Emerson and the Civil War"
VII. July 30-31	Prof. Amos Emerson Dolbear on "Emerson's Thought in Relation to Modern Science" Julia Ward Howe on "A Century from the Birth of Emerson"

EMERSON AND GERMANY

Their Debt to Each Other Under Consideration

Affinity of Emerson and the German Character

Fifth Day of Emerson Memorial School

Today's Interesting Paper by Professor Kuno Francke

Special to the Transcript:

Concord, Mass., July 17—"Emerson's Debt to Germany and Germany's Debt to Emerson" was the topic of a very discriminating and thoughtful paper by Professor Kuno Francke, at the Emerson Memorial School this morning.

Mr. Frank B. Sanborn, in presenting the essayist, said that, in arranging the programme, it had been thought well to have treated the mission and work of Emerson outside of his own country. "Of all such countries in the world," said he, "that which is the most akin to the spirit of Emerson and that from which he also derived a part of his own inspiration, is Germany—that very broad term which,

like charity, covers a multitude of sins as well as virtues. We have the privilege of having with us this morning a gentleman from that part of the world, who is very familiar with his native country and also with ours, and also with their literatures. He will discourse to us this morning on a subject which will be new to most of this audience— "Emerson's Debt to Germany, and Germany's Debt to Emerson." (Applause.)

SYNOPSIS OF PAPER

Lecturer's Salient Points Noted and Summarized Below

Professor Francke began by pointing out the inner affinity existing between Emerson and German character, the German insistence on intellectual personality in particular. "It would be futile to deny," he said, "that the pressure exerted upon the individual by official authority is greater in Germany than in America, England, France or Italy. Indeed, there is good reason for thinking that this very subordination of the individual to superior ordinances has had a large share in the extraordinary achievements of German statecraft, strategy, industry and science of the last fifty years. What I maintain is this: In spite of the intense supervision of personal conduct, in spite of the supremacy of drill and regulation, in spite of the overwhelming sway of historical tradition and class rule, in spite of all this, there is to be found in Germany a decidedly greater variety of individual views, convictions, principles, modes of life, ideals; in short, of individual character than in America. I do not wish here to analyze the causes of this remarkable phenomenon, beyond stating that one of these causes seems to me to lie in the very existence of those barriers which in Germany restrict and hem in individual activity. It seems as

though the pressure from without tended to force to light the life within. Certain it is that the German, while submitting to external limitations which no American would tolerate, is wont to guard his intellectual selfhood with a jealous eagerness compared with which the easy adaptation of the American to standards not his own come near being indifference. His inner life the German wants to shape himself; here he tolerates no authority or ordinance; here he is his own master; here he builds his own world.

"It is easy to see how closely allied Emerson's whole being was to this side of German character. The moderation and harmoniousness of his temper preserved him from the angularity, the oddities and eccentricities which often go with the German insistence or pronounced intellectual personality. On this personality itself he insisted with truly German aggressiveness. Indeed, it may be said that his definition of the scholar as being, not a thinker, but man thinking—a definition which is at the root of Emerson's whole view of intellectual life —is an essentially German conception and places Emerson in line with those splendid defenders of personal conviction which have embodied German thought with all its rugged pugnaciousness, from the days of Luther to Lessing and Fichte, and finally to Schopenhauer and Nietzsche."

The speaker next dwelt on four important consequences of this German insistence on individuality, namely, the German contempt of sham, the German delight in small things, the German sense of the infinite, and the German disdain of intellectual compromises, showing how closely akin Emerson was in all these respects to the German temper. He then passed on to a characterization of the fundamental thought of the great German idealists of the eighteenth

century and traced its influence upon Emerson. Continuing he said:

"It is easy to see that here are found side by side all the essential elements of Emerson's spiritual world—his freedom from tradition, his deep interest in man, his belief in moral freedom and in the moral order of the universe, his pantheism, his optimism, his trust in the perfectibility of the race. But it is worth noticing that in the application of these principles there is a decided difference between Emerson and his masters. The great German idealists, while embracing the human race in their thought, while glorying in the idea of a strong and free popular life, addressed themselves in reality to a small circle of elect spirits; these they hoped to influence, to them they adapted their manner of presentation; with the people at large they had little to do. They were, in other words, with all their democratic sympathies, at heart thoroughly aristocratic; they lack, for the most part, simplicity and the direct appeal to the popular heart. It must further be borne in mind that the condition of the German people at that time was one of utter political disintegration, that the very foundations of national existence were crumbling away, one after another, before the onslaught of the Napoleonic invasion, and that the task of the future was nothing less than a complete reorganization of public life. Whatever there is, then, in German literature of that time of popular appeal is dictated by distress, by the bitter need of the hour, and has to do with the death-agony of a social order sinking into ruin, and the birth-throes of a new order not yet fully formed.

"Emerson, on the other hand, although his life was spent amid the most refined circles of New England culture, although his own utterances never fail to appeal to the finest and most elevated aspirations of the human heart, yet always looked beyond his own cultivated surroundings into the wider spheres of common, ordinary life. With all his aristocratic bearing and predilections, he was at heart thoroughly democratic. And the people to which he gave his life's work was not a nation threatened in its existence, crippled, defeated; but a nation that only recently had won its freedom, a healthy young giant, teeming with untried power and latent vitality, unexperienced but perfectly normal, untouched by disappointment, a vast future in his loins. Is it a wonder that Emerson's application of German idealism should, on the whole, have been more sane, more normal, more vigorous, more genuinely popular, more universally human than German idealism itself?"

After illustrating this point by a detailed comparison between Emerson and Fichte, Professor Francke finally considered Emerson's influence upon contemporary German life. He spoke of the decay of German idealism in the second half of the nineteenth century, the ascendency of Schopenhauer and Nietzsche, the rise of industrialism, the absence of spirituality in scientific investigation. But a reaction against the pessimism of Schopenhauer, the cynicism of Nietzsche, the soulless monotony of specialization has in a reaction closely bound up with the rising influence of Emerson. To Herman Grimm belongs the credit of having first acquainted Germany with Emerson and of having held him up as a leader in the spiritual awakening which is surely coming. The speaker closed by saying:

"The signs of the time are full of promise. The extraordinary success of such a book as Harnack's 'Essence of Christianity'; the widespread influence of such a university teacher, such a wise, free, kindly man of ideals as Frederick Paulsen; the devoted efforts of Pastor Naumann, of Bruno Wille, Wilhelm Bölsche and others to win the masses back to spiritual hope and an enlightened faith; the new life kindled in poetry and the drama—all this is conclusive evidence that we are on the very verge of a new era of German idealism. And when it comes, there will come with it the demand: less Nietzsche and more Emerson; and a new intellectual bond between America and Germany, will have been established.

THE DISCUSSION

Interesting Debate Which Followed the Paper

After the great and prolonged applause which had greeted the conclusion of Professor Francke's extremely interesting paper had subsided Mr. Sanborn said the ignorance of the average American of German literature, in its formative period at least, was extraordinary. He supposed no country—not even England, which is the slowest in the world to receive ideas from other countries—was, up to 1825, so densely ignorant of what Germany was thinking as was the United States. This might account for Emerson's slowness in becoming acquainted with German idealism, though in its essentials he had it in himself.

Mr. George Willis Cooke said that Professor Francke had not thoroughly recognized the element of idealism in New England. In Emerson's lecture, delivered in 1842, on "The Idealists," in his course of lectures on "The Times," he indicated that idealism as it then existed was indigenous to New England. Emerson's idealism was not formed from any knowledge, second, third, or fourth hand, of the German authors, but from his reading of a wide circle of thinkers in all ages—Plato and others. In German literature he found more complete, more philosophical, more systematized, that which he had already conceived; and it was made more familiar to him.

Mr. Charles Malloy said he had read Emerson and did not read Goethe.

Mr. F. B. Hornbrooke said the signal value of Emerson was, not that he said an especially new thing, or uttered a new thought—nobody ever did that—but that he gave expression to what was beginning to be in the air, and what was always in the air. Ideas were like microbes—always in the air. Emerson had the advantage over the German idealism, that he said what he had to say in the very best form, and gave it a classic expression; and that was why what he said lived. Emerson was also independent—the mouthpiece of no party or church, and therefore could always say what he said and thought. (Applause.)

EMERSON'S PHILOSOPHY OUTGROWN

George Willis Cooke Says Its Individualism, Though the Greatest Single Intellectual Phase of American Thought, Is Outdated

George Willis Cooke's lecture on "Emerson and the Transcendental Movement," delivered at Huntington Hall last evening in the Emerson memorial course, was a new essay toward the definition of the term. It was of necessity a discussion of Emerson's philosophy, around whose name has crystalized most of what the transcendental movement meant. Mr. Coke left transcendentalism, in his conclusion, an outgrown and outdated philosophy, though historically recognized as the greatest single intellectual phase of American thought.

The lecturer showed transcendentalism to be, first of all, a religious movement, relying in no way upon agnostic or unbelieving types of thought. Rather there was a considerable demand on human faith, founded on the belief in a set of ideas common to humanity that are not born of experience; something that comes by intuition—a spiritual sense that "transcends" the intellect. To this Emerson applied the term "oversoul," and used as he used it, the word is a substitute for God, a term, in its popular sense, that to Emerson implied limitations he would not admit. As a further development, there was introduced the element of self-reliance, as opposed to what may be called a God-reliance, in the sense that man possessed in himself resources for spiritual and ethical regeneration. The only condition prescribed was a free receptivity and acceptance of the teachings of intuition; transcendentalism being, then, the oversoul plus self-reliance. There was nevertheless the limitation that man, while self-contained and independent of other men, was by no means a free agent, as against this intuitive philosophic element. The whole modern conception of the sociality of man, as opposed to the individuality so earnestly preached by Emerson, has made transcendentalism an outdated philosophy.

The Concord of Emerson

One of the most interesting of the special Emerson lectures was attended by about two hundred people yesterday afternoon in Huntington Hall. The lecturer, Rev. Dr. Gleason, was enabled from personal acquaintance with Thoreau and from familiarity with the Concord woods to treat his subject, "Thoreau," with exceptional interest and authority. The stereopticon views of the noted spots in Concord and the homes and haunts of Emerson and Thoreau brought the famous Concord authors vividly before the audience.

Notes of the School

The Emerson Memorial Meeting will be held at the Hillside Chapel, Concord, next Wednesday, at 3 P. M. At the conclusion of the exercises there—probably at about 4.30—Mrs. Lothrop ("Margaret Sidney") invites all attendants upon the Concord and Boston lectures to a reception at her residence (which adjoins the Hillside Chapel), "Wayside," Hawthorne's old home.

There will be no lecture, either in Concord or Boston tomorrow. The sessions of the school will be resumed Monday morning.

TOWN HALL, CONCORD
At 10 A. M.

July 20—Edwin D. Mead, "Emerson's Message in Education."
" 21—Rev. Charles E. Jefferson, "Emerson and Carlyle."
" 22—Dr. Edward W. Emerson, "The Religion of Emerson."
" 23—Prof. Charles F. Richardson, "Emerson's Place in American Literature."
" 24—Percival Chubb, "Emerson's Spiritual Leadership in England."
" 27—Prof. Nathaniel Schmidt, "Emerson and Oriental Thought."
" 28—Charles Malloy, "The Sphinx."
" 29—Rev. John W. Chadwick, "The Simpler Emerson."
" 30—Moorfield Storey, "Emerson and the Civil War."
" 31—Mrs. Julia Ward Howe, "A Century from the Birth of Emerson."

HUNTINGTON HALL, BOSTON
At 7.45 P. M.

Tonight—Rev. Samuel A. Eliot, "Emerson and Harvard."
July 20—William R. Thayer, "Emerson's Gospel of Individualism."
" 21—Dr. Francis E. Abbot, "Emerson the Anti-Imperialist, or Prophet of the Natural Rights of Man."
" 22—Rev. R. Heber Newton, "Emerson the Man."
" 23—Henry D. Lloyd, "Emerson's Wit and Humor."
" 24—William M. Salter, "Emerson's Aim and Method in Social Reform."
" 27—Rabbi Charles Fleischer, "Emerson, the Seer of Democracy."
" 28—Rev. Benjamin F. Trueblood, "Emerson and the Inner Light."
" 29—William Lloyd Garrison, "Emerson and the Anti-Slavery Movement."
" 30—Prof. A. E. Dolbear, "Emerson's Thought in Relation to Modern Science."
" 31—Rev. Edward Everett Hale, "Emerson's Gospel for His Own Time and for Ours."

Emerson, the Anti-Imperialist

Dr. Francis E. Abbott Attacks a Recent View of Emerson and Touches on Current Political Questions

"Emerson, the Anti-Imperialist, or Prophet of the Natural Rights of Man," was the subject of the Emerson Memorial School lecture in Huntington Hall last evening. Dr. Francis E. Abbott, the speaker, reviewed Emerson's career as an agitator, and discussed his views on the duties of a citizen and the doctrine of democracy in general; the latter turning chiefly upon certain criticisms recently made upon Emerson, as having taught a different sort of equality than appears in the Declaration of Independence. Emerson was described as being, throughout his life, too original and independent a character to join as a member in organized efforts, though when the time for action came there was no one more prompt or earnest in seeking out the nodal points of conflict.

In Emerson's connection with the anti-slavery movement, to which Dr. Abbott referred, this would be found to be a prevailing character of his activity. In his utterances, whether on anti-slavery or political problems as they enlisted his attention, or in problems more strictly ethical, his conception of Americanism was pointed out as entirely in accord with the teachings of Jefferson and Lincoln, in urging at all times an equal freedom under the law for all. His teaching was everywhere a paraphrase of Lincoln's, that government should be "of the people, by the people, for the people"; not the Jefferson Davis conception of a purely white man's rule. Emerson everywhere urges this conception of the unimpeded, equal freedom of all men; the sovereignty of nature; to equal opportunities and equal security, in the attainment of individual aims. Nowhere does he do aught but condemn the modern contempt for moral law that grows indignant at restrictions on the game of exploiting other men. He has repeatedly taught that progress was always in successive ameliorations of conditions, from the emancipation of privileged classes to the emancipation of all from whatever conditions of servitude.

from the Boston Evening Transcript, July 22, 1903.

FRANK SANBORN'S PHILIPPIC

Harvard University Sharply Excoriated

For Early Treatment of Ralph Waldo Emerson

"Red Letter" Day at the Memorial School

Lecture on "Emerson's Religion" by His Son

Special to the Transcript:

Concord, Mass., July 22—This has been a "red-letter" day in the history of the Emerson Memorial School. This morning, in the Town Hall, Edward Waldo Emerson, son of Ralph Waldo Emerson, lectured on "The Religion of Emerson." This afternoon, in the Hillside Chapel, on Lexington road, where the famous Concord School of Philosophy used to meet, and where Emerson, Alcott, Harris, Sanborn, Davidson, Snider, Julia Ward Howe, Ednah Dean Cheney, Elizabeth Peabody and others lectured, a "memorial" meeting was held. Mr. Frank B. Sanborn presided. His address was largely an excoriation of the treatment of Emerson by Harvard University from 1838 to 1863. Mr. Sanborn did not spare his own and Emersons' alma mater. The North American Review and the "Respectable Daily," as the Boston Advertiser was called—then the two mouthpieces of Harvard—came in for their share of this well-known journalist and free lance's sarcasm. Mr. Samuel H. Emery, Jr., of Quincy, Ill., sent some interesting recollections of Emerson and the School of Philosophy. Rev. A. N. Alcott of Minneapolis, a distant kinsman of A. Bronson Alcott, sent some reminiscences of the latter and the school. There were other interesting oral and written contributions, among them a quotation from a recent letter in the London Times from its brilliant correspondent, Mr. Smalley, eulogizing Emerson.

After the exercises, a reception was tendered those in attendance upon the school by Mrs. Lothrop ('Margaret Sidney"), at her residence adjoining the chapel grounds, "Wayside," Hawthorne's old home.

FRANK SANBORN'S REMARKS

Sharp Criticism of Harvard's Treatment of Emerson from 1838 to 1863

Mr. Sanborn, speaking from the heart upon a subject with which no man is more thoroughly imbued, said:

"Friends of Philosophy and Literature: We are assembled here today, not only to pay a personal tribute to Emerson, the man and the neighbor, but to remember him in his long and fruitful activity as the Thinker, the Teacher, and the Reformer. So far extended was his life on earth that he had seen the bigotries, the stupidities, the small prejudices and immense egotims which greeted or ignored the first thirty years of his literary life, so far overcome, that even the university which neglected and ridiculed him from 1838 to 1863, has come to regard him as one of its treasures, and has called a stone structure, hereafter to be dedicated to Philosophy, by his illustrious name. Yet when he was sent to their shadowy and insignificant Coventry by the Philistine majority of the fellows, faculty and alumni of his alma mater, in the long years that produced his most epoch-making books, Emerson was the same wise and serene influence that he is today, when his fame has extended over the whole civilized world.

"In his endurance of long neglect and aversion, Emerson only followed the experience of all grand leaders of thought. To be great is to be misunderstood by those who stand near. Pliny, and who knows how many ancients before him? said: 'To confer benefit and get a bad name for it is the prerogative of the princely,' Bene facere et male audire, regium est; Emerson knew this as well as Pliny did, and had counted the cost of his bold venture, when he left the traditional pulpit of his ancestors, and appealed to the public at large, outside of churches and colleges. He knew what awaits the advanced believer, and he said in his essay on Montaigne: 'Great believers are always reckoned infidels, impracticable, fantastic, atheistic—or really persons of no account. Presently, the unbeliever, for love of belief, burns the believer.' This did not happen to Emerson, because burning heretics had gone out of fashion; but the unbelievers sent him to Coventry, as they thought. They woke up after a generation, and found themselves there.

"Harvard University, the alma mater of Emerson, singularly mischose the objects on which it turned its eyes and its candelabra, after it found Emerson setting up as a thinker for himself. Until 1828, it had a certain pride in him as a son who might do it credit; asked him to read a Phi Beta poem in 1834, and to give an oration in 1837; but there it stopped, and became an unjust stepmother for the next thirty years. He was invited by a few students to give in Divinity Hall the address of 1838, which brought so much opprobrium on him. Andrews Norton attacked the address in the daily organ of Harvard, the Boston Advertiser, as 'the latest form of infidelity;' the faculty of Divinity College, in whose chapel and presence he had spoken, disowned him, and for about twenty years after he was the subject of attacks in public places, or public prints, by professors of the university, which now honors his memory and is building the sepulchres of other prophets.

"Emerson stood by his colors, and after many years the mob opposed to him gave way. But they kept up the attack as long as they could. The two mouthpieces of Harvard at that period were the North American Review, always edited by a college professor, and the 'Respectable Daily,' whose owner was a kinsman of Edward Everett, then president of Harvard University. I have cursorily glanced through the quarterly, for twenty years, and cannot find that it ever reviewed or otherwise noticed Emerson's 'Nature' of 1836, though it had praised his centennial address of 1835; as for the Advertiser, I have not

burrowed through its heaps of indifference to see; but I fancy it was set against Emerson by his gallant defence of Alcott, whom the 'Tiser had denounced for folly and blasphemy. Nor did the North American pay any heed to the Essays as they came out, nor to the reprint of 'Nature' in 1849. But in April, 1847, after sharpening his tusks on the novel of 'Margaret' and George Eliot's translation of Strauss, the rejecter of pearls in the North American (afterwards my college professor in what Harvard was then pleased to call 'philosophy'), rent and chawed up Emerson's 'Poems,' which had come out the winter before.

Five years after the North American had discharged its pop-squirt, I entered Harvard College (1852), and had occasion to know by personal observation what Philistinism reigned there. Of the 500 students and faculty in the college proper, it would be a large estimate to guess that a fifth part had read Emerson to any great extent; most of them had only heard his name, if even that. The faculty would as soon have thought of asking Wendell Phillips to lecture to the students on constitutional law, as of inviting Emerson to give instruction on any subject.

As the slavery contest grew warmer, and the slaveholders contemptuously tore up the Missouri Compromise, in order to push Negro-slavery into Kansas, the slow and timid conscience of Harvard began to stir and writhe in pain; but in September, 1856, when Emerson made his indignant plea for freedom in Kansas, not a half-dozen of the instructors of youth were there to hear and second him, in the village of Cambridge. It took her more than seven years to come out of her transformation; for even in 1862, a good share of her professors were unwilling that Lincoln should free the slaves. But her own darling sons dying on the field of battle brought her to her senses—and darkness.

"With this regeneration her appreciation of Emerson rose to something like justice; she invited him, after an interval of thirty years, to sound once more in her hearing that eloquence against which she had stopped her ears in 1837. No doubt she was helped to this sober second thought by the praise of him she heard from our own country and foreign lands."

OTHER CONTRIBUTIONS

Tribute to Emerson from Mr. Smalley and to Alcott from a Distant Kinsman

After reading Mr. Emery's reminiscences, Mr. Sanborn said the testimony to Emerson's uniform courtesy and simplicity of manner was cumulative, and quoted from a recent letter of Mr. Smalley's in the London Times, detailing his first interview with Emerson, when he visited him in Concord, with his nephew, William Emerson, which said: "Nothing could be more charming than his manner. He had that air of high breeding which comes from consideration for others. There was not a trace of condescension or superiority of any kind in his welcome to the two boys who stood on his threshold. I saw him often afterwards, in many various circumstances, in America and England, and his manner never altered. There was a quaint benignity which never forsook him. His tall, slight figure was not quite straight, but easy in movement. Heroic, either in stature or feature, he was not; but the stamp of distinction was on both, and of abso-

lute simplicity. Of affectation he was incapable."

"Bronson Alcott and the Concord School of Philosophy" was the title of a contribution from Rev. A. N. Alcott—a distant kinsman of Bronson Alcott—who now resides at Minneapolis, Minn., but formerly at Fredericksburg, Ohio, at which place Bronson Alcott visited him in 1880. This letter contained interesting descriptions of Mr. Alcott's personal appearance at that time and numerous anecdotes. "If," said the writer, "Pythagoras of Crotona, or Empedocles of Agrigentum had been reincarnated, and presented himself then and there, he could not have filled my ideal of a philosopher better. Notwithstanding the aspect of age given by his long white locks falling well down to his shoulders, Mr. Alcott's step was strong, quick and elastic. I knew at once that New England transcendentalism had arrived; yes, the modern Plato was there! No man native to Ohio or to the whole West could match that appearance. Under the ample brim of that tall hat I saw a broad, benevolent countenance, serene and placid as a summer sky; his demeanor was that of one evidently schooled in the great world and accustomed to men.

"But such a guest as he was! So royally graceful and courtly in his manners, so charming, so instructive, and, best of all, so absolutely at home, and making us feel entirely at home with him."

The letter went on to speak eulogistically of Mr. Alcott as presiding over a conversation, and the grace with which he then took the intellectual throne, of the two eloquent discourses which he preached to delighted congregations, and of his addressing the school children and how instantly they became his friends because of his benignant manner and evident knowledge of their nature. "As our acquaintance grew, I asked his opinion of the Bible, of religion and of miracle. For answer I obtained very little; perhaps he feared to offend. He seemed to avoid such themes. As we were accustomed to have family worship every morning after breakfast, I at first asked him to read the scriptures and lead in prayer (the next morning after his arrival). He declined, and proposed to unite with us. I afterward came to know that a stated form was not his idea of worship. Forms were little to him." The writer closed with an account of his visit to the Concord School of Philosophy, in July, 1881, and quotes from the journal which he kept at that time.

"THE RELIGION OF EMERSON"

Interesting Paper Before the Memorial School by Edward Waldo Emerson, Son of the Philosopher—A Breeze in the Discussion

Special to the Transcript:

Concord, July 22—By far the largest audience that has attended the Emerson Memorial School was present this morning, notwithstanding the threatening weather, to hear Dr. Edward Waldo Emerson, the son of the Concord seer, speak on "The Religion of Emerson."

Dr. Emerson said that he might more properly speak of his father's religious life than of his "religion," for there was no separation between them. Freedom was more easy to him than religion. He always delighted to address young people. He desired, above all things else, that they should not later on become mere deniers.

He always laid emphasis on the thought that "man in the bush with God may meet."

The Old Book always had its charm for him. He chafed at the traditional work in the church of his day, and, coming in from the woods, he felt suffocated by it. When he came to the Unitarians of his day, without enthusiasm even in their work, he found worship dwelling on the plane of the understanding rather than of divine reason. He left his pulpit as a man of honor and even questioned his fitness for the pastoral duties of a minister. Nature was his shrine. His constant advice to the young was "listen." If Mr. Emerson seldom attended church it was because he found that the church, as it then was, was seldom helpful to him, and was occupied with the very things he had left behind. Yet he was always more reverent than many regular church attendants. The late Dr. Bartol said of Mr. Emerson that his besetting spirituality was his only ecclesiastical sin.

His address to the young was: "Do not speak much of God." His intolerance was not for the devout worshipper, but for the stupid absence of wonder and faith in the presence of nature. He was as sorry for the minister whose idea of God had not got beyond the Jehovah of the Pentateuch as he would be if he had not got beyond Zeus or Thor. On the lecture platform he found the opportunity that he could not in the pulpit. People, in the middle of the week, at the lecture, were not on their guard against supposed heresy.

After the Divinity School address, Mr. Emerson was denounced as an atheist. This was untrue. If he did not attack a personality to God, it was because he thought too much of God, and not too little. He was cleaving to God, and not to a name. "God everywhere" was his thought. As regards the future life, the soul should not be too curious. He was too manly and sensible to be a recluse. He loved mankind; he loved his poor. To be isolated, to him, was to be so far dead.

Mr. Emerson never sincerely enjoyed a sermon, but orations and addresses he did enjoy. The disagreeable word "sage" would never have pleased him. "Seer" was certainly better. He strove to report what he saw simply and beautifully. There is no doubt where he would have stood today. The matter of color would be nothing to him today, whether in the South, the Malayan or the Hawaiian Islands. The eternal law must be heard by America in time, for it will vindicate itself. He wrote not for 1857 but for today and all time. Mr. Emerson did not grieve very much over Harvard's treatment of him because of his Phi Beta Kappa oration and the Divinity School address, because he knew the truth was with him. He abhorred self-consciousness; the truth was the thing—not the individual. He did dislike the notoriety, the discussions in the newspapers and the sympathy offered to him by his friends.

In the discussion that followed the applause which followed, Dr. Emerson's paper, Rev. Charles F. Carter, pastor of the Congregational Church, Lexington, said that to affirm an appreciation of Emerson's religion was like trying to prove the beauty of the lily. All Emerson's writings were permeated with true religion. He was most essentially religious. We found his spiritual credential on every page of his works. There was the basal faith that God was revealing himself to every soul, and that the part of each man was to hold himself attentive to the revelation. Emerson was a first-hand reporter of the living God, and that was the very essence of religion.

Mrs. Anna Garlin Spencer said she owed to Emerson the greatest debt that one human being could woe to another, when it was impersonal, and she expressed her gratitude therefor.

Professor A. E. Dolbear of Tufts College, Rev. Loren B. Macdonald, minister of the First Parish (Unitarian) Church, Concord, also spoke briey in appreciation of Emerson and Dr. Emerson's paper.

There was quite a breeze toward the end of the discussion. It was created by the remarks of Rev. Henry K. Hannah, rector of the Episcopal Church in Concord, who declared that Mr. Emerson was not a Christian, because he did not recognize the existence of sin and because he did not recognize the scheme by which sin was to be put out of the world.

Professor Maulsby of Tufts College differed from Mr. Hannah, defending Emerson from the foregoing charge. He said that the essence of Christianity did not consist in what Mr. Hannah thought it did.

Mr. Mead said that if anyone thought that Emerson did not recognize the presence of sin in the world he, the speaker, would like to furnish a list of one hundred sinners whom Emerson had already judged.

Mr. Sanborn, while not participating in the discussion, said afterwards in conversation with the Transcript representative that Emerson's doctrine would be found almost word for word in St. Augustine, who was the father of Calvinism.

from the Boston Evening Transcript, July 27, 1903.

EMERSON SCHOOL

Essay on Emerson and Oriental Thought

By Professor Nathaniel Schmidt of Cornell

This Morning's Very Instruction Essay

Followed by Lively Discussion in Concord Town Hall

Special to the Transcript:

Concord, July 27—This is the third and the closing week of the Emerson Memorial School. The lecturer this morning was Professor Nathaniel Schmidt of Ithaca, N. Y., professor of Semitic languages at Cornell University, and his topic was "Emerson and Oriental Thought." It would be impossible to find anyone better fitted to treat of this topic—always somewhat obscure to the lay mind—than Professor Schmidt. His paper was listened to throughout most intently. It was enlivened with keen flashes of epigrammatic wit, which caused ripples of laughter to sweep over the company. Here is one of his epigrams that illustrate the foregoing statement. Having declared that Emerson was not a historian and had no passion for facts, the essayist said: "He knew not the delirious delights of chronology." Professor Schmidt has a resonant voice and a most fascinating extempore delivery. This was most especially noticeable when he quoted, with fine effect, from "The Problem" and other poems of Emerson.

SYNOPSIS OF PAPER

Lecturer's Salient Points Noted and Summarized Below

"It is not easy to define Oriental thought. One is apt to fence out as much as one fences in. What constitutes the Orient? No meridian can be safely followed and no line of latitude. If we set out upon the blue Pacific to greet the rising sun, no wind or star will tell us when we shall leave the Orient behind. Japan must be within the circle. But the neighboring Aleutian Islands are in our eWstern home. New Zealand is more occidental than New York. We dare not cross the bleak Himalayas for fear that our previous definitions born on the banks of the Ganges shall freeze to death in the snows of Thibet. The common ancestors of Semite and Egyptian may have risen to higher destiny among the luxuries of an African environment. What a splendor of Driental life once spread over the gardens of Andalusia! eYt in the Spanish caliphotes there were nine Moors to every Arab. In another aspect, it was not Indus that fashioned into Orientals the Aryan invaders of India. Nor is the Atlantic broad and deep enough to wash away the strain of Orientalism from the descendants of those who once roamed with their herds between the Baltic and the Caspian. Blood is thicker than water. Father Rhine himselm could not prevent the genius of Germany from leaping to embrace the thought of India a century ago. Thus throbs the heart of man when a forgotten melody of childhood's days comes back again. Oriental thought cannot be forced within geographical boundaries or confined within the terms of a definition. But it is possible to select some lands, some men of genius, some songs, some sentiments that may roughly represent this vast, mysterious world of the Levant. Emerson's own works furnish a guide. One must be aware, however, of lusty inferences. Every great man is himself a world imperfectly explored. Many a secret we would be fain to worm out of his books he has carried with him into the eternal silence. We may never know what Japan gave to Emerson, whether the strains of Cudraka and Kalidaska ever gladdened his heart, how justly he could judge the Tear of Mount Hira, whether he could look with eyes like Goethe's upon the Book of Job, how deeply he was affected by the parable of Jesus. The lore of Egypt and of Babylon was quite unknown to him, and so was early Arabic and modern Turkish poetry.

"Tree gates that open the palace of Oriental thought were closed to him—language, history and travel. Translations at best sow only the wrong side of the tapestry. Eerson depended on such. He was not a historian. He knew not the delirious delights of chronology. His soul was never thrilled by feeling the naked vertebrae of this backbone of history. He had no passion for facts. No sooner did he discern a fact than he transuted it into a sybol. He never visited Asia and seems almost to have made a virtue of staying in the home-land. What cared he for Arabia, when Monadnock gave him visions such as no man ever saw from Sinai? However, there are two ways of reading a translation—the thorny path of the scholar beset with harrowing suspicions of inaccuracy and a parching thirst for the original, and the airy path of the bee in search of honey, the poet's highway to the heart of things. The gathering and classifying of details may not have been to his taste, but Emerson knew how to weigh massive personalities and great events. When the air is clear, one can sit in Concord and survey with naked eye the beauties of Maj Total and the Alhambra."

The speaker discussed in detail the translations of Chinese, Indian, Persian, Arabic and Hebrew authors known to Emerson and likely to have been used by him. Special importance was given to the versions of Bhagavad gita, the poets or Bidpai, the laws of Mann, the Persian poets Sardi, Hajz and Yai, the Qoran and the Hebrew Bible.

He also examined at length the German and French works through which Emerson is likely to have gained insight into Oriental thought. Goethe's importance as an exponent to Emerson of the deepest thought of the East was especially emphasized.

"Living in an age," Professor Schmidt continued, "when every movement of thought on the continent of Europe is quickly felt in England and America, we are scarcely able to realize how Germany could have been so deeply affected by the thought of India and experienced such a revolution in the view of Hebrew antiquity without aparently leaving any but the faintest impression in English literature. Strauss made little stir in 1835, Bruno Bauer appears to have been observed by nobody in 1841. But even among educated Englishmen and Americans, German seems to have been a rare accomplishment.

"Emerson felt the Oriental impact in another direction. He realized how the ancient Hebrew world had superimposed itself upon the Occident as to some extent a foreign and heterogeneous lement. He chides Swedenborg for his 'boyishness' in preserving 'the scarf of Hebrew antiquity.' Yet his spirit was too receptive, his wental disposition too generous, to be satisfied with a purely negative and problemical attitude. Individualist as he was to the core of his being, he yet could not gaze upon the mighty institutions of Christianity, its systems of thought, its churches, rites and sacred customs, its organized efforts for the amelioration of mankind, without feeling that, if this frozen music could be thawed out by the genial warmth of the spirit of life, sweet soul-refreshing melodies would escape.

"This survey of the sources through which Emerson became acquainted with oriental thought would be of little value, if the contention were true that he only used it to illustrate his own, but that it in no wise influenced his conception of life. But we do not honor our heroes by ascribing to them an originality which would have made them insensible to the noblest impressions. The greatest spirits of the orient visited the bard of Concord and whispered their secret in his ears. Shall we think well of him by assuming that he learned nothing from them? The magi of the East no doubt brought to him gold and frankincense and myrrh, but they also carried with them their knowledge of the stars. It consists of thought swept through him from the silent stars of the sky, he was still more deeply affected when the sons of the morning sang together in the human firmament. If, with a poet's wonder and joy, he

looked upon mountains, trees and rippling waters, he gazed with greater delight upon the majestic grandeur or the delicate charm of a human soul.

"Confucious impressed him deeply. He marvelled at the supremacy of moral principles in the Chinese civiliation. It may be doubted, however, whether any of those principles came as a distinct addition to the ethical perception of Emerson. Buddhism does not seem to have had a special attraction to him, though he recognized its moral earnestness and ethical insight. Emerson appears to have been less capable of appreciating these cries of the soul ex profundis, these agonizing struggles, these plaintive yearnings for redemption.

"No phase of Oriental thought influenced him more profoundly than Brahminism. It was a fortunate circumstance that he ~made acquaintance with this subtlest thought of India through Bhagavalgita. Here philosophy is poetry and poetry is philosophy. We are still in the midst of a process of thought. Great ideas irradiate the landscape with a glacial light; they do not yet flood its with their almost blinding sheen. Three thoughts—perhaps the most stupendous ever concerned by the human mind—come to view. These are the identity of God and nature, the overcoming of evil with good, and the law of compensation. The Saṇkhya philosophy looks upon the idea of a god sitting on a throne above the world or immanent in it as a crude survival of the childhood of the race. Nature is conceived to be infinite in space, eternal, exhaustless in energy, inherently right, spiritual and good.

Evil, then cannot belong to the essence and reality of the universe, but is good in the making. The highest good to man is the realization of his spiritual ascendancy, freedom and power. This comes of knowledge dispelling ignorance, love conquering hatred, good overcoming evil. By abstraction from the world of sense and concentration on the highest, the Yogin approaches to perfection. But all existence is subject to the law of Karma. Karma is the deed. The deed flows from the truer disposition, makes character and creates destiny. Retribution is not an everlasting hell for a few years of sin, nor an everlasting dream for a few moments of repentance, faith or goodness. The character formed is a brief section of the soul's existence, fashions an outward form in harminy with its nature, and this in turn issues in another. Thus there is the possibility of a perpetual rising and sinking in the scale of being. That this most marvelous adjustment of character and form of life must itself ultimately become a burden and make the mind gratefully accept the prospect of deliverances from the endless wheel of existence in the Nivorna, does not diminish the intrinsic value of so noble an attempt to solve the great mystery. It measured retribution in terms of character, and here and there the greater thought looms up that the good deed and disposition and character are themselves their own reward.

"It is obvious to every reader of Emerson that this is to a marked extent the work of thought in which his spirit moved. 'Brahma' is a translation and interpretation, but the

"The living heaven thy progress respect,
House it over and architect,
Quarrying men's rejected hours,
Builds therewith eternal towers."

as well as numerous passages in 'The Over-Soul' and other essays show the pentheistic thought of Emerson. This he did not get from Platon, or Spinoza, nor from his own unaided contemplation of nature.

Mozoomda knew him for his own, and Vlockananda saw in him a kinsman. This was not merely the feeling of a sympathetic personality. It was the thought of India that met them in Emerson. It may be asked whether there are not Arabaptists, Quakers, quietists enough to account for the outcropping of the doctrine of non-resistance in a Western Quaker. The essay on war might indeed have been read with joy by Fox, and Laborie, and Spencer. But none of them would have understood the higher cosmic bearings of the principle in Uriel. And Emerson did not know Johannes Denek. In his essay on compensation, Emerson tells us how this subject had occupied his mind since childhood. His reflections upon the good parson's sermon were certainly not influenced by philosophical speculations from without. It is also noticeable that the idea of a future state, limited or otherwise, as the issue of the character formed, plays no part in Emerson's thinking. The immortality of the soul is a matter of indifference to him. But the thought of a retribution is terms of character so infinitely exact that in each moment of existence the account is balanced finds fine expression. How far this trend of thinking was influenced by the similar ideas in India must be left unsettled.

It was not the Persia dominated by Zarathustra's thought that left an impression upon Emerson. It was the later Persia that chafed under the restraints of the Coran, rebelled against the authority of the Prophet and asserted its spiritual independence. Hafiz was dear to Emerson because he was a nonconformist, sincere and true to himself. tI is profoundly interesting to watch the influence of the Persian poet on this son of the Puritans. Hafiz taught him that it is not the drunkard who loves wine, and the debauchee can neither love nor sing the praises of love. "Good Saadi dwells above." his would be a sufficient tie to bind his soul to Emerson's even if he were not so demonically wise.

"Trees in groves,
Kine in droves---but—"

In a thousand generations how many men are htere who dare to dwell alone, away from creeds and rites and sacred customs, removed from greed, lust and ambition, facing the universe and the Sphinx within?

"The Church spoiled for Emerson the Bible. It was a book with seven seals, and most of Emerson's energy seems to have gone into the effort to break them. Could he have lived today and enjoyed the fruits of critical investigation, he would have gladly listened to the charming story-tellers of Bethel and Beersheba, to elders in the gates and priests at the shrines proclaiming laws of life and social ideals. His rebellious spirit fled from ancient oracles to whose fallibility he saw only too clearly, to prophets not spoiled by being canonized. Henever knew the greatness of Amos and Hosea, Isaiah and Jeremiah. His strange indifference to the Book of Job is perhaps to be accounted for by his general lack of appreciation of the tragic element in life Goethe knew the value of the greatest poem the Semitic world has ever produced, and paid it the sincerest compliment of imitation. Emerson shrank from this abyss of mental agony and spiritual defeat. It is of interest that Emerson's critical insight led him to discuss the true character of Canticles. With all his mysticism he rejected here, as in the case of Hafiz, the allegorical interpretation, and declared the song to be of earthly love.

"The only Jew whom Emerson really understood was Jesus. Supreme greatness attracted him, as the magnet does the needle. The Nicene creed did not prevent him from giving his heart to Jesus. He revered him too sincerely for adulation; he loved him too tenderly for genaflexion. He was not astonished and overwhelmed by Jesus as strangers to his spirit are, but comforted and inspired as is a friend. No fiction of sinlessness put a barrier between them. How deep his spiritual insight was, his parting address to his chuch shows. This lucid discussion of Jesus's last meal also reveals his remarkable critical acumen. Nevertheless, 'the might that lurks in reaction and recoil' made Emerson emphasizer against the artificiality of dogma, with force no longer needed, the independence of the human soul.

"Emerson has not unjustly been charged with being responsible for the strong hold of Oriental speculation upon our Western World, and for what men are pleased to call 'the vagaries of anti-imperialism.' If there is today in ever-widening circles among us a disposition to listen with reverence to all the great teachers of religion in the world and to emphasize the ethical contest of each form of religion, this is in no small measure due to Emerson. If there is a broader outlook upon humanity, a kindlier feeling among the representatives of its different races, a fellowship not based on creed or ceremony, a recognition of the value of religious mysticism, Emerson's share in bringing forth these fruits of the spirit is great. His hospitality of Orential thought did not make him less the prophet of American demoracy. Have the doctrines of the supremacy of manhood, the worth of spiritual independence, the overcoming of darkness with light, peace and good will on earth come from the East? There are good reasons for a generous reception. For the recognition of the worth of man, the liberty of conscience, the simple, well-poised life, the advance through peaceful growth are also the foundations of our Commonwealth. The healthy opposition to the pomp of empire, to war and subtle statecraft is not a vagary. But the dangerous disregard for the fundamental principles of the rebpublic, the strenuous effort to advance the nation's fortunes at the expense of the nation's character, threaten us with the common fate of empires. Salvation lies in a return to those great convictions to which our Concord sage gave so courageous and unwavering expression. It is not the citizen's part to despair of the republic. However dark the clouds may seem the splendid optimism of Emerson will help to win the day.'

THE DISCUSSION

Lively Remarks by Mr. Sanborn, Rev. Henry K. Hannah and Others

After the prolonged applause which followed Professor Schmidt's concluding sentences had subsided, Mr. Sanborn said it would be difficult to go deeper into the subject than had been done "in this most remarkable paper which we have just heard."

Rev. F. B. Hornbrooke, D. D., said it would be an impertinence to try to supplement the essay. The essayist had told them something definite and (referring to the essayist's fine delivery) had told it in a way that gave pleasure.

Mr. Sanborn said that but few critics realized what an early and profound reader Emerson as. The Baghavad Gita was the core of Emerson's thought.

Rev. George Willis Cooke said that two things should be remembered: In the first place, Emerson had gotten so far away from Christianity as ordinarily interpreted in his time, that his mind was free for the

consideration of other forms of faith than that with which he had been made familiar by the churches. In the second place, Emerson did fundamentally recognize the fact that all religions are essentiallly the same in their origin and nature.

Mr. Sanborn referred to the assertion made in last Wednesday's discussion by Rev. Henry K. Hannah, rector of the Concord Episcopal Church, that Emerson was not a Christian because he did not understand the presence of sin or evil in the world or the scheme for putting evil out of the world. Mr. Sanborn declared that Emerson's doctrine of sin and Evil in the world could be found almost word for word in the writings of St. Augustine.

Rev. Mr. Hannah rose in his seat near the rear of the hall. Mr. Sanborn invited him to take the platform. Mr. Hannah declined to do so. "I rose," said he, "to speak for Miss Leavitt, but she cautions me. What I desired to say for her was that she wants to correct Mr. Sanborn in regard to St. Augustine."

Mr. Sanborn. "I should be glad to be corrected."

Mr. Hannah—"She (Miss Leavitt) says that, at one time, St. Augustine did hold the view of evil which Mr. Emerson practically held; but he (St. Augustine), I believe, gave it up. That leads me to say the only thing I want to say this morning, and that is this: I question the legitimacy of that method of substantiating the view of any man. You should not go to a man like St. Augustine, whose entire philosophy and view of life were, it seems to me, so different, and take any single thing that he may have said at any time, to substantiate any of Mr. Emerson's doctrines.

The only thing I should question in the paper would be this: I doubt whether the lecturer has a right to lump, under the title of 'Oriental Thoughts,' the whole system of thought which would come with the Old and the New Testament. True, it is Oriental thought. But, if my own thought and reading is at all true, and comes anywhere near the truth, it seems to me that there is developed in that great system of thought, something which is decidedly different from what we ordinarily know as 'Oriental thought.' While it is true, as Mr. Cooke has said, that religion is the same because we are all searching for the same God, let us keep the distinction as clear as we can. I think it would be very interesting to have the essayist say a little something on this point.

V

from the Boston Evening Transcript of July 29, 1903.

"THE SIMPLER EMERSON"

A Feeling That He Was the Only Emerson

Interesting Paper by Rev. John White Chadwick

Before the Memorial School at

Concord

His Simplest Means Always Secured Eloquent Effects

Special to the Transcript:

Concord, July 29—"The Simpler Emerson" was the topic of this morning's very interesting paper by Rev. John White Chadwick of Brooklyn, N. Y., at the Emerson Memorial School. One of the largest audiences of the school was present to hear the distinguished preacher, and recent biographer of Parker and Channing; and they were well rewarded for coming out on the lowering and sultry morning. With all his learning and talents, Mr. Chadwick is himself one of the "simplest" of men, in the best and highest sense of that word. It was fitting, therefore, that, in choosing his own topic for his essay, as he did, he should choose, for what proved to be a graphic and convincing portrayal, the "simpler" Emerson.

SYNOPSIS OF THE PAPER

The Essayist's Salient Points Noted and Summarized Below

Mr. Chadwick began by saying that one of Emerson's most interesting and attractive perceptions was that there are several audiences in each particular audience. So there were several Emersons and more in Emerson. There was the poet, the psychologist, the humorist, the orator, the friend, the domestic person, the Concord citizen. And there was the simpler Emerson and the more difficult. Mr. Chadwick related his first experience in reading Emerson: "The book was 'Representative Men,' the time was 1858. When I read in the first paragraph of the men who tasted the earth and found it deliciously sweet, I seemed to be repeating their experience. What I could understand seemed to me better than anything that I had read before. To this day there are parts that baffle me, especially in the earlier essays. Here and there Emerson seems to use a cryptic terminology, of which he has the key, but does not lend it, nor explain the use of it, to me. In other places I appear to understand, but not to be able to interpret. If a friend asks, 'What does this mean?' I answer, 'It is so perfectly expressed that to change a word would be to change the thought.' I find in such sentences illustrations of the principle of necessity in art. The beautiful building or statue has to be so and not otherwise.

"The simpler Emerson is much more in proportion to the whole of Emerson than the simpler Browning to the whole of Browning. Reading the whole body of his writings continuously within the course of a few recent months, I was wellnigh persuaded that the simpler Emerson was the only Emerson; that the proportion of his difficult to his simple matter was that of Falstaff's bread to Falstaff's sack—hardly an appreciable quantity. At the outset the novelty of Emerson's view of man's relation to the world, so fluid in comparison with the hard-and-fast conceptions of the Lockian school, staggered a great many persons. But now science having come to the support of the idealistic view, Berkeley and Huxley having kissed each other, there is much less bewilderment. Moreover Emerson speaking ten times as the poet to once as the metaphysician, and sometimes using that superlative which he deprecated in his more deliberate moods, did sometimes seem to dissipate the objective world into a shadow of the perceiving mind. In his reaction from 'the window theory'—that the soul looks out through the senses, on the external world—he sometimes seemed to accord to nature no reality except as a reflection of mind, our mind. But he corrected this exaggeration more and more as time went on, until at length he wrote, "There is in nature a parallel unity which corresponds to the unity in mind and makes it available. Not only man puts things in a row, but things are in a row, . . . nature being formed everywhere after a method which we can well understand, and all the parts, to the most remote, allied and explicable.'

"The simplicity of Emerson's discourse suffered much less deduction from its formlessness than is asserted by his harsher critics and conceded by his friends. That he lacked 'wholeness of tissue,' as Matthew Arnold discovered with his habitual light and insisted on with his habitual sweetness, is obvious, and yet if Arnold had known Emerson better he would have made less of this. Many of the Essays, lacking formal unity, have an organic unity which is better. There are degrees of this, the Divinity School address representing the most strict coherency and the most orderly development. Architectonic he was not, and yet he liked to have a steeple to his church, a climax to his essay or address."

Mr. Chadwick particularized the Thoreau address, the first he heard Emerson deliver, and that upon Lincoln's anticipatory emancipation proclamation of September, 1862. Mr. Chadwick said: "I had heard Lincoln at his best; I had heard Everett, of whom Emerson had written, 'All his speech was music and with such variety and invention that the ear never tired'; I had heard Sumner magnificently thundering. 'Let my people go'; but till I heard Emerson saying, 'Do not let the dying die; hold them back till you have charged their car and heart with this message to other spiritual societies announcing the amelioration of our planet,' I had not heard the best that human speech could do.'

"And always with Emerson the simplest means secured the eloquent effects. Never was voice more magical, but from those sloping shoulders slid off too easily the honors of distinguished oratory which he might otherwise have won. It is only a small part of the beauty of Emerson's writing that has the eloquent note, but beauty is everywhere his most commanding trait, and, in proportion as his expression is more beautiful, it is always less obscure. The simpler Emerson is the purveyor of beautiful thoughts, the poet not submitting his poetry to prosodic forms, but expressing it in his choice and novel use of words, in cadences more musical than many of his formal rhythms, in passages of such haunting loveliness that once read they can never be forgotten. With Thackeray and some others he goes far to convince us that prose is the most beautiful form of writing possible, more beautiful than the most lovely verse.

"The fable of Emerson's difficulty has been encouraged by the character of a few poems even more, perhaps, than by a few essays among which 'The Oversoul' enjoys a particularly bad eminence. But Emerson's essay, 'Poetry and Imagination' exhibits him as a careful student of the forms of poetry, its artifices and devices, and as extremely sensitive to these. With this knowledge of his art how could he so frequently permit himself to be as harsh as Donne? His defect is the more curious because he could be, and often was, quite perfect in the music of his

lines." Quoting several examples, Mr. Chadwick said: "That the same hand that moulded these perfections shaped others rough as frozen stubble is a strange thing no doubt. We must believe for one thing that the muse he courted was a fickle muse, that the goddess was sometimes 'invita;' for another that his chief concern was with his thought, not with the form. Much of Emerson's verse has, equally with his prose, the note of eloquence the sonorous, resonant quality that invites to audible expression. And by this sign we have the simpler Emerson, for where there is eloquence there must be simplicity.

"John Burroughs says that Emerson cared for ideas not for things." Mr. Chadwick doubted whether Burroughs cared for "things" so much. "Emerson's books are full of them, and so vividly expressed that we seem to be in contact with the things themselves, no mere report of them. He never tires of sitting by that loom which weaves of things the garment of the Eternal Thought and listening to its joyous whirr. He thinks much of the garment. 'O mother!' said Robert Collyer's little daughter, 'when you were away from home I went into the closet and just hugged your dresses.' Not less was Emerson's affection for the living garment of the never-absent spirit of the world."

Mr. Chadwick found other manifestations of the simpler Emerson in his liking for the homelier forms of speech and in his delicious humor which is not so much here and there as everywhere in his writings. "But it is when we pass to the more general aspects of Emerson's teaching that his simplicity is most conspicuous; he is plainest in proportion to the elevation and importance of his thought, its relative significance in the range of his principal ideas. We have in his own words 'the first simple foundation' of his 'belief that the author of nature has not left himself without a witness in any sane mind.' It is that 'the moral sentiment speaks to every man the law after which the universe was made; that we find parity, identity of design through nature, and benefit to be the uniform aim; that there is a force always at work to make the best better and the worst good.' Here is the optimism of Emerson, but it is everywhere. It is so obvious that it is frequently invoked in justification of that contemporary optimism which is characteristically a gross and sordid satisfaction in the social and political conditions of the time, a fat and lazy acquiescence in its tendencies to lower and the lowest things. But nowhere can we find sterner accusation of this bastard optimism than in Emerson. He never despairs of the republic, but, if no one cherishes a better ultimate hope, no one is keener to detect the present rottenness. Seeing the national folly and defect, he saw beyond it to the better coming time. He did not think it possible for us to defeat by any ingenuity the blessed purposes of God. At the same time he could wish that our will and endeavor were more active parties to the work.'

"As with his national, so with his universal optimism. Perfectly simple in its fundamental cheerfulness, it is not exclusive of the ugliest fact that seems to militate against its validity. Further, the simplicity of Emerson declares itself in his attitude of habitual worship, his sense of God as everywhere present, urgent, insistent, informing all things with his thought, touching them all with his beauty, embracing them all with his law, saturating them all with his love.

"If Emerson could not see, he felt the 'private amity' of everything with any other, and he took a long step forward and

placed himself among the evolutionists who stood eager and tremulous upon the threshold of Darwin's generalization. But the parity and identity which delighted him in nature had their best use for him as type and illustration of the parity and identity of all things natural with all things spiritual, 'the identity of the law of gravitation with purity of heart.' 'One world at a time' for him, and all the time a moral world, all things making for the good, and hence all things having in it their root and ground. 'Religion,' said Dr. Channing, 'is the worship of goodness,' and the whole body of Emerson's thinking resolves itself into a great 'Amen.' The moral sentiment was his 'sky that holds them all,' God, nature, man. And the door that opens on the invasions of this sentiment is self-reliance, the surrender of the soul to the highest leadings which it knows. If there was a simpler Emerson than the prophet of this burden, it was the Emerson who pleaded for the simple life and in his own person made such a life as real as the granite ledges of his ancestral town. It is the simplicities of his character, even more than the sublimities, that draw after him so many hearts and make possible the grateful reverence of his centennial year."

THE DISCUSSION

Mr. Sanborn and Mr. Mead Express Their Differences Concerning the American Scholar

After the prolonged and very general applause which followed Mr. Chadwick's closing period had subsided, Mr. Sanborn said the school welcomed any attack upon what Mr. Emerson was, or even upon what anybody thought he was. Mr. Sanborn said that the educated class never led the multitude, but always followed. He called upon Mr. Mead, who said he was sorry that he had been called upon.

"But, so long as I have been," said he, "I wish to take up the brief for the scholar. I do not quite agree with Mr. Sanborn. Emerson and his generation are conspicuous illustrations of the other side of the shield. I cannot help remembering that it was a man, learned of all the Egyptians, who led Israel out of Egypt and that it was Paul who sat at the feet of Gamaliel who did more to spread the gospel than did the fishermen of Galilee. And, as one comes right down to the great struggle for the English Commonwealth, it was Hampton, Pim, Cromwell, Milton, Vane and all those students of Cambridge and Oxford who led the movement for the Commonwealth, and the leaders of the Commonwealth were scholars. The leaders of the American Revolution were chiefly graduates of Harvard and of William and Mary. The scholar has been too often recreant, but the scholar has done great and splendid service. With reference to Lincoln, this homely man, I cannot help thinking that, just as Oliver Cromwell found his great panegyrist in Milton, so it is a blessed thing that Lincoln lived in the Golden Age of our poetry and that every one of our great poets has paid to him so great and wonderful a tribute.

"The scholar can always be kept right and encouraged to be kept right by the fact, and the statement of that fact, that so many scholars in the progress of radicalism and history have kept right.

"As to Mr. Chadwick's criticism I will say that I do not disagree with him even in what he thought I said about Emerson's poetry being always the best possible. He probably refers to something in my recent book. If so, that was not quite what I

said. I simply expressed my feeling that many of those works which annoy the machine versifier and the lover of equal verse grow to us gradually to have a peculiar charm, definiteness and propriety."

Mr. Sanborn, replying to Mr. Mead, said, with his most sarcastic smile wreathing his lips and with a manner impossible to convey by the printed word:

"The American scholar! Ha! Ha! It reminds me of the saying that all the deacons are good, but there is a difference in deacons. The trouble with the American scholar is that he must be with the majority and does not feel easy with the minority. He cannot get out of this servitude to the Government. The business of the scholar is to support the Government when it does right and denounce it when it does wrong. When he gets down on his knees instead of standing up on his feet, he betrays his own order. He will have to repent for his want of incupidity in caskcloth and ashes. Emerson — peculiarly a man of courage."

Words of appreciation of the paper on the debt to Emerson were uttered by Colonel Nort; and Señorita Carolina H. Huidobro, a former resident of Chile, now living in Boston.

THE DEFECT IN HIS PHILOSOPHY

As Seen from the Standpoint of the Sect of Friends Is Pointed Out by Rev. B. F. Trueblood

Rev. Benjamin F. Trueblood, secretary of the American Peace Society and one of the leading Friends in America, was the speaker at last evening's session of the Emerson Memorial School in Huntington Hall. His topic was "Emerson and the Inner Life," and his views were from the standpoint of a Friend. The address contended against what the speaker considered as a deeply religious mind for maintaining a light that was too "inner" for the attainment of aims cherished by Emerson.

The lecturer argued that the trying difficulty in a study of the theological conceptions was Emerson's talent as a phrasemaker—in the best sense of the term—probably the greatest that has ever written in English prose, as Tennyson was the greatest phrasemaker among English-speaking poets. Many of Emerson's phrases are so great, so pregnant with meaning, that they "move the world" and make one feel that a new order of things is coming to light. But not infrequently his temptation to turn a fine phrase for the mere mystic beauty of the thing is so great that he sacrifices sense to form, and it is impossible to be sure of what he is trying to say. This is particularly true of some of his expressions about God.

Emerson's simple, living faith in God was doubtless arrived at, he said, from his ancestors, and he read it into himself from English, German, Hebrew, Persian and Hindu literature, but recast it in his own mould. His faith could not harmonize with the cults and creeds and practices about him, and in his inflexible honesty he withdrew; possibly not being able to justly estimate the utterances of other men in these fields. He felt compelled to trust his own faculties and his own conscience, through those processes he came to a knowledge of the universal moral system.

EMERSON AND THE WAR

Moorfield Storey Before Concord School

Boston Lawyer Delivers an Interesting Address

How Poet's Anti-Slavery Feeling Grew

Tomorrow the Sessions of the School Will End

Special to the Transcript:

Concord, July 30—"Emerson and the Civil War" was the topic of this morning's very interesting and stirring paper before the Emerson Memorial School by Moorfield Storey. The lecturer declared that the Civil War was the culmination of a long struggle against a gigantic wrong—slavery. It was not a sudden explosion like the Spanish War. It was, therefore, impossible to present adequately Emerson's attitude toward that war without considering his attitude toward the anti-slavery agitation that preceded it. For many years now slavery had found no defender, but it was a very different world into which Mr. Emerson was born. Even then, however, there were men who looked beneath the surface and realized the true nature of slavery. Between the great mass of the people who, as Emerson had declared, "permitted themselves to be ranged with the enemies of the human race," and the militant agitators who devoted their lives to attacking slavery —Garrison, Phillips, Sumner and others— there was a middle ground. Mr. Emerson adopted this course, and in 1852 stated in his journal, as his reason, that he had "quite other slaves to free than these Negroes—to wit, imprisoned spirits, imprisoned thoughts, far back in the brain of man, far retired in the heaven of invention, and which, important to the republic of man, have no watchman or lover or defender but I." There were anti-slavery orators enough, but there was only one Emerson, and we know that he chose wisely. He was like Sumner, in that he did not take an early interest in the slavery question. His mind was occupied with questions of philosophy and religion, but he does not seem then to have been stirred deeply by anything in the condition of the Negro. He kept close to his own work, and used slavery and the struggle against it, as he used other evils, to illustrate and point his argument. The methods of the anti-slavery leaders seem at times to have irritated him, and his sense of humor was not blind to their foibles.

Yet, when the Abolitionists were most despised, in the winter of 1838, Emerson said, in his lecture on "Heroism": "Human virtue demands her champions and martyrs, and the trial of persecution always proceeds. It is but the other day that the brave Lovejoy gave his breast to

the bullets of the mob for the rights of free speech and opinion, and died when it was better not to live." In 1844, in his address on "The Young American," he stated his true position thus: "We cannot give our life to the cause of the debtor, the slave, the pauper, as another is doing, but to one thing we are bound—not to blaspheme the sentiment and work of that man, nor to throw stumbling blocks in the way of the Abolitionist, the philanthropist, as the organs of influence and opinion are swift to do."

Yet no man foretold the inevitable punishment of our national sin more clearly than he. It would seem impossible that he should not have applied to slavery the doctrine which he taught in "Compensation."

As the combat grew fiercer, Emerson was gradually drawn into more and more active sympathy with the opponents of slavery. In 1831 he invited Samuel May, the well-known Abolitionists, to preach from his pulpit. In 1837 he made his first speech on the subject of slavery, which was, however, rather a plea for free and charitable discussion than an expression of strong anti-slavery feeling.

After this deliverance the position of Mr. Emerson was clear to all the world; but he was content to be silent, until the compromise measure of 1851, including the fugitive slave law, intended and expected to end forever the agitation against slavery, brought the Civil War nearer by exhibiting the brutality of the slave hunter in the very heart of the free States. This measure and Webster's support of it aroused him to fierce indignation, which he was not slow to express.

The lecturer quoted from Emerson's Concord address in 1851 to show this. He declared that the policy which Emerson proposed was that of the Republican party, which was founded when the fugitive slave law was passed. From that time on, Emerson, while he was not an organizer of the movement or a leader in anti-slavery councils, he was ready to speak when occasion required. It was because slavery was no longer mendicant, but aggressive and dangerous, that Emerson became aroused. It was the acts of the slave power which roused Emerson to realize that his post was on the firing line of the anti-slavery army. From Emerson's recognition of the Anti-Slavery Society, the Cassandras of today, whom men call pessimists, may like some comfort, and their countrymen may wisely remember that Cassandra prophesied truly and that the Trojans might have saved their city had they heeded her warnings. Eemrson subscribed $100 in aid of the Free State Letters in Kansas. He entertained John Brown at his house and after his attempted invasion of Virginia had failed spoke of his as "that new Saint awaiting his martyrdom, and who if he shall suffer, will make the gallows glorious like the cross." After Harper's Ferry no man in the North was more thoroughly aroused against slavery than Mr. Emerosn, he was satisfied it must be extirpated, and he saw in the war, which had now become inevitable, at once the result of slavery and the means of destroying it. Disunion had no terror for him, as compared with any compromise which should make a false peace and postpone the day of freedom. As the war was the knife to extirpate our national cancer, he was anxious to see it do its work quickly and thoroughly. He was anxious to have Lincoln attack slavery immediatel; and when, in 1862, the preliminary emancipation proclamation was issued, he was prompt to praise. The lec-

turer quoted from Emerson's Boston address at that time, and from his "Boston Hymn," closing:

"Be just at home; then write your scroll Of honor o'er the sea."

"How full of inspiration," exclaimed Mr. Storey, "are these words to every lover of freedom and justice! How ineffably sad it is to read th in now and to reflect, as we listen to the cries of the mob in Wilmington and Evansville, and read of the horrors committed in Luzon that ours is a less moral age, and that punishment waits upon our sons as it did on the sins of our fathers!" (Great applause.)

Emerson was not a soldier, but he could keep up the courage of the people. Said Lowell: "To Emerson more than all other causes together did the young martyrs of our Civil War owe the sustaining strength of thoughtful heroism that is so touching in every record of their lives." Emerson was not a campaign orator, nor a political leader, but a prophet seeing with clear vision the sin of the nation and foretelling the wrath to come. The deep indignation that burned ebneath his calm exterior, the very fact that such a man was deeply stirred gave wonderful power to his words. Emerson's view of the war in retrospect was shown in his address at the dedication of the soldiers' monument in Concord, the closing words of which were: "A gloom gathers on this assembly, composed, as it is, of kindred men and women, for, in many houses, the dearest and noblest is gone fro mtheir hearthstone. Yet it is tinged with light from heaven. A duty so severe has been discharged, and with such immense results of good, lifting private sacrifice to the sublime, that, though the cannon volleys have a sound of funeral echoes, they can yet hear through them the benedictions of their country and mankind." (Great applause.)

Mr. Sanborn, Señorita Carolina H. Huido bro and others spoke briefly. The attendance was one of the largest of the session.

EMERSON AND ANTI-SLAVERY

William Lloyd Garrison Tells How He Changed from Dislike of Abolitionists to Praise of John Brown

In the evening session of the Emerson Memorial School in Huntington Hall yesterday, William Lloyd Garrison spoke on "Emerson and the Auti-Slavery Movement."

"It is undeniable," said he, "that Mr. Emerson first viewed the abolitionists through the medium of his fastidious instincts and prejudices. Eccentric individuals who gravitate to every new reform were inseparable from anti-slavery meetings and gave excuse for the aloofness to the hostile and the cowardly.

"The anti-slavery leaders often winced when Emerson's utterances gave aid and comfort to the enemy. Every such phrase was seized upon and quoted fully by the newspapers, where not a line of his real wisdom would find a place. But these sentiments of Emerson's twilight disappeared, as owls and bats before the sunlight. It may be quoted to show the vital change that overtook him when, in storm and stress, he stood side by side with the "amiable enthusiasts." Emerson reached the point of agreeing to pay slaveholders for emancipated slaves, but when Fort Sumter had clarified his vision, as it did that of many others, he could say in his Boston hymn:

Pay ransom to the owner
And fill the bag to the brim?
Who is the owner? The slave is the owner
And ever was. Pay him.

"What the fanatics saw at the outset, the North was then slowly coming to discern, but Emerson had not awaited this tide of opinion. When the John Brown days arrived, how gloriously Emerson rose to the height of a great argument. 'That new saint,' he said, speaking of John Brown, 'than whom none purer was ever led by love of men into conflict and death; the new saint awaiting his martyrdom, who, if he shall suffer, will make the gallows glorious like the cross.'"

Y, JULY 31, 1903

EMERSONIANS' FINAL DAY

Concord Memorial School's Last Proceedings

Mrs. Julia Ward Howe Was Today's Speaker

Progress During a Century Her Subject

Dr. Hale Will Give the Closing Address Tonight

Special to the Transcript:

Concord, July 31—Today the Emerson Memorial School ends. This morning the last Concord lecture was delivered in the town hall by that "grand old woman" of this Emerson century—or, to use her own phrase, member of the "octogenarian phalanx"—Mrs. Julia Ward Howe. Tonight, in Huntington Hall, Boston, Rev. Edward Everett Hale, D. D., will utter the final word. Mrs. Howe's topic was "A Century from the Birth of Emerson." Dr. Hale will speak on "Emerson's Gospel for His Own Time and for Ours." No more fitting voices to "pronounce the benediction" could be imagined than those of the authors of "The Battle Hymn of the Republic" and "The Man without a Country"—literature which has done so much to inspire the true patriotism and the high ideals for which Emerson himself stood.

The course as a whole has been highly successful, and reflects great credit upon the Free Religious Association of America, of which Emerson was one of the founders and vice presidents, and under whose auspices the "school" has been held. Great credit, too, is due to the committee, consisting of Edwin D. Mead, George Willis Cooke, John C. Haynes, Frank B. Sanborn, William R. Thayer, Moorfield Storey and David Greene Haskins, Jr., who have had the "practical" arrangements directly in charge. Mr. Mead, as president of the association, presided at the opening, and a few other of the Concord lectures in his usual felicitous manner. For the rest, Mr. Sanborn has been in the chair. In that position and as a leader in the discussions he has fairly shone. Never have his wide general knowledge, his keen wit, caustic sarcasm and fund of anecdote been made more manifest. If his sar-

casm and his reiterated attacks on he "Harvard professors and the educated classes" have not always been a sauce thoroughly palatable to all his hearers, yet they have added a piquancy to the meetings that has caused the listeners to forget their disagreement and to finally join in the wave of laughter that has rippled over the hall. If any hostile criticism were to be made upon the lectures—and it is the farthest possible from the desire of the present writer to seem ungracious—it will be the monotony of the laudation heaped upon Concord Seer. Indeed, Professor Schmidt deprecated in one of the discussions the lack of genuine debate. He confessed that he was somewhat wearied by the constant adulation, and longed for the scent of the woods and the pine trees. During this last week, however, there has been some debate, due to a difference of opinion between Rev. Henry K. Hannah, rector of the Concord Episcopal Church, and Mr. Sanborn and others as to whether Emerson was a Christian, whether he recognized the problem of sin and evil in the world and the scheme for putting it out of the world, and whether Emerson's views of sin and evil were the same as and substantiated by those of St. Augustine. Rev. John White Chadwick, to be sure, spoke more discriminatingly of Emerson's work. Once again Mr. Mead and Mr. Sanborn "broke a lance"—a mild one—over the educated classes, Mr. Mead "taking a brief" for the American scholar. While, as Mrs. Malaprop said, "comparisons are odorous," this may perhaps fairly be said: Emerson was such a many-sided man that one side of him appeals more strongly to a given admirer than another; so one lecture has doubtless afforded greater pleasure to one hearer than another essay. Perhaps, however, it would not be unfair to single out two lectures, besides that of this morning, which have impressed the many. They are widely contrasted. One was that of Professor Nathaniel Schmidt of Cornell University, on "Emerson and Oriental Thought." The other was that of Rev. John White Chadwick of Brooklyn, N. Y., on "The Simpler Emerson." It was to be expected that great stress would be laid upon Emerson's passion for political righteousness, and that anti-imperialism would figure largely in the lectures. The expected has happened; and, though the word "anti-imperialism" has not been uttered, its essence has cropped out in nearly every paper. The applause which always followed such utterances showed that there were many anti-imperialists present.

Today was indeed a "field day" here. The town hall was crowded with the largest audience of the "school." Mrs. Howe arrived in town yesterday afternoon, and was accompanied by her daughter, Mrs. Florence Howe Hall. They are the guests of Mr. and Mrs. Frank B. Sanborn. Mrs. Hall and Mrs. Sanborn sat upon the platform, leaning lightly upon Mr. Sanborn's arm, there was loud applause and the entire audience arose and stood until she had become seated. In presenting her, Mr. Sanborn said she was no stranger in Concord, and had visited the village long ago; now she came to add to its fame. Mrs. Howe, who was again heartily applauded, then read her paper. It was closely listened to throughout, and again applauded at the close. Its prevailing tone was that of Emerson's own abounding optimism of thankfulness for the progress made in the nineteenth century and of joyful prophesy for the future. Mrs. Howe stood throughout her entire delivery, the silvery and musical notes of her voice penetrated to the rear

of the hall, and she showed no signs of fatigue as she sat down. Her manner would have put many a younger woman to shame. An abstract of her paper follows:

SYNOPSIS OF PAPER

Lecturer's Salient Points Noted and Summarized Below

"With halting and uneven steps we attained the year of our poet's birth, 1803, children of hope, still somewhat overbound by the traditions of the fathers, and yet led onward by champions who combined a noble enthusiasm with a nobler courage. In view of the great material exansion which then awaited us in the latter part of the century, what could have been more providential than the Transcendental movement which preceded it? When Dives was destined to amass his millions, how instructive were the simple lives of those who gladly accepted poverty as the condition of following their heart's love, philosophy! Emerson said: 'Things are in the saddle, and ride mankind!' Yes, but the Ideal was in the saddle also, and its steed had wings.

"The nineteenth century and the one preceding it as well, were, above all, periods of question. In our modern civilizations, Luther began the religious question, Goethe the aesthetic, Napoleon the military. The question of justice, pure and simple, was left for the new continent to propose and to solve. The nineteenth century witnessed a combination of these questions, and our dear poet's manhood awoke to consciousness while this combination was approaching its height. He, entering upon man's estate, finds the whole range of polite literature within his reach. His first utterances, though in the guise of 'woodnotes wild,' have in them the rythm of the Puritan conscience. He gradually studies and annexes the civilized world, which belonged to him before he belonged to it. What was his theme? Nature—a topic trite enough, but Nature as she had been interpreted before. His communings with her led him to contrast with her steadfast calm the turbulence of society, the cruel uncharity of priestly rule, the degradation of humanity in the person of the slave, most of all, the unthought of the age.

"In the generation of which I was fortunate in being one, who has done more than the beloved centenarian of our present consideration? His question throughout is: 'How about this so-called philosophy of thine? Has it made thee more really wise, more energetic in fulfilling the duties, civic and personal? Does it interpret for thee beauty and glory of life in such wise that thou dost take highest pleasure in highest things? How does it reason, for example, between the slave and his master? W have emblazoned the device of freedom upon our flag—does this flag consent to sanction th desecration of its pledge? How about religion? Is it to show the worship of any king really to be esteemed divine, or does it consist in ordinances and prescriptions which bear witness more to man's native ignorance than to the achievements of his educated reason?'

"Among the latent forces which the last wonderful century aroused to efficient action, I must include the sphere of woman's activity, as today conceded and even established. Need I say what a beneficent power has hereby been added to man's struggle with the brute force of nature? Making allowance for all the evils which we still see and deplore, I must think that the ethical and spiritual progress of the century now under consideration is its most

astounding feature. The growth everywhere visible of religious tolerance does not appear to me to mark a stage of indifferentism, but one combining faith in the power of divine things with belief in man's power of apprehending them. I seem to feel in the various religious bodies a growing directness of relation to the central source of religious power which enables, and indeed obliges, one sect to make room for others in the periphery of the circle, whose bounds are not for us to determine. How are the mighty strongholds of uncharity fallen! In respect of the relation of Philosophy and Religion, may we not find distinct evidence of the progress of the age in the present appreciation of one whose message to mankind was once difficult to read, but is now adopted in the common thought? Incarnation, the embodiment in everyday life of our best hopes and aspirations—is not this a feature of our true philosophy, married to religion? And is it not present with us in the writings of our dear friend? The familiar things of every day are woven into his beautiful verse. This twofold priesthood of man as an interpreter of nature and man as an exponent of nature, belongs eminently to our dear friend. He surely felt more deeply than most the office of culture in common human life. Mr. Emerson knew, no man better than he, the delights of study, the desk of solitary labor, the instruction of the lonely ramble in the woods, or by the seashore. In his rapt mood, he seems remote from us, a creature

"too bright and good
For human nature's daily food."

But when the cry of human need reaches him, he is with us, he is one of us, helpful and brotherly in our midst, giving, not as the world gives, of his inmost and best.

"Originality consists largely in freshness of view. This freshness of vision was conceded to our sage, and this it is which enables him to cast so new a glory over the visible world, with whose aspect we are so familiar, but in the interpretation of which we have made so little progress. This freshness, Mr. Emerson carried into his studies. Old scriptures had a new message for him and through him for us. The monumental literature of the East sang for him its cradle song. And all this newness of interpretation our sage gave to a generation wearied with logic and reason, with pounding of pulpit cushions and proving of the theo-metaphysical problems.

"In all that I have known of the Emerson century, the new form of freedom takes itself felt, freedom of question and answer, of assertion and denial, of association and disassociation. This freedom it is which gives to the intellectual life of today so bright a colony. Under the impulse much which was formerly sealed with mystery has been brought within the domain of positive knowledge. Much, on the other hand, which was imposed upon other generations as irrefragable dogma is today happily relegated to the region of the much that we cannot know. Although we still have wars and rumors of war, the prevalence of the peace-promoting qualities over the fighting spirit is an unmistakable feature of our time. I notice this sensibly in the changed relations between young people and their elders. Teachers now intend to train their pupils by sympathy and attraction, and if parents are often overlax in the discipline of their children, the child can fly to them without encountering the chevaux de frise of terror which in old times separated them.

"Concerning the questions which precede and accompany human progress the Emerson century has given us some important lessons. Timid souls fear to seek to know anything beyond what has been delivered to them of the fathers. This age, so full of interrogation, has done much to convince all that honest question, even of things most sacred, in always safe. Shall we dread to grow irreverent in proportion as we seek to understand the true inwardness of things eternal? Shall we expect to find the nearer aspect of Truth less majestic than her remote disguise? No! a thousand times, no! Of this reverent daring, our dear friend has given us an eminent example. Who has attacked more daringly than he the false commonplace which contented the social world of his time? Yet so discriminating was his touch, so delicate his perception, that not a feature of any availing belief was marred or disturbed by him.

"The rehabilitation of the Present is to me a welcome feature of the century which we are now reviewing. The apotheosis of the ancients dimly shadowed forth a truth which we more clearly recognize today, viz.: That the spiritual significance of a man's life-work does not fully realize itself until it is ended. As I stand in this place, where we have so often seen our beloved sage, I must feel that he is honored and even understood now as he would not have been in his lifetime. To me today his seat is not empty, his voice is not silent. The golden trumpets of world power carry far and wide his glowing syllables in which is distilled so much of the wisdom of the world, so much of individual fire and fervor. The beneficent countenance associated with these utterances smiles upon us with an earnest which coming ages will neither dim nor deny. A new century opens before us whose youth will soon forsake us of the octogenarian phalanx. In its inevitable course new exigencies will develop new resources. The coming hundred of years may surpass the last as far as the last one has gone beyond the wildest dreams of its predecessor. We elders think with dear affection of the generations which we shall never see with mortal eyes. If, in their onward sweep, they should pause to take account of us, let them remember us as foes of all tyrannies, as the friends of all true progress. We have made war on the supremacy of stereotype and tradition—we leave for our parting word our unalterable faith in God and man.

"In all our homage, let us remember that no man is so great as the truth which belongs to all men, the truth which it is our prerogative to pursue with our thought and to embody in our life." (Great applause.)

THE DISCUSSION

Mr. Mead, Mr. Sanborn, Mrs. A. G. Cooper and Others Speak

In the discussion that followed the paper, Mrs. Francis H. Brown of Boston said: "We came here to honor a prophet and stay to honor a prophetess," referring to Mrs. Howe. Then she went on to express her appreciation of Emerson. Mr. Sanborn read some impressions of Emerson published in the London Spectator by David MacRae, a Scotchman. John T. Michau, of St. Joseph, Mo., said that Emerson had been the lighthouse in our sea of time that points us forward in that pathway that leads us to the stars. Mrs. A. J. Cooper of Washington, D. C., a very intelligent colored woman, said that she could not sit still, having been stirred as she had been by the words of Mr. Chadwick the other day and of Mrs. Howe today. She referred to Emerson's—

"Do not let the dying die,"

and characterized it as a "grand pæan," a "great gloria in excelsis," a "just and fitting companion piece to Mrs. Howe's own

"As he died to make men holy
Let us die to make them free."

Continuing, Mrs. Cooper said: "I wondered if these disciples and letters of Emerson were not ready nowadays to say: 'Do not let the dead hear it; do not let them wake up.' I wondered if those souls that flitted out with those glad tidings on their lips might not be saddened by the thought that those tidings were not all that they thought they were; that many were crying 'peace' when there was no peace." (Applause.)

George H. Albert Meyer of Paris, France, denied strongly that Emerson did not sympathize strongly with the common people.

Mr. Mead said: "These lectures will not have done their proper work unless they prove an inspiration to churches and societies in coming days to continue the study of Emerson's character. Mrs. Howe has emphasized the word 'unthought.' That was the great vice against which Emerson stood. Emerson put it in another form, and pleaded for a 'revival of the human mind.' Our danger is that, in the plentitude of material resources, we shall come to rely upon the materialities, and not upon the spiritualities, upon those forces for which the 'machine' and the dollar and the gun stand, instead of those ideals which are along the sure salvation of nations as of men. (Applause.) There was not half so much war in the nineteenth as in the eighteenth century. If our 'unthought' ceases, if our reliance upon the spiritual arm is stimulated in America as it should be, then the record of this century will be brighter still. Let us take hope; but let us not forget the words just uttered by Mrs. Cooper, which seem so solemn upon the lips of one of her race."

At Mr. Mead's suggestion, Mrs. Howe, after speaking briefly of Emerson's beautiful benignity, recited her famous "Battle Hymn of the Republic" so impressively and beautifully as to elicit great applause.

On motion of Rev. Mary Safford, pastor of the First Unitarian Church of Des Moines, Io., a rising vote of thanks was tendered to the committee who have had charge of the lectures. Mr. Sanborn then declared the Concord school at a nend.

Mrs. Howe, her daughter, Mrs. Hall, Miss Julia Osgood and Mrs. Lucia Ames Mead were the guests at luncheon of Mrs. Daniel Lothrop, at her home, "The Wayside."

Through the kindness of Miss Ellen Emerson, her father's study was opened this afternoon for the inspection of all attendants upon the school who wished to visit it. Many availed themselves of the opportunity.

WAS A TRUE SCIENTIST

Emerson Formulated Theories Which Science Has Itself Accepted Decades Afterwards

It had remained for Professor A. E. Dolbear to consider before the school the subject of "Emerson's Thought in Relation to Modern Science." The speaker declared that the philosophy of Emerson was wholly scientific and proceeded to explain that Emerson had arrived at a theory of nature which is wholly in keeping with the tenets of modern science made decades afterwards.

"It is easy nowadays to believe in any of the great scientific generalizations that have been established in the nineteenth century, but it was not so seventy years ago, when Emerson was presented with the problem," Professor Dolbear explained. "Then the world was dominated by the conception of a special creation; of some power

interpolating factors in the series, by flat, altering or controlling by supreme will or other quality, the processes of nature. The Bible was a book of final reference and nothing was so firmly established as its infallibility—on no evidence. Emerson, a child of that age, came to disbelieve in creation; to disbelieve the historical accuracy of the Bible.

"There is no other recourse for a thinking mind than to substitute a theory of nature, working by law, where the processes were continuous and miracles were not. If he was like most men of his or any age, the present included, he would not have worried a moment about theories of nature or attempt to account for the beginning, the progress and the end of things. He was not like them, but more like Socrates, or Newton, or Kepler or any of those rare, great spirits, who are not content with passive inertia in intellectual effort.

"His time-honored conceptions falling, he sought the alternative and, without necessarily following the paths of science, saw by philosophic insight that all in nature was governed by laws that were permanent and sufficient for all the manifestations presenting themselves. Such a man is a scientist."

THE FIRST PARISH MEETING HOUSE — Rebuilt in 1901, after a fire, on the site of the old church where the Provincial Congress met before the Revolution

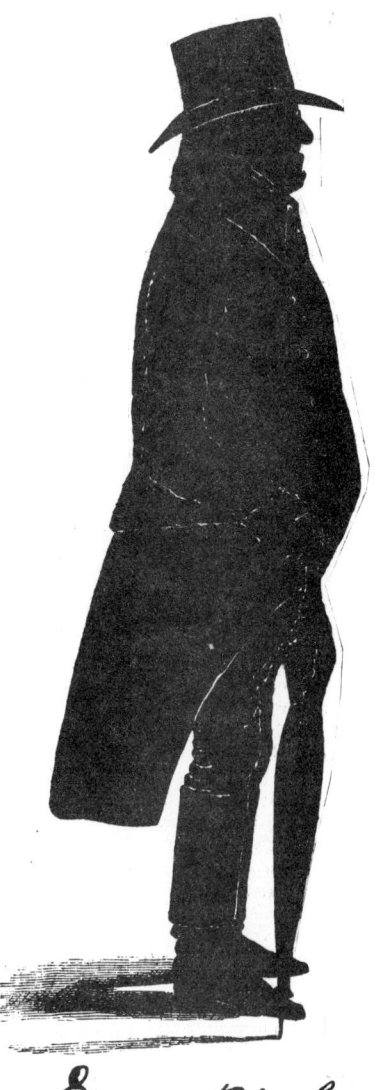

Ezra Ripley

GRAVE OF BRITISH SOLDIERS — On the field where they fell. Verses by James Russell Lowell were written for the 1875 celebration.

EMERSON'S PROPHETIC ROLE IN SCHOOLS OF THE ETHICAL MOVEMENT

[The New York Society for Ethical Culture was founded
by Felix Adler, educator and ethical reformer, six
years before Emerson's death——in 1876.]

Emerson's Prophecy

"The progress of religion is steadily to its identity with morals. ❧ ❧ ❧ It accuses us that pure ethics is not now formulated and concreted into a cultus, a fraternity with assemblings and holy-days, with song and book, with brick and stone. Why have not those who believe in it and love it left all for this, and dedicated themselves to write out its scientific scriptures to become its Vulgate for millions? ❧ ❧ ❧

"America shall introduce a pure religion. ❧ ❧ ❧ There will be a new church founded on moral science; at first cold and naked, a babe in a manger again, the algebra and mathematics of ethical law, the church of men to come, without shawms, or psaltery, or sackbut; but it will have heaven and earth for its beams and rafters; science for symbol and illustration; it will fast enough gather beauty, music, picture, poetry. Was never stoicism so stern and exigent as this shall be. It shall send man home to his central solitude, shame these social, supplicating manners, and make him know that much of the time he must have himself to his friend. ❧ ❧ ❧ The Laws are his consolers; the good Laws themselves are alive; they know if he have kept them; they animate him with the leading of great duty, and an endless horizon."

Emerson's Prophecy of a New Religion for America

We have printed on the preceding page, as our little memorial tablet on this Centennial occasion, a few brief passages from Emerson's writings, giving the gist of his prophecy of the coming Ethical Religion. These passages are not unfairly wrenched from the body of his work. They express no merely tributary current of his thought, but its very main stream. He here casts into prophetic form the burden of his message from the first to the last of his utterances. What he says in his maturity, in the essay on "Worship," is, in its general substance and spirit, what he said in his first writings and addresses; while in the other essay from which we draw, his still later "Sovereignty of Ethics," he but obeys at eve the voice obeyed at prime—to use his own beautiful words; the voice which, as he echoes it, has grown clearer and mellower with his advancing years.

The spirit of the future was strong in Emerson. He felt a definite call from the outset to be the mouthpiece to his countrymen of a new religion. He records, after his first visit to Europe, his conviction that it was for New World men to answer the Old World men what the new religion was to be for which mankind was waiting, and the hour was ripe. This new religion the passages we print clearly announce. They leave no room for the criticism brought against Emerson, that his meaning is never clear. Some things in his teaching and in his life are so decisively clear and consistent that there can be no doubt as to what they meant. It was, for instance, a clear and decisive step, actuated by clear and decisive thought, which led him in his early life to sever his connections with a Christian Church and Christianity. His son records that, after he had gone alone to the mountains to consider his duty in relation to his religious doubts, he came down and explained to his people that he had decided to resign his charge, not because he had objections to prayer and the sacrament on the score of texts or of history, but because of "the witness against these rites in his own breast." Forever after his appeal was from tradition to this witness in his own breast. And similarly when, after settling down in Concord, he declared: "Henceforth, I design not to utter any speech, poem, or book that is not entirely and peculiarly my work,"—he announced those principles of self-reliance and self-justification which were the key-notes of the Ethical Religion of the future which he foresaw. Our citations, therefore, express but the fruition of early insights and convictions, and of that spirit of the years to come which would not let him rest in the old but made him in his life and in his utterance the prophet and exemplar of the new.

As the American Revolution and the establishment of the American Republic was but a transatlantic version of the ferment of liberal thought and tendency in Europe, so this new religious revolution which Emerson heralded was but an expression on American soil of the religious awakening and clarification which had manifested itself throughout Europe, and especially in the great transcendental philosophers of Germany—Kant, Fichte, Schelling, and in great German writers like Herder, Goethe, and Schiller, whose thought and sentiment reverberated in England through Coleridge, Wordsworth, and Carlyle. The common tendency everywhere was toward a simplification of religious belief; the common effort, to disengage from the religious impulse natural to man, and seated in the depths of his moral personality, all those extra-beliefs which were felt to be indifferent to true religious belief and deep religious life. Emerson did but announce to his own countrymen in terms suited to their time and place, and in a manner that was for the first time truly American by reason of its consciousness of America's new mission in the world, this new religious thought and aspiration. His message to them was that the so-called supernatural voice which had spoken through creeds and sects, through churches and scriptures, was, after all, only the natural but muffled and stammering voice of man's deeper yearning, dreaming, troubled self. His aim was to liberate that self.

And here we may fittingly correct a misapprehension that we find commonly current as to the historic relation of the Ethical Movement to preceding phases of religious development. Ethical Religion and the Ethical Movement are all too frequently spoken of as if they were a sort of by-product of the religious development of our time. In truth, they are but a natural fulfillment of the tendencies of preceding phases of religious development, especially as these find their culminating wave in this country in Emerson. In other words, the Ethical Movement comes to fulfill, and not to negate or destroy. It signalizes not a baffled and despairing, but a victorious and exultant faith: faith in the ultimate moral intention and destiny of things; faith in the inevitable triumph of truth and right, justice and love: faith in the illimitable moral possibilities of man.

Emerson, like every great nature, points beyond himself. He does not all-express the new religion, of course. If there is one element of it in particular which he does not adequately represent or announce, it is that element—more abundantly represented, be it said, in his contemporary, Whitman—of a robust, human love and a large, social passion, without which there can be no realization of the aims of Democracy.

THE
ETHICAL RECORD

PERCIVAL CHUBB, Editor

VOL. IV　　　　　　JUNE-JULY, 1903　　　　　　No. 5

CONTENTS

THE ETHICAL RECORD, a magazine of practical ethics, is published bi-monthly, except August-September. It appeals to all those who are interested in the treatment of the problems of personal and social life from the ethical point of view. Its contributors are not confined to adherents of the Ethical Movement, but include those who are especially qualified to deal with current issues from this standpoint.

SUBSCRIPTION PRICE.—One dollar a year, with Lecture Supplement (10 issues), payable in advance; foreign postage, 25 cents extra. Twenty cents a copy, including Lecture Supplement.

SPECIAL OFFER TO SUBSCRIBERS.—By arrangement with the publisher, we are able to offer the two publications—the INTERNATIONAL JOURNAL OF ETHICS, published quarterly ($2.50), at the joint subscription rate of Three Dollars per year.

MANUSCRIPTS, books for review, newspapers, etc., should be addressed to the Editor,

BUSINESS communications should be addressed to THE ETHICAL RECORD. Rates for advertising on application.　　　THE ETHICAL RECORD, 48 East 58th Street, New York

THE ETHICAL RECORD

A Magazine of Practical Ethics

RECENT ISSUES IN VOL. IV

February-March, 1903

April-May, 1903

The Ethical Record

HAS a threefold purpose, and addresses a threefold public. Its controlling aim is to promote the profounder and steadier application of ethical standards and ideals to life, public and personal; to interpret, clarify, and deepen the ethical consciousness. It seeks to do this: First, by dealing sympathetically and critically with the ethical issues and interests, the ethical thought and effort—religious, social, political, philanthropic, educational, and literary—of the time. Second, by bringing itself into closer touch with those distinctively ethical organizations that have a similar purpose, it endeavors to promote more effective and helpful union with them. Third, more specifically, it aims to advance the ethical movement and cause, here at home, through the corporate, institutional expression of it in The Society for Ethical Culture of New York. It makes appeal, therefore, at once to all those who are interested in the treatment, from the ethical standpoint, of the urgent problems of civilized life; to all adherents and friends of the ethical movement in this country and abroad; and, more directly, to the members of the New York Society.

THE ETHICAL RECORD

Vol. IV   June–July, 1903   No. 5

Emerson's Presiding Idea

As a thinker Emerson takes rank rather among the poets who are thinkers than among the philosophers. And yet a poet in the fullest and highest sense of the word Emerson never was. In his verse, instead of molding noble form, sensuous and passionate, to embody his thought or his emotion, he attempts to transmit a ray from his own spirit—keen, fine, and intense—directly to the spirit of his reader. He does not live with delight in the medium of expression, but parts it asunder or passes through it, as if it were an obstruction instead of an aid to the idea. If, however, we use the word poet in an extended sense, so as to include the rhapsody of the seer or the sage, we may call Emerson a writer of lofty hymns in prose. He is often alone with his idea, and what we overhear is a kind of divine soliloquy. Many of his most impressive passages are voluntaries, rendered in a temple not made with hands, voluntaries which uplift the spirits of the hearers, and which are inspired by the moral sentiment in man. But all these hymns and voluntaries, however various may be their several themes, group themselves around one common center; and this it is which permits Emerson to write without an elaborate or a strict design. "Here I sit and read and write," he says, "with very little system, and, as far as regards composition, with the most fragmentary result; paragraphs incompressible, each sentence an infinitely repellent particle." Yes, for system and construction are a kind of manufactured unity; we attain to them by calculation, by manipulation. But the unity which we discover in Emerson's writings is that of the breathing of the spirit.

What is the one dominant and persistent idea of which Emerson is the organ and the envoy? It is this—that each man may find within him, if he will but seek, something more than what is merely personal, something impersonal and universal, the divine impulse and the divine law, and that this—this, and not any kernel of hard individuality—is the very center of his being. Deep in the consciousness of every man may be found the meeting-point between the individual will and the universal law, the universal life; there lies the quickest center of personality, and there, too, is that something making for righteousness which, while a portion of our being, yet transcends our personality. Let us fall back upon this source and center of our life; let us grow from it; let us recognize the fact that our truest self reposes upon and flows forth from the universal. Let us lose and find ourselves in this tide of God, of universal being, which is ever present, and at times seems to flood the soul of each of us. Emerson does not attempt to define this power in which we live and move and have our being; names and descriptions and definitions are but shadows. The Psalmist may name it "the Lord"; the Evangelist may name it "our Father"; the Positivist may tell us it is "Humanity"; the Stoic philosopher may style it "the moral law." That our life should be its organ and agent is more important than that we should give it a name.

It is in the applications of this idea—an idea common to many religious minds—that Emerson's originality largely lies, and these applications remove it from the region of abstractions, and render it eminently practical and fruitful. We are not carried into remote regions or distant ages in search of what is best; we find what is best in the present moment and in all that lies nearest to us, in common things and in "the earnest experience of the common day." For our work in the world we need a sane self-reliance. Well, here is the true foundation of such self-reliance: "We lie in the lap of immense intelligence, which makes us receivers of its truth and organs of its activity. When we discern justice, when we discern truth, we do nothing of ourselves, but allow a passage to its beams." In its highest form this self-reliance becomes genius, which is ready to oppose the whole world, but in no spirit of egoistic revolt; rather in the faith that what is true in a solitary, private heart "is true for all men," and that in the end the assertion of an individual heart and brain will vindicate itself as part of truth universal. Whoso would be a wise man, Emerson tells us, must be a nonconformist; but our nonconformity, we learn, is not mere revolt or whim; it must be practised only for the sake of a deeper and wider conformity.

I turn over the pages of the "Essays" for other applications of the writer's central principle. Surely, it may be said, we grow out of the past; the history of the human race has determined for us what we are and what we are to be. Shall we not consult authority? Yes, but the historical Plato can speak only to the Plato that is within us. And it is only in so far as each individual possesses something of the universal mind that the history of the past becomes intelligible to him. It is only in so far as some common life or common mind circulates between us and the great spirits of former ages that we can have any profitable communication with them. Thus, instead of reading history passively and loading his memory with lifeless facts, the student should "esteem his own life the text and books the commentary." All public statements of history must be made vital in the personal life of each of us, and all private experiences of our own lives must be generalized, and so seen as part of the common life which flows through the past and the present toward the future.

So much for History and the Past. But how great is the risk of losing our best selves, and the soul of goodness that is in the world, amid the meaningless tangle of circumstances through which we move! To restore this confusion to order we must look for the meaning of what seems so chaotic, and this Emerson finds in the law of immutable justice, by which the deed returns to the doer, light and strength of heart to the righteous, darkness and ill to the doer of evil deeds;

"the dice of God are always loaded." And trusting in the universal laws work-ing in us and through us, we shall not vex ourselves with a fussy activity, striv-ing with heated forehead and blind hands to set the whole world to rights. Let us, if we can, work in joyous serenity, pro-viding an unobstructed channel for the higher life of which we should be the or-gans. Half of our bustle and vexations are unnecessary. Find the right place in relation to the center, and all will go well: "Place yourself in the middle of the stream of power and wisdom, which ani-mates all whom it floats, and you are without effort impelled to truth, to right, and a perfect contentment."

Among the passions which seem, and which are, most personal to each of us we reckon those of love and friendship. All readers of Emerson will remember that even here he justifies the private pas-sion by discovering in and behind it the presence of something that is everlasting and universal. Heroic lovers recognize after a time that all which first drew them together is deciduous, the scaffolding by and by to be removed from the building, and that "the purification of the intellect and the heart from year to year is the real marriage, foreseen and prepared from the first, and wholly above their conscious-ness." Of friendship Emerson writes with enthusiasm; nothing is more sub-stantial in the whole universe than such an alliance of souls; and it is so because the friend is an envoy of the glory that lies behind him; he stands out splendid and hardy upon a background of higher splendor; a friend is but "the harbinger of a greater friend."

It would be easy to point out the presence and the influence of Emer-son's presiding thought in the essays on Prudence—the "outmost action of the inward life," and false only when de-tached—on Heroism, "the answer of the soul to a clarion-cry," of the divine spirit within the soul, on Intellect, on Art. But enough has been said to show that Emerson, if not a builder of systems, has that unity which comes from one steadfast inspiration, a pure and con-stant gale of the spirit. "Faithless, faithless," he cries, in the lecture on the Times, "we fancy that with the dust we depart and are not; and do not know that the law and the perception of the law are at last one; that only as much as the law enters us, becomes us, we are living men—immortal with the immor-tality of this law." The strain seems so lofty as to be remote from practice; yet in truth it may quicken and illuminate every act of humblest duty.

EDWARD DOWDEN.

Channing, Emerson and Parker

IT is an interesting fact that the cen-tennial anniversary of Emerson's birth is very nearly that of Chan-ning's installation in his Boston minis-try. Emerson was born, as everybody knows by this time, May 25, 1803, and Channing was installed June 1, of the same year. But these men had vital af-filiations that would make even a more exact coincidence a matter of compara-tive indifference. Channing, Emerson, and Parker are the three now acknowl-edged leaders to whom American Uni-tarians lift up their admiring eyes. (When the survey includes England, Martineau, of course, is added.) One needs hardly to be told that, much as they are honored now, they were much feared, disliked, disparaged, and con-demned in their own time; Channing first by the orthodox party, then by some of his own sect; Emerson pre-eminently by Unitarians; Parker by Unitarians and orthodox alike. Three sermons preached by these men are the three tallest landmarks of the Unitarian history — Channing's Bal-timore sermon of 1819, Emerson's Di-vinity School address of 1838, Parker's South Boston sermon of 1841. It is generally believed and stated that there was a genetic relation between the sec-ond and the third of these, that Parker's sermon was the translation of Emerson's address into concreter form; but no such genetic relation is conceived between Channing's sermon and Emerson's. Yet it was actually there. In the Baltimore sermon there was an appeal to reason as the final standard in religion which enfolded all that was most vital and pro-gressive in Emerson's address and Parker's brave discourse.

The mutual regards of these religious leaders are so interesting that I could easily exhaust on them the space as-signed to me. Emerson's respect and reverence for Channing were great from his youth up. He characterized his Dudleian Lecture (1821), a consistent piece of supernaturalism, as "the highest species of reasoning upon divine sub-jects; the fruit of a sort of moral im-agination." The best expression of Emerson's opinion of Channing is in his "Historic Notes of Life and Letters in New England." There we read that Channing's articles on Napoleon and Milton were our first specimens of large criticism and made a deep impression. "He could never be reported, for his eye and voice could not be printed." "He left no successor in the pulpit." "We could not spare a single word he uttered in public, not so much as the reading of a lesson in Scripture or a hymn." "A poor little invalid all his life, he is yet one of those men who vindicate the power of the American race to produce greatness." For Emerson, twenty-three years his junior, Channing had a recip-rocal appreciation. He praised his "severe sincerity and moral independ-ence" in declining to administer the Lord's Supper in the habitual manner, at the same time resigning his charge. Prevented by deafness from hearing Emerson's early lectures, his daughter brought him home the manuscripts and he read them with avid interest. To the main purport of the Divinity School Address he responded heartily, and he did not find the lack of divine personal-ity in it that troubled Henry Ware, Jr., and other Boston Unitarians.

Thirty years Parker's senior, Chan-ning lived to hear the painful echoes of Parker's South Boston sermon and died in 1842, when Parker's relations with his conservative brethren were strained un-til they broke. He deprecated Parker's indifference to the miraculous in Chris-tianity, but said, "I wish him to preach what he thoroughly believes and feels. . . . Let the full heart pour itself forth." Parker, on the other hand, had a boundless reverence for Channing. To be near him that he might seek his

counsel, which he often did, was a principal reason for his settling in Roxbury. He declared that a new-comer with Channing's principles could not secure a Boston settlement. He hailed him as the head of a Unitarian liberal party, the "Unitarian orthodoxy," which Channing deprecated, having no head. When Channing died, Parker laid a wreath upon his tomb that surpassed every other in the freshness of its sweet and homely flowers.

Parker was Emerson's junior by seven years. His sermons and other writings make frequent mention of him, always in terms of lofty admiration. Once he said, "The little town of Concord is the center of his sphere; its circumference—that great circle—lies far off, hid underneath the horizon of future centuries." Emerson probably had this in mind when he said, after Parker's death, "He was capable of the most unmeasured eulogies on those he esteemed, especially if he had any jealousy that they did not stand with the Boston public as highly as they ought." In the memorial address wherein this expression occurs, Emerson paid to Parker one of the loftiest tributes of admiration that he paid to contemporary character. When he denied him the poetic quality he was perhaps thinking of his defective appreciation of Emerson's own verse. "It was," he said, "his merit to speak tart truth, and when there were few to say it. But his sympathy with goodness was not less energetic . . : and it is well known that his great hospitable heart was the sanctuary to which every soul conscious of an earnest opinion came for sympathy." Parker was one of the favored "few persons besides the [half-dozen] students" who heard Emerson's Divinity School Address. He walked back to Roxbury in the clear moonlight resolved that he would straightway preach two sermons on the character of the Bible, which for some time he had been holding back.

The relations of these men's ideas and principles are more important than their mutual personal regards. Parker and Emerson broke with the supernaturalist tradition, which Channing never did. Yet Channing's interpretation of the traditional opinion was so generous and expansive that it brought him into closer sympathy with Emerson and Parker than were some who echoed their denials. Philosophically it was those elements in Locke and Hartley that leaned to the intuitional side of the debate that attracted Channing. Hence his admiration for Dr. Price and his distaste for Priestley. Emerson and Parker were not more disinclined to accept any materialistic conception of the world or any necessarian conception of morals. Theologically he laid the axe at the root of the tree for Emerson to sharpen and for Parker to swing with his stout farmer strength, when he said, "I am surer that my rational nature is from God than that any book is the expression of His will." Formally subjecting himself to the authority of Christianity, he was virtually as self-reliant as Emerson. So it was simple truth that Dr. Gottheil spoke of him, "Though he always meant to be a disciple, he, in truth, spoke as a master. You feel, when you read him, that he was much bolder than he knew, and that all his thoughts have the force and freshness of a spontaneous mind and do not state what he found in the Book but in his own reason and conscience." Emerson could have learned his entire doctrine of individualism and self-reliance at Channing's feet. Channing said, "There is no moral worth in being swept away by a crowd, even towards the best objects." . . . "What many of us have to dread chiefly from society is not that we shall acquire a positive character of vice, but that society will impose on us a negative character; that we shall live and die passive beings; that the creative and self-forming character of the soul will not be called forth in the work of our improvement." . . . "Could a perfect individual be found, we should injure ourselves by indiscriminate and servile imitation." Such expressions are not narrowly isolated in Channing's writings; they are sporadic. We pass from his doctrine of self-reliance to Emerson's without any shock of difference.

And what they thought they lived. Their individualism made them both hostile to organizations of all kinds. Hence, with increasing sympathy with the abolitionists, they never joined themselves formally to their assembly. They maintained a similar attitude toward other reform organizations. Personally Channing had a much more isolating temperament than Emerson, who accounted him "the most unprofitable private companion." Here, perhaps, the shadow of some personal misfortune falls upon the page. Others had better luck, and it is by no means certain that Emerson's "aloofness" was not more central than Channing's, who, superficially repellent, admitted a few persons to his deepest mind as Emerson never did or could.

With much of agreement there was much of difference between the Boston preacher and the Concord seer. Emerson made no mistake when he conceived himself to be essentially a poet. Channing was of another kind. Quite as different was the abundance of Emerson's humor compared with Channing's almost total lack. Emerson's was the more abstract philosophy, but in the presentation of his thought he was much more concrete than Channing. His was the more observant, Channing's the more meditative mind. Their different methods are admirably illustrated by the Lenox Address on West India Emancipation, which Channing gave in 1842, and Emerson's on the anniversary of the same event in 1844. Emerson's abounds in "wise saws and modern instances"; Channing's in broad generalizations. Of the two, Channing was the more idealistic in his humanity. That the slave was a man obliterated for him every racial and acquired defect as it could not for Emerson, who was always checking his universals with the inexpugnable facts.

Emerson's "Sovereignty of Ethics" is a doctrine that is very dear to the representatives of Ethical Culture. The doctrine should attract them to Channing with an equal love. Martineau was a disciple of Channing, but in his doctrine that morality is obedience to "another person" he fell short of Channing's teaching, "There is but one ground for virtuous affection in the universe, but one object of cherished and enduring love in heaven or on earth, and that is Moral Goodness." And, again, he said: "The adoration of goodness—that is religion."

If Parker was not more the Reformer than either Channing or Emerson, he had not their aversion to organized activity; reading as they never read, a de-

vourer of libraries, a scholar in many languages, he was in his ultimate expression more the man of action than the man of thought, and he knew the joy of battle upon theological and political fields. Even his transcendental philosophy was shaped for practical exigencies, so much more concrete was it than Emerson's, with its equal certainty of God, the Moral Law, and Immortality — a philosophy which took counsel less with Kant and Schelling and other masters than with his own naturally affirming and believing soul. His social contacts were as much more frank and jovial than Emerson's as were Emerson's more easy and gracious than Channing's. In Emerson's there was more of intellectual curiosity, in Parker's more of human sympathy. The fact is that Parker had a liberal education, denied to both Channing and Emerson, in that he was a farmer's boy, and was brought up on a farm and in a carpenter's shop. So it happens that he writes of the smacks of the soil as they do not; and when he writes of the comeliness of the potatoes with the brown earth clinging to their sides, and of the ripe apples plumping down in the still moonlight, as we get nearer to the facts than in Emerson's more deliberate approach. It is impossible to conceive of either Channing or Emerson working in Parker's fashion to thwart the Fugitive Slave Law and the enslavement of Kansas. He translated their ideas into events. He beat their plowshares into swords in a time when without shedding of blood there was no remission of the nation's sin. Where Channing with wise thrift saved himself that he might give himself more effectively, Parker flung his life with glorious abandon into the enemy's lines and died untimely, yet not with his work undone.

The individual members of this great triumvirate differed in many ways, but they had more in unison than in difference, and they will be joined together in the reverence and affection of mankind for a much longer period than many of much noisier fame.

JOHN WHITE CHADWICK.

Emerson As a Reformer

THE popular idea of the idealist is that he lives in a sort of cloud-land. But Emerson's idealism consisted in believing in ideal possibilities in this world—in human society. Such idealism and active reform are closely connected. For reform in essence is nothing but the attempt to bring ideas into the realm of fact, or to transform facts so that they become an image of the idea. Emerson says that the history of reform is always identical; it is the comparison of the idea with the fact. Again, "Out of the fair Idea in the mind springs the effort at the Perfect. It is the interior testimony to a fairer possibility of life and manners." He finds the origin of all reform in the mysterious fountain of the moral sentiment, which, he says, amidst the natural, ever contains the supernatural for men.

Indeed, if men could see it in its wholeness, and present no opposition to it, it would be beautiful like all creation of order out of chaos. Reform is made arid, noisy, fanatical, because it is opposed, and because men see only a part of it: they become advocates of one virtue, partisans of one idea.

Religion itself tends in the direction of reform according to Emerson. To quote his words, religion does not "tend now to a *cultus*, but to a heroic life." We find him even speaking of the reformers of his time as "the visible church of the existing generation." The leaders of the crusades against War, Negro-slavery, Intemperance, Government based on force, Usages of Trade, Court and Custom-house oaths, and so on, to the agitators on the system of Education and the laws of Property, he called the right successors of Luther, Knox, Robinson, Fox, Penn, Wesley, and Whitefield. "They have the same virtues and vices, the same noble impulse, and the same bigotry." Though there are two sides to every question, or two standpoints from which it may be viewed, Emerson says that if we take our stand on necessity we shall go for the Conservative; but if on ethics, for the Reformer.

Emerson witnessed with exhilaration the growth of the reform spirit in his time. It actually seemed, he said, as if the higher inspirations that had been assigned to poetry and music, to prayers and sermons, without much thought of their getting a footing in real life, were about to be executed. So strongly did he feel, that he was classed among the "new lights" himself. He had welcomed anti-slavery speakers to his pulpit. His later lectures before the Lyceums of the country were full of a subtle radicalism. In private life he manifested an uneasy conscience about the "dubious problem" of domestic service, wished to "co-operate" with his less fortunate neighbors, and felt that he ought to labor with his hands.

This deep view of the matter marks one of the characteristic traits of Emerson. He often speaks of the partiality and one-sidedness of reformers; but he does not forget the underlying motive; his writings are one of the most subtle and powerful influences for reform that the last century produced. "What," he once exclaimed, "is a man born for but to be a *Re-former*, a *Re-maker* of what man has made?" Reform becomes something natural in this view, something poetic, a part of ascending life.

The ills he was sensible of in our social system were at bottom internal; the only remedies in which he had absolute faith were internal, too. Selfishness vitiated government, property, religion itself, and the only cure was new principles in the heart. We must become lovers, he said, and what is impossible becomes possible. There are intermediate steps between principles and concrete action; and as to ways and means Emerson does not always give us light, and sometimes himself went astray—as in what came near to an advocacy of anarchy; but if the souls of men could have his vision of principles, they would soon and inevitably find the way to successfully incorporate them into life. We go to Emerson for impulse, not for instruction; and no one for a century has struck higher or deeper notes than he.

WILLIAM M. SALTER.

Personal Reminiscences of Emerson

IN one of the many fine tributes recently paid to Emerson's influence, it has been stated that to see a great man face to face is worth more than to have read all his books or an account of all his doings. That there is some truth in this broad assertion is brought home to me when I recall my own personal impressions of Emerson, about which I have been asked to say something here.

When I was a student at the Harvard Divinity School in the years 1876 to 1879, I used to see Emerson at various meetings; and I remember vividly what a strong impression his face and eyes made upon me as he passed close by me once coming out of Sander's theater after one of the Commencement exercises. But this strong impression made by the living Emerson was no doubt largely due to the fact that I had read and been inspired by the two volumes of his "Essays," which were among the first books I added to my library on going to the Divinity School, and which had a more abiding influence on me, I think, than all the other books I read during my three years' course.

Those years were rich in personal experiences with the distinguished leaders of the Transcendental and Free Religious movements, whose lectures I took every opportunity to attend, and whose writings I eagerly read. But the three whose influence upon me at that time stood out above all others were Ralph Waldo Emerson, Francis Ellingwood Abbot, and Felix Adler: the first, the great spiritual inspirer; the second, the great stimulator of clear thought and clear conscience; the third, the great prophet of the new way—the builder of the new type of the ethical and spiritual church of the future.

But, to return to Emerson, every association connected with him was precious at the time, and has been precious ever since. The fact that the room I occupied one year at the Divinity School was said to have been once occupied by him, was not without its influence upon me when I looked upon him as one of the world's great ethical inspirers.

Emerson's presence made a deep impression wherever he went. On one occasion, at a great public meeting I attended at Tremont Temple, at which Wendell Phillips and others spoke, the audience, discovering that Emerson was on the platform, called upon him to make a speech. He only got up and bowed; but that presence and that bow vied with Wendell Phillips's eloquence in their effect upon the audience.

A more personal and more important reminiscence remains to be told. Our class in the Divinity School took the initiative in having Emerson invited to give his address on "The Preacher" in 1879—an event which has been referred to by the Rev. George Gordon, of Boston in his recent article in *The Atlantic*. Emerson was introduced by our distinguished teacher of Church History, Dr. Hedge (who had himself as a young man met Goethe face to face); and the impression made upon me by his introduction was very different from what it appears to have made upon Dr. Gordon. I sat next to Dr. Gordon in Prof. James's course in Psychology that winter; and, remembering from incidental conversation how far we were apart in our attitude toward liberal religious thought, I am not surprised that Dr. Gordon's impression of that evening differed so widely from my own. When Dr. Hedge said that we were to listen to the one man whose writings would probably outlast those of any living American, and be a source of inspiration to men centuries hence, certainly one of those who crowded the Divinity School chapel that evening believed that he was not paying Emerson a flattering and unmerited compliment, but was sincerely foretelling what future historians and scholars as distinguished as Dr. Hedge himself would be affirming as an actual fact of history. Although that address on "The Preacher" is not as soul-stirring as some of the other essays and addresses, yet, listening to Emerson deliver it was assuredly a *most inspiring* experience—an experience that no one who was present could ever forget.

Perhaps I may be allowed to refer to one incident of that evening which was connected with a much-prized personal possession. The light on the desk in the Divinity School chapel being inadequate, a lamp was necessary for Emerson to read by; and it was my privilege to bring my student's lamp from my room near by and place it on the desk. I still have the lamp, with Sidney Morse's bust of Emerson, in my rustic camp in the Adirondacks; and, while the forest fires have recently been threatening it, I have frequently thought that the one thing in the camp I should most wish to be saved from destruction was the lamp by the light of which Emerson read his address on "The Preacher."

Emerson's death occurred while I was a student at Berlin, and I learned of it in a most interesting and impressive way. I was at the time attending a course of lectures by Hermann Grimm (the distinguished interpreter of Emerson to his countrymen, whose correspondence with Emerson has just been published); and I remember well how, one morning, before proceeding with his lecture, Professor Grimm referred most feelingly to the news which had just come of Emerson's death, and how glowing a tribute he paid to Emerson's influence both upon himself and upon the world.

S. BURNS WESTON.

Philadelphia.

___

"There is no end to the suffering of character. It can afford to wait, it can do without what is called success; it cannot but succeed. To a well-principled man existence is victory."—EMERSON.

* * *

. . . "What this country longs for is personalities, grand persons, to counteract its materialities. For it is the rule of the universe that corn shall serve man, and not man corn."—EMERSON.

* * *

"All good conversation, manners, and action come from a spontaneity which forgets usages, and makes the moment great."—EMERSON.

Emerson's Interpretation of Nature

EMERSON, we know, was deeply influenced by Wordsworth; and there is so much kinship between the two poets that they may well be coupled in our memory as great prophets of natural piety. They both extolled, by their lives as well as their writings, the virtues of simplification and of the life near to nature, and both made a powerful plea for a "wise passiveness," as contrasted with the busy, excited, fretting life which modern civilization thrusts upon men. Moreover, Emerson and Concord play much the same part in the map of man's spiritual territory in America as Wordsworth and Grasmere do in England. Concord must be to the American lover of wisdom and beauty, of health and joy, the most memorable spot in his country. There flows the most musical and most cleansing of the streams that freshen and fertilize the thought and the virtue of a people. The heart of the pilgrim to this Mecca must rejoice in the beautiful river that waters the meadows and scented woodlands of Concord Plain; but it must ever be the symbol of that other mystical stream of Time and Fate and Godhead which its poet heard flowing, not alone through Concord, but

Through years, through men, through nature fleet,
Through passion, thought, through power and dream.

It is in one of Emerson's perfect poems that these two streams blend their currents:

Musketaquit, a goblin strong,
Of shard and flint makes jewels gay;
They lose their grief who hear his song,
And where he winds is the day of day.

So forth and brighter fares my stream,—
Who drink it shall not thirst again;
No darkness stains its equal gleam,
And ages drop in it like rain.

And everywhere in his poetry the two streams of Nature and Spirit, the real and ideal, mix their music. The poet takes a genuine delight in the real river and woods and fields about him; but they speak not only to the outward eye and ear; they "pipe ditties of no tone" to the spiritual ear. Walk through the woods or by Walden pond with Emerson, and you will not only see the shy squirrel on the boughs, not only hear the laughter of the leaves, but you will be surprised by a fugitive glimpse of some hiding wood-god, and hear occasional strains of music from some hidden world.

While Emerson has marked affinities with Wordsworth, especially in feeling a didactic purpose in Nature and in sympathizing with the almost humanly conscious life in things; and whilst he has a few affinities with Shelley in filling nature with human-like presences above and behind the outward forms—it is nevertheless obvious that his interpretation and his attitude are quite his own. There is in him very little of Tennyson's sensuous delight in Nature, and it is very seldom that he can, like Tennyson, enshrine the beauty of things in suggestively beautiful words. Occa-

sionally he manages it, as in the line,

"As in broad orchards resonant with bees;"

but that is a rare effect. He was not trying for that sort of thing.

He is only secondarily concerned with Nature on her sensuous side. Being a vast allegory, a series of symbols to him, he does not rest in the sensuous exterior she presents, be it ever so fair, but presses on to her occult meanings, her second intentions. Not that he has no eye for fact, no love of form and color, no ear for sound. Mr. John Burroughs cites many instances of his closeness of observation, and happy characterization praising the "Humblebee" and the "Titmouse," and his lines about the wild geese and many other passages in "May Day" and elsewhere. But his realistic touches are, comparatively speaking, light and scarce. Nevertheless, he does manage to get a fragrant atmosphere of the woods and fields into both his poetry and his prose. It is always out of doors. The pages are redolent of pine scents, the most delicately pungent of odors; birds and flowers are never far to seek, and sunlight flickers upon the pages as we read.

Emerson goes to the woods not to be lulled by the dreamy music of summer in the boughs or the rich pageant of summer in the grass, but to catch some notes of the mystical celestial Song of Nature. For him

Æolian harps in the pine
Ring with the song of the Fates.

Nature is always chanting a choral song in praise of her own wonders and the mysteries of the universe:

Wandering voices in the air,
And murmurs in the world,
Speak what I cannot declare,

Yet cannot all withhold.

* * *
* * *

Let me go where'er I will,
I hear a sky-born music still;
From all that's fair, from all that's foul,
Peals out a cheerful song.
It is not only in the rose,
It is not only in the bird,
But in the darkest, meanest things,
But in the mud and scum of things
There alway, alway, something sings.

The poet is all the time haunted by a desire to make these wandering voices and murmurs deliver up their message. They have secrets which, if known, will shed auroral light on things. The joy of wandering in the woods comes of the sense one has of getting close to the heart of the world. A feeling of oneness with nature and the universe, a sort of intellectual rapture born of feeling oneself in harmony with the World-Soul that animates all, seizes one, abolishes the barriers between self and the World-Soul, and mingles the finite with the infinite in an ecstatic union. To be sure, certain conditions of right living are essential to these experiences: you must be pure of heart; your manner of living must be clean and upright; you must have renounced the baser allurements of the world.

When one analyzes carefully the impression of external beauty which Emerson's verse indubitably leaves, one finds that he had a special eye and love for the fugitive, delicate, evanescent effects of Nature. He loves movement; the quick gleam of light; the flash of the jewel; the sparkle and radiance of the lake; the spreading rings on disturbed water; the melting changes of dawn and sunset; the impalpable sensitive bloom on things. His ideal poet, as he wanders in the woods, is found

Pondering shadows, colors, clouds,
Grass-buds and caterpillar-shrouds;
Boughs on which the wild bees settle,
Tints that spot the violet's petal.

Again, we have kindred preferences sketched in the poem entitled, "Beauty":

Was never form and never face
So sweet to Seyd as only grace
Which did not slumber like a stone,
But hovered gleaming and was gone.
Beauty chased he everywhere,
In flame, in storm, in clouds of air.
He smote the lake to feed his eye
With the beryl beam of the broken wave;
He flung in pebbles well to hear
The moment's music which they gave.

It sorts with Emerson's lack of response to rich, sensuous beauty that he should be attracted by these finer fleeting things, by the transient blushes on Nature's cheek, by her rapidly changing expressions, by

    the sun-spark on the sea,
And the cloud-shadow on the lea,

or it may be by the red-bird flashing his side of flame as he flies, or by

The frailest leaf, the mossy bark,
The acorn's cup, the rainbow's arc,
The swinging spider's silver line,
The ruby of the drop of wine.

The same fact is brought out in the fragments on "The Poet and the Poetic Gift." Saadi figures again in these fragments, and the references to places are Oriental; and I suppose we may say that this very love of the daintier, gemlike, gleaming things of the world has a characteristically Oriental quality. At any rate, this poet, Saadi, loves such things as

    harebells nodding on a rock,
A cabin hung with curling smoke,
Ring of axe or hum of wheel,
Or gleam which use can paint on steel.

He loved to watch and wake
When the wing of the south-wind whipped the lake

And the glassy surface in ripples brake
And fled in pretty frowns away,
Like the flitting boreal lights,
Rippling roses in northern nights.

He came to the green ocean's brim
And saw the wheeling sea-birds skim
Summer and winter o'er the wave,
Like creatures of a skyey mold.

It is by reason of his peculiar responsiveness to these effects and his apt expression of them that Emerson enlarges one's sense of beauty in a new direction. But let us return now for a few moments to our poet in the woods, hearkening to the woodnotes. He is beneath his favorite, the pine tree, with its "waterfall tones." He has discovered the soul and secret tongue of the tree: it is the giver of honor, the genius of hardihood, the symbol of strength, endurance, and simplicity. We listen with the poet at the foot of the tree, and we hear:

Whoso walks in solitude
And inhabiteth the wood,
Choosing light, wave, rock, and bird
Before the money-loving herd,
Into that forester shall pass
From these companions power and grace.
Clean shall he be, without, within,
From the old adhering sin.
He shall be happy in his love.

But the pine has other meanings and messages. Not only does he sing in his lower branches the lay of the natural life; but his song mounts higher, and the green top branches break forth into a mystical song of the beginnings of things. The music alters somewhat:

Hearken! Hearken!
If thou wouldst know the mystic song
Chanted when the sphere was young.
To the open ear it sings
Sweet the genesis of things,
Of tendency through endless ages,
Of star-dust and star-pilgrimages.
The rushing metamorphosis
Dissolving all that fixture is,
Melts things that be to things that seem,
And solid nature to a dream.
O listen to the undersong.

And this undersong the pine tree keeps on singing, uttering the music to which it and the whole universe moves; the wisdom of the woods, the perfection of nature's every part, the sorrowfulness of man's exile from her. Then the poet hears the tree's invitation to the worldling to accept its ministering help:

Come lay thee in my soothing shade
And heal the hurts that sin has made.

All these melodies of the pine might find a commentary and amplification in the essays of Emerson—those essays which are so much the more powerful because behind them, as behind the poems of Wordsworth, is that beautiful life of simplicity, of modesty, of labor, of piety, and duty. It is the life of a man who found so much joy in simple things that he could proudly exclaim, "Give me health and a day, and I will make the pomp of emperors ridiculous."

Emerson's love of nature does not lead him, as it has led some weaker men, into extreme and violent reaction against society and civilization. He is not pleading for solitude with Nature as against the intercourse of society. He has said: "We require such a solitude as shall hold us to its revelations when we are in the street and in palaces." What stirs him to his strictures on the life of men in cities—as it stirred Wordsworth and other poets of kindred perceptions—is his recognition of the fact that the tendency of the tide of civilization setting toward a massive and complex urbanism, is away from Nature, away therefore from simplicity and innocence and modesty, poise and self-possession.

It is by reason of his criticism of life from the vantage point of his own simple career, with its abundant joy and wealth, that he moves us. This is partly expressed in the poem, "The Day's Ration," in which the poet tells us

When I was born
From all the seas of strength Fate filled a chalice,
Saying, "This be thy portion, child; this chalice,
Less than a lily's, thou shalt daily draw
From my great arteries—nor less, nor more."

And he goes on to say how little suffices to fill the chalice; and how the cunning chemist, Time, heedlessly overbrims his little cup. Instead of having to go far to seek for beauty and interest, there is near at hand in common things too much to appropriate. Hence the questions:

Why need I volumes, if one word suffice?
Why need I galleries, when a pupil's draught
After the master's sketch fills and o'erfills
My apprehension? Why seek Italy,
Who cannot circumnavigate the sea
Of thoughts and things at home, but still adjourn

The nearest matters for a thousand days?

And then we turn a page to the autobiographical poem, "Musketaquid," in which the poet lets us into the secret of his own happiness, and gives us a picture of his simple life of rustic contentment.

with Mother Earth, and that they have reason to rely on her, as did Antæus.

Because I was content with these poor fields,
Low, open meads, slender and sluggish streams,
And found a home in haunts which others scorned,
The partial wood-gods overpaid my love,
And granted me the freedom of their state,
And through my rock-like, solitary wont
Shot million rays of thought and tenderness.

And so the recipient of so much grace from Nature can express his gratitude by declaring that

the great

Would mortify me, but in vain; for still
I am a willow of the wilderness,
Loving the wind that bent me. All my hurts
My garden spade can heal. A woodland walk,
A quest of river-grapes, a mocking thrush,
A wild rose or rock-loving columbine
Salve my worst wounds.

Thus have we patterned for us with stimulating and renervating power a simple life lived according to Nature, and very near to Nature's heart. It was not a bare or a narrow life. It had an amplitude and dignity as of the hills and skies; a fullness and fragrance as of rich summer days; a lovely serenity as of deep and tranquil waters. Moreover, it was a life which demanded and conserved with man and human affairs a converse as high and as august as that which it kept with Nature herself.

PERCIVAL CHUBB.

Emerson's Influence in Germany.

EMERSON absorbed the essence of the German spirit through many a channel of his nature. We Germans owe a great debt to his memory. With subtle penetration, remarkable in a non-German, he commended Goethe to English readers, and has interpreted certain sides of his genius in the most convincing words we possess. He presented the classic philosophy of Germany to his own country as the outcome of one of the most glorious epochs of human research, and thus made it a common possession of all civilized lands. He testified to the mysteries of German mysticism with the illumination of one who gazes on a wonder, and yet surrounded it with the common sense of his American nature, so that our glory is now clearly mirrored from his own shining countenance.

Let us now, in our turn, assign to Emerson the place he deserves to fill in Germany. Many of us have paid tribute to him, but little attention has been paid to those words. The various German editions of certain of his books or essays are old and forgotten, although they came from men of authority, such as Julian Schmidt, Dietrich Spielhagen, Hermann Grimm. Of late his name has again been heard, and this is possibly due to the appearance of cheaper editions of his works as well as to the activity of Nietzsche and Maeterlinck in his behalf.

I intend no discredit to the great influential men of our time, when I say that it was Emerson who was the inspirer of Nietzsche and of Maeterlinck. It is especially the essay on "Fate" in Emerson's "Conduct of Life" which proves clearly that Maeterlinck is a humble version of Emerson—humble as being without the stirring courage with which the American sweeps us along so irresistibly. The merit of the European lies in the fact of his having exhibited visibly, by means of the drama, how subtle are the relations existing between individual and individual. Emerson, though gifted with marvelous imagination, could not acquire the plasticity of the true artist, because he had to fulfill the mission of the prophet with the flaming sword to his dollar-mad American people. He acted thus as their judge; but at the same time he understood how to be also, as Maeterlinck puts it, "the kind, cheerful shepherd on the gentle, green meadow of a new, natural, intelligible optimism"—an optimism which teaches us that we must go on living, because there is not an hour which does not reveal inner wonders and ineffable meanings. This trait in Emerson is praised also by Nietzsche, whose coarse masculinity, however, leads him to add the sarcastic words, which I think undeserved: "At times he comes close to the cheerful transcendentalism of the jolly fellow who returns from a carousal." To me, he is not lacking in a robust, manly strength, that has its earthly ideal in the "healthy mind in a healthy body." His thoroughly sound nature does not permit him to despair or curse. In his relations with the outer world he resembles Faust in his Easter wanderings, who discerns above the shouts of the peasants the basic strains on which his life's harmony is built. At the same time we see in him also the mature Faust, who can attain to the loftiest heights of human accomplishment only by remaining within the limits imposed on him through his having been born human. He loves the men of action—engineers, cautious merchants, undaunted dealers in earth's products, practical sages like Montaigne, and, above all, those persons whose garments betray by their smell that the wearers are one with Mother Earth, and that they have reason to rely on her, as did Antæus.

Emerson liked wine and the prized things of life; and yet he could forego them smilingly without parading before us as an ascetic. In one word, he exerts over us the remarkable attraction of men strong in action, who associate kindly with us, "as though they were leading Might, their good steed, gently by the bridle, preferring to go on foot, although they are such splendid horsemen." Proud and self-reliant though Emerson was as a personality, yet in him the kindliness of the spiritual shepherd had become incarnate. Like Böcklin, he teaches us that only what is in us can we find outside of us; and while we are exulting in the discovery of new light, believing ourselves to be on the highway to progress, he admonishes us to still nobler effort, because, as says Angelus Silesius: "We must pass from one light upward to another."

WILHELM SPOHR.

(*Translated by Mrs. Hellman.*)

The Emasculation of Emerson.

ONE is struck, on reading the genteel tributes almost everywhere paid to Emerson this centennial year, by the lack of sturdiness and reality, by the evasiveness and thinness of men's thinking and feeling about him on the religious side. What—one rubs his eyes and asks—did then Emerson mean so little? Did he so daintily scratch the surface of the old, thick-skinned orthodoxies that all trace of his incision is gone? Did he so amiably and harmlessly promulgate that new idealistic, democratic faith of his?—the faith which de-

clares that man is divine in his own right, and should now walk alone without the cumbersome prop of tortured Christ-God and moss-grown church, without priest or prayer? Is he who was for so many a vigorous and uncompromising emancipator become a respectable Christian parson and apologist? We dishonor his name and fame by such attitude, or by allowing such an attitude to pass without a protest. Here was a man who definitely cut himself loose from the most advanced Christian body and Christian thought of his time; discarded the Christian name; and proclaimed a new religion for a new world, to harmonize with its new polity and destiny of a nation that had dared to plant itself on the great truth of man's independence and equality.

We amiably discourse of our "poet" and "sage" with an eye blind to what was distinctive and epochal in his message and his mission. We pay high tribute to him for having given us (in the catching phrase of his polite Bostonian biographer) America's Declaration of Spiritual Independence in that startling Divinity Address of his; and then we proceed to go our ways along the old, rutty, dusty tracks in which he refused any longer to travel; and we make our bows to the old shrines and idols, the old parchments and paraphernalia which he had the insight and splendid courage to forsake for untried paths in a vast unexplored continent.

We are perforce led into striking too negative a note in introducing the thought that rules our mind. Our purpose is to do justice to what was positive and prophetic in Emerson's work.

What he did was to assert the religious implications of Democracy, to give Democracy religious meaning and consecration. Democracy did not mean for him cutting adrift from kings and aristocracies, from feudalism and the fictitious distinctions of senile civilizations; it meant fealty to the inward sovereign who commands through conscience and reason and love. For him the act which emancipated from this political and social bondage of the old world, at the same time emancipated any consistent nature from a kindred bondage to the dogmatic creeds and authoritative Churches, the priests and the books, of feudal and mediæval religion. These had shackled the thought and had done violence to the religious nature of man, just as those secular bonds had tied his hands and feet, and coined the sweat of his body and his brow.

Emerson, as Carlyle said, was a new man in a new country. More, he preached and prophesied this new man —new by virtue of a religion based on the larger and deeper conception of selfhood which this great democratic and republican enterprise involved. He announced the birth, the liberation, and transfiguration of what we may call the democratic self. Politically speaking, Democracy meant self-government in which all men should have equal share; and it justified itself by a faith in each man's trustworthiness and recognized power of personal self-government. In other words, it assumed a moral power, operative or latent in each—be his creed any or none, his race or color what it might—sufficient for this difficult task of self-determination and of social and political co-operation with other similar selves.

But Emerson did not separate this political self from the religious self. They were one. Self-trust, self-reliance, self-sufficiency for all purposes, is his keynote. Consult this self, he said, and it will guide you, because it is no merely private self, but universal and divine. It is the same self that has spoken through history and the great heroes of history, that still speaks through Man and Nature. God hides the whole world in thy heart and brain; and the ultimate authority for conduct speaks in the still, small voice of thy own conscience and reason.

He began, in his first work, "Nature," to upbraid his countrymen for relying too much on the past and on tradition. "We build the sepulchers of the fathers," he said. But the divine and authoritative facts are Here and Now—self-witnessing, self-authenticating. "Why should not we enjoy an original relation to the universe? Why should not we have a poetry and philosophy of insight, and not of tradition, and a religion by revelation to us, and not the history of theirs?" And he concluded in the same strain with an announcement of a new revelation to the new man in the new world —the revelation of his own moral selfhood, in the light of which the old revelation through miracle and special dispensations of Providence seemed superfluous and irrelevant.

This is the evangel we need to-day. We do not lay our sins to the charge of man's moral self. He feels no sufficient burden of moral responsibility. He still hides behind the excusing fictions of outworn creeds. He still pleads a shameful weakness and insufficiency. He still relies on charms, incantations, magical words, books, or what not. Help and increase of strength come after the valiant effort and painful deed. By such signs do we know the self-sufficiency of the moral life—it brings accession of strength, joy, inspiration.

The sick world needs—not the all-conceding Emerson, whom so many are eulogizing—but the sturdy Emerson, who, in trumpet-tones, summoned men to a life of greater idealism, greater consistency, greater courage, greater faith, greater consecration to that righteousness which alone can save from the many perils that hang like clouds above us to-day.

We are glad to present to our readers of this issue of the ETHICAL RECORD a portrait of Emerson, reproduced by the courtesy of Messrs. Houghton, Mifflin & Co. It is, on the whole, we think, the most satisfactory of the presentments of the Concord Sage. Not wanting in the benignity and charm of his early self, he wears here the mature, sage-like and seer-like look of his ripened age. It is the image that we fain would have dwell with us.

To those who desire a more substantial portrait, may be commended the excellent dry point etching by Mr. G. Kruell, which may be seen at either Keppel's or Wunderlich's, and may be obtained there or by writing to Mr. Kruell himself at 331 Main Street, East Orange, N. J.

International Journal of Ethics

1305 ARCH STREET, PHILADELPHIA

Yearly, $2.50   Single Number, 65c.

EDITORIAL COMMITTEE

HENRY C. ADAMS, Ph.D., Ann Arbor
FELIX ADLER, Ph.D., New York
GIACOMO BARZELOTTI, Ph.D., Naples
STANTON COIT, Ph.D., London
ALFRED FOUILLÉE, Ph.D., Paris

HARALD HÖFFDING, Ph.D., Copenhagen
FR. JODL, Ph.D., Vienna
J. S. MACKENZIE, Litt.D., Cardiff, Wales
J. H. MUIRHEAD, M.A., Birmingham
JOSIAH ROYCE, Ph.D., Cambridge, Mass.

Managing Editor, S. BURNS WESTON, Philadelphia

COMBINATION SUBSCRIPTIONS

International Journal of Ethics, Ethical Record, and Ethical Addresses $3.00
Ethical Record and Ethical Addresses 1.00

Foreign postage extra: Journal of Ethics, 20 cents; Ethical Record, 15 cents; Ethical Addresses, 10 cents

Address S. BURNS WESTON, 1305 Arch Street, Philadelphia

Ethical Addresses

Lecture Supplement to the Ethical Record

Published Monthly (except July and August)

TENTH SERIES—1902-1903

September—Ethics and Culture, FELIX ADLER
October—The New Attitude toward Others, FELIX ADLER
November—Morality as a Religion, WILLIAM M. SALTER
December—Changes in the Conception of God, by FELIX ADLER
January—What Makes Life Worth Living? WALTER L. SHELDON
February—Society and Its Children, with Special Reference to the Problem of Child Labor, WILLIAM M. SALTER
March—Revelation, DAVID SAVILLE MUZZEY
April—"Everyman;" or, the Higher Possibilities of the Drama, WILLIAM M. SALTER
May—The Negro Problem: Is the Nation Going Backward? WILLIAM M. SALTER
June—Tolstoi's "Resurrection," PERCIVAL CHUBB

Work of the New York Society for Ethical Culture

SURVEY OF PROGRESS DURING THE PAST YEAR, SUMMARIZED FROM THE PRESIDENT'S ANNUAL REPORT

The history of the Society for Ethical Culture for the past year has been one of varied experiences, but of decided growth in the clearer conception of ideals, in firmer grasp upon the members of the Society at large, and the possibilities of taking its stand on the pressing issues and complex problems of our day. The first and most significant event in this direction was the acceptance by Dr. Adler of the Chair of Political and Social Ethics at Columbia University, this new dignity calling him away from the lecture platform only for the Sundays of three months, during which time the place was occupied by influential leaders in education and ethics—Prof. Nathaniel Schmidt, Prof. Edward Howard Griggs, Mr. William M. Salter, Mr. Walter L. Sheldon, Mrs. Anna Garlin Spencer, Dr. Elliott, and Mr. Chubb.

The second important change was the decision to transfer the care of the School from the United Relief Works directly into the keeping of the Society for Ethical Culture.

This year the Sunday School has successfully organized work for the older girls, thus offsetting the failure of the regular Sunday School to reach the high-water mark of attendance which friends of the Society hope to see realized.

The HUDSON GUILD in uniting with the Children's Guild has coördinated the interests of both, and has proved itself more and more equal to meeting the needs of the neighborhood as a social center. There has been conspicuous growth in the work of the Kindergarten and the Library.

In its work of interpreting the ideals and aims of the Society to the people, the DOWN-TOWN ETHICAL SOCIETY, at 310 Madison Street, has made encouraging strides. The clubs now number eighteen; and the house is becoming more and more of a neighborhood center, and increasingly useful in ministering to the moral and intel-

lectual needs of the East Side, and in giving to the foreign population the ideals of American citizenship.

The WOMEN'S CONFERENCE takes no undue credit to itself in calling the attention of the community to the work it has done in starting the Manhattan Trade School for Girls, at 233 West Fourteenth Street, which has come to a successful termination of its first year's experiment. In addition to its varied and philanthropic work, the lecture courses this year included one by Mrs. Anna Garlin Spencer on "Modern Philanthropy," and the second by Mr. Chubb on "The Literary Study of the Bible." For next year the Conference proposes the following program:—November: "The Religious Problems of the Adolescent," Dr. Adler. January: "Co-Education in High Schools." February: An Evening Meeting: "The Rights of the Individual against the Rights of the Family." March: Symposium—"Educational Ideals as Exemplified by the Ethical Culture Schools;" speakers, Dr. Adler, and others. Lecture Course by Mrs. Anna Garlin Spencer, and Monthly Conference with her in Philanthropy, in connection with the Committee on Philanthropy. The scheme is given in detail below.

THE OUTING AT FELICIA

A debt of gratitude is due to the members of the Young Men's Union and to the Council for the inspiration which resulted from the successful Outing at the Summer Home at Mountainville on May 24th. The occasion was commemoratory of the twenty-seventh anniversary of the Society, and the beautiful farm purchased by the Young Men's Union for their Fresh Air work, situated in the heart of the mountains (proof of the earnestness of those young men who have espoused the Society's ideals of work for humanity), seemed a most fitting place in which to bring together in pleasant social intercourse the varied interests of the Society and their

representatives. Nor could the leaders of the Society forget that, by happy coincidence, the day was also being celebrated throughout the country as the Centennial Anniversary of the birth of the great sage and prophet of the Ethical Societies, Ralph Waldo Emerson, whose picture was unveiled after a tribute rendered him by Mr. Chubb. The ideals of the work were set forth by the Chairman of the Young Men's Union, Mr. Charles J. Liebmann. Dr. Adler spoke on the value to young men of work done for children and of the splendid influence which the surrounding country has upon city boys and girls. The value of associated life and enterprise in such an environment in developing the character of the city boy was the topic of Dr. Elliott's address; and after varied musical contributions by the members of the Chorus, Mrs. Adler planted a bit of ivy commemoratory of the dedication of Felicia to the ideals of service and happiness.

Books That Concern Us

LIFE AND DESTINY: Thoughts from the Ethical Lectures of Felix Adler. McClure, Phillips & Co. 1903. $1.00.

"A great man," we find it written on one of the pages of this little book, "helps us by what he earnestly tries for, and by what the standard which he sets. . . . He helps us by what he suggests to us that we should try for; he helps us, not so much by what he achieves, as by what he reveals, by the insight which he gives us into the nature of good." This stress laid on the value of effort and of ideals is the keynote of Dr. Adler's teachings and beliefs, and all the thoughts gathered together in these excerpts from his lectures cluster around the central idea of the lasting strength that comes with earnest endeavor and the lasting beauty that resides in ideal thought. The surcease of sorrow depends largely on individual will and character, and the answer to despair and pessimism is the eternality of "the nature of good." Joy is made more beautiful and life is given meaning by this view of individual destiny inseparably inwoven with the destiny of man.

The thoughts in this book are so arranged and expressed as often to reach very intimately those who are in need of sympathetic moral and spiritual support; and if by the very nature of such a compilation, it does not possess the philosophical weight and sense of completion to which a larger volume would aspire, it keenly stirs the old desire of so many of the author's friends for that *magnum opus* which shall in printed form conserve for future men and women his whole philosophy of life.

G. S. H.

WILLIAM ELLERY CHANNING, MINISTER OF RELIGION. By John White Chadwick. Houghton, Mifflin & Co. $1.75 net.

Mr. Chadwick, who had put all Liberals under obligation by his life of Theodore Parker two years ago, now does us another service in drawing the portrait of perhaps a still greater religious pioneer, Dr. Channing. It is a singular proof of the logical necessity of the general movement in which Channing was a leader, that though orthodoxy reacted against it and raised up able champions to attack it, it is itself now being gradually permeated with the spirit it once combated. It is a question whether there is enough left of the old doctrines to produce another reaction.

In his particular theological opinions Channing did not go as far as many of us feel obliged to go to-day. For instance, he deprecated Emerson's indifference to the miracles and other supposed facts of the New Testament narratives as evidenced in the famous Divinity Address of 1838. All the same, he declared his essential agreement with Emerson, and no one upheld the rights of the mind more absolutely than he. His "one sublime idea"—the "greatness of the soul"—became that of Emerson. The idea of the intimate connection of the human and divine, which Emerson wrought out with such wonderful persuasiveness and charm, we also find in Channing, who once wrote: "We do not discern him [God] because he is too near, too inward, too deep to be recognized by our present imperfect consciousness. And he is thus near, not only to discern, but to act, to influence, to give his spirit, to communicate to us divinity." This is very near the doctrine of the Over-soul. Emerson's adoration of character, of the ethical laws, is anticipated by Channing's assertions: "The adoration of goodness—this is religion," "To love God then, is to love morality in its most perfect form." In his deeper views Channing is thus ahead of our time as well as of his own. "Channing Unitarianism" is a misnomer—it recalls what was temporary and accidental in Channing's teaching.

Particularly in his social teachings—for goodness and morality were no abstractions to him—does he tower above us still. No keener or more searching words about modern social and economic conditions have ever been said than were said by him. He belongs among the reformers and seers and prophets of the race. It is a pity that some of his addresses on social topics are not gathered into a volume by themselves.*

Mr. Chadwick has drawn a sympathetic and adequate portrait of him, giving a notable chapter to "The Social Reformer"—indeed he has so truly caught Channing's spirit and applies it in passing so faithfully to the political and social conditions of to-day, that his book might almost be called a "tract for the times."   WILLIAM M. SALTER.

EVERY DAY WITH EMERSON. Compiled by Harriet A. Townsend. Buffalo: White-Penfold Co.

Mrs. Townsend, in a dainty little volume which it is a pleasure to handle, gives every lover of Emerson a chance to receive inspiration and impulse in starting afresh every day. Her passages are well selected, with an eye to the central motives of Emerson's thought.

LECTURES ON THE ETHICS OF T. H. GREEN, MR. HERBERT SPENCER, AND J. MARTINEAU. By Henry Sidgwick. Macmillan Co.

This is a volume for the close student of ethical theory. The lectures which are reproduced here are, as Miss E. E. Constance Jones, the editor, explains in her Preface, virtually supplementary to Sidgwick's great work on "The Methods of Ethics," and were necessitated by the fact that, when that work was produced in 1874, the three representative treatises of Professor Green, Herbert Spencer, and Dr. Martineau, representing respectively the latest and most influential versions of the Transcendental or Idealist, the Evolutional, and the Intuitional Schools, had not appeared. It almost goes without saying that these criticisms of the doctrines of Green's "Prolegomena to Ethics," Spencer's "Principle of Ethics," and Martineau's "Types of Ethical Theory," from a critic so searching and sincere as Sidgwick, and from the standpoint of modern utilitarianism, must be taken into account by every student as being of first-rate importance. The most considerable...

IDEAS OF GOOD AND EVIL. By W. B. Yeats. The Macmillan Co.

"We love nothing but the perfect, and our dreams make all things perfect that we may love them."

Mr. Yeats, as the exponent of the Celtic race, in this series of literary essays interprets the ideals of the writers of poetry as being at last the great human ideals. There is a touch of freshness, a certain magic in the style, and the writer has succeeded in such essays as "Symbolism of Painting," "Symbolism of Poetry," in weaving into the intellectual imagery the feeling of humanity. Shelley he distinguishes as a mystic and revolutionist, but explains that the liberty for which he pleaded was more than one of political justice, including also intellectual beauty. Wagner, Keats, Blake, Rossetti, Whistler, Maeterlinck, Verlaine, have all been symbolists.   "Our imaginations are but fragments of the universal imagination, portions of the universal body of God, and as we enlarge our imagination by imaginative sympathy, and transform with the beauty and peace of art, the sorrows and joys of the world, we put off the limited mortal man more and more and put on the unlimited 'immortal man.'"

WHERE THERE IS NOTHING: A Drama. By W. B. Yeats. The Macmillan Co. $1.25.

Mr. Yeats's plays have been criticised for the slightness of their theme and the looseness of their structure. Certainly this one is less interesting as a drama than as a psychological study, while it has much incidental literary and poetic charm. In it the hot Celtic temper is offset by the spiritual revelation to Paul Ruttledge, revolutionist and mystic. He is a revolutionist who contends mystically that all phenomena fail to reveal to man the deepest and highest aspirations. These are known only in that state of superconsciousness declared by the saints to accompany the turbulent scene in the tavern, this strangely compounded hero has a magistrate and a colonel bound and put on barrels, while he taunts them with failure to live up to the Christian teaching of turning the other cheek to the smiter; forgiving one's enemies; giving away one's cloak with the coat, etc. In the next act he is revealed in the state of trance, from which his brother friars fail to call him. The mob pursue him and his friends for heretics, and he dies a martyr to his teaching that "Where there is nothing, there is God."

ALCOTT

AND THE CONCORD SCHOOL

OF PHILOSOPHY

A Paper Read at a Meeting
of the Concord Antiquarian Society
By FLORENCE WHITING BROWN
May 28, 1923

Privately Printed
Aug. 1926

"Greatness abides not *here*; her home
is in the clouds, save when she descends on the meadows of Concord."

From a letter written by Mr. Alcott while in England.

ALCOTT

AND THE CONCORD SCHOOL

OF PHILOSOPHY

IT was with the greatest reluctance that I consented to prepare even as modest a paper as this upon so ponderous a subject. I con-clude that there were two reasons why I had this honor thrust upon me:—first, that I bear a somewhat close relationship to your Chairman* whose duty it is to provide this Society with an occasional literary effort on some subject of local interest; and second, because circumstances made me somewhat more closely connected with the early sessions of the Concord School of Philosophy than perhaps almost any one now belonging to this Society. I have also two reasons for consenting—after much definite urging—to attempt this rather difficult task,—one, that I have had such long training in yielding my ideas of things to those of your Chairman that I can hardly do otherwise at this late day, and the other reason,—that I can find nowhere any definite and complete account of this interesting phase of Concord's history such as should be preserved in manuscript by this Society for future inquirers. Accounts many have been written: some very, *very* serious, some humorous, but *all* dealing with certain phases only, or over-emphasizing the importance of *some* facts, and minimizing the influence of certain others.

As I understand it, what the Society will wish is a comparatively brief and impersonal narra-tive of the purpose, the maintenance, and the accomplishment of the Summer School which held its sessions here in Concord for a few weeks every year from 1879 to 1888 inclusive, a period of ten years, although the last few sessions were desultory and almost unnoticed by the public.

There are several ways that occur to me in which I might deal with this subject. I might approach it with awe and give you synopses of the very abstract and metaphysical utterances which were effective, perhaps, in the exact ratio of the impossibility of any of the audience being able to answer them at short notice, or possibly, at any notice at all. I *could* manage to do this, I suppose, as nearly everything that was pub-lished is in my possession. Or I might endeavor to collect the many funny stories and jokes which some of the townspeople, and many writers for the newspapers and current maga-zines, thought the most appropriate kind of notice of the School. Or I might give you my own impressions, which being those of a very young and untrained girl could have no value except as an eye- and ear-witness of any event gives a certain amount of interest to a narrative. As this last seems the least important, I will begin with it, and then proceed to material more worthy of your attention. As a young girl, I was somewhat debarred from the usual active life of young people by delicate health. This made me depend much more on books than on society, and also threw me much more with older people whom, at that time, I preferred to my *young* friends. (I might say here, in parenthesis, that nature had her revenge and I now like my friends to be as young as they will permit.)

My mother, before her second marriage, had been the Alcotts' family physician, and between her and Miss Louisa Alcott there grew up a very close friendship so that the Alcott home was almost as familiar to me as my own, and Miss Louisa was the same as a very dear relative to me. I have an idea that she would have taken even more interest in me if I had been a jolly normal kind of *boy*, for she never made any secret of her preference for boys to girls, and I cannot think that a young girl, very self-centred and rather given to morbid imaginings and nervous fancies, could have really appealed to her very strongly. But she was deeply attached to my mother, as a great quantity of letters now in my possession testify, and for her sake, she had me with her a great deal. I was spending some weeks with her at a summer resort the very

* Percy W. Brown, son of the writer, and then President of the Con-cord Antiquarian Society.

season that the Concord School was taking shape, and heard her racy comments on the people connected with the plans. I owe her much on the line of good advice and pleasant, wholesome companionship. It was, of course, because I was so much in the Alcott home that I was asked to attend the Conversations which were the prelude to the Concord School of Philosophy. In 1878, Dr. H. K. Jones, the lecturer on Plato, came to Concord for a few weeks, probably attracted to our little town principally because it was the home of Mr. Emerson, but also acquainted with Mr. Alcott, and Professor Harris who was shortly to live in what we now call the Orchard House, although he did not buy it until 1884. A few words about Dr. Jones will not come amiss here. He was a Southerner, being born in Missouri of Virginian ancestry, but he lived and died in Jacksonville, Illinois, where he had held classes and conferences on the philosophy of Plato and kindred subjects. Having taken a degree in a Medical School, he might have been supposed to favor Aristotle rather than Plato in his philosophic speculations, but it was not so. He may be called the reviver of the study of Platonism in his time and land. Of course, Mr. Alcott had found his way to this congenial spirit in his western journeys and they had counselled together as to a possible larger circle to be gathered together some time and some where for the study of philosophical subjects. When Dr. Jones came eastward, he was of course warmly welcomed by the choice company of thinkers in Concord, and Mr. Emerson, then beginning to withdraw himself more and more from public discourse because of failing memory, opened his house for conversations, as did Mr. Alcott in his Main Street home, and Mr. F. B. Sanborn.

Mention is made of Dr. Jones thus early, not because he was the most important figure in the subject we are considering, but because it seems probable that his coming to Concord just when he did caused the School of Philosophy to assume its definite form and being. I can learn nothing of Dr. Jones' life after the year 1882, at which time I suppose he delivered his last lecture in Concord; but as he died in Jacksonville, Illinois, and as he is not especially mentioned in any Biographical Encyclopedia that I can find, I presume that the Concord School may have been the high-water mark of his experience.

To return to my small share in the situation: —Mr. Alcott having become very familiar with my presence in his home, and often talking *to* me (not *with* me, for that was not his forte!) on weighty and abstruse matters of which probably I comprehended very little, invited me to attend these symposiums, which I did. I remember no one of my own age ever being present, and I had the grace to sit always in some remote corner, and was, probably, no more remarked than a piece of furniture in the room. After the wise ones had given utterance to their ideas in more or less oracular form, questions were encouraged, but although never a shy person, I had the sense not to ask any; if I had, perhaps I might have a more definite remembrance of these occasions, and what I learned from them. I should not suppose I could have brought away much, except a general impression of a number of serious-minded people, striving to gain more light on the things of the spirit and no two of them able to agree entirely as to how the light was best obtained. *The rooms* were never very well lighted according to present day ideas, and there was no attempt at entertainment, and certainly no refreshments! The occasions were serious, and anything like frivolity or light conversation would have been distinctly out of place. I presume Dr. Jones was the guest of honor, but I remember distinctly that Mr. Alcott did the largest part of the talking, as probably he felt constrained to do. All of you who remember Mr. Alcott will have no difficulty in believing that he talked if there was any one to listen, that being distinctly his long suit, so to speak.

And perhaps this is as good a place as any to speak of his peculiar gifts and of his unusual experience, for without him, the real originator and principal lecturer, the Dean of the School and its presiding genius for the first four years, there would certainly have been no Concord School of Philosophy. Whether the world would have been any the poorer, I am not prepared to say; but tonight, at least, we are taking for granted that Mr. Alcott's cherished dream as it took shape in Concord forty-four years ago under the pine-clad hill in the little brown chapel, was an epoch-making affair.

Personally, I have the pleasantest memories of Mr. Alcott. A very young person likes to be treated with some consideration, and he, finding me a docile listener, may be said to have tried out, as it were, many of his ideas on me. Fortunately he required no response and no stimulus of opposition, and I had aesthetic sense enough to enjoy this silver-haired philosopher among his books, uttering sonorous and well-rounded sentences which certainly sounded like the very essence of beauty and truth. I do not remember his ever trying to guide my faltering steps in the rugged paths of speculation, for of course by this time I was trying to read books that were far beyond me; and I don't remember his ever giving me any practical advice on any subject whatever, but his talk affected me in *some* way, making trivial matters seem less worth while, and impressing me with a love of study and of the value of living in the realm of the mental. All the poverty and hardships of the Alcotts which our practical townspeople attributed to the lack of industry and common sense of the husband and father, were long before my time. I did not know the family until Miss Louisa's

success had changed all that.

This prophet certainly had not much honor in his own country. It is rather hard work to be an avowed idealist in a New England Community, and the philosopher's willingness to let someone else support his family while he soared into the infinite did not meet with the approval of the practical every day men and women who paid their debts and their taxes, and believed that if they assumed the responsibilities of a family, such responsibilities could not be shifted on to the neighbors. We can easily imagine some of our practical townspeople remarking that while Mr. Alcott wrote in his Diary "All day occupied with endless infinite themes" *Mrs. A.* was doing the endless *finite* chores.

Thoreau wrote to Mr. Emerson in 1847: "Mr. Alcott seems to have sat down for the winter. He has got Plato and other books to read. If he would only stand upright and toe the line, though he were to put off several degrees of largeness, and were to put on a considerable degree of littleness!"

Perhaps we need no better record of the family's feeling than Miss Louisa's definition of a philosopher, given in quick response to a question: "A man up in a balloon, with his family and friends holding the ropes which confine him to earth, and trying to haul him down."

Many very bitter and critical things were said about the head of the Alcott family, and these things, as I happen to know, were never forgiven or forgotten by the daughter Louisa. Her own attitude toward him was a curious mixture of reverence and humorous criticism. I have often heard her make fun of his soarings (as in the balloon illustration) but woe be to any one else who did not accord him all honor and esteem. Mr. Sanborn has written the only good biography of him, and a good one it is, sympathetic, and in the main, I think, written with judgment and discrimination.

If this paper seems to give undue prominence to his personality and career, it is because it seems necessary to form a definite picture of the person who formulated the idea and the plan of the Concord School of Philosophy. Without him, and his somewhat peculiar ideas as to the value of the teaching prophet, there would have been no such School. Dr. Harris and Mr. Emery, the younger men, Mr. Sanborn and Mr. Emery, were the practical helpers, but there is no doubt that Mr. Alcott had never ceased to hope for such a gathering of truth seekers since he began his talks to a few choice spirits in the Boston of 1840.

Born in Connecticut in a small country town in the closing years of the 18th century—Nov. 29, 1799—of plain-living parents, but with a rather distinguished ancestry, he seems to have possessed certain refinements and aspirations which set him apart from the youths of the farming community, where education was confined within narrow limits, and the social life was simple and primitive in the extreme. There was very little money in the home, and books were few, but it is said that young Amos spent his Saturday afternoons (a boy's natural playtime) walking to the farmhouses within a reasonable distance to examine the small collections of books which they contained,—always the Bible, and usually works like Pilgrim's Progress, Young's "Night Thoughts," Hervey's "Meditations" and Burgh's "Dignity of Human Nature." The bookish lad borrowed and read Pilgrim's Progress every year. At 12 years of age he had somehow acquired Paradise Lost, the Robinson Crusoe, and Thomson's Seasons, the beginnings of his own library. At the age of 14, he went with his father to New Haven for a short visit. One can imagine him looking wistfully at the college buildings whose privileges were not for him, and longingly at the book

stores, the first he had seen. Even at this early age, he was musing on theories of education, and his head was more or less "in the clouds," but stern necessity forced him to earn something toward the family exchequer. It is hard to picture him whom we knew as the white-haired scholar, serene, benignant, *satisfied*,—ever being a peddler of notions, a clock-maker, a book-agent, but these occupations were those of a few years only.

To one who loved the sound of the spoken word—especially when *he spoke* it—and was serenely secure that he had ideas of imparting knowledge far in advance of his contemporaries, there was one calling to which he was destined, —school-teaching. The public schools of the first half of the 19th century certainly needed improvement. Alcott quotes in the Diary which he kept in 1826 the opinion of a college professor that little good could ever be done in common schools, and that it would be well if the Connecticut School Fund could be applied to the use of colleges. Exactly how the young were to be prepared for the advanced education, is not stated! Alcott evidently pondered much on necessary reforms in the common schools, and whether we follow with approval all the methods which he employed to work out his ideas in the schools which he formed in later life, we must acknowledge that he made the Connecticut schools with which he was connected in those early years, very different seats of learning from what they had been previously.

Mr. Sanborn says that "he anticipated most of the changes afterward wrought by Horace Mann and others in the public school system, and without any intimate knowledge of what had been done by Pestalozzi in Switzerland, he followed the same ideal path and accomplished similar results in his small field of action." As early as 1823, he had decided, evidently, that

teaching was to be his life work, and we hear no more of the mechanical and commercial pursuits of his earlier youth. Various little schools employed him, but his methods were ahead of the times and he seems to have lacked the *savoir faire* and a certain tact which would have smoothed his way and convinced the town committees that his ideas were practical. One school for which he applied was far from home and he walked there, having no means of transportation. This was in Paris, New York State, then pronounced by the home-keeping inhabitants, *Pay-ris*. There is a funny story told about this village, and as my subject is so extremely serious that I fear the audience may soon be overtaken with slumber, I am going to venture to insert this bit of comicality here, though it has little to do with philosophy. One of the residents was trying to promote a real-estate boom—they seem to have had those things even in the 1820's—and when calling upon a possible buyer, he said that the town had so many advantages as a place of residence that the only things they really wanted in Payris were *water* and *good society*. The reply was "I believe that is all they really feel the need of in hell!"

The school in Cheshire, Connecticut, where Alcott found himself in 1825 and where he remained for two years is the first where he was really appreciated, and given a free hand to work out his theories. Here he established a school library,—one of the earliest in New England—filling it with books never before brought to the notice of common school pupils. And now the educational journals of the day—such as they were!—began to praise this school and to call it the best one in the country. It is pleasant to know that the young man had this small amount of appreciation, for the days were approaching when he was to meet with little but criticism and ridicule.

The scope of this paper does not warrant too much detail concerning Mr. Alcott's domestic life, or even his experiments in the line of plain living and high thinking, his literary efforts, or his struggles with adverse circumstances and an unappreciative world, though this last must be touched upon. I take it that our purpose is to follow the development of his peculiar ideas of teaching which found their final expression in the Concord School, where in his old age, he certainly attained the fulfillment of many dreams. His marriage with the daughter of so prominent a man as Colonel Joseph May caused him to become better known than formerly; and after various teaching experiences in different places we find him established in Boston, and beginning to be known as a man of advanced, if peculiar, ideas, and fitted to put them in practice. Up to this time, his public had been very limited. He had taught in many schools, more or less (usually *less!*) successfully both in New England and Pennsylvania, as well as in several small ones in Boston. He had lectured when he had opportunity concerning the absolute necessity of redeeming mankind through the right kind of education of children, and he had written a little on philosophical subjects for certain liberal publications, but through the School in the Masonic Temple in Boston, known as the Temple School, he was to become a prominent and much-discussed person. We have now come to the year 1834, and while Mr. Alcott is arranging to open his own school, after his own plan, where he would be accountable to no one, we will see what sort of a Boston he has come to.

It would be quite impossible to understand certain phases of this period without taking into account the general unrest in the political and religious world. It seemed as though nearly every thoughtful person had his or her special theories as to every kind of subject. Emerson

has facetiously described the attendants at a convention of the period:—"Mad men and women, men with beards, Dunkers, Muggletists, Come-outers, Groaners, Agrarians, Seventh-Day Baptists, Quakers, Abolitionists, Calvinists, Unitarians, and Philosophers." All the radical thought of the time was by no means confined to what we know as the Transcendental Movement, although the leaders of that were held responsible for many of the vagaries that to the ordinary person appeared to *transcend* common sense. So much has been written about the Transcendental Movement—and perhaps there are those present who had an inside knowledge of the days of which we are speaking (though I think everybody here is too young!) that it would ill become me to attempt an extensive elucidation of it. But as Transcendentalism was in a sense behind our Concord School, and if there had been no such movement, there would have been no School, it will not be out of place for us to touch lightly on a few of its features.

As is the case with most radical reforms in religion or medicine, the fundamental ideas of those reforms gradually become incorporated in the general thought—sometimes in a modified form—until no one remembers the violent opposition which their introduction caused. Briefly speaking, this philosophy taught the unity of the world in God and the imminence of God in the world. But a more popular definition would be the divine authority of the intuitions of the soul. In a certain sense, every man was to be a law unto himself; he must trust his instincts which were the voice of God guiding and teaching him. The Movement, of course, was a protest against the materialistic philosophy of Locke and others who claimed that the soul was governed only by what it had learned through materiality or the evidences of the senses. The Transcendental Movement originated with Im-

manuel Kant, with Fichte, with Schelling, and some French thinkers; their works were becoming known through translations. In 1838, George Ripley began to publish his Specimens of Foreign Standard Literature; these books opened a new world to the untravelled American reader, usually little skilled in tongues.

In preparing this paper, I read again with some care O. B. Frothingham's book "Transcendentalism in New England," not so much as a philosophical study, but with the wish to get into the atmosphere of the '30s and '40s, when the men whose names have since become household words were throwing down the gauntlet in the contest with the materiality of the times. Emerson's "epoch-making sermon," as it has been called, was preached in 1832; in 1836 he published "Nature," which has been called the Bible of Transcendentalism. There was idealism in New England prior to these days, of course, for idealists are of no age or clime, but they were of no philosophical school, and they recognized immediately—those of *this* period—that their leader and organizer had appeared. But Emerson had no desire to organize; it was for lesser men to do that, or to *seem* to do it for a time. In reality, the Movement was never organized; its very nature prevented organization; it was a great wave of spiritualization of thought; "it affected thinkers, guided moralists, inspired philanthropists and created reformers." As a form of mental philosophy, it was at its height from 1835 to 1845, ten years only; but long enough to give a distinct character to American thought and life. Its literary achievements are best exhibited in the quarterly magazine called The Dial, without any question the most remarkable periodical ever published. It had a brief life of only four years and it reached but a limited public, but a partial list of its contributors fixes its standard at once,—Emerson,

Margaret Fuller, Thoreau, both Channings, George Ripley, James Freeman Clarke, Theodore Parker, John S. Dwight, Cranch the poet, names that have lived and will live as long as there is real literature in the land.

New England furnished an ideal location for the working out of transcendental theories in practical life, because here the sentiment of individual freedom was active, and a feeling was still in the air that all new things should be welcomed in a new world. To quote for a moment O. B. Frothingham: "The philosophy of sensation (of material evidence), making great account of circumstances, arrangements, customs, usages, etc., was alien to people who, having emancipated themselves from political dependence on the mother country, were full of confidence in their ability to set up society for themselves." "The philosophy that laid stress on the capacities and endowments of the mind was as congenial as the opposite system was foreign."

Just when the term Transcendentalism was applied to the opinions of Emerson and his circle, Alcott, Thoreau, Channing, Theodore Parker, Margaret Fuller, etc., no one seems to know. It is said that they did not much favor the word. This may have been because very soon the name took on somewhat of that significance which it has had for the popular mind ever since. To the average person, it was synonymous with *flighty, above the clouds*, impractical, visionary, perhaps even egotistical, self-sufficient. That is the way that advanced thinking may be misunderstood by the man in the market-place.

Now we will return to Mr. Alcott and his new plans, and again, let me say that if undue space seems given to him and to the Temple School in this little paper, it is because in the brain of one and in the mechanism of the other, we find the beginnings of the Concord School which took

shape more than forty years later.

Boston has always been fond of self-contemplation and not unwilling to believe that those persons whom it distinguishes with its approval are very much worth while. At this time—1834 —Dr. Channing—who never was unpleasantly prominent in the new school of thought and did not accept its extreme phases—was the idol of the liberal thought of Boston and his favor counted for much. He had, in a sense, discovered Mr. Alcott, and the two had found that they held many opinions in common. Everything looked most favorable for Mr. Alcott's educational plans. He opened his school in a large and handsome room in the Masonic Temple on Tremont Street, which was one of the finest buildings in Boston architecturally. He was able, perhaps with assistance, to furnish it suitably, and, as he expressed it, "to surround the senses with appropriate emblems of intellectual and spiritual life." Paintings and busts were to help bring external circumstances into harmony with serenity of spirit. These ideas seem natural enough now, but were an innovation in those days when school rooms were usually places to study books in, regardless of anything to develop the aesthetic side of child nature.

For a year all went well. His income from the school was about $1800, which in those days was sufficiently ample for a simple family. Miss Elizabeth Peabody, one of the most interesting women of her time, came to assist him in teaching and was at first delighted and enthusiastic. She kept a Journal of Events which she published a year or two later, calling it "The Record of a School." This book is as quaint reading in this year 1923, eighty years later, as can be imagined.

With no one to check him, Mr. Alcott certainly rode his educational hobby nearly to absurdity. It is hard for us moderns to believe

that there was nothing priggish and unnatural in the replies which the children learned to give to the amazing questions concerning life, death, and the vast forever, which Mr. Alcott asked them. His teaching was always by the Socratic method, and his questions had to do with the weighty matters of spiritual law. The utterances of young Josiah Quincy, aged seven, concerning matter and spirit and the souls of dead infants are decidedly precocious, and rather appalling. Mr. Alcott maintained that from a circle of twenty well-selected children, he could draw forth in their conversation everything that is in Plato!

As time went on, Miss Peabody got a little out of step with Mr. Alcott's ideas of education and did not hesitate to try to convince him of the disadvantages of some of his methods; but although he listened to all opposition with perfect courtesy, I have yet to find that anyone ever convinced Mr. Alcott of anything contrary to his own opinion. The second year showed a marked falling off in the attendance and the income from the School, but the hopeful idealist kept on, looking for the gradual melting of prejudice and awakening of dormant minds. In this second year, Sunday Readings were established in the Temple, and though the meetings were simple and reverent, they aroused much criticism. In the third year, the attendance was still smaller and the burden of debts contracted in his youth complicated the plans, if it did not weigh on the mind, of this unworldly sage.

But in 1837, matters had gone from bad to worse financially. Mr. Alcott was now the reputed leader of the Transcendentalists "none being more active than he in diffusing the ideas of the Spiritual Philosophy, and none being so uncompromising in his interpretations of them." He was one of the founders of the Symposium, a somewhat indefinite sort of club which held meetings at private houses from 1836 to 1850. It had little organization and no such mundane things as By-Laws, but the influence of its discussions and interchange of ideas is not to be calculated. It is probable that Mr. Alcott's *extreme* stand on many lines was not congenial to his friends,—his theories as to animal food, non-payment of taxes, etc. But he was appreciated by such men as Emerson, Hedge, and Dr. Channing, who understood that the principles by which he lived work out differently with different temperaments, but always *toward* freedom, purity, and the development of the power of spirit over material conditions. It has never been disputed that Mr. Alcott had not the slightest sense of humor; this sad deficiency is in itself quite enough to entitle him to our profound sympathy. Even the faithful friend Mr. Emerson once called him "the *tedious archangel.*" How discerning is Carlyle's description of him! "The good Alcott; with his long lean face and figure, with his gray worn temples and mild radiant eyes; all bent on saving the world by a return to acorns and the golden age; he comes before me like a kind of venerable Don Quixote whom nobody can even laugh at without loving."

In 1837, when the walls of debt were closing around him, when his school was dwindling away, and he had been obliged to sell all his fine furnishings, he published his "Conversations with Children on the Gospels" and Boston, the city where freedom of opinion was strongly advocated, (though seldom practised!) arose in wrath to rebuke this apostle of the *Newness.* The newspapers took up the matter and printed much adverse criticism of Mr. Alcott and his methods of teaching, as well as his religious views.

Mr. Emerson, whose acquaintance with Mr. Alcott was comparatively recent, wrote him a most sympathetic letter, one paragraph of which was—"I hate to have all the little dogs barking at you, for you have something better to do than attend to them." He also sent a strong article to one of the papers—the Courier—advising that the Conversations be read thoroughly before being so unjustly criticized. Here might be a suitable place to speak of Mr. Emerson's faithful and practical friendship for Mr. Alcott and his family from the year 1835 when they first met to the end of his life,—a period of nearly fifty years. Louisa Alcott pays loving tribute to the family friend, as the man who understood her father best, and helped him in so many ways. But it is not probable that he could do much for Alcott at this time; in a letter written in April 1837, Mr. Emerson says "I never regretted more than in this case my own helplessness in all practical contingencies. I was created a seeing eye and not a useful hand." Nevertheless, the friendship and moral support of a man like Emerson can not be over-estimated. And Alcott was naturally calm, composed, sure of himself and of his mission, *and*—perhaps not entirely averse to being in the lime-light. There were rumors that the symposiums which Mr. Alcott was already conducting would be broken up by a mob, but no such disturbance occurred.

Three hundred copies of his Gospel Conversations were sold almost immediately, but interest in the book was confined to so small a class of persons that the demand soon ceased, and it might be added that a few years later 750 copies (without covers) were sold to a trunk-maker for linings, for $50—900 lbs. at 5½ cents a lb.! Quite enough had been said against Mr. Alcott's innovations to injure his school, and two other things assisted in its downfall. One was Miss Harriet Martineau's caustic account which seems to have been considered most unjust by the friends of the school, and the other was the

admission of a colored girl in 1838, on an equal standing with the other pupils. One by one, the children were withdrawn until only five were left, which number included his own daughters and the colored child. All Boston at that date was hostile to the social equality of the white and colored races except a little band of abolitionists including Garrison and Philips, who stood by Mr. Alcott but had not sufficient influence to prevent the disaster. So the school came to an end in 1839. It might be of interest to observe its financial decline: in 1834, the income from it was $1794; in 1835, $1649; in 1836, $1395; in 1837, $549; and in 1838, $343. The anxiety and hardships of this period seriously affected Mr. Alcott's health for a time, and again his good friend Mr. Emerson writes him an affectionate letter, begging him to visit him in Concord, a capital place for resting! Mrs. Alcott's letters to her own family at this period are full of indignant feeling, but never waver in admiration for her unsuccessful spouse. To quote one sentence: "It is a low state of moral discrimination which will give the man an honorable discharge who has been twenty years gambling in fancy stocks, but drives into the regions of starvation an exalted spirit whose desires and efforts for the twenty best years of his life have been to elevate and improve the moral and intellectual condition of mankind."

It was thus that the Alcott family was frozen out of Boston and it was natural that their thoughts should turn to Concord, the home of Mr. Emerson who seemed to really appreciate the genius of Alcott and had aided him in so many ways. Also, Concord was at that time well adapted for a life of plain living and high thinking and contained a small but cultivated society of persons wholly of English descent, the foreign immigration not beginning till some years later. Perhaps no sweeter verse in praise of Concord has ever been written than the sonnet composed by Mr. Alcott when he was 82 years of age:—

"Calm vale of comfort, peace, and industry
Well doth thy name thy home-bred traits express!
Considerate people, neighborly and free,
Proud of their monuments, their ancestry,
Their circling river's quiet loveliness.
Their noble townsmen's fame and history.
Nor less I glory in each goodly trait,
Child of another creed, a stricter state;
I chose thee for my haunt in troublous time,
My home in days of late prosperity,
And laud thee now in this familiar rhyme;
Here on thy bosom the last summons wait
To scenes, if lovelier, still reflecting thee,
Resplendent both in hope and memory."

To the Hosmer cottage just above the rail-road crossing on Main Street came the Alcotts in March 1840, to make, as Mrs. A. wrote her brother "another experiment in the art of living." Mr. Alcott describes in a letter his new home in such characteristic phrases that we quote them: "My little cottage and garden lie low in the landscape, but there is the broad sky overhead and something still of its depth of azure in my hopes." Whether he means that his hopes continue vast and beautiful, or whether he has the "blues" symbolized by the sky's color, is problematical. Mr. Alcott always expected the other man to know what he was talking about; if he didn't, so much the worse for the other man. The letter closes with a truly pathetic sentence, easily understood "And must I own that sometimes in our straitened moments, I have even wished some portion of the gifts with which I have been blessed had been withheld if I might thereby have been brought into closer sympathy with the ordinary pursuits of mankind!" In this rural retreat, Mr. Alcott designed to support his family by manual labor, but he toiled with a divided mind and there were many days of extreme poverty and some hardship during this period. In the old Hosmer homestead next door lived a dear good woman, Mrs. Lydia Hosmer, the mother of my step-father; she had been left a widow with five little children, the oldest at this time being only thirteen, and was obliged to practise a rigid economy in order to feed and clothe her own flock, but she was the kind who could always find something to spare for any one in need and many were the loving deeds which helped to keep her poorer neighbors from absolute want.

It is pleasant to think that the daughter Louisa later never forgot these benefits, but always spoke of old Mrs. Hosmer with the tenderest respect and gratitude. It was about this time that Mr. Alcott had conscientious scruples concerning paying his town taxes and when big-hearted Sam Staples, the constable, came to arrest him and carry him off to jail, he assured the tearfully-protesting wife that he'd see that Mr. Alcott "had a good square meal on the way anyhow." So much impressed was he with the sincerity of his prisoner that he said to a questioner "I vum! I believe it was nothin' but principle, for I never heerd a man talk honester!"

Meantime, Mr. Alcott had friends in England; no reform as radical as the educational one in which he was conspicuous could be untalked of by kindred thinkers. These friends had started a school in England near Richmond and had named one of their buildings Alcott House. Imagine Mr. Alcott's longing to leave his potato patch and his wood-chopping to go and see for himself the progress in his own line of thought made in another land! The journey would have seemed to be well-nigh an impossibility, but through the interest of Mr. Emerson a fund was raised, and in May 1842 Mr. Alcott set sail. The story of his English experiences does not belong here, neither does that of the Fruitlands

episode which grew out of them. More akin to our subject are the frequent tours westward, after these years of experience, where the philosopher at last found open parlors and small lecture halls, and little groups of attentive listeners when he expounded his views. It would seem that all idea of really earning his living had departed from his mind if, indeed, it had ever really found lodgment there, and there is a tragi-comic description of his return to his ever-welcoming family with one dollar in his pocket as the result of several months talking. But a legacy from her brother had enabled Mrs. Alcott to buy the house now known as the Wayside, Mr. Emerson again helping out with what more was needed. But more than a roof over them was necessary in order to live, and the family left Concord and drifted about until 1858, when they returned to buy the Orchard House, at that time a forlorn and neglected building, most unpromising and for sale at a small price. The whole family took part in its renovation, and it became a charming home where they lived for many years. The "little women" were growing up, and the faithful Louisa, finding a better market for her mental wares than her father ever found, set herself to work out the family problem. Through her success, prosperity came to them; her father could "swim in seas of talk" without anxiety about where his supper was coming from when he floundered to shore; her mother had every comfort in her old age, and the sisters were helped on in many ways. Mr. Alcott found listeners in the West and went there at least each year. He was keen enough to realize that his daughter's fame swung many doors open to him and said once in a letter home "I am having a delightful time riding about in Louisa's chariot, and being adored everywhere, not for myself or my beliefs, but as the grandfather of 'Little Women'."

There is hanging on the wall at the Orchard House a framed notice of one of Mr. Alcott's Conversations; his name is written in *small* letters as Dr. *Brunson* Alcott the sire of Louisa May Alcott (in *large* letters) and the public is invited to come and hear the "Socrates of America." He who runs may read the reason why the good gentleman brought home a thousand dollars from one of these late Western trips in contrast to the one dollar of thirty years earlier. Not every dreamer in this busy world finds his declining years so pleasant and comfortable. If Mr. Alcott had not done his practical duty by his family, it is certain that they had only love and veneration for him. Always some one was smoothing the way,—the devoted wife, the faithful daughter, the kind neighbor-friend. Surely there must have been great beauty and gentleness of character to bind these superior natures so closely to him. There is a pretty story of Mrs. Alcott's joy and pride when in these later years an elaborately bound volume arrived by post from Germany. It was written by a then well-known German philosopher. Imprinted upon the cover was a bust of Mr. Alcott and beneath it in gold letters one of his Orphic sayings. It is said that Mrs. Alcott trod on air for many days, so delighted was she at this "token of recognition from a high authority of her husband's fitness to rank among the famous thinkers of the day." Before we leave Mr. Alcott as an individual and take him up as the Dean of the school, one or two anecdotes may not come amiss.

Once in their days of extreme poverty, Mr. Emerson gave Mr. Alcott a present of $25. He immediately expended it for a great quantity of fine stationery which he carried home smilingly like a child with a new toy. This reminds me of a woman in this town who received a Christmas donation to relieve her great need; she immediately purchased a pound of nutmegs saying she was going to have enough of *something* for once in her life. Possibly Mr. Alcott felt like that and I confess to a great sympathy with this attitude of mind, never having owned in my life as much *paper* as I really wanted!

Mr. Alcott sometimes sowed his ideas on stony ground as must often be the teacher's fate. Once arguing a point with a man of the world "he urged as a reason for abstinence from animal food that one thereby distanced the animal. For the eating of beef encouraged the bovine quality, and a pork diet would bring out a swinish element. The friend replied that according to that theory, a potato diet would eventually change a man into a potato and how if the potatoes proved to be small?" The philosopher's reply is not recorded.

It is probable that as years went on and life became easier and more prosperous, Mr. Alcott's thoughts often turned again toward establishing a school where he could talk as much as he wanted to. Indeed, he and Mr. Emerson had frequently discussed the subject though I can not think that Mr. Emerson's heart was in the matter; it does not seem characteristic. It is more probable that his friendly courtesy impelled him to lend a kindly ear to Mr. Alcott's planning. A winter session was at first considered —a sort of small university devoted wholly to philosophical study—and Concord and Hyannis were both mentioned as the place. (Why Hyannis, I do not know.) Of the men who in the '40s had created such a sensation in Puritan Boston, several were still living in 1878, and younger men had come into the field. Mr. Alcott's many Western tours had brought him in touch with a company of persons who were studying philosophical systems with definiteness. Prof. W. T. Harris, through his classes in Hegelian philosophy, and the Journal of Speculative Philosophy which he edited, had a large

and intelligent following. It has been said that as Acton provided the men at the North Bridge, so Illinois furnished the patrons for the Concord School; but this is no more strictly true in one case than in the other. A goodly number of our townspeople attended one or more Sessions of the School, though it cannot be said to have appealed to the general public. The very fact that Mr. Emerson lent his sanction to the School and occasionally lectured there gave it a certain standing here, for no citizen of Concord has ever been more beloved and revered in his own town. It was rather *the thing* for the first two or three years to have a season ticket and be known as one who could at least *seem* to comprehend the profound utterances of the sages.

Let us turn back in our thoughts to the Concord of forty-five years ago, before the days of the automobile, the trolley car, and the ubiquitous telephone. In an English magazine of some years still earlier there is an article on the town which was then called the Mecca of the Transcendentalists, which article includes these words: "It is known among the manufacturing towns around it as Sleepy Hollow! and is just too far from Boston to be an inviting place of residence to those having business in the city." This certainly would not apply to our town today. Neither would it have applied to the village in 1879, for the number of inhabitants had sensibly increased and the era of modern improvements had begun. Still it was a quiet village with varied interests of the more refined and scholarly sort; and as another English magazine says (for somebody has always been writing about Concord), "With shady streets very considerate to the meditative mood." The days of the long-haired men and the short-haired women who sojourned here for short periods at one time, attracted by the literary atmosphere, had passed away. Transcendentalism as a system had faded into oblivion, although what it stood for was, in large measure, immortal, and many of its ideas have become accepted.

As we have seen, Dr. Jones and his Platonic wisdom had been the reason for the season of Conversations in 1878 and these were the preface of the Concord School of Philosophy, so to speak.

I have had access to the bound volumes of letters sent to Mr. Alcott in the spring of 1879, after the plan of the school had been made public, inquiring more about it, and asking for the price of board and the possibility of securing accommodations near the School. Some of them are very amusing, as of course a plan of this kind would appeal to cranks and innovators as well as to serious students. One letter was sent from the Office of the Heir to the World, Brooklyn, N. Y., and began "I am at present engaged in editing a magazine which advocates the theory that the Ten Lost Tribes of Israel are found in the Anglo-Saxon race."

A certain Mr. Kennedy sends this poem as a sort of advance agent before he appeared himself.

POEM

NATURE—A FRAGMENT
A Tribute to the Concord School of Philosophy and Literature

"Tirelessly weave
The million-armed, iron-sinewed Laws
With dim and delicate shuttles
Knitting thoughts and colors and voices.
Looms the vast mirage
And topples mid the stars;
Slow turns the kaleidoscope
During the ages
Revealing new landscapes
And golden geometry
While through its myriad eyes
Looks the ineffable One,
Breathes in its perfumes
Smiles in its dimpling seas."

What better introduction could a man offer than that?

In 1879, two students of Prof. Harris of St. Louis came to live in Concord, Mr. S. H. Emery Jr. and his brother-in-law, Edward McClure. To them as a guest came Prof. Harris, and after a little, settled here, buying the Orchard House. These men were naturally greatly interested in the prospect of a School of Philosophy, and a Faculty was soon formed,—Mr. Alcott as Dean; Mr. Emery, Director and Presiding Officer; Mr. F. B. Sanborn, Secretary and Treasurer, and Prof. Harris. The plan was to have a six weeks session with five principal lecturers and incidental lectures on Saturdays. The first course was divided as follows: Mr. Alcott, Dr. Harris, Mrs. E. D. Cheney, Dr. Jones, and Mr. David Wasson. Mr. Alcott's talks were largely on Personality and on the *Lapse* as he called his theory that all sin, ugliness, and discord of every kind in the universe was caused by the lapse of mankind from the ideal of divine perfection.

Dr. Harris's talks were on the philosophy of Hegel, of which he was an earnest student. Mrs. Cheney's were on different phases of Art. Dr. Jones's on Plato, Mr. Wasson's on Ethics and Social Conditions. As a relief (so-called) from this strain of severe thought, Prof. Pierce talked on Cosmogony, T. W. Higginson on American Literature, Mr. Davidson on Athens, Mr. Emerson on Memory, Mr. Sanborn on Social Science, Dr. Bartol on Education, and Harrison Blake read from Thoreau's manuscripts.

This first session opened July 15, 1879. Miss Alcott wrote in her diary the day before: "The philosophers begin to swarm and the buzz starts tomorrow. How much honey will be made is still doubtful, but the hive is ready. People laugh, but will enjoy something new in this dull old town."

Another year she wrote: "The town swarms with philosophers and they roost on our steps like hens waiting for corn. If they were philanthropists, I should enjoy it, but speculation seems a waste of time when there is so much real work to be done. Why discuss the unknowable till our poor are fed and the wicked saved?" Her attitude toward the gathering may be inferred by an earlier entry in her diary concerning a gathering of seekers for truth elsewhere. "The Club was a funny mixture of rabbis and weedy old ladies, the 'oversoul' and oysters. Papa and B. flew clean out of sight like a pair of Platonic balloons, and we tried to follow, but couldn't."

The attendance at the first session of the Concord School was larger than was expected and hopes of a permanent organization rose high. We began to hear that a certain Mrs. Elizabeth Thompson would build a chapel for the School. As I had never met anyone who could tell me anything about this lady, I was glad to obtain, recently, some facts concerning her which should be recorded here. I do not know whether she ever attended the sessions of the School, but it is probable that at least she was an occasional visitor.

The building cost $512 and the rest of the $1000 which was her contribution was used for furniture and upkeep. It was here that the school sojourned after its first year.

Mrs. Thompson was born in Vermont in 1821, the daughter of a poor farmer. She went into service with a neighbor at the age of nine years, earning twenty-five cents a week! She was a strikingly handsome girl and while on a visit to Boston, captivated a millionaire named Thomas Thompson who married her and later left her all his money. She gave large sums for scientific purposes and in charity. She purchased the painting of Lincoln signing the Emancipation Proclamation in the Presence of his Cabinet and presented it to the U. S. Congress who hung it in the rotunda at the Capitol. For this she was given the freedom of the floor of the House of Representatives, the only woman who had that honor till very recently.

The little chapel needs no description to Concord people. Simplicity was its keynote, as might be expected when in one of his addresses of welcome, Mr. Alcott informed the audience that the chapel had few ornaments since a holy life was the only true beauty, and also that the eye itself and not what it sees, is Beautiful. Nevertheless, there were always a few flowers, and we were able to gaze on the busts of Plato, Pestalozzi, Emerson, and Alcott, and also at an engraving of Raphael's School of Athens.

I saw the other day all that is left of the low platform where the lecturer sat and some of the wooden chairs and benches where the listeners were grouped. The seats were hard and the air was hot, but a company such as met there were soaring above all such minor discomforts. Those of us who were not yet freed from these physical limitations, kept very quiet about it, and who knows how much good just that may have done our youthful souls?

In 1880, the program of the School included Mr. Alcott on Mysticism, Dr. Jones and Prof. Harris again on their specialties, Rev. Mr. Kedney on the Philosophy of the Beautiful and Sublime, Mr. Denton J. Snider on Shakespeare, Rev. W. H. Channing on Oriental Philosophy, Dr. Mulford on The Personality of God, and various other lectures, including Mr. Emerson on Aristocracy and Mrs. Julia Ward Howe on Modern Society. Dr. Hedge had a thrilling one on Ghosts. This was the session which I attended most constantly. I remember it was a hot summer and I suppose the hottest place in Concord was that small wooden building under the hill on Lexington Road. How our brains must have sizzled in that July torridness! But as I have said, it was not correct to mention it.

The program in 1881 included Alcott, Jones, Harris, Snider, Kedney, Mulford, a few new ones and Prof. Watson on The Critical Philosophy in its relation to Realism and Sensationalism.

In 1882, Dr. Harris included such subjects as Gnosticism and Turner's paintings, ranging far afield for subjects. Miss Peabody gave a lecture on Childhood; Dr. Holland one on Atomism; Dr. Howison on Recent German Philosophy; and Mr. George Lathrop on the Symbolism of Color. This being the summer after Mr. Emerson's death, there was a commemoration day at which time was read, among many other tributes, Mr. Alcott's beautiful poem "Ion; a Monody." This poem was Mr. Alcott's last literary effort; he never recovered from the shock of his friend's death and it was while correcting this memorial poem that he was stricken with apoplexy. His contributions to the school ended here and Mr. Emerson's passing away removed the two great inspirers of the School.

Nevertheless, in 1883, Harris, Sanborn and Emery carried on the work with regular courses and nearly all the former names are on the list as well as others like Julian Hawthorne, Mr. Edwin Mead and Mr. John Albee.

The year 1884 was largely given up to Lectures on the Genius and Character of Emerson and these were published with a preface by Mr. Sanborn.

The sessions were now growing much shorter and the one in 1885 covered but two weeks and was largely devoted to Goethe. These lectures were also published.

I have not been able to find any program or account of the session of 1886. I myself was an invalid that summer and have no remembrance of attending, or of any of my friends speaking

of attending. I think there was a short session. I have the prospectus for 1887,—a two-weeks course largely devoted to Aristotle, Masters of the Drama, and Ontology,—a somewhat curious mixture.

In 1888, the School closed with a Memorial meeting to its Dean and Founder, Mr. Alcott, who had died in the spring of that year. The little Chapel has been opened a few times since for centenary exercises in honor of Emerson and Hawthorne, for a memorial service for Sanborn, etc. Today it stands untenanted, and in partial ruin, under the sighing pines (having been moved a little from its first location) waiting quietly for some further pleasant using, an object of interest to the tourist—as a part of what he ought to see on the Blue Line Tour, but little known or cared about by the present generation.

It will be observed that the most prominent lecturers at the school were Emerson, Alcott, Jones, Harris, Kedney, Snider, Davidson, Mrs. Cheney and Miss Peabody. The first three need no further word. Prof. Harris's Life, I understand, is to be written by one of our townsmen in the near future; we older people remember him well and are proud to think so great a man became one of our citizens for nearly ten years. Born in Connecticut, he was a graduate of Yale and was active all his life in educational supervision. His special study was the philosophy of Hegel, and he had many students.

Of Dr. Kedney, I can find nothing except that his home was in Faribault, Minnesota. His line was the philosophy of Ethics.

Dr. Snider is still living and has quite recently published a book. He was born in Ohio in 1841 but now resides in St. Louis. He has been always a profound student on philosophical and psychological lines. Mr. Sanborn alludes in his Reminiscences to some disagreements between Snider and Prof. Harris, and it would be singular if no two of these gentlemen had found it impossible to preserve perfect equanimity when free discussion allowed their cherished convictions to be assailed. Dr. Davidson aroused considerable contradiction in his audience it is said; he was a fine Greek scholar and a remarkably handsome man.

Mrs. Ednah Cheney was known to many of us and was one of Boston's splendid women, given to all sorts of progressive and philanthropic movements, and a friend of many eminent persons.

Miss Peabody is so closely connected with Concord that she needs no words of mine. Her long life covered ninety years of America's progress and she lived to see many of her cherished theories concerning the education of children accepted and improved upon. She was a constant attendant at the School and frequently led the discussions. Her talk was always good, though often rambling and disconnected. We younger women used to look after her appearance a little, for *dress* did not occupy much of her thoughts; her bonnet was always crooked, her collar was sometimes forgotten, and apparently she never could find but one glove at a time. I remember once sitting directly behind her and trying to get courage enough to lean forward and remedy some rather glaring discrepancy in her costume before she took the stage; at last I did it and I shall never forget her unconcerned, absent-minded smile and her "Never mind, dear!" It seemed best that somebody *should* mind on that occasion. Dear Miss Peabody was not thinking about herself. One morning when Mr. Alcott came in to the Chapel after an absence of some days because of illness, she rushed forward and threw her arms around his neck in the exuberance of her welcome. It is a sad commentary on human nature that perhaps we young hearers remember more concerning the number of peppermints she could consume during a session than her words of wisdom.

One result of having the School here was a pleasant social life outside the hours for attendance at the lectures which were usually in the forenoon and the evening. As time went on, the students found many boarding places in the town and made friends among the citizens. Many were the water picnics and the good times both in woods and on the river. In 1882, Miss Alcott writes: "The town is full of ideal speculators. Penny has a new barge; we call it the 'Blue Plato' (not the 'Black Maria') and watch it rumble by with Margaret Fullers in white muslin, and Hegels in straw hats, while stout Penny grins at the joke as he puts money in his purse."

A verse of hers was published in the New England magazine.

"Philosophers sit in their sylvan hall
And talk of the duties of man,
Of Chaos and Cosmos, Hegel and Kant,
With the Oversoul well in the van;
All on their hobbies they amble away
And a terrible dust they make;
Disciples devout both gaze and adore,
As daily they listen and bake."

As a little talk on Cosmogony was supposed to lighten up the regular course of lectures, perhaps a few of Mr. Alcott's Orphic Sayings would relieve the seriousness of this paper. They were printed in the Dial in such numbers that even Margaret Fuller, the Editor, had to cry "Hold! Enough!" Perhaps this accounts for his saying about The Dial, in characteristic phrases, "It satisfies me not; it measures not the meridian but the morning ray; the nations wait for the gnomon that shall mark the broad noon."

NORTH BRIDGE — "Here once the embattled farmers stood
And fired the shot heard round the world"

These Orphic sayings have been called "an amazement to the uninitiated and an amusement to the profane."

It may be asked by those of this generation how much of the lecture-material was ever published; nearly all the tributes to Emerson and the lectures on Goethe; and most of the material used in 1882, a Mr. Bridgman being authorized to publish a volume at that time. Some lectures were reported in part in the newspapers and I have here a little book, originally a treatise on some kind of an electric battery, but used by some student-philosopher for pasting in lectures column by column. The owner had evidently either lost interest in the matter, or had gone where we suppose philosophical problems will be less difficult and the book had drifted to Goodspeed's and thence to me. Mrs. Anagnos, Mrs. Julia Ward Howe's daughter, published in 1885 a sketch of the doings of 1883 and 1884, very serious, very flowery, and of little value except as a literary curiosity. All the names are disguised, as for instance, Mr. Alcott is Venerabilis, Miss Peabody Nestoria, etc.

I wish very much that I had attempted this account of the School while Mr. Sanborn was with us, for his mind must have been a storehouse of anecdote. I was fortunate in being one of the persons who was on speaking terms with him, perhaps because I did not belong to the Concord Bank, and had nothing to do with the sewer.

The school closed free from debt and with 31 cents in the treasury which Mr. Sanborn pocketed as his salary for ten years as Treasurer. It has been estimated that nearly 2000 persons attended the school during its ten years of existence. The best attended lectures were those of Mr. Emerson and Mrs. Julia Ward Howe; Mr. Alcott's listeners decreased steadily in numbers but never entirely deserted him.

If I have been able to make a little more definite to the younger people this phase of Concord life before they were born, and at the same time bring pleasant and amusing memories to those who shared in it, I shall feel amply repaid for having undertaken what seemed a well-nigh impossible task.

FLORENCE WHITING BROWN

ORPHIC SAYINGS

Spirit is derivative, identity; Unity is actual, merely. Identity halts in diversity.

The poles of things are not integrated; creation globed and orbed. Yet in the true Genesis, Nature is globed in the material, souls orbed in the spiritual.

The metamorphosis of the body and the metempsychosis of the soul.

Sin is the abstract side of nugatoriness.

PHILOSOPHIÆ QUÆSTOR;

OR,

DAYS IN CONCORD.

BY

JULIA R. ANAGNOS.

BOSTON:

D. LOTHROP AND COMPANY,

No. 32 FRANKLIN STREET.

Copyright by

D. LOTHROP AND COMPANY

1885

STEREOTYPED BY

C. J. PETERS AND SON, BOSTON.

CONCORD.

I love the Sages' cradle and their grave,
  I love the dwelling of their earthly joy,
The air that to their high thought pinions gave,
  The sky that's robbed them from their fond employ.

Here let me pace with gentle step and hushed,
  Where feet have trod that lead my own forever,
Where the great war of Right first nobly blushed,
  Nor Truth's new champions from the older legend sever.

Placid retreat! so shy, so leafy-veiled,
  Girt by the river that no murmur giveth;
Only the breath of long-stemmed lilies paled
  Upon its surface, where sweet shadow liveth.

Concord, I hail thee! and I prize them glad
  Who rest them 'neath thy shades in peaceful living;
The pilgrim leaves thee, lingering, yet not sad,
  To others still thy benison outgiving.

The names of places, associations, and persons of a venerable renown only have been placed in this diminutive key.

The names of the younger philosophers, as belonging more to the world's immediate present, are not translated; but the reader will easily recognize them for himself.

KEY.

HARMONY . . . . Concord.
THE ACADEME . . . . . . The School of Philosophy.
BOTOLPHSBOROUGH . . . . Boston.
VENERABILIS . . . . Mr. Alcott.
NESTORIA . . . . Miss Elizabeth Peabody.
THE ROOT AND BRANCH MEN . . . The Radical Club.
TRANSPONTON . . . . Cambridge.

PREFACE.

IN making the following unpretentious sketch of two of the seasons of the Philosophical School of Concord, a sketch written rather for enjoyment than with any idea of a reporter's résumé, I have taken as a sort of half heroine the shadowy figure of a young girl, through whose eyes the school appears in the light of a *coup d'œil*, and not of an exact scientific history.

What this slenderly-drawn personage saw and heard, in looking on as a silent spectator at one of the great dramas of modern thought and intellectual aspiration, has been told as simply as the nature of the occasions described would permit, and I shall be very glad if the portrayal (which I offer more in the sense of a free-hand drawing than of a matured dissertation) proves of interest to the reader. The picturesque elements which the school presents have struck me as only requiring a frame to complete them, and this frame I have carved with a light hand, and without the addition of superflous ornaments or gilding. Hoping, then, that, as all thinkers have earnestly watched the very important developments which have been occur-

ring at Concord for the past five years, some interest may also be awakened by this presentment of the aspect which they wore to the young traveller whom I have here made memory's mouthpiece, I will introduce the reader at once to the *milieu* presented by the Hillside chapel and its assemblages.

CHAPTER I.

1883.

THE young Eudoxia thought the village of Harmony the most simply dignified place she had ever been in, in all her life, as she drove up toward the Academe on a splendid morning in July, enjoying the glimpses which she caught of the charming, peaceful *entourage*, in which the noble institution which she was seeking as a very humble, silent disciple, had taken root and sprung up, — a plant worthy of the surroundings and atmosphere which nourished it, and had given it vigor and energy. The noble trees, the graceful girlish forms flitting about beneath them, the dwellings, with their air of ease combined with simplicity, — all blended together in that lovely atmosphere to impress the mind of the beholder with calm and happiness, the golden legacy of its king-citizen, Emerson, but recently passed away.

But what was this external impression, compared with the atmosphere of the Academe itself, now entered for the first time by this new aspirant for philosophic wealth, come to drink of the fresh fountain of a wisdom worthy of the thought-schools of the older world? The gentle Eudoxia passed the groups of smiling waiters, sitting under the sheltering trees, or chatting genially by the hospitable doorway, and, crossing the mystic, world-famed threshold, entered the philosophic Chapel.

If walls have ears, and retain impressions of all that passes within them, as a distinguished psychic scientist has said, what treasure-keepers, richer than the heavy-lintelled doors of Atreus' house, those vine-grown walls must be! All arabesqued with thought and inspiration — crusted with gems, chased by no earthly jeweller, they were full of the echoes with which the centuries were to ring.

In flocked the eager auditors, some hushed, some whispering and expectant, — in knots, single, social, or abstracted, grave or gray. There were greetings and surmises, handshakings, and inquiries for absent friends, — all the preparatory bustle which announces that a great event is coming. Gradually the looks of anticipation on the faces of the waiting audience deepened. Taller forms were seen hastening toward the speakers' door. The many-colored groups still lingering without in the charming grounds, began to seek the Chapel itself. The lively, alert little doorkeepers (children of one of the elect thinkers within) inspected tickets and admitted students. The school was about to begin. The busts on the pleasant, summery walls of pine within smiled down benignly on the seat-seekers. The fresh greeting of flowers was placed upon the desk, and the lecturer of the day, — Professor Le Sérieux, — began his discourse.

Resting very strongly on the opening sixteen verses of the Johannian Gospel (denied by some scholastics), Professor Le Sérieux proceeded to develop his philosophic doctrine of the Trinity like an opening rose.

It was such a beautiful rose, and offered to the Professor's hearers with such an angelic sweetness, that even the Unitarians in the audience did not like to refuse it, although they could not feel quite sure that the exposition was wholly free from theology, as its honored author

sincerely affirmed.

Le Sérieux was a man with all the dignity of study fresh about him. His countenance and mind alike suggested the scholastic, — nay, almost the recluse. His eloquence was at times quick, nervous, and sharp, as he displayed his clear-cut definitions and positions. As he raised the vast structures of his logic and of his philosophic imagination, Le Sérieux looked like a doctor of the early Church, half student and half saint, whom all the glories of paradise could not deter from the enjoyment of a good debate.

The whole scene was inexpressibly touching to Eudoxia. The lovely trees peeping in like nodding friends through the windows, the grassy stretches and murmuring sounds of Summer without, the younger intelligence-beaming faces, and the august snowy heads, all bent alike in rapt attention toward the eloquent speaker, — all made the scene a most marked, intense one to the eye of youth and vigor, coming in upon this little unexpected heaven, and looking down upon it with the bird's-eye glance of health and of a worldlier activity. Here was 'other-worldliness' enough, indeed. Many churches might be stocked from the faith in the transcendental, the unseen, of one of these thought-circles ; and when the earnest speaker, in his exalted mood, took into his hands a jewel lost by some vainer member of the congregation, — and left upon the desk for recognition, and expounded it as an emblem of time, the acme of uniqueness seemed to the new auditor to be attained. Then came a pause, when Nestoria, the Old Woman Eloquent, put in some silvery supports or protests, as the case might require.

No one could care whether she rebuked or praised him, if she would only forever wear that child-like, beaming smile, — that appealing,

irresistible glance, which she brought straight from heaven, whence she certainly was born, whether the other children of Men have taken their descent thence to earth (as she hypothesizes, in her all-loving, all-hoping theory of the origin and destiny of the soul) or not. Nestoria seemed to be the embodiment of Memory, — to combine within herself (like a cameo stone) the various ages of New England's truth and beauty, — to join them all in the magical circle of her own existence, like a silvery century-plant.

————

The next time that our novice entered that temple, she thought herself in Greece. For there sat Doctor Hilary, whose refreshing vigor of thought and utterance was devoted to the cult and exegesis of the mighty song of the world's most ancient bard. How he glorified Homer, and 'happified himself' in the glory of his master, it was refreshing to hear.

The liveliest of the philosophers, he was none the less true and sincere for this exhilarating quality. His mind seemed like the presence of the fair philosopher, Hypatia of old, allegorizing and interpreting from the Homeric account of the gods, or like the heart of an implicit Swedenborgian, with his 'internal meaning of the Word.'

Hilary constructed a whole temple of what he considered the true meanings and real intentions of Homer, — a city of thought in which he wandered with joyful steps, and where he expected his acolytes to follow him implicitly. He was the architect of a system of Homeric exposition, characterized both by a great poetic and philosophic ingenuity, and by a towering though amiable positiveness. He made of the ancient singer, whom the world is ever ready to pause and listen to, in the midst of all its cares

and spites and turmoils, a sister-Bible, one of a chain of four mighty links, four giant books containing the World's great words of prophecy. By the vicissitudes and developments of the Hellenic race in that great crisis of the Trojan campaign, he typified the progress of Man from individual into institutional life. His eagerness of thought and of inference had in it a certain *entrainant* character, although his hearers well might doubt, with regard to some of his interpretations, as to whether they had ever occurred to Homer himself, — whether the great singer would not have looked at them with wonder and amaze.

Hilary's method, as we have said, resembled that of Hypatia, in that he shared her enthusiasm for the inspirations not only which Homer had, but for those which they both alike imagined him to have had. They worshipped not only the Poet's divinity, but those attributes which their own hands had laid at his feet. Their attitude was almost like that of a sculptor-monk adoring in a chapel-shrine the saintly statue of his own creation.

A lady who loves to extend to her friends the hospitality which the name of her amiable city (Providence) renders so appropriate, whether at home or abroad, was waiting at the door of the Chapel with an ample conveyance to carry off guests to the home of Thoreau. Through the silvery moonlight they drove into the silvered woods, and found the hidden lake, the cairn of stones that marked the hermit's valiant effort against an unfriendly climate, that marked him for its own.* Eudoxia could not help classifying Thoreau's instinct of seclusion (original though he was) with that of hermits seen abroad, — the soli-

---

* The death of Thoreau followed eighteen months or so after an attempt which, though most interesting and poetic in itself, was yet and must ever prove, a suicidal one in our unfriendly climate.

tary monk in his cell on the summit of the Mount Lycabetus (afterward struck by lightning), — the recluse who looked down from a Mediterranean hillside, and others who loved solitude better than they loved man. She could not help asking herself what they had lost and what they had gained, these worshippers of the element of solitude which we all love at times so dearly, — what their fate would have been had they lived in the world, and whether they were ever homesick for all that they had left — whether the memory of their abnegations chained them down to regrets which even the most powerful heart cannot shut out, — and other doubts and ponderings on their behalf. Did they ever feel a reactionary impulse to that which had first directed their incloistration, and which bade them flee from the solitude which they had courted, and had once found a strong inspirer, as from an oppressive power, obstructive to the outgrowth and development of the mind's more social element (ever its highest gift, since in itself comprehending and embracing not only all other gifts, but their highest inspiration as well)? — or was the deaf and dumb goddess (Solitude) always a genial, kindly friend, and richly-rewarding hostess to these her guests and devotees?

In any case, lay the universal tribute of a friendly stone upon this cairn, that marks so long an absence of the philosopher from dependence upon his fellows: for, as the old peasant says in the song, —

'''T was a famous victory!'

The next day the Battle of Hastings was fought over again, at the School, by a gentleman whose countenance was carved in Norman arches, — and who, having chosen for the subject of his essay the contrasting of the Norman

and Anglo-Saxon elements in English literature, certainly had the caprice to be unjust toward the more immediately Germanic factor,— toward everything that dared to be English without being Norman, that is to say; for he seemed to regard Canute the Great as a sort of historical rowdy, and Alfred as merely falling somewhat short of an ignoramus. In brief, the orator of that morning should have taken for his motto,—

'Dym Sassenach,'

the reply of the old Welsh people to De Quincey.

Mr. De Rouen seemed wholly to forget the glories which Saxon England still wears in her crown among the proudest of her most treasured jewels,— undimmed by the brilliancy of the Norman gems. Where was the long row of early ascetical kings and queens, calendared for their virtues? Where their beautiful theologic sayings, full of the child-tones of the world's infancy? Where the grand battle of Harold against the king of Norway? Where the noble, undefeated glories of King Edmund Ironsides?

Next came the presence, both august and sweet, of a lady who gave an eloquent Buddhistic study,— a glimpse into the sphere of Nírvana, the embodiment of the Buddhist idea of annihilation. Beautiful verses adorned this thought-structure: but so impossible is it for Man, in himself the negation of all negations, to conceive of nothingness, even while his very breath is uttering the word, that the realization of such a condition is the Impossible for him. Man is the great positivist of the universe, the acme of reality, since he is amphibious synchronously to the material and ideal worlds. He does not visit the two elements alternately, like some vast pachyderm of the Nile; but

draws the air of both with every breath.

Genially as they enjoyed the noble essay of Firma, and the shining smile and warm, friendly presence of the giver, the audience did not seem converted to a wish for annihilation. On the contrary, they appeared extremely flourishing, and went to a musical party that very afternoon. The music gave rise to philosophic discussion, quite as eagerly attended to as the art which called it forth. No piece was considered complete without the ringing out of a silvery voice in exposition of its meaning; and the blending of the metaphysical with the artistic and social thought-factors on this occasion, was felicitous in the extreme.

Sometimes, in the leisure hours, sketchers from the School would stray with reverent steps up to Sleepy Hollow, a favorite resort of those who sought solitude, or who wished to find conversation in the whispering of the pines.

Ay! Visit them as often as ye list, those graves august, and don your brightest robes to enliven their rest, gentle wanderers. Bring flowers for the tomb of the great name which there remains unwritten,* in vocal dumbness. Climb that fair hill, lightly as the bird climbs its cool, towering pines to listen to their voices aloft, and stand among mourning monuments over the bodies of the departed, thyself a joyous monument that towers to hail their souls.

Go on, and tread with awe-hushed pace the stone-laid footpath to the Old Manse, that gave its name to the sweetest book ever brought by elves and angels out of the realms of fiction.

* Emerson.

Here, too, was spent the honeymoon of the ideal pair, the romance-weaver Thorncroft and his bride. Here Una's name is written in diamond on the pane. Here pen and pencil lovingly wrought together, wielded by loving hands. Here, too, thou once wander'dst with Nestoria with the marble curls, to the river's brink, and heard'st from the lips of Age all the wise sweetness of the child-soul guided by the master-mind. Here thou saw'st the gentle Saint Scholastica, mild and surprised amid her honors. Now wander onward to where the first blood of the old conflict was shed, and the Minute Man towers above the spot of his divine struggle, eternized in the artist's breathing bronze.

> 'He left his life that we might live,
> He gave us all was his to give:
> His home, his farm, his child, his wife,
> And fell amid the sacred strife.
>
> 'And if that strife should come again,
> That clarion-call to blood and pain,
> He from his grave would rise once more,
> And drive the foeman from our shore.'

Remember, too, how the tall theocratic form,* known in childhood's far-off mists, towering above them like Mount Washington above its clouds, used to say with infinitely more pride than in the Jovian bolts of sacred invective which none could wield and hurl like himself, 'My grandfather took down his gun to fight at Lexington.' Could that simple grandfather have beheld him, his mighty descendant, girding him for a yet more glorious fray, in which all chains were to be broken, and the suffering Slave go free, gladder yet would have been his heart, and readier his hand.

As to that strife of yore, first waked at Concord, generous France sent her warm-blooded legions, her gallant cavaliers, so she sends to-day to Concord a *chevalier preux* whose generous

ardor wakes the native hearts to yet warmer love for their great Sage,* whose ghost beckons its worshippers from afar.

But we anticipate.

Nestoria discussed Milton at the School, and a severe tournament followed her mild address. Milton was arraigned as the poet of Calvinism by a new-comer, who was, of course, rebuked by the philosophers on behalf of Milton, and by one of their number (who thought Milton shallow,) on behalf of Calvin himself.

The son of the great novelist-magician, whom Harmony and the world will always revere and admire, gave a very interesting, well-conceived essay on the writing of Romance. Young Thorncroft showed the same vigor in the analysis of Romance which his great father had shown in its construction. His was a striking presence, his deep voice, with a touch of pathos to match that which dwelt upon his face, had fine, arresting tones. His whole bearing was marked and remembered, and all the Harmonians always flocked, when he spoke, to hear the child of their mighty romancist.

One day the presence of Margaret Fuller was invoked in a conversation devoted to her honor.

Could she only have heard it all, could she only have sat among them, only have broken the spell of tragedy which cut her off forever from the world! But she died in the full glory and maturity of her power, as was pointed out long since, before any one could say, 'She has diminished!'

'So, too,' thought Eudoxia, 'may it perhaps be with the School' (whose wider range of ac-

------

* Theodore Parker.

* Emerson, in 1884.

tivity at this time threatened to be drawing to its close), 'No one can look on and say, if she die in the full meridian of her powers, "She has diminished!" And, if the philosophers should be drawn to follow their work in other spheres, the School will yet live, like the form of Margaret Fuller, in the hearts of all who have ever heard its voice.'

Thus thought Eudoxia one morning; but that night she dreamed of the Phœnix, with the light of eternity shimmering in gold and silver upon its wings; and she awoke with fresh faith in Valhalla.

Doctor Michaelmas came up one day and gave a poetic discourse, on the whole. The doctor had been the president of an older thought-circle in Botolphsborough (the Root and Branch Men,) whose members, with less structural completeness in the processes of their mental architecture than that displayed at Harmony, had always distinguished themselves by great breadth of pinion and fulness of intellectual scope.

Eudoxia became more and more firmly convinced that an institution of this order must not be allowed to die out. Viewed from some points, it seemed to her almost more important than a church.

Of course, it was essential that sermons and sacraments should go on, as important mileposts, pointing, like the resurrection of the Saviour, to immortality beyond; but one especial church (*i. e.*, parish) was in reality a monarchy, while here certainly was

'THE NEW REPUBLIC.'

The most perfect courtesy, and a beautiful, sincere ignoring of inequality, prevailed in the School. The Alpine summits kindly conversed with the little hills. She felt also that it would be good for the champions of theology and those of philosophy to intermingle more freely. Each system had its own annals and archives, which would enrich the other.

Most strongly of all, it seemed to her that it would be insincere to pray for the coming of the kingdom of Heaven, and then to let such a heavenly institution as this die out.

She thought less regarding self; but, having once breathed that 'diviner air,' she felt that the world could never seem the same to her as before going there. The solitude of the soul was broken.

Labor seemed to grow light for all who were associated with these seekers after the divine idea, — even for those who good-naturedly purveyed for their more material well-being. Even the rustics of that pleasant region wore a certain simple garb of dignity, all their own.

The Hillside Chapel stood on rising ground, like an aspiration.

The charm of the former home of Venerabilis, the Orchard House, was very great. Embowered in trees, roomy and ample, it looked a combination of home and study-house most grateful to the eye.

Not far away rose the exquisite home of the vanished great one already so often named, seeming to the delighted guest a temple of loveliness; and, on the other side, separated from the Orchard House by a whispering wood, was the home of the fairy of America, the wizard in whose tales, perhaps, is found New England's truest history.

They were heart-delighting, these homes, shrines of visitation to some faithful pilgrims.

Eudoxia felt that she stood on an elevated oasis (if the expression may be employed), above the

world, on whose sordid pursuits and ambitions she looked down with a wonder and amazement never felt before. A beautiful simplicity of aim, an entire absence of any clinging rags of worldliness, characterized all who had come to worship wisdom in this higher clime.

A tribute to the brilliancy and power, perhaps, of the principal actors in the heavenly scene, rather than to the quality above described, was seen in the ardent interest felt by people in the outer world regarding what transpired in that inner, upper circle. They would hang on their words, perhaps from afar, — wish that they could listen personally, and daily look for more.

Our novice-friend felt a certain pride in her own discovery of the new Pantheon of the West, which had sent so many delegates to this Congress of the soul, and which is, by a singular paradox of fate, in so great measure *terra incognita* to the East. Here were great halls of thought, and long galleries of portraits, which to her New England compatriots usually were undreamed of. It seemed to her as if she had discovered a Mammoth Cave of thought.

Nothing was more interesting than the fact of its magical subterranean connection with the Eastern thought-centre of Harmony, which had helped (cryptologically, as it were), to create it, — while Botolphsborough and its friend and neighbor, Transponton, had only vaguely realized the fact of its existence.

Sometimes Eudoxia feared that an eclipse might take place in the thought-firmanent, when too extended a divergency of opinion impended among the thinkers. Instead of such a catastrophe, however, only a more shining planetary conjunction ensued as a result.

On her return into the social life of everyday circles once more, our heroine began to realize that she had been on a far journey, to lands whose full scope and climate were unknown to the outer world.

She seemed to herself like a sort of dumb Dante, who could not explain what he had seen, and yet who knew that it was all there.

CHAPTER II.

1884.

THE EMERSON SEASON.

'As when a father dies, his children draw
  About the empty hearth, their loss to cheat
  With uttered praise and love, and oft repeat
His all-familiar words with whispered awe,
The honored habit of his daily law,
  Not for his sake, but theirs whose feebler feet
  Need still that guiding lamp, whose faith less sweet
Misses that tempered patience without flaw ;

So do we gather round thy vacant chair,
  In thine own elm-roofed, amber-rivered town,
Master and father ! For the love we bear,
  Not for thy fame's sake, do we weave this crown,
And feel thy presence in the sacred air
  Forbidding us to weep that thou art gone.'

With these words from a Jewish maiden, the next season of the Academe opened, a year after, — a breathing of aspiration and invocation, which gave the keynote to the assembly, as they sat around to raise the silvery ghost of the great dead.

The fair Rebecca's devout and loving tribute was listened to with tenderest thoughts and tearful eyes, and all hearts responded with a tuneful consonance to her gentle, ardent words.

As Eudoxia turned her eyes toward the casement, that the passing breeze might dry her rising tears, the birds and boughs which Emerson had loved so well said and sang to her:

EMERSON.

The moonlight of thy silver brow,
Methinks I see it, even now;
The tender music of a voice,

Which but to hear was to rejoice,
Still rings for me through distant years,
Undimmed by Time, unwhelmed by tears.
The Hero's message, "Ever Dear!" *
The World would echo, could'st thou hear:
He spoke for that full sphere of hearts,
Whence thy sweet image ne'er departs:
Nor shall it ever — Exquisite
As Dawn, ere Day hath grown too bright, --
Such was the light thy spirit shed,
Such the mild halo of thy head,
Too thoughtful e'en to claim its crown,
Too gentle e'en on foes to frown,
Such thy fair spirit's atmosphere,
The greatly pure, the sweetly clear.

* The dying Sumner said: "Tell Emerson I always loved him."

Gleanings from the exquisite diary of Venerabilis followed. These had everywhere the magic, sacred touch — that which gives ease, and never weariness to the reader : that which distinguishes the delicately chased silver from the rough ore.

A halo spread over the atmosphere of the reverent assembly. They felt that once again Emerson, the man with the rainbow smile, stood in their midst.

That smile, proclaiming the death and end of all the storms and troubles the world has ever seen, was an angel's greeting to the world from God.

It contained loveliest promises, of which we are now reaping the splendid fulfilment in the present progress of to-day's growing and advancing world.

———

All the old feeling of coming into another atmosphere came back to Eudoxia with her delightful, long-anticipated return to Harmony. The air was clear and full of angels' voices.

From all the different avenues and branches of Philosophy to which the guests of the year before had been invited, came forth a note of homage to Emerson, which, blending into a majestic unity, rose in a chorus of far-reaching beauty to seek the skies.

The speakers all came forward, and took the spirit of Emerson by the hand, as it were, — each greeting the august guest by the name by which he was dearest to each:

'I 'll call thee King, — Hamlet, — father, — Royal Dane!'

It was the opposite of Shakespeare's terrific scene before the dawn of Bosworth, when each of the dead ghosts comes, and clasps Richard to him by some more and more hideous accusation. Here it was the living, instead, who visited the ghost, and called him by all divinest names — king, and friend, and prophet!

The gentle priest comes too, and claims this all-beloved spirit as his own. He takes his hand and fastens it again to the altar from which conscience (falsest of demons when she chooses to be out of tune) had dragged the gentle Emerson away. He says, reversing the Bible word, —

'Thou wentest forth from among us, and yet thou *wert* of us!

'Thou wert all too mild to rend even the veil of the Temple, as thou rushedst forth into the outer air. Thou didst not even fray the fringe which blindlings stigmatize as ceremony. Our priests now swing their censers towards thee, as towards the pictures of the saints. For art thou not their image? And all the fairer because thou knewest it not?'

A carriage passes, and the shadowed smile of suffering Venerabilis is seen from within, as his faithful acolyte-friends greet him.

De Rouen, whose ultra-Normanism offended the ear last year (in spite of his good will), now uses his Norman architecture to build high

a stately temple in Emerson's honor, piling it to the clouds, till his language takes on, in many ears, almost the tone of the master whose name he invokes.

The discussions of that morning bring with them an energy that awakens in the mental atmosphere of the place thoughts of fire, and turns the torch of the animated discussion into a halo for the head of Emerson.

———————

Next day the gentle Musa came up from the far seaside, where Narragansett's blue waters greet Atlantic; and, looking out with her eyes of ocean-color from beneath her fair brow, all of snow,—gave her glowing, opal-like tribute of tenderness and delicacy to Emerson's great memory. Her greater works seemed to the on-looker to be peering over her shoulder, like mighty columnar shadows, listening to her gentle, silvery voice. They seemed to whisper:

'We, too, are of thy family.'

But no fairer act was Musa the mild ever seen to do, than this gentle laying of a blooming, living wreath upon the high altar of her great compeer, who had taken her hand in youth,—even as she now, all flower-crowned with happy years of achievement and adornment, took his cold hand of marble.

———————

Sunday steals in with its startling, all-pervasive stillness, seeming the spectre of the group of days. She lays her finger on the busy hand that relaxes not, and says, 'Toil not: for I am come. Therefore be happy.'

Van Antwerp's eloquence flocks the little Anglican sanctuary. He has brought his message from the far South, and it is a celestial one. He fully responded to the question which is ever in the soul regarding the Hereafter.

Such a sermon carries its own pearl of great price with it, whether all hear it, or whether it is shut up in the pearl-shell of a little chapel.

———————

Flowers and garlands heralded the morning on which two fair ladies (fairer than with the fairness of youth) were to give the inspirations which they had each received from the great Master, whom all had gathered together there to honor.

Their discourses, to both of which the listeners attended with rapt countenances, harmonized like the chime of two lovely bells, each of which has, nevertheless, its own song, yet to each of which it would be impossible to give forth a note which should not be in perfect harmony with that of its twin sister.

Firma spoke first; and her clear accent, splendid head, piercing eye, and decisive presence, rendered her on all occasions a speaker upon all of whose words it is especially easy to attend. Her tribute of retrospection glowed with all the energy of her own firm, fine nature. Firma would have appreciated Emerson just as strongly, loyally, and thoroughly, had she been born a thousand years his junior, instead of in the next generation to his own.

Firma never knew, in her so proudly organized and constructed nature, one shade or shadow of disloyalty toward any cause or person she revered. All the more refreshing, from this cause, were her enthusiasm and her homage. She seemed to bring all the beauty and holiness of Emerson with her on that inspired, happy morning. It clothed her about like a mantle of purple and gold.

Hers was a nature to realize to the fullest all the augustness of her Master's; and, with her strong, majestic presence, bringing out in yet greater relief the excellence of her speech, it

seemed as if some firmly sculptured figure from the groups that upheld a memorial monument of memory and glory had spoken.

Sweet Nestoria, though bearing on her head the silver crown of so many honored years, bravely began to deliver her thesis in strong, well-pitched tones. Her voice was clearer than when last it had been heard within those walls. She stood and spoke like to an aged Mnemosyne; and could say with truth of those times of which she narrated, —

'Et quorum pars magna fui.'

She had been in the companionship of Emerson, as of Channing; had sat at the feet of both Gamaliel and St. Paul, and could 'tell the wondrous story' of all their gestes and speech. Nestoria was tended with an exquisitely delicate care by the philosophers, — all her juniors by at least a generation or two. She was listened to with tearful interest, as if her mind had been the only archive of the precious past; and all hung most eagerly upon her lips.

She had seen the mighty generation in whose van Emerson stood; had heard them, as Earth shall never see or hear them again. She had been their companion, friend, pupil, fellow-student, had been a sympathetic onlooker at their joys and sorrows, had received all the suggestion and consecration of the lives the world still worships: and, freely having received of the wine of their presence and existence, she freely, nay, generously, gave it forth to the waiting, listening echoes of a later — a less privileged — Age.

That Age looks back with tearful homesickness to the days when it was yet a stranger on the earth.

'Why was I not born then?'

It cries, —

'Why could I not have seen them, known them, called them mine?'

Patience, O Age! They spoke for thee. Of thee they prophesied, to thee they sang, from thee they await their most peerless pæans and unbroken homage.

Therefore, O Age! take heart of grace unto thyself. Thou art not, shalt not be, a dwarf among the eras. For thou, too, hast thy mission among the times and centuries. Thou art not the great thought-creative age of fifty years ago, nor yet the hero age of twenty years syne; but thou art an age of the development of the many, in contradistinction to the time of the few: and thy chorus shall give forth grandeur, blended with guilelessness.

Very powerful was the song of Emerson, as heard on these occasions, when the speakers brought large, sparkling draughts from that perennial fount of inspiration.

EMERSON AND GRAY.

Alǎcer, one of Emerson's own acolytes, a most faithful disciple-friend, arose to antidote the absurd onslaught made by Matthew Arnold since last the philosophers had met together.

Would that he could likewise have erased the record of that most futile attack from Arnold's own shield, with that same breath wherewith he blew away his batteries into thinnest air. It had been an act of double magnanimity; and it was sad to us Transatlantics to see one so honored as Arnold (nay, may we not say, so threefold honored, in father, brother, and self?) come over the ocean to us empty-handed, or bearing a gift that was less than nothing in his hands.

Welcome as was the apparition of Alǎcer, in the character of refuter and champion, nevertheless was it a less pleasant challenge when he turned upon a dead knight, gone to his reward

ere the century dawned, — the gentle Gray.

While this satiric stroke was given in order to exalt in yet bolder relief all the mental heroism, in its grand, perennial freedom from all bathos, of his own hero, Emerson, — yet to pull down the statue of one god in order to erect that of another must ever be an irrelevant iconoclasm.

Alăcer had the gentle elder-brother poet of his all-beloved Emerson at an unfair advantage in the first citation which he elected to make from his works; yet even from these too keenly chosen excerpts there peeped forth lines of a commanding beauty, to chide and silence all impeachment, made with however loyal an intent, of Gray's really great, ever-enduring loveliness and beauty of spirit. The fine quotation which Alăcer afterwards read, to raise again his slaughtered victim, only served to show how unnecessary had been the wounding him, — was not needed to set forth that Gray was fair, for we all knew that of old. The gentle poet need not tremble. For Emerson, however, Alăcer is the perfection of the dauntless banner-bearer, holding his master's ideals aloft with an unswerving hand.

GOETHE AND EMERSON.

Now comes Hilary again from the West, and with a vigorous counter-action overturns the thoughts which would slay Goethe on the altar of Emerson.

This appearance of Hilary in the character of a knight-errant was most opportune. One star differeth from another star in glory. Then why mangle Goethe in order to exalt Emerson yet further? Would you make of the gentle lamb himself a butcher toward one whom he never thought to rivalize?

It was all very well for Samuel to hew Agag to pieces before the Lord: but if Agag had been as nice as Samuel, not to say quite as clever, the world would have thought less of him for so doing.

Firma also stood up well and nobly for Goethe, the great Greek god of the modern world.

Firma belonged to those who would emancipate Goethe, the great ancient and modern in one (who, as the generations recede, still shines on them like an unset sun, from the West), from the prison of Prejudice, that vast house of captivity, over which should certainly be written:

'Lasciáte ogni speranza,
Voi ch' entrate.'

To know that Emerson is of the truly Great Ones must only ever serve to remind, in this connection, that Truth (the friend of all the True) and her deathlessly devoted disciple, Goethe, are great likewise.

EMERSON AMONG THE POETS.

Gallus, on the evening of this day, rose, youthful and enthusiastic, to pour forth his own abundant testimony of gratitude and delight in Emerson. A perfect 'Hymn of Praise,' to use the Mendelssohnian dialect.

Young and erect, with a noble brow and speaking eyes, Gallus stood upon the little platform of the chapel to bear his witness, in his own fluent, beautiful mother-tongue, and looked a strange transplantation to our shores.

(Mozoomdar, the more distant exotic, the Hindoo littérateur, had not come from his far-off India, to grace the pale assembly with the darker coloring and vivid thought of a warmer clime than ours.)

Gallus was himself a poet, and his unwritten oration (traced only on the hidden tablets of his mind,) was all beflowered with exquisite

leaflets from his own field of verse, — gems which he did not acknowledge as of his own origination, modestly leaving the fact of his authorship in them dumb; though, like all things silenced, it awoke in echoes the next day.

Beside him on the dais sat Fitz-Caledon, who, when the address was over, gave an able and very interesting commentary in English; and, being requested to recite one of his own Scottish ballads, gave a part of the exquisite old ballad of the sea, — *Sir Patrick Spens*, always so fresh in its historic allusions, as well as in the tragic pictures which it paints upon the tablets of that quaint, sad time.

'I am the Doubter and the Doubt,
  And I the hymn the Brahmin sings.'

What though they may read to us kindred lines from the Hindoo books? Was not the inspiring poetry which pervades them still in great part Emerson's own? Emerson only borrowed, like the jeweller who wishes to reset the precious stone in more exquisite encasements.

That Thoreau, too, was a poet, and that Channing likewise wore the undying bays, who can doubt, who was present on that Olympian morning, when the lays of the august trio were read? Let the three stand together, and the rays of each illumine and lend to the other. Hand in hand, let them walk the woods still, whether as solid or as faded shadows!

Up to the high, skyey window one looked, while the breath of the wild flowers seemed to exalt itself, and try to rise as high as the casement itself, — or through the aperture all filled with the green shadows of the towering pines, like tall foresters clothed in ever-living green.

Why Channing's poems, all alive with beauty and a daring, lovely quaintness of expression, — published in thinking Botolphsborough ere the last forty years of war and strife, politics and martyrdom, earthquakes and tidal waves had passed over the groaning earth, have never since been read, remains a problem. None could give the key. Here was true beauty: but where was the eye to see it? What is blindness? What the voluntary blindling's loss? How touchingly might such a poet exclaim to his deaf generation, without a shadow of ear for music so far as his singing is concerned, 'Have I been so long among you, and yet have ye not known me?'

With loving regret was the time devoted to drawing down among us Emerson's exquisite presence once more brought to a close. It had been a season of enchantment mingled with holiness, like the poet-philosopher's own smile; and we could no more bear to see it fade away than to bid farewell to that world-conquering smile, — the dawn, as we have said, of better days for the weary planet.

DAYS DEVOTED TO THE DISCUSSION OF IMMORTALITY.

Now blossoms forth the noble tree of Thought into the glorious field of Immortality, — so that there is, in real truth, no parting from the reverentially-loved figure, after all: but only a meeting with the spirit of Emerson upon a yet higher plane, where the other angels of the just made perfect may be beheld and worshipped together with him.

Athānatos appeared from Transponton to

bear his witness, on the first morning devoted to the discussion of the noble problem of Immortality, — the utterance of whose very name wakens echoes all through Heaven's far-off corridors, where sweet spirits listen, to hear if they be remembered or forgot.

Bravely Athānatos avouched for the Testament, so new even in its present age (and only just beginning, like a century plant which should bloom once in a *thousand* years, to cast off, sleepily rousing to its vast awakening, the husks of misconception — the tangles of souls sent to a hell, did not the good Creator forbid one, through linguistic ignorance), left by his Master to His world. Athānatos carried his hearers with him, both in plaudits and in tears, as he pursued his touching discourse. Withal, his exposition was luminously exact and in brilliant accordance with all the dictates of Science. Yet could it not strip itself of the tenderness of the pastor of the old school, still a father to his people. May they never be orphaned!

Numerous tributes to the same noble cause were afterward given. Professor Le Sérieux launched forth into a rapid, dazzling exegesis, of vast profundity, in the course of which he alluded very interestingly to the great atomic theory.

Fitz-Caledon rose, and vindicated Immortality from the implied necessity of the support of Religion. In himself Fitz-Caledon was also an ardent defender of the new Revelation. Nevertheless he conceived that the fact of Immortality ought to be able to stand solidly upon its own basis, neither asking nor receiving aid from the religious powers.

There was a vast fund of consolation in this entirely new position, hitherto unheard of in the spheres of metaphysic disquisition, — as

well as a whole world of thought. One word drawn from so deep a source of conviction, and so full of faith, had in it power enough to scatter all the armies of Skepticism.

———

Van Antwerp disagreed with Doctor De Forest regarding the vitality of the necessity of the abolition of capital punishment, and its concomitant system of rewards and prizes in the hereafter toward which Athānatos had been leading the little world within the chapel, on that bright day on which the discussion of Immortality was opened to the ear of a World which sometimes falls asleep to the fact that it does not sparkle as a solitary gem beneath the velvet curtains of the skies: but that it is rather one of a family, albeit it forgets often to listen to the footsteps of its sister-planets, as they wander on together through the immeasurable halls of space.

———

By a curious coincidence, Transponton sent, on the evening of that self-same day, another of her delegates, McMasters, to plead for the great gem of Immortality, which the heavens have never refused to rain down upon the Earth like a great and precious tear-drop, which shall make amends for all the miseries endured in the waiting for it.

McMasters might with justice be denominated a stalwart. Not one iota of materialistic derivation was he willing to bate, even in so spiritual an assembly; but, having stated the case of his belief in these particulars, he gave a very glowing and well-developed peroration on Immortality, of which he hoped to be a partaker, although he had called both himself and his race by all manner of names, borrowed from a menagerie with which Barnum would

no doubt be very glad to have dealings, — at the beginning of his discourse.

McMasters' kindly — nay, even gentle — face, rosy and good-natured as that of a child, belied his resolute onslaught in behalf of saurians and elephants. He might, indeed, conscientiously believe it to be his duty to defend them; but the question which arose in the onlooking mind was whether, in avoiding all cruelty to animals, the powerful advocate of evolutionary principles were not committing a certain cruelty toward men, himself included? Here Science steps in, and, laying her great hand warningly on the questioner's shoulder, says: —

'Let Cæsar manage his own affairs; and do you deal with the spiritual world.'

Now was old Father Time speedily rolling the hours of inspiration and enjoyment toward the close of that high festival.

Wistfully asked the pilgrims if the curtain were to be closed forever on its joyful solemnities. Would its directors give Past or Future as its watchword? — Memory or Hope, the Recording or the Prophetic Angel?

Welcome whisperings then were heard of another season, in which the lovers of true thought might again assemble in this little home of truth and wisdom. All intent of putting a period to the discussions which had attracted so many listeners and enjoyers from so far, was silenced by the evident desire on the part of delegates from all thoughtful communities for its continuance. A chorus from all the well-wishers of the truest and purest thought ought to respond to this decision, so eminently in the interests of the higher progress, and of the furtherance of a more exquisite culture and of a refined, aspiring taste.

Dr. Van Antwerp, whose thought came next in the rapidly revolving kaleidoscope of mental contrasts and colors, opinions, shades, and differences, both pleaded for the great cause of Immortality, and exhorted eloquently on its behalf; and was listened to with the interest and response which his powerful word was well fitted to command.

The essay of Fitz-Caledon was like some vast columnar front of a Grecian temple, yet withal had something of the fortress-quality in it likewise. Fitz-Caledon claimed for Immortality the privilege of standing on a basis of its own, nor stretching toward religion the hand which asks a helping hand.

His oratory, all bristling with strong philosophic facts, as lightly handled and placed as if they had been toys instead of towers, partook of the nature of the forest, in that every inch of ground was covered by some powerful growth of fact and deduction, and with the vast experience of widely extending and overspreading demonstration and corroboration.

But the last day must dawn at length, bring with it as many regrets as it may.

The certainty, however, of the School's renewing its hospitable invitation for the ensuing Summer was now assured, and its guests were therefore gladdened with the thought of a return to those delightful shades, and to the voices of truth and beauty resounding to the ears of the faithful in that abode of the higher wisdom.

The eloquent Le Sérieux speaks on the closing morning to welcoming ears and minds

And now, how can we thank Harmony enough for the glorious opportunity of listening to the noble philosophic presentments with which the last ten days have been so full? How leave a tribute on her altars 'that can express the half' of our gratitude for all that she has given us? 'T is but a poor garland that mortal hand can weave to tell her fame; but it is offered heartily.

Good-bye to little Eudoxia; but not good-bye to all that she has seen and told us of; for that is undying and 'eternal in the heavens.'

PHILOSOPHY.

Tell me not that she is silent, tell me not that she is dead,
Tell me not that she would leave us, thousand blessings on her head!

Tell me not that she is silent, tell me not that she is dead,
All the groves of ancient sweetness shed their laurels for her meed!

Tell me not that she is silent, tell me not that she is dead,
Show me else all music, sculpture, poetry to Hades sped!

Tell me not that she is silent, tell me not that she is dead;
Rather say the sun is gloomy, and the gentle stars have fled!

Henry D. Thoreau, age 39.
From a daguerreotype by B. D. Maxham, of Worcester, Mass., taken in 1856.

MEMORABILIA

of

THOMAS DAVIDSON

Selected chapters from the Memorials of Thomas Davidson, the Wandering Scholar, collected and edited by Wm. Knight, London, 1907.

CHAPTER IX

THE NEW YORK BRANCH OF THE NEW FELLOWSHIP

One of the first things that Davidson did when he reached New York was to found an American "Fellowship of the New Life"; not exactly a branch of the English society of that name, but one similar in character, aims, and tendency. It was founded in 1884, and as its prospectus contains a declaration of principles, differing in some points from that set down in the London programme, it may be reproduced with advantage, along with an official statement on the religion of the Fellowship, and a letter from its founder concerning the "Vita Nuova."

I. DECLARATION OF PRINCIPLES

NAME AND DOMICILE

The Name of the society shall be THE FELLOWSHIP OF THE NEW LIFE, and its Domicile shall be wherever two or three persons animated by its spirit shall unite and meet.

SPIRIT

The Spirit of the Fellowship, in all its sayings and doings, shall be intelligent love, that love which Jesus meant when he commanded his disciples to love one another, that love whereof the fruits are "joy, peace, long-suffering, gentleness, goodness, faith, meekness, temperance," and perfect purity and simplicity of life.

PURPOSES

The Purposes of the Fellowship shall be the cultivation of character in the persons of its members, and the attainment of whatever follows from high character. The ideal of character shall be perfect purity or holiness, including perfect intelligence, perfect love and freedom — that freedom which springs from perfect obedience to the divine laws of the spirit. Truth and love alone shall have authority in the Fellowship, and in all cases the material and fleshly shall be subordinated to the spiritual.

METHOD

The Method of the Fellowship shall be coöperation for the ends of holiness. Unwilling to stand or fall with the success or failure of any practical undertaking, it shall not, as a body, identify itself with such, but shall seek to remain a center of religious life and inspiration. At the same time, it shall encourage its members to form, in connection with it, and in its spirit, societies which shall do practical work in the way of lecturing, teaching, discussing and in other ways aiding in the elevation of all whom they can reach.

BRANCHES

The Fellowship may have branches wherever persons are willing to unite on the basis of its spirit, purpose, and method. Each branch shall regulate its own affairs.

II. THE RELIGION OF THE FELLOWSHIP OF THE NEW LIFE

THE FELLOWSHIP OF THE NEW LIFE is essentially a religious society, that is, a society whose members seek to order their lives in accordance with the Supreme Will (by whatever name it may be called —God, Holiness, Intelligence, Love), in so far as that can in any way be ascertained. Its religion, however, in contradistinction to other religions, is purely one of attitude; attitude of the whole human being, mind, affections, will. It seeks, through the persons of its members, to be receptive toward all truth, whatever its mediate source, responsive with due love toward all worth, and active toward all good. It believes that this triple attitude comprises the whole duty of man, and that this belief is at once the all-sufficient and unassailable creed. For, surely, no one can doubt that every human being ought to pursue all truth, to love duly all that is lovable, and to further, as far as he may, all good. And, again, the man who did these three things, would be performing his whole duty as a man. In one word, it may be said that the religion of the Fellowship consists of a determined endeavor to know well, to love well, and to do well.

In endeavoring to know well, the members of the Fellowship, far from depending solely on individual reason or experience, seek light

and aid from every quarter; from every age and people; from religion, science, and philosophy; from nature and art; from reason and faith. Knowing that their own mental and moral status, the very conceptions by which they interpret experience, and the thought by which they unite them into a known world, as well as the language by which they express all this, are not their own products, but are the outcome of a process of mental unfolding dating back far beyond the dawn of recorded history, and are to be understood only through a knowledge of this process, they can look only with pity upon those persons who, having no comprehensive acquaintance with the history of human conceptions, rashly undertake, with their crude notions, to pronounce upon the great problems of life and mind. They are, therefore, neither dogmatists, skeptics, nor agnostics, but reverent students of the world of nature and of mind, seeking to supplement their own experience and conclusions with the experience and conclusions of the serious men and women of all time. Inasmuch as they are not called upon to accept any special beliefs, but only to be honest and circumspect with themselves in accepting any belief whatever, it follows that no honest belief or unbelief need prevent any one from being a member of the Fellowship. The man who finds cogent reasons for believing in the doctrines of transubstantiation and the immaculate conception, and the man who finds it impossible to attach any definite meaning to the word *God*, are equally in their place in the Fellowship, provided they are equally sincere. But sincerity is not possible apart from a living desire for ever deeper insight, and a sympathy with those who sincerely hold opinions different from our own. There is no sincerity in accepting or maintaining a belief that has not been tested to the limits of our powers. The proper names for such acceptance are credulity and fanaticism. Knowing how often it happens that old and long-exploded doctrines reappear in new forms and become for a time fashionable, by reason of popular ignorance, the members of the Fellowship are not liable to be found among the followers of new prophets, or the purveyors of patent remedies for social ills. Their aim is to stand firm on a basis of knowledge amid the tumultuous sea of conflicting popular prejudices.

In their endeavor to love well, the members of the Fellowship seek to love wisely, — not only to cultivate the power to love, but to distribute love in proportion to the spiritual worth of things. Just as only a feeling, thinking being can truly love, so only a feeling, thinking being can properly be loved; and the deeper and broader the feeling and thought which being has, the more it is a being, the more it is capable of loving, the more worthy to be loved. Mere indiscriminate loving, vague philanthropic sentiment, and enthusiasm for abstractions, such as

humanity, law, etc., it rejects as unprofitable and wasteful. True love is that which seeks the highest good of its object, and rejoices in that good. It is merely another name for a desire to realize and abide with perfection.

By doing good, the Fellowship means acting in accordance with the best knowledge and the widest, most discriminating love. It is only when a man has his head and heart well trained that he can act well. Without a comprehension of the end of all action, and of the various tendencies of different actions, he will act blindly from prejudice, passion, or impulse; without well-regulated sympathies, all his actions will have a wrong emphasis and hence be abortive. Such wrong emphasis we see in all those philanthropic movements whose chief aim is men's physical comfort and the indiscriminate removal of that powerful natural corrective, suffering. With such movements the Fellowship, realizing how beneficial suffering may be, has no sympathy. Better to suffer and be strong, than to be comfortable and weak. While the Fellowship seeks to foster coöperation for good works, it hopes for its best results from individual character and effort. It seeks to avoid all publicity and to do its work quietly and unobtrusively in the hearts of men. It calls upon each of its members to be a living power for good, not only in one way or in one connection, but in all ways and in all connections, in the smallest things as well as in the greatest. Its ultimate aim is the good man and the good woman, the intelligent, loving, vigorous character, that seeks good and good alone.

Such is the Religion of THE FELLOWSHIP OF THE NEW LIFE, such attitude its only bond of union.

III. EXTRACT FROM A LETTER FROM MR. DAVIDSON CONCERNING THE NEW LIFE

The way to begin the New Life, I believe, is to try to forget oneself, one's sorrows, one's annoyances; to count oneself happy, if he can have the approval of a good conscience and the sense of having furthered the good. The New Life, as I conceive it, is a new attitude of the intelligence, the feelings, the will — a desire to lay aside all prejudice and to know the absolute truth, a wide, sweet sympathy, recoiling at no sin, no suffering, no hardness of heart, but only at selfishness and meanness and lying, a firm resolution to do the best, as far as that is known, in the spirit of love. Such a life, *I know*, is worth living. It is a life in which all wounds soon heal, and all scars are but brands of victory — legal tender for future blessedness.

But the New Life is, in its outward form, more than this. It is an association for the *cultivation* of true insight, boundless sympathy, and devoted helpfulness. It is the absence of these that makes the old life so blind, so dreary and lonely, so unblest. Every human being ought to be a providence to every other, ready, as far as his powers go, to solve every dark problem, sympathize with every joy and every sorrow, however deep and agonizing, and satisfy every need. We are still living in willful ignorance of our own nature and in barbarous isolation with respect to each other. We wither in silent pain because we have not confidence in each other. In our agony we invent a God to do for us what we are too miserable and selfish to do for each other. We are so sluggish that we try to make a virtue of faith, instead of laboring in earnest to find out and communicate the truth. We are so selfish that we allow our neighbor to suffer, when we have the means to help him. We are so low spiritually that we doubt the infinite possibilities of being, and sink down into a contented or discontented materialism. We do not rise to a firm and abiding sense of our own dignity and infinite worth. All this, I hope, will be altered in the New Life, whether I succeed in doing anything to further it or not. I have only a clear insight as to what is necessary and a desire to do the best I can. I see that, if ever life is to be again wholesome and inspiring, we must have a new social order and a new education; an order in which each shall feel the burdens of all, and all of each; an education which shall aim at producing perfect characters, rich in insight, in love, in energy, scorning selfishness, impurity, and wrong.

I see no way in which these things can be reached but through a strong, combined effort on the part of those that firmly and earnestly believe in them, through a society, realizing in itself and in the relations between its members, that ideal which it recognizes as the highest. Such a society cannot be formed in a day, nor by any general vote or resolution. It must be done slowly and quietly, through the gradual formation of a nucleus of earnest men and women, resolved to live a noble life and to make the redemption of humanity from ignorance, selfishness, and vice the end of all their efforts, and ready to search out and communicate the means whereby this may be done. In the great work we need association, with division of labor. There must be some to discover principles, others to apply them; some to teach, others to labor with their hands. What we can do at present is to keep these ends steadily in view and try to make them clear to others; to interest other people in them and to form little societies for the study of the highest things, for religious sympathy, for mutual aid. All this we can do now —to-day,— before to-morrow.

And what if it be true that all great attainment calls for suffering, that such is the law of our being? Shall we slink back and tremble, and drug ourselves, like craven cowards? Never! The pure metal rings when it is struck, and the true soul finds itself and its own nobility often only in the throbs of pain and utter self-sacrifice. One true act of will makes us feel our immortality: alas! that we so seldom perform an act of will. In the face of an act of real will, heredity counts as nothing. What makes heredity tell is our own cowardice and sluggishness in not forcing children to conquer it, and also in not conquering it in ourselves. Heredity, like corruption, acts only when the soul is gone. It is utterly debasing to be bullied by heredity. The belief in its power "shuts the eyes and folds the hands," and delivers the soul in chains to the demon of unreality. The reason why people doubt about the freedom of the will is because they never exercise it, but are always following some feeling or instinct, some private taste or affection. How *should* such persons know that the will is free? Our time is dying of sentimentality— some of it refined enough, to be sure, but sentimentality —which destroys the will.

We are on our way to all that heart ever wished or head conceived. But the greater gods have no sympathy with anything but heroism. When we will not be heroic they sternly fling us back to suffer, saying to us: Learn to will! The kiss of the Valkyre, which opens the gates of Valhalla, is sealed only upon lips made holy by heroism even unto death.

The hosts of Ahura-Mazda are still fighting, and **woe** to us if we do not join them! It is the custom among the wise men of the world to laugh at all great heroism, all thirst for self-sacrifice; but we can afford to let them laugh. Somewhere in the shadow there are spectators who laugh at them, and will laugh when these have lost the will to laugh. The sons of Ahura-Mazda laugh forever, and there is no uneasiness in their laughter. Their laugh is the beauty of the universe.

But this will, perhaps, weary you and seem mere poetry to you. Poetry it is; but, as Aristotle said long ago, "Poetry is more earnest and more philosophical than history." The true poetry of the world is the history of its spiritual life, and is as much truer than what is *called* history as spirit is truer than outward seeming. When shall we learn this?

Several societies for study, instructions, and practical work in connection with the Fellowship were soon organized, and series of lectures arranged.

CHAPTER X

THE SUMMER SCHOOLS AT FARMINGTON AND GLENMORE

To carry out the idea of summer study—in philosophy, literature, sociology, and religion—away from the turmoil and distractions of city life, Mr. Davidson selected the small New England town of Farmington, where he gathered together a few friends in the year 1888.

Farmington is thus described in the prospectus which he issued at New York:

FARMINGTON

Farmington is a quaint, old, shady New England town, overlooking the Farmington and Pequabuck rivers, and affording beautiful and extensive views in many directions. It is on the New Haven and Northampton Railroad, about 30 miles from New Haven, 46 from Northampton, and 10 from Hartford. The town is about two miles from the station. The rugged hills and broad valleys about Farmington afford excellent opportunities for pleasant walks, rides, and drives, while the rivers are very convenient for bathing and boating.

The following is the prospectus for the third year (1890). The experiment lasted for three years. In 1891 it was absorbed in the school at Glenmore.

FARMINGTON LECTURES ON PHILOSOPHY AND ETHICS
1890 (third year)

THE FIRST MORNING COURSE will be devoted to the *Philosophy of the late Professor T. H. Green.* This philosophy takes a bold stand against the agnosticism and materialism of the time, seeking to show their inconsistency and insufficiency, and to replace them by a doctrine of reason and spirit, offering a solid basis for religion and ethics.

THE SECOND MORNING COURSE will treat of *Functions of a Church and its Relation to the State.* The six lectures will be given by six

The prospectus of the seventh year gives a list of papers read, followed by discussion on "Theories of Ethics." Seven were devoted to ancient ethics, two to mediæval, and sixteen to modern ethics. That of the eighth year gives a list of twenty-five addresses and discussions on the "History and Science of Religion."

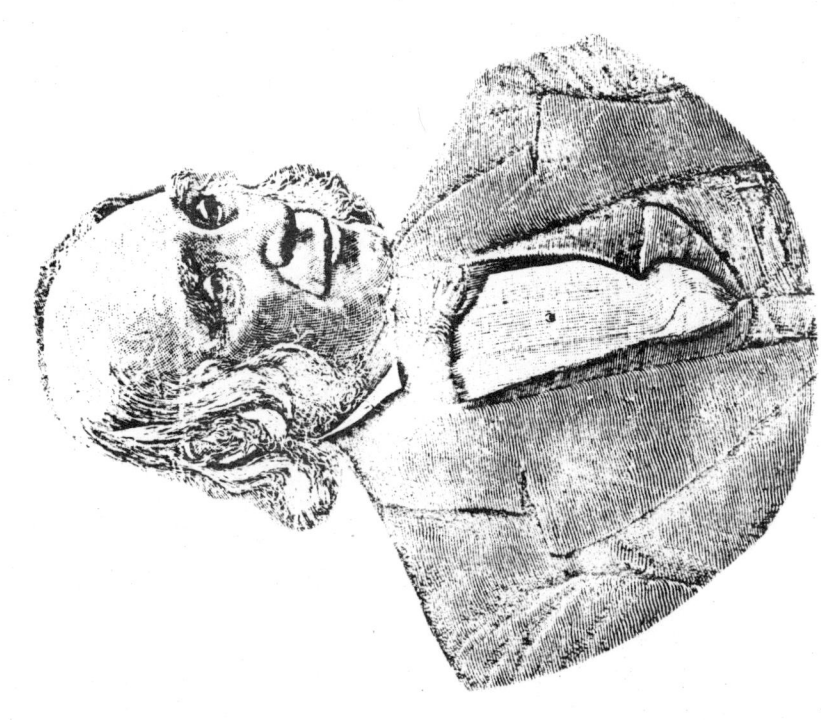

different persons representing as many different views, and will form a kind of symposium.

THE FIRST EVENING COURSE will be devoted to the Greek Moralists,—(1) Æschylus, (2) Socrates, (3) Plato, (4) Aristotle,—and will attempt to show how the Greeks gradually rose from the conception of a life governed by external fate and authority to that of a life guided by internal insight.

THE SECOND EVENING COURSE will deal with *Some of the Primary Concepts of Economic Science*,—(1) Wealth, (2) Value, (3) Property, (4) Land, (5) Labor, (6) Capital,—and will aim at clearing these of the vagueness which at present attaches to them, and showing that they involve a recognition of man's moral nature. It will follow from this that economics cannot be divorced from ethics.

After each lecture an opportunity will be given for free discussion in which it is hoped that all persons present will take part.

MORNING COURSES

I. THE PHILOSOPHY OF T. H. GREEN

June 17. Green's Theory of Cognition and its place in the History of Thought. By Thomas Davidson of New York.

June 18. Green's Treatment of the Relation of Feeling to Reality. By H. N. Gardiner, Professor of Philosophy in Smith College, Northampton, Massachusetts.

June 19. Green's Ethical System. By Stephen F. Weston of New York.

June 20. Green's Ethical System viewed in its Relation to Utilitarianism. By W. Douw Lighthall, B.C.L., of Montreal, Canada, author of *The Young Seigneur, Sketch of a New Utilitarianism.*

June 23. Green's Political Theory. By Percival Chubb of London, England.

June 24. Green's Religious Philosophy. By John Dewey, Ph.D., Professor of Ethics, History of Philosophy, and Logic in the University of Michigan, author of *Psychology,* etc.

II. THE RELATIONS OF CHURCH AND STATE

June 25. The Politico-Philosophical View. By Professor John Dewey, Ph.D.

June 26. The Free-Religious View. By Reverend W. J. Potter, D.D., of New Bedford, Massachusetts.

June 27. The Historical-Philosophical View. By W. T. Harris, LL.D., Commissioner of Education, Washington, D.C. Editor of the *Journal of Speculative Philosophy,* etc.

June 30. The Humanitarian View. By H. D. Lloyd of Chicago, author of *The New Conscience,* etc.

July 1. The Scholastic or Roman Catholic View. By Brother Azarias of the Brothers of the Christian Schools, New York, author of *The Culture of the Spiritual Sense,* etc.

July 2. The Unitarian View. By the Reverend A. N. Alcott, of Elgin, Illinois.

EVENING COURSES

I. THE GREEK MORALISTS

(By Thomas Davidson)

June 17. Æschylus. The Ethical Interpretation of Mythology.

June 18. Æschylus. Ethical Theory. Man's Relations to Family, Society, State, and God.

June 19. Socrates. The Relation of Intelligence to Moral Freedom.

June 20. Plato. The State as the Embodiment of Reason and Justice.

June 23. Aristotle. The Good. The Golden Mean. The Ideal Life.

June 24. Aristotle. The State as a School for Life.

II. PRIMARY CONCEPTS OF ECONOMIC SCIENCE

June 25. Wealth. By Percival Chubb.

June 26. Value. By W. M. Salter, Lecturer to the Chicago Society for Ethical Culture, author of *Ethical Religion,* etc.

June 27. Property. By Percival Chubb.

June 30. Land. By Stephen F. Weston.

July 1. Labor. By Stephen F. Weston.

July 2. Capital. By W. M. Salter.

During the summer of 1889, while the work was going on at Farmington, Mr. Davidson and a few friends informally visited the district of the Adirondacks, above and beyond the village of Keene, in order to prospect the locality, and see if

it was a more suitable place for the formation of a summer school of study, than Farmington had been. In the succeeding year (1890) the scheme matured, although it still remained in a tentative state, and the following prospectus was issued.

A SUMMER COURSE OF STUDY IN THE ADIRONDACKS

Last summer a small number of persons gathered at Glenmore, in the Adirondacks, and freely arranged their days in a way which was found to yield at once rational enjoyment, instruction, and physical exercise. The mornings were devoted to private study and reading, the afternoons to exercise — walking, driving, mountain climbing, tree felling, etc., and the evenings either to the discussion of some important work upon philosophy, art, ethics, or religion, or to music. Many of these evenings were spent round a camp fire. Among the works thus discussed in whole or in part were:

(1) Aristotle's *Nicomachean Ethics.*
(2) Professor Robertson Smith's *Prophets of Israel.*
(3) Professor Drummond's *Philo-Judæus, or the Jewish Alexandrian Philosophy, in its Development and Completion.*
(4) Goethe's *Faust* (three lectures).
(5) St. Bonaventura's *Soul's Progress in God.*
(6) T. H. Green's *Prolegomena to Ethics.*
(7) Mr. Edward Carpenter's *England's Ideal.*
(8) Mr. W. M. Salter's *Ethical Religion.*

The advantages of spending the summer in this way were so great that it has been proposed this year to extend them to a larger number of persons, that is, to offer them to all serious students, and particularly to teachers, who may desire to pass an agreeable and profitable summer at a very moderate expense. The instruction will consist of private aid to study, and of lectures. The former will be given in the forenoon, or during walks in the afternoon; the latter on four evenings in the week, and on Sunday morning. Three evenings a week — Wednesday, Saturday, and Sunday — will be devoted to music and conversation. For the present the subjects of study will be limited to what, in contradistinction to the natural sciences, may be called the culture sciences — philosophy, religion, ethics, economics, politics, art, language, and literature — and their history. The choice to be made this year among these will, in large degree, depend upon the wishes of intending students and the capacity of obtainable instructors. It will materially aid the directors in making out their programme if intending students will communicate their preferences to the secretary as soon as possible.

Provision has already been made for instruction in the theory and history of philosophy, religion, ethics, economics, politics, art (Greek sculpture and piano music), language (comparative philology, Greek, ancient and modern, Latin, Italian, French, German, Anglo-Saxon, and Old Norse), and literature (Homer, Æschylus, Sophocles, Lucretius, Dante, Shakespeare, Goethe, and the English writers of this century).

The summer course will be divided into two parts, one covering July and August, the other September and October. The fees for instruction and lectures will be low, but must depend somewhat upon the numbers who attend. About April a detailed programme will appear, giving all necessary particulars in regard to instruction, accommodation, travelling, camping out, etc. Meanwhile persons desiring further information are requested to communicate with Thomas Davidson, 239 West 105th Street, New York.

GLENMORE

Glenmore is a farm of one hundred and sixty-six acres, on East Hill, in the north end of Keene valley. It lies in the wilderness, on the foothills of Mount Hurricane, about two thousand feet above the sea level. Of its very uneven surface two thirds are covered with forest, while one is under cultivation. The farm is traversed by a large trout brook of the most picturesque kind, and is remarkable for the number of cold springs which water it. The neighborhood offers every opportunity for healthy exercise of all sorts. The scenery of the whole region is grand, and much of it can be enjoyed from different points of the farm. The air is pure and bracing and the heat moderate. Mosquitoes are rare. Altogether, it would not be easy to find a more delightful summer retreat.

I have seen the prospectuses for the seasons 1890, 1891, 1892, 1893, and 1894. It is unnecessary to extract anything from them except a portion of the statement issued for sessions 1891 and 1892, the lists of "Lectures and Interpretations" (as they were called) by Mr. Davidson. The latter may be useful to many a lecturer of the future; they are therefore included in the appendix to this volume.

GLENMORE SCHOOL

The subject of culture is man's spiritual nature, his intelligence, his affections, his will, and the modes in which these express themselves. This culture includes a history, a theory, and a practice, a certain familiarity with which must be acquired by every person who seriously desires to know his relations to the world and to perform his part worthily in those relations. The aim of the school, therefore, will be twofold,—(1) scientific, (2) practical. The former it will seek to reach by means of lectures on the general outlines of the history and theory of the various culture sciences, and by classes, conversations, and carefully directed private study in regard to their details. The latter it will endeavor to realize by encouraging its members to conduct their life in accordance with the highest ascertainable ethical laws, to strive after "plain living and high thinking," to discipline themselves in simplicity, kindliness, thoughtfulness, helpfulness, regularity, and promptness.

In the life at Glenmore an endeavor will be made to combine solid study and serious conversation with reinvigorating rest and abundant and delightful exercise. It is hoped that this may become a place of annual gathering for open-minded persons interested in the serious things of life, so that, being thrown together in an informal way, they may be able to exchange views and initiate sympathies better than in the class room or at the hurried annual meeting. The retirement and quiet of Glenmore seem especially favorable for such things, and the numerous picnics and evening bonfires in the woods offer provision for the lighter moods. Last year two plays were acted by members of the school, and it is hoped that a Greek play may be brought out this year.

The members of the school will have access to a large, well-selected library. Every meal at Glenmore will be opened with a few minutes' reading.

In the *Scottish Review* for January, 1892, there is an article by Professor John Murray of Montreal, entitled "A Summer School of Philosophy," which gives an interesting account of the work at Glenmore. The first summer school, which was an American invention, was held at Concord, in Massachusetts, where the editor of the *Journal of Speculative Philosophy*, Mr. Harris, now the United States Minister of Education, took an active part, along with Thomas Davidson and others. It was pioneer work, and its success led Davidson to attempt a somewhat similar school at Farmington, in Connecticut. For several reasons the second experiment did not succeed so well; and a third was started, and carried on with fresh missionary zeal by its founder, at Glenmore, in the Adirondacks. Glenmore is some twenty miles west of Westport, on Lake Champlain, and two thousand feet above the sea level, at the northern end of the Keene valley. The attractions of the scenery were great, hill and dale, field and forest intermingled. The original farmhouse of Glenmore was bought, with extensive acreage around, and additional wooden cottage buildings were put up, while some of the students camped out in tents. Interesting descriptions of the place and its attractions are given by some of the students in these pages (see Chapters XI and XII). The teaching session lasted only for the two months of July and August, but arrangements could be made for earlier or later residence. It was a home of simple living, assiduous study, and bright fellowship. There was a morning call by horn at half-past seven, breakfast at eight o'clock, preceded by two or three minutes' reading by the dean. Lectures began at half-past nine. Two were given in the forenoon and one in the evening, each followed by half an hour's familiar discussion of the question that had been raised. The subjects of lecture were various; for example, Aristotle's Metaphysics and Politics, Hegel's Philosophy of Spirit, The Comparative History of Religion, Spenser's *Faërie Queene*, Tennyson's *In Memoriam*, The Psychology, the Ethics, and the Metaphysics of the Will. In the lecture room the following device was inscribed on the wall : Ἄνευ φίλων οὐδεὶς ἕλοιτ᾽ ἂν ζῆν, ἔχων τὰ λοιπὰ ἀγαθὰ πάντα (*Nic. Eth.*, VIII, 1) (Without friends no one would choose to live, even with all other good things). Perhaps the chief characteristic of the teaching given in this school was the thorough discussion of *the great books themselves*—the books that were referred to and commented on, not the mere reading of a written commentary upon them. There were

CHAPTER XI

RECOLLECTIONS OF GLENMORE BY MARY FOSTER

The work of Thomas Davidson in his Summer School of the Culture Sciences at Glenmore can best be recorded by those who were pupils, or comrades, in it. I therefore give that record very largely in the words of those who were members of that school, rather than weave their detached reminiscences together in a restatement of my own. Two of the women students—Miss Mary Foster and Miss Charlotte Daley—have sent me extensive notes from which I make extracts, Miss Foster's notes being concerned more especially with the daily life at Glenmore, and Miss Daley's with the teaching.

Miss Foster spent four summers at the school, and knew most of the people who surrounded Mr. Davidson in these years. From her paper, which she calls "Mr. Davidson and the Life at Glenmore," I take the following:

"I first met Mr. Thomas Davidson in New York in 1890, and at a meeting of the New Fellowship I made acquaintance with the friends who had entered actively into his endeavors after higher aims in life.

In the previous year Mr. Thomas Davidson had purchased a farm at East Hill, near Keene in the Adirondack Mountains, and a preliminary informal meeting had been held there that summer. He was now about to go up into the mountains to prepare the camp, which he had named 'Glenmore,' for a more formal gathering of students; and with this in view the members of the Fellowship presented him with a large tent, for use until additional buildings should be put up and

conversational lessons in French, German, and Italian. Then there were afternoon walks, Saturday rambles, and evening concerts. There was no pedantry of any kind. Unconventionality reigned. Students dressed in easy summer attire. There was no display and no flirtation. The stimulus of the life of the place was immense.

One of his student friends at Glenmore writes to me:

"When I first met Thomas Davidson he was interested in the Nationalist movement, a kind of socialism that had arisen from the publication of Bellamy's *Looking Backward.* He left it immediately afterwards, because his name had been published with regard to some action in connection with it, without his being consulted; and he afterwards became antagonistic to every form of socialism, considering that it was a return to militarism, and subversive of true liberty of the individual. . . .

There were inconsistencies in his likes and dislikes; e.g. I sometimes wondered why he objected to Marcus Aurelius, and to Matthew Arnold. Kind as he was to children, he was a stern disciplinarian; and nothing roused him more than to hear it said, 'Poor child, let her have a good time!' A time of laziness, a do-nothing-ness was a bad time. He occasionally made fierce attacks on frivolity in conversation as indicating low aims in life, and so unsparing was his censure of it that women students sometimes thought it scarcely polite!"

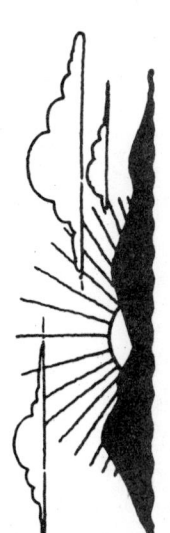

made available for such guests as desired outdoor life during their sojourn.

It was an interesting experience to come into contact with this group of people and their remarkable leader, devoted as they all felt themselves to be to high social and intellectual ideals. Their hope was by individual effort to promote simplicity of life, together with a sincere pursuit of truth, and by association to increase their capacity for such work. 'The Religion of the Fellowship consisted,' they said, 'of a determined endeavor to know well, to love well, and to do well.'

Mr. Davidson was in many ways eminently fitted to devise and carry out such a scheme, being endowed not only with a remarkable personality but with a power of influencing others intellectually which I have never seen equaled.

I have always felt that the first year at Glenmore (in 1889) must have had a peculiar charm of its own, the charm incident to pioneering. The community 'waited on itself' to a much greater extent than in later years, and there seems to have been a very pleasant feeling of fraternity among them. The farmhouse parlor had to be used as lecture hall, dining room, and general sitting room; and I think that many of the guests slept in the barn on balsam boughs. The ladies often made pillows of the balsam needles, while reading was going on; and they all experimented in cooking and washing. In the afternoons they united in such undertakings as deepening the bathing basin in the brook, cutting through the fallen trunks on the Hurricane trail, and clearing certain spots in the woods of old stumps and underbrush so that social gatherings could be held, or tents erected there. There was also the whole surrounding region to be explored, and choice spots were to be discovered and opened out.

Many of the evenings were spent round a camp fire, and works on Philosophy, Art, Ethics, and Religion were freely discussed. Other evenings were devoted to music, or recitation; and all the proceedings were on a less formal scale than was necessary later on, when the number of students had increased.

It was in the third year of the work at Glenmore that I paid my first visit to the place. I went up the Hudson by boat, then by train from Albany to Westport on Lake Champlain; thence a drive of about twenty miles carried me into the heart of the mountains, through lanes thick with flowers and ferns, to the hearty greeting awaiting me at Glenmore.

The only buildings at first noticeable were the log farmhouse, a plain modern building opposite,—which was the dining hall, with four bedrooms over it, built in 1890,—and an old barn. Some friends, who were lodging in the farmhouse, received me, while a servant blew a horn; upon which Mr. Davidson descended the hundred and twenty foot declivity, from his abode in higher regions, to add his warm welcome. I was immediately invited to ascend the hill to the lecture hall; this could be done by the steep face of the cliff, or partly by the road leading to the trail up Mount Hurricane. One thus reached a level open space, in the front of which, and commanding a magnificent view of the mountain and valley, the lecture hall had been erected that spring. Like all the other buildings it was of wood. It contained a spacious room having a large open fireplace, with dogs for burning large logs, and a brick chimney. Behind this, on the south side, were two bedrooms, and stairs ascending to Mr. Davidson's private rooms, which opened on a large veranda, and also to seven other bedrooms designed for the accommodation of guests. On two sides of the building there was a wide piazza, where hammocks could be swung. From here, later on, we often watched the sunset clouds or the aurora borealis, and listened to the boys' singing of college songs. A few paces to the south, in the shade of the wood, was the simple two-roomed cottage in which Mr. Davidson had lived two summers with Mr. Percival Chubb.

The road by which I had come led immediately into the woods clothing the ravine (or gulf, as it was called) and made a gradual descent, crossing the stream below by a picturesque bridge; then, doubling upon itself, it passed in front of the Willey House, a local hotel, and descended parallel to the stream, until it reached the village of Keene — the post and shopping town — 1100 feet below.

Just above the bridge was the meeting place of two streams, and in the main stream further on was an island, the space round which had been cleared of underwood and fallen branches. Here, under high trees and among rugged boulders, with the brook leaping by in a series of small cascades, wooden seats had been constructed, and it was amid such surroundings that festive gatherings were held. Directly above this spot the bed of the brook had been deepened so that an excellent basin for bathing was formed. That it was not spacious enough to swim in mattered little, since even in the warmest weather the water, running under trees all the way from its numerous sources, was of so low a temperature that no one could remain in it for many seconds at a time. For a quick plunge, however, it was most invigorating and delightful, and the basin was a favorite resort.

I arrived on June 26, and found a fair number of guests already assembled. Several ladies had built cottages for themselves on the estate. There were two of these halfway up the hill, between the farmhouse and the lecture room, and at the top of a clearing on the north side was a hut, afterwards owned by Dr. W. T. Harris. Several more sprang up later and added much to the picturesqueness of the settlement. On the margin of the gulf Mr. Stephen Weston's tent was pitched. Two boys with their tutor occupied another, and Professor John Dewey had built a house on his own land low down on the other side of the stream.

The school opened on July 1, and lectures were given in the mornings of five days in the week at 10 and 11.15 A.M., as well as in the evenings at 8 P.M. Meals were served in the dining hall, breakfast being at 8 A.M., dinner at 1 P.M., and supper at 6 P.M. Dairy produce, eggs, and wild fruit were abundant, but meat was sometimes difficult to get, and by many deemed unnecessary in the pure, bracing air of the mountains.

On the first Saturday — a day when no lectures took place — there was a housewarming at the lecture hall. This was decorated for the occasion, chiefly with various trailing species of club-moss common in the woods, and a bonfire was lighted outside.

Mr. Davidson's Sunday lectures were on Tennyson, Goethe, or Dante. He also gave some readings, and the singing of hymns or poems was arranged before the lecture. Sometimes at these Sunday gatherings he would expound a psalm, or other portion of the Hebrew Scriptures.

People staying at the Willey House, or summer boarders at any of the neighboring farms, would also attend, so that there was quite a large congregation. The inhabitants of the district were all either Roman Catholics, or Seventh-Day Baptists, and there were no places of worship except of these denominations. Even when the school was no longer in session, Mr. Davidson always gave some teaching on Sundays, generally in the evenings, to the smaller audience that still surrounded him.

On Saturdays, if there was no festive function at Glenmore, the guests could arrange excursions to the lakes, mountains, and waterfalls of the district. Lake Placid, Whiteface Mountains, Ausable Lake, John Brown's grave, and many other places of interest were within a drive; and a neighboring farmer had set up an extra 'team' to accommodate the guests on these occasions, as well as to fetch them to and from the station.

The walks in the immediate vicinity were also very delightful. Opposite Glenmore, beyond the Willey House,

were two round-topped hills, called Great Crow and Little Crow. Irreverent students of the first year at Glenmore had attempted to fix upon them the names of Soda and Potash, much to the disapprobation of Mr. Davidson, who suggested Ben More and Ben Ledi. On the edge of the woods that crowned Little Crow was a huge boulder as big as a small cottage, with wooden steps by which to ascend it.

On rare occasions a general walk or stroll would be taken, with the privilege of Mr. Davidson's company; and it was then amusing to notice the behavior of his beautiful collie, named Dante, who, true to his instincts as a shepherd's dog, did all he could to keep the party together, and objected to their straying or lagging behind.

In these regions very little wheat or barley is grown, but buckwheat and oats are common, and on every farm we saw long rows of Indian corn. Between these rows pumpkin vines flourished, and in the autumn left their splendid golden balls over the whole field.

The primeval forest still held full sway on the more remote slopes of the hills, but near the farms the younger growth consisted of the paper birch, the common poplar, spruce firs, and the sweet balsam firs. Pine trees were not so common. At the borders of the woods there were maples and other soft-wood trees.

By 1893 a new dining hall had been built, and on the walls were hung many interesting pictures, with portraits of people who had come into contact with Mr. Davidson. All these perished in the fire that destroyed the block of buildings a few years ago.

It was outside this building that we assembled for the eight-o'clock breakfast, and the guests were not often visible before that hour. Occasionally an early bather might be seen, or those few who invited health by walking barefoot in the dew,— a delightful practice inaugurated by a German doctor, who had been at Father Kneipp's sanatorium in Austria. In the

first years a horn, as used on the farms around, and later, a bell, summoned the visitors from tent, cottage, and lecture hall to breakfast. All meals were preceded by a brief reading by Mr. Davidson from some work on Ethics, Philosophy, or Religion. By 8.30 we were away at our studies, or tidying up our dormitories, until 10 o'clock, when the lecture began, often with a second at 11 o'clock. Dinner was at 1 o'clock, after which Mr. Davidson and many of the party took a short rest before engaging in further study, or in the outdoor exercises of the afternoon. There were plenty of charming places for hammocks among the trees, and sometimes private-study groups met in the woods or at some one's hut. Supper was at 6 o'clock, leaving more spare time, which was often employed in watching the sunset, and in talking or singing until the hour for the evening lecture. The students were not expected to attend all the lectures, five a week being the minimum exacted of them. Young people, not sufficiently advanced for the courses in Philosophy and in the Culture Sciences, were expected to pursue other studies under the tuition of some of the older members.

In the short American summer evenings it was generally dark when lectures were over, so that lanterns were neces-sary. Dr. Mann proved himself a benefactor to the commun-ity by making a better path through the wood that lay between the lecture hall and the lane, and by adding a railing at one side. This bore the inscription at the foot, 'The Ascent of Man,' and at the top, 'The Descent of Man.'

After the session of the school was over, and while per-haps eight or a dozen guests still lingered at Glenmore, Mr. Davidson would give many delightful informal talks on mat-ters philosophical. It is never to be forgotten how in those quieter times we sat listening to his conversation at the break-fast table, sometimes for two hours after that meal was really over,— a delight that was never ours when many guests were present.

The delivery and the dispatch of letters were irregular at Glenmore, and few cared whether or not they got any newspapers. For our mail we depended upon the convenience of the neighboring farmers, who frequently had errands to Keene; or upon the willingness of some guest to walk down the 1100 feet into the valley, and to return through the silent woods after nightfall, a weird and impressive experience.

Saturdays were, as I have said, our free days, and they were often devoted to long walks. A favorite excursion was the ascent of Mount Hurricane. There were three miles of walking along through Glenmore. There were three miles of walking along a narrow forest path with occasional crossings of a rushing stream, till you reached a height, often swathed in clouds, where the lichens hung thickly on the trees, and the mosses underfoot were deep. At the last spring, before leaving the woods to ascend to the summit, we used to stop to fill our water cans. Then we would emerge upon the open face of a mountain 3763 feet high, whence one of the finest views in the Adirondacks is to be obtained. Toward the north lies Canada; Lake Champlain and the hills of Vermont are to the east; while on the south, and west, a splendid range of local mountains stretches before you. The botanist can enjoy the Alpine vegetation which is to be found at this height.

Sometimes a party arranged to sleep on the summit of Hurricane, so as to see both sunset and sunrise. Blankets were brought up, and the boys collected fir branches for beds, and other wood to keep a fire during the night. There were several bonfires each summer on the island near the bathing place as an accompaniment to singing and other entertainment. A few concerts were also given in the lecture hall, at which the songs of Scotland were sung; and occasionally Mr. Davidson indulged us with his inimitable recitations of Scottish ballads. One year he gave a charming account of the life and poetry of Lady Nairne, illustrated with music. Discussions were also held on special subjects, such as free

will, socialism, and vegetarianism. It was an interesting occasion when the boys at Glenmore gave a masquerade in the woods round the spring, near which Mr. Davidson's bungalow was afterwards built.

Mr. Davidson often entertained, under his own roof, friends from Keene valley or the Willey House, as well as the students at Glenmore; and there was frequent interchange of courtesies between our camp and friends near St. Hubert's, Keene Heights, twelve miles off, where many members of the 'Ethical Society,' surrounded Dr. Felix Adler. They had a lecture hall in which Mr. Davidson was in request, and he used to speak there at least once in the summer.

It was in the early summer of 1893 that Mr. Davidson's bungalow was built in a retired spot in the wood on the other side of the trail from the lecture hall. It was finished before the school opened, and those who were spending June at Glenmore helped him to carry across his extensive library. A path less abrupt than the very steep one to the farmhouse was needed, and another one diverging from it to the lecture hall. These works were undertaken by some of the residents. Trees were cut down, and the path along the sloping side of the hill was shored up. Large stones were found to bridge the rivulet that trickled down by the side of the lane, and pathways were soon made for philosophers to walk in.

An open glade stretches along the crest of the hill from Mr. Davidson's bungalow to the east, and it is on the border of this that his body now lies buried. In the autumn the place is a blaze of golden-rod, and there is a picturesque rock at the further end where harmless snakes make their home. Part of this glade is very swampy, and at night fireflies may be seen pursuing the small water insects that rise from it. The carriage way to Mr. Davidson's house crossed this swamp in an uncomfortable and unsafe manner; and it occurred to the members of the school to build a wooden bridge, which would not only improve the road, but be a pleasant feature

in the landscape. Large trees were felled by Mr. Davidson, Dr. Edward Moore, and others; while the ladies sawed smaller branches into lengths suitable to form crosspieces in corduroy fashion. The railing on each side was constructed in an elaborate pattern of the choicest branches of paper birch that could be found, and finally a Virginia creeper was brought up from the valley to grow over it.

It is not easy to sum up the methods and results of Mr. Davidson's teaching. Delightful as a lecturer, he was even more charming in conversation. A strong personal magnetism enabled him to become a welcome vehicle for the conveyance of truth and the disclosure of wisdom.

In the years 1891 to 1895, when I saw most of him, he discoursed much on the universality of Spirit, and on the necessity for each individual to evolve an ordered world in his or her own consciousness, the ethical life depending on the completeness and harmony of such a world.

His aim in organizing a school of philosophy was to impart the instruction of which he felt that the educated classes stood so greatly in need; and he wished to do this in healthy and beautiful surroundings, under simple conditions of life. He hoped that the good of the whole school would be striven after by each individual, and that through mutual helpfulness, and by pursuing work and pleasure together, an unselfish spirit would be fostered. He used to refer to the ideal of life among the Greeks, pointing out that this implied the free enjoyment of life apart from its practical side; which included such things as earning a livelihood, politics, education, and religious observances. On the other hand the ideal life was a contemplative one, and was to be distinguished from mere play and amusement; there was no phrase he objected to more than 'having a good time.' All free enjoyment was to be rational. It was not easy to get together many people who were able to live up to this ideal; and it must be feared that the embodiment of his School of the Culture Sciences fell far

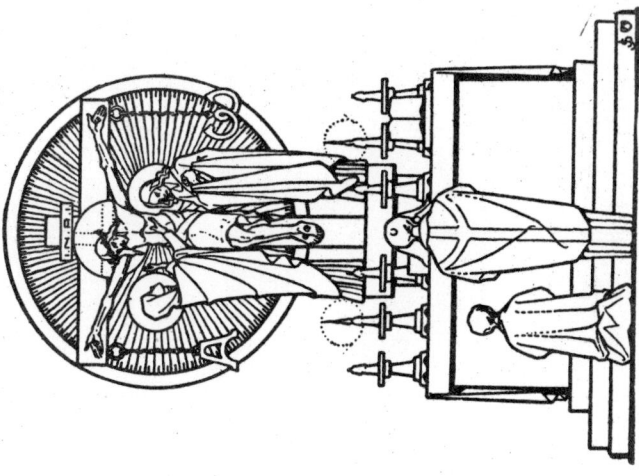

short of his conception of what it should have been. But it is certain that, in the course of his busy life and frequent travels, he came into contact with many individuals who derived much inspiration from his teaching and conversation; and that they were by him imbued with a new, and higher, conception of their responsibilities in life."

CONTENTS.

PORTRAITS.

THE

LIFE AND GENIUS

OF

GOETHE

LECTURES AT THE CONCORD SCHOOL OF PHILOSOPHY

EDITED BY

F. B. SANBORN

BOSTON

TICKNOR AND COMPANY

1886

University Press:

JOHN WILSON AND SON, CAMBRIDGE.

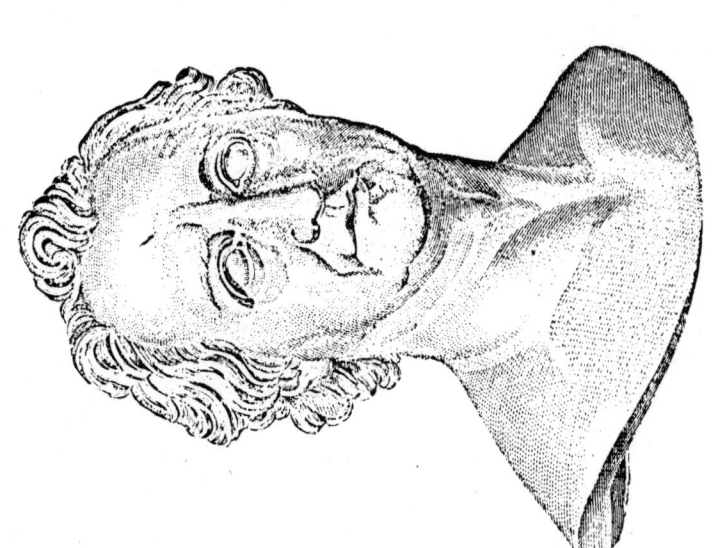

GOETHE IN AGE.

From the bust by Rauch about 1820.

INTRODUCTION.

THE Lectures on Goethe here printed are not the whole of those delivered at the School of Philosophy in July, 1885; for several of the lecturers have either published their essays elsewhere, or withhold them for other uses. Much also that was said in the conversations which followed the Lectures, and which threw light on the text as here printed, is necessarily omitted; although the lecturers, in revising their manuscripts, have sometimes included remarks that were thus made. Mr. Alcott, the founder of the School, although several times present during these sessions, (as he had not been since 1882,) was unable to make his comments in the conversations; and therefore some passages from his Diaries have been inserted in the lecture of Mr. Sanborn. On the other hand, Mr. Snider and other lecturers have omitted, in revision, some of the comments made in the spoken lectures.

Professor Hewett, of Cornell University, whose lecture on "Goethe in Weimar," expanded, will form part of a series on the "Homes of the German Poets"

vi

in Harper's Magazine, and is not available for this volume, has kindly furnished for this Introduction an account of the newly discovered Goethe manuscripts which were mentioned in his lecture. It is based on the reports of Professor Geiger and Dr. Brahm, and is as follows.

THE GOETHE SOCIETY AND THE GOETHE ARCHIVES.

Walther von Goethe, Chamberlain of the Grand Duke of Saxe-Weimar, and the last descendant of the poet, died in Leipzig, April 15, 1885. By his will he bequeathed the Goethe house, its art and scientific collections, to the Grand Duke; its literary treasures were left to the Grand Duchess Sophie, a princess of the house of Orange, whose intelligence and interest in literature make her a worthy successor of the Duchess Amalia. On the 9th of June a call was issued, inviting all friends of Goethe literature to unite in the formation of a Goethe Society in Weimar. The meeting was held on June 20 and 21, in the guild house of the Crossbowmen, an organization of which the poet was a member. More than one hundred eminent scholars and university professors assembled from all parts of Germany and Austria to honor to the poet. The Goethe archives, which had been so long the object of ardent interest to all scholars, had at last been opened, and the results of the investigation were to be made known. The Society was constituted with a long list of active members, including the Empress of Germany, the granddaughter of Carl August, the Princes and the Grand Duchess of Saxe-Weimar, the Princes of Reuss-Gera, of Meiningen, and of Saxony; the Ministers Von Gossler of Berlin, Von Gerber of Dresden, and numerous foreign scholars of Naples, Rome, Athens, and America. The Grand Duke Carl Alexander of Saxe-Weimar

vii

accepted the office of patron of the society. Dr. Simson, President of the Imperial Court of Leipzig, formerly President of the German Parliament, was chosen the first President. The Executive Committee consists of Professor W. Scherer of Berlin, First Vice-President; General-Intendant Von Loen of Weimar, Second Vice-President; Professor Kuno Fischer of Heidelberg; Paul Heyse, the novelist, of Munich; Von Loeper of Berlin; Von Beaulieu-Marconnay of Dresden; Rumelin, Chancellor of the University of Tübingen, of Stuttgart; Professor Erich Schmidt of Vienna; Eggeling, Curator of the University of Jena; and Ruland of Weimar. A business board was also selected, Herr Commerzienrath Moritz was appointed Treasurer of the Society.

The objects of the organization are to promote a knowledge of the whole domain of Goethe's intellectual activity and influence, and to promote special investigations in Goethe literature. Annual meetings will be held for the presentation of papers and interchange of views. The Goethe Jahrbuch will become the organ of the society, in which will be published much of the fresh material discovered in the archives. The volume for 1886 will contain the letters of Goethe to his sister Cornelia, and to Behrisch in Dessau; also, the hitherto unpublished letters of the Frau Rath (Goethe's mother) to the Duchess Amalia, from the state archives, the arrangement of which has been entrusted to Archivrath Burkhardt. A subsequent volume will contain the letters of Goethe from Italy to the Frau von Stein, and also his correspondence with his wife. The Society will establish a Goethe museum and library, with facilities for investigation, and seek to complete the Goethe archives.

The Grand Duchess has determined to inaugurate two monumental works: (1.) A complete life of Goethe, based on his diaries and the additional material contained among his papers. This has been undertaken by that most eminent Goethe scholar, Privy-Councillor von Loeper. (2.) A new authentic edition of his works, based upon the collation of all

viii

existing manuscripts, which will devolve upon Von Loeper, Scherer, and Erich Schmidt, the last of whom has resigned his professorship in the University of Vienna to accept the Directorship of the Goethe Archives.

At a later session of the Society, Herr von Loeper and Professor Scherer presented the results of their examination of the archives. Six cases were filled with the manuscripts. One contained accounts of domestic expenses, the bills of butchers and bakers, preserved with that order which was characteristic of the poet; a second contained careful notes, from the highest authorities, together with the results of his own observations in science; two other cases contained manuscripts of his works, journals, and letters. Von Loeper gave a general view of the contents of two cases out of the six, which he had been able to examine. The material may be divided into three parts: (1.) Manuscripts of Goethe's works; (2.) Letters; and (3.) Diaries.

I. The existing manuscripts, while not presenting new and complete works, reveal the methods of study of the poet, the vast field of his intellectual activity, and the origin, growth, and connection of his various writings. They begin with the unique copy of the "Höllenfahrt Jesu Christi," written in 1765, and published in "Die Sichtbaren" in 1766, and end with his last great work, the Second Part of Faust, in 1831, thus covering a period of sixty-six years. Many manuscripts most eagerly anticipated were not found, among them the original of Faust. Count Friedrich Stolberg, in describing a visit to Weimar in 1775, speaks of a glorious afternoon when Goethe read "his half-completed Faust, a noble poem," to the Duchesses and himself. This manuscript, which Goethe carried with him to Italy, would settle many questions in Faust criticism. The preliminary sketch of "Wilhelm Meister," spoken of by Herder, and its earlier form, as well as the first version of "Tasso," are missing. Among the treasures revealed, however, from the pre-Weimar days, are a fine manuscript of "Der Ewige Jude"; the first manuscript of "Götz von

ix

Berlichingen"; a hitherto unknown collection of dialogues, in one of which Frau Aja plays a part (October 14, 1774); and a volume of youthful poems, parts of which are known through copies in the possession of the Herders and Frau von Stein; also, three versions of the "Mitschuldigen" (probably later revisions), and several manuscripts of "Prometheus," one copied by Lenz, and one by the Fräulein von Göchhausen. Belonging to the period of his residence in Weimar are copies of his minor dramatic works, among them three manuscripts of the "Triumph der Empfindsamkeit."

From the period of Goethe's residence in Italy there are versions of the "Iphigenie" in prose and in iambics, "Tasso," and the "Roman Elegies" complete, in his own autograph. Of later date are three autograph manuscripts of the "Venetian Epigrams," with many hitherto unpublished; some of these are of an erotic nature, others were directed against Lavater, and still others were anti-clerical in spirit. A manuscript of the "Grosskophta" as an opera was also found, and "Elpenor" in two versions. Of the period of Goethe's connection with Schiller, there is the manuscript of "Hermann und Dorothea," copied probably by A. W. Schlegel, with corrections by Goethe. There are also numerous smaller works and fragments,—among the latter the beginning of a tragedy in five acts, called "Das Mädchen von Oberkirch," in which Goethe treats the phenomena of the French Revolution. He located the action in the Alsatian village of Oberkirch, with the surroundings of which he was familiar. There is also a beautiful manuscript of that ambitious fragment, the "Achilleis," in which Goethe, filled with the spirit of his Homeric studies, undertook a classical epic, in continuation of the Iliad, but stopped with the first canto. A plan, however, has been found, embracing the action of the six books originally contemplated. Goethe's enthusiasm for Homer is further shown by essays in the translation of various passages in hexameters, and even a critical interpretation of an obscure passage.

x

His productivity is shown by the vast materials accumulated in his later studies. Among these are poems and *collectanea* for the "Divan," all in autograph, and nearly all supplied with dates. These exhibit various readings and rejected passages, and are of great value in the interpretation and historical criticism of the verses as they stand. He even attempted a "Historisches Volksbuch" (1808). Numberless minor poems and fragments were found, occasionally recreations of the charming evenings of the literary "circles," but more often the records of more serious work. Among them are additional *Zahme Xenien*, invectives, political stanzas, attacks on persons, *Erotica*, etc. There is an attack upon Wolfgang Menzel, whose bitter hostility could not always leave Goethe unmoved. He is called a "Potenzierter Merkel." There is also an addition to the poem, "Es ist ein Schuss gefallen," with references to Friedrich Schlegel, and Müller, the romanticist and publicist, who followed his friend to the Roman communion.

Professor Scherer, in his investigations, gave especial attention to the manuscripts of "Faust." He found, what cannot be a surprise, from Goethe's own expressions, that the poet himself had attempted an adaptation of the First Part to the stage. His plan for its representation included in the first act the Dedication, Prelude, and Prologue in Heaven. Music was

xi

introduced skilfully and effectively in many passages; as in the abridged monologue, and in the scene of Faust's covenant with the evil spirit, when the choir of spirits is heard contending with one another, "He will sign," "He will not sign," singing in chorus, until Mephistopheles cries,

"Blut ist ein ganz besonder Saft."

Goethe's taste for the opera, and his estimate of the capacity of music to heighten dramatic effect, are shown by this treatment. This scheme or arrangement is often styled in the manuscript "melodrama." As early as 1810, Goethe considered the presentation of "Faust" on the stage, and requested Zelter to write the music for the Easter Song and the Slumber Song of the Spirits, "Schwindet ihr dunkeln Wölbungen droben"; but the musician declined, and Goethe dropped the matter for the time. Later, he was very angry at the proposed production of "Faust" in Weimar in 1829, before consultation with him, "as though he were no longer alive, and without asking what view he might have in the manner of its presentation." For the Helena scenes there is the most abundant material, and there is a manuscript, "Helena im Mittelalter, ein satyrisches-Drama," which later bears the odd title, "Satyr-Drama, eine Episode zu Faust." The inference is drawn from this, that Goethe's earliest work on the "Helena" continued, in the ancient metres, until the appearance of "Faust." The results of this examination are in no respect complete or final.

II. The second division includes the letters to and from Goethe. These cover an extended period,—from his student days in Leipzig to his late Weimar days. New and unexpected materials are here presented. Of high value in determining the history of Goethe's life, and his relations to his family, are his letters to his sister Cornelia. Strehlke, in his catalogue of Goethe's letters, recently completed, says, "No single letter of Goethe to his sister or his father is known"; but here we have a welcome collection of letters to his sister, the companion of his first triumph, whose loss he so greatly mourned. There are also letters to Behrisch in Dessau, the friend of his university days in Leipzig, from whom he parted with so much regret. There are also three letters written while an advocate in Frankfort, and thirty-eight letters to the Minister von Fritsch. The series of letters which will attract most attention are those to his wife, covering twenty-five years in an unbroken succession, from 1792 to her death in 1816. They are described as evincing a "constant ardor and sincerity of feeling, and to afford an irrefutable view of Goethe's domestic happiness. He communicates to her all the interests of his life, his poetic undertakings, visits, and moods, and shows a faithful interest in her domestic duties. He is always the kind, loving, attentive husband. Amid the

xii

excitements of his campaign in France, he longs for his home, and, for his highest happiness, wishes his dear one with him in Verdun." There are a hundred and eighty letters from Goethe's mother, in one collection, and additional letters incorporated in the current correspondence of each year; also, numerous letters, mostly notes, from Frau von Stein; serving to show the character of their later intercourse. There are letters of Frau von Grotthus, Frau von Eybenberg, Amalie von Imhof, and F. Caspers, and single remembrances from Lotte Buff (1798) and Lili Schönemann (1801).

Goethe's letters from the Grand Duke Carl August are preserved intact in the collection, and show how unsatisfactory the present edition is. This correspondence, edited by Dr. Vogel, was published in 1863 in an incomplete form. It had been withheld, owing to two expressions of Goethe,—one in a letter of November 17, 1787, from Rome: "Burn, I pray you, my letters at once, that they may be read by no one; with this hope I can write more freely." Before his departure for Switzerland in 1797, he said: "I have burned all the letters sent to me since 1772, from a positive disinclination to the publication of the silent march of friendly intercourse." His views afterward changed, and he published parts of his correspondence covering this period. The letters preserved in the Goethe archives show that the destruction of his correspondence was not so general as his language would imply. Of particular interest at the present time is the discovery of Carlyle's letters to the poet, and copies of Goethe's letters in reply.

The Schiller correspondence suffered from the arbitrary and capricious suppressions of its editors, and the fourth edition was necessary to give it in substantial correctness. Even in its present form there is much to be desired. Goethe himself says that letters are the most valuable memorial of a man. His correspondence grew with his fame; his interest extended to the most varied branches of literature, art, antiquities, and science; and letters from scholars, poets, and artists multiplied

xiii

during the later period of his life. They present his relations to individuals, the growth of his opinions, his judgments of men and things, and the inception and progress of his works. Political events in Europe do not escape him. Discoveries, facts, and theories are mirrored in his all-reflecting mind; the works of contemporary and past writers are estimated; and thus his letters become a contribution to a knowledge of the literary history of his time.

III. The third division contains Goethe's diaries. These begin in 1776, before the first year of his residence in Weimar had passed, and extend to the 16th of March, 1832, but six days before his death. They present a rich material for estimat-

ing the poet's life, the existence of which was entirely unsuspected. Meagre and inaccurate extracts from certain portions had appeared, limited in range and time; but the originals are presented here entire. There is, however, a blank between the years 1782 and 1796, interrupted by two brief beginnings in 1791 and 1793. These journals are at first short, condensed notices, which increase in fulness and richness of contents as his life advances. From 1817 they average nearly four volumes a year. Important events are recorded with great accuracy. Days like those which followed Schiller's death contain no entry. These diaries furnish means for determining the dates of Goethe's works, since little that the poet wrote went at once to the press. Many works were for years under his hand; they were begun, discontinued, resumed, modified, and completed, and their final form differed greatly from the original plan.

The art collections are extensive, and of great interest. They contain plaster casts; original drawings of the old masters, Netherland art being especially represented; and even sketches of early Italian painters; many drawings of personal friends, such as Tischbein, Meyer, Hackert, Kraaz, Angelica Kaufmann, and Kniep; a rich collection of majolicas; Italian medals, two thousand in number, some of which are unique; numerous plaques, two hundred Italian and German bronzes,

xiv

antiques, and a large number of engravings. To these general art collections have been added, by gift of the heirs at law (the families of Count Henckel von Donnersmark and the Vulpius family), the personal memorials of the poet, consisting of portraits, busts, medallions, and casts of the same. Among these are portraits of Goethe by Angelica Kaufmann and Tischbein, and also a graceful portrait, probably representing Christiane.

Two portraits of Goethe are given in our volume; one representing him in youth, before the publication of any except his earliest works; the other engraved from Rauch's bust, which was made in August, 1820, when Goethe was seventy-one. Both are interesting, and neither is much known in America, although reduced copies of the bust are common.

A partial bibliography of works relating to Goethe's youth will be found at the close of Professor White's lecture. We add here a more general, but still very incomplete bibliography, compiled by Mr. John Edmands of the Philadelphia Mercantile Library, for the benefit of the frequenters of that institution.

xv

READING NOTES ON GOETHE.

The following notes and references will be found pertinent, and will be useful to any who may wish to pursue a course of reading on these subjects:—

A.—WORKS OF GOETHE.

Autobiography; or, Truth and Poetry, from my Life, edited by P. Godwin. New York, 1846-47. 2 v.

Bride of Corinth, with Anster's Faust.

Campaign in France, translated by R. Fairie. London, 1858.

Same, in his Miscellaneous Travels, pp. 71-247.

Correspondence between Schiller and Goethe from 1794-1805, edited by L. D. Schmitz. London, 1877. 2 v.

Dramatic Works; comprising Faust, Iphigenia in Tauris, Torquato Tasso, Egmont, and Götz von Berlichingen. London, 1851.

Egmont; a Tragedy in Five Acts. Boston, 1841.

Elective Affinities. Boston, 1872.

Same, in Novels and Tales. Reviewed in Revue des Deux Mondes, C. 863.

Eleonora, with a Poetic Epistle from Werter to Charlotte. London, 1787.

Essays on Art, translated by S. G. Ward. New York, 1862.

Faust, eine Tragöilie. Stuttgart, 1867.

Faustus, a Dramatic Mystery; the Bride of Corinth, the first Walpurgis Night, translated and illustrated with Notes by J. Anster. London, 1835.

Faust; a Tragedy in Two Parts, translated by J. Birch, with engravings by Brain after Retsch. London, 1839.

Same, translated, with Notes, by C. T. Brooks. [Part I. only.] Boston, 1856.

Same, translated by L. Filmore. London, 1847.

Same, translated into Verse by J. Galvan. Dublin, 1860.

Same, translated, with Notes, by A. Hayward. Boston, 1859. Part I. "Previous to Taylor's translation Hayward's prose rendering was the leading work consulted by scholars on account of its full notes and lengthy introduction." — *Literary World*, XII. 273.

Same, translated by T. Martin. Edinburgh, 1865. Reviewed in North British Review. XLIV. 50.

Same, translated in Rime by C. Kegan Paul. London, 1873. Reviewed in Revue des Deux Mondes, CXLIII. 921.

Same, translated into the Original Metres by Bayard Taylor. Boston, 1871. 2 v. Has a Preface and extended Notes. "Bayard Taylor's notes and comments are exhaustive, and *must* be consulted by any student of the subject who wishes to go to the bottom of disputed points. His translations are quoted even by the latest and best German commentators in proof of the meaning of doubtful passages." — *Literary World*, XII. 273.

xvi

Same. The Text, with English Notes, Essays, and Verse Translations, by E. J. Turner. London, 1882. The First Part only.

Same. Shelley's Translations of the Prologue in Heaven and of the May-day Night scene, may be found in his Poetical Works. London, 1877. IV. 284.

Same. The Liberal. London, 1822. I. 121.

Boyesen's Goethe and Schiller has a full and elaborate Commentary on the two parts of Faust, pp. 151-285.

The original Faust-Legend may be found in Roscoe's German Novelists, I. 256.

Faust and Marguerite. V. 35.

German Emigrants *in his* Novels and Tales.

Good Women *in his* Novels and Tales.

Götz of Berlichingen, with the Iron Hand, an Historical Drama. Dublin, 1799.

Götz von Berlichingen *in his* Dramatic Works.

Herman and Dorothea, translated by Ellen Frothingham. Illustrated. Boston, 1870.

Same, translated into English Hexameters, with an Introductory Essay. London, 1849.

Same, translated by T. C. Porter. New York, 1854.

xvii

Iphigenia in Tauris, translated by W. Taylor, *in his* Historic Survey of German Poetry. London, 1830. III. 249.

Same *in his* Dramatic Works.

Margaret Fuller *in her* Life Without, p. 51, gives a sketch of this Drama, with Extracts.

Letters from Switzerland, *in his* Miscellaneous Travels, pp. 1-67.

Letters to Leipzig Friends, edited by O. Jahn, translated by R. Slater. London, 1866.

Meister's Travels; or, The Renunciants, a Novel. Boston, 1851.

Memoirs written by himself. New York, 1824.

The same as the Autobiography above, but another translation, and contains only fifteen of the twenty books. It contains biographical notices of the principal persons mentioned in the memoirs. "A most wretched and unfaithful translation." — *Quarterly Review*.

Minor Poetry, a Selection from his Songs, Ballads, and other lesser Poems, translated by W. G. Thomas. Philadelphia, 1859.

Miscellaneous Travels; comprising Letters from Switzerland, the Campaign in France, the Siege of Mainz, and a Tour on the Rhine. London, 1882.

Novels and Tales: Elective Affinities, Sorrows of Werther, German Emigrants, Good Women. London, 1854.

Poems and Ballads, translated by Aytoun and Martin. New York, 1859.

Poems, translated in the Original Metres by Paul Dyrsen. New York, 1878.

Poems and Translations from the German, by C. R. Lambert. London, 1850. pp. 81-98.

Reynard the Fox. London, 1845.

Sämmtliche Werke. Stuttgart, 1850. 30 v. in 18.

Schriften. Reutlinger, 1784. 2 v.

Select Minor Poems, translated by J. S. Dwight.

Select Poems, in Baskerville's Poetry of Germany. New York, 1857. Contains a number of Goethe's Poems in the original, with English verse translations on the opposite page.

Selections from Dramas, translated, with Introduction, by A. Swanwick. London, 1843.

Siege of Mainz, in his Miscellaneous Travels, pp. 251-287.

xviii

Sorrows of Werter, translated by W. Bender. London, 1801.

Stella : a Drama in Five Acts, translated by Benjamin Thompson. German Theatre, v. 6. London, 1801.

Torquato Tasso, in his Dramatic Works.

A Tour on the Rhine, etc., in his Miscellaneous Travels, pp. 291-424.

Truth and Poetry, same as the Autobiography above.

The First Walpurgis Night. (The English version by W. Bartholomew.) Compiled by Felix Mendelssohn Bartholdy. Boston [no date].

Werther, Trad. nouv. et Notice biog. et litt. de L. Enault. Paris, 1855.

West-Easterly Divan, translated, with Introduction and Notes, by J. Weiss. Boston, 1877. Reviewed in Blackwood, CXXXII. 742.

Wilhelm Meister's Apprenticeship. London, 1873. Reviewed by D. A. Wasson in Atlantic Monthly, p. 16.

B. — Works on Goethe.

De Staël, Madame. Goethe and his Dramas in her Germany. London, 1814. I. 265, II. 138.

Taylor, W. Review of Goethe's Works in his Historic Survey of German Poetry. London, 1830. III. 242-379. Contains a Translation of Iphigenia entire, and large portions of other works.

Carlyle, T. Death of Goethe, in his Criticisms and Miscellaneous Essays. London, 1872. IV. 42.

——. Goethe in his Criticisms and Miscellaneous Essays. London, 1872. I. 172.

——. Goethe's Works and Character, in his Criticisms and Miscellaneous Essays. Boston, 1888. I. 220.

——. Goethe's Helena, in his Criticisms and Miscellaneous Essays. Boston, 1888. I. 162.

——. Same. London, 1872. I. 126.

——. Goethe's Works, in his Criticisms and Miscellaneous Essays. London, 1872. IV. 132.

Life of Schiller. New York, 1846. Describes the friendship between Goethe and Schiller, pp. 111, 273.

xix

Eckermann, J. P. Conversations with Goethe in the Last Years of his Life, translated by S. M. Fuller [Ossoli]. Boston, 1839.

Menzel, W. Goethe, in his German Literature, translated by C. C. Felton. Boston, 1840. III. 1.

Austin, S. Characteristics of Goethe, from the German of Falk, von Müller, &c., with Notes. Paris, 1841. 2 v.

Retsch, M. Illustrations of Goethe's Faust. London, 1848. Characteristics of Men of Genius. Goethe. London, 1846.

Jeffrey, Francis. Goethe's Wilhelm Meister, in his Contributions to the Edinburgh Review. Paris, 1846. p. 104.

Ulrici, H. Goethe in Relation to Shakespeare, in his Shakespeare's Dramatic Art. London, 1846. p. 512.

Longfellow, H. W. Goethe, in his Hyperion. Boston, 1849. p. 155.

Moschzisker, F. A. Goethe, in his Guide to German Literature. London, 1850. II. 95-170.

Emerson, R. W. Goethe, or the Writer, in his Representative Men. Boston, 1851. p. 209.

Döring, H. J. W. von Goethe's Biographie. Jena, 1853.

Bancroft, G. The Age of Schiller and Goethe, in his Literary and Historical Miscellanies, p. 167. New York, 1855. Contains translations of several of Goethe's poems, p. 231.

Lewes, G. H. The Life and Works of Goethe, with Sketches of his Age and Contemporaries. London, 1875. 2 v.

——. Same. Boston, 1856. 2 v.

"Mr. Lewes's main work was done a long time ago, when comparatively few of Goethe's letters were printed. And the revision mentioned in the Preface of 1875 was not a thorough, adequate revision." — T. W. Lyster.

Masson, David. Shakespeare and Goethe, and The Three Devils, in his Essays, Biographical and Critical. Cambridge, 1856. pp. 453.

——. The Three Devils. London, 1874. pp. 1-124.

Godwin, Parke. Goethe, in his Out of the Past, p. 341. New York, 1870.

Taillandier, Saint-René. Goethe, in Nouvelle Biographie Générale. Paris, 1857. XXI. 27.

Metcalfe, Frederick. Goethe, in his History of German Literature. London, 1858. pp. 431-453.

xx

Arnim, Bettine von. Goethe's Correspondence with a Child. Boston, 1859. For a review of this work, by M. E. W. Sherwood, see Atlantic Monthly, XXXI. 216.

Ossoli, Margaret Fuller. Goethe, in her Life Without and Life Within. Boston [1859]. p. 23.

De Quincey, T. Goethe, in his Biographical Essays. Boston, 1860. p. 227.

Heine, W. The Romantic School. New York, 1882. The chapter on "German Literature to the Death of Goethe," treats largely of Goethe and his relations to Herder, Lessing, the Schlegels, and others.

Steffens, H. Story of My Career. Boston, 1863. This book was subsequently issued as "German University Life."

Merivale, Herman. Voltaire, Rousseau, and Goethe, in his Historical Studies. London, 1865. p. 130.

Caro, E. La Philosophie de Goethe. Revue des Deux Mondes. Paris, 1865-66. LIX, LX. 147, 301, LXI. 623, LXII. 386.

Belani, W. C. R. Goethe und sein Liebeleben. Historischer Novellenkreis. Leipzig, 1866. 3 v.

Calvert, G. H. Goethe, in his First Year in Europe. Boston, 1866. pp. 165-198.

——. Goethe: His Life and Works. An Essay. Boston, 1872. pp. 276.

——. Goethe, in his Coleridge, Shelley, and Goethe. Boston, 1880. p. 261.

Conway, M. D. A Hunt after Devils, in Harper's Magazine, March, 1869. XXXVIII. 540. Contains notices of places and incidents connected with Faust and with Goethe's house.

Robinson, H. Crabb. Diary, Reminiscences, and Correspondence. Boston, 1869. 2 v.

Blaze de Bury, H. Madame de Stein et Goethe. Revue des Deux Mondes. Paris, 1870. LXXXVI. 900.

Konewka, Paul. Illustrations of Goethe's Faust. Boston, 1871. Twelve silhouette designs with Taylor's translations.

Mendelssohn-Bartholdy, K. Goethe and Mendelssohn (1821-1831), translated, with additions, by M. E. von Glehn. London, 1872.

Mézières, A. Une Page de la Vie de Goethe. Ses Affinités Electives. Revue des Deux Mondes. Paris, 1872.

xxi

Gostwick, James, and R. Harrison. Outlines of German Literature. London, 1873. pp. 221-299, 440.

Helmholtz, H. On Goethe's Scientific Researches, in his Popular Lectures on Scientific Subjects. 1st ed. London, 1873. pp. 33-59.

——. Ueber Goethe's naturwissenschaftliche Arbeiten, in his Populäre wissenschaftliche Vorträge. Braunschweig, 1876. pp. 33-53.

Phelps, Almira L. Life and Writings of Goethe, in her Reviews and Essays. Philadelphia, 1873. p. 180.

Lazarus, Emma. Alide : an Episode of Goethe's Life. Philadelphia, 1874.

Hutton, R. H. Goethe and His Influence, in his Essays in Literary Criticism. Philadelphia, 1876. pp. 1-97.

Sime, James. Lessing. Boston, 1877. 2 v. Exhibits the literary relation of Goethe and Lessing, with the latter's criticisms on Goethe's Works.

Hayward, A. Goethe, in Foreign Classics for English Readers. Philadelphia [London, 1878].

Arnold, M. A French Critic on Goethe, in his Mixed Essays. New York, 1879. p. 274.

Barine, Arvide. La Légende de Faust. Revue des Deux Mondes. Paris, 1879. CXLII. 921.

Boyesen, H. H. Goethe and Schiller : their Lives and Works, including a Commentary on Faust. New York, 1879.

Browning, Oscar. Goethe, in Encyclopedia Britannica. 9th ed. London, 1879. X. 721. Contains an extended list of German authorities on Goethe.

Taylor, Bayard. Goethe, and Goethe's Faust, in his Studies in German Literature. New York, 1879. pp. 304-387.

Goethe, Catherine E. (Goethe's mother). Correspondence with Goethe, Lavater, Wieland et al., translated, with Biographical Sketches and Notes, by Alfred S. Gibbs. New York, 1880. pp. 263.

Grimm, H. Life and Times of Goethe, translated by S. H. Adams.

nal of Speculative Philosophy" for October, 1885, except Mr. Fiske's on "The Idea of God," which has been published as a separate volume by Houghton, Mifflin, and Company, who published in the same way, in 1884, Mr. Fiske's Lecture on "The Destiny of Man." The Lectures of 1884, on "The Genius and Character of Emerson," were published in a volume by J. R. Osgood and Company, and are now sold by Ticknor and Company, who publish the present volume; and members of the School are requested to order the volumes of the publishers, and not of the Faculty of the School.

The *Eighth* Session of the School will open on Wednesday, July 14, 1886, and will continue two weeks. The lectures and conversations of the first week (July 14–21) will be on *Dante and his Divine Comedy*; those of the second week (July 22–29), on *Plato and his Influence in Philosophy.* The Lecturers will be mainly the same as in 1885, but with some omissions and important additions. It is intended to publish a volume of the Lectures on Dante in 1886.

F. B. S.

Concord, December 1, 1885.

CONCORD SCHOOL OF PHILOSOPHY.

SEVENTH SESSION.

LECTURES AND SUBJECTS, 1885.

I Goethe's Genius and Work.

July 16. *Goethe's Self-Culture.* By Mr. John Albee, of New Castle, N. H.
" 18. *Goethe and his "Märchen."* By Rev. Dr. F. H. Hedge, of Cambridge, Mass.
" 24. *Goethe's Relation to Kant and Spinoza in Philosophy.* By Dr. F. L. Soldan, of St. Louis.
" 20. *Goethe's Faust.* By Professor Harris.
" 21. *Goethe's Faust.* By Professor H. S. White, of Cornell University.
" 17. *The "Ewig - Weibliche."* By Mrs. E. D. Cheney, of Boston.
" 22. *Goethe's Faust.* By Mr. D. J. Snider, of Cincinnati.
" 20. *Goethe's Relation to English Literature.* By Mr. F. B. Sanborn.
" 28. *Goethe as a Man of Science.* A Conversation conducted by Mr. Snider and Professor Harris.
" 27. *The Novellettes in "Wilhelm Meister."* By Professor Harris.
" 28. *"Wilhelm Meister" as a Whole.* By Mr. D. J. Snider.
" 18. *Goethe and Schiller.* By Rev. Dr. Bartol, of Boston.
Aug. 1. *The Women of Goethe.* By Mrs. Julia Ward Howe, of Boston.
July 22. *The Elective Affinities.* By Mr. S. H. Emery, Jr., of Concord, Mass.

xxiv

July 25. *Goethe's Titanism.* By Professor Thomas Davidson, of Orange, N. J.
" 23. *Goethe at Weimar.* By Professor W. T. Hewett, of Cornell University.
" 21. *Child-Life as portrayed in Goethe's Works.* By Mrs. Caroline K. Sherman, of Chicago.
" 27. *Goethe as Playwright.* By Mr. William O. Partridge, of Brooklyn, N. Y.
" 29. *The Style of Goethe.* By Mr. C. W. Ernst, of Boston.

II. A Symposium : Is Pantheism the Legitimate Outcome of Modern Science?

Lectures by Rev. Dr. A. P. Peabody (July 29) and Mr. John Fiske (July 29) of Cambridge, Professor Harris (July 30), Dr. G. H. Howison of California (July 31), Dr. F. E. Abbott (July 31) of Cambridge, and Dr. Montgomery of Texas (July 31). Readings from Thoreau, July 24, by Mr. H. G. O. Blake, of Worcester.

The Lectures on Pantheism appeared in the "Jour-

Boston, 1880. pp. 559.
Japp, Alexander H. Goethe, *in his* German Life and Literature. London [1881] pp. 269-379.

xxii

Stevens, Abel. Madame de Staël : a Study of her Life and Times. New York, 1881. The second volume contains notices of Weimar and its literary celebrities.
Blackie, J. S. Wisdom of Goethe. Edinburgh, 1883. pp. 246.
Düntzer, H. Life of Goethe, translated by T. W. Lyster. New York [London], 1884. pp. 796.
Lewes, M. A. Three Months in Weimar, *in her* Essays and Leaves from a Note-Book, by George Eliot. New York, 1884. p. 226. Gives an account of Goethe's life and associations at Weimar.
Nevinson, H. Herder and His Times. London, 1884.
Seeley, J. R. Goethe, *in* Contemporary Review. August, October, November, 1884. XLVI. 166, 488, 653.

C. — Papers on Goethe, in *The Journal of Speculative Philosophy.* (D. Appleton & Co., New York.)

Goethe's Theory of Colors, by W. T. Harris. I. 63.
Goethe's Faust, Letters on, by H. C. Brockmeyer. I. 178, II. 114.
Rosenkranz, Johann Karl Friedrich. On the Second Part of Faust. Translated by D. J. Snider. I. 65.
——. On the Social Romances. Translated by T. Davidson. II. 120, 215.
——. On the Wilhelm Meister. Translated by T. Davidson. IV. 145.
——. On the Composition of the Social Romances. Translated by D. J. Snider. IV. 268.
——. On Goethe's Märchen. Translated by Anna C. Brackett. V. 219.
——. On the Faust. Translated by Anna C. Brackett. IX. 48, 225, 401.
——. On Faust and Margaret. Translated by Anna C. Brackett. X. 87.
——. On the Second Part of Faust. Translated by Anna C. Brackett. XI. 113.
Goethe's Essay on Da Vinci's Last Supper. I. 243.
Goethe's Essay on the Laokoön (tr.). II. 208.
Goethe and German Fiction, F. G. Fairfield. IX. 303.
Goethe's Song of the Spirit over the Water, F. R. Marvin. X. 215.
Goethe's Das Märchen, by Gertrude Garrigues. XVII. 383.

xxiii

THE Lectures actually delivered at the School of Philosophy in the summer of 1885 were those in the following list, in the order indicated by the dates.

GOETHE IN YOUTH.

I.

GOETHE'S YOUTH.

By HORATIO S. WHITE.

IT will readily be observed that Goethe's life may be divided into distinct periods, each defined by some change in his outward relations, and each characterized by some change in his inner development. The great divisions which would naturally be made are: his youth before the removal to Weimar; the decade in that Thuringian capital preceding his departure for Italy,—a journey which forms the most significant epoch in his life; the period of mature manhood following, which was passed in the society of Schiller; and, finally, the long and fruitful old age during the first third of the present century. Leaving to others the task of tracing Goethe's later achievements in diverse fields,—where his tireless energy and his perennial vigor of spirit display him as the master of prose, the incomparable poet, the

2

literary despot, the histrionic magnate, the faithful prime-minister, the profound investigator and gifted discoverer, and the unwearied sage,—it shall be my attempt to depict him in his early youth, and in that perhaps most fascinating time of his young manhood embracing the dawning consciousness of varied powers which came to him at Strassburg, the stimulating intercourse with Herder, the impulse toward the study of Greek and English literature, the fleeting fervor for Gothic architecture, the sad but lovely idyl of Sessenheim, the tempestuous ardor of the Wetzlar entanglement, and the first flush of creative genius breaking forth in "Götz," in "Werther," in his matchless lyrics, and in the beginnings of "Faust."

For the study of this period we have ample sources. It is but a few years since a work appeared under the title, "Der junge Goethe," edited by Professor Bernays of Munich, and comprising the correspondence and literary proceeds of the first twenty-five years of Goethe's life. The editor had consulted the original manuscripts and first editions, and had in most cases carefully restored the early orthography, which had been modernized in the later revisions. All the spice and raciness of Goethe's youthful style, the strongly flavored South-German vernacular, the erratic spelling and still more erratic punctuation, have been preserved in their primitive freshness. Specially valuable is the series of letters in which his whole outward and inner life is mirrored with

3

all the warmth of unreserve which marked the epistolary literature of the last century.

To this useful work let us add Goethe's Autobiography, covering precisely the same period, but composed at a much later date.

"The question whether one should write his own biography," says Goethe, "is quite malapropos. I consider him who does so to be the most courteous of men."

In his Autobiography he reports that throughout his life he could not refrain from embodying in a written form his personal experiences, whether to relieve his soul, or to establish his conceptions of external things. "Everything which has hitherto been known as mine," he concludes, "forms therefore a great fragmentary confession, to make which complete this trifling work is a daring attempt." To Eckermann he said, in 1824: "The most important part of the individual's life is his development, which in my case is comprised in the detailed account of 'Wahrheit und Dichtung.'" And in 1831 he declared that the particular facts narrated in his Autobiography served merely to confirm a general reflection, a higher truth.

It is interesting to note, from a comparison between that work and the original sources, that, apart from some unessential inaccuracies and inconsistencies, Goethe's memory retained a trustworthy impression of his early experiences. It is true that discrepancies of detail have often crept into the relation; that

4

events may have been described in a manner somewhat different from that of their actual occurrence; that a character may have been idealized, and the outlines softened and harmonized to accord with the poet's purpose. But with all this, the portrayal of his youthful days must be considered thoroughly faithful to the inner meaning of his life.

Other contemporary accounts of Goethe's early career exist, together with a vast mass of commentary; but these two sources are sufficient to present him to us both as he unconsciously depicted himself at the time, and as he afterwards consciously depicted himself to the world.

It may be appropriate at this point to recall the principal features of Goethe's earlier years. We find in them an exceptional concurrence of fortunate circumstances. Born into an advantageous environment, an independent citizen of a free municipality, endowed with great natural gifts, possessed of varied accomplishments and acquirements, with comfortable if not affluent means, coming into contact with many of the illustrious people of his day, and viewing many of the notable events of that period, his life assumes more than an individual interest, and becomes important and significant as typifying and illustrating his times. The Lisbon earthquake touches his young heart, and forces him to question the goodness of the Creator; the French occupy Frankfort, and he is initiated into the political quarrels of the Seven Years' War; in his rambles

5

among the common people at their labors and their pastimes in that curious old town, he imbibes the spirit of their walk and conversation, which is afterwards reflected with fidelity in the popular scenes of his dramas; the coronation of Joseph the Second unrolls before his eyes the pageantry of the pompous but hollow Empire; as a student at Leipzig he skims round the circle of knowledge, and chants,

"Da steh' ich nun, ich armer Thor,
Und bin so klug als wie zuvor."

The Dresden Gallery attracts and charms him with its pictorial treasures; in Frankfort the gentle and devout mystic, Fräulein von Klettenberg, pursues with him studies in alchemy, and imbues him with the doctrines of pietism; and in 1770 he arrives at Strassburg, in season to behold the daughter of Maria Theresia crossing the Rhine on her triumphal and fateful journey toward the French capital.

Let us here note a few characteristic passages from his earlier letters. Writing in 1764, at the age of fourteen, he describes himself as follows:—

"One of my chief defects is, that I am somewhat impulsive. You know of course the choleric temperament; on the other hand, no one forgets an affront more readily than I. Furthermore, I am quite accustomed to be imperious; but when I have nothing to say, I can let things go. However, I am quite willing to submit to authority when it is exercised as should be expected. One thing more, I am very impatient, and do not like to remain long in uncertainty."

6

To a home friend he writes from Leipzig, in 1765, describing his college life:—

"What am I studying? Is it worth while asking? *Institutiones imperiales. Historiam juris. Pandectas,* and a private course on the first seven and last seven titles of the Codex. For one does not need any more, the rest one forgets anyway. No, your obedient servant! That we will let well alone.—Next week the courses in philosophy and mathematics begin.

"Gottsched I have not yet seen. He has married again. You know it though. She is nineteen and he is sixty-five. She is four shoes tall and he seven. She is as thin as a herring and he as stout as a sack of feathers. —I'm cutting a great figure here, but am no dandy yet, nor shall I become so. I have to be rather clever in order to get time to study. To parties, concerts, the theatre, at banquets, suppers, excursions, no end! Ah, it's a precious time, but a precious business too! It costs! The deuce, but my purse feels it.

"Stop! save us! hold on! Don't you see them flying? There go two Louis d'or marching off! Help! There goes another. Heavens! a couple more. Dimes with us are like cents with you. But yet one may live very cheaply here. I hope to get through the year on three hundred thalers.—what do I say?—with two hundred thalers. N.B. Not counting in what has already gone to the dogs."

At the end of his Leipzig course he writes back, in 1768, a grateful letter to Oeser, one of his instructors:—

7

"What do I not owe you, dearest Professor, that you have shown me the way to the true and beautiful, that you have rendered my heart susceptible to all that is beautiful, my knowledge, my insight,—do I not possess them all through you? How true and clear the strange, almost unintelligible saying has become to me, that the workshop of the great artist develops the budding philosopher, the budding poet, more than the auditorium of the sage and the critic! Teaching does much, but encouragement does everything. Who among all my teachers has ever deemed me worthy of encouragement save you? Either all blame or all praise, and nothing can so destroy one's capacity. Encouragement after blame is sun after rain, fruitful growth.

"You have taught me to be humble without being cast down, and to be proud without presumption. I could find no end of saying what you have taught me; pardon my grateful heart this apostrophe; I have that in common with all tragic heroes, that my passion would fain pour forth in tirades, and woe to the one who gets in the way of my lava!"

These earlier years yielded an abundance of literary composition, the remnants of which reveal not indistinctly the coming lyric poet, while the two little comedies of that date betray the influence upon their composer of the lighter French dramatists, and perhaps of Wieland, with whose writings he was then quite captivated. One may also detect reflections in thin disguise of Goethe's juvenile *affaires de cœur*, the confession of which has already begun.

8

To Strassburg he comes at twenty. Of deep import was his sojourn in the quaint Alsatian city. It gave him the Cathedral, Herder, and Friederike.

At Leipzig Goethe had been led to regard the term *Gothic* as the Greeks did *Barbarian*. An ignorant but declared enemy to that style of architecture, he is now confronted in silent reproach by the mighty and impressive minster. His conversion is as sudden and complete as that of Saul of Tarsus; and in the

rhapsodic essay, "Von Deutscher Baukunst," a memorial to the noble architect, Erwin von Steinbach, is contained his recantation. He bursts forth:—

"With what an unexpected sensation did its aspect surprise me! My soul was filled by an impression of grandeur and completeness, which, consisting of a thousand harmonious details, I was able indeed to taste and enjoy, without recognizing or explaining it. They say it is so with the joys of heaven; and how often have I returned to partake of this joy of heaven upon earth, to comprehend the giant spirit of our elder brothers in their works! How often has my eye, wearied by its searching inspection, been refreshed in cheerful repose by the evening twilight, when the countless parts melted into entire masses, and these, simple and grand, stood before my soul! Then was revealed to me in gentle premonitions the genius of the great master. And how freshly it dawned upon me in the vaporous splendor of the morning! How rejoiced I was to behold the great, harmonious masses enlivened into numberless minute details, as in works of eternal nature, down to the slightest fibre, every-

9

thing form, and everything adapted to the whole! how the firmly founded monstrous structure rises lightly into air! how like network all, and yet for eternity!"

If these early and enthusiastic impressions gradually faded, and well-nigh were extinguished by the stay in Italy, at the end of Goethe's life they were once more revived, less ardent, but with greater clearness, and again through the influence of his study of another worthy and imposing structure, the Cathedral at Cologne.

Before meeting Herder in Strassburg, Goethe had not come into contact with a mind of the first order. Herder was five years older, had already gained reputation as a writer, and had recently returned to Germany from an extended tour in France and Holland. He writes to his Riga friends, that, whereas before he had been frothy, vain, erratic, and whimsical, they would now find him more manly, ripe, developed, cosmopolitan, more of a Briton, and perchance thrice as ardent, instead of frivolous, Frenchy, and unstable. His relation to Goethe was similar to Goethe's rela-

tions with Schiller at the first meeting in 1788, after the Italian journey. Said Schiller, in describing to Körner this interview: "Goethe is so far ahead of me, less perhaps in years than in experience of life and in self-development, that we shall never come together while en route." Goethe felt toward Herder the same modesty of immaturity; nor did Herder, to whom his young admirer seemed then but a wild fledgling, seek to spare his sensibilities. Mercilessly

10

caustic, lashing Goethe's foibles and conceits, establishing no such relations of mutual admiration and mutual palliation as then existed among many prominent German litterateurs, yet holding him by force of lofty character and a reach and range which Goethe fully acknowledged, a moral pedagogue of the finest type, and already a literary critic and historian of independent and original stamp, his was an influence to correct, to guide, and to inspire his fervid young follower. It is Herder, then, who expounds to Goethe the bearings of modern literature, who rails at the weaknesses of the contemporary native authors, who, fresh from Paris, yet sated with French materialism, turns away from Voltaire and the philosophers, although for a time singling out Rousseau alone as

the apostle of the day, and aids Goethe to check and overcome his own early tendencies, who introduces him to Swift, to Goldsmith, to Ossian, and to Shakespeare anew, who teaches him to know the Greeks, to appreciate the Hebrew bards, and to realize that poetry is not the possession of a learned caste, but the heritage of all mankind.

In that initial year of their acquaintance Goethe thus addresses his new correspondent:—

"I am compelled to write to you in the midst of my first sensations. Away with mantle and collar! Your spicy letter is worth three years of every-day experience. There is no answer to it, and who could answer it? My whole self is thrilled,—that you may imagine, man,—and the vibration is still too great for my pen to move steadily.—

11

Herder, Herder, abide to me what you are to me. If I am destined to be your planet, I will be so, will be so

gladly, will be so loyally. A friendly moon to the earth. But this—feel it absolutely—that I should rather be Mercury, the least, the smallest rather among seven, revolving with you around one sun, than the first among five turning about Saturn.

"Adieu, dear man! I will not let you go. I will not leave you. Jacob wrestled with the angel of the Lord. Even if I should grow weary at it!""

The later relations of Herder and Goethe at Weimar are beyond the scope of this paper, but we may recall that it was the latter's influence which secured for Herder his summons to the principal ecclesiastical position in the Duchy, and that, if their subsequent association was not always of the most cordial description, the fault or the misfortune must be laid chiefly at the door of the Herders.

Before leaving Strassburg, a word on Friederike. The well-known incidents of the story may be briefly narrated[1] A young man, fresh from the perusal of a literature of poetry and sentiment, wanders away on horseback with a student friend over the smiling meadows. In the picturesque little village of Sessenheim he is presented to a pastor's family, whose situation to his quick imagination soon reproduces, with strange parallelism, the environment of the Wakefield group in Goldsmith's "Vicar," a work which Herder

12

was introducing to Strassburg circles. Received with full rural cordiality, he lingers and returns, and returns and lingers, until a fair heart is fatally his own. The end of his academic course is the end of the idyl. The world demands him, and to the world he yields himself; and a summer of perilous sweetness has saddened one joyous life, and left in another a lasting sting of remorse. Traces of this remorse one may find in the long deferred confession which Goethe's narrative contains,—a narrative which the aged poet could not dictate without signs of deep emotion. He depicts his conscious feeling that a withdrawal would be indefensible, his inability to break away from the beloved object even when he had in purpose re-

[1] Cf. "A Pilgrimage to Sesenheim," Lippincott's Magazine, February, 1884.

nounced her, the pain of the final parting, and the heart-rending answer of Friederike to a farewell in writing. "Here for the first time," he continues, "I was guilty, I had keenly wounded a most beautiful soul; and the period which followed was an almost unendurable time of gloomy repentance." He seeks for aid in poetry, and acknowledges that the two Marys in "Götz" and "Clavigo," and the sorry *rôles* which their lovers play, are the results of his remorseful contemplations. In the Gretchen of "Faust," too, one may recognize traits of the unaffected village maiden; and some of the most irresistible of Goethe's earlier poems were directly inspired by his acquaintance with Friederike Brion. What a gust of stormy fervor sweeps through the stanzas of "Willkommen und Abschied"!

13

"Es schlug mein Herz; geschwind zu Pferde,
Und fort, wild, wie ein Held zur Schlacht!
Der Abend wiegte schon die Erde,
Und an den Bergen hieng die Nacht;
Schon stund im Nebelkleid die Eiche,
Wie ein gethürmter Riese, da,
Wo Finsterniss aus dem Gesträuche
Mit hundert schwarzen Augen sah.

"Der Mond von seinem Wolkenhügel,
Schien schläfrig aus dem Duft hervor;
Die Winde schwangen leise Flügel,
Umsausten schauerlich mein Ohr;
Die Nacht schuf tausend Ungeheuer—
Doch tausendfacher war mein Muth;
Mein Geist war ein verzehrend Feuer,
Mein ganzes Herz zerfloss in Gluth."

And again in the glad "Mayfest," where every line is a joyous heart-beat:—

"Wie herrlich leuchtet
Mir die Natur!
Wie glänzt die Sonne!
Wie lacht die Flur!

"Es dringen Blüten
Aus jedem Zweig,
Und tausend Stimmen
Aus dem Gesträuch.

"Und Freud' und Wonne
Aus jeder Brust.
O Erd! O Sonne!
O Glück! O Lust!"

But Sessenheim was not enough; for this waywardness of Goethe ceased not with maturer years. That the poet has been his own accuser cannot ren-

14

der one's censure less severe. For this censure is undoubtedly induced by the feeling that, if a great genius should not need to be governed by the same laws perhaps as the ordinary mortal, this must happen by reason of his rising superior to those laws, not by his falling subject to their jurisdiction and then claiming exemption by a special act of grace. Such censors feel that Goethe's life, despite its great intellectual sweep, does not mirror a moral career correspondingly pure and lofty. To guard an artless maiden against the involuntary deviations of her unshielded heart, to observe not merely the visible and outward, but the invisible spiritual sanctities of betrothal and wedlock, to despise not, even in externals, the righteous formalities of the marriage tie,—this much, at least, may be demanded of that man before whom we are to bow the head. It is this fine "sense of conduct," to borrow a happy phrase of Matthew Arnold, the lack of which many severe Western Puritans deplore in the author of "Stella," and such a lack to them fatally mars Goethe's character.¹ Whether this lack arose from the constitution of society in Goethe's day, or was an innate defect of his own, we shall leave for others to decide. Yet a faithful chronicler of Goethe's early years may not write, as the English Laureate of his friend,

"A passion pure in snowy bloom
Through all the years of April blood."

15

Nor in spite of Goethe's ardent human praise of woman, and the many exquisite feminine portraits which he has drawn, do we find that reverential and ethereal adoration in thought and act of which types are not wanting in modern literature and life. While conceding, then, the wide sweep of his sympathies and of his intellectual powers, it must not be considered unjust to Goethe to deny him, not moral eminence, but that moral pre-eminence which is the mark of the finest spiritual organizations.

The four years, from 1771 to 1775, between Goethe's departure from Strassburg and his arrival in Weimar, were filled with varied experiences and with the most active literary productivity. It was a whirl of journey upon journey, of friendship added to friendship, of love affair and tender attachment. On one side, Schlosser, Merck, Gotter, Kestner, the Stolbergs, Leuchsenring, Lavater, Basedow, Klopstock, the Jacobis, Knebel, and the Weimar princes; and on the other, Lotte, La Roche and Maximiliane, Fräulein von Klettenberg, Anna Mönch, the Countess Stolberg, and Lilli von Schönemann; while the restless youth ycleped the Wanderer went roaming through the woody solitudes about his native place; or visited the courts at Wetzlar to pursue anything but law; or strayed up and down the Main and Rhine and Lahn, or through the pleasant South-German cities, or into Switzerland and over the St. Gothard; and again from Frankfort setting out for Italy, but turning back at Heidelberg, and onward at last to Weimar.

16

Equally nomadic, too, his intellectual career. Ostensibly trained for the legal profession, his studies had spread over a far wider field. His note-books at the University disclose an interest in medicine, chemistry, anatomy, physics, philosophy, and general literature. Nor were music and art neglected. "To regard things carefully, to store them up in memory, to give good heed and let no day pass without collecting something, this," writes Goethe from Strassburg, "is what we now have to do." And again: "Jurisprudence begins to please me. After all, it is like Merseburg beer,—the first sip, you shudder, but after a week you cannot do without it. And chemistry still remains my secret mistress."

His first months in Frankfort give him a distaste for the practice of the law, as well as a prejudice against the aristocratic philistinism of the place. He institutes a Shakespeare celebration, and pronounces

¹ Cf. Das Goethe-Jahrbuch, 1884, p. 237, "Goethe in Amerika."

an ecstatic oration.

"The first page which I read in him," he exclaims, "made me his own for all my life, and when I had finished the first piece I stood as one born blind, to whom a miraculous touch has in a moment restored his vision. I recognized, I felt most keenly, that my existence was infinitely broadened. All was new and unknown to me, and the unaccustomed radiance pained my sight. I doubted not a moment to renounce the regular theatre. Unity of place seemed to me so oppressively confining, unity of action and time burdensome fetters for our imagination!—And now that I saw how much the men of

17

rules in their prison pen had wronged me, my heart would have burst if I had not declared war against them, and daily sought to storm their towers."

It was his "Götz von Berlichingen" which led the assault. No cold and stately hero from classic antiquity, but a valiant mediæval German knight, bluff and honest, fuming and fighting, and dying bravely.

Goethe waits for Herder's judgment. "Shakespeare has quite ruined you," exclaims impatiently Herder. "Enough," cries Goethe. "It must be melted down, freed from dross, furnished with nobler material, and be recast. Then shall it appear before you again." It is done, and with the several draughts before us we can watch the work and note the change. At last, a fresh, vigorous drama, or series of spirited dramatic tableaux and staccato dialogue, distinguished by no unity of design nor historic accuracy, but, with all its ragged edges, a healthful, breezy, patriotic outburst.

In 1772 the "Frankfurt Gelehrte Anzeigen," a semiweekly journal, was founded by friends of Goethe, and created a great sensation. He, as well as Herder, becomes at once a collaborator, and a remarkable series of critical reviews is issued. Pungent, racy, epigrammatic, slashing away at all pretence however dignified, dealing fearless censure and wholesouled praise,—we need no acquaintance with the writings examined to appreciate and enjoy the clear view, the bubbling extravagance, the lusty blows,

18

the wit, and withal the sound judgment which is displayed.

Snatches only can we quote, from the collections of Bernays and of Scherer, for our space forbids longer and perhaps more significant passages.

On a work entitled "Letters regarding the most important Truths of Revelation," he comments :—

"These letters are directed principally against the haughty sages of our century who see in God something else than the penal judge of degraded humanity, who believe that the creature of his hand is no monster, that in the sight of God this world is something more than the antechamber of the future state, and who peradventure even presume to hope that he will not punish to all eternity. We pass by the attacks upon the foes of revelation, which often are blows in the air; the argumentation regarding the history of mankind at the time of the Redeemer, and the many accumulated proofs of Christianity of which one can no more demand than from a bundle of rods that they should all be of equal strength. But we ask all fanatics on both sides to consider whether it be seemly to maintain in a spirit of persecution that what it is claimed is regarded by God as good or evil on our part is good or evil in his sight too, or whether that which is refracted in our sight into two colors may not flow back to him in one ray of light. In this we all agree, that man should do that which we all call good, whether his spirit be a muddy pool or a mirror of beautiful nature, whether he has strength to journey along his way, or is sick and needs a crutch. Strength and crutch come from one hand. In that we agree, and that is enough!"

19

The following notices illustrate what may be called the summary process :—

"Address to his Royal Highness, the Grand-duke Paul Petrowitsch. Petersburg, 1772.—Alexander used to take a poet along with him, to whom he would give on contract a coin for every good verse and a cuff for every poor one. We trust that this poetic spokesman made other conditions for himself, and we admire the patience and vigilance of the young Duke, if he heard the address through without falling asleep."

"The Brother. By a Lady. 2 vols.—We desire that this brother may remain the only son of his father; for the work is beneath criticism."

"The Praise of Fashion, an Address delivered and printed à la Mode. 1772. . . . And also written à la mode; that is, as badly as possible."

"Wolf Krage, a Tragedy, by Johannes Ewald, from the Danish. 1772.—Night, high treason and fratricide, abomination and death, and gloom, horrors, pains of love and pains of dissolution, so that with a devout 'Heaven preserve us!' we began to think about going home betimes!"

"Lyric Poems by Blum. Berlin, 1772. . . . We wish the composer a first-rate girl, days of leisure, and the pure poetic spirit, without the spirit of authorship. The best of poets degenerates when he has the public in mind while composing, and when filled more with a desire for fame, especially newspaper fame, than with his subject."

"Enlightened Times; or a Contemplation of the Present Condition of the Sciences and Prevailing Customs in

20

Germany. Züllichau, 1772.—A tedious academic discussion. The composer, who is probably quite young, at least quite inexperienced, knows the world only from the four faculties, and must have heard somewhere that we live in enlightened times. Now this vexes him, and so he proves that the philosophers are not enlightened because some still defend the best world; nor the doctors, because so many men die; nor the lawyers, because there are so many laws without lawsuits, and lawsuits without laws; nor the theologians, because they are so obstinate, and because one falls asleep so often when they preach; nor the humanists, because they do not pursue Latin and Greek with sufficient earnestness, make Hebrew so hard, write so many verses, and the like. Enlightened times! If the fellow had only written about the man in the moon, or the polar bear! That was his calling! Any one who presumes to consider our times enlightened again, must read this whole work as a penalty; and he who considers them enlightened because he lives in them himself, must learn it all by heart."

And finally one more extract, from a review of a work entitled, "A Characterization of the most refined European Nationalities. In Two Parts."

Leipzig.

"Character of refined nations! Throw the coin into the crucible if you wish to learn its worth. From the stamp you will never find it out to all eternity. What then is the character of a polished nation? What else can it be than the reflection of the religion and the civic constitution in which a nation is set; drapery, regarding

21

which the most that one can say is how it may fit the nation. Perchance a philosophic observer might have produced a tolerable characterization. But the composer complacently made the grand tour through England, France, Italy, Spain, Germany, and the Netherlands, looked into his Puffendorf, talked with fine ladies and gentlemen, and took his book and wrote. Unfortunately there is nothing in all the world more devious than fine ladies and gentlemen, and so his portrayals were also out of focus; the Englishman he always defends against the Frenchman; the Frenchman he always contrasts with the Englishman; the former is simply frivolous, the latter simply strong, the Italian pompous and sedate, the German guzzling and counting up his ancestors. Everything by hearsay, on the surface, an abstract of 'good society.'

"And this he calls a characterization! What different judgments he would often have passed if he had condescended to view the man in the midst of his family, the peasant on his farm, the mother among her children, the journeyman in his workshop, the honest burgher by his tankard of beer, and the scholar and merchant in his club or café! But it did not even occur to him that there were any people there; or if it did occur to him, how was he to have the patience, the time, the condescension? To him all Europe was a fine French drama, or, what amounts to pretty much the same thing, a puppet play! He peeped in, and peeped out again, and voilà tout!"

22

An important and perhaps somewhat neglected phase of Goethe's earlier years is his attitude in matters of religion. We sometimes hear him called

"the great Pagan," a shallow echo of the reactionary romanticists and the strict ecclesiastics of sixty or seventy years ago. But the paganism of Goethe, as Heine cleverly says, is marvellously modernized; and if the middle period of his life betrays a drift toward classic heathendom, his youth, like his old age, bears the stamp of strong religious views, and a faith which in these days would simply be termed liberal. His home training introduced him to catechism and dogma, and he was encouraged to report the sermons heard. The New Testament he learned to read in Greek, and the Old Testament in Hebrew. Stealthy hours were devoted to memorizing Klopstock's "Messias,"—a work which evidently inspired one of his earliest efforts, the poem on Christ's descent into hell,—and a Biblical epic in prose was partly accomplished. Much in the religious life of his day, and some peculiarities of the official representatives of the Church, did not appeal to his nature, nor did he seem to possess what are called "settled convictions"; but he honored the sacraments, and for many years pursued an independent and sober study of the Scriptures.

A previous quotation has given the tendency of his thought regarding the truths of revelation. In a criticism of the history of Count Struensee's conversion, he remarks further:—

23

"Of the worth of a conversion, God alone may judge; God alone can know how great the step must be which the soul has to take here in order yonder to draw near to a communion with him, to the abode of perfection, and to the intercourse and friendship of higher beings. Thousands of open and secret foes of religion exist, thousands who would have loved Christ as their friend if he had been depicted to them as a friend, and not as a sullen tyrant, ever ready to crush with the thunderbolt where the highest perfection is not found."

Goethe's youthful standpoint is still more clearly indicated in a short publication, dating from 1771, in the form of a letter from an aged pastor to his new colleague. Some people, he writes, find no pleasure in being Christians unless all the heathen are to be roasted forever; but for his part he hurries over that doctrine as over red-hot iron. He has grown old in contemplating the ways of the Lord, and finds that God and Love are synonymous. He has no ground for doubting any one's salvation; it is enough to believe in Divine Love revealed in Christ. Controversy he avoids; it is easier to hold an eel by the tail than a sophist with reasons; the divine nature of the Bible cannot be proven if it be not felt; Augsburg and Dordrecht make as little essential difference in the religion of man as France and Germany in his nature; the confession of faith was a formula necessary in order to establish something, but leaves him his Bible; if one creed comes nearer the Word of God than another, so much the better for its confessors; to force opinions upon one is cruel, but to require that one must *feel* what one cannot

24

is tyrannous nonsense. Luther labored to free us from spiritual bondage, yet the Romish Church has preserved much of divine truth; suffer it to be, and give it your blessing!

In a word, the essence of Goethe's creed was *toleration.*

It was during this early period that Goethe became at least partially familiar with the writings of Spinoza. Herman Grimm ranks the latter with Homer, Shakespeare, and Raphael as one of the four great minds which had a lasting effect upon Goethe, regarding them as representatives of Greece and Rome, with all the treasures which those names imply and include, and of the Germanic and Hebrew tradition. Goethe acknowledges to Eckermann, in 1831, how well adapted to his own youthful necessities were the views of the great Jewish thinker, in whom he found himself. Unable to distinguish between what he brought to Spinoza's "Ethics" and what he took away, it was yet enough for Goethe that he there discovered that which calmed his emotions,—a grand and open survey of the sensuous and the moral world. But it was the boundless disinterestedness of the contemplations of Spinoza which specially attracted him, as well as the lesson of renunciation, the distinction between knowledge and

faith, and the thought of the unity of creation. To these contemplations Goethe repeatedly recurred in later years, and in his old age the "Ethics" was still by his side.

25

If we seek for traces of pantheistic views in Goethe's writings, we are at first embarrassed by the necessity of defining the term Pantheism itself. According to a recent English historian of this subject, (C. E. Plumptre,) Pantheism, in the generally accepted meaning of the word, is the name given to that system of speculation which identifies the universe with God. This explanation presents a good working definition, allowing the author to trace the presence of pantheistic ideas in various philosophic systems from ancient times. But much depends upon the manner of the identification; and in his summary and conclusion Mr. Plumptre becomes more precise, and describes the form of pantheism which he has been discussing as that which, discarding anthropomorphism on the one hand, and naked materialism on the other, conceives God to be a Power, Eternal, Infinite, disclosing itself alike through every form and phenomenon of nature. It does not identify God with perishable matter; but rather conceives him to be related to matter somewhat as the soul is to the body. More concise is the definition of Dr. Hedge: "God, the creative and ruling power of the universe, distinguished by reason alone from the universe itself." In this sense Goethe, who was the last remove from an atheist, viewing the Finite only as the "living garment" of the Infinite, will be found fully in harmony with the spirit of Tennyson in his profound and beautiful poem styled "The Higher Pantheism."

26

A discussion of the many proofs of this view which Goethe's works afford, would carry us far into Goethe's manhood and old age. One illustration only may perhaps be permitted, from the "Proœmion," in 1816:—

"Was wär' ein Gott, der nur von aussen stiesse,
 Im Kreis das All am Finger laufen liesse,

Ihm ziemt's die Welt im Innern zu bewegen,
Natur in sich, sich in Natur zu hegen,
So dass, was in ihm lebt und webt und ist,
Nie seine Kraft, nie seinen Geist vermisst."

The ante-Weimar days witness only the beginnings of Goethe's growing interest in Spinoza's ethical and pantheistic theories, and of the irreconcilable conflict thereby induced between Jacobi and himself; but we are able to pick out from his letters and reviews of that period, from "Werther," and from those portions of "Faust" which evidence an early origin, fragmentary but significant passages which bear witness to this interest. It was his unfinished drama of "Prometheus," indeed, which, containing seeds of Spinozism, incidentally occasioned the famous colloquy between Lessing and Jacobi upon Spinoza, rousing an extended controversy regarding Lessing's opinions;—a controversy from which the serious study of Spinoza, and the important philosophic conclusions which proceeded from that study, are considered to date.

We have reserved till now any mention of the work which Goethe is said to have rated next to "Faust,"—"Die Leiden des jungen Werthers."

27

Shakespeare has been quoted by Doctor Bartol as describing the phenomenon of sleep-walking in Lady Macbeth better than any modern physiologist; and recently a prominent German professor of psychiatry has gravely analyzed Goethe's work as an accurate pathological study of a diseased mind. Werther indeed was an illustration, somewhat over-wrought, of his time. He is the super-sensitive soul, whom the rough world only bruises instead of bracing. Disappointment in love, combined with a social affront which cripples his ambition, proves too heavy a burden, and he turns his back upon the world and seeks in suicide an escape. The weak side of Werther—the unhealthy sentimentality in place of healthy sentiment—is specially repugnant to the present age, which is schooled to control, if not to conceal, its emotions; and although the pure and powerful fancy, the warm affec-

tion for nature, are fascinating traits in the work to this day, no sound mind can peruse the narration without a continuing inward remonstrance and impatience. This feeling, however, extends not so much to Werther as a creation as to Werther as a character. But it was precisely because Wertherism was then so common a psychological phenomenon that the work gained so enormous a success. The mirror was held up to human nature, and the distorted likeness was at once recognized. The personal experiences upon which the story was based are now common property, and it will scarcely be necessary to

28

describe in detail the framework of society in which the story is set. The Storm and Stress period forms the background, a period whose leading characteristics indeed are peculiar to no special time or place. In its limited application to the last third of the eighteenth century in Germany, the movement which this phrase describes was a general revolt against conventionality and the restraints of oppressive authority, both in society and in letters. Herder and Goethe are the leaders in literature, the former as a pioneer in criticism, the latter as the embodiment of the poetic spirit. Goethe feels the far-reaching, penetrating agitation, and through his soul quiver and thrill the subtle and potent forces which are at work to fashion the coming era. He gathers up the tangled threads of life, and weaves them into a brilliant tapestry of song and tale and drama, which faithfully depict the universal fortunes of mankind. So Goethe required first experience before he might poetically create. But not solely in order to create. He was receptive, ardent, impressionable, blending warmth of heart with strength of intellect. To the younger Goethe, as well as to the elder Goethe, sweet human intercourse, encouragement, and sympathy were needful. Solitude, save for brief intervals, he could not suffer. He knew little of those heights of loneliness on which the impatient soul of Lessing was so often forced to dwell. For even if his mental outlook was far wider than the glance of most of his associates could comprise, even

29

if he had often to endure bitter criticism and personal hostilities, his motives and his aims alike misunderstood, he was also assured of ample appreciation, aid, and applause.

Thus he rounds out his first quarter of a century. The principal features of his youthful prime we have here endeavored briefly to sketch, indicating the various influences which shaped or modified his course, and outlining his multifarious mental activity. We have found him in his youth already a perfect lyric poet; for all that follows,—the luxuriant elegiacs, the fresh and natural ballads, the splendid harmonies of "Gott und Welt," the tender, melancholy yearning of Mignon, the melodious Oriental imageries, the elaborate elegies of Marienbad, the numberless variations of the Faust stanza,—is but a differing manifestation of the same spirit; we find him already penning a warm and vigorous prose, which, pruned and perfected, is to become the standard of modern German; we find him as the author of "Götz" already vying with Klopstock in arousing a national sentiment in the German mind by restoring to his countrymen a consciousness of their manly past; as an essayist and reviewer, we find him already laboring to rebuke vain wordiness and false or artificial canons of taste, to unfetter the judgment and to awaken a catholic sympathy; already in "Werther"

30

"He took the suffering human race,
He read each wound, each weakness clear,
And struck his finger on the place,
And said, *Thou ailest here and here.*"

And finally his masterpiece of "Faust" is growing under his touch and gaining some of its rarest passages. Thus endowed with this potent promise of his brilliant past, we leave him at Weimar, on the threshold of his long and beneficent career in that his final home.

APPENDIX TO "GOETHE'S YOUTH."

IN order to convey some idea of the peculiarities of Goethe's youthful style, the exact text of the letter from which the extract on page 6 has been translated is here given:—

AN JOH. JACOB RIESE IN FRANKFURT.

Leipzig 20. Oktober 1764.
Morgens um 6.

Riese, guten Tag!   den 21. Abends um 5.

Riese, guten Abend!
Gestern hatte ich mich kaum hingesetzt um euch eine Stunde zu widmen, Als schnell ein Brief von Horn kam und mich von meinem angefangnen Blate hinweg riss. Heute werde ich auch nicht länger bey euch bleiben. Ich geh in die Commoedie. Wir haben sie recht schön hier. Aber dennoch! Ich binn unschlüssig! Soll ich bey euch bleiben? Soll ich in die Commödie gehn?— Ich weiss nicht! Geschwind! Ich will würfeln. Ja ich habe keine Würfel!—Ich gehe! Lebt wohl!—

31

Doch halte! nein! ich will da bleiben. Morgen kann ich wieder nicht da muss ich ins Colleg, und Besuchen und Abends zu Gaste. Da will ich also jetzt schreiben. Meldet mir was ihr für ein Leben lebt? Ob ihr manchmahl an mich denkt. Was ihr für Professor habt. & cetera und zwar ein langes & cetera. Ich lebe hier, wie —wie—ich weiss selbst nicht recht wie. Doch so ohngefähr

So wie ein Vogel, der auf einem Ast
Im schönsten Wald, sich, Freiheit athmend wiegt.
Der ungestört die sanfte Luft geniesst.
Mit seinen Fittichen von Baum zu Baum
von Bussch zu Bussch sich singend hinzuschwingen.

Genug stellt euch ein Vögelein, auf einem grünen Aestelein in allen seinen Freuden für, so leb ich. Heut hab ich angefangen Collegia zu hören.
Was für?—Ist es der Mühe wehrt zu fragen? Institutiones imperiales. Historiam iuris. Pandectas und ein privatissimum über die 7 ersten und 7 letzten Titel des Codicis. Denn mehr braucht man nicht, das übrige vergisst sich doch. Nein gehorsamer Diener! das liessen wir schön unterwege.—Im Ernste ich habe heute zwei Collegen gehört, die Staatengeschichte bey Professor Böhmer, und bei Ernesti über Cicerons Gespräche vom Redner. Nicht wahr das ging an. Die andere Woche

32

geht Collegium philosophicum et mathematicum an.— Gottscheden hab ich noch nicht gesehen. Er hat wieder geheurathet. Eine Jfr. Obristleutnantin. Ihr wisst es doch. Sie ist 19 und er 65 Jahr. Sie ist 4 Schue gross und er 7. Sie ist mager wie ein Häring und er dick wie ein Federsack.—Ich mache hier grosse Figur!—Aber noch zur Zeit bin ich kein Stutzer. Ich werd es auch nicht.—Ich brauche Kunst um fleissig zu sein. In Gesellschaften, Concert, Comoedie, bei Gastereyen, Abendessen, Spazierfahrten so viel es um diese Zeit angeht. Ha! das geht köstlich. Aber auch köstlich, kostspielig. Zum Henker das fühlt mein Beutel. Halt! rettet! haltet auf! Siehst du sie nicht mehr fliegen? Da marschierten 2 Louisdor. Helft! da ging eine. Himmel! schon wieder ein paar. Groschen die sind hier, wie Kreuzer bei euch draussen im Reiche.—Aber dennoch kann hier einer sehr wohlfeil leben. Die Messe ist herum. Und ich werde recht mengeus leben. Da hoffe ich des Jahrs mit 300 Rthr. was sage ich mit 200 Rthr. auszukommen. NB. das nicht mitgerechnet, was schon zum Henker ist. Ich habe kostbaaren Tissch. Merkt einmahl unser Küchenzettel. Hüner, Gänsse, Truthahnen, Endten, Rebhüner, Schnepfen, Feldhüner, Forellen, Hassen, Wildpret, Hechte, Fasanen, Austern u. s. w. Das erscheinet Täglich. nichts von anderm groben Fleisch ut sunt Rind, Kälber, Hamel u. s. w. das weiss ich nicht mehr wie es schmeckt. Und die Herrlichkeiten nicht teuer, gar nicht teuer.—Ich sehe, dass mein Blat bald voll ist und es stehen noch keine verse darauf, ich habe deren machen wollen. Auf ein andermahl. Sagt Kehren dass ich ihm schreiben werde. Ich hore von Horn, dass ihr euch ob absentiam puellarum forma elegantium beklagt. Lasst euch von ihm das Urteil sagen dass ich über euch fällete.

GOETHE.

33

In a letter to his friend Schönborn, consul in Algeria, occurs a noteworthy passage in turbulent praise of Herder:—

Frankfurt am 8. Jun. [1774.]

Herder hat ein Werk drucken lassen: *Aelteste Urkunde des Menschengeschlechts.* Ich hielt meinen Brief

inne um Ihnen auch Ihr Theil übers Moor zu schicken, noch aber bin ichs nicht im Stande, es ist ein so mystisch weitstrahlsinniges Ganze, eine in der Fülle verschlungener Geäste lebende und rollende Welt, dass weder eine Zeichnung nach verjüngtem Maasstab einigen Ausdruck der Riesengestalt nachschäffen, oder eine treue Silhouette einzelner Theile melodisch sympathetischen Klang in der Seele anschlagen kann. Er ist in die Tiefen seiner Empfindung hinabgestiegen, hat drinn alle die hohe heilige Kraft der simpeln Natur aufgewühlt und führt sie nun in dämmerndem, wetterleuchtendem hier und da morgenfreundlich lächelnden, Orphischen Gesang vom Aufgang herauf über die weite Welt, nachdem er vorher die Lasterbrut der neuern Geister, De- und Atheisten, Philologen, Textverbesserer, Orientalisten etc. mit Feuer und Schwefel und Fluthsturm ausgetilget!

Appended is a short bibliography of works relating to Goethe's youth.

General Subject.

Der junge Goethe. Seine Briefe und Dichtungen von 1764–1776. Mit einer Einleitung von Michael Bernays. 3 Theile. Leipzig, 1875.

Goethe's Dichtung und Wahrheit. Mit Einleitung und Anmerkungen von G. von Loeper. 4 Theile. Berlin, 1879.

34

Briefe und Aufsätze von Goethe aus den Jahren 1766 bis 1786. Zum erstenmal herausgegeben durch A. Schöll. Weimar, 1846.

Deutschlands politische, materielle und sociale Zustände im Achtzehnten Jahrhundert. Von Karl Biedermann. 2 Bde. Leipzig, 1854–1880.

Geschichte der deutschen Literatur im achtzehnten Jahrhundert. Von Hermann Hettner. 3 Bücher. Braunschweig, 1872.

Goethe. Vorlesungen gehalten an der Kgl. Universität zu Berlin von Herman Grimm. Zweite durchgesehene Auflage. Berlin, 1880. [Translated by Sarah Holland Adams. Boston: Little, Brown, & Co., 1881.]

Goethe's Leben von H. Düntzer. Leipzig, 1880. [Translated by T. W. Lyster. Macmillan, London, 1883, and Estes and Lauriat, Boston.]

Goethe in den Jahren 1771 bis 1775. Von Bernhard Rudolf Abeken. Zweite Auflage. Hannover, 1865.

Werther und seine Zeit. Zur Goethe-Literatur. Von J. W. Appell. Neue Ausgabe. Leipzig, 1865.

Aus Goethes Frühzeit. Von Wilhelm Scherer. [Quellen und Forschungen xxxiv.] Strassburg, 1879.

Goethe's Werther und seine Zeit. Eine psychiatrisch-litterarische Studie von Prof. Dr. Ludwig Wille. Basel, 1877.

Herder.

Herder nach seinem Leben und seinen Werken dargestellt von R. Haym. 1. Bd. Berlin, 1877.

Herders Lebensbild. Sein chronologisch-geordneter Briefwechsel. Herausgegeben von seinem Sohne. 3 Bde. Erlangen, 1846.

35

Aus Herders Nachlass. 3 Bde. Frankfurt am Main, 1857–1858.

Herder. By Karl Hillebrand. N. A. Review, July and October, 1872, April, 1873. Vol. CXV. pp. 104–138, 235–287, 389–424. (Reprinted in part as Monograph IV. Bangor, Me.)

Friederike Brion.

Der junge Goethe. (Letters and Poems in Vol. I.)

Dichtung und Wahrheit. (Books 10, 11, and 12.)

Friederike Brion von Sessenheim. Geschichtliche Mittheilungen von Phil. Ferd. Lucius, Pfarrer in Sessenheim. Strassburg, 1877.

Friederike Brion von Sessenheim. (1752–1813.) Eine chronologisch bearbeitete Biographie nach neuem Material aus dem Lenz-Nachlasse. Von P. Th. Falck. Berlin, 1881.

Deutsche Rundschau, November, 1878, pp. 218–226: Wallfahrt nach Sesenheim. Von Heinrich Kruse.

Goethe's Youthful Reviews.

Der junge Goethe. Vol. II. pp. 405–504.

Studien über Goethe von Professor Wilhelm Scherer in Berlin. Der junge Goethe als Journalist. [In the Deutsche Rundschau, October, 1878, pp. 62–74.]

Goethe's Religious Views.

"Der junge Goethe" and "Dichtung und Wahrheit," passim.

[For the later period, see his works in general. Note specially Sarah Austin's "Characteristics of Goethe: from

36

the German of Falk, von Müller, etc.," (3 vols., London, 1849,) Vol. I. pp. 65–103. Also, "Gespräche mit Goethe in den letzten Jahren seines Lebens. Von J. P. Eckermann. Sechste Auflage. (Edited by Düntzer.) In drei Theilen." (Leipzig, 1885.) II. 30, 100–101, 200; III. 253–258. In Bohn's translation, pp. 54–55 (passage suppressed by translator), 411–412, 524–525, 566–570.]

Goethe's Stellung zum Christenthum. Von Julian Schmidt. (In the Goethe-Jahrbuch, II., 1881, pp. 49–64.)

Der Gang der Kirche in Lebensbildern dargestellt von K. Fr. Aug. Kahnis. Leipzig, 1881. (pp. 410–426: Goethe und das Christenthum.)

Goethes religiöse Entwickelung bis zum Jahre 1775. Von R. Fr. A. Jobst. (Programm.) Stettin, 1877.

Spinoza and Pantheism.

Benedicti de Spinoza Opera quæ supersunt omnia. 3 vols. and supplementary vol. (1862). Lipsiæ, 1843. [Spinoza's Works are translated into English in the Bohn series.]

Spinoza's Ethic. Translated by W. H. White. London, 1883.

Spinoza, his Life and Philosophy. By Frederick Pollock. London, 1880.

Ways of the Spirit, and other Essays. By F. H. Hedge. Boston, 1877. [pp. 252–284: Pantheism.]

General Sketch of the History of Pantheism. By C. E. Plumptre. 2 vols. London, 1881.

Schöll, (v. supra,) pp. 193–229.

37

II. GOETHE'S SELF-CULTURE.

By JOHN ALBEE.

The theory of education at present is to offer an all-embracing outline of studies, from which every

talent may select, may specialize itself, and receive its appropriate training. Universal culture, that is, knowing or affecting a variety of intellectual interests, is not now much encouraged, and is seldom marketable. Even the phrases, "a great scholar," "a learned man," have ceased to carry their ancient significance. And the opponents of classical studies would say it is well it is so; for the terms meant an acquaintance with Greek and Latin and the contents of libraries merely. Scholar, learned man, do not well describe the modern proficient, their successor, whose claim and place can be exactly defined when one inquires, "What does he know?" This was sometimes a difficult question to answer in the case of the former class, when one praised them and provoked curiosity and inquiry. The answer was as vague and general as the supposed accomplishments. Universal culture we no longer encourage in the individual; in the accumulation of studies, in their clear

38

demarkations and the demand for thoroughness, there is required a more or less close following of particular lines. Universal culture must now be confined in meaning to the possibilities, or opportunities, embraced within the plans and under the teachers everywhere offered, and to their distributed results. The education now most insisted upon is that which qualifies a man to maintain himself by his usefulness to others, — to possess and to be able to apply that knowledge which has its practical value and its equivalent money value, like any other commodity. You may know too little to be wanted anywhere by anybody; and you may know too much to meet the wants of sagacious employers.

The bounds of knowledge — to sum up what has been said and to make clearer what follows — have been so extended, and the demand for application is so strenuous, that only by devotion to one single department can a man hope for any degree of completeness or usefulness.

At the same time, this accomplishment in one thing, with its professional or private application, gives to its disciple a limited development which

is not in harmony with the highest philosophical or spiritual revelations of the being and aim of man. For man is a unit, a whole, in himself, whatsoever component place he may consent to fill temporarily and with a detached portion of his being. He wishes to know all, grasps at all. He can learn all; but he can teach, can communicate, only a part. Now all

39

that which cannot be taught, but which every earnest, striving spirit wishes to know and succeeds in knowing through his own power and will, and in his own way, that is, as his genius guides him, I call self-culture. And inasmuch as I speak of Goethe's self-culture, I am anxious that my definition should be considered, in a peculiar manner, as applicable to him, for it has grown out of a study of his life and activities. I hope it is capable of generalization, and useful to every one who has taken his education, his cultivation, into his own hands; but it is beyond the scope of this paper to make applications and draw the obvious moral. It is simply the way which one man, already by natural endowment great, found to supplement a usual education, such as was available in his youth, to pass from known and distcovered ground to original, and to satisfy the impulse of his genius. Nor do I wish to lower or confuse the definition of self-culture, by connecting it in any manner with the history or experience of those commonly called self-educated men, of whom we have enough and hear enough; men who struggle up out of the masses, and who are sufficiently honored and wondered at for their striving and their triumph. Self-culture as now to be considered must be held up and measured upon the Goethean plan; and as the sermon ever and anon comes back to its text and the song to its refrain, so must we to the definition, which is to be the clue in studying one chief characteristic of Goethe: all that which cannot be taught, but

40

which every earnest, striving spirit wishes to know and succeeds in knowing through his own power and will and in his own way, — that is, as his genius guides him, — is self-culture; and Goethe is the

eminent and peculiar example of it, and of its most extraordinary results.

It is hard to keep hold of Goethe as a whole, he turns himself in so many different directions. And who is competent to estimate a man who was poet, novelist, art critic, translator, editor, lawyer and councillor of state, dramatist, stage manager and actor, the most voluminous correspondent we know of, — over nine thousand letters known to be now procurable, and one half of them already published, — besides his special scientific pursuits in botany, mineralogy, anatomy, and optics? To some of these departments he added valuable contributions; in some he made original discoveries, and his literary work has become already the property of mankind. All the while, as we read his life as known to the persons among whom he moved, his diaries and letters, we are struck with the attention and time bestowed on private and official concerns, which could leave no profitable results, and which would seem to interfere with the concentration requisite for enduring performances. But for the explanation of the amount and quality of his literary legacy, we must study his characteristic literary methods; and in addition, remember his fortunate circumstances and his long life, productive to the end.

41

It is claimed, and it is a valid claim, that Goethe's life and work make an epoch in world history. Whether we know it or not, we now see through his eyes when we come to certain points in our studies and experiences. And although unable, and indeed incompetent, as most men are, to follow and appreciate the whole range of his contributions, yet any interested and careful reader can feel everywhere the Goethean characteristic in his style and method; and, more than all, in the comprehensive sweep of his mind, which looks out upon things in a large, infinite way, gathering as it labors on vast materials, overflowing in almost every instance the receptacle he had planned for them. He was almost too great and active a man to be a writer; it is condescension in him to write. After the Frankfort period, he

needed urging to prepare anything for print. He was indebted to his friends, and especially to Schiller, for stimulation in this direction. He loved to accumulate, to sketch out plans, to read to friends an incompleted design, and then put it away for more light. Thus all his work seems a means to some other end, — a preparation, — an exploring expedition, returning with abundant results, but how to be finally distributed and arranged, somewhat in doubt; and in fact it is lucky if anything more than a roof is erected over them. Much appears to be unfinished, fragmentary, all sorts of things interjected between the covers of his books; and this not from want of good structural idea, but either because of some

42

difficulty in keeping within its limits, or because he found no conventional literary form quite adapted to his peculiar genius. So he overflows in all his longer works; yet in his shorter is perfectly restrained and unified.

It was especially hard for Goethe to bring any of his more important books to end, because his accumulations were so large and continuous, and because he filled his writing with his life, which flowed on, and could only be complete by the arrest of life. It must also be remembered that he waited upon his moods, and was not independent of physical aids and hindrances. He used wine and love as stimulants, but not tobacco. He consulted the barometer to know the weather in his brain; and he knew what seasons, sleep, diet, change, and music could do for the mind. However, there comes a time when we can no more rely upon these charming coadjutors. The problem came to the aged Goethe how to complete works which for the most part had been thrown off in periods when his genius was susceptible to outward influences, responding involuntarily and warmly. His solution was that by which most men are obliged to labor from beginning to end, namely, to finish what needed finishing by energy and resolution, no longer waiting upon Muse and season. Still we must say that in much of Goethe's

work there were additions rather than completions, and it marks a characteristic trait, the cause of which we have already indicated. The Second Part of

43

"Faust" is a completion, but not a dramatic completion; it is a religious reinvestment of the whole conception. The Second Part of "Wilhelm Meister" follows vaguely and in a lower atmosphere the same lines; nothing is brought to an issue after the manner of ordinary fiction. In Goethe was the extraordinary sense of the progressive character of all that concerns human life; it appears as merely succession oftenest; and in either case the highest art must deal with it as without limitations. No end is conceivable to it, but only transitions. Thus while Goethe lived the period could be, and generally was, changed into a semicolon; whatsoever conclusion, it was provisional; ceaseless self-culture added chapter after chapter, rewrote, inserted missing leaves, and gave to the god Terminus feet and arms. There should be a dash at the end of most of his writings, to signify that he was interrupted, or was waiting for more light, a new experience, a fresh impulse. This intellectual exuberance was in part the fruit of a habit of self-culture, which accompanied step by step the writings given to the public.

The creative power in him seems to have been exactly commensurate with the opportunities of self-culture; and in the latter we must include, besides various studies, all kinds of personal contacts, experiences, and employments. These came forth again as images, characters, or generalizations, in poetry or prose, and tantalize us at once with their likeness and unlikeness to their originals. And it may be

44

noticed in passing that he appears to reveal most of the germs out of which grew his literary works. It is true he was a little fond of mystification concerning them, and himself, doubtless, as we all do, connected the image created independently in the mind with some material, actual counterpart subsequently. This, otherwise, is to give to what we

call real existences, facts, or even experiences, too much credit. These have no creative power; the mind, the imagination, create them. We may admit only this: that the relation of Goethe's creations to their originals, or beginnings, is similar to the genesis of life. There is a cell of some sort; it little resembles the final form of independent being, which at any other stage than this is perishable.

Goethe was a realist in a certain distinguishing sense; that is, there must be for him firm realities, but such as were intimately interwoven with his own life. He hated the vague, the subjective, and that which attempted to make something out of nothing. He strove for such a universal expression as could not be literally interpreted, but so flexible as to have in it a manifold adaptation. In some degree, favored by the German intellectual tendency to minute and critical study of masterpieces, he achieved in a short space that which time and chance have given his compeers, Homer, Dante, and Shakespeare, — the possibility of many meanings and many applications. He founded himself upon the internal real; so that his realism differs greatly from that which among some

45

writers is practised and championed in our time. They claim to give us pictures of life as it is, still calling their work fiction. Nothing that does actually, literally exist, is worthy of portraiture. "The spirit of the real is the true ideal"; and this alone is all that man recognizes and cherishes forever.

There is, however, a deeper objection than this to the surface realism of our present literary art. In the moral world, as in the natural, we shall not go far wrong, if we seek for truth and reality in the direct opposite of what appears. The apparent is something adjusted to the measure of the senses. Although Goethe laid strong hold of this apparent, there was for once a man who turned it, not half or quarter, but clear round, and saw the other, the real spirit, or ideal face.

He turned the plant clear round, and discovered its secret, the law of its life. And as ever appear-

ances are confusing, while the reality is simple and satisfying, so now-botany, which, when one looks into a text-book or upon a garden of flowers, is the most bewildering of studies, becomes by Goethe's discovery as clear and beautiful as a remembered single line of perfect poetry. In fact it is poetic; and it distinguishes nearly all of his scientific investigation that it is resolved into poetry. He is the first modern man who has well succeeded in working this transformation; thus restoring for us the manner of the most ancient natural philosophers, who rendered everything in verse. It seems to have been his

46

aim in natural science to satisfy the desire for a productive thought,—one that should be a further means of self-cultivation. His investigations in osteology resulted in nearly the same law as in botany,—a simple principle on which the structure of animals and plants is built up alike. What is its value? Chiefly to the imagination in man. There is no final good in scientific discoveries unless they furnish us something beyond the useful; this also has its value, but not the entire. As Goethe himself said, "Whatever is useful is only a part of what is significant." When a simple, pregnant generalization, like Goethe's in botany, is given us, we are not hindered by default of technical knowledge from the highest possible perception of the central idea in the plant world. We no more stand before the simplest flower ashamed of our ignorance because we cannot call it by name; or when we can, satisfied with our knowledge. But there is now freedom for the imagination, and an invitation to reflection. Then truly pansies will be for thoughts; and the "flower in the crannied wall" will answer, not what God and man is, but as much as it knows about itself. And though some flowers recommend themselves by their beauty or rarity, and others by their commonness, and some even because they are fashionable, all of them, when we are acquainted with the law of their inward being, help us to draw nearer to the spiritual symbols and resemblances which connect each province of nature with every other, and all with man.

to know all sides of himself, the weak, the strong, the excellent, and the evil. He confessed that his striving to become an artist was a mistake, but added that mistakes also give us insight. This calm, quite superhuman characteristic has prejudiced many good people against Goethe; they think that he sacrificed everybody to his own selfish purposes. The French call love the egoism of two; but some say Goethe's love was still no more than that of one,—self-love, in short.

47

Goethe teaches us after a method, and to a point where we can teach ourselves. In every direction to which he turned his mind, this is one of his chief merits, that he takes you where you can go alone if you will. This makes him for adults, for poets and writers especially, the most helpful master that has ever lived. How he becomes so is easy to see; it is because he is trying to teach himself; in short, we come again upon his self-culture as the fruitful source of his achievements and influence. His studies and investigations were private, unprofessional, with no worldly or ulterior aim. What he puts into the mouth of Makaria in "Wilhelm Meister's Travels" expresses his habit very nearly: "We do not want to establish anything, or to produce any outward effect, but only to enlighten ourselves." When therefore Goethe, a man of ample acquirements and genius, sits down to study something that he wishes to know, and gives us not only the results, but the steps and the method of his effort, he becomes a great teacher.

48

Yet we do not wish to follow any master too far; he is the best who leads us from himself to self-reliance. A man needs many, to whose influence he can surrender himself, and recover himself again and again. In Goethe's self-cultivation it is striking how often he meets with persons and objects, and gives himself up to them until he has learned all they have to impart which can help him, or discovers his own false tendency or position. Then he abandons them without regret or apology. Without regret, except the poetic, inspiring regrets of his love affairs, which cannot be omitted from the account of the sources and circumstances of his inward culture. In these there were usually two productive phases or periods; one while elevated by passion, the other when tormented by remorse. It is said by H. Grimm that Margaret grew out of the latter. But usually he had no time or taste for repenting himself of anything that had happened. In his self-complacent way he foresaw compensation, and was not afflicted

One of the essential contrasts between Goethe and most literary creators—let us say, for instance, our own Shakespeare—is that Goethe found his material, his suggestions, his impulse, in his own experiences; while Shakespeare and his contemporaries, and also the greater Greek poets, take what has happened to others as the primary motive of their work. Goethe embodies states of feeling, workings of the intellect; consequently they have not that charac-

49

teristic or historical consistency which is common among other creators. I venture to call their consistency *ideal*; and I would refer its manifestations more to the personality of Goethe than to that of the characters themselves, which in most works of the imagination are made effective by sharply drawn limitations. I do not know a character of Goethe's that stands for much more than his mouthpiece; that one thinks of as a person, as in the creations of many even inferior novelists and dramatists. In truth, one may say,—or perhaps here it is better to inquire whether nearly all the most famous characters of poets and dramatists have not something vague and impersonal about them; while it is left to the inferior to come before us with their impressive, although very limited personality. The great are great without being peculiar, and indeed by contrasts to it; they fill a great place, symbolize the total conception, and must be drawn with a few and the simplest lines; while about them move all manner of subordinates, of narrower yet more striking idiosyncrasies. It is these latter we make ourselves free with; they pass into proverb, yes, into language, and

have the honor to become nouns and adjectives.

Goethe wrote in the modern temple, where all the Muses were real women. He transformed them back to their ancient estate. This his temple was of glass, so that the transformation could be seen, the original clay be detected after it was winged. Doubtless other poets, his predecessors and compeers, also drew

50

much out of their own lives, fashioning their creations out of real, present images; but it is concealed from us by our meagre information concerning their personal history and character. In Goethe's case all is open, all is revealed, by his own disclosures and innumerable testimonies. We know the avidity of the public concerning everything which connects personal affairs with a poem or story, — its liability to mistake, and its haste to censure; and as the world is full of literalists, as well as of those who conceive of all as if existing in the present and among themselves, forgetful that every age "determines and fashions both the willing and unwilling," they hear of Goethe's relations to his time, to its persons, ideas on religion and politics, with some scruples of conscience; their most serious charge being that he immolated, and then dissected, living, loving human beings for the purposes of literary art. It should be remembered that, so far as Goethe's own confessions are summoned against him, they cannot be fully admitted; for he did not confess himself in print until the matter which entered into it had become poetry in its first stage. He used it over and over, and gave it endless additions and transformations. In truth, the literal experience, the actual fact, do not exist for a moment, or but just a moment, in his mind.

In his first attempt at verse, when he was in love with Gretchen, he says he first "mystified himself." You cannot detect him writing anywhere except sym-

51

bolically. Thus, in working the chief miracle given man to perform in his earthly life, the changing the water which he draws out of the common reservoirs into the wine of song and story, Goethe had a wonderful, almost supernatural power. In tracing back this gift, it becomes clear that it grew out of his genius for self-culture. We can observe that it had a twofold or reciprocal character, not uncommon to all men, but in the highest degree to him; namely, being taught by his own faculties, unconsciously at first, and then in return consciously and earnestly teaching them. It may be said, that when a man arrives at the latter stage, he is free; he, by the same means, liberates others; he becomes a self-determined being, and can wholly exterminate what is obstructive in himself, and perfect what is productive and best. This consciousness becomes distinct gradually; and the interesting point in Goethe's intellectual history is to observe its development.

But now what shall we say on behalf of those lovely, and, as some think, wronged ladies, sacrificed to make the images of Gretchen, Ottilie, Iphigenia, Sulieka, who now seem to have an independent being? Were Friederika, Lottie Buff, Lillie Schönemann, Von Stein, and the others, but the rough stone in which sleeps the statue? or did they breathe, suffer, feel the chisel and polisher of the artist? And which endured most, they or Goethe himself? It is permitted to women to heal themselves by sensible attachments and marriage, which all seem to have

52

done, with one exception; while he poetized his woes. It is too much to expect of every man that he shall commit suicide to show that he was in earnest in love. Yet I know of no other course that would thoroughly satisfy the world of Goethe's sincerity and unhappiness. Must we, however, exercise ourselves in passing some kind of judgment in the business? For this present, all such controversies must be renounced; and once for all let us summarize the supposed defects of Goethe's nature, which, as comprehensive and yet condensed as we can make them, are religious, domestic, and political.

In conclusion of this element in Goethe's manner of self-culture, that is, the embodiment in imaginary forms and relations of not only actual people and events, but as well his various internal moods, reflections, and tendencies, I will add, that it grew into a habit with him to want to know, first of all, in regard to the productions of other writers, and even scientific labors, out of what kind of personal character and experience they had been evoked. In this, as critic and student, is to be observed his leaning toward the historical and objective method. One might suppose, after all that has been divulged respecting his own way of drawing from his experience and circumstances, that it might properly be called the subjective method, and that he would use approvingly, in describing others, the same term. I shall not insist on the distinctions in the use of these terms by Goethe which I have endeavored to find; but I

53

have made the attempt in order to read his critical works especially, and maxims scattered all through his other writings, with better understanding. In the first place, then, there are two essentials to all intellectual efforts and products. These two essentials may be called by several terms; as, broadly, nature and art; or, specifically, reality and imagination, truth and symbol, yourself and the world. These cannot be separated; the objective method does not separate them; but the subjective method undertakes to exclude, sometimes one, sometimes the other. To this must be added that he often employed the term *subjective* in speaking of egotists, mannerists, and dilettants.

The terms *dilettant* and *dilettanteism* grew up alongside of this enlargement of the meaning of art and artist, and were the necessary negative or antithetical expressions. The looser meaning of dilettant is one who amuses himself, or cultivates not too seriously any art, or science, or literature, and does not pretend to success or excellence. He is judged in proportion to his intention, and we give our applause graciously, because it is not demanded of our head, but our heart, in return for a casual pleasure, or because there has been displayed to us some unexpected natural, though untrained talent.

But if the effort be serious, yet a failure; if it make a demand to which we do not, cannot yield, then, in the usage of Goethe, Schiller, and their friends, the effort is dilettanteism, and the agent is a

54

dilettant. In short, when one undertakes to gain the height, as Goethe said, through admiration of it, but not the steps to it; or feels himself from any impulse, inward or outward, disposed to something for which he has, perhaps, a little, but no effective talent; there is the delineation of numberless individuals who pretend much, who even labor industriously, yet with no praiseworthy results. However, we must not apply these significant words empirically, or too harshly. We have had many single gifts, precious and enduring, from men of this class; and we cannot forget the contributions of many untrained observers of nature.

It is inevitable that Goethe must believe in recovery after never so many false steps and tendencies. Being men out of the earth, going through the world for a brief period, looking forward constantly, and in the crises of life upward, it is necessary we should make our mistakes help us. In the "Annals" of Goethe, which are a sort of epitome and continuation of the "Autobiography," he declares that he meant in "Wilhelm Meister" to delineate the career of a dilettant, whose "false steps may at last conduct to an invaluable good."

One word more of his manner of coming to conclusions respecting the work of other minds. We have recently here, in last year's study of Emerson, been led through various special points of view to one agreeing opinion,—that character was the source of his activities, and that it is reflected in them with few reser-

55

vations and no pretensions. Always, when we can find no clue to the private life of the great men of the past, we attempt to construct it out of their times, their contemporaries, and the whole personal environment, as far as we can reproduce it. It was this objective spirit in Goethe that made him wish to come into the closest relations with all that interested

him,—men, women, and nature. If there was known to him good fruit anywhere, he was not satisfied with eating, but wished also to see the tree that bore it,—its root, its climate, and the soil out of which it had grown. In this way a book became to him something more than a dry fagot of sticks from the still living tree; it became an expression of life, and contributed something to his own living and reflecting nature. Thus he absorbed the large circle of extraordinary persons whom at first he took pains to know, and who at length took equal pains to make themselves known to him, and to communicate whatever they were able. His own account of what we here but hint at must be given, that it may become more clear to the reader:—

"From the standpoint where God and nature had been pleased to place me, and where, next, I did not neglect to exert my faculties according to my circumstances, I looked all about me to mark where great tendencies were in operation and lastingly prevailed. I, for my part, by study, by performances of my own, by collections and experiments, endeavored to reach forth towards those tendencies, and, faithfully toiling upwards, to the level of

56

the achievements I could not myself have accomplished; in all simplicity, innocent of all feeling of rivalry or envy, with perfectly fresh and vital sense, I presumed to appropriate to myself what was offered to the century by its best minds. My way, therefore, ran parallel with very many beautiful undertakings, till it would next turn towards others. The new accordingly was never foreign to me, nor was I ever in danger either of adopting it in a state of unpreparedness, or, by reason of old-fashioned prejudice, rejecting it."

On such a text as this confession offers, one might gather together all the articles and story of his self-cultivation. On one point we must here add something, so that we may keep in mind that results were never wanting to complete the full measure of this absorbent genius, to show that the productive kept an equal pace with the receptive effort. The stream of influences flowing to Goethe received in their passage the most earnest inspection; he took up all that were

allied in any manner with his nature, and bodied them forth again in suitable forms, enhanced by art and the fulness of a thus multiplied life. This design, which personified a tendency or feeling. Often he belongs more strictly to confessed allegory, ends in Goethe rather tamely, so far as we look for character-drawing. The symbolical man has a too diversified nature, as well as field of action. I say man, for it is the men in his books that generally fail to live in our memory as independent beings. It is quite different with his women; they are simple or sensuous; some

57

have the elusive feminine charm which no poet before has known how to depict so well; some are the women of men's imagination, who all in his writings turned out so well; others are downright saints, whose spiritual introspections are graphically portrayed. To all these representative types he gave such human forms as well satisfy our love of the beautiful, within artistic limits. Let us listen to his own opinion of his women characters for a moment, in order to mark the difference between his creative method and that of the writers who draw from the life, and beg of us to be pleased to recognize our acquaintance in their gilded frames:—

"My idea of women is not abstracted from the phenomena of actual life, but has been born within me, God knows how. The female characters which I have drawn have therefore all turned out well; they are all better than could be found in reality."

Mark here the logic of the ideal method,—"*therefore* all turned out well." Of his men it may be said that they are all also parts of himself, but from a very different realm than his women. In them there is more objective treatment, and yet they are not so distinct. But in all and each may be seen how well he had resolved all his materials into his own life before reproduction.

Man is an imitative animal, is the received axiom and basis of all art. This unconscious impulse accompanies, nay, is commonly the means of setting free, of delimiting, what is nature's particular gift to

58

each man. Too often, we are aware, it is the finished production, the feeling raised in us by it, that we would at once imitate. The deep-seeing Goethe very early found that not this was the true path of self-cultivation, and a substantial, abiding fountain of literary activity; but that it might be attained with fortunate circumstances, by study of all previous conditions, and the life and art out of which great masters and their work had sprung, and upon which they had impressed themselves in return. So from early life he began to grasp and to imitate, not the finished works themselves, which would have resulted only in something less than his models and ended in disgust, but the foundations and elementary conditions of a rich, self-developing, and continuous mental activity. This was why he was so receptive; and being so became many-sided without the usual fatality of accomplishing nothing to justify the name. He was, in truth, both actively and passively many-sided.

59

But now it should be noted with what certainty he drew back from influences and studies when they threatened to absorb and restrict him. It seems as though he looked upon them all as but preparatory; a means of cultivation, not an end in themselves. And his peculiar genius led him on to know many things up to a certain limit, rather than the one which always flatters the specialist that it is without limit, because it has obtained possession of him rather more than he has of it. What was this limit which Goethe observed? Spinoza had shown him the boundary of investigation in respect to divine things; which, it has been often said, had a powerful and soothing influence upon his reflections. Whether it was that early impress, or a native tendency, the limit of the surrender of his mind and interest was reached when the method, the *how*, of nature had been reached, and when the next step would involve a recourse to metaphysics to resolve the *wherefore*.

In a similar manner, in all which he denominated Art he stopped short at the vague, the inexpressible, and the subjective. Even the romantic he thought no adequate expression, because it confused the moral and artistic sense. He must work where there was reality, freedom, such as the Greek outline denotes; and upon that which was not already a shadowy and uncertain symbol, but so universal and inevitable that it could be symbolized in a thousand pleasing and instructive ways. Many a time he abandons himself to a mood; seldom to the formal choice of poetic theme; and he believes that the occasional poem, the fruit of the former, is our best modern poetry, while the latter labors in a vacuum. He yields to personal influences, intellectual and passionate, until they become noxious and are likely to submerge his individuality. And he follows the study of natural sciences as far as the human senses, unaided by microscope, scalpel, laboratory, and prism, can penetrate.

60

Artificial contrivances introduce artificial relations. But the chief objection, from the standpoint of Goethe's self-culture (which would coordinate the visible world with man), to the technical and mechanical methods of investigation, is again this, to which I have already alluded; namely, that in science and in philosophy we should not attempt to search the inaccessible, the great mystery, but keep ourselves on the hither side, where we can labor fearlessly and to some purpose. This, one may well say, is a poet's doctrine; since it gives up one world to his sharpest outward senses, and consecrates the other to the imagination. In Germany more than anywhere else, in Goethe's time, such a belief appeared as the natural reaction from the innumerable attempts of philosophers and theologians to formulate systems which should explain by ratiocination what, having been long accepted by faith, was beginning to be shaken by those inquiries that we now stand in the full stream of. A great deal in "Faust" has a symbolic or ironical reference to the current discussions. These discussions were bold and vehement, and went so near the verge of profanity that a man of Goethe's sense of proportion reacted against them.

61

Fichte's conclusion of one of his lectures, whether true or false, hits off the height of the fashion of philosophical agitation: "To-morrow, gentlemen, I shall create God."

I have said that Goethe disliked all mechanical contrivances for extending the reach of the five human senses. It is well known how much he interested himself in the theory of colors. He came in the course of his investigations more near to being moved off his usual calm balance than by any other affair of his life. His theory was not accepted, and still is not, save by a few men. Yet who would know Goethe must know it; for even in its supposed errors is more clearly shown than in his accepted faith, in the unity of Nature and the simplicity of her operations. In optics, as in other pursuits, he would have no aids but the natural eye; and his chief distrust in Newton's theory of colors came from that philosopher's use of the prism in experiments. There is here a curious coincidence in sentiment between Goethe and Keats, which seems to reveal the poetic temperament the same in two otherwise infinitely different natures.

One day, at a merry meeting of poets and artists in London, Keats proposed the toast, "Confusion to the memory of Newton." Charles Lamb refused to drink until it had been explained. "Because," said Keats, "he destroyed the poetry of the rainbow by reducing it to a prism."

62

Nature, as if to reward the poet who would tolerate no mediatory artifices for access to her mysteries, endowed him with a natural second-sight. Still he must deliver what he saw by symbol. Thus were both nature and art satisfied.

The unity of Nature was an early vision, and the last supreme certainty of his old age. This, being well established in him, became an active, efficient idea. The apparent manifold parts and diverse manifestations of Nature being but adaptations of her-

63

self to external mutual conditions, every one was the symbol of the other; and the typical form was that which self-culture and art should bend themselves to produce.

We left behind one Goethean characteristic, of which some mention should be made. This was his special studies as a means of self-culture, rather than for the purpose of becoming a specialist. Just as he released himself from personal influences when he found them like to be overpowering or barren, so in studies he stopped at the point where it would be necessary for going on with one to give up all the others. Had his inclination been other, he would have become a learned professor, or a great authority in minerals, anatomy, and botany; or a poet and only a poet. But he never could lose himself in anything. Perhaps one of the reasons of this, besides the motive of self-culture, was, that though a poet and much else, he was also a critic. Indeed, the chief limitation of Goethe's temperament is, that reflection interferes too much and too often with spontaneity. As he grew older, he became more and more didactic and Orphic. The early fruitage and flowers had been plucked; he now began to harvest the seed-corn. There is something in the oracular wisdom of his maturity which resembles the poetic effect, but we miss the morning-red. The dæmonic

influences of his youth are in abeyance; they are in his cabinets now, strung upon wires. They are moved at length by determination and energy, and help him to complete his unfinished works, where they reappear disembodied and passionless. The apotheosis of that which had lived in him, all glowing, sensitive, creative, took place.

Although much given to symbolizing throughout all periods of his life, and to a reliance upon moods and circumstances, as well as a secret leaning toward poetic superstitions, presentiments and omens, in general he held firmly to realities, and insisted that divining-rods could only be found on the tree of knowledge. As the closing result of these two tendencies he became in prose didactic; and in

poetry, there being for him not much else left to undertake, he attempts to reveil symbols in a deeper mystery. In this he still adhered to his life-long habit of leaving one world to action and reflection, the other to invention and imagination. In the former, his treatment and subjects are various and suggestive; in the latter, there are plentiful masterpieces, ample invitations to study. We can make personal applications here and there. Yes, it is plain that Goethe foresaw the needs of this generation, and left some sealed, almost personal messages. These are, I dare say, such as most would vouch Goethe never intended. But a reader who finds no more in any book than the writer intended is a poor reader, or he is reading a poor book. A good book

64

is the author plus the reader. I say this by way of preparation for the inevitable questionings which must arise in the coming week as to whether Goethe intended all that we shall hear from our speakers in their interpretations. We shall hear profitably what each one finds in which we can all agree. For the rest, the unconscious element, that is in every great work of man's mind, it lies before us like a friendly, rich banquet, where there is enough for all and something for every taste. This unconscious element is no doubt an extensive portion of Goethe, and especially fascinating as it appears in every sort of figurative form. Never believe that in Goethe you are getting your truth without poetry. The naked truth is verily naked, and had better remain in the bottom of its traditional well. Give to it its relations, its adaptations, put it into action and thought, and as it is a liberating, divine thing, it clothes itself in joyful, beautiful forms, and becomes poetry. The higher the truth, the more poetic; and all men prefer illumination, the opening of the intellectual and spiritual sense, to any other light. For it takes them out of their limitations, which higher truth challenges as facts. These a low, earth-dwelling understanding has erected into institutions, social, religious, political, which our study of Goethe may expose and help us to resist.

65

The sacred treasure, the accumulation of a long life of activity, upon which Goethe turned constantly reflection and imagination in due proportions and

with an infallible discrimination, has been handed on to us in various vessels; some translucent, always visible; some to be seen only in the night, like the castle of Avallon, by the light of certain stars, reckoned lucky in the horoscope of the beholder, under which his vision is clearer in some seasons and epochs of life than at others. To speak without metaphor, if we live, experience, suffer, love, and think, we come in succession to pages of Goethe where, having once been dark, we now find he has left a lamp burning for us; like a friendly host, who divined better than ourselves the hour of our arrival.

As we have said, the unity of nature was Goethe's constant perception; every seeming diversity but adaptation, in whose processes are all the semblances of motive, cunning contrivance, sympathy, sex, motherly forethought, as in the cotyledonous leaf, love of beauty and final purpose. It appears to me he took a lesson here; yielding himself, like a plant, to the external conditions of man's world. But then he reversed the operation, and made all conform to an inward shaping mind. Herein we come to that which distinguishes man from plants and animals, and also, it must be said, man from man; one living wholly in the external, and forever guided and moulded by it; another receiving it, but reacting upon it, and impressing his own inward being in typical forms that draw us from the fashion that passeth away to the permanent and true.

66

Self-culture, therefore, by means of the external surrender and the internal shaping, is a good part of the philosophy and religion of Goethe. To separate them is a sin in literary ethics, and is to want the philosophical substructure of all creative literary art.

It was in delineating these two aspects of man's

nature and destiny, morally considered, that he found man's greatest good and worst evil. Meister blunders, Faust sins, in the endeavor to satisfy themselves with the external world, — to conquer, to possess it. All along they are not sinners, but exceedingly desirous of wisdom by means of self-cultivation; but they have taken wrong roads. This, then, their bungling was their error. And as in Faust we have a new sort of devil, so in Meister we have a new kind of sinner; both much needed to instruct and convict the modern world, hotly in pursuit of every means, culture included, to possess itself of external advantages, to live more splendidly on the surface, to feel, like the fly on the wheel, that they cause all the movement and the dust. Our age had outgrown the interpretations of the good parish priest; Satan did not embody for us any wickedness with which we were practically acquainted, and most vulgar sins were provided for by the law. We needed a more subtle, refined, and familiar devil to affright us, and a corrected catalogue of those errors in which we were involved, scarcely however knowing it, because long without prophets. Goethe came, and having first

67

taught and saved himself, in a manner demanded by modern life, he then left us the method and the useful precepts.

When we use the words *sin* and *devil*, the implication is too often of some outward act or some incarnation of it; when we find it in French, we suspect a woman not far off. In Goethe it is a little nearer; it has many marks, many metonymic names; but false tendencies and vague, and impatience, negation, egotism are some of them. The great human effort and act is renunciation; the final issue, reconciliation. For these self-culture in its broadest meaning is the instrument and preparation, and its purpose justifies its means.

Whenever the nations of the North, and especially the Teutonic, have reached certain stages in civilization, they have been bowed down under the feeling that there was something wrong in the universe,

68

which it was their mission to set right. Goethe was born into a chaotic time, when this feeling was at its height throughout Europe. He was endowed by nature with a highly organized being, susceptible to every impression, to such a degree that he cherished superstitions in regard to it. As great care is taken that those who can suffer shall, he felt to the full the maladies of his age. He wrought his own cure first, by self-culture, there being no outward helps; then he turned to the relief of others, and became the great intellectual and spiritual physician of mankind.

III.

GOETHE'S TITANISM.

By Thomas Davidson.

Two things become clear to men as they advance in spiritual life: first, that there is no rest for the soul anywhere save in the Absolute and Infinite; and, second, that this rest can be attained only by the persistent and heroic efforts of the soul itself. Although the facts corresponding to these truths are eternal, although the life of the soul, unconscious as well as conscious, is a striving toward the Absolute and Infinite through infinite evolution, the truths themselves come but slowly and late into consciousness, and the former comes much earlier than the latter. Indeed, the former has been impressed by all the great world-religions, as well as by some of the great world-philosophies, whereas the latter is in many quarters, even of the civilized world, counted little less than blasphemy. Looking merely at the Western world, we find that, in the religion of ancient Greece, the greatest impiety of which a man could be guilty was ὕβρις, or insubordination; that is, any intent or endeavor to place himself on an equality with the gods. This we find forcibly illustrated, not only in the

69

myths regarding the Titans, but also in those related of Tantalus, Ixion, Niobe, etc. To the Greeks, as to the Hebrews, the divine powers are jealous, standing upon their rights and claiming unquestioning obedience, after the manner of Oriental despots. The heaven, as Aristotle hints, is always a copy of the earth, and men's gods are never very much better than themselves. No doubt, both in Greece and in Judæa, there were men who had a nobler and truer conception of the Divine Power, and this conception finally attained currency in that powerful movement called, after its chief promoter, Christianity. Jesus, "being in the form of God, thought it not robbery to be equal with God;" or, as the revised version has it, "being in the form of God, counted it not a prize to be on an equality with God." More clearly expressed, this means that Jesus, though essentially deiform, held that equality with God was not a thing to be obtained by robbery.

It was a great step for men to have come to recognize that they were deiform, and still a greater step to have realized that that form could be actualized, and that they might be perfect, even as the Father which is in heaven is perfect. This view is by no means peculiar to Christianity. We find it repeatedly stated by heathen philosophers in the clearest terms. Hierokles, the Pythagorean, for example, tells us that "each ought to become, first a man, and then a god." It is true that the Hellenic view, having its root in polytheism, is not identical with the Christian

70

view, which is founded in monotheism; but the two agree in this important respect, that they recognize the end of spiritual life to be the attainment of the Absolute. The most fundamental difference between the two views is this: that, while the philosophic Greeks held the way to the Absolute to be through the exercise of the speculative or theoretic virtues, the Christian Fathers placed it in the practical virtues, which the Greeks held to be merely the conditions of arriving at manhood. In later Christianity, which is quite as much Hellenic as Hebrew, the two views were

united. The motto of the greatest of all the monastic orders, the Benedictine, which, roughly speaking, was founded in the year 500, is, *Ora et labora*, "Pray and labor,"—in other words, combine the practical with the contemplative life. As has recently been pointed out in an admirable way by the Bishop of Foggia, St. Benedict combined in himself the practical wisdom of the Roman (he was the son of a Roman patrician) and the contemplative spirit of the Christian monk.

But, besides the above-mentioned difference between the Hellenic and Hebrew views, there was another, hardly less pregnant in its effects. In the Hellenic view, man was destined to attain divinity, if at all, through his own efforts, through self-purification and devotion to that contemplation which, as Aristotle says, "we sometimes enjoy, God always." In the Hebrew view, on the contrary, man was to be raised to perfection equal to that of the Father, in large measure by grace, that is, by a free transient

71

act on the part of the Divine itself. The doctrine of special grace is an abiding portion of the Christian creed. Christians, therefore, following the example of Jesus, were expected to empty themselves and wait till God filled them and exalted them, while the Greeks were expected in all ways to strive and help themselves. As a natural consequence, the characteristic Christian virtue is Oriental self-abasement or humility, whereas the characteristic Hellenic virtue is self-respect or personal dignity. While the Christian claims nothing for himself, but looks for everything as a free gift from God, powerful and pitiful, against whom he has no rights, the Greek, conscious of his own potential divinity, makes infinite claims, and labors in every way to make these good.

The success of Christianity and the downfall of Hellenism mean that the world accepted the Christian view and rejected the Hellenic. It has done this in large measure, at least in theory, for some eighteen hundred years. Still not altogether even in theory, and very imperfectly in practice. Though the Hellenic spirit slumbers, it does not die.

"The vine-wreathed god,
Rising, a stifled question from the silence,
Fronts the pierced Image, with the crown of thorns."

At no time has this spirit been entirely inactive; but its mightiest revolt took place in the sixteenth century, in what is known as the Pagan Renaissance, which again was closely connected with the Protestant Reformation. In the former there is an asser-

72

tion of the rights of the natural, as over against the spiritual; in the latter, an assertion of the rights of human reason, as over against faith; in both, a revolt against the spirit of historical Christianity. In the last three hundred years, Hellenism has been making rapid strides. Freedom is the order of the day, just as submission was in former times, and there can be but little doubt that this tendency will go on increasing.

And it is right and well that this should be so. In spite of all its great worthiness, in spite of its unexampled success, in spite of its manifold adaptation to human weaknesses and needs, the Christian ideal is not a perfect one. It is essentially one-sided, and needs to be supplemented by the Hellenic ideal, which contains elements both of manliness and truth which the Christian ideal lacks. It is in every way more manly for the deiform human being to work out his own perfection by his own free efforts, than to place himself in the position of a dependent mendicant and accept it from another. Moreover, such perfection, even if desirable, is not possible; for perfection is not something that can be imparted or received; it is something that must be worked out through a long series of free acts, and these no being, not even a god, can perform for another.

That the Christian Fathers should have adopted a view at variance with this, only shows that they understood the nature of spirit and of spiritual things much less perfectly than the contemporary

73

Pagan philosophers. This difference becomes very apparent, when we compare the Christian concep-

tion of God with the later Hellenic philosophical one. The Christian conception is still mythological to a considerable extent. According to this, God is still only a large man, with all the finite attributes and passions of man, an individual among individuals, a being who loves and hates, plans and repents. The Greek conception, on the other hand, is profound and philosophical. According to this, God is above all individuality, being its essential correlate and condition. None of the attributes of individuality apply to him. He is neither one nor many, although he is the essential condition of both. He performs no transient acts, inasmuch as time does not exist for him. He is nowhere, and yet everywhere, because space does not exist for him. He is without variation. In a word, he is; he is that which is. He is not a reality, since all reality is of necessity finite and capable of performing transient acts in time and space. That is what we mean by reality. He is the pure Ideal, of which the attributes are Absoluteness and Infinity. In the material world he appears as space, the prime condition of all corporeal existence; in the intellectual world he objectifies himself as being, the condition of all thought; in the moral world he diffuses himself as pure love, or as the good, the condition of all morality, heroism, and self-sacrifice. The sensible manifestation of God was recognized by the early Aryans, when they made Dyâus, that is

74

Zeus or Jupiter, their chief god; for Dyâus is merely the open sky, which these early thinkers confounded with pure space. The intellectual objectification of God as Being we find first in the Vedas and in the Mosaic records. In the former we read: "He who established the six worlds,—is he that One which exists in the form of unborn Being?" In the latter, God is made to speak of himself as *I am that I am*, or as *I am that am*. It is not until after the rise of Christianity that we find the clear statement made that God is Love; but centuries before that, as early at least as Aristotle, we find what is virtually the same thing, the affirmation that God is the highest

good, that is, the object of the highest love.

We thus find that all the three modes in which the Divine Being reveals itself — the real, the ideal, and the moral — have successively and at long intervals of time been discovered, and even stated with almost philosophical precision. Unfortunately, this philosophic statement has never attained currency, but has always been reduced to terms of the imagination. The Infinite has been made finite; the Absolute, relative; the Ideal, real; the Eternal, transient. Dyâus became Jupiter; *I am that am*, Jehovah; Love, the angry divinity of Christianity. The truth is, the philosophic conception of the Spiritual and the Divine cannot be made intelligible to the popular mind, which thinks almost entirely in terms of the imagination. Since, however, even the popular mind craves, and, for moral reasons,

75

requires, some notions of divinity, an attempt is made to accommodate the philosophic conception of it to the imagination. These fanciful conceptions of the Deity after a time recoil from the people upon philosophers themselves, and turn these into theologians, who employ all their efforts in order to make the popular notions of divinity acceptable to pure reason or thought. This is the real source of all that is mythic in religion, as well as of all that is purely dogmatic. It is, consequently, the source of all those systems of religious thought which arise from time to time and become popular in the world; for example, Buddhism, Christianity, Mohammedanism. Such systems, though essentially unphilosophical, and necessarily containing much that is erroneous, are in many ways of very great value. Indeed, it may be said that practically they are of more value than the pure truth would be. The error contained in them is like the nitrogen in the atmosphere, which prevents the oxygen from destroying the human frame by too rapid combustion. But, after all, no religious system whose god or gods are to any degree conceived in terms of the limiting imagination can be perpetual. The error involved

will, sooner or later, make itself felt, in thought by contradiction, and in life by disorganization, and then will follow something in the form of a revolt, both in thought and life. The revolt in thought will come from philosophers — not necessarily from propounders of systems, but from men intimately ac-

76

quainted with the aspirations and intellectual needs of their time, probably from poets or literary men. The revolt in life will come either from men who have suffered deeply from the institutions among which they were born, like Rousseau, or from men in whom the "enthusiasm of humanity" is an overpowering passion, like the inspired founders of the great religions.

It is this revolt against established conceptions of the divine and the institutions founded thereon that we call *Titanism*. But, inasmuch as new conceptions of God are practically new gods, Titanism always seems a revolt against God himself, a violence, an impiety, whereas it frequently turns out to be the very opposite. When such a revolt is crushed, the revolters are spoken of as atheists and traitors; when it succeeds, they may be counted as prophets and religious heroes. As John Harrington puts it,

"Treason doth never prosper : what's the reason ?
For when it prospers, none dare call it treason."

All revolts against the established order of things are due to one form or another of radicalism, — some attempt to secure a more perfect expression of the fundamental being or nature of things. This is just as true of those great religious reformations that have ended in giving to mankind a nobler and truer conception of the divine, and in bringing this conception to bear upon human life, as of those wild revolutions that seek to overturn law and order in favor of anarchy and license. There are, indeed, two entirely

77

distinct forms of Titanism, just as there were two orders among the mythical Titans themselves. The Titans are simply personifications of the brute forces of nature and the fundamental forces of spirit. The

former of these always tend to revolution and anarchy; the latter, even in their revolt against order, to a higher order. The former in man we call the lusts of the flesh; the latter we call the aspirations of the spirit after the Divine, the Infinite, the Absolute. Aristotle (*De Anima*, B. IV. 2; 415^{b} 1) says that "all things reach out toward the eternal and the divine, and it is for the sake thereof that they do all that they do according to nature." Whatever acts, then, do not tend toward the Divine may be said to be unnatural; whatever acts do so tend, to be natural. All nature, as such, tends to the highest order, to the Divine. At the bottom of all revolutions lies a conception of man as a material being; at the bottom of all reformations, a conception of man as a spiritual being, striving to realize the Divine in himself

Having thus distinguished the two fundamental forms of Titanism, we may now ask, Under which of the two must we class Goethe's Titanism, — under that of Kronos, who rose up in rebellion against his own nobler offspring, Zeus, in order to restore the world to an older and less spiritual condition, or to that of Prometheus, who rebelled against Zeus, in favor of something more spiritual than even *his* dominion? One may answer this question without

78

hesitation. The Titanism of Goethe is for the most part the Titanism of Prometheus. And it is so in a very marked and striking way. One can hardly read Goethe's best works without being continually reminded of Prometheus. The similarity did not escape Goethe's own notice. Prometheus was a favorite figure with him, and there is perhaps no portion of his writings in which his own true character comes out more clearly than in the powerful fragment bearing the name of the great Titan. In this we find Prometheus, after having served Zeus for many years, engaged in open, outspoken rebellion against him, and yet enjoying the special favor of Zeus's daughter, Athena, the personification of wisdom. In a conversation with her the Titan says:

"Hast thou not seen me oft,
In self-elected servitude,
The burden bear, which they
In solemn earnest on my shoulders laid?
Have I the labor not completed,
Each daily task at their behest,
Because I thought that
They saw what has been, and what shall be,
Within the present,
And that their guidance, their command,
Was first, primeval and
Unself-regarding Wisdom?"

79

Prometheus has found the limitations of the gods in whom he has been taught to believe. They know no more about the past and the future from the present than he does; they are blind leaders of the blind, and their blindness is due to the fact that

they are selfish, looking for their own enjoyment, instead of being universally diffused to bless. Prometheus has been able to discover these limitations of the reigning gods, because he has won the love of a younger and nobler divinity, — the *ewig-weibliche* of Athena. A declaration of this love on the part of Athena, coupled with an expression of respect for her father, —

"Ich ehre meinen Vater,
Und liebe dich, Prometheus," —

draws from the Titan these remarkable words: —

"And thou art to my spirit
What it is to itself.
Even from the first
Thy words have been celestial light to me.
Ever, as if my soul spake unto itself,
It opened wide,
And harmonies, born with it at its birth,
Rang forth, from out itself, within it,
And a Divinity
Spoke when I seemed to speak,
And when I thought Divinity did speak,
I spoke myself.
And so with thee and me,
So one, so intimate,
Endless my love to thee!"

Here we find expressed in its most intense and naked form the Titanism of Goethe. It is a revolt against the outward gods of tradition and dogma, the individual gods of the current religion, in favor of the God in his own heart, the God whose kingdom of heaven is within him, who is not distinguishable

80

from his own inmost being, who is at once wisdom and love and the desire to be utterly diffused in creation and blessedness. When Athena blames his hatred for the gods, and reminds him that they have power, and wisdom, and love, Prometheus replies:

"All that belongs not
Unto them alone:
I too endure like them.
Eternal are we all! —
Of my beginning memory have I none,
To end I have no call,
Nor see I any end.
Thus am I eternal, for I am,
And wisdom! —

(*Directing Athena's attention to his statues.*)

Look upon this brow!
Has not any finger
Fully moulded it?
And all this bosom's might
Bares itself to meet
The universal danger round about.

(*Looking at a female statue.*)

And thou, Pandora,
Thou sacred vessel of all gifts
That are delicious
Under the broad heaven,
Upon the infinite earth,
All that e'er thrilled me with emotion sweet,
That in the shadow's coolness
Poured refreshing on me,
All spring delight that ever the sun's love,
All tenderness that e'er
The sea's warm wave
Around my bosom poured,

81

All that I e'er of pure celestial glow
Have tasted, or of joy of spirit-rest —
This all, all — my Pandora!"

Prometheus feels that he has within himself all the divine attributes that he knows of, or can conceive, — power, wisdom, love. In only one thing does he seem inferior to Zeus, in that he has not the power to give life to his creations. Zeus has offered to ani-nate them for him, if he will bow down and worship him; but Prometheus contemptuously refuses any such condition, and Athena, that is, the divinity within him, hastens to assure him that Zeus, whatever he may pretend, has not the giving or the taking away of life in his power. That belongs to a higher power, whom Athena calls Fate. She will herself guide Prometheus to the spring of life, and his creations shall live through him. Prometheus replies:

"Through thee, O my goddess,
Shall they live and feel them free.
Live! Their joy shall be thy thanks."

Let us linger a moment upon this word Fate, which the inner Wisdom declares to be higher than the gods, to be the source of life, and to impart that life through the Titanic spirit. The thought expressed by the word is a very profound one, and one that has occupied the attention of the greatest thinkers and poets. Among the Greeks it had many names, corresponding to different aspects of it, Μοῖρα, Αἶσα, Πεπρωμένη, Εἱμαρμένη, Κῆρ, Ἀνάγκη or Necessity. In their minds it generally lay, as a dim, illimitable, inscru-

82

table background, behind the brilliant array of their numerous gods, as something superior to the gods and against which they had no power. This thought occurs in several passages of the Homeric poems (Il. XVIII. 117, XIX. 417, &c.), but is perhaps most clearly expressed in a passage from the third book of the Odyssey (236–238):

"The gods themselves have not the power to save
Whom most they cherish from the common doom,
When cruel Fate brings on the last long sleep."

It is hardly necessary to say that the same thought permeates and dominates the whole of Æschylus's tragedy of "Prometheus." Prometheus, "the high-spirited son of right-counselled Justice," is more humane than Zeus himself, and farther-seeing. The conception of divinity embodied in Zeus does not satisfy him. Before his mind floats a higher conception, and he has learnt from his mother, Justice, that this higher conception shall one day be realized, and Zeus hurled

perfectly consistent philosophical conception of God, it had made very considerable advances in that direction, when the event of Protestantism once more imposed upon a large portion of the world an intensified mythical concept of the Divine. The popular god of Catholicism, or rather the god of popular Catholicism, a very different being from the god of philosophic Catholicism, became the supreme god of Protestantism. We all know, probably but too well, the conception of God ordinarily held in Protestant churches, and how little it differs from the old Greek popular conception of Zeus. We all know, too, to what an amount of narrowness, bigotry, intolerance, uncharitableness, misunderstanding, oppression, and spiritual pride and deadness it has given rise. We know how compatible it is with almost every form of selfishness and every form of economical and political abuse. The Calvinistic form of this conception has been stated, with a scathing force that can hardly be excelled, by Burns, in his famous "Holy Willie's Prayer," which begins:

86

> " O Thou, wha in the heavens dost dwell,
>   Wha as it pleases best Thysel'
> Sends ane to heaven and ten to hell,
>   A' for thy glory,
> An' no for ony guid or ill
>   They've done afore thee."

Burns too was a Titan, and despised this monstrous God with all his heart.

It was not merely against the cruel and blasphemous conception of God entertained by Calvin that Goethe's Titanic scorn was directed, but against the entire Protestant conception of him, and against everything that followed naturally from that conception. The words which he puts into the mouth of Prometheus, as he sits forming men in his workshop, after having refused all offers of a compromise with Zeus, no doubt accurately express his own feelings with reference to the Protestant conception of God. He says:

> " While I was yet a child,
>   Not knowing out or in,

from his throne by one "who will find a flame mightier than the thunderbolt." What is this but another way of saying that Prometheus rebels against the external god of the popular fancy in favor of that God whom justice proclaims in his heart? He knows and feels that he is rooted in a power deeper and mightier than Zeus, a fate by whose eternal decree he lives and must live forever. He boasts, "What should I fear, who am fated not to die?" The result is that Zeus is finally compelled to release him from his cruel torment, and to rise to the height of that

83

ideal which Prometheus had conceived. That inscrutable fate whose mouthpiece is Justice is greater than any god conceived or conceivable in the image of man. The same thought we might easily find, more or less clearly expressed, in many passages from the other Greek poets. We find, indeed, in some of them, and still more frequently in the philosophers, that the impersonal Fate is identified with the highest god, that is, with Zeus; but this does not alter the character of that fate. When Zeus becomes identified with Fate, he loses his capricious, tyrannical attributes, and becomes that which no imagination can conceive and no tongue adequately express,—in a word, he becomes the Absolute and Eternal. For, after all, the Greek conception of Fate or Necessity is, at bottom, a rude conception of the Absolute. The Greeks, as we have already said, were far on their way to a true conception of the Divine under all its forms, extension, being, and love,—when popular Christianity, with its Oriental, mythological concepts, took possession of the world and once more imposed upon it a mythical Deity, conceived in the image of man.

In proportion as Christianity found its way among philosophers and thinkers, the notion of God fostered by it became less and less mythical and more and more philosophical, and, indeed, it would not be difficult to find among the writers of the two great ages of ecclesiastical thought—that of the Fathers and that of the Schoolmen—expressions for the Divine

84

as philosophical as any that occur in Plotinus or Porphyry. In no case, of course, is the expression adequate; for every expression for the Divine must, to a large extent, be negative.

The attempt to conceive God philosophically is especially marked in the works attributed to Dionysius the Areopagite,—the first bishop of Athens and the patron saint of Paris,—works which in reality were produced about the end of the fourth century of our era, under strong Neo-Platonic influences. Here we are told, for example, that "the supra-essential One limits the existing one and all number, and is itself the cause and principle of the one and of number, and at the same time the number and the order of all that exists. Hence the Deity, who is exalted above all things, is praised as a monad and as a triad, but is unknown to us or to any one, whether as monad or as triad; in order to praise the supra-unified in him, and his divine creative power, we apply to him, not only the triadic and monadic names, but we call him the Nameless One, the Super-essential, to indicate that he transcends the category of being." We might find similar expressions in Augustine and other influential writers of the patristic period. Similarly, in that most famous of all medieval theological manuals, the "Sentences" of Peter the Lombard, we find it said: "The Trinity is a supreme thing and common to all that enjoy it, if, indeed, it can be called a thing and not rather the cause of all things, or if, indeed, it can be called so much as a cause."

85

Similar expressions might be found scattered through the schoolmen, down as late as the time of Suarez, who was contemporary with Descartes.

Dante, whose conception of God was eminently philosophic, tells us that Holy Writ, in condescension to our powers,

> "Doth hands and feet

> Ascribe to God, still meaning something else."

Although Catholic thought, being trammelled by mythical dogmas, could hardly ever have arrived at a

I turned my straying eye
Sunwards, as if above me were
An ear to hear my plaint,
A heart like mine
To pity the heavily-laden.

87

"Who helped me
Against the Titans' arrogance?
Who rescued me from death,
From slavery?
Hast thou not all achieved thyself,
Heart of sacred glow?

And, young and good, didst glow,
Poor dupe, with gratitude
To him who sleeps above?

"I honor thee? Wherefore?
Hast thou e'er soothed the anguish
Of the heavily-laden?
Hast ever wiped away the tears
Of the grief-oppressed?
Have I not been forged into a man
By almighty Time
And by eternal Fate,
My lords and thine?

"And didst thou fancy
I should hate life
And flee to deserts
Because all blossom-dreams
Did not bear fruit?
Here sit I and mould men
After mine own image,
A race to be like me,
To suffer and to weep,
To enjoy and to be glad,
And pay no heed to thee,
Like me."

88

This poem was written in 1773, two years after the heroic radical "Götz von Berlichingen," and one year before the still more radical "Werther," in which the worst part of Goethe's Titanic tendencies culminated. "Prometheus" gives us Titanism in the classic world; "Götz," Titanism in the mediæval world; "Werther," Titanism in the modern world, or rather in the seething world of the eighteenth century, previous to the French Revolution. Of the three works, "Prometheus" is the one that repre-

sents best the spirit of Goethe's own Titanism, that Titanism which remained with him through life. The hero of "Götz" comes to an untimely and disappointed end, to a death of admitted defeat, through the pressure of outward circumstances. The hero of "Werther" does still worse, for he puts an end to his own life. Prometheus alone remains Titanic to the last, defying, and with impunity defying, all external circumstances, strong in the strength of that divinity which glows with a holy flame in his own heart. And, indeed, from the point of view of poetic justice, this is as it should be. The Titanism which struggles for individual freedom through mere physical courage and strength, without due regard to existing institutions and moral conditions, must necessarily suffer defeat. Independence for an individual baron would be a retrogression toward barbarism and anarchy. On the other hand, that Titanism which seeks personal satisfaction in passive sentiment, however refined, instead of in rational activity, must not only necessarily fail, but must end by making life worthless to the person who attempts it. He needs no outward circumstances to destroy him: the outraged god within him will be quite sufficient for that. Prometheus, whose delight is in creative activity, in loving obedience to the Divinity within him, can alone safely and defiantly carry out his Titanism to the end. Naught can touch him who himself gives up all.

89

It is a significant enough fact that the drama of "Prometheus" was never completed, much as the central figure was a favorite with Goethe. And the reason of this is curious. Goethe himself somewhere tells us that his different works represent stages in his own culture, and that the completion of each work marked the completion of the stage. No doubt his individual Titanism ended with "Götz," and his sentimental Titanism, in large measure at least, with "Werther." But his Promethean Titanism never ended, until the last day of his life. It was an abiding fact in his life, indeed perhaps the most

important fact in it, the source of all other important facts. But Goethe, whose spiritual progress was very rapid in those years, could not but soon come to see that the conflict between Prometheus and Zeus, the envious thunderer, could in no adequate way express the depth and extent of his own Titanism. Zeus could not be made to do duty as the conservative Philistine God of Protestantism, and Prometheus could not be made to represent all the forms of opposition which had to be directed against that God.

So Goethe, after writing two brief acts (and part of a third) of his "Prometheus," abandoned it, and in the following year set to work upon another theme, in which he must have felt that his own Titanism could be much better embodied,—a theme drawn from the annals of Protestantism itself,—the story of Faust. This theme had several advantages over the other, besides modernness and adaption to Goethe's

90

own state of mind. It enabled him to show the gradual growth of the true Titanism, out of the many forms of false Titanism, to develop its positive and beneficent side, instead of its negative and defiant side, and to depict the nature of its ultimate triumph.

In "Prometheus" the narrow jealous Zeus, the god of popular fancy, still reigns supreme, while the Infinite God "whose throne is in men's hearts" occupies an unrecognized position of patient defiance, moulding men after his own image. In "Faust," on the contrary, the inner, the Infinite God is already supreme lord of heaven and earth, seated in power among the cherubim and seraphim, while Zeus, or the god of narrow selfishness, is relegated to a small sphere in the affairs of human kind. He is, in fact, "der kleine Gott der Welt," the little god of the world, or rather of worldliness, who, as Mephistopheles says, "always remains of the same fashion, and is as queer as on the first day." To be sure he has a glimmer of heaven's light,—even Zeus had that; but he uses it only to be more beastly than every other beast. The Supreme God, on the contrary, the Lord, so far from being jealous of any one, can

afford to tolerate the very devil, and even finds a use for him. His amenity is so great as to surprise that dignitary, who remarks, at the end of his interview with him, that

> "It is quite handsome in so great a lord
> To speak so kindly with the devil himself."

91

The dethroned divinity, the god of worldliness, does not appear anywhere in the poem as a distinct person, nor indeed does the Supreme Divinity, except in the Prologue. The Deity, who reveals himself in the conscience, and the little god of the world, who for the most part directs human institutions, alike appear only as tendencies working silently. The former shows his power by continually preventing Faust from yielding to the allurements of Mephistopheles, the latter appears in the form of official religion, which finds its most striking embodiment in the Astrologer at the imperial court. This dignitary is ready at once to enter into close alliance with Mephistopheles, even when the latter plays the part of court fool, so much so, that, when asked how things look in heaven,—"Wie sieht's am Himmel aus?"—he replies in a mock-serious, meaningless speech whispered into his ear by Mephistopheles.

The difference between the relative positions of the great and the little deity in "Prometheus" and in "Faust" really marks the difference between the relative positions of conscience and human law in ancient and modern times. In ancient times, the laws of the state and of society, both written and unwritten, were held to be superior to the individual conscience, whose exercise in opposition to them, as in the case of Sokrates, could be regarded only as ὕβρις, insolence, or insubordination. In modern times, on the contrary, it is universally held that conscience, when sane, has a higher claim than any human decree.

It was doubtless this fact among others that made Goethe select Faust, rather than Prometheus, as the representative of his own Titanism. It must be remarked, too, that Faust's consciousness of the Su-

92

preme Divinity is at first very slight compared with that of Prometheus. He appears in all his splendor to the latter from the first, in the person of Athena, and draws forth his most ardent love and consequent activity. Faust is hardly conscious of him at all, except as a vague feeling that somehow directs him in the midst of his dark strivings. The Lord says to Mephistopheles, speaking of Faust:

> "Though but confusedly he serves me now,
> Yet will I soon conduct him into clearness."

Goethe's Titanism, then, is Prometheanism, only with the relative position of the two deities, the great and the little, changed, and the vision of the former dimmed in the soul. Whereas Prometheus lives to obey the Supreme God, whom he knows and loves, and is, therefore, supremely happy in his defiance, Faust toils on in darkness, seeking the vision of this highest God, whom he finds at last, when he reaches the philanthropic position (φιλάνθρωπος τρόπος, as Æschylus says) of Prometheus. Though Faust is by no means Goethe, yet Faust's problems are those which most profoundly occupied the mind of Goethe. Goethe's life, with all its activities, in so far as they had his own approval, was a Titanic struggle against the god of the world, under the inspiration of the God whom he felt in his own soul, and whom he

93

recognized as speaking out of the very depths of being, with the voice of Fate and Justice, which in the last result are one. The conception of this God which we find in Prometheus is not materially altered in Faust, except that in the latter more emphasis is placed upon the fact that the wisdom which speaks with authority in the human heart and intellect is also Lord of the universe. Further we cannot go; at least, further Goethe could not go. He deprecated all attempts to define God as a person, or as anything else. When Margaret asks Faust concerning his belief in God, the latter replies:

> "My darling, who dare say,
> I believe in God?
> Mayst question priest or sage,

And their answer seems to be
But mockery of the asker."

And when Margaret persists with

> "Then you do not believe?"

Faust replies in the much admired speech, of which I shall quote only a part:

> "Mishear me not, thou gracious countenance!
> Who dare name him,
> And who confess
> I believe in him?
> Who can feel
> And have the courage
> To say, I believe not in him?
> "Doth not all crowd
> Into thy head and heart,
> And pulse in everlasting mystery

94

> Invisible, visible, beside thee?
> Fill full thy heart therewith, in all its bulk,
> And when in feeling thou art wholly blest,
> Then name it what thou wilt,
> Say bliss! heart! love! God!
> I have no name
> For it! Feeling is all;
> Name is sound and smoke,
> Beclouding heaven's glow."

This speech has been very much admired, as embodying the highest conception of divinity possible for man. I think it is the highest conception of divinity to which Goethe ever attained, and the one under the influence of which he played the Titan against the God of popular tradition and worldliness. But it is by no means the highest conception of God, and its limitations mark Goethe's own limitations, and the defects in his Titanism. Two elements, and perhaps the most important of all, are omitted,—truth and right,—in one word, holiness. The God of Faust, who is in the main the God of Goethe, is not a moral God, and Emerson was entirely right when he maintained that Goethe was incapable of a surrender to the moral sentiment. The simple fact is, that the moral sentiment, pure and simple, found no utterance in Goethe's heart, and hence could not appear in his God, who was but the bearer of the

utterances that were found there.

It may perhaps be objected, that it is unfair to attribute to Goethe a conception of God put into the mouth of Faust at a time when that hero was still

95

far from God; and this would be correct, if it could be shown that Goethe ever attained to any higher conception. Such, however, I have not been able to find in his works or in his life. Faust himself attains to no riper conception, even in heaven. We find many instances in which Goethe shows his comprehension of the divine nature, by declaring it to be in things, and not outside of them, and by refusing to define it in the imperfect forms of speech. In a short series of poems called "Gott und Welt," he writes:

"What were a god that pushed but from without,
And let the world about his finger spin?
God must be one who moves the world within,
Nature in Him, Himself in Nature holding,
So that what in Him lives and moves and is
May never miss His power, His spirit never."

And again:

"There is a universe within the soul,
And hence all nations laudably permit
Each man to call the best he knoweth God,
Yea, his God, to deliver to Him earth
And heaven, to fear, and, if he can, to love Him."

In "Wilhelm Meister's Wanderjahre," in speaking of the three forms of reverence, (1) for that which is above us, (2) for that which is below us, (3) for

96

that which is on a level with us, he says:—

"These three produce together the true religion. From these three reverences springs the highest reverence, reverence for oneself, and this again is the source

of the other three. Hence man arrives at the highest of which he is capable, by being allowed to consider himself the best that God and Nature have produced."

In 1813, writing to Jacobi, he says:—

"I, for my part, with the manifold tendencies of my nature, do not find one aspect of the Divine enough. As

a poet, I am a polytheist; as an investigator of nature, I am a pantheist, and both in the same degree. If I require a personal god for my personality as a moral being, that also has been provided for in my mental constitution."

This last is perhaps the most explicit declaration we have of Goethe's theological belief, and it is a most important one, as showing the character of the Divinity under whose inspiration he played the Titan against the popular Divinity of his time. This Divinity is conceived as above number, equally capable of being conceived as one and as many, as occasion may require. In so far as he is a person, he is identical with Goethe's own personality, the very inmost core and essence of that. The notion of an individual, personal God, existing outside of him, Goethe rejected with the utmost scorn, and in so doing returned to the philosophic position of developed Hellenism,— to the position of the Neo-Platonists,—as opposed to the mythical view of Christianity, and especially of Protestantism.

It has often been said that Goethe was a Pagan. Even his biographer Düntzer gives him this appella-

97

tion. This is not only correct, but it is correct in a deeper sense than is generally known. We have seen that the three forms under which the Divine has been conceived are space (or extension), being, and love. These appear in Christian theology in the mythical forms of the Father, who is being, the Son, who is space, the condition of creation, and the Holy Ghost, who is love, the source of all action in the world, as even Empedokles saw. The aspect of the Divinity which most struck the Hebrews, and which, consequently, is uppermost in Christ's teaching, is that of being, or of the Father. Now, it is just this aspect of him that is the ground of morality; for morality has its foundation, not in extension or in love, but in the very depths of being. Even love itself has a moral significance only in so far as it is distributed in accordance with the recognized exigencies of being. For this reason the Hebrews were pre-eminently a

moral people, a people ready to bow before the authority of the Divine, a people, when at their best, obedient even unto death, for the sake of the right. Job can say (I quote from the revised version): "Behold, He will slay me; I have no hope; nevertheless, I will maintain my ways before Him. This also shall be my salvation." (xiii. 15, 16.) Now it was just the moral aspect of Divinity that was wanting in Hellenism. The Neo-Platonists were careful to say that God was above being ($\epsilon\pi\epsilon\kappa\epsilon\iota\nu\alpha$ $\tau o\hat{\upsilon}$ $\check{o}\nu\tau o\varsigma$), and hence above the good. In saying this, they thought they were honoring Him; but in truth they were losing

98

the moral aspect of Him; for the ground of all morality is being. The immoral is simply that which contravenes the essential laws of being, that which strives to be and cannot.

This failure to recognize God as being and as the ground of morality was the essential weakness of Hellenism from first to last, although, as one might have expected, it was formulated only when that system was near its close. Movements formulate themselves only at their close. Goethe then, in being a Pagan, as he was, failed to see the moral aspect of the Divine. He saw it as omnipresence and as love, but not as authority. His highest god was not the absolute right and good; it was rather the beautiful. Nay, it was not even the highest kind of beauty, that

"In loveliness of perfect deeds
More strong than all poetic thought."

It was rather the half-sensuous beauty which is capable of being expressed in symmetry and rhythm, the two forms in which harmony displays itself in space and time. Calm, serenity, balance, freedom from strife, from Sturm und Drang,—these were the attributes of that perfection which Goethe aimed at, and which therefore was his God. The still, adamantine strength which speaks out the truth without thought of consequences to self, that courts strife as the life of the world, that is so strong as to be ready to accept suffering unflinchingly, which seeks satisfaction in service and self-diffusion,—this was not Goethe's ideal.

99

Goethe was an artist, his spirit and temperament were those of the artist, not those of the martyr. Like an artist, he labored for finish, for completion, which has a term; not for perfection, which stretches away into the eternal. He saw what was in process around him and divined a good deal more; but that which lay behind the process he did not see. He saw evolution, but caught no glimpse of that which evolves. In one word, he lacked what Parmenides called faith, the vision of the eternal, of that which is, of God. He could see some of God's relations,—those to art, nature, and his own personality,—but God himself he could not see. Hence in Goethe there is none of the martyr spirit. The thought of dying to make men holy, or even to make them free, could never enter into his calculations. He wished to make his own life a complete poem, finished and harmonious in this world, and it was for the sake of this harmony that he demanded renunciation of the discordant elements. The utter renunciation of self, of the natural self, in order to find a self that is above nature, above process, individual, yet infinite and perfect as the Father which is in heaven is perfect, was a state of mind he could not rise to. He could not, in a word, combine Christianity with Hellenism, which is the problem of our time, but remained essentially Hellenic. The god in whose name he titanized was still an imperfect god, a duality, not a trinity.

The reason why Goethe failed to find the highest God, when men like Dante, that mightiest of the mod-

100

ern Titans, succeeded, is not hard to discover. It lay partly in his own temperament, which was sensuous and made heavy demands. It lay partly in his education, which did not go far to curb that temperament and subject it to divine law. But it lay also in the philosophical atmosphere of his time, in the clouds of Spinozism and Kantianism that went to darken the atmosphere. Say what it may to the contrary, modern philosophy from Descartes to Spencer is atheistic in the deepest sense. It is essentially a philosophy of process, not of being,—of genealogy, not of ontology.

Now God, essential being, is just that which lies outside of all process, that transcends all evolution, that imparts all movement, but does not itself move. We may call other things God,—the process of events, the current that makes for righteousness; but in doing so we are idolaters, setting up the idols of our imagination for God. And the idols of the imagination are far worse gods than the graven images of men's hands. When the pure intellect and its object, essential being, are banished from philosophy, God and the true ground of moral being will soon be banished from life, and false gods, or no god, will soon take His place.

But, besides the three causes mentioned as preventing Goethe from attaining to the highest consciousness of Divinity, there was still a fourth,—the direction of his studies, which was toward nature and the emotional or sensuous side of spirit. Goethe rather despised logic and metaphysics, the sciences

101

of pure spirit, but these sciences had their revenge, as they never fail to do, and as his own Mephistopheles, as conceived in his youth, knew that they did.

> "Only despise intelligence and science,
> The highest powers accorded unto man !
> In things of glamour and of magic let
> Thyself be hoodwinked by the spirit of lies,—
> Then have I thee at once without condition."

Of course, no one would think of saying that Goethe fell a prey to Mephistopheles, or that he was a bad man. On the contrary, Goethe was a good man, in very many senses a great man: he was a Titan, trying to steal divine fire to better human lives, and in a large degree succeeding. But, after all, it was not the purest fire that he stole, but a fire dimmed with the smoke of sweet incense.

Let us now try to sum up the character of Goethe's Titanism, and to show wherein it was manly and beneficent, and where it fell short of the highest. Its greatness consisted mainly in this, that it warred against the external enslaving god of tradition and conventionality, with all his belongings in the shape of human institutions, and did so in the name of the internal, freeing God whose kingdom is within us, whose being is our being, who exists in every human soul, making us one with the Father and capable of being perfect as he is perfect. Its shortcomings were all due to the fact that Goethe was unable to conceive this inner God in his full majesty of absolute insight, love, and diffusive power. And this

102

inability again was certainly due to the fact, that in Goethe himself the inner God was not revealed in all his majesty. Only the pure in heart see God, and this for the reason that the heart is the eye wherewith God is seen.

But though this is strictly true, it must be admitted that Goethe struggled manfully during his long life to remove the film from his eye, and obtain a clearer and ever clearer view of the Divine. If he did not at any time entirely succeed, that was his misfortune, in the garb indeed of fortune, rather than his fault.

And this leads me to say a word of the different stages of Goethe's Titanism, which I have intentionally left to the end. It is generally said that it was confined to the early part of his life, and practically ended with his visit to Italy. Now in a certain superficial sense this is true, but only in a superficial sense. It was considerably transformed before he started for Italy; but it did not altogether cease at any period of his life, though it tended ever more and more to become a compromise. The "little god of the world," under the influence of the great God, has become much wiser since the days when Zeus sent Prometheus to the limits of the world, to be riveted to a rock and to have his liver torn by vultures. He now not unfrequently takes the new Prometheuses into his service, and makes them privy-councillors, thus rendering them in large measure innocuous and obtaining from them much good for themselves. To drop metaphor, Goethe's persistent good fortune, in

103

the course of time, tamed and soothed his Titanism and ever made him more desirous of finding a reconciliation between the world-spirit and the supreme in-

ward God. This tendency assumed the form almost of homage to the world-spirit in the later part of Goethe's life, especially during that reactionary period which followed the excesses of the French Revolution, when men, wearied with Titanic struggling and in a measure cheated of its results, turned back with a kind of pathetic fondness to the obsolete systems of the past, seeking for rest anywhere, even in a monastery. It would be wrong to say that Goethe at any time proved a traitor to the highest God, and did homage only to Baal; but that he was deeply affected by the reactionary spirit that prevailed during the last decade of his life, there can be no doubt. More and more he became averse to Titanic revolution, more and more in favor of quiet evolution. He disliked the volcanic theory even in geology, and said that the Protestant Reformation had disturbed quiet evolution (*störte ruhige Bildung*). This tendency becomes apparent more or less in all that he wrote after Schiller's death, but especially in the closing scene of the Second Part of "Faust." Here, in the summing up of his greatest work, a work begun in the Promethean spirit, some sixty years before, he altogether abandons the Titanic position, and seems to revert to the submissive attitude of Roman Catholicism. Faust reaches heaven, not by his own efforts, and by bringing the reigning Divinity to terms, but

104

by the help of good angels, conceived as the Middle Age conceived them, and by the levitating power of the purified spirit whom he had once wronged. He not merely effects a reconciliation with the popular God, but he makes entire submission to him, allowing himself to be carried to heaven, like a mediæval saint from the cloister. No doubt Goethe allowed Faust, as a man of the sixteenth century, to do things which he himself would not have done; but there can be no doubt that, as Goethe became an old man, his early Titanism tended to lose itself in compromise and even submission. "The wise indifference of the wise" unfortunately often takes this direction.

But, after all, this tendency in Goethe's case is not a matter for surprise. His Titanism had not at

any time been of that kind which imparts perfect satisfaction to the Titan, and can therefore endure forever. In that Titanism there was always an artistic and somewhat sensuous element of self. He could never entirely surrender himself to the God within him, in utter self-forgetfulness, careless of happiness. He is said to have asserted, with some pathos, toward the end of his long and marvellously fortunate life, that he had never, in all that life, known more than an hour's happiness. This shows what he had been seeking for, shows the defect in his Titanism, shows why it ended in compromise and submission. It shows also why his literary work is, after all, so fragmentary, and why many of his contemporaries condemned him as a renegade to progress and humanity.

105

Had Goethe, in the days of his early Titanism, seen God, the inner God, as authority, as being, and not merely as omnipresence and love, the case would have been different. No compromise would have been needed, the want of happiness would not have been felt, his works would have had the glorious unity of the "Divina Commedia," and he would have been recognized as the uncompromising Titan, the manifestation of Very God.

The truth is, Goethe wavered between the Christian spirit and the later Hellenic spirit, without ever being able to unite them, for the reason that he never seized either in its purity. This union is the great problem of our time. To reject the outer god of mythology, and all his works, — to cling to the inner God, who is the very life of our life, the self of our self, — to crush out mercilessly the little temporal self in ourselves, in order that the great, the eternal, the divine self may be free to manifest itself, — that is our task; a task to be performed titanically by ourselves and by none other. There is no salvation anywhere but in our deepest selves, no light anywhere but in the hidden shrines which we call our own souls. No outer God, with the best of wills, can save us; for salvation means being strong in and through ourselves. It is a poor charity that pampers weakness, instead of making strong, that tries to make depend-

ents, suppliants, and thralls, instead of free, pure men and women, obedient only to the laws of that kingdom of heaven which is within them, and striving

106

to be perfect, as the Father which is in that heaven is perfect.

That Goethe did not attain to this point of view is a matter to be regretted, but not one for which we can afford to blame the great poet. For many a long year he struggled manfully, with all the power that was in him, against the aggressive blandishments of good fortune, which continually reinforced the smaller self in him, and, though he did not altogether conquer in the end, he has left much work that will go far to help others to conquer. For such help, and such help alone, one man can give to another. He can point out the whither and the why of a religious life, and make it clear that there is no ultimate blessedness save in that uncompromising Titanism which fights in the name of the inner God of truth and love and right, — above all, of right.

107

IV.

GOETHE AND SCHILLER.

BY CYRUS A. BARTOL, D. D.

"Words are good, but they are not the best. The best is not to be explained by words. The spirit in which we act is the highest matter. Action can be understood and again represented by the spirit alone. No one knows what he is doing while he acts aright, but of what is wrong we are always conscious." —*Wilhelm Meister's Indenture.*

THE authorities of the Concord School of Philosophy demand of me to measure the incommensurable, to compare a literary accident with an intellectual necessity, to make an equation of an event with an element. To group and paint on one canvas two so unlike characters and incomparable minds were a rash attempt, which yet must share its presumption between the assigners of such a trust and the incompetent assignee, however unduly bold the latter may

be in handling it, giving less his reasons than impressions leading to the conclusion that the genius of the two foremost German poets is too diverse for any common scale. Goethe's superiority is not in degree, but in kind. They lie together; so do Chamouni and Mont Blanc. Schiller might have been or not,

108

Goethe must have been. He was a necessity. He was hewn out of the rock he proceeded to hew from. He re-created the language his tongue lisped in the cradle. He reconstituted the nation of which he was born. To take out Goethe were to take out Germany from modern history. Napoleon, who said he found but two men in Italy, found but this one in Germany, and bluntly said to him, "You are a man," as he said to his military staff, "There is a man." But how little Napoleon dreamed that the man he nodded this compliment to would by his thinking and writing so unite his divided and distracted country as to be the prophet of Bismarck and Moltke, and, as the Jews fancied of their Elias, reappear after a generation, and in turn overcome the empire Bonaparte transmitted to his dynasty, at Sedan and the gates of Paris, without sight of the conqueror's tomb! Goethe was denounced as no patriot because he did not personally withstand the invader, but declared him too strong to resist. He was blamed that he did not seize the trumpet and throw away the harp. He replied, that military songs might be composed by Körner amid the neighing of horses, but not by himself sitting in a room. "When I was in love, I wrote love-songs; why should I write songs of hatred when I did not hate?" His contribution to freedom was his thought, and every word from his pen, though no summons to arms. That in aught beside the doctrinary devotion to native soil, which is so cheap on the Danube or the Merrimack, Schiller surpassed him, does not appear.

109

In the purely intellectual realm, they are to be rather contrasted than compared. Schiller's poetry is regular, often magnificent in its bursts; Goethe's is inspired from the universal law and order, as much part of nature and human nature as the landscape is of the world. Schiller has a fine plot, with able and admirable execution. He produced pieces adapted to the stage. He has more personal ambition and ingenious contrivance to compass, by managing the public, his literary ends; knows how to play the game, and instructs Goethe in it, when they become a sort of business firm and a literary coalition against common foes; but a deeper than any aim at popularity, or wish to win or please had the elder companion,—too great to be a compeer, above being rewarded, and scorning to be bribed or pre-empted; witness to the truth of things, advocate of the universe, with but from his Creator a retaining fee. Schiller's verse is clear and sweet, and shows a rare constructive gift. He excels in the speeches he puts into his heroes' and heroines' mouths. He is quotable in many a splendid passage. His printed oratory is superb. But declamation is for the hour, and its platform does not abide. Eloquence, below the supreme pattern, cannot endure the test of pewter types. It is an effervescing glass, to be drunk at the moment. It is manna, that will not stand over to the next day.

110

It is not lack of reflection that sets Schiller in the second rank. Rather his philosophy entangles and drowns his Muse. Nor is a basis of fact in his compositions the want. He is historical, as for a singer he is metaphysical, to excess. He is not the warbler that Goethe is, and has not the pitch. Goethe is as the bobolink that flies and sings at once, its transporting music subsiding into a short chirp as he lights on a bough, or fence, or swaying stem in the field. No master, ancient or modern, more triumphantly than Goethe has cloven the atmosphere of our common breath with lyrical airs. Of the transcendent bards, Homer, Dante, Shakespeare, he is the last. Homer—be it said without offence to the traditional father of song—begins to look gray with the world's longevity and the antiquity of letters and religious myths. Dante is supra-mundane, vexed with Italian feuds, provincial in his scope. He loves Beatrice and other divine creatures, with the Supreme Head; but he hates many men and spirits, for whom he fashions his dread converging circles of the pit. He makes his Inferno his masterpiece. He spends himself on that, —and more on the Purgatory than the Paradiso; writes the sentence "No hope," as the frontispiece of hell, and throws the earth into eclipse with the awful shadows of other spheres. Shakespeare and Goethe are the two great poets for the modern mind, for humanity, for the hour that is coming and that now is. Goethe posts the books up to date; insists that everything shall be natural, real, and true, present to the faith and experience of mankind. Milton treats us to stately and sonorous lines, that march in

111

perfect step. They are as an army at whose even and solid tread the earth trembles, while banners flaunt and sounds of drum and trumpet pierce the air. But his manner is more than his theme. He surfeits us with fabulous celestial doings, fancied diabolical rebellions, extra-terrestrial battles, and *feux d'artifice*, pyrotechnics, however by the tragedy they illustrate made sublime, yet shot off to accompany a theology that no longer can fit our condition or content our moral sense. The Satan he shows issuing from the far-off under-world portals for his travels, with brave equipment, to compass the ruin of a distant planet, precursor of all Alexander-like conquerors, Goethe with a drop of ink depicts in the shape of a poodle, starting up in a study or a street, let in or out at the corner of a diagram, dressed and talking like a gentleman, up to all the tricks of trade, plausible and persuasive as any huckster or broker, a dealer in jewelry, ready to enter a maiden's chamber, captivate a duenna, spur to a quarrel, and lay down on any counter the coin for the price of a human soul. He lives next door, and is at our own and our neighbor's service. We suspect his lodging in our breast. Ever since Goethe wrote, in all lands we say of any cunning man-shaped devil he is a perfect Mephistopheles. Demons, angels, or mortals Goethe makes familiar spirits, domesticates and plants them on the earth. Natural or supernatural, they are always real; and many of

Schiller's characters beside them are as stuffed figures of tradition, or paper silhouettes cut by metaphysical scissors.

112

Goethe's gold brightens, Schiller's lacquer tarnishes and fades, with use. Why are the moth and rust at work on compositions which the school-girls thirty years ago were mad over, Don Carlos, Marie Stuart, the Robbers, and William Tell, while Wilhelm Meister, Elective Affinities, Hermann and Dorothea, multiply their constituents and strengthen their hold, and, as readers appreciate, are insured against accident? Schiller has fared better than Goethe on the playhouse boards; but the world is the stage on which Goethe's men and women are players of his *dramatis personæ*, the scene being life, and society the panorama unrolled. Goethe knew good work, and therefore did it. He said, I thought I should have done some things differently from Shakespeare, but soon learned what a poor sinner I was, and that he is Nature's prophet: and Goethe is the same: Faust and Hamlet coequal in date, although, in the Second Part of Faust, Helena can never be popular even among scholars.

113

The women are alike good from the English and the German draughtsman, however honestly either acquired his skill Margaret and Mignon are not copies of Ophelia or Desdemona, and their colors are as fast. Shakespeare did not, perhaps could not in his lordly age, glorify like his successor a humble peasant lot. Both were close to nature, witnesses faithful and true; and Goethe is the chief example in history of critical and creative faculty combined. Art, he says, consists not in making beautiful descriptions, but in describing beautiful things. Without being intimately present for a long time with a special object, he adds, the artist cannot succeed. With Schiller rhetoric prevails over reality. He is a performer whose expression is sacrificed to his technique. "The Song of the Bell" is a fine poem; Wallenstein and Thekla are noble characterizations, but fashioned by conventional rules. The author lacks the artless graces, knows too much. Goethe, with all his skill and information, obeys the genius he does not pretend to understand or guide. "I prefer," he says, "that the power which works in and through me should be hidden from me. I have never thought about thought. I have metaphysics enough to last me for life." Nature to him is God's anteroom and audience-chamber. He does not try or expect to reach the Sovereign Presence by climbing up some other way, or presume at the King's shoulder to dictate or suggest, but humbly pores over his handwriting to peruse or spell it out. He is as physical, as much of a naturalist, including the soul, in his poetry as in his science. When Schiller complains that a lecturer had shown Nature not in her unity, but in specimens and bits, Goethe eagerly expounds to him that unity in the metamorphosis of plants, each portion as a transformed leaf. Schiller replies, that this is not an observation but an idea. Goethe rejoins, that he is glad to have eyes to behold such

114

ideas in nature. He says, "When I look, I see all there is." So he saw the topmost vertebra expanding into the skull, and the seven colors as mixtures of light and shade. Schiller did not consider that we can see, with eyes, only what the frame of nature tends to. Newton does not see the fall, as an apple, of the sphere: Kepler does not see the planetary approximations, nor Darwin the animal evolutions: they see indications and draw conclusions which the facts and motions require. Nature refuses to be caught in the very act. Goethe saw the live robe of God which the earth-spirit weaves; and he held all the bright and dark yarn in some extra pair of hands. He portrays man, the living, moving body of the race; not, like our Emerson, the individual mind or the Holy Ghost alone. Emerson spins a thread, Goethe weaves a web. Emerson snatches a trumpet from some angel's grasp, Goethe greets us with an orchestral symphony. Emerson fetches the top-stone of a monument or pinnacle of a temple before the structures are reared and ready; Goethe builds from the ground with vast and complete design. Emerson arrives a pilgrim and stranger after long sojourn in a foreign land, angelic visitor from some heavenly sphere, and, shrewd though he be, gets but half-acquainted with this world; Goethe is native to the soil, and knows every earthly mother's son and daughter by heart. None higher in aim than Emerson, more a prince among the fine spirits that have lighted up this earth with a celes-

115

tial gleam: none more true to his call, which was not, like that of Shakespeare and Goethe, to set forth this human membership which we are. He is a soloist at the concert, his performance slenderly related to the choir. He imperfectly appreciates the functions of church or state. He gazes at Goethe as an antelope, gazelle, or camelopard might at Behemoth or the great Pan. He is the zenith which from a scornful altitude surveyed the nadir and the poles. Yet Emerson draws from Goethe.

> "And e'en the grass shall plot and plan
> What it will do when it is man,"

comes after Goethe's encouragement to the Proteus Delphis in "Helena," —

> "Through myriad forms of being wending,
> To be a man in time thou 'lt rise."

So hard it is to be original. The last shall be first and the first last. Emerson and Darwin are anticipated, exceeded, and included by Goethe. The most generous of admirers, Emerson notes the merits of his senior contemporary without justice to his supreme human representative claim.

"Faust," the crowning product of the nineteenth century, is to his dainty mind a disagreeable book, as if a poem, epic or dramatic, could be made of the leavings when all the sad and dark passages of the worldtale should have been erased; the critic not seeing that it is only against the facts or materials of the tragedy that his objection holds. He complains that

116

Goethe neither surrenders himself to the torrent of inspiration nor devotes himself to the absolute truth; cares for art for the sake of culture, and is not even

an artist because not incorporating all the matter of his pages in artistic form; the censure from other quarters being that Goethe is artist too much with determination of blood to the head at the cost of the heart. Puritan clashes with cosmopolitan. Emerson writes to Carlyle, "Goethe can never be dear to me"; and, in his "Representative Men," that he can never be dear to mankind. Sterling wrote to Carlyle that Goethe is not to be loved, and Carlyle cries back, "Who has the right to love him?" "Goethe was a wicked man," exclaimed a lady lecturer; and a bad man he was long before pronounced to be by a Cambridge orator, who describes him as inwardly felicitating himself on the rich accession to his artistic domain from discreditably precious experiences, and deriving material for poetry from sufferings wantonly caused. That moral worth is essential to intellectual success was the orator's point, which he declared he would not give up for a hundred Goethes,—as if the earth had not labored in bringing forth one; and that it was too soon to conclude that Goethe as a man of letters does succeed; that the love and enthusiasm of the German heart ran to Schiller, the true, earnest, whole-souled man with his great, glowing, outpoured heart. Forty-one years are gone since this conscientious prevision, and time as yet gives no backing to the seer, who did not foresee. Time cannot be so cheaply subsidized

117

and suborned. Time seems to be of the opinion, that a man may have faults or defects, or commit immoralities, as Moses and David and Solomon did, and as in some way and measure all men, the harsh judges included, do or may have done, and yet not be reckoned as refuse for the dunghill; but repent and be pardoned, even be exalted, like him who slew the Egyptian in a passion, or like the Hebrew Psalmist, or his son, with his bitter-sweet proverbs for part of the canon; or like St. Augustine, head father of the Church, when a boy; or, to take illustrations from our own day, like some platform speaker, Christian professor, or occupant of a presidential chair. The condonings of history make a strange chapter when mixed with the decrees of the moral sense. To say that

Goethe gloated over the sin, while he gathered up the lesson, is a calumny. Sin would play all of us a worse trick than it does, if we learned nothing from it. Shall we revile Peter for turning with beautiful petrifaction his inconsistencies into a rock, or Paul for making fuel of his persecutions to kindle his devotions to super-heat? When we assail Goethe for his fifty-first penitential Psalm, issue of his adultery, it will be in season to attack Goethe for the pathetic strains that accompany or follow his unhappy slips of like sort. Stones will not be so plenty and at hand if the innocent, who are never known to throw them, are commissioned to cast the first. "That," said the visitor, pointing to a picture on the wall, "is a St. Cecilia." "No," replied the lady, "a Magdalen." "Pardon

118

me, my eyes are so poor," he answered, "I cannot tell a sinner from a saint." An ill opinion of human virtue exaggerates, both in individuals and the community, the sum of sexual vice, till a malaria of suspicion confounds the general virtue, and covers like a baleful fog the land. Goethe, born with immense susceptibility, bred in an atmosphere which French license and German sentiment mixed for his breath, and becoming like a city set on a hill, erred too often and conspicuously to be hid. History must mark him, not as treacherous or insincere in his affections, but volatile, inconstant, lacking that consecration whose mutuality between two persons, man and woman, is the right, duty, and glory of both. But it demoralizes society to decide that the unmarried may not have friendships as pure as they are dear.

Great men are too scarce to be thrown away, even for grievous faults. Consult proportion in what you judge. Measure the mountain, as well as the rift in its side. We accept vast benefits from and for them own our debt to Webster, Hamilton, as factors and benefactors; and to Samuel Johnson, mournfully confessing, "Ah! I have not lived as I ought." Schiller's record appears to be free from this particular blot, to which, by his cleaner or less passionate constitution, he was not exposed. But how his loyal wife befriended Goethe, and promoted confidence in the two

identified homes! But Schiller's early pen left some stains; and he had sins, of as deep a dye as his friend's, in the jealousy which made him say of

119

Goethe, "This man stands in my way"; in the ambition which proposed his own honor for his object, as well as, if not more than, the common good, and the indirection with which he sometimes brought his purposes to pass,—in contrast with Goethe's simplicity, royal generosity, and the modesty with which he accepted criticism of his own writings for more than it was worth. His ability at such a multiple distribution as he made of his own heart is a flaw. The two parts of God's image whose sundering is sex tend, run, fly together, and collisions occur. The ever-womanly draweth us on; the ever-manly too, what woman will not add? But desertion of another, even for the sake of one's own supposed destiny, is a crime; and doubtless there are eyes fine enough to see where Goethe's work suffered for his mistake.

Among the appreciators of Goethe, why such warmth in Thomas Carlyle, a man so pure, so slow to praise and quick to blame? Was it that he found in Goethe, for once, no sham, but a veracity without parallel in the literary guild,—words like those nails in the Bible by the Master of assemblies fixed, fastened, driven in a sure place, written on an iron leaf,—and an originality unmatched in this age? We can find a touch of Carlyle and of Emerson in Wordsworth, in Thomas Browne, and in Montaigne. But, says Dr. Hedge, Goethe lighted his torch at the sun. Perhaps Carlyle, resembling Goethe in his truthful testimony, admired also what he wanted himself, and never quite attained, the serenity of the great author, as if he sat

120

in the star Sirius with a pen reaching to the earth,—from the subjects he was identified with so wondrously remote! But he was wicked? No, such an altitude as his is impossible for a bad man! Satan, the Devil or evil one, is restless, goeth up and down, seeking whom he may devour. Says Miss Shepherd, author of "Counterparts,"—"Show me poetry of a bad man, and I will show you wherein it is not poetry." The

inquires, divines from the silence of those around him that the end has come, says Schiller is dead, covers his face with his hands, and laments an irreparable loss. In the delirium preceding his own death he sees a bit of paper on the floor, and asks why so careless as to leave Schiller's letters in that fashion lying round loose,—his affection, as the living wave ebbed in his bosom, showing its unsounded depth.

In England the man who has rated Schiller highest and studied Goethe most is Thomas Carlyle. It is like the praise of Sir Hubert Stanley when he makes Goethe of modern literature the head. Schiller was but the Mercury to that Jupiter, with whom Carlyle might be in some sense and measure a competitor had he become as peaceful and sunny as he was strong; could he have spoken the *Yea* of his own "Sartor Resartus" and left behind him the everlasting *No*, to learn the power of ideas as well as of will, and to perceive how mighty Goethe was, not in tak-

125

ing a partisan side in whatever affair was in question, but in thinking it all out and with glad content; not wishing to be brilliant, doing justice in his portraits to things and persons the most dull and commonplace, but genuine in every way, because he discerned how the repetition of forms and phrases ossifies the organs of intelligence. Goethe was a son of the morning; he wrought as the elements, he changed the climate and emancipated the human mind. Carlyle wielded the hammer of Vulcan, struck Cyclopean blows, and heated, to fashion anew and better, the old metal of the earth's annals. Standing round the strong and sweating craftsman, we feel like boys in whose faces fly the sparks and cinders from the blacksmith's forge. But, as he looks up, his honor for the unfallen German Lucifer is not less trustworthy by reason of the limits of his own position. He especially delights in the easy and airy style in which by his superior the miracle is done. But let me give specimens, such as translation of German into English allows. Take Mignon's death-song, in her gala attire, as she declines to be undressed.

"Such let me seem till such I be,—
Take not my snow-white dress away!
Soon from this dusk of earth I flee
Up to the glittering lands of day.

"There first a little space I rest,
Then wake so glad to scenes so kind;
In earthly robes no longer drest,
This band, this girdle, left behind.

126

"And those calm shining sons of morn,
They ask not who is maid or boy;
No robe, no garments, there are worn,
Our body pure from sin's alloy.

"Through little life not much I toiled,
Yet anguish long this heart has wrung;
Untimely woe my blossom spoiled,
Make me again forever young."

Lynceus, charged by Faust with neglect of warder duty when Helena arrives, explains his dereliction:—

"Let me kneel and gaze upon her,
Let me live or let me die,
Pledged to serve with truth and honor
The god-given dame am I.

"Watching for the morning, gazing
Eastward for its rising, lo!
In the south, my vision dazing,
Rose the sun, a wondrous show.

"Neither earth nor heaven-ward turning,
Depth nor height my vision drew;
Thitherward I gazed, still yearning
Her the peerless one to view.

"Eyesight keen to me is granted,
Like to lynx on highest tree;
From the dream which me enchanted
Hard I struggled to be free.

127

"Could I the delusion banish?
Turret, tower, barred gateway, see!
Vapors rise and vapors vanish,—
Forward steps this deity.

"Eye and heart to her I tender,
I inhale her gentle light;
Blinding all, such beauty's splendor
Blinded my poor senses quite.

"I forgot the warder's duty,
I forgot the entrusted horn;
Threaten to destroy me,—Beauty
Tameth anger, tameth scorn."

Let me add the "Chorus of Nymphs":—

"He draweth near!
In mighty Pan
The all we scan
Of this world-sphere.

All ye of gayest mood advance,
And him surround in sportive dance.
For, since he earnest is and kind,
Joy everywhere he fain would find.
E'en 'neath the blue o'erarching sky
He watcheth still with wakeful eye;
Purling to him the brooklet flows,
And zephyrs lull him to repose;
And when he slumbers at midday,
Stirs not a leaf upon the spray.
Health-breathing plants, with balsams rare,
Pervade the still and silent air.
The nymph no more gay vigil keeps,
And where she standeth, there she sleeps.
But if, at unexpected hour,
His voice resounds with mighty power,
Like thunder or the roaring sea,
Then knoweth none where he may flee.
Panic the valiant host assails,
The hero in the tumult quails.
Then honor to whom honor is due,
And hail to him who leads us unto you."

128

In a different strain, like Tennyson before the time, is "Peneios surrounded by Waters and Nymphs":—

"Sedgy whispers, gently flow,
Sister reeds, breathe faint and low;
Willows, lightly rustle ye,
Lisp each trembling poplar tree."

Goethe knew himself. He could measure himself. When some of the Romanticists preferred Tieck, he said, "I speak freely, I did not make myself; it is of no more use to compare Tieck with me than if I should compare myself with Shakespeare." This latter comparison, however, with a greater nature than his, some scholars in Germany make; and consider Faust a more commanding peak to observe human life from than Lear, Othello, or Macbeth.

Goethe, like Thackeray and Victor Hugo, tried sketching as well as writing, as Michael Angelo was painter, sculptor, architect, and poet, and Leonardo da Vinci could turn his hand to any art, painter, sculptor, architect, engineer. But there is a law against coveting. Rare is success in more than one calling. The Apostle Paul would not go beyond his own into another man's line of things. God and Nature grudge us any perfection. It might be too much for hope of progress without end were there a man who did not lack, and need eternity to mend. Schiller is the poet of a section and season; Goethe, of ages and the world. In personal relations, not intellectual merits, they meet. The putting their names together in a lecture, for one theme, reminds

129

me of the Soothsayer's talk with Antony in Shakespeare's play.

"*Ant.* Say to me,
Whose fortunes shall rise higher, Cæsar's or mine?
"*Sooth.* Cæsar's.
Therefore, O Antony, stay not by his side.
Thy demon, that's thy spirit which keeps thee, is
Noble, courageous, high, unmatchable,
Where Cæsar's is not; but near him thy angel
Becomes afeared as being o'erpowered; therefore
Make space enough between you."

I see Schiller in his customary pacing about in his composing-room through the night, rousing himself to his stint with some stirring of exercise as he spouts a passage and resorts from time to time to the stimulating draughts at his side; and I find cause for whatever may be strained or unnatural in the literary result. Goethe is started from healthy slumber by the Musagetes, which he celebrates, the flies that bring the Muse as they buzz and sting. Schiller thunders and lightens, Goethe brings music and light. Michael in the "Prologue in Heaven" describes the swift destructive storms, and adds, as if to hint Goethe's genius,

"But, Lord, thy messengers revere
The mild procession of thy day."

If they *think* not, Landor tells us, the gods stride and thunder in vain. We have declaimers and decorators enough! Goethe is a continental upheaver, a world-force; not by reason of his knowledge alone; but, to adopt Horatio Greenough's title for one of his marbles,

130

by the genius of love. Supreme in self-love he has been called. A man working so hard for near fourscore years, he felt entitled to another body. Is the Creator selfish, living in what he creates, losing himself in his works, making the smallest creature large enough to eclipse Himself, wearing a veil which he cannot, like Moses, put off, — making all nature glow with the presence no burning bush can bound, and conscious only in his children's souls? I stand with some awe before the likeness realized by a human author with the Divine, when I see that he exists, as no egoist can, in *his* offspring, and that the least and lowliest of them is as dear to him as any duke or pope.

Ideality is neighbor to Benevolence on the phrenological chart. So we speak of the good Homer, because by a sympathetic imagination he gives all his gods and men, goddesses and women, a fair chance, which from poets alone the latter as yet have had; and from no poet more than Goethe, not better even from Shakespeare. With what just spacing his pencil draws! We have a sense of room in all his work, as when we read in the Book of Genesis of the succession of days and dividing of the firmament, — and what an observer he is of the sphere he projects, never getting himself into his own object-glass as a mote or blur! Yet he surveyed himself apart as a natural curiosity. The guests are many, the entertainment great, the host unseen; and the keeper of this vast inn for the weary foot-sore humanity of yet to

131

be reckoned generations is not evil, but good; but of being a perfect model of righteousness he comes short. We have heard much of what is called the artistic temperament as explaining, if not excusing, fretfulness and self-indulgence as besetting sins. Charlotte Cushman said to me, in palliation of an artist's errors, "Artists do not take the moral point of view." But certainly she did. Washington Allston needed no cloak of charity. We read no list of exceptions for bards or actors in the law from Sinai, or the larger code of good news. The moral constitution cannot be nullified God is no respecter of persons. Gifts enhance obligations.

Goethe is one of the magi or wise men. He says, only by knowing others can one know himself. But only by loving others as he did, can we know them. The best knowledge goes with loyal love. Cover him, as Othello begged of Emilia, Gratiano, Lodovico, and Cassio to be protected!

"Speak of me as I am; nothing extenuate,
Nor set down aught in malice: then must you speak
Of one that loved not wisely but too well."

Must we not say not *well* enough? Could Johann Wolfgang Goethe, the youth, have cast his own horoscope, or could he have known to what a Brocken of witch and will-o'-the-wisp certain paths would lead, and could he have seen his own image magnified on the screen of time, he might not have had always the same choice of things on which, in his demeanor, the light should fall.

132

In his drama or broad farce of "Mitschuldigen," the Fellow Culprits, all sinners in divers ways, of whom was he thinking for his characters but the race of mankind, of us all who pass sentence on him? Says Lear to Gloster, "Change places, and, handy dandy, which is the justice, which is the thief?"

"Compound for sins we are inclined to,
By damning those we have no mind to."

The just disclosed letters of Goethe are said to present his social loyalty in a more favorable light. On the sliding-scale of iniquity we can never for individuals anticipate the ultimate decisions. A certain act, word, spirit, we may condemn: the actor, speaker, person, we dare not doom. As the poet Burns tells us, we can know what is done, not how much is resisted.

Goethe and Schiller: yes, but Goethe has Schiller

in tow. The association is not intrinsic, but accidental. Schiller is behind Goethe, not as one of two racers, runners, or regatta yachts; he is inferior in kind, as a ruby is to a diamond, or a garnet to a pearl. Schiller moulds, Goethe makes. Schiller composes, Goethe crystallizes. Goethe is a projectile like a planet, Schiller a spent ball, or rather like the swiftly spinning top that begins to waver on the floor. Goethe is one of a handful whom God and Nature hold for immortal fame; Schiller is among the thousand lesser luminaries. Goethe was self-luminous and conscious, like Cæsar or Bonaparte, of an end he was born for; Schiller was brilliant, adventurous, and con-

trived to carry his points. Goethe had the poise as well as brightness of the sun, Schiller shone more by reflected light. Goethe was a reporter or private secretary of the King, and without an intention utters no word. He is the granite, Schiller the secondary, yielding, friable trap-rock.

When Daniel Webster was urged to make a special effort, he said, "I will not strain myself to kill a fly; I reason not from worlds to atoms, but from atoms to worlds." The mark of greatness is ease, because then not the man, but the supreme power in him, is at work. The best work is unconscious, as the shellfish carves and paints its house. It is the Divine Wisdom rather than energy that Goethe represents: so there is less grandeur of motion and of rising to the sublimer heights than in Shakespeare's Muse. He is, in the way of rushing strength, outstripped by Homer and Dante too. Yet his like their scripture bears being translated into every tongue. He sees, and helps us to see, more than he stirs and inspires. But his name seems chosen to announce his nature, and somewhat of the Deity is revealed when his instrument is handled and played. His eyes shed serene light over all. His works are an illustrated edition of the world.

Schiller is one of the great poets below the first rank. Put with Goethe, he is like some hill fair and noble by itself, but dwarfed by the neighboring height

by which it is overtopped. As a singer, even by Heine he is surpassed. He is of a youthful quality, which

recommends him to young Germany and America more than to the old in either land; and I am content that youth should, if it please, put what it may consider as any detraction from him to the score of the prejudice of age. Schiller is ardent: with a tranquil fervor, Goethe is warm, but instructive above all. If I may use the figure, drawn perhaps from a grape-laden wain, "his paths drop fatness." His pithly sayings are not protruded with any conscious superiority, but fall without conceit and almost unawares by the way, in the large handling of his themes. Accused of egoism, as an author he is eminently free from that fault, which clings rather to writers of the oracular, transcendental, or radical school. The prophet or renewer of the time and the race must, however innocently, yet be loftily sensible of his momentary mission, as he towers an object of attack from the world he assails. But the dramatist, which such a man as Goethe is, alike in his verse and his prose, finds no room to scold or scream at what he portrays. He paints a Madonna, like Correggio, or a scene of dicers and drunkards, after the coarse style of some Dutch artist, with impartial concern. He leaves sinner and saint in the hand of that other Author who creates or permits both to exist.

V.

GOETHE'S MÄRCHEN.

BY FREDERIC H. HEDGE, D.D.

In the summer of 1795, Goethe composed for Schiller's new magazine, "Die Horen," a prose poem known in German literature as "Das Märchen," *The Tale;* as if it were the only one, or the one which more than any other deserves that appellation.

It is not to be supposed that the author himself claimed this pre-eminence for his production. The

definite article must be taken in connection with what precedes it in the "Unterhaltungen Deutscher Ausgewanderten"; it was *that* tale which the Abbé had promised for the evening's entertainment of the company.

Goethe gave this essay to the public as a riddle which would probably be unintelligible at the time, but which might perhaps find an interpreter after many days, when the hints contained in it should be verified. Since its first appearance commentators have exercised their ingenuity upon it, perceiving it to be allegorical, but until recently without success. They made the mistake of looking too far and too deep for the interpretation. Carlyle who, in 1832,

published a translation of it in "Fraser's Magazine," and who pronounces it "one of the notablest performances produced for the last thousand years," says, "So much however I will stake my whole money capital and literary character upon, that here is a wonderful EMBLEM OF UNIVERSAL HISTORY set forth," etc.

But Goethe was not the man to concern himself with such wide generalities. He preferred to deal with what is present and palpable, and the inferences to be deduced therefrom.

Dr. Hermann Baumgart, in 1875, under the title, "Goethe's Märchen, ein politisch-nationales Glaubens-bekenntniss des Dichter's," wrote a commentary on "The Tale," which gives what is probably the true explanation. If it does not solve every difficulty, it solves more difficulties and throws more light on the poem than any previous interpretation had done. I follow his lead in the exposition which I now offer.

"The Tale" is a prophetic vision of the destinies of Germany, an allegorical foreshowing at the close of the eighteenth century of what Germany was yet to become, and has in great part already become. A position is predicted for her like that which she occupied from the time of Charles the Great to the time of Charles V., a period during which the Holy

Roman Empire of Germany was the leading secular power in Western Europe.

137

That time had gone by. From the middle of the sixteenth century until near the middle of the nineteenth, Germany declined, and at the date of this writing (1795) had nearly reached her darkest day. Disintegrated, torn by conflicting interests, pecked by petty rival princes, despairing of her own future, it seemed impossible that she should ever again become a power among the nations.

Goethe felt this, he felt it as profoundly as any German of his day. He has been accused of want of patriotism, and incurred much censure for that alleged defect. He certainly did not manifest his patriotism by loud declamation. During the War of Liberation he made no sign. Under the reign of the Holy Alliance he did not side with the hotheads, compeers of Sand, who placed themselves in open opposition to the government. He could not echo their cry. They were revolutionists; he was an evolutionist; and they hated him, they maligned him, they invented all manner of scandal against him. They accused him of abusing the affections of women for literary purposes. They even affected to depreciate his genius. Börne pronounced him a model of all that is bad. Menzel wrote: "Mark my words; in twenty, or, at the longest, thirty years, he will not have an admirer left; no one will read him." Well, near sixty years have elapsed, and here we are, on the other side of the globe, devoting these summer days to the reverent consideration of the man and his works.

138

But in the thirties and forties of this century those slanders had crossed the sea, and found ready acceptance on this side. There was nothing too bad to be said of Goethe; he was publicly held up for reprobation and scorn. It was as much as one's reputation was worth to speak well of him.

Goethe, I say, was charged with want of patriotism. He was no screamer; but he felt profoundly his country's woes, and he characteristically went into himself and studied the situation. The result was this wonderful composition, "*Das Märchen.*"

He perceived that Germany must die to be born again. She did die, and is born again. He had the sagacity to foresee the dissolution of the Holy Roman Empire, an event which took place eleven years later, in 1806. The Empire is figured by the composite statue of the fourth King in the subterranean Temple, which crumbles to pieces when that Temple, representing Germany's past, emerges and stands above ground by the River. The resurrection of the Temple and its stand by the River is the *dénouement* of the Tale. And that signifies, allegorically, the rehabilitation of Germany.

The agents that are to bring about this consummation are the spread of liberal ideas, signified by the gold of the Will-o'-wisps; Literature, signified by the Serpent; Science, signified by the Old Man with the Lamp; and the Church, or Religion, signified by his wife. The Genius of Germany is figured by the beautiful Youth, the disconsolate Prince, who dies of

139

devotion to the Fair Lily. The Lily herself represents the Ideal.

Having premised thus much, I now proceed to unfold the Tale, with accompanying comments, omitting, however, some of the details, and presenting only the organic moments of the fable.

In the middle of a dark night (the dark period of German history) the ferryman asleep in his hut by the side of a swollen river is awakened by the cry of parties demanding to be ferried across the stream.

Here let us pause a moment. The Hut, according to Baumgart, is the provisional State (*Nothstaat*), the government for the time being. The Ferryman then is the state functionary who regulates and controls civil intercourse. The River represents that intercourse, the flow of current events, swollen by the French Revolution. Now a river is separation and communication in one. The Rhine, which separates Germany from France, is also a medium of communication between the two. What is it, then, that the River in the *Märchen* separates and medi-

ates? This is a difficult question. No interpretation tallies exactly with all the particulars of the allegory. The most satisfactory is that of a separation and a means of communication between State and people, between official, established tradition and popular life.

To return to the story. The Ferryman, roused from his slumbers, opens the door of the hut, and sees two Will-o'-wisps who are impatient to be put across.

140

These are the bearers of the new ideas which proved so stimulating to the German mind, giving rise to what is known in German literature as the *Aufklärung* (enlightenment). Why called Will-o'-wisps? They come from France, and the poet means by their flashes and vivacity, as contrasted with German gravity, to indicate their French origin.

They cause the Ferryman much trouble by their activity. They shake gold into his boat (that is, talk philosophy, the philosophy of the French Encyclopaedists); he fears that some of it might fall into the stream, and then there would be mischief; the stream would rise in terrible waves and engulf him.

The new ideas were very radical, and, if allowed to circulate freely in social converse, might cause a revolution.

He bids them take back their gold. "We cannot take back what we have once given forth."

The word once spoken cannot be unspoken.

When they reach the opposite shore, he demands his fare. They reply that he who will not take gold for pay must go unpaid. He demands fruits of the earth (that is, practical service), which they despise. They attempt to depart, but find it impossible to move.

Philosophy without practical ability can make no headway in real life.

He finally releases them, on their promise to bring to the River three cabbages, three artichokes, and three onions.

141

I am not aware that there is any particular significance in the several kinds of vegetables here speci-

fied. The general meaning is, that whoever would work effectually in his time must satisfy the necessities of the time, must pay his toll to the State with contributions of practical utility.

The ferryman then rows down the stream, gathers up the gold that has fallen into the boat, goes ashore and buries it in an out of the way place in the cleft of a rock, then rows back to his hut.

Now in the rock cleft into which the gold had been cast dwelt the Green Serpent. The Serpent is supposed to represent German Literature, which until then had kept itself aloof from the world, had wandered as it were in a wilderness. But the time was now come when it was to receive new light and be quickened with new impulse.

She hears the chink of the falling gold pieces, darts upon them, and eagerly devours them. They melt in her interior, and she becomes self-luminous,— a thing that she had always been hoping for, but had never until then attained.

Proud of her new lustre she sallies forth to discover if possible whence the gold which came to her had been derived. She encounters the Will-o'-wisps, and claims relationship with them.

"Well, yes," they allow, "you are a kind of cousin, but you are in the horizontal line; we are vertical. See here." They shoot up to their utmost height. "Pardon us, good lady, but what other family can

142

boast of anything like that? No Will-o'-wisp ever sits or lies down." The Serpent is somewhat abashed by the comparison. She knows very well that although, when at rest, she can lift her head pretty high, she must bend to earth again to make any progress. She inquires if they can tell her where the gold came from which dropped in the cave where she resides. They are amused at the question, and immediately shake from themselves a shower of gold pieces, which she greedily devours. "Much good may it do to you, madam."

In return for this service they desire to be shown the way to the abode of the Fair Lily, to whom they would pay their respects.

The Fair Lily represents Ideal Beauty.

The Serpent is sorry to inform them that the Lily dwells on the other side of the river. "On the other side!" they exclaim, "and we let ourselves be ferried across to this side, last night, in the storm! But perhaps the Ferryman may be still within call, and be willing to take us back." "No," she says, "he can bring passengers from the other side to this, but is not permitted to take any one back."

The interpretation here is doubtful. It may mean, that, while a jealous government is willing to assist in the deportation of questionable characters, it will have nothing to do with them on its own ground.

But besides the government ferry there are other means of getting across. The Serpent herself, by

143

making a bridge of her body, can take them across at high noon.

Literature in its supreme achievements, its meridian power, becomes a vehicle of ideas which defies political embargo.

But Will-o'-wisps do not travel at noonday. Another passage is possible at morning and evening twilight by means of the shadow of the Great Giant. The Giant's body is powerless, but its shadow is mighty, and, when the sun is low, stretches across the River.

Here all commentators seem to agree in one interpretation. Says Carlyle, "Can any mortal head, not a wigblock, doubt that the Giant of this poem is Superstition?" This is loosely expressed. Unquestionably superstition, in the way of fable or foreboding, stretches far into the unknown. But it is a *shadow* according to the Tale, which possesses this power. Now, to make a shadow two things are needed,— light, and a body which intercepts the light. The body in this case is popular ignorance; that is the real giant. Superstition is that giant's shadow, strongest and longest, of course, when the sun is low.

Thus instructed, the Will-o'-wisps take their leave, and the Serpent returns to her cave.

Now follows the scene in the subterranean Temple, the Temple of the Four Kings, — by which we are to understand historic Germany, the Germany of old time. The Serpent has discovered this temple, and,

144

having become luminous, is able to see what it contains. There are the statues of four kings. The first is of gold, the second of silver, the third of bronze, the fourth a compound of several metals. The first King, who wears a plain mantle and no ornament but a garland of oak leaves, represents the rule of Wisdom and acknowledged worth. The second, who sits and is highly decorated, — robe, crown, sceptre, adorned with precious stones, — represents the rule of Appearance (*Schein*), majesty supported by prestige and tradition. The third, also sitting, represents government by Force. The fourth, the composite figure in a standing posture, represents the Holy Roman Empire of Germany. The Serpent has been discoursing with the Gold King, when the wall opens and enters an old man of middle stature in peasant's dress, carrying a lamp with a still flame pleasing to look upon, which illumines the whole temple without casting any shadow. This lamp possesses the strange property of changing stones into gold, wood into silver, dead animals into precious stones, and of annihilating metals. But to exercise this power it must shine alone; if another light appears beside it, it only diffuses a clear radiance, by which all living things are refreshed.

The bearer of this lamp is supposed by Baumgart to represent Science (*Wissenschaft*), but it seems to me that his function includes practical wisdom as well. What is signified by the marvellous properties of the lamp must be left to each reader to conjecture.

145

"Why do you come," asks the Gold King of the Man with the lamp, "seeing we already have light?" "You know that I cannot enlighten what is wholly dark," is the reply.

Wisdom does not concern itself with what is unsearchable, with matters transcending human ken.

"Will my kingdom end?" asks the Silver King. "Late or never." The answer is, "Soon." "With whom shall I arise?" The Brazen King asks, "When shall I combine?" "With your elder brothers." "What will the youngest do?" inquired the King. "He will sit down," replied the Man with the lamp. "I am not tired," growled the fourth King.

The Empire, even at that date, was still tenacious of its sway.

Again the Gold King asks of the Man with the lamp, "How many secrets knowest thou?" "Three," replied the man. "Which is the most important?" asks the Silver King. "The open secret," the man replies.

It sometimes happens that a truth, or conviction, is, as we say, "in the air," before the word which formulates it has been spoken; it is an open secret. Thus, in the closing months of 1860, "Secession" was in the air; it was our open secret.

"Wilt thou open it to us also?" asks the Brazen King. "When I know the fourth," replied the Man. "I know the fourth," said the Serpent, and whispered something in the ear of the Man with the lamp. He cried with a loud voice, "The time is at hand." The temple resounded, the statues rang with the cry; and

146

immediately the Man with the lamp vanished to the west, the Serpent to the east.

Here ends the first act of this prophetic drama. The Man with the lamp returns to his cottage, where the Old Woman, his wife, greets him with loud lamentations. "Scarcely were you gone," she whimpers, "when two impetuous travellers called; they were dressed in flames, and seemed quite respectable. One might have taken them for Will-o'-wisps. But they soon began to flatter me and made impertinent advances." "Pooh! they were only chaffing you. Considering your age, my dear, they could n't have meant anything serious." "My age indeed! always my age! How old am I then? But I know one thing. Just look at these walls! See the bare stones! They have licked off all the gold; and when they had done it, they dropped gold pieces about. Our dear pug swal-

lowed some of them, and see there, the poor creature lies dead."

The Old Woman represents the Church, the accepted, traditional religion. There is a beautiful fitness in this symbolism. Science and religion, knowledge and faith, are mutually complemental in human life. The little pug may mean some pet dogma of the Church; Baumgart suggests belief in the supernatural, to which modern enlightenment (the gold of the Will-o'-wisps) proves fatal. The little pug dies; but a doctrine which perishes, which becomes obsolete as popular belief, may become historically precious as myth.

147

This is what is meant when it is said, farther on, that the old man with his lamp changes the pug to an onyx. Moreover, when such myth is embraced by poetry, it acquires a new, transfigured, immortal life. Thus the gods of Greece still live, and live forever, in Homer's song. In this sense, with this aim, the Man with the lamp sends the onyx pug to the Fair Lily, whose touch causes dead things to live.

The Old Woman had incautiously promised the Will-o'-wisps — in order, we may suppose, to get rid of them — to pay their debt to the River, of three cabbages, three artichokes, and three onions.

But why did they visit her cottage at all, and why so intent on the obsolete gold on its walls? The answer is, modern culture knows full well that the Church is the depositary of many precious truths, which, though no longer current in the form in which they were once clothed, approve and justify themselves when restated and given to the world in a new form. So they, the New Lights, say in effect to the Church, "Old Lady, you are somewhat out of date; if you mean to keep your place and vindicate your right to be, you must throw yourself into the life of the time, you must contribute something useful to forward that life. It is through you that the new philosophy must discharge its debt to the River" (that is, to the life of the time).

The Man with the lamp approves and seconds the commission intrusted to his wife by the Will-o'-wisps, and at dawn of day loads her with the cabbages, the

artichokes, and the onions destined for the River, to which he adds the onyx as a present to the Fair Lily. The first part of her mission is a failure. On her way to the ferry she encounters the Shadow of the blundering Giant stretching across the plain. The Shadow unceremoniously puts its black fingers into her basket, takes out three vegetables, one of each kind, and thrusts them into the mouth of the Giant, who greedily devours them.

Some freak of popular ignorance intercepts and impairs the practical benefit which the new culture, through the Church, had hoped to confer on the age.

The Ferryman refuses to accept the imperfect offering as full satisfaction of the Will-o'-wisps' debt, and only consents at last to receive it provisionally, if the Old Woman will swear to make the number good within twenty-four hours. She is required to dip her hand in the stream and take the oath. She dips and swears. But when she withdraws her hand, behold! it has turned black; and, what is worse, has grown smaller, and seems likely to disappear altogether.

The apparent dignity of the Church is impaired by contact with vulgar life.

"O woe!" she cries. "My beautiful hand, which I have taken so much pains with and have always kept so nice! What will become of me?" The Ferryman tries to comfort her with the assurance that, although the hand might become invisible, she would be able to use it all the same. "But," says

149

she, "I would rather not be able to use it than not have it seen."

Here is a stroke of satire on the part of the poet, implying that the Church cares more for the show of authority than for the substance.

Sad and sullen the Old Woman takes up her basket and bends her steps toward the abode of the Fair Lily. On the way she overtakes a pilgrim more disconsolate than herself; a beautiful youth, with noble features, abundant brown locks, his breast covered with glittering mail, a purple cloak depend-

ing from his shoulders. His naked feet paced the hot sand; profound grief appeared to render him insensible to external impressions. The Old Woman endeavors to open a conversation with him, but receives no encouragement. She desists with the apology, "You walk too slow for me, sir. I must hurry on, for I have to cross the River on the Green Serpent, that I may take this present from my husband to the Fair Lily." "You are going to the Fair Lily," he cried; "then our roads are the same. But what is this present you are bringing her?" She showed him the onyx púg. "Happy beast!" he exclaimed; "thou wilt be touched by her hands, thou wilt be made alive by her; whereas the living are forced to stand aloof from her lest they experience a mournful doom. Look at me," he continued, "how sad my condition! This mail which I have worn with honor in war, this purple which I have sought to merit by wise conduct, are all that is left me by

150

fate,—the one a useless burden, the other an unmeaning decoration. Crown, sceptre, and sword are gone; I am in all other respects as naked and needy as any son of earth. So unblest is the influence of her beautiful blue eyes; they deprive all living beings of their strength, and those who are not killed by the touch of her hand find themselves turned into walking shadows."

This is finely conceived. The Youth, the Prince who has lost sceptre and sword, represents the Genius of Germany, once so stalwart and capable in action, now (at the time of Goethe's writing) enervated and become a melancholy dreamer from excessive devotion to the Lily, that is, excessive Idealism; whereby

"Enterprises of great pith and moment
. . . . . their currents turn awry,
And lose the name of action."

Such was Germany in those days. And even later, Freiligrath compared her to Hamlet, in whom

"The native hue of resolution
Is sicklied o'er with the pale cast of thought."

The travellers cross the bridge which the Serpent makes for them. The Serpent herself straightens out her bow and accompanies them. On the way the Will-o'-wisps, invisible in broad day, are heard whispering a request to the Serpent that she would introduce them to the Lily in the evening, as soon as they should be any way presentable. The Lily

151

receives her visitors graciously, but with an air of deep dejection. She imparts to the Old Woman her recent affliction. While her pet Canary-bird was warbling its morning hymn, a Hawk appeared in the air and threatened to pounce upon it. The frightened creature sought refuge in its mistress's bosom, and, like all living things, was killed by her touch.

The Hawk represents the newly awakened, impatient spirit of German Patriotism, which scared into silence the lighter lyrics of the time.

The Old Woman presents the onyx púg, and the Lily is delighted with the gift. Her touch gives it life. She plays with it, caresses it. The melancholy youth who stands by and looks on is maddened with jealousy at the sight. "Must a nasty little beast be so fondled, and receive her kiss on its black snout, while I, her adorer, am kept at a distance?" At last he can bear it no longer, and resolves to perish in her arms. He rushes towards her; she, knowing the consequence, instinctively puts out her arms to ward him off, and thereby hastens the catastrophe. The youth falls lifeless at her feet.

Here ends the second act. The Genius of Germany is apparently extinct. Can it be revived? The third and final act foreshows its revival,—the political rehabilitation of Germany. I am compelled by want of time to omit, in what follows, many of the accessories, such as the female attendants of the Lily, the mirror, the last desperate freaks of the

152

Giant, etc., and to keep myself to the main thread of the story.

The first object now, on the part of those inter-

ested, is to prevent corruption, which would make resuscitation impossible. So the Serpent forms with her body a cordon around the lifeless form of the Youth to protect it. "Who will fetch the Man with the lamp?" she cries, fearing every moment that the sun will set and dissolution penetrate the magic circle, causing the body of the Youth to fall in pieces. At length she espies the Hawk in the air, and hails the auspicious omen.

Shortly after, the Man with the lamp appears. "Whether I can help," he says, "I know not. The individual by himself cannot do much, but only he who, at the proper moment, combines with many."

All who have their country's salvation at heart must join their forces in time of need.

Night comes on. The Old Man glances at the stars and says, "We are here at the propitious hour; let each do his duty and perform his part." The Serpent then began to stir; she loosened her enfolding circle, and slid in large volumes toward the River. The Will-o'-wisps followed. The Old Man and his Wife seized the basket, lifted into it the body of the Youth, and laid the Canary-bird upon his breast. The basket rose of itself into the air, and hovered over the Old Woman's head. She followed the Will-o'-wisps. The Fair Lily with the pug in her arms followed the Wo-

153

man, and the Man with the lamp closed the procession. The Serpent bridged the River for them, and then drew her circle again around the basket containing the body of the Youth. The Old Man stoops down to her and asks, "What are you going to do?" "Sacrifice myself," she answers, "rather than be sacrificed." The Man bids the Lily touch the Serpent with one hand and the body of the Youth with the other. She does so, and behold! the Youth comes to life again, but not to full consciousness. Then the Serpent bursts asunder. Her form breaks into thousands upon thousands of glittering jewels. These the Man with the lamp gathers up and casts into the stream, where they afterward form a solid and permanent bridge. The Old Man now leads the party to the

cave. They stand before the Temple barred with golden lock and bolt. The Will-o'-wisps at the bidding of the Old Man melt bolt and lock with their flames, and the company are in the presence of the four Kings. "Whence come ye?" asks the Gold King. "From the world," is the reply. "Whither go ye?" is the reply. "Whither go ye?" asked the Silver King. "Into the world." "What would ye with us?" asked the Brazen King. "Accompany you," said the Old Man. "Who will govern the world?" asked the Composite King. "He who stands on his feet," is the answer. "That am I," said the King. "We shall see," said the Old Man, "for the time is come."

Then the ground beneath them began to tremble; the Temple was in motion. For a few moments a fine

154

shower seemed to drizzle from above. "We are now beneath the River," said the Old Man. The Temple mounts upward. Suddenly a crash is heard; planks and beams come through the opening of the dome. It is the old Ferryman's hut, which the Temple in its ascent had detached from the ground. It descends and covers the Old Man and the Youth. The women, who find themselves excluded, beat against the door of the hut, which is locked. After a while the door and walls begin to ring with a metallic sound. The flame of the Old Man's lamp has converted the wood into silver. The very form has changed; the hut has become a smaller temple, or, if you will, a shrine, within the larger.

Observe the significance of this feature of the Tale. The hut, as was said, represents the existing government. New Germany is not to be the outcome of a violent revolution forcibly abolishing the old, but a natural growth receiving the old into itself, assimilating and embodying it in a new constitution.

When the Youth came forth from the transformed hut, it was in company with a man clad in a white robe, bearing a silver oar in his hand. This was the old Ferryman, now to become a functionary in the new State.

As soon as the rising sun illumined the cupola of the Temple, the Old Man, standing between the Youth

and the Maiden (the Lily), said with a loud voice, "There are three that reign on earth, Wisdom, Show, Force." When the first was named, up rose the Gold

155

King; with the second, the Silver. The Brazen King was rising slowly at the sound of the third, when the Composite King (the Holy Roman Empire) suddenly collapsed into a shapeless heap. The Man with the lamp now led the still half-conscious Youth to the Brazen King, at whose feet lay a sword. The Youth girded himself with it. "The sword on the left," said the mighty King, "the right hand free." They then went to the Silver King, who gave the Youth his sceptre, saying, "Feed the sheep." They came to the Gold King, who, with a look that conveyed a paternal blessing, crowned the Youth's head with a garland of oak leaves, and said, "Acknowledge the Highest."

The Youth now awoke to full consciousness; his eyes shone with an unutterable spirit, and his first word was, "Lily." He clasped the fair maiden, whose cheeks glowed with an inextinguishable red, and, turning to the Old Man, said, with a glance at the three sacred figures, "Glorious and safe is the kingdom of our fathers; but you forgot the fourth power, that which earliest, most universal, and surest of all, rules the world, — the power of Love." "Love," said the Old Man, smiling, "does not rule, but educates. And that is better."

And so the Temple stands by the River. The Old Woman, having at the bidding of her husband bathed in its waves, comes forth rejuvenated and beautified. The Old Man himself looks younger.

Husband and wife, Science and Religion, renew

156

their nuptial vows, and pledge their troth for indefinite time.

The prophecy is accomplished. What Genius predicted ninety years ago has become fact. The Temple stands by the River, the bridge is firm and wide. The Genius of Germany is no longer a sighing, sickly youth, pining after the unattainable, but, having mar-

ried his ideal, is now embodied in the mighty Chancellor whose state-craft founded the new Empire, and whose word is a power among the nations.

157

VI.
GOETHE'S RELATION TO ENGLISH LITERATURE.

BY F. B. SANBORN.

IN that triangulation and speculative mensuration of the greatest German intellect which we have this year attempted, I have been assigned to a single field, "Goethe's Relation to English Literature." If this were understood to mean the influence upon Goethe's own work of the antecedent literature of England, one could almost treat this theme as the old writer did when describing Iceland. One of his chapters contained this and nothing more: "Chapter VI. *Concerning Serpents in Iceland.* There are no serpents in Iceland."

When Handel, the great German musician, went to Ireland about 1722, he carried a letter of introduction from some of his English Tory friends to Dean Swift, then living near Dublin. As soon as the Dean heard he was a German musician, he declined to see Handel; but when his servant added that the bearer of the letter was "a great genius," Swift cried out, "What! a genius and a German! show him up

158

this instant." Such was the reputation which the intellectual character of the Germans inspired in Great Britain thirty years before Goethe was born; and such it continued through much of the lifetime of Frederic the Great, who made Germany so respectable in matters of war and state-craft. That singular and useful tyrant, whose life Carlyle has so brilliantly related, had the greatest contempt for his country's literature, which he would not read, and for its clumsy language, which he did not know how to spell. He had contracted this prejudice in his youth, before Goethe was born, and he continued in it after Goe-

the, who even more than Handel was "a German and a genius," had begun to publish his youthful works. Goethe was born at Frankfort, outside of Frederic's dominions, in 1749; he published his first important work, the play of "Götz von Berlichingen," in 1773, and about this time Frederic wrote an "Essay on German Literature,"[1] in which he said:—

159

"To convince yourself of the little taste which prevails in Germany, you need only go to our theatres; there you will see the abominable works of Shakespeare exhibited, in German translations, while the whole audience almost die with delight, as they listen to ridiculous forces, worthy of American barbarians. Shakespeare perhaps may be pardoned his caprices, because the birth of an art is never its point of perfection; but here we have a 'Götz von Berlichingen' making his appearance,—a detestable imitation of these wretched English productions. The pit applauds, and enthusiastically demands a repetition of such disgusting dulness."

Even in 1777, when "The Woes of Young Werther" had captivated Europe, and "Faust" and "Iphigenia" were begun by Goethe, who was then twenty-eight years old, and at the height of his poetic creativeness, neither Frederic nor the old Voltaire, who constantly wrote letters complimenting each other, valued this rising star in the least degree. Frederic wrote to Voltaire, December 17, 1777: "As to works of the imagination, I am convinced that we must get along with Homer, Virgil, Tasso, Voltaire, and Ariosto; for the human mind seems to be withering in all countries, and no longer produces either fruit or flowers." Of these poets thus named the Prussian King preferred Voltaire, to whom he had written two years before: "You are the rival of Ariosto. We do not know much about Homer's life, but Virgil was nothing more than a poet. Racine did not write prose well, and Milton was but the slave of his country's tyrant. You alone have united tal-

[1] This Essay was communicated by Frederic to D'Alembert in January, 1781.

ents so various."

Yet the great Frederic, with all this blindness to the genius that was before his aged eyes, did finally predict the triumph of German literature, which Goethe and Schiller were to create. In one of his papers, which first saw the light after his death, in 1786, appear these prophetic words:—

160

"We shall have our classic authors; our neighbors will study German, and it will be spoken in the courts of princes. Our language, polished and improved, may haply, in the books of great writers, extend over all Europe. These summer days of German literature approach. I foretell them, but shall not see them. Age deprives me of this hope; like Moses, I have a view of the promised land, but may not enter it."

Frederic was, of course, as ignorant of Schiller's genius as of Goethe's. In 1781, the year that Schiller brought out his popular play, "The Robbers," which still keeps the stage after a hundred years, the old King sent to D'Alembert, in Paris, his "Essay on German Literature," already cited, and in his accompanying letter said: "Our language does not deserve to be studied till good authors have first rendered it famous; and of these we are entirely destitute. They will perhaps appear when I am walking in the Elysian fields, where I intend to offer to Virgil the idyls of a German named Gesner, and the fables of Gellert."

But to return. Goethe, unlike Schiller, but in this like Milton, whom he did not much read, drew more from the Greek fountain than from Shakespeare's "well of English undefiled"; and his "Iphigenia," like Milton's "Samson," follows closely in the steps of Greek tragedy, while his "Faust" in no way resembles the "Dr. Faustus" of Marlowe, who was Shakespeare's only brother in English tragedy, but has a rich Gothic exuberance of its own in the first part,

161

and a broad philosophic conspectus, broken by strains of lyric melody, in its long-delayed and confusing conclusion. In fact, the form of Goethe's "Faust" is no less original, I might say individual, than his

conception of Satan, who, as Mephistopheles, sets at defiance every preconceived type of the Evil One.

Doubtless there has been no such poetical genius since Shakespeare as this German dramatist and poet, who is also novelist, art critic, man of science, and philosopher. But his versatility, and the whole strain of his genius, are not in the English manner, nor bred in any English school. That inward vision of thought and nature,—that profound conception of the world's symbolism,—which is so wonderful in Shakespeare, and in other English poets exists in a less degree, is coupled in Goethe's case with a plodding, patient, almost pedantic research into the laws and methods, and even the smallest details, of nature and of thought. Having flown to his height of imagination on the wings of poesy, Goethe must needs build a stairway therefrom downward to the merest, most beggarly elements; so that he and others shall go up and down as they please, counting every step of the way. Moreover, while Shakespeare and other great poets content themselves with setting forth the ideal, —flashing it out perhaps for a single moment upon our mind's eye,—Goethe insists on realizing his ideal in every form and institution of society. In this respect he resembles Plato more than any of the moderns; yet he does not resemble Bacon, that English

162

truncated Plato, except in some of those superficial points of similarity which do not touch the real character of the two men. Goethe, like Bacon, "took all knowledge to be his province"; like Bacon, he delighted in state and splendor, in the completion of his theory until it should fill out and touch at every point the circumference of man's world; but then in that poet's eye which, with fine frenzy,

"Doth glance from heaven to earth, from earth to heaven,"

Goethe excelled the English Chancellor even more than he did in that terrestrial prudence or fortune which so handsomely convoyed him through life, while Bacon fell into disgrace and belittled himself by complaints and entreaties. Indeed, the good fortune of Goethe was something almost appalling, and

must have often made him think of Polycrates and his ring; it went beyond the felicity of Shakespeare's life, which consisted partly in his obscurity; while Goethe was at once conspicuous and safe,—admired, and not ruined by admiration. Goethe suffered spiritually from this good fortune, and I must say that, when compared with the best English and-American authors, the finest aroma of our literature—which proceeds from a magnanimous and adventurous character, displayed now in love, now in war, now in the heroism of private life or in the sanctities of religion—is perpetually wanting in Goethe. I do not speak now of Shakespeare, in whom this magnanimity had its widest and highest range, but of lesser poets and prose

163

writers, who sometimes in very humble spheres of literature display the same winning quality. It is this which gives immortality to Sidney's youthful essays in verse and prose,—which makes Herbert memorable, Marvell more than a wit, and poor Dryden respectable even in his degradations; this gleams in Donne and Jeremy Taylor, in Gray and Dr. Johnson; in Burns and Wordsworth, Shelley, and Byron; in Thoreau and Emerson, in Walt Whitman, and among Americans Carlyle among the Scotch, and others of less note. It is by virtue of an untamable energy that English literature is capable of rising so high, and sinking so low, and is incapable of that measured and deliberate excellence of which the books of Plato and of Goethe are perhaps the best examples.

In the writings of Goethe, not less than in his life, we see the limitations which egoism imposes, and which not his great genius even could remove. "A man," said Cromwell to the French Ambassador, "never rises so high as when he knows not whither he is going." Although Goethe would fain follow his intuitions, and yield himself to the impulse of the moment, his very intuitions had prudence and self-love in them, so firmly implanted that he could never escape from worldly considerations. But the old belief of mankind is wisest, which declares that the poet's inspiration is greater than any worldly prudence, and that the oracles are sincere.

164

Goethe's relation to German literature was something different from Shakespeare's relation to our own, of which he is the head and front, but which he did not create, nor did he sustain it in his own time. Without Shakespeare there would still have been an important and universal English literature, though it would be far less significant and poetic than it is. Without Goethe, not only would the literature of his fatherland be less poetic and less significant, but it would not have extended so swiftly over Europe, and led to that rapid extension of German philosophy, and German science also, which our century, now closing, has seen and profited by. Goethe lived to be nearly as old as Voltaire, dying in 1832, at the age of eighty-two; and his period of authorship covered more than sixty of those years. His greatest work, "Faust," was only completed in its present form a short time before his death; his next greatest book, "Wilhelm Meister," was in fact left unfinished, although he had been at work on it for thirty years. Besides these books, which are everywhere known, he published more than forty other volumes; while his letters and conversations, printed since his death, and his manuscripts at Weimar, soon to be published, will make twenty or thirty volumes more. Hardly any author, even in Germany, has written so much; and no German author—not even Luther, whose books are the foundation of German prose literature—is now so indispensable to those who would know what German

165

many has thought, or what modern culture is and has been for a hundred years past. He is the greatest poet, though not the best dramatist, of Germany; and he is one of the few great prose-writers in a language that does not readily lend itself, as the French does, to graceful prose, or, as the English does, to vigorous and picturesque prose.

When Goethe began to study and to write,—and it is hard to say which came first with him,—the literatures that lay before him as models were the Greek, the Latin, the French, the Italian, and the English; in later years, he tasted something of the Oriental thought and literature. Of all these we should hold that English literature was the greatest, when Shakespeare is taken into account,—as he was, and very fully, by Goethe,—yet the Greek, the Latin, and especially the French, exercised apparently a more potent sway over the young poet's mind, and were better known to him. For it is difficult to find in Goethe's fifty volumes any serious traces of English influence from the literary side, although he read and admired Shakespeare and Marlowe, knew something of Bacon, Newton, and Milton, praised Goldsmith, and extended a respectful patronage towards Byron. But it is impossible to say that English literature impressed him and moulded his own work as did the classical literature, the Oriental, or even the French and Italian. In this respect, as in so many others, he presents a contrast to Schiller, who was deeply influenced in his dramatic forms of expression by Shakespeare, as he

166

was by Kant in his philosophic theories and rules of criticism.[1]

If ever men are self-forgetful, it is when they are in love,—at least for a brief period of that passion,—and it is the magnanimity thence proceeding which gives worth and dignity to characters otherwise frivolous or brutal, like those of Antony and Cleopatra, who, like Othello, "loved not wisely but too well." Goethe, as Dr. Bartol has said, loved not well enough, but too wisely; he lacked that magnanimity which men and women much less gifted have displayed in

[1] It should be remembered that Kant, the greatest of all the German philosophical writers, was an older contemporary of Schiller and of Goethe, having been born at Königsberg in 1724, a quarter-century before Goethe, and dying there in 1804, the year before Schiller's premature death. There was another person of the same name at Königsberg earlier, whom Frederick the Great praised (in 1739) for his eloquence, and his graceful use of the awkward German language, saying: "I confess I never heard better German, more beautiful phrases, nor a style more flowing and embellished. M. Kant is, past dispute, the first man in the kingdom for uttering nonsense with dignity." See Frederic's letter to Jordan, August 3, 1739.

their affection, though himself magnanimous in the other relations of life. And I must accuse him of another great fault, which he never learned of the English poets; he would "kiss and tell." Shakespeare has so well disguised his affairs of the heart, that it will always remain a question, not only whom he loved, but whether it was love or friendship of which he wrote so wonderfully; but Goethe has related what he should not about Gretchen, and

167

Annette, and Emilia, and Lucinda, and Frederica, and Heaven knows how many more. To be sure, he has given them an immortality thereby, and by idealizing them in his plays, and novels, and poems; but even there we feel that he has taken an unfair advantage of these fair ones, by drawing their pictures for the world to see, when they were turning their faces toward him alone. Whether these love affairs were innocent or not,—and I am disposed to give them always the most favorable construction,—there is here a betrayal of confidence, against which one of the minor English poets of Shakespeare's time had warned him. Donne says:—

> "If, as I have, you also do
> Virtue in woman see,
> And dare love that, and say so too,
> And forget the He and She,—
>
> "And if this love, though placéd so,
> From profane men you hide,
> Who will no faith on this bestow,
> Or, if they do, deride,—
>
> "Then you have done a braver thing
> Than all the Worthies did,
> And a braver thence will spring,
> Which is, to keep that hid."

168

Goethe was born of a wealthy burgher family in Frankfort, ten years before Schiller; and they both grew to manhood at a time when England, through Pitt and his son, had much to say and do in the

affairs of Germany. Yet the connection of the two countries in literary matters was of the slightest.

"Pathless the gulf of feeling yawns,"—

and the great abyss that is fixed between the sentiments and daily opinions of Germany and England was quite as wide when England had a German king as it is to-day. France was nearer spiritually, as well as geographically, and we find the young Goethe far more affected by French than by English books. He read Shakespeare early, and felt his vast powers; he also read Richardson and Goldsmith, and found pleasure, perhaps inspiration, in "The Vicar of Wakefield"; but the daily influence of French thought and the French style did more to modify the strong native impulses of Goethe than any impressions that came to him from England. No sooner did he begin to become known in England however, than he exerted an influence of his own on English literature, which has been growing stronger ever since, and has had some remarkable results,—chiefly by indirect radiation through Carlyle, Emerson, Matthew Arnold, and a host of lesser writers or translators. The first and most eminent of his translators, until Carlyle appeared, was Walter Scott, who, in 1799, published in Edinburgh a version of "Götz von Berlichingen," which Goethe himself had published twenty-six years before. In itself this play is of little value, as compared with the later works of Goethe; but it has a peculiar significance, as the first of those

169

feudal romances which, forty years afterwards, in the hands of Scott, became such an important part of European literature.

The real work of Goethe, indeed, was not to vary the existing forms of literature, however much he might do this, but to inspire in all literature a deep conviction of the unity of Nature and the absolute activity of spirit. This, once done, is nothing less than regeneration of the inner life of literature, which may thenceforth take any form, old or new, and yet be true to the inworking spirit. Carlyle seems to have been the first of British writers to seize this perception of Goethe's mission, and he was certainly the first to enforce and insist upon it in ways that

soon wrought an actual, if incipient, revival in the English-speaking world of letters. With him was soon associated our own Emerson, who, arriving at the same insight, not through Goethe's illumination, but by his own, nevertheless found his inward light extended and clarified by the writings of both Goethe and Carlyle. The period of Goethe's death (March, 1832) may be taken as the time when Carlyle and Emerson distinctly perceived that they stood at the opening of a new era; and it was not long afterwards, when they met at Craigenputtock, that they also became aware of the unity existing between them upon vital issues, and that they were appointed to carry forward Goethe's work in their own lands, and with reinforcement of each other. What Carlyle thought at Goethe's death he has left on record,

170

and we may be sure that in essentials Emerson would have said the same things. Carlyle wrote in "The New Monthly Magazine" for 1832:—

"So then our Greatest has departed. That melody of life, with its cunning tones, which took captive ear and heart, has gone silent: the heavenly force that dwelt here, victorious over so much, is here no longer; thus far, not farther, shall the wise man, by speech and by act, utter himself forth. . . . Goethe, it is commonly said, made a new era in literature; a Poetic Era began with him, the end or ulterior tendencies of which are yet nowise generally visible. This common saying is a true one; and true with a far deeper meaning than, to the most, it conveys. . . . It begins now to be everywhere surmised that the real force, which in this world all things must obey, is Insight, Spiritual Vision and Determination. The Thought is parent of the Deed, nay, is living soul of it, and last and continual, as well as first mover of it; is the foundation, beginning, and essence, therefore, of Man's whole existence here below. The true sovereign of the world, who moulds the world, like soft wax, according to his pleasure, is he who lovingly *sees* into the world; the inspired thinker, whom in these days we name Poet. The true sovereign is the Wise Man."

Some years later, Emerson added his testimony as follows:—

"The Greeks said, Alexander went as far as Chaos; Goethe went, only the other day, as far; and one step farther he hazarded and brought himself back. He has clothed our modern existence with poetry. Amid little-

171

ness and detail, he detected the genius of life, the old cunning Proteus, nestling close beside us, and showed that the dulness and prose we ascribe to the age was only another of his masks.

'His very flight is presence in disguise.'

Goethe, the head and body of the German nation, does not speak from talent, but the truth shines through; he is very wise, though his talent often veils his wisdom. However excellent his sentence is, he has somewhat better in view. The old Eternal Genius who built the world has confided himself more to this man than to any other.'

Emerson is not always to be construed literally, any more than other poets are, — and he did not mean to say that Goethe was nearer to the old Eternal Genius than Shakespeare had been. His portrait of these two men, side by side, was given to the world later, (in 1867,) in those remarkable verses called "Solution," in which he guesses the riddle of the Muse who asks, —

172

"Have you eyes to find the five
Which five hundred did survive?"

Yes, says Emerson, the five great writers are Homer, Dante, Shakespeare, Swedenborg, and Goethe; and thus he portrays the English and the German poet: —

"Seethed in mists of Pennaunmaur,
Taught by Plinlimmon's Druid power,
England's genius filled all measure
Of heart and soul, of strength and pleasure,
Gave to the mind its emperor,
And life was larger than before;

Nor sequent centuries could hit
Orbit and sum of Shakespeare's wit.
The men who lived with him became
Poets, for the air was fame.

"In never days of war and trade,
Romance forgot and faith decayed,
When Science armed and guided war,
And clerks the Janus-gates unbar, —

When France, where poet never grew,
Halved and dealt the globe anew,
Goethe, raised o'er joy and strife,
Drew the firm lines of Fate and Life,
And brought Olympian wisdom down
To court and mart, to gown and town;
Stooping, his finger wrote in clay
The open secret of to-day.'

Among the friends of Emerson, while he was studying Goethe, none was more intimate than Mr. Alcott, whose diaries preserve much that was common to the thought of the two friends. I will therefore read from the diaries of 1847 and later years some of his comments on Goethe as he read him from time to time. Mr. Alcott writes (date uncertain): —

"Life is but a Werther's Sorrows to many, with an end as tragical; nor can it be otherwise till we come forth from our woes to speak peace to the wailers. The chaos about us is but the confusion within us; first place ourself, and all things then take place around us. Hitherto, for the most part, men have been bad economists of life, and spendthrifts of themselves. Few have deserved the epithet 'illustrious,' — and yet life itself

173

might be a lustre so dazzling that to have hidden its flame were almost to quench it."

(1847.) "Goethe has treated the strife of the worst for the best, in nature, more cunningly than either of his predecessors, Moses or the author of the Uzzian Job. And for this old-world fable he was better fitted than any one of his time. He has an eye for subtleties. He is a discerner of spirits, a draughtsman of guile. His faith in nature was so entire that it held all fine gifts at his service, nor could he, fortified and equipped as was his genius, but render faithful copies of what he so clearly saw and learned to portray. 'The demons sat to him,' and we have before us the world he knew so well, and also the one in which almost all are conversant. For this demon of the temptation is as old as man, and thus far the catastrophe has been disastrous to individuals in conflict with multitudes. None has come off victorious with his life; the world-spirit, Mephistopheles, bribing even the Faust, or the will, proffering the present delights for the future pains as at first."

(1851.) "Dipped here and there into 'Faust' (Anna Swanwick's translation), and am admitted more intimately than by Hayward's or Anster's version into the subtleties of the modern Satan, the world-spirit of the nineteenth century. Our devil has partaken of the cosmopolitan culture; he, too, is a scholar and a gentleman, scarcely distinguishable in a crowd from any mortal else, — his complexion sallower by a shade, perhaps, and, if surveyed closely, some show of hoofs in his boots. . . . Faust's dealings with him are infinitely suggestive and profitable, and inclusive of the whole range of guile. 'The demon

174

sat gladly, — the portrait is sketched by a master, and is exhaustive of the subject. Goethe knew too much to paint well anything else; and this, his masterpiece, remains as the last likeness, finished up to the latest dates. Yet he lived too early to sketch this Western democratic shape, some fifty or more years later. Apropos of him, just now and here in this Western hemisphere everybody is putting down the dark Webster as the latest and best devil, concrete and astir in space perhaps, — certainly in these American parts, — clearly responsible for the sins of life, North and South, — a Satan of national type and symmetry. 'T is a great pity that Goethe should have come too soon. Head, shoulders, all, all of Webster should have gone into the picture, and this legal, logical, constitutional Mephistopheles of the States had justice done him by his master. . . . Perhaps Goethe is the most remarkable instance in literature of an intellect holding its eye quite coincident with the plane of things, — endowed likewise with an aptitude to seize at the nick of time every aspect of the demonic forces, as these emerged from their hidings in Nature. But he was held, by consequence, to the mundane plane and the fatal moment, — an intellectual describer, but never a partaker at heart of what he saw and sketched so inimitably. His aloofness from life and from the spirit of permanence; his inability to identify himself with the heart and whole of things, the soul of souls; the duplicity of his genius, one may say, left him the sport of a cunning which partook, at once, of the fate that drives, and of the freedom that controls life's motions. We feel that this eye, mighty as it is and miraculous, escapes not the spell that holds it fixedly on the features he is portraying. There is never

175

the elevation of lid and fluency of light, telling of raptures and of the world's saints, seen and felt,—the sure sign of victories won from nature and one's self. Goethe was cunning, but he was never wisely wise. Too noble for mere prudence, he was coeval with fate; but never magnanimous and Fate's victor; and as the Fates made, so they slew him too, but by incantations soft, siren-like, and prolonged, melodizing his muse, and intimating (although most persuading us the while) his claim to a perpetuity of genius which was not theirs to give. All he was his Faust has taken and celebrates. Faust is admitted to heaven as Goethe to mortality, without the fee of a divinity which alone opens honestly the gates. So the clandestine wins by defeats, from the beginning of evil till its ending here."

176

(1851.) "There is adequate justification for Goethe's treatment of Evil in his great poem, about which so much has been said and written,—most of this quite wide of its drift and province. It is one of the auspicious signs of these latter times that men are beginning to canvass and account for everything that turns up in the world. Nothing remains unquestioned; the popular inquiry is, 'Who are you? what are you here for? Account for your existence,—show us, on penalty of forfeiting it, what right you have to be,—and away with you, if you cannot do it!' Even the Devil, his place and functions in the world, are under discussion, and he too will have to show what he is here for, or quit forthwith. That is a question altogether new, first raised on its proper grounds and poetically argued by Goethe in the 'Faust.' But now the thinkers everywhere are fast hold of it; and it

must render up its secret, so long hidden from the faith of men. Modern judgments seem to be far more tolerant of the Devil than at any former period of the world; his claims are fairly admitted, and his right to be here and take part in mundane affairs is unquestionable. Tolerance is taking place of the old prejudices, and it is becoming quite evident that his presence is indispensable. The most enlightened minds go still further, entering fearlessly into the darker counsels of Providence, and relieving the old superstitions by some sensible and even religious reasons for his existence and place in nature. Say what we will to the contrary,—and it is creditable to

the heart of man that it does doubt the final necessity of his existence and functions, and proves these only transient and mediatorial,—the Devil is felt to be a vast benefit to the present multitude, who could not get on at all without him. The Lord needs and so suffers an agent for the administrative ends of mortality,—a whipper in and secretary. The Devil is a friend in the guise of an enemy. We need him to measure our strength and weakness, to prove our virtue. Life, for the most part, is a contest, a devil's duel, with seconds few or many to provoke and stand sponsor for us, to each according to his mettle and provocation. An imp or two, if no more, is pitted against every one of us,—is one of us, if we knew it. To some there are seven of them, we read, and our merits and demerits are measured precisely by our management of the enemy, whether one or many."

177

In these remarks of Mr. Alcott reference is constantly made to that dramatic poem of Goethe's which

he had just been reading, "Faust," in which the Satanic element is shown as constantly present in a modern and realistic guise. Shakespeare, except in his "Othello," has hardly treated this theme at all; nor is there much common ground in the subjects chosen by these two great poets. Goethe was above all things wise, and in nothing does his wisdom appear more striking than in his estimate of Shakespeare as far above himself, and in his fixed resolve not to imitate one so unlike. He might almost have used in this connection the pregnant query of Emerson, "Why should I forego my own excellence to come short of Shakespeare's?" He had gifts of his own, many and great ones,—but not those of Shakespeare, whose nature was in so many points the opposite of his own. Ben Jonson could not measure Shakespeare, but he saw him, and in some particulars has well described him, in terms that could never be applied to Goethe:—

"The players have often mentioned it as an honor to Shakespeare," says Jonson in his Discoveries, "that he never blotted out a line. My answer hath been, Would

he had blotted a thousand! which they thought a malevolent speech, who chose that circumstance to commend their friend by, wherein he most faulted. He was indeed honest, and of an open and free nature; had an excellent fantasy, brave notions, and gentle expressions; wherein he flowed with that facility, that sometimes it was necessary he should be stopped. His wit was in his own power: would the rule of it had been so too."

178

It could never be said of Goethe that he had not the rule of his own wit in his own power; for no man of genius was ever so deliberate and methodical. Jonson adds,—with that tone of patronage which the intervening centuries have made so amusing to us,— "But Shakespeare redeemed his vices with his virtues. There was ever more in him to be praised than to be pardoned." This mild encomium is increasingly true of Goethe, as we withdraw more and more from the immediate conditions of his life, and judge him by the standards of genius and of benefit to mankind. Tested by these, Goethe must be greatly praised, and his influence on English literature, whether indirect or direct, has been every way salutary. For Goethe, even where he is pedantic, is profound; wherever he deals in small and trivial concerns, there is something just and wholesome in his method, and though he may check and discountenance spontaneity, this can do little harm to our literature, which is spontaneous rather than profound, except in those rare examples like Chaucer, Shakespeare, and Wordsworth, where it is both profound and spontaneous.

179

I do not find that Goethe had any knowledge of Chaucer; yet of all English authors this ancient poet was the nearest to Goethe's serene and tolerant temper, and he rose too, as Goethe did in Germany, from a dead level of mediocrity in his own age, to the very heights of humor and insight. There is a just judgment on this good old poet by Sir Philip Sidney which deserves to be quoted,—written in 1581,

and found in his "Defence of Poesy." "Chaucer," says Sidney, "undoubtedly did excellently in his Troilus and Cressida; of whom, truly, I know not

whether to marvel more, either that he, in that misty time, could see so clearly, or that we, in this clear age, go so stumblingly after him."

One was soon to come who would no longer stumble in following Chaucer, but would overtake and pass him by, so that even Shakespeare's contemporaries would have no doubt what his rank was. An obscure poet of that period, of whom we know almost as little as of Shakespeare himself, William Basse by name, commemorated Shakespeare's death in 1616 by this elegy, which is one of the best, though seldom quoted:—

180

"Renowned Spenser, lie a thought more nigh
To learned Chaucer; and, rare Beaumont, lie
A little nearer Spenser, to make room
For Shakespeare in your threefold, fourfold tomb.
But if precedency in death doth bar
A fourth place in your sacred sepulchre,
Under this sable marble of thine own,
Sleep, rare tragedian, Shakespeare! sleep alone:
Thy unmolested peace in unshared care
Possess as lord, not tennant of thy grave.
That unto us and others it may be
Honor hereafter to be laid by thee."

Here the elegist recognizes, what time has fully attested, that Shakespeare is the lord paramount of English literature, holding a rank higher than Beaumont's, or Spenser's, or Chaucer's. A similar rank must be given, and has long been joyfully conceded,

to Goethe, among German writers. I do not agree with Dr. Bartol in the comparison which he drew between Schiller and Goethe, so disparaging to the former; but it is in accord with that severe Scripture which says, "To him that hath shall be given, and from him that hath not shall be taken away." In the higher meaning of poetic greatness, Schiller "hath not," and therefore must surrender some part of his recent or present renown to the more masculine and original Goethe. In one respect, however, and an important one, he will always be superior to his friend,—in his recognition of that wholesome sexual morality which Goethe at all times considered too lightly, and in his youth and middle life so habitually transgressed. It will be long before English and

American literature becomes accustomed to the tone of Goethe on this subject,—a coarse and worldly habit of mind, which came to him partly by nature, and partly from the French, Latin, and Greek books which he read in his youth far more than he read the better English or German authors. Indeed, there were few good German authors before Goethe and accessible to him; while Ovid and Catullus and Martial and the Greek poets, were open to him, and the amusing literature of France was in every German household where books were read at all. Goethe brings it almost as an accusation against Herder at Strassburg, that he made him think less favorably of Ovid than Goethe had been accustomed; but the "Roman Elegies," written at the age of thirty-eight, show that Ovid

181

was then his model much more than Herder. He had studied the more profound classical poets with profit, and his most perfect drama, so far as form and language go,—the "Iphigenia in Tauris,"—is the best result of this part of his education. It would be impossible to find in English literature so vivid a reproduction of the antique spirit, reinforced by the veracity of the Teuton, as this drama exhibits. Milton's "Samson," which in some points may be compared with it, is so strongly Hebraized that it little resembles in spirit the Greek dramas on which its form was modelled; while the "Prometheus" of Shelley, the "Atalanta" of Swinburne, and the pseudo-classical poems of Landor and of Browning, almost wholly lack the calm dignity of Goethe's "Iphigenia." As those who have preceded me have made little mention of this drama, I will quote a single passage in the earliest American translation, that of Dr. Frothingham of Boston, made some fifty years ago, when Goethe was almost an unknown name in America.

SONG OF THE PARCE IN "IPHIGENIA."

IPHIGENIA (soliloquizing).

Within my ears resounds that ancient song,—
Forgotten was it, and forgotten gladly,—
Song of the Parce, which they shuddering sang
When Tantalus fell from his golden seat.

They suffered with their noble friend,—indignant
Their bosom was, and terrible their song.
To me and to my sisters in our youth
The nurse would sing it,—and I marked it well.

182

THE SONG.

"The gods be your terror,
Ye children of men!
They hold the dominion
In hands everlasting,
All free to exert it
As listeth their will.

"Let him fear them doubly
Whome'er they've exalted!
On crags and on cloud-piles
The altars are planted
Around the gold tables.

"Dissension arises;
Then tumble the feasters
Reviled and dishonored
In gulfs of deep midnight;
And look ever vainly
In fetters of darkness
For judgment that's just.

"But They remain seated
At feasts never failing
Around the gold tables.
They stride at a footstep
From mountain to mountain;
Through jaws of abysses
Steams toward them the breathing
Of suffocate Titans
Like offerings of incense,—
A light-rising vapor.

"They turn—the proud masters—
From whole generations
The eye of their blessing,—
Nor will in the children

183

The once well-beloved
Still eloquent features
Of ancestors see.

So sang the dark sisters!
The old exile heareth
That terrible music
In caverns of darkness,—
Remembereth his children,
And shaketh his head.

The Greek doctrine of divine vengeance and of irresistible destiny here set forth, (but which is beautifully softened in the play by the devotion and truthfulness of Iphigenia,) has scarcely found an entrance into English literature, where tragedy assumes a character more personal. The deepest sufferings of Shakespeare's heroes grow out of their own acts, and are not the result of foreordained or inherited guilt, as we may see in "King Lear" and "Othello." Goethe also gives this personal turn to all the tragedy which he brings forward; but his "Iphigenia," with its deep realization of the antique tragic motives, may serve as a connecting link between ancient and modern tragedy. And so strong in his mind was the ancient form of presentation, that he adopted it to some extent in his next important work, his "Tasso,"—which was mainly written in Rome, in 1786-88, as the "Iphigenia," was finished and privately brought out there. His "Egmont," on the other hand, the most dramatic of his plays, but far from the best, has nothing of the antique about it; and still less has the first part of

184

"Faust," which, though dramatic in form, is rather a succession of declamations, spectacles, and songs, than a drama, strictly speaking. This fits it for operatic representation, in which it is most successfully and constantly given to the public. In itself, as a closet drama, or what Mr. Snider calls a "literary Bible," it is extremely foreign to the English and American mind, and there is nothing really akin to it in our literature, notwithstanding Marlowe's "Dr. Faustus" and the octogenarian Philip Bailey's "Festus,"—which was "Faust" emasculated, trimmed and scented and sent forth on a harmless round among the circulating libraries, forty years ago.

Mr. Snider has so well set forth the origin and spirit of the Faust legend, and this exposition has been so well supplemented by Mr. Davidson, that I need only call attention to the manner in which it burst forth in English literature,—a single flash and explosion of flame and smoke from the Titanic cave of Christopher Marlowe's genius. This man—who, if he had lived, might have disputed Shakespeare's

pre-eminence in dramatic poetry, as he was in fact Shakespeare's teacher and coadjutor during their hot youth in London—seems to have caught at the Faust myth almost as soon as it appeared anywhere in Europe in a printed form—though it had circulated from mouth to mouth at universities and among the people for more than half a century, when, in 1587, there appeared at Frankfort the "History of Dr. Johann Faust, the far-famed [weibeschreiter] Sor-

185

cerer and Black-Artist [Schwarzkünstler]." From an English translation of this book, made in 1592, Marlowe is supposed to have taken his play, "The Tragical History of Dr. Faustus," which must have been written in 1592-93, for in June, 1593, Marlowe was killed in a tavern brawl. This fact and Marlowe's own character, which was that of an unbeliever and sensualist, gives a peculiar significance to his version of the Faust myth, which Goethe had thoughts of translating into German. Crabbe Robinson, when visiting Goethe in 1829, read to the old poet for the first time Milton's "Samson," and mentioned Marlowe's "Dr. Faustus." Goethe did not admire Milton so much as Byron, but of Marlowe's play he said, bursting out into an exclamation of praise, "How greatly is it all planned!"[1] The Diary of Crabbe Robinson, and the remarks and letters of Goethe after the visits of this indefatigable Englishman in 1829, give some anecdotes and remarks which will show how imperfect was Goethe's knowledge of English authors. Robinson says:—

"I took an opportunity to mention Milton, and found Goethe unacquainted with 'Samson Agonistes.' I read to him the first part, to the end of the scene with Dalila. He fully conceived the spirit of it, though he did

186

not praise Milton with the warmth with which he eulogized Byron, of whom he said that 'the like would never

[1] It is curious that Meissner in his recent book, "English Actors of Shakespeare's Time in Austria," not only proves that Marlowe's "Dr. Faustus" in a German version was played at Grätz in 1608, but offers evidence to show that it was played in Frankfort in the autumn of 1592.

come again; he was inimitable.' Even Ariosto was not so daring as Byron in the 'Vision of Judgment.' Goethe preferred to all the other serious poems of Byron the 'Heaven and Earth,' though it seemed almost satire when he exclaimed, 'A bishop might have written it.' He added: 'Byron should have lived to execute his vocation,—to dramatize the Old Testament. What a subject under his hands would the Tower of Babel have been! Byron was indebted for the profound views he took of the Bible to the ennui he suffered from it at school.' . . . It was with reference to the poems of the Old Testament that Goethe praised the views which Byron took of Nature; they were equally profound and poetical. 'He had not, like me, devoted a long life to the study of Nature, and yet in all his works I found but two or three passages I could have wished to alter.'" Robinson objected to the then common comparison of Manfred to Faust, and said, "Faust had nothing left but to sell his soul to the Devil, when he had exhausted all the resources of science in vain; but Manfred's was a poor reason,—his passion for Astarte." Goethe smiled and said, "That is true." But then he fell back on the indomitable spirit of Manfred. Even at the last he was not conquered. And the impudence of Byron's satire he felt and enjoyed. Robinson pointed out "The Deformed Transformed" as really an imitation of "Faust," and Goethe especially praised that piece. Byron's verses on George IV, he said, were the sublime of hatred.

Returning to Milton, Goethe said to Robinson, as afterwards to Zelter, "Samson's confession of his guilt is in a

187

better spirit than anything in Byron. There is fine logic in all the speeches. Dalila's vindication of herself is capital; he has put her in the right." To one of Samson's speeches he cried out, "O the parson!" He thanked Robinson for making him acquainted with the "Samson," saying, "It gives me a higher opinion of Milton than I had before; it lets me more into the nature of his mind than any other of his works." To Zelter he wrote that "in Samson we acquire knowledge of a predecessor of Lord Byron who is as grand and comprehensive as Byron himself; but then the successor is as vast and wildly varied as the other appears simple and stately." Again he said, that "he never before met with so perfect an imitation of the antique in style and spirit" as in the

"Samson." He told Robinson that Schiller's rendering of the witch-scenes in Macbeth was "detestable,"—"but that was his way. You must let every man have his own character."

I do not find that Goethe had much to say of Landor, the man of England who most resembled him in some traits, and who valued highly and early, for an Englishman, the greatness of Goethe. In 1819, Southey wrote to Landor that a contributor to the county paper had spoken of Landor in "The Westmoreland Gazette" as the English poet who most resembled Goethe; adding, "I do not know enough of Goethe to judge how far this assertion may be right." Considering that Southey was the poet-laureate of England, and Goethe then seventy years old, the remark indicates how far apart were

188

English and German literature when Carlyle began to write. Landor did not read the "Iphigenia" till after Goethe's death, when he praised and criticised it. In 1837 he said of Goethe: "He was the wisest man of his time, as he was the most poetical. Drops hang from every work of Goethe's (that I have seen) of the very purest brightness, such as will never dry up nor fall. I admire much of his poetry and all his prose."

It is a pity that these two men could not have known each other, living as they did for half a century within a few hundred miles, and both engaged in the lonely pursuits of thought and imagination. They were not too much alike to have quarrelled,—except as Landor quarrelled with everybody,—while Goethe would have met that pettish trait by his wise habit of quarrelling with nobody. The English-man, true to his national character, had more magnanimity, but ill-regulated; the German had more wisdom, and deserved better than Landor that closing epigram which the Englishman wrote on himself,—styling it "The Dying Speech of an Old Philosopher":—

"I strove with none, for none was worth my strife;

Nature I loved, and next to Nature Art.
I warmed both hands against the fire of life, —
It sinks, and I am ready to depart."

189

VII.

GOETHE AS A PLAYWRIGHT.

By WILLIAM ORDWAY PARTRIDGE.

WE may affirm without arrogance that we of the present day are better informed with regard to the highest artistic effects of the drama and the use of technical methods than were Lessing, Schiller, and Goethe. These are the words of Gustav Freitag, a German writer standing in all but the first rank of literary men and dramatists, and in the very foremost rank of dramatic critics. In writing a criticism upon the work of a man of Goethe's eminence, some part of which, at least, must be unfavorable, one is fain to take refuge under the shield of so great a critic, and thus avoid all possible charge of arrogance. Not only as a shield, however, have I quoted the above passage; it is of great significance as pointing out the two distinguishing characteristics of the successful playwright: (1.) A clear conception of highest artistic effects; (2.) The power to apply the best technical methods for the production of these.

We must here make a careful distinction between a playwright and a playwriter. And in the present

190

paper we wish especially to insist upon this distinction. It is not our intention to criticise Goethe as a writer of plays, or his plays as mere literary productions, or what are called closet dramas; but to consider him strictly as a playwright, and his plays as productions intended for representation on the stage. The dramatic value of a play is its effectiveness upon the stage. Whatever other merits a play may have, psychological, philosophical, or ethical, if it is not effective upon the stage, it lacks the first essential of a good drama. A psychological, philosophical, or ethi-

cal discussion may be cast in the form of dialogue, or even of a drama; as, for example, the Dialogues of Plato, but these are not dramas in the proper sense. In order to arrive at clearness in this matter, we must first inquire what kind of effectiveness we have a right to expect from the drama, and, secondly, through what technical methods this effectiveness may be best attained. Of course we must not expect from the drama every kind of effectiveness, as, for instance, the effect of a philosophical argument, sermon, or oratorio; we must not look for the effect produced by an intoxicating draught as Niagara.

First, then, let us consider what constitutes dramatic effectiveness. The question might be answered by one word, viz. the term "drama," which properly means action, so that a drama without action is a contradiction in terms. The essential element, then, in dramatic effectiveness is action. It must, however, be action of a peculiar kind,—in a word, it must

191

be motivated action, and the motive must at once be rational and apparent to the spectators. This Goethe himself believed, and has admirably expressed in words put into the mouth of Wilhelm Meister with regard to Shakespeare's characters: "These very mysterious and composite creatures of nature act before us in his plays, as if they were clocks with cases and dial-plates of crystal; they show in their determination the lapse of the hours, and at the same time we can recognize the wheels and springs that drive them."

The drama, then, in its true sense, is an action, a rounded and complete action, whose various parts or moments are evolved and connected by intelligible motives.

These motives may have two sources, that is, they may be either in the characters or in the exigencies of the action itself. For example, the fortunate termination of "Iphigenie" finds its motive in the perfect sincerity of Iphigenie's character. In "Egmont" also, as well as in "Götz," the hero's fate is plainly due to defects in his own character. On the other

hand, the task imposed upon Hamlet of putting his uncle to death plainly arises from the exigency of circumstances,—the moral demands of his time,—and can in no wise be laid to the charge of Hamlet's character. It may here be remarked that the ancient differs from the modern drama, in the source from which it mainly draws its motives. The ancient dramatists looked for their motives chiefly in the

192

exigences of circumstances, which to them were synonymous with necessity, destiny, or Fate, whence the majority of ancient plays are Fate-dramas. Modern dramatists, on the other hand,—and pre-eminently Goethe,—seek their motives chiefly in character, whence most good modern plays are, to a very large extent, character-dramas. This difference accounts, in some measure, for the superior effectiveness of the ancient drama, inasmuch as motives originating in external circumstances are far more easy to represent than those drawn from character. Probably the highest type of drama is that in which the motives are drawn equally from circumstances (not necessarily conceived as Fate) and from character. This balance of motives we find in Shakespeare's best plays, for example, "Hamlet" and "Romeo and Juliet." In a word, we may say that the prime and fundamental condition of dramatic effect, as such, is perfect motivation. A series of brilliant scenes, however effective otherwise, are not dramatic. In this the drama differs from history, that in the former the events are connected by perfect motivation; in the latter, merely by time and imperfect, often non-apparent motivation.

Although motivation is the first essential of dramatic effect, it is not, by itself alone, sufficient to insure that effect. Other and secondary conditions are requisite. In the first place, the motives must be of a particular kind, since all motives are not dramatic. True dramatic motives are such as an au-

193

dience feel to be human and rational,—such as men like themselves in similar circumstances would act upon. Consequently, all motives that affect only ec-

centric or exceptionally good or wicked characters, must be used sparingly, if at all. The same is true of all motives of a miraculous, revolting, or fantastic kind. What is regarded as miraculous, revolting, or fantastic, is not the same in all ages or among all peoples; for which reason every dramatist must keep very steadily in view his own time and public. For example, some things that the Greeks forbade to be represented on the stage as revolting, such as assassination, murder, and suicide, we permit, and applaud. The stabbing of Cæsar, the suicide of Brutus, the death of Romeo and Juliet, of Gretchen, etc., are examples of this.

In the second place, dramatic motives, in order to be effective, must produce certain results.

(1) They must produce passion and action, and not merely dialogue, however philosophical, beautiful, or moral it may be.

(2) The motivated action must be so arranged and rounded as to arouse a steadily increasing sympathy, expectation, and anxiety — or, as Aristotle puts it, pity and fear — on the part of the audience, and then to satisfy these emotions.

(3) The ultimate result of the whole action must be to solemnize the mind by revealing to it the workings of the human heart and the moral order of the universe, and to send an audience forth refreshed,

194

strengthened, and inspired for the duties of life,—in a word, it must result in what Aristotle calls *Purification*.

Having thus stated, in general terms, the true artistic effect of the drama, we come next to consider by what technical methods these results are to be obtained. Inasmuch as the first condition of artistic effectiveness in the drama is complete and thorough motivation, our first inquiry must relate to the mode in which this may be reached. It is evident that this will in large measure depend upon the choice of subject, the fact being that it is much easier to find motives for certain lines of action than for others. Indeed, however this choice may be influenced by fashion or by the intellectual and aesthetic idiosyncra-

sies of the author, the subject must always be one capable of being transformed into a dramatic idea,—that unital and initial germ from which the whole drama is developed. There is hardly any point in which the genius of an artist is more apparent, than in this ability to see what subjects are capable of being permeated with the living, causative, formative dramatic idea.

And this is especially true of the dramatist. The question of what is really dramatic has been much agitated, but one may affirm that dramatic, and more especially tragic subjects, are those containing the elements of some great moral collision, taking place in a sphere of life in which the characters must be supposed capable of expressing this collision in speech

195

and action. This collision itself must be of a kind to give ample opportunity for the display of passion and action. This regulation effectively excludes all subjects containing collisions which are fought out within the breast of the individual, or in philosophical and moral discussion with others. Moral collisions that lead to no outward action, but only to monologues or conversations, are essentially undramatic. It would follow, of course, that a subject could not be chosen from among a people of a low degree of culture, or a people whose lives are not dramatic. Granting now that the subject is properly chosen, the conditions specified being fulfilled, the question arises how the subject is to be developed so as to produce these dramatic effects, we have mentioned above; viz. (1.) abundant display of action and passion in the character; (2.) the excitement of a steadily increasing sympathy on the part of the audience, and the satisfaction of the same; (3.) the moral inspiration and physical refreshment that come from the clear presentation and solution of moral problems. To exhaust this question is not easy, and, in a brief lecture like this, only the more prominent means for producing effectiveness can even be mentioned

In the first place, then, care must be taken to concentrate interest, and this can be done only by preserving the unity of action, which action must not be

understood to mean a single event, but a connected series of events, or, as Aristotle says, a praxis. In every drama the action must be strictly *one*,—undivided. It

196

must then revolve about a single character, or a single group of characters, involved in the conception of the subject. What is true of the drama is true of every other art. A picture, for example, must have a single point of interest, about which everything else is grouped. It follows from this, that those accessory characters and groups which are necessary to the development of the plot, and as foils to the principal characters, must be subordinated, and not receive any prominence beyond what they derive from their relation to these characters. Any attempt to give them prominence on their own account would only distract attention, scatter interest, dilute sympathy, cause confusion, and diminish effectiveness.

We must here note that the unity of the actions so essential to the effectiveness of a drama, does not depend solely upon the unity or oneness of the characters, or central group. Actions belonging even to a single character do not necessarily form a dramatic unity. A drama is never a biography, nor a series of adventures or episodes. In other words, a mere historic or personal connection between events is utterly different from that relation which produces dramatic unity. A dramatic action, therefore, is one which not only has its centre in a single character, but must be a single action in the sense that all its parts are connected as cause and effect, and every event must tend to advance or relieve the progress of the action. And not only so, but the action must have a natural beginning in a *deed* or juncture forming the collision of the

197

piece; and an ending, in which the problem involved in the collision is naturally solved. *Naturally* solved, I repeat, because there are unnatural solutions, and these are essentially undramatic. A natural solution is one whose elements are found in the action and characters of the piece itself. An unnatural solution is one violently introduced from without, in the shape of miracle, chance, or some catastrophe of

nature. Each of these is a *Deus ex machina*, or, as the Italians say, a *salto mortale*, which is forever interdicted in art as nullifying its true purpose. Other unities have, at certain times, been insisted upon, especially those of time and place; but these are unessential, and have almost universally been discarded.

In the second place, it is not only necessary to concentrate and sustain interest, but to arouse it properly. And this can be done only by putting the audience in possession of facts sufficient to enable them to understand the nature of the collision involved, and the relation of the different characters to it. This Aristotle happily calls the δέσις, or tying of the knot. This must be done in the opening scenes of a play, which in a certain sense must always be introductory. Any attempt to put the audience in possession of the necessary facts by means of a prologue,—though favored and practised by some dramatists, such as Euripides, Seneca, and Alfieri,—is inartistic, and bespeaks incapacity on the part of the dramatist. A prologue hardly becomes more artistic even when it

198

takes the form of a mere explanatory dialogue, in no way advancing the action of the play. The opening of a piece which puts the audience in possession of the necessary facts will, by a good artist, be so arranged as to be brief, and a part of the action of the play, for only in this way can it arouse the highest interest.

In the third place, the interest, once aroused, must be steadily sustained; which means, not that it must be kept uniformly at the same degree of intensity, but that it must gradually increase until it reaches its climax and satisfaction in the solution of the piece. In a word, we may say that the interest must be compound interest. At the same time, care must be taken to retard the interest until the climax can be fairly reached. This is perhaps the most difficult task imposed upon the playwright, inasmuch as it involves a profound knowledge of psychology and an immense power of grading and directing all the parts of his play to a single end. With this in

view he must carefully avoid introducing anything, however tempting, not bearing directly upon the action of the play, and also the placing of less interesting scenes after more interesting ones; or in any way introducing mere explanatory matter without action. For this reason, long messages interrupting the action of the play, and similar things, should be avoided. A play in which scenes can be omitted or transposed, without affecting the interest of the piece, is by that fact alone a poor play, and argues an

199

inferior playwright. Perhaps the worst of all possible plays is one consisting of a series of scenes in which the action does not advance, or the characters are not brought into any different relation to each other at the end from that which they occupied at the beginning. Such plays are the "Hecuba" of Euripides, and the "Brunhilde," written some years ago for the actress Janauschek.

In the fourth place, the interest, having been aroused and sustained throughout the play, must in the end secure complete satisfaction. Such satisfaction we are wont to call poetic justice. By this we mean that every one of the principal characters must at the conclusion of the piece meet with the just reward of his deeds; thus impressing that most profound of all moral truths, often so dimly visible in our actual lives, namely, that there is an inexorable moral law ruling in the world, and giving to each man the exact reward of his deeds. Only in this way can a play produce that exhilaration and moral inspiration which are the ultimate tests of the value of a drama. But although a play, like every true work of art, ought to produce a moral effect, the artist's intention to produce this effect should never be apparent. In other words, a drama ought not, either in whole or in part, to be a sermon or moral lecture.

The moral effect, on the contrary, ought to be apparent in the very construction and action of the play, and to be deduced therefrom by a spontaneous action under the influence of emotion on the part of

200

the audience. We ought no more to look for a sermon in a play, than we do in the Venus of Melos or the Hermes of Praxiteles. True works of art, like lofty characters, exercise their influence, not through what they do or say, but through what they are. As Schiller puts it, "There is nobility even in the moral world. Common natures pay with what they *do*,—noble natures with what they are."

Such then are some of the principal and essential conditions of dramatic effectiveness: (1) choice of subject, noble and capable of being developed and motivated into scenes of action and passion,—in other words, into a dramatic unity; (2) absolute unity and probability of action; (3) interest artistically enlisted, sustained, and satisfied, at last, by poetic justice. In order to deal with Goethe as upright judges, and not arbitrarily as tyrants, we have now only to apply the principles laid down, in all their rigor, to his dramatic productions,—or, at least, to such of them as may be supposed in any way to determine his position as a playwright.

In doing so, we shall deal mainly with those plays which may be regarded as marking stages in his dramatic development,—"Götz von Berlichingen," "Egmont," "Torquato Tasso," "Iphigenie," and "Faust." Although Goethe had previously written some smaller pieces for special occasions, his career as a serious playwright begins with "Götz von Berlichingen." This play, of which the first draft was written in six weeks, in the year 1771, was con-

201

ceived under the influence of a powerful enthusiasm due to the reading of Shakespeare. With respect to the effect of this first acquaintance with the work of the English dramatist, Goethe himself says, speaking through the lips of Wilhelm Meister:—

"I cannot recollect that any book, any man, any incident of my life, has produced such effects on me. . . . . They seem as if they were performances of some celestial Genius, descending among men to make them, by the mildest instructions, acquainted with themselves. They are no fictions! you would think, while reading them, you stood before the unclosed awful books of Fate, while

the whirlwind of most impassioned life was howling through the leaves, and tossing them fiercely to and fro. The strength and tenderness, the power and peacefulness of this man, have so astonished and transported me, that I long vehemently for the time when I shall have it in my power to read further."

It was in this frame of mind that Goethe wrote "Götz," drawing his theme from the autobiography of the old national hero of the Iron Hand, a theme capable of being treated in the manner of Shakespeare. He wrote under the influence of an imitative enthusiasm, and not in accordance with any theory of dramatic art. Indeed, at that time he had not arrived at any such theory. This fact accounts in great measure for the merits and the defects of the work. The defects are very great; but it has real merits, and, indeed, from a purely dramatic point of view, this piece, though the earliest, is unques-

202

tionally the most popular and effective of Goethe's plays.

Nor is this fact difficult to explain. Shakespeare's influence upon Goethe had been of a most healthy and stimulating kind. It had roused the spontaneity of his genius, which was naturally great, and supplied him with admirable models, without subjecting him to any aesthetic rules or theories. And this last negative advantage was perhaps as valuable as the other two positive ones. For so strong in all Germans is the tendency to work according to rules addressed to the understanding,—and so fatal is this tendency to all German artists, even those of high genius,—that Goethe could hardly have failed to be injured in his work by any such restrictions.

This indeed, we shall see, actually took place with much damage to Goethe's dramatic work, after he became interested in dramatic theory. Not only will theory never make an artist, but it may even damage one, especially if he be a German.

"Götz von Berlichingen," in spite of its popularity and its extraordinary value in the history of German literature, will not stand the test of vigorous dramatic criticism. The subject, indeed, is well chosen,

being one in which the unity of action might easily have been preserved, strict motivation introduced, and abundant opportunities offered for scenes of action and passion.

But unfortunately Goethe was unable to permeate this subject with a dramatic idea, and hence the

203

work remains a series of interesting but disconnected scenes, which do not form in any sense a dramatic unity. The interest is scattered and broken into fragments, with neither proper gradation, climax, nor satisfactory solution. Much crude historical matter, connected, as historical matter usually is, by mere chronological succession, instead of dramatic motivation, remains to burden the play. The result is, that the catastrophe does not follow necessarily from the conditions of the piece, and leaves the demands of poetic justice unsatisfied. Götz, it is true, is a tragic character, and this for two reasons. The former of these is his thoughtless, incautious, and fond confidence in Weislingen, a man who had abundantly proved himself fit for a place in the lowest circle of Dante's Inferno. The latter was his failure to see that his efforts were directed against the natural advance of civilization, and in favor of an obsolete feudalism. At the same time, these defects are not sufficient to reconcile us to the hero's dying as a coward might, with a feeling that his whole heroic life had been worse than vain. This inartistic ending is the more to be regretted, inasmuch as it might easily have been avoided. The fault is due in part to Goethe's following too closely the facts of history, in defiance of the aesthetic law which demands poetic justice; that is, a recognition of a man's virtues as well as of his defects. But it was due perhaps even more to the circumstance, that, when Götz was written, the author was in revolt against

204

the German political system, just as Schiller was in revolt against the social system when he wrote "The Robbers," and wished to excite popular indignation against that system by making Götz appear as a martyr to it. This purpose to excite indignation

must be set down as inartistic, as all tendentious purpose in art is.

In spite of all these great defects, the play has a certain amount of confused effectiveness, both in the action, and in the characters. Notwithstanding Götz's lamentable ending, he and his little group of associates remain inspiring characters; and this is so true, that the play has always, perhaps more than any other of Goethe's works, been a favorite upon the stage. This is certainly only in a small degree due to its artistic merits, since the interest which it excites is not, strictly speaking, a dramatic interest; nevertheless, the general tone of the play is so healthy, and its action so full of varied life, that the ultimate effect is in a large degree inspiring and exhilarating. As early as 1799, the drama of "Götz von Berlichingen" was thought worthy of a translation into English by so great an artist as Sir Walter Scott. It ought perhaps to be remarked that Goethe wrote three, if not four, editions of "Götz," and that only the third was really intended for the stage.

205

"Götz von Berlichingen" can claim two great merits. It was the first truly national German play, and it was also the play in which was first fully realized what Lessing and others had so earnestly striven for without completely achieving,—a breach with traditional rules, and the complete liberation of the German stage from the artificial and conventional drama of France, which had so baneful an influence on the literature and morals of Germany. The work has thus the merit of marking a most important epoch in German literature.

There must have been considerable outcry on the part of the critics against this departure from dramatic rules and precepts,[1] and this must have come, in part at least, from critics whom Goethe felt bound to respect; for we find him writing to his friend Kestner: "I am now engaged upon a drama for the boards, in order that the fellows may see that, if I please, I can observe rules and portray morality and sentimentality." To what drama Goethe here refers we cannot say with certainty. It may have been "Faust," the idea of which was fermenting in his mind at this time. Be this as it may, the first draft of "Faust" which, in the main, was written shortly after "Götz," though not published till many years later (1790) corresponds accurately with Goethe's description, inasmuch as it follows dramatic rules perhaps more than his other dramas, and deals with morality and sentimentality. And although "Faust," as a completed work, did not appear till sixty years later, we may here insert what has to be said concerning its dramatic properties. Paradoxical as it may seem, "Faust" is a drama to which the standard of dra-

206

matic criticism should not be applied, if we do not wish to make it appear a failure, as, indeed, Vischer and other eminent critics have shown it to be. Indeed, as a whole, it does not belong to the class of acting plays, but to that of literary and philosophical dramas. The dramatic idea in itself, though well and profoundly chosen, is far too vast for a single drama, and almost even for a trilogy. Moreover, many of the scenes are almost incapable of being presented on the stage, such as the two *Walpurgisnächte* and the Prologues. It is true that the whole is now annually played at Weimar, but under circumstances altogether exceptional, and such as are hardly possible on any ordinary stage. Moreover, the dramatic unity is frequently violated, the scenes being often bound together, not by dramatic motivation, but by the personal identity of Faust. In fact, it is largely a series of episodes in the life of an individual, Faust; and according to Aristotle, the episodic drama is the worst of all. The only part that lies within the sphere of strictly dramatic criticism is the original fragment, published in 1790, founded on popular legend and embodying Faust's relation to Gretchen. This part will stand the severest dramatic criticism. The subject is well chosen, and capable of being thoroughly permeated by the dramatic idea. It also affords excellent motives for scenes of action and passion. It rises naturally to a climax, and descends as naturally to the catastrophe, which satisfies all the claims of poetic justice. The interest is sustained

207

throughout, and the final effect is, in the highest degree, solemnizing and purifying. It cannot be otherwise than a matter of regret that Goethe did not complete his "Faust" in accordance with his original conception; for the additions which, after his metaphysical and critical studies, he made even to the first part, not to speak of the second, essentially injured the unity of the *action*, and considerably impaired its effectiveness for the stage.

The other three plays of Goethe which we purpose to criticise as typical productions are "Egmont," "Iphigenie," and "Tasso." These dramas were written nearly at the same time,—between 1777 and 1789, when Goethe was in the full possession of his highest dramatic efforts. First came "Egmont," 1777 to 1785. The subject is an event in the rebellion of the Netherlands against Spanish domination, and therefore may be considered a *national* subject. Indeed, it is said that the play was intended as a companion to "Götz." Here, for the first time, we see the baneful effects of Goethe's attempt to apply dramatic rules in a comprehensive way, and the result as a whole is a mechanical production, devoid of dramatic unity.

This criticism may appear unjust, especially as the play has held the stage for so many years, and possesses a certain effectiveness. But, after all, this effectiveness is not truly dramatic, being due, in great part, to a few graceful love scenes scattered through

208

it, and in some degree also to a certain historic and political interest, which has no artistic bearing. The chief effectiveness is derived, not from the dramatic idea, which is political, but from a series of domestic scenes utterly foreign to his idea. For the fundamental idea, or collision, is this: A nobleman finds himself placed between duty to his conquered and rebelling countrymen, and fealty to their conqueror,

[1] See the scoff of Frederic the Great, cited on page 158.

under whom he has accepted service. Being of a generous, brave, tender, reckless, and unreflective character, fond of pleasure and popularity, he countenances his countrymen in their seditious practices, thereby giving offence to the conquerors, from whom, nevertheless, he has not sufficient patriotism or foresight, as Orange had, to disconnect himself.

This tragic weakness brings about his destruction. To such a political idea, the domestic scenes between Egmont and Clärchen are plainly alien, and, as a matter of fact, they have no bearing upon the action of the play, and in no way tend to relieve or develop it. Indeed, the only case when she in any way enters into the main action of the drama is after the catastrophe is certain, when her ghost appears as a *Deus ex machina* in the garb of Freedom, from a supernatural world, whose introduction is not justified by the plan of the play. It is a rule of dramatic art, that the miraculous and supernatural should not be introduced into a play unless they have been suggested as credible agents early in the plot, as they are in the case of the witches in "Macbeth," the ghost

209

in "Hamlet," and others. Indeed, the introduction of Clärchen in the winding up of "Egmont" is inartistic, being unmotivated, and, as Schiller said, operatic.

Beside the weakness of the termination, the play has other glaring defects. Many of the scenes are too prolix, and so loosely connected that they not only could be, but actually are, transposed when the play is represented; which shows that the interest is not properly graded. A number of the scenes consist of mere padding of talk: indeed, Goethe might, without impropriety, have called those scenes, in which the citizens so fortuitously meet to gossip, the choric part, and assigned to his play a chorus of Netherlanders. There is no binding and loosing in the play, and of course no Peripeteia. On the whole, then, in spite of its popularity, from the standard of just dramatic criticism the play must be regarded as a failure.

In passing from "Egmont" to "Iphigenie," we

suddenly enter a new world. "Iphigenie" is almost in every respect a complete contrast to the play we have just considered. Here Goethe was dealing with a subject which had already been dramatized by two great playwrights, Euripides and Racine.

The main incidents of the play, therefore, were already given in the title, "Iphigenie in Tauris," and a new motivation alone, remained to be supplied. This, it must be admitted, Goethe has accomplished with admirable taste and success. In fact, the mo-

210

tivation is so entirely his own, that he has given us one of the best of character-dramas, instead of a fate-drama. The dramatic unity is preserved throughout: the tying and untying of the knot, although classically simple, are managed in a masterly way. Strangely enough, although the characters are in large measure foils to each other, they are all noble and dignified. The character of Iphigenie, combining princess and priestess, is perhaps the purest and stateliest that Goethe or any dramatist ever conceived. One lingers before it with ever-increasing delight, as he does before the Venus of Melos, or the Immaculate Conception of Murillo. One especial feature of the "Iphigenie" is the limpid flow of its stately language, which has, perhaps, never been excelled. To use the words of Keats, it reads like the large utterance of the early gods.

Though entirely modern and un-Greek in tone and sentiment, in form it is as perfect and self-contained as the Parthenon of Iktinos; and, like the Parthenon, its effect is calculated for an audience of highly developed taste. The play contains little external action or violent expression of passion to attract a popular audience. Its strength lies mainly in its psychological *truthfulness*, which in the hands of highly cultivated actors can be made very impressive. Although exception might be taken to a few features of the play, such as the Euripidean prologue, and the somewhat too epigrammatic and philosophical character of the dialogue, "Iphigenie" must be regarded as the

211

most finished of Goethe's dramatic efforts; and this is clearly shown by its ultimate effect, which leaves the mind in the attitude of solemnity, purity, and lofty courage.

From "Iphigenie" we pass to the last of Goethe's typical plays, "Torquato Tasso," finished in 1789. In the choice and development of this subject, Goethe had to depend upon his own resources; and, when we compare the play with "Iphigenie," we see at once how much he owed in the latter to his Greek predecessor, especially in the matter of incident. "Tasso" is almost purely a character-drama, and is well motivated from beginning to end. Nevertheless, the result in the two cases is very different. What in "Iphigenie" was pure, living classical stateliness, has here become rigidity, coldness, formality. Instead of a Parthenon of lucent Pentelic marble, we now enter the ice palace of a Russian autocrat. The cardinal defects of this play are largely due to a false choice of subject, which does not lend itself to dramatic development. An almost sure test of a good play is that its dramatic idea, or collision, can be fully stated in a few words. "Macbeth," "Hamlet," "Iphigenie," may be cited as examples of this.

In "Tasso," on the contrary, it is extremely difficult to state, even in a prolix way, the dramatic idea. The truth is, Goethe took an incident from the life of an historic character, and was unable to lift it out of its historic wording into the refinement of a living dramatic idea. A plebeian poet of passionate tem-

212

perament finds patronage and high favor at the court of a powerful prince. In the moment of his highest triumph, he is brought face to face with another favorite of the court,—a nobleman of practical and diplomatic turn of mind. In the conflict which follows between the two natures, the one-sidedness of each is brought out. A dispute arises, which has to be settled by the prince according to a purely conventional and unjust standard; bringing disgrace upon the poet, who was really blameless, and acquitting the culpable nobleman. Partly under the influence of the prince, the nobleman is induced to

admit his wrong, and sue for reconciliation, which he ultimately effects, and draws from the poet an enthusiastic acknowledgment of his superiority. This story, though long, does not really state the entire plot of the play, for it does not include the very important *rôles* played by the two heroines. But this fact only bears out the statement that the idea is undramatic. And indeed these *rôles* are almost unrelated to the main collision,—so much so that at the end the relation between Tasso and the Princess is left entirely unsolved. The same inferior and fragmentary art to which we called attention in "Egmont" reappears here. The effectiveness of the play when represented is due in large measure to a few delicately constructed and tender love scenes, which have no real relation to the dramatic idea. In the arts of the playwright and the novelist, love scenes are too frequently the refuge of the destitute.

213

They are the refuge of the destitute, because they are sure to interest a large public, whatever the character of the work may be in which they appear. In introducing such scenes Goethe shows that he was a true German himself, and knew the character of his countrymen. In a similar manner, a French painter who cannot attract attention by legitimate means will frequently resort to the introduction of nude figures, sure that under any circumstances this will appeal to something in his countrymen, if not to their artistic sense. To sum up the dramatic characteristics of the play, we must say that, although conforming in many ways to the rules of art, as a drama it is a distinct failure, and was so considered even by Goethe's contemporaries; and at the present day the play has almost disappeared from the stage.

This ends our consideration of the acknowledged typical dramas of Goethe. If time permitted, other minor dramas might have been considered with interest, but the general result would not thereby be materially affected. What, then, we may ask, is that result? Is it such as to justify us in affirming that Goethe was a great playwright? Without detracting

from Goethe's greatness in other directions, and indeed heartily acknowledging it, we must, in accordance with the verdict of rational criticism, answer the question in the negative. And in order to justify this answer, we have only to generalize what we have already stated in particular. Goethe's short-

214

comings as a playwright may be said to be four in number:—

1. A fundamental lack of the dramatic sense,—which in great measure prevented him from recognizing what subjects were capable of being transformed into dramatic ideas, and so becoming dramatically effective.

2. A fundamental lack of constructive power,—which prevented him from producing works distinguished by organic unity; thus leaving his dramas, either a series of almost disconnected scenes, like "Götz" and "Egmont," with an operatic termination like the latter, or united only by an abstract notion, not arising out of the dramatic idea, but essential to it, as in "Tasso" and in "Faust."

3. The lack of passionate expression and vigorous action, leading him to dwell upon descriptions of characters and scenes, rather than upon living actions and stirring events.

4. His inability to deal with the legitimate rules of dramatic art,—at one time leading him to set them aside altogether, at another time allowing him to be completely overmastered by them.

Of these cardinal defects some may be attributed to Goethe's nationality, while one, at least, namely, the lack of constructive power, must be ascribed to Goethe himself. As compared with the other leading nations of Europe, the Germans may be said to be an undramatic people, deficient in passionate expression, overflowing energy, and above

215

all in the keen dramatic sense of the ludicrous and incongruous,—which is the salt of active life and which is incompatible with their phlegmatic temperament and extreme sentimentality. That these national drawbacks were not necessarily fatal to a great

dramatic genius, when relieved by a strong constructive ability, was shown in the case of Schiller, and in a lower degree by Lessing and Iffland; all of whom, though inferior to Goethe in other respects, are superior to him as playwrights. Goethe's failure as a playwright, therefore, was due in large measure to his lack of constructive power,—that is, of the ability to hold many things together and reduce them to a living organism permeated by a dramatic current. This defect appears not only in Goethe's dramatic books, but also in his works,—notably in "Meister,"—and may account for his failure in the plastic and graphic arts. As a poet Goethe was essentially epic and lyric, but not dramatic. Germany owes him her best modern epic, namely, "Hermann and Dorothea," and a large number of the best lyrics in the language. And, in confirmation of this, it is a curious fact that Goethe's most perfect drama, "Iphigenie," is, like the Greek plays which he imitated, a combination of epic and lyric elements.

If we were to look into the facts and habits of Goethe's life for an explanation of his failure as a playwright, we might perhaps find it in three things: (1) his tendency to allow a long interval to elapse

216

between his first conception of a piece and its execution and completion, his views respecting life and art changing materially in the mean while; (2) his exceptional good fortune, which left him untouched by many forms of human experience; (3) his ever-increasing withdrawal from the world of human strife and suffering, which is pre-eminently the dramatic world. The first of these facts accounts for much that is fragmentary and inorganic in "Faust," while the second furnishes a sufficient reason for Goethe's inferiority as a playwright to the poor, much-tried Schiller, who during the most of his brief life was deep in the world's hardships and sufferings. It remains forever true, that "we learn in suffering what we teach in song."

But if, in a technical sense, we cannot speak highly of Goethe as a playwright, we must not fail to ac-

knowledge his other great merits in connection with the drama, and his abundant efforts to raise it from coarseness, conventionality, and thraldom to French ideas, and to make it an integral part of the national literature of Germany.

By his long-continued personal efforts in connection with the stage at Weimar, he raised the standard of acting in Germany, and by his admirable and sympathetic criticisms he elevated the standard of dramatic taste; and last, but not least, by introducing Shakespeare to the notice of his countrymen, he gave a lasting impulse for good to German literary effort and life.

217

Besides all these great merits, his failure as a playwright — insist upon it as we may and as we have a right to do — seems but a spot on the face of the sun, which we mention oftener in order to excuse something in ourselves, than to detract from the life-giving fulness of that luminary.

218

VIII. DAS EWIG-WEIBLICHE.

By Mrs. E. D. CHENEY.

> Alles Vergängliche
> Ist nur ein Gleichniss;
> Das Unzulängliche
> Hier wird's Ereigniss;
> Das Unbeschreibliche
> Hier ist es gethan,
> Das Ewig-Weibliche
> Zieht uns hinan.[1]
>
> FAUST, *close of the Second Part.*

THESE words are the ripened fruit of the whole study, thought, love, and life of the greatest poet and

[1] Translations: —

All that is changeable
 Is but a fable!
Lo, the intangible
Reached here and stable!
More than we humanly
Dreamed, here is done,
While the Aye Womanly
Wafteth us on.

The Indescribable
Here it is done,
The Ever Womanly
Beckons us on.

     J. S. DWIGHT.

All that doth pass away
 Is but a fable;
All that eludes is made
 Here true and stable.

All things transitory
But as symbols are sent;
Earth's Insufficiency
Here grows to event
The Indescribable
Here it is done, —
The Woman-Soul leadeth us
 Upward and on!

     BAYARD TAYLOR.

219

thinker of our century; of one who did not alone receive and repeat traditions of the past, — deeply as he studied their meaning, — but who fully accepted the scientific method of investigation, and dared to confront every question that suggested itself to his mind. They are not the expression of youthful fancy, nor the impulse of early passion. We may almost say they are the last important utterance of his mind, the climax of all his thought, all his experience. They are the final summing up in his thought of human life. Sin is forgiven, the meaning of this world's experience as symbol of eternity is declared, all that the human heart has longed for is promised, and the whole closes with the words that seem to include everything, —

> "Das Ewig-Weibliche
> Zieht uns hinan."

220

What a promise of continued life and fresh creation is there in these words! what abounding love, what infinite hope! They are the closing words of the great drama of "Faust."

Faust was the burden of Goethe's life, — a task long delayed, but never relinquished; and in the final Chorus into which the whole grand symphony is resolved, as the simple Hymn of Joy concludes Beethoven's glorious Ninth, occurs a noble fugue, and the same thought is repeated in differing form, as Faust is released from his slavery to evil and welcomed into new life. As in the First Part of "Faust" the Chorus of Angels and of Women first awaken human love and sympathy, so in the Second they again minister to him; and it is finally the same Margaret who asks to teach the soul escaping from sense and sin,[1] and it is the *Mater Gloriosa* who points out the path:

> "Komm hebe dich zu höhren Sphären!
> Wenn er dich ahnet, folgt er nach.[2]

[1] Vouchsafe to me that I instruct him:
  Still dazzles him the Day's new glare.
[2] Rise thou; to higher spheres conduct him,
  Who, feeling thee, shall follow there.

Let us pause to note that Goethe gives to his expression in this last verse the abstract form; he uses the neuter article and noun, — *Das Ewig-Weibliche.* It is not the masculine or feminine personified. The whole drama has been drawing out the most abstract ideas into expression in its varied and motley groups, and in the previous verse, Doctor Marianus has raised the feminine personality to its very utmost expression, — *Jungfrau* (maiden), *Mutter* (mother), *Königin* (queen), *Göttin* (goddess). But the mystic

221

Chorus goes a step further, and carries the thought out of personalities again into the supreme abstract idea of womanhood. This seems intentional on the poet's part. Faust has learned at last the meaning of mortal life, the value of human relations, but this is not the end. What has glorified and blessed it all becomes now immortal and infinite: it is no single loved one, but the Eternally Womanly which is henceforth to lead him upward and on.

We are tempted to ask, Did Goethe know what a great sentence he had penned? Did he mean all that can be extracted from this line? Every great poetic word is a flower which folds up in itself and brings to ripeness precious seed innumerable, and capable of producing even fairer flowers and richer fruit, and this was a flower of genius, full of infinite, inexhaustible meaning. Goethe himself says of the Second Part of Faust: "If it contains many problems, (inasmuch as, like the history of man, the last-solved problem ever produces a new one to solve,) it will nevertheless please those who understand by a gesture, a wink, a slight indication. They will find

And finally the Chorus Mysticus sums up the meaning of the drama in the pregnant lines:

> "Alles Vergängliche,
> Ist nur ein Gleichniss;
> Das Unzulängliche
> Hier wird's Ereigniss;
> Das Unbeschreibliche
> Hier ist es gethan,
> Das Ewig-Weibliche
> Zieht uns hinan."

in it more than I could give."

Doubtless this line sounded for years in Goethe's soul as a prophecy and inspiration, not as a rigid formula; but that he spoke it with full sense of its deep meaning and truth is plain from the place which he has given it, and the relation it bears to all his thought. It is not an isolated statement. It is not the dramatic utterance of an individual mind, it is the

222

word of the mystic chorus which sums up the whole drama of life. Goethe might have used the more general term; he might have sung the Divine Humanity which is expressed in Christian thought. Why does he find his true expression in "Das Ewig-Weibliche"? Why does he use this word, which implies difference of sex, and the eternally directing function of one aspect of the eternal thought, instead of employing a phrase that would express the whole?

Goethe's habitual thought was as far as possible from any Indian idea of reabsorption in Divinity and the loss of personality. He recognized that when a life was achieved, it became a living force,[1] although he questioned whether every apparent human life accomplished this purpose.[2] It is not, therefore, from any thought of the extinction of personality as the final consummation of life is approached, that Goethe uses this abstract term, but to express the essential nature of the power which he thus invokes. It is not the feminine in its manifestation, but in its original character.

223

In our effort to develop the meaning of this line, let us trace out, so far as brief limits will allow, Goethe's thought of Woman. In many an old mythologic story, Woman is the tempter, the embodiment of the material side of life, — that which prevents the soul from finding its true relation to the Divine. Can it be that this is the reversal of the truth? that it is by the influence of the womanly that man alone can be saved from being cut off from the Eternal, the Universal, the Divine, — from the only damnation possible, the breaking of the bond which binds all together? The light in which Woman is regarded is always significant of the philosophy and character of a people, and whether she is revered and honored as helper and sanctifier, or courted as a pleasure, or despised as an inferior, shows the quality of the soul. To man's feeling for Woman might well be applied Wordsworth's thoughtful lines:

"Who feels contempt for any living thing
Has faculties which he has never used,
And thought with him is in its infancy."

224

I find nowhere in Goethe's writings an expression of contempt for Woman as such. If there are any seeming exceptions, they are simply dramatic utterances, appropriate to the coarse or frivolous persons who utter them. But he does not shrink from as thorough analysis and as realistic treatment of women as of every other subject. He depicts women as he has seen and known them, studying them in all classes and conditions. We find the holy Saint, whose life is in rapt communion with God, — Mignon, who has wandered from some far-off land, an unbidden guest, and finds herself lost in this strange world, where even love fails her as a guide, — the stately Iphigenie, the practical Theresa, the commonplace Frau Melina, the unimpassioned Charlotte, — Lotte, the good sister, — the flippant Phillina, and Margaret, the child of Nature, — all are women, and he recognizes them as souls following out the law of their own natures, and influencing those with whom they are connected by force of character and will. They are not women alone, they are living wholes. He always recognizes the value of Woman's own life in relation with, but not simply as supplementary to, that of man. When he glorifies the household, it is not merely as a place for man to rest from past labors, and fit himself for new ones, but it is as the kingdom of the most precious life, to which all other service should be subordinate; — to rule here is to rule at the centre. That a woman's life should be fully wrought out from her own centre of being, is just as important as that a man's should be, — as is shown in Theresa, in Natalia, and in the whole tenor of his thought.

How earnestly he sought to understand Woman's life from her own stand-point, and not as men look at it, is shown by his interest in "The Confessions of a Fair Saint," which is introduced, seemingly somewhat irrelevantly, into his "Wilhelm Meister," though

225

she is found to have deeply influenced the other characters. It is a genuine experience of a woman's soul, of which a mystical religious feeling has taken possession, without driving out the natural thoughts and feelings of her sex. As such, he gives it without comment, as he might a scientific discovery. She is a striking instance of a most womanly woman finding ultimate satisfaction in spiritual life, without its full expression in human relations.

In an early article of Goethe's, published in 1772, when he was but twenty-three years old, appears his thought of the profound influence of Woman. It is a notice of the poems of a Polish Jew, who seems to have been a young and fickle lover. He says: "O Genius! be it publicly known that neither shallowness nor weakness is the cause of his fickleness. Let him but find a maiden who is worthy of him." Goethe then describes the maiden full of charms and home graces: —

"Should these two find each other, they at once divine what an embodiment of bliss each has secured in the other, and that they never can be parted. Then let him stammer — foreshadowing, hoping, enjoying — what none with words have ever spoken out, none with tears, none with the long lingering look and the soul in it. Truth and living beauty will then be in his songs, not the glittering baubles floating in so many German melodies."

[1] In a letter to Zelter, Goethe says: "Let us continue our work until one of us, before or after the other, returns to ether at the summons of the World Spirit! Then may the Eternal not refuse to us new activities, analogous to those wherein we have been tested! If He shall also add memory and a continued sense of the Right and the Good, in his fatherly kindness, we shall then surely all the sooner take hold of the wheels which drive the cosmic machinery." — Bayard Taylor's notes, p. 532.

[2] He said to Eckermann: "I do not doubt our permanent existence, for Nature cannot do without the entelechie. But we are not all immortal in the same fashion, and in order to manifest one's self in the future life as a great entelechie one must also become one." — Taylor, p. 516.

Lotte, in "The Sorrows of Werther," is one of those wonderful creations of genius whom you cannot analyze more than a beloved child. Grimm says:—

226

"Up to the time of her appearance, Klopstock's Fanny had been the highest ideal of womanhood in Germany; but Lotte at once won all hearts. After the appearance of Werther, young girls named Lotte refused to be called so any longer, feeling themselves unworthy to bear the name. . . . Lotte is the most simple and lovely German maiden, of whom nothing special is to be said. She enjoys dancing, she loves poetry, she *can be* enthusiastic; but she only needs to hear the slightest noise in the house, and she leaps down from the heavens into her wonted sphere, and is nothing but a housewife."

How sanitary must have been the influence which made this the ideal of German girls!

In Goethe's own life the influence of Woman predominates. His "Wahrheit und Dichtung aus meinem Leben," the review of his own development, dwells upon his relations of love and friendship to various women, far more than upon matters of statesmanship or learning. He was truly born of his mother's nature. Her traits are reproduced in him, while from his rich, pedantic father came the formality, the net-work of convention, the shell of worldly environment, which surrounded and obscured his life. Grimm says: "Goethe's father can be set aside: we do not need him to understand Goethe. But his mother is inseparable from him; she forms a part of his being; she understood him from the beginning, she divined him." Educated with his sister, a noble type of the intellectual woman, says Grimm, "he was from youth better acquainted with women than with men." But in spite, or more truly in consequence, of this strong influence from genuine women, Goethe was decidedly a masculine man. The feminine by its polarity developed the full force of his character. The calmness and self-poise, the absence of self-devotion in his nature, the joy in pursuit rather than fruitful delight in possession of the desired object, the centripetal force which made all

227

things serve him,—intellectual traits which led to the false appearance of moral selfishness and coldness in affection,—mark this development of the masculine. But they never prevented him from recognizing the great truth of that relation whose leadings he steadily followed through all his life and thought, until he expressed it in the immortal line,—

"Das Ewig-Weibliche
Zieht uns hinan."

It is for the truth of relation that we come into mortal existence,—not to know ourselves, not to save ourselves, not to be ourselves except in relation,—so that the individual is bound again to the universal. The relation of Man to Woman is typical of this great law. As light and darkness show forth each other, so Man and Woman are fully revealed only in their relation to each other. Throughout the universe, only relation is creative. Goethe sees that not identity; but union in difference, is the attitude of Man and Woman. When Man and Woman see each other, they begin to apprehend the Universe.

228

"When I saw thee, all other things
Appeared to me more bright;
I looked not on thee, but on them
In thy reflected light;
Nor knew if it were they or thou
That filled me with delight."

"When each the other loves, and loves himself no more."

Then each learns that its own self is not complete, can only be perfected by fitting itself to others, accepting the welfare of others as more its own than its own personality,—

This is love and piety; and the Masculine and Feminine, however embodied, do ever this service to each other. As a noble woman thus serves man, so says Dante,—

"The like in lady doth a man of worth."

Separation is the first step which makes creation, development, life, possible,—not one, but two. We must conceive of two before we can have relation, however we may still see that the two are one. How constantly this thought of relation runs through all Goethe's study and life! "Nothing is fair or good alone." It must be judged by all Grimm says, "Goethe was persuaded that all phenomena stand in mutual relation, and therefore nothing can be demonstrated by the study of isolated parts."

"Truly doth Nature all things tell,
Nature hath neither shell nor kernel,
Whole everywhere, at each point thou canst learn all;
Only examine thine own heart
Whether *thou* shell or kernel art."

229

"Wouldst thou truly study Nature,
Seek the whole in every feature."

Newton taught the doctrine of a definite number of independent colors; but with Goethe color is the relation between light and darkness; white is the color of light, and black of darkness. All its beauty and variety come from the fact that light is never wholly lost, darkness never wholly escaped. It is a grand generalization, if it has not yet been corroborated by analysis. So too, in his great biological discovery, he cannot accept an independent creation of leaf, flower, and seed. They stand in relation to each other not alone by mutual utility, but by development and the possibility of exchange of function and reconversion into each other.

"All in their forms are kindred, and yet no one like another;
So this wonderful choir points to a half-hidden law."

How deeply he felt the spiritual significance of this law, as running through all spheres of being, is shown by the poem which he addresses to his beloved one, in which he carries up the analogy from the plant to friendship and love. After a description of the flower, as scientifically true as it is poetic, he concludes:

"O, bethink thou then too, how, out of the germ of acquaintance,
Day by day between us mutual interest grew;
How in the depth of our hearts Friendship revealed its full power,
And how Love came last, bringing the blossoms and fruits.
Think what manifold hues and shapes, now this, now another,
Nature in quiet unfolds, and to our feelings imparts.
Now enjoy thyself fully to-day! for holy affection

230

Strives for its highest fruits, strives for congenial tastes,
Similar views of all things, that, through harmonious insight,
Firmly united, the pair thus the true heaven may find."

So the naturalist is prepared for the great mystery of sex, which we recognize to be neither identity nor unlikeness; for the sexes are like stamen and pistil, different modifications of the same type, and so perpetually varying that it is impossible to make any statement of distinguishing characteristics, which will be invariably true. We trace analogous polarity even in the inorganic world; yet although one may fancifully claim the sharp acid or the inert base as dimly representing one or the other sex, no one will seriously claim that this distinction is clearly recognizable, for the characteristic function of creation is not found. In the vegetable world, where the function is in many cases performed by the whole organism, it is difficult to trace any clear lines; but as we find more developed specimens, the functions of parts become more distinct; the root will no longer perform the duty of the leaf, nor the leaf that of the flower. In the more complex classes of both the vegetable and animal world, we separate the sexes broadly by the functions of reproduction; and these are generally accompanied by secondary characteristics, in many cases so strongly marked as at once to indicate sex. But throughout these kingdoms, these secondary characteristics are very changeable. The females excel in size in the lower orders, and either sex in brilliancy and depth of color according to their sur-

231

roundings. Among fishes the male often builds the nest and cares for the young,— in some cases even on his own body. The female is capable of as great violence as the male, and the male, under stress of circumstances, can be as devoted and tender as the mother. In the animal world sex is less differentiated in the lowest forms of life; but the analogy does not hold in the spiritual world. In the highest types of human life, we always find a blending of the characteristics of the sexes. The illustrations are almost too numerous for selection.

Jesus, Buddha, Fénelon, Dürer, Charles Lamb,— even Michel Angelo and Dante,— blend strong feminine traits with their masculine powers; and no less in Deborah and Zenobia, in Joan of Arc, Isabella of Castile, Elizabeth Frye, Lucretia Mott, and Margaret Fuller, do we find their full womanliness reinforced by powers commonly esteemed masculine. In our own immediate circle we can easily trace out the same law; we find the boy-girl and the girl-boy in almost every family. The father of the Fair Saint "often with suppressed joy called her his misfashioned son." Coleridge expresses the greatest scorn for the man who recognizes no sex in soul; but the difference is so subtile that it has never been well stated in words. And yet so rooted in thought is this distinction that the most religious souls have felt the necessity of recognizing it as existing within the bosom of Divinity itself. Theodore Parker would not accept Coleridge's dictum, because he knew that

232

in a semi-barbarous civilization, such as ours still is, it became the pretext for a claim of sovereignty, and a power of oppression; but he felt the necessity of expressing the thought in the beautiful formula with which he was wont to begin his prayer: "O God! our father and our mother both." So the apostle of the Brahmo Somaj,— the most original and sincere religious movement of our day, though it be still vague and undefined, like its Indian predecessors,— recognizes this truth, and the Divine Maternity is one of the leading doctrines of its faith. In fact, this idea, mystically expressed in so many old mythologies, is to be the guiding star of the better civilization yet to come. George Sand says, in one of her letters, "There is but one sex"; yet in spite of her masculine name the *ewig-weibliche* is revealed not only in the motherly heart, but in the longing for human love and the infinite tenderness for humanity expressed in all her work.

How easy to accept, but how impossible to carry out, the distinction of sex in the spiritual life! In externals, in the realm of form, it is easy enough to

make divisions, but in any finer sense it can only be felt, no analysis has ever been keen enough to detect it. In intellectual life this is shown by the constantly repeated occurrence of the fact that woman's mental work has been wholly accepted as that of man. Three of the greatest novelists of our time, George Sand, George Eliot, and Currer Bell, while known only by the products of their genius, found

233

no eyes keen enough to detect their feminine traits. Thackeray, an eminently masculine man, was sure George Eliot was of his sex. Dickens was the first to detect her secret. The acute critics of Jena declared "Agnes von Lilien," written by Caroline von Lengefeld, to be an anonymous work of Goethe, the master mind of Germany. In our own society Charles Egbert Craddock found no recognition as a woman till she appeared in person to her astonished publishers. Had the same outward reasons existed to lead Edgar Poe, or Charles Lamb, or Dickens, to masquerade under a woman's name, we might have found the caprice and unregulated fancy of woman in "The Raven," the tender sensibility and beauty of her sex in "The Essays of Elia," and the warm humanity, the morbid sentimentality, and the utter incapacity of woman to represent the passion of love, in "Oliver Twist" and "Little Dorrit."

Hermann Grimm, in his "Essay on Goethe and Suleika," tells a remarkable and pleasing instance of such an interchange of thought between Goethe and his young beloved friend, Marianne von Willemer. Grimm quoted as one of Goethe's finest poems the song,

"Ach, um deine feuchten Schwingen
West, wie sehr ich dich beneide,"

and found to his amazement that it was written by the lady; and he says, "The Divan from which this poem was taken was almost carried on like a duet between them." Yet who has distinguished

234

the masculine and feminine voices in the various lines?

Open any book in physiology, and it is set down for you in broad characters, "Man is strong, reasonable, governed by his judgment; Woman is weak, emotional, swayed by her feelings." But take this formula with you as your chart in active life, and you will soon find it a delusive cheat. Witness the excitement of the Stock Exchange, and the ease with which a cyclone of confidence draws all men into its fatal grasp, or a sudden blast of doubt scatters the trust of the whole business community. Even the British House of Commons, the sanest body of men in the world, goes into wild delirium at the defeat of a liberal ministry. After thirty years' experience in various reformatory and benevolent works where men and women took part together, I have never been able to trace a dividing line, on one side of which were the men guided by judgment, and on the other the women swayed by feeling. Goethe's men are very men, and his women always women, yet he has given us almost every shade of character in womanly form. In "Elective Affinities," Ottilie is so absolutely feminine, according to the recognized type, that she is unfit for human life; like Ophelia, she has no self-directing power, and is crushed by the world about her, as the simple pressure of the common air breaks the fragile glass, exhausted of its resisting medium. In her exquisite purity and loveliness sin cannot

235

touch her, yet she is incapable of virtue, and can only fly from the battle which she is unable to win. Charlotte, too, is womanly, in her calm sense, her cold unselfishness, ready to resign all her rights, all her happiness, to another's wishes, or a sense of duty; but by that very want of self-assertion, incapable of strengthening others, and holding them to good by the bond of justice. And what has Edward of the Masculine but that self-centring thought which in its good and evil is characteristic of man? The puzzle of the book is in his unfitness to mate with the lovely girl. Sweetness of temper, a crystalline frankness of manner, refinement of deportment, and a capacity for intellectual enjoyment, make him a delightful companion. His early attraction to Charlotte is renewed when both are freed from outward constraint, and can look forward to a life of intellectual companionship and aesthetic enjoyment. How devoid of passion the relation is, becomes evident from Charlotte's having planned his marriage with Ottilie. But Charlotte is very wise in her own domain, and she knew well the danger of destroying this happy balance of friendship. Without jealousy on her part, it is his friend's introduction into the home which she opposes, not Ottilie's. She is the self-restrained, reasonable being; he is the rash and self-willed one, who will let nothing stand between him and his desire. And it is this warmth of desire alone which redeems his nature: he does recognize that the beloved one is more than himself;

236

and this alone makes it comprehensible that Goethe can recognize an eternal union for them. "So lie the lovers, sleeping side by side. Peace hovers above their resting-place. Fair angel faces gaze down upon them from the vaulted ceiling, and what a happy moment that will be when one day they wake again together." He has blindly loved, but he has recognized Love, and

"Das Ewig-Weibliche
Zieht *ihn* hinan."

Tasso is more poetic and lovely than Edward, but is he not equally self-centred? His life is not wrecked on sensual desire, but on the morbid sensitiveness of his soul, which never enters into the life of others, into the generous activity of the Duke, or calm wisdom of Antonio, but measures everything by himself. His love was as narrow as the learning of Faust. He had not learned the secret of relation. The Princess sees his need:—

"Willst du genau erfahren was sich ziemt
So frage nur bei edlen Frauen an."[1]

She will have him find, in a love that gives itself wholly up, the freedom that he needs. Antonio also sees his need of relation, but bids him seek it in active life:

"Der Mensch erkennt sich nur im Menschen; nur
Das Leben lehret jedem was er sey."[2]

237

"Wilhelm Meister" is the study of the development of a human mind. What a part does Woman play in it! Goethe seems striving to find the true type of Woman to call forth the noblest in man. How loving, fresh, and natural is poor Mariana! Wilhelm's boyish affection rashly indulged, and as he believes betrayed, is never forgotten, and only through this love is the joy of paternity known. The wise men say, "The child is thine, and in our opinion the mother was not unworthy of thee." He never fully loves again, but is ever seeking for this lost Eden of unconscious trusting affection. His feeling for Mariana was loving, fresh, and genuine, but regardless of law and duty to others. It was like his passion for the stage: when the illusion passed, much of the truth and poetry went also, yet it left behind remorse never silenced, and regret never satisfied. How striking is the tenacity of this feeling, and the facility with which a fancied resemblance makes him believe that a fateful past can be recalled! Varying impulses play over him, yet there is an evident progress in the development of his ideal. He enjoys only superficially the toying of Phillina, sensuous and graceful as it is. She only "pressed to the door of his heart, but never entered." He meets with fatherly care the unearthly love of Mignon; he longs to bring into his life the strong practical good-sense of Theresa; he is fascinated by the beauty of the Countess, the spiritual grace of Natalia,— but they are only shadows of things to come, which never come. He

238

is ever a scholar, trying all phases of life. He has never become a Man, and so has never found his true relation to Woman. Yet keeping his ideal high and pure, we still watch for his unfolding, sure that the Eternally Womanly is leading him up. In Macaria, who appears only towards the conclu-

[2] Man knows himself only in Men; only Life
Teaches every one what he is.

[1] Do you wish to learn truly what is becoming,
Ask it only of noble women.

sion of "Wilhelm Meister's Wanderjahre," (if there be a conclusion to a work so wandering,) we have a type of woman whose influence approaches that of "das Ewig-Weibliche." She has nothing of the attributes of passion, the sensuousness of sex; but by her unselfish wisdom, by the power which she has gained from suffering and thought, to look clearly upon human affairs in their largest relations, she becomes confessor and counsellor to all within her range,—always leading them to be true to themselves, while in her "light do they see light." This function belongs to the post-maternal period of life, and has ever been recognized in the Virgin becoming the Seeress. Macaria's mystical relations to heavenly bodies indicate the universal reach of her influence and central source of her inspirations.

The deep sense of the overpowering sanctity and importance of the relation of Man to Woman appears in many of the minor dramas, I might perhaps say in all of them. Goethe places it in every light. Eugenia, in "Die Natürliche Tochter," finds herself suddenly placed in an exceptional position. She will be raised above the multitude by rank and power. She grasps at the outward signs of it; to find it slipping from her grasp. She has been false to the relation of the individual to the whole, and the whole, represented by the Church and the State, threatens to crush her. How can she be saved? Only by the acceptance of the marriage relation, whose sanctity and power are set forth by the simple burgher:

"Im Hause wo der Gatte sicher waltet,
Da wohnt allein der Friede, den vergebens
In weiten du, da draussen suchen magst." [1]

And again:

"Als Gatte kann ich mit dem König rechnen." [2]

He too recognizes the function of the wife:

"So führt ein edles Weib ihn leicht ans Ziel.

[1] In the house where the husband surely directs,
There alone dwells peace, which in vain in the distance
Thou out there in the world mayst seek.
[2] As husband can I reckon with the king.

240

Hinauf zur höchsten Frauen kehr er sich." [3]

The marriage which can save is of the heart and soul, as the monk expresses it:

"Den Wunsch der Liebe, die zum All das Eine,
Zum Ewigen das Gegenwärtige
Das Flüchtige zum Dauernden erhebt,
Den zu erfüllen ist sein göttlich Amt." [4]

In the Old Harper's history we have the unconscious violation of a natural law, bringing intense tragedy, but not destruction of inward purity. In "Die Geschwister" we have the sweet regard of a sister unconsciously intensified by the difference of sex, and changed into happy love when the true relation is revealed. In "Die Wette," a pretty little comedy, the lighter characteristics of the two sexes are very pleasantly painted, and the lesson of mutual forbearance and concession gently taught.

In "Clavigo," Goethe reproduces in tragic form what was not so tragic, his love for Frederika; and here is the same thought which ever haunted him,—it is the womanly which tests man. Clavigo had failed to stand this test, had been untrue to love, and only tragedy is possible. Repentance does not help. The young, romantic heart does not accept any salving of sores, any of nature's processes of filling up chasms with new growth. Repentance cannot heal this sin, for no reparation is possible; relation is broken, faith is destroyed. Even in the moment of hoped for reunion, Marie recognizes that the old tie cannot be restored. Clavigo has passed into another mood: the opportunity is gone. Death alone, resolving the mortal back into the immortal, can restore this relation, and only when the Eternally Womanly leads him upward can he leave sin behind? So also in "Stella," Fernando has placed himself in the conflict between passionate love and recognized self-imposed duty. He has dared to play with this greatest of

[3] So does a noble wife easily lead him to the goal.
Up to the highest women does he strive.
[4] The wish of Love, which raises one to the All, the present to the Eternal, the fleeting to the Everlasting, that to fulfil is her godlike office.

human relations, and he is overwhelmed by the forces he has set in motion. For this wrong no earthly reparation is possible; property may be restored, slander may be refuted, anger may be atoned for, but this wrong cannot be righted. No unselfishness, no magnanimity, on the part of his victims, avails aught: each would sacrifice to the other, but neither can give what she cannot hold, and only Death, which dissolves all earthly ties, can make new life possible. In the novelettes in "Wilhelm Meister," Goethe seems to put this relation of love and marriage in every possible light: they are like the changes of a kaleidoscope, beautiful but fleeting. He seems to warn against his own besetting sin of mistaking the transient for the permanent. With this intense feeling of the mission of love and the sanctity of marriage, Goethe himself never had a full and perfect relation to a woman. The force of his being was expended in those transitory affections which, as Tennyson says,

"Are but embassies of love
To tamper with the feelings, ere he found
Empire for life."

242

With Frau von Stein his intellectual yearning for sympathy found full satisfaction, and his Christiane gave him for a time the homelike content, more often known in the cottager's hut than in the palace, which he had never had before. But the tragedy of his life, so often referred to as a wonderfully fortunate one, was just here. He never found the true family life, and, as husband and father, shared little of the joy which makes so many humble lives infinitely blessed. Is it for this reason that he has never been able to paint a successful, happy love, but in the simplicity of peasant life in "Hermann und Dorothea," or "Die Geschwister," or in the dim perspective of history in Götz and his faithful wife?

In his own life, domestic love took on a very quiet and humble form. How his heart must have longed for this life,—he who was so sensitive to tenderness, and had such a thirst for human relation! Where shall we find a more concise and comprehensive ex-

pression of family love and life as representing the eternal mysteries of creation, than in the words of the Chorus after the birth of Euphorion?

"Love in human wise to bless us
In a noble pair must be;
But divinely to possess us
It must form a precious Three."

And the all-sufficiency of Love is told in simplest words:

"All we seek has therefore found us,
I am thine and thou art mine;
So we stand as Love hath bound us,
Other fortune we resign."

In the family is the most perfect expression of the Eternal Trinity, that great mystic doctrine running through many religions, which has been so dwarfed and narrowed by being made individual and dogmatic. But it runs as the simplest, plainest law through mechanics and chemistry, as well as biology and met-

243

aphysics,—the One, the Two, the resulting Third,—the union of differences in likeness producing a new creation. Goethe saw this, and if he fails to paint it fully, it is because he had not known it in his own experience.

In the First Part of "Faust," the great work in which Goethe sought to read the riddle of life, failing, as all will fail till life is fully accomplished, *das Weibliche* is the moving power. Faust is the unrelated man, devoted to knowledge only for himself. He exhausts every source of learning and thought, only to find himself wholly unfed and unsatisfied, and is ready to grant any terms on which he may secure a consciousness of life and joy. He makes the hasty compact to buy what a true faith would have given him. Woman by her beauty first calls him out of himself, and he seeks union with others. In the First Part he asks only his personal gratification, and he cannot enter into true relation with others, for he has not found himself. He is the sport of unformed desires, he does not recognize the necessity or beauty of law. The Devil is his guide, the incarnate spirit that denies. How can he lead him to true love?

It is the simplest feeling of attraction to a person, not any ideal relation to the universal, which leads him on.

Heedlessly he breaks the highest law of love, which bids us seek not our own good, but the welfare of the beloved; and the human law which should represent the inward principle revenges itself upon him.

244

How? Not by direct infliction of outward punishment, but through the misery of the beloved one. Woman's misery, man's degradation, is the result of the broken law of love. The redeemer buys with his own sacrifice the redemption he works for others.

Faust is still free to follow his selfish course; but never again unconsciously: the gadfly of conscience is aroused, which will not cease to sting him till he is elevated into true life. Yet in spite of his selfishness and sin he has loved; he has recognized that self is not all; he has known the highest human relation; he has acknowledged the existence of something not himself, yet to which he is eternally bound. So he is led out of abstraction into personality. Even through sin, still more through suffering, he has learned the lesson of relation to others, which in the Second Part is to be worked out, not in the simplicity of individual love, but on the broad scale of Humanity. Through all the wild masquerading of its many scenes, we find him learning this lesson. He seeks to become a benefactor to mankind, but at first how wildly,—with the help of the Devil! The scheme of spreading universal happiness by producing an abundance of paper money, devised by Mephistopheles and since followed by his successors, while it is undoubtedly a satire on South Sea and other wild financial schemes, may also fitly represent that selfish benevolence which finds pleasure in beholding the transient enjoyment of those around us, whether it is based on good or evil. The women see the char-

245

latanry of the great mask, and mock at the false magician who is—nothing; not even feeling when one pinches him. Here in homely form is a hint of the quality of Woman which is expressed in the

last line. The Womanly tests life by a more delicate analysis than masculine logic supplies. Woman considers things in their relations. This is the quality of judgment which we recognize as specially womanly, and which has been manifested on a large scale by queens and empresses, as in every-day life in the management of a household and the control of children.

The mystical charm with which Goethe loved to surround the feminine, while keeping its peculiar function ever in mind, is shown by his introduction of the Mothers in "Faust." This passage has been the despair of commentators. An obscure phrase in Plutarch, calling the Goddesses "the Mothers," seems to have excited his imagination, and he uses this term as the most powerful and suggestive of names, without feeling called upon to offer any explanation of it. Yet it has a power for Faust, and a terror even for Mephistopheles, who may well feel it to be utterly outside of his realm. The various metaphysical analyses of this phrase seem very wide of the mark; it is the all-including comprehensiveness of the expression which gives it a charm and terror. As the little child believes that the mother can answer all questions and satisfy all wants, is it strange that man should come back to a longing for the motherly

246

power? Goethe has said, "Express thyself, and 't will a riddle be,"—this simplest of all words is full of mystery and terror. Why should Faust be appalled at their very name? What is the meaning of the key which is to lead him to them? Is the key the childlike trust which Faust has lost, and which would make motherhood an attraction, and not a terror? When we can carry our desires into the presence of the Divine Motherhood, they must have become righteous and holy. Faust goes to the mothers to grant the fulfilment of his longing for beauty and love.

Here his escape from the power of Mephistopheles seems to begin. It has already become another love than that to which Mephistopheles first led him. It is not he in his individual being who is

wedded to a beautiful maiden. It is the spirit of his country, German thought, which seeks after Greek beauty, and from this union is born the modern poet. This love does not become tragic in its results, like his attraction to Margaret; it is indeed only an image of love, but it truly represents it as not for themselves alone, but for the whole of Humanity.

If we take Helena in the literary sense for Classic culture, while Faust represents the German, may not the appeal to the Mothers represent that return to the old primitive thought, the universal source, which always accompanies every new radical movement in thought? We must relate our special movement to the universal, and the new must strike its roots deep

247

into the old. It seems hopeless to attempt to fathom the precise meaning with which Goethe uses this phrase, yet it is certain that it meant a great deal to him, and that when interpreted by his own voice and manner it strongly impressed others. Eckermann writes:—

"To-day, as a supplement to the dinner, Goethe gave me a great enjoyment by reading to me the scene where Faust goes to the Mothers. The new, unsuspected character of the subject, together with the tone and manner in which Goethe recited the scene, took hold of me with wonderful power, so that I found myself at once in the condition of Faust, who feels a shudder creep over him when Mephistopheles makes the communication. I had heard and clearly comprehended the description, but so much of it remained enigmatical to me that I felt myself forced to beg Goethe to enlighten me a little. He however, according to his usual habit, assumed a mysterious air, looking at me with wide-open eyes, and repeating the words,—

'The Mothers! Mothers! It sounds so strange.'"

This Second Part of "Faust" seems at first like a wild chaos. In it are the riches of a hundred dramas, but it is not crystallized into clearness and symmetry. It was Goethe's study of life, and he could not marshal it all into line, as a lesser man might do his lesser riches. Yet there is one simple thought running through it all, and, as he expresses it in the last grand verse, we see it is the plainest

religious truth,—that which enters into every faith,—that which underlies the beautiful in art, the ideal in

248

philosophy, the essence of morality, the meaning of life. It is the sense of the relation of the individual to the universal. We never think, never can think, of the feminine alone. It is not what separates her from others, but what gives the power of union, which makes her feminine, and so creative. And the masculine knows itself only in its relation to the feminine. So it is that the eternally feminine "draws us by sweet leadings" of beauty to love, to union, to new creation. But in using these words, we must remember that these human forms which we live among, and which fit past us like the changing phantoms in Goethe's half-mocking drama, are but shadows and types. Sex, as we see it gradually evolved out of the chemical relations of the mineral world, the fertilization of flowers, the wooing of the oriole and the bobolink in the spring-time, the chivalry of the cock, and the fierce jealousy of the tiger, to its beautiful outcome in the highest human relation, which is the never-wearying theme of romance and poetry, is a shadowing forth of the duality in the original spirit out of which comes the creative energy manifested in the universe. As we have seen, this double strand is woven in and out throughout nature, and in trying to trace it we are constantly bewildered by finding its place and attitude changing. We cry, "Lo here! and, Lo there!" but like the kingdom of God, it is within us and found everywhere. If it represents duality, it equally represents unity and universality, and we may as well

divide the rainbow by arbitrary lines, as seek to put asunder those differing phases of His creative agency which God has so closely joined together. Yet the difference of sexes is as expressive and necessary as their unity, and their functions cannot be confounded. Mythology has made woman the representative of attraction to evil, because it had not learned that life is good; but Goethe's inspired Muse,

249

who knew that secret, and held the Faust to be redeemed who had at last found it good, taught that woman leads indeed through varied and dangerous paths, but still leads to life; and it is a grand acceptance of life, and its experience and its teachings, which bids him close his great drama with a recognition of this truth,—*Das Ewig Weibliche zieht uns hinan.*

N O T E.

As the various reports of the School have made it apparent that the doctrine of this lecture was misunderstood, I have added the following Synopsis:—

There is, even in the Divine Nature, as we are forced to conceive it, a polarity, or power of differentiation which is eternal,—*ewig.*

This polarity running through all nature, even the inanimate and inorganic, appears as sex,—suggested in the vegetable kingdom, and slowly evolved in the

250

animal world, taking its most complete form in the Human Being.

Its distinctive characteristics appear as impulse and attraction. Its function is creation, and while the masculine is stimulating and life-giving, the feminine is receptive and productive.

This central difference, complicated with all the circumstances of existence, produces many secondary characteristics illustrative of sex; but these secondary characteristics are in the process of evolution unstable and interchangeable. These principles, though separated in our ultimate thought, are constantly blended in manifestation. Nature works to produce embryo wholes, and not ever-widening monstrosities. Hence, while our ideal of *das männliche* and *das weibliche* may be sharply defined as force and attraction, or centrifugal and centripetal, or Justice and Mercy, its manifestation in persons is rarely distinct; but by the double descent the two are blended in every individual, and in the highest natures the most perfectly.

The office of mortal life is to develop the spiritual nature by the constant manifestation, action, and reaction of these principles on each other, so as to attain the widest universality, and the most perfect unity. They play an equal part in the great drama of Life; but as the feminine represents attraction, this is the leading principle which draws us upward and on.

251

IX.

THE ELECTIVE AFFINITIES.

By S. H. EMERY, JR.

THIS special creation of the great artist, whose genius and work are the principal theme of this session of the Summer School of Philosophy, belongs to that particular form of art which is named "The Novel." Perhaps it is the only work of our author which can properly be so classified. Goethe himself seems to have been in doubt about the appropriateness of the title to this work, for he is reported by Eckermann as saying, with reference to the sketch of the Child and the Lion, called "A Tale" in Dr. Hedge's edition of Goethe's Works:—

"I'll tell you what, we will call it 'The Novel'; for what is a novel but a peculiar and as yet unheard-of event? This is the proper meaning of this name; and much which in Germany passes as a novel is no novel at all, but a mere narrative, or whatever else you like to call it. In that original sense of an unheard-of event, even the 'Elective Affinities' may be called a novel."

Goethe's definition of the novel does not distinguish it from the romance, nor from short tales and

252

sketches, such as the work the name for which he was considering. A brief consideration of the place of the novel in the system of art is not impertinent here.

The novel, as a work of art, belongs to the domain of Poetry, and therefore, so far as the material it uses is concerned, is capable of the most complete expression of the highest ideal in art. It has the external characteristics of the prose form, but is essentially poetic. Goethe says that the "Elective Affinities" is a poetic production. The fundamental art element in poetry is not the rhyme, the rhythm, or the harmony of the verse, but the image. The true is therein represented in an image; not an actually existent, external, spatial image, but an internal form of the imagination,—"images preserved in the spirit and recalled by it"; this makes the whole in the part. Art manifests the whole in the part. This fundamental element of art is the basis of the novel in point of form.

In point of content, it belongs to that phase of art which is called by Hegel "Romantic Art." It portrays the individual working out the problem of his spiritual development,—either, on the one side, subjective passions, caprices, desires, even good but mistaken intentions, on the other side the universal and eternal verities, into harmony with which the individual must come; or, with equal validity, on the one side the universal and eternal as realized in the individual spirit, on the other side, the exter-

253

nally capricious and accidental: but in either case it portrays a struggle for spiritual harmony.

The novel proper is of modern English origin, dating from about the beginning of the eighteenth century. It is distinguished from the romance, which is a narrative of wonders, strange, improbable events; while the novel accommodates itself, for the most part, to ordinary society and the ordinary course of human affairs, seeking to draw attention to, and excite our interest in, the collisions of the subjective with the objective. A writer in the Encyclopedia Britannica mentions as a fact that the rise of the novel is coincident with the decline of the drama, and attributes both to the change in the spirit of the age. Goethe in "Meister" expresses the true distinction between the novel and the drama in point of content and method. He says:—

"In the novel as well as in the drama, it is human nature and human action that we see. ... But in the novel it is chiefly sentiments and events that are exhibited; in the drama it is character and deeds. The novel must go slowly forward, and the sentiments of the hero, by one means or another, must restrain the tendency of the whole to unfold itself and to conclude. The drama, on the other hand, must hasten, and the character of the hero must press forward to the end; it does not restrain, but is restrained."

There can be no doubt that for the modern English mind the novel is a more effective form of art than the drama; perhaps because the novel, as being

254

nearer to the verge of art, is better adapted to a prosaic age and nation. The wider range of incident and more minute analysis of character are more in accordance with the disposition and taste of a highly civilized people, than the strong situations and powerful effects which are necessary to the drama. The picture of life presented is also more true to the present reality, and therefore takes hold of the interest more readily.

The "Elective Affinities" has then a special interest, as an example of a form of art more distinctively peculiar than any other to our time, and to the English consciousness. I have said, also, that it is perhaps the only work of our author which is, strictly speaking, a novel, as we ordinarily understand the term. The novel proper falls between the romance and the disquisition, and the "Elective Affinities" seems to occupy this middle ground more consistently than any other work of Goethe. It has a variety of place, time, action, and persons, to distinguish it from a sketch or tale; it presents a picture of life, which seems true to the ordinary conditions of the place and time wherein the scene is laid; its incidents are for the most part commonplace, rather than romantic, in the sense of startling, wonderful, unreal; and its story does not impress the reader as a merely artificial and external thread, on which the author has strung disquisitions upon every imaginable subject. On the contrary the story furnishes, as

in a novel it should, the necessary field for the collisions sought to be portrayed. A critic has said of Goethe's novels generally:—

255

"They are ingenious speculations on painting, agriculture, landscape-gardening, etc., connected by a thread of mystical narrative, and introducing us to a set of beings without the least trace of reality about them, who all appear to be playing some theatrical part in a dreamy representation of life, which seems to have no intelligible object."

But this criticism is entirely inappropriate to the "Elective Affinities," though that has episodical passages, which might be called "ingenious speculations" on gardening, architecture, painting, chemistry, and other subjects; and it doubtless in a deep way justifies Goethe's statement that it is a novel because it is a before unheard-of event. The critic proceeds to say:—

256

"A novel which does not explain its purpose without a commentary seems to violate the essential laws of such compositions; but a novel in regard to the object of which no two commentators agree, is an anomaly in literature."

If this criticism were to be accepted as final, it would dispose of the claim of the "Elective Affinities" to be considered a novel, for there has certainly been a wide disagreement among the commentators as to its purpose; but it very naturally occurs to one that this result may rather be the fault of the commentators than of the novel. It must have been surprising to Goethe, for he seems to have doubted whether he had not made his meaning too plain, to the detriment of his art. Soret reports him as saying,—

"The only production of greater extent, in which I am conscious of having labored to set forth a pervading idea is probably my 'Elective Affinities.' This novel has thus become comprehensible to the understanding; but I will not say that it is therefore better. I am rather of the opinion, that the more incommensurable and the more incomprehensible to the understanding a poetic production is, so much the better it is."

You will notice that Goethe's conception of the proper aim of the artist in this regard differs fundamentally from that of his critic; hence, it is not surprising that the critic should not have been pleased with the results.

With these preliminary general observations we will proceed to an examination of the "sentiments and events" which Goethe has portrayed in the "Elective Affinities," reserving our consideration of the special content of this novel for the conclusion. We have it on the authority of Goethe, that the novel was written with a conscious pervading purpose, and we must try to ascertain what the purpose was, or better, perhaps, what has really been done; for the purpose in and of itself might be accidental and temporary.

257

The title "Elective Affinities" Goethe justifies, early in the work, in a conversation between Edward, Charlotte, and the Captain, in the course of which it is explained that "elective affinity" is the technical scientific term applied to those instances of chemical action where, on the presentation to a compound substance of a third, one of the elements of the compound will leave its combination and combine with the third, thus exhibiting a natural election between the two possible combinations. The most important and remarkable cases of this action are where the separation and uniting are both double; that is, where two compounds, on being brought together, each divide and reunite with change of partners. This is chemically analogous to what sometimes happens in human society, when the casual introduction of a third person utterly destroys a connection, apparently indissoluble, between two, through presenting opportunity for a new and naturally more urgent combination; but Charlotte warns us that man is placed many steps above chemical elements, and that he will do well to consider carefully the validity of the analogy as applied to himself. The incidents of the novel exhibit the workings of a double elective affinity in the human sphere: hence the name. The scene of the story is the estate of a German nobleman, and the time probably contemporaneous with the writing. Neither year nor real location is anywhere mentioned.

Solger wrote, in a letter to Tieck, an elaborate criticism of the "Elective Affinities," which interested and pleased Goethe, who says, "It would not be easy to say anything better about that novel." In the

258

course of this critical survey Solger said, "The facts of the 'Elective Affinities' had their germ in the nature of all the characters." We will therefore consider the principal characters before examining the incidents. They interest us, not only in themselves, but as general types.

Edward was the only, and consequently spoiled, child of wealthy parents, from whom large possessions had descended to him. In early life he had met and loved Charlotte, who loved him. He married, however, through the persuasion of his parents and while dissatisfied with Charlotte's reserve, a wealthy lady far older than himself, who petted and indulged him in every way, and, dying, left him free, in the prime of life, to return to Charlotte, whom he married; and he is introduced at the beginning of the story as living with Charlotte alone, soon after their marriage, at his ancestral castle. He is apparently "equal to all contingencies and changes, with desires never excessive, but multiple and various; free-hearted, generous, brave, at times even noble"; he has had large experience of life, at court, in the army, and in travelling, but has never been thwarted, and has not learned self-restraint. His return to Charlotte was due to a sort of romantic remembrance of their early love, and to a desire to settle down quietly to a delicious leisure with a pleasant companion, rather than to a strong, absorbing passion. He is of good disposition, and has not fallen into vices, but he has little constancy or perseverance; even his

259

flute-playing is not good, because, although he would for a little while prosecute it with industry, he would soon tire of the effort. His favorite method of decision as to courses of action, where decision is difficult,

is to submit the matter to chance. He is amiable and considerate, but impulsive, ardent, and youthful; without substantial character, settled convictions, or high purposes. He is in danger of becoming a drunkard when things go against him. He has never learned to forego his immediate desire, is vehement and obstinate, and thinks life valueless unless he can have what, at the moment, seems to him a necessity of his nature. Hence, he is essentially extravagant, sacrificing always the distant to the near. He prefers death to disappointment in love. Goethe says, speaking of Solger's criticism of Edward:—

"I do not quarrel with him because he cannot endure Edward. I myself cannot endure him, but was obliged to make him such a man in order to bring out my fact. He is, besides, very true to nature; for you find many people in the higher ranks with whom, quite like him, obstinacy takes the place of character."

Charlotte is a quite opposite character. She is a prudent, wise, fore-looking person. Her instincts are conservative and tenacious of institutional requirements, and she recognizes that the family is woman's special institution. She is domestic, careful, and economical; she keeps the accounts and pays the bills. Perhaps she is more excitable and quicker to feel

260

even than Edward, but with power of self-restraint, and always ready to subordinate her feelings to her judgment. She does not willingly allow herself to be surprised into emotion. With tact and self-possession to see and do the right thing in any emergency she unites self-sacrifice, so that she is willing to do what she believes to be right, at whatever cost to herself; with fortitude also, so that she can insist upon the present suffering of those she loves, for their ultimate best good, even in spite of their shrinking, added to the pain of her own heart. She is a constant and reserved, not a passionate and effusive, lover. One can believe that when she gave her hand, after Edward's first marriage, without any special motive, to an excellent man, whom she could respect if she could not love, she did it, not because she

had forgotten Edward, but because she thought it unwise to sacrifice her life to a hopeless passion. It would seem that she should have been a devoted mother, yet she is not; and possibly Goethe means thereby to intimate that maternal love and devotion are dependent upon supreme love for the father, which was lacking in Charlotte's case. However this may be, Charlotte is a conscientious mother, but not passionately fond of her children. Her chief weakness lies in allowing herself to be over-persuaded against her instincts and judgment. When Edward returned to her, and urged marriage, she hesitated: she felt that it was not prudent; that during the interval of their separation she had outgrown him,

261

though they were of about the same age, and that the love of their youth had changed to friendship; yet his urgent solicitation overcame her doubts. So too when Edward impulsively proposed the introduction of a third person into their home, she said, "My feeling is against this plan; I have an instinct which tells me no good will come of it"; yet she yielded From these two concessions arise the complications of the story.

The Captain is a man of affairs, reserved, laconic, sedate, accomplished, and self-restrained. Up to the time when Edward invites him to the castle, he has found no situation in life which he considers worthy of his own ability and accomplishments; and although he is not wealthy, finding strict economy and occasional assistance from his friend Edward necessary to the maintenance of his accustomed style of living, he will not accept offered positions which seem to him not suitable to enlist all his energies, in directions where he can accomplish substantial, permanent benefit to the world. He is orderly, methodical, industrious, persistent, laborious, tireless, and conscientious in his work; never willing to leave undone what he has begun, or to surrender a position into incompetent hands,—despising a man who wishes to insure that he shall be appreciated and missed through the failure of those who have displaced him. His passions are substantially under his control, and

we are not surprised to find him urging upon Edward the claims of institutions and society as paramount

262

to individual inclination, by all the arguments of a mature, self-poised man of the world, though success would destroy the Captain's own hopes.

Ottilie is the most interesting and the most attractive character in the novel. She is introduced to us as a young girl at school, and Goethe describes her character as it appears to the Mother Superior, who does *not* love her, and to the Assistant, who does. She is an orphan, has been adopted by Charlotte, who is her aunt and was her mother's most intimate friend, and has been placed at the school with Luciana, the daughter of Charlotte. The Lady Superior says of Ottilie, "She is always unassuming, always ready to oblige others; but it is not pleasant to see her so timid, so almost servile." She thinks her too abstemious as to personal comfort and adornment, in her eating, drinking, and dressing; but says, "She keeps her things very nice and clean." The Lady Superior's suggestion as to Ottilie's habit of abstinence from proper food is obviously intended to prevent the misapprehension that Ottilie, at the crisis of her life, wilfully committed suicide by starvation.

At the school examination Ottilie utterly fails, and the Assistant tells us why. She is very slow to learn, and cannot learn at all by rote. Everything must come to her by slow, successive steps, and with the logical connection perfectly explicit and fully seized. She learns like one who is to educate, and her progress, though slow, is sure. But brilliancy at an

263

examination is not possible to her. She is inevitably behind her companions in superficial acquisition, and besides, when she is asked a question about what she *does* know, she seems to know nothing; even her handwriting exhibits this slowness and stiffness, though it is not without character. The Assistant excuses the examiners for their lack of appreciation of Ottilie, for it is their function to appraise accomplishments, not capabilities; yet he is sure that she

has been born for the good and happiness of others, and assuredly also for her own, and that the fruits of her labors will develop themselves sooner or later into a beautiful life.

Goethe brings the saintliness of Ottilie into prominence by the Assistant's description of a saintly gesture, which is habitual to her; and he tells us that when, in the Young Architect's tableau, she appeared as the Mother of God, "she excelled all that any painter has represented." We find that Ottilie is beautiful in person, affectionate, and appreciative; that she has that exceedingly agreeable faculty of entertaining one by her listening; that in the domestic sphere she is very quick to learn and very skilful in directive power, knowing how to direct, and able also to set right herself anything undone or wrongly done; very methodical she is too, dividing her day and assigning to each division its own labors. The whole management of the household is soon given up to her; even Charlotte's child is her especial care. She is a delightful companion for both women and men, and

264

at Charlotte's request makes for herself most tasteful dresses. Goethe says she becomes thus more and more a delight to all who behold her, for human beauty appeals both to the outward and to the inward sense, and "whoever looks upon it is charmed against the breath of evil and feels in harmony with himself and with the world." She is exceedingly and increasingly anxious to be of service,—half a word is enough for her here; "with her calm attentiveness, and her easy, unexcited activity, she is always the same; sitting, rising up, going, coming, fetching, carrying, returning to her place again, all in the most perfect repose,"—constant change, constant agreeable movement, yet always a calm placidity. Her desire to serve is excessive and needs restraint, appearing servile to one not appreciating its motive, as it did to the Lady Superior. She alone, of all the characters, unless perhaps the Young Architect, seems to have religious sentiment; she feels the pervading presence of God, sees His hand in her afflictions, and asks His aid and comfort. Her artistic talent is quite remark-

able, though it does not rise to genius. She has the clairvoyant temperament, can see her lover by second-sight, and feels buried treasures. She is so attractive to men that in any company she is the centre of attraction. The Captain, the Count, and the Baron all seek her society, and the Assistant and the Young Architect, besides Edward, are her lovers. Yet their love is unsought, and is a surprise to her. There is no trace of the coquette in her character. Goethe

265

indicates the universality of her fascination by making her so attractive to such different men.

Ottilie's love is so unselfish that she could surrender Edward willingly, if his best good demanded the sacrifice, while Edward's love is intensely selfish. It seems as if Goethe gave to Ottilie every characteristic of body, mind, and spirit which he considered desirable in a woman. When Ottilie died, all the people followed, or rather crowded around, her bier; men, women, boys, and especially the girls who had been her pupils,—there was not one among them all unmoved. Even her lifeless body had the saintly virtue of healing, so that he who touched it was restored to health, and great crowds made pilgrimages to her tomb as to the shrine of a saint.

Lewes says of Ottilie's Diary, that it gives us, instead of the impassioned feelings of a young girl, the thoughts of an old man. Goethe himself says that the larger proportion of the sentences could not have arisen from her own reflection, but must have been copied from something which took her fancy. There are parts of the Diary, however, which are evidently intended as revelations of Ottilie's own feelings, and these exhibit the patient waiting which is characteristic of her. There are no passionate longings for immediate possession of her lover; she is content to look forward to lying side by side with him in the grave. The impetuous, vehement Bettine writes to Goethe, in regard to Ottilie: "It is not maidenly for her to leave her lover, and not to wait from him the

266

unfolding of her fate; it is not womanly that she does not consider his fate alone." It were evident

enough without this criticism that Bettine is not the original of Ottilie. It lies in Ottilie's nature that her very innocence should expose her to the fatal entanglement of a love impossible of realization on earth. With her deep, undemonstrative nature, her surrender to the guidance of others, her desire to do right, her little self-reliance, but great capacity silently to endure, she is sure, if she love unwisely, to die for love. One feels her fascination, and can pardon her mistake.

The four characters already considered are the principal persons of the story; their sentiments are the theme, and the events are important only as they affect these persons. The other characters, though subordinate, are very interesting, and worthy of serious study, but we must at this time dismiss them hurriedly.

Mittler is a unique creation, and one would suppose hardly to be met with in real life; yet Goethe says of this character, that "a person whom he had never seen or known in his life had supposed the character of Mittler to be meant for himself." He adds, "There must be some truth in this character, and it must have existed more than once in the world." He is, as his name indicates, a mediator, (his only business in life being to settle disputes,) and he serves two important purposes. Into his mouth Goethe puts his own views of the marriage relation,

267

In some of its aspects, and, through Mittler's inability to give any real assistance when it is most needed, Goethe exhibits the insufficiency of external mediation for the solution of internal problems.

The Assistant is a laborious, pains-taking teacher, who loves Ottilie, not with vehement passion, but with deep-seated regard, based on association and careful observation of her character. He thinks she would make an excellent teacher's wife. He can wait however, and does wait forever, without apparently being much the worse for it. He would undoubtedly have made Ottilie a good husband, but would hardly have satisfied any heart-hunger. His great gift is to talk well, and to treat in his conversation of men

and human relations, particularly in reference to the cultivation of young people. He is absorbed in his vocation, and Goethe attributes to him many profound observations on teaching.

The Young Architect, though a subordinate character in the incidents of the story, is placed by Solger "*high above all*; because while all the other persons of the novel show themselves loving and weak, he alone remains strong and free; and the beauty of his nature consists not so much in this, that he *does* not fall into the errors of the other characters, but in this, that the poet has made him so noble that he cannot fall into them." Goethe, commenting on this, says to Eckermann, "that is really very fine"; and Eckermann responds, "I have felt the importance and amiability of the Architect's character; but I

268

never remarked that he was so very excellent, just because by his very nature he could not fall into those bewilderments of love." To which Goethe replies, "No wonder, for I myself never thought of it when I was creating him. Yet Solger is right; this certainly is his character." So Goethe bears testimony to that unconscious element in the creative activity of the artist by which he "builded better than he knew." It is true, therefore, that it is much wiser to seek the content of the created work of art in the work itself, than to search the memoirs of the artist for his purpose, though that may have human interest also. It is the function of the Young Architect to *restore*. He has a great collection of imitations of and designs from old monuments and vases, and of outlines and figures traced from original ancient pictures. The character of the collection indicates that purity, reverence, tranquillity, are the prominent characteristics of the collector. The fantastic and sentimental in art are not in accordance with his taste, but he delights in reproducing the placid, innocent, satisfied, pious happiness of the saints. In this spirit he restores the church and chapel; but as he is only a dilettante in painting, he makes no attempt at originality, and he is so susceptible to the influence of his companionship with Ottilie, that all the faces he paints resemble her. To

him Ottilie is the saint; in her the right thing is innate. His devotion is so deep and true, that one feels his love ought to have been requited. Certainly, of Ottilie's lovers he was far the most worthy of her

269

love. But Solger's estimate of his nobility, which protects him from the errors of the other characters, seems justified. When his work is done, he departs, lingering to be sure till he forces himself away, feeling that he can endure his disappointment better at a distance; yet he goes with only a half-melancholy feeling, bravely resolving, one can believe, to conquer what cannot be satisfied. He returns to stand, "in the vigor of youth and grace, with his arms drooping and his hands clasped piteously together, motionless, with head and eye inclined over Ottilie's inanimate body," and to think of "the rare, sweet, lovely virtues whose peaceful workings the thirsty world had welcomed, while it had them, with gladness and joy, and now was sorrowing for them with unavailing desire"; but as he sees "his beautiful friend floating before him in the new life of a higher world," his tears cease flowing, his sorrow grows lighter, and, reverentially taking his leave of Ottilie, he rides away into the night, we hope, consoled.

Luciana, the daughter of Charlotte and the excellent man whom she "respected, if she did not love," is a foil to Ottilie. Ottilie is modest, retiring, unassuming, undemonstrative, considerate, and helpful. Luciana is bold, brilliant, superficial, pushing, utterly reckless of the feelings of others, utilizing all persons and things for the gratification of her caprices, born to command, but not to command gracefully. Wherever Luciana comes, she turns everything topsy-turvy; yet notwithstanding the arbitrariness of her caprices,

270

she has a certain skill for winning people to herself when she thinks it worth while, by making each believe himself the most favored by her; and she has many admirers, even adorers. She has no success with the Young Architect, however. She is satirical, wilful, and thoroughly selfish, though with occasional capriciously benevolent impulses; and her feelings

toward Ottilie have a genuine bitterness. Luciana is an essentially unlovely and distasteful character, even though the Lady Superior regards her as a little divinity, and one wonders how the combination of Charlotte and the excellent man produced such result; yet Charlotte with a parent's hope believes that the discipline of life may make her amiable and charming.

Nanny interests us as enabling the author to exhibit the attractiveness of Ottilie in the relation of mistress and servant. Nanny is a wild, wayward, lively little village girl, who seems to have no capacity for work at home, but devotes herself body and soul to Ottilie, and in her service is active, cheerful, never-tiring. Nanny's devotion does not always restrain her covetousness and greediness; but she is driven distracted by the thought that she had killed her mistress by concealing the fact that, at Ottilie's command, she had eaten the food prepared for Ottilie, remembering with remorse that she had enjoyed the eating. The touch of Ottilie's lifeless hand worked a miracle in Nanny's soul, as well as on her broken body; for we find her, after, addressing the Young Architect in his sorrow with such truthfulness and

271

power, such kindness and such confidence, as to astonish and comfort him.

The Count and Baroness are distinctively "society people," and while recognizing the validity of marriage, and respecting it in their own case as a social and legal requirement, they have no deep conviction of its rationality. Curiously enough, Goethe makes them instruments to separate the Captain from Charlotte, and Ottilie from Edward, though the latter scheme does not work out as the Baroness intended.

The Earl and his friend have only an episodical connection with the story; but here, as always, the more carefully we examine the episode, the more thoroughly we feel its real artistic connection with the main work.

We will next examine the events in which these characters are involved, confining ourselves, however, for the sake of brevity, to the two principal

threads. The story opens with a picture of domestic contentment. Charlotte and Edward, having been married a few months, have settled down to a country life by themselves, in a beautiful home, with ample wealth, spending their days industriously in the improvement of the estate, and their evenings in pleasant conversation, writing, reading, playing duets for flute and piano, and arranging and completing Edward's old journal,—perfect domestic tranquillity. But even Adam and Eve, who had had no experience of anything else, and had no social world over

272

against them, found a garden life irksome; while these persons have spent their youth at court, have been accustomed to gay society, have many ties which connect them with the social world, and are still in the prime of life. They have experienced also a youthful, mutual attachment; each has made a marriage of convenience, and they have now united themselves in a marriage of friendship. From what we have seen of the two characters, we know that Charlotte could spend her life contentedly under her present circumstances, but that Edward will soon become discontented, will desire a change, and will be entirely carried away by the first strong passion which change of circumstances may give occasion to. This tranquil life is only the point of departure, therefore Goethe provides for its destruction in the very first chapter; indeed, Edward has the invitation to the Captain in mind as he lays down his gardening tools in the opening paragraph. Edward proposes inviting their old friend the Captain to visit them. Charlotte opposes to his excellent practical reasons for the change her feeling that the introduction of a third person will break up their scheme of life disastrously. She feels, what Edward does not, that a marriage of friendship is not secure, and is sure that the intervention of a third person is a matter of very great moment. However, she yields at last to Edward's vehemence and obstinacy, concealed by the warmth and sweetness with which he urges his scheme, and is even finally over-persuaded by him into solving her difficulty

273

about Ottilie by sending for her as well. Edward's crowning argument is, that it would be selfish in them to decline to help those who have the closest claim upon their affection, lest some danger should come to themselves. And so the foundation is laid for the collisions of the story. We notice, however, that Edward does not intend any harm; he has seen Ottilie, but has hardly noticed her, and wonders that Charlotte can think her particularly attractive.

The limits of a single paper will not permit me to stay upon the details of the story. I must content myself with the slightest outline, assuming that you are already familiar with the details, or will become so if your interest is excited. The first part of the work is devoted to portraying with consummate art the rise and development of the passion of love between Edward and Ottilie, the Captain and Charlotte. Love scenes, of the ordinary English novel variety, are scarcely to be found at all in this novel. They are managed with great delicacy for the most part, and the growth of passion is indicated mainly by slight artistic touches, rather than by broad delineation. In each of the personages the sentiment takes form and is dealt with as the character of the individual determines. Edward begins to fall in love with Ottilie the first evening after her arrival, and yields himself wholly to his passion, with utter disregard of every other consideration; yet even he, as a lover, finds himself in his beloved, and can make sacrifices for her. Ottilie's love is as pure and innocent as the

274

unfortunate circumstances will permit. She began to love Edward (Charlotte contriving to bring them together) before his marriage to Charlotte; but Edward, with characteristic obstinacy and singleness of view, was at that time so intent upon securing Charlotte that he did not notice Ottilie. So it was his own wilfulness, not an external fate, which placed the insuperable barrier between them. Ottilie is persuaded by Edward that Charlotte desires a separation that she may marry the Captain, and, accus-

tomed to rely upon the judgment of others, does not reflect farther, but allows her whole soul to become devoted to her love. Goethe says that, "led by the sense of her own innocence along the road to the happiness for which she longed, she only lived for Edward; and, strengthened by her love for him in all good, more light and happy in her work for his sake, and more frank and open toward others, she found herself in a heaven upon earth." Our author very carefully preserves Ottilie from any wilful, deliberate transgression of the laws of God or man.

Charlotte and the Captain are drawn together by similarity of tastes and occupation, and by mutual respect and esteem. Between them there is at no time violent passion, but only sincere regard. They co-operate in renunciation and separation, and each strives heartily to reinstate the divided family; but Edward's headlong impetuosity renders all their efforts futile. He insists upon a separation from Charlotte, refuses to allow Ottilie to be sent away, abandons his

275

home; and when he learns that Charlotte is about to become a mother, instead of being recalled to duty and family, he is overcome by despair, joins the army, and, recklessly fighting, seeks to solve by death the difficulties of his situation, or to find in his escape an assurance that fate favors his love. Charlotte recovers her spirits and cheerfulness, and does all she can to help Ottilie, providing full employment for her, and advising her wisely and considerately. Ottilie enters as best she may into the various activities suggested by Charlotte, teaching the village girls, and superintending the house and gardens; but does not succeed in overcoming her passion. "She had first found in Edward what life and happiness meant, and in her present position she feels an infinite and dreary chasm of which before she could have formed no conception." So, at the end of the first part of the story, all the tranquillity is destroyed, the family is divided, and the chief personages are out of true relation to each other and to the world. Goethe's universal panacea, activity and diversion, seems inadequate here. In the second part a solution is sought. We shall see

how it is effected.

We will pass over the discussion about burial-places, which would alone furnish suggestion for an entire essay, as well as also the restoration of the chapel, the social whirlpool stirred up by Luciana, and other very important episodes, which have not however essential bearing upon the principal content of the story. The evident devotion of the Young

276

Architect, the prudent desire of the Assistant, and the round of gay entertainments devised by Luciana, make no change in Ottilie's absorbing passion. The Assistant finds her, "in respect of a freer carriage, of an easier manner of speaking, of a higher insight into the things of the world, altered much for the better." But "it seemed to her as if nothing in the world were disconnected, so long as she thought of the one person whom she loved; and she could not conceive how, without him, anything could be connected at all." She is docile, and does her part everywhere, but without essential change. The child of Charlotte and Edward, the heir to the estate, is born, and Ottilie, devoting herself to it for Edward's sake, begins to realize the ethical requirements of the family. She sees how desirable and necessary it is that the child should grow up under the eyes of the father and mother, "and renew and strengthen the union between them." It becomes clear to her that her love, if it would perfect itself, must become wholly unselfish; and there are moments in which she believes that she has already attained this elevation, and thinks herself able to resign Edward and never see him again, if she can only know that he is happy: "the one only determination she forms for herself is never to belong to another." Charlotte has so far succeeded in her renunciation that she begins to plan the marriage of the Captain with Ottilie. So it seems as if the family were to triumph, and all were to be set right by the

277

But Edward, who has survived the perils of the war, reappears, and neither his own sense of duty nor the arguments of the Captain (now the Major) restrain him. He listens to what the Major says about his duty to his wife, to his family, to his own position, and to the world, but they are all naught to his love. He is still determined upon separation from Charlotte. He says fate has brought them into their present situation, and the only solution is by a reconstruction of their relations. He will not quite promise to reconsider, even if it can be shown that Ottilie can be happy without him; but no other consideration will have any effect upon him. The most the Major can secure is a slight delay, and he is finally prevailed upon to assent to Edward's plan. Edward goes to Ottilie, tells her that the Major has undertaken to persuade Charlotte, and begs and implores her acquiescence, but is met by a reference to the child, and a firm determination to abide Charlotte's decision, though he succeeds in getting fresh assurance of her love.

Here interposes an accident which destroys all hope of solution by means of the child. Goethe makes the agitation produced in Ottilie by Edward's impetuosity cause the child's death. Charlotte sees in this the determination of destiny, and consents to the separation. She believes that the good of Edward and Ottilie requires the sacrifice at her hands. To the Major's urging of his own suit, she says, "Do not ask me now! I will tell you another time. We have

278

not deserved to be miserable; but neither can we say we have deserved to be happy together." The Major and Edward are both inclined to regard the death of the child as "a convenient accident." Now, however, when all has conspired apparently to free Ottilie from restraint, she comes to full consciousness of her mistake. She says, "I will never be Edward's wife. In a terrible manner God has opened my eyes to see the sin in which I was entangled. I will atone for it, and let no one think to move me from my purpose."

But our personages are not to escape from their entanglement easily. Though Ottilie by her repentance and resolution feels herself freed from the burden of her fault and her misfortune, and has forgiven herself, yet the self-forgiveness is conditioned solely on the fullest renunciation persisted in for all time to come; and her own weakness, which she cannot wholly conquer, and Edward's pertinacity, make a tranquil life of renunciation impossible. Only the death of the lovers can bring peace. Ottilie determines to return to the school, never willingly to see Edward again, and to devote herself to God; but Edward compels an interview and destroys her plans, though she remains firm in her renunciation, and subdues him by the saintly attitude which the Assistant noticed as so characteristic of her when she would not be further urged. She returns to the castle, as does Edward also. The Major too and Mittler come frequently. They endeavor to resume their old relation outwardly, without bitterness or cross purposes,

279

but with the new relations in some way taken up into it; but Ottilie neither speaks nor eats, and gradually fades away, till Mittler's rude, though unintentional, portrayal of her sin against the bond of marriage destroys her life. Edward lived on mechanically; he seemed to have no tears left, and to be incapable of any further suffering; his power of taking interest in what was going on diminished every day; sometimes he would follow Ottilie's example, and neither speak nor eat; then his restlessness would overcome him, and he would desire to eat, and would begin to speak again; then he would bewail his inability to follow in Ottilie's footsteps, and say, "Genius is required for everything, even for martyrdom, as well as the rest."

At last they found him dead; Charlotte feared that he had committed suicide, but the circumstances of his death prove that he died naturally. He died with his memorials of Ottilie spread out before him, and, falling asleep "with his thoughts on one so saintly, might well be called blessed." Charlotte gives him his place by Ottilie's side. The novel concludes: "So lie the lovers, sleeping side by side. Peace hovers above their resting-place. Fair angel faces gaze down upon them from the vaulted ceiling, and what a happy moment that will be when one day they wake again together!"

This meagre sketch of the incidents omits innumerable artistic touches with which the artist charms

280

the reader, and the limits of this essay forbid my calling attention to them. I have intended only to present what is necessary for a consideration of the ethical content of the work; incidentally observing also how the characters ground the facts. It is evident that the passion of Edward and Ottilie, and its collision with the family, are the main theme of the novel. Everything else is incidental thereto. The principal element of the content of this novel is therefore love, and more especially that love of man for woman, and woman for man, on which the family is founded. As it is the special function of art to excite in the beholder a *feeling* of the true, and as it accomplishes its purpose by reducing the true to a form which appeals to the feeling, it is evident that it will use spirit in its internality mainly on the side of sentiment. Love as the paramount sentiment in some form — as religious love, parental or filial love, or love in which the difference of sex is an important factor — is therefore a favorite element of the content of works of Romantic Art. This is especially true of novels, so that it has been said that no novel could possibly be successful without at least one pair of lovers; and the artist usually considers that number insufficient. Goethe in the "Elective Affinities" furnishes several pairs.

In the devotion of one person to another of the opposite sex, the deepest thinkers have seen a manifestation of the highest phase of love. The utter surrender of self to find and know one's self for the first

281

time in another manifests the infinity of personality. The infinite character of love appears in that the true lover exists only in his beloved. It is evident that the collisions, in real life, of a sentiment so absorbing, with domestic, civil, and political relations, and with itself as manifested in different individuals, with duty, honor, and fidelity, furnish abundant material for the imagination of the artist. Then there appear an indefinite variety of grades of manifestation of the sentiment, from the shallowest and most sensuous passionate desire to the highest and truest devotion, determined by the temperament and character of the lover. No two of the lovers in the "Elective Affinities" exhibit the passion in the same form. There is also an inherent imperfection in the sentiment itself, in that the loved object is a special individual. Baron Bunsen, dying, recognized and repudiated this limitation, when he said to his wife, "We shall meet again, for I have loved the eternal in you"; but ordinarily we love the special and particular. Hegel has expressed with his accustomed vigor and completeness the limitation of the special phase of love which is the principal element of the content of the work we are considering; and he furnishes the key to the ethical validity of Goethe's treatment of the situation, in the consideration of love, under the general heading of Chivalry in his "Aesthetik."[1] The obstinacy with which the lover insists that only the one particular individual he has selected can possibly meet the

282

requirements of his nature, lays the foundation for distressing collisions. In this novel the principal collision is with the monogamic family which God and man have instituted as the fundamental secular institution. The institution has *its* limitations. The true family should have for its foundation true love, and then no collision of the kind here portrayed would be possible; but there are marriages of convenience, marriages of vanity and ambition, and marriages of friendship, and none of these are secure against love. Goethe has given us four instances of marriages of convenience; namely, the first marriages of Charlotte and Edward, which were entered into at the solicitation of family and friends; and (we may assume) the respective marriages of the Count and Baroness. The first two continued peacefully to their natural termination, not through any inherent validity, however, but because no occasion for collision occurred. The second two were not so fortunate, but Goethe is careful of the legal bond. The Count and Baroness must wait, however unwillingly, till the death of the Countess sets the Count free. Luciana's marriage with the Baron is a marriage of vanity and ambition, and we can readily see that trouble between Luciana and the Baron is very sure to arise. The marriage of Charlotte and Edward is a marriage of friendship. Their early love was a mere childish affection, and the respect and esteem which had succeeded are not the ideal foundation of marriage. Hence it is not inartistic to present a collision between this marriage

283

and true love, as it would have been had true love existed between Charlotte and Edward.

In considering the validity of the "Elective Affinities" as a work of art, the question arises primarily, Ought the artist to have selected this particular collision as a theme? If it is a truth of human experience, that is surely some justification; and Goethe says: "Indeed, there is not a line in the 'Elective Affinities' that is not taken from my own experience, and there is more in it than can be gathered by any one from a first reading. ... No one can fail to recognize in it a deep, passionate wound, which shrinks from being closed by healing, a heart which dreads to be cured. In it, as in a burial urn, I have deposited, with deep emotion, many a sad experience. The 3d of October, 1809, set me free from the work, but the feeling it embodies can never quite depart from me."

In a letter to Bettine he says: "The poet was, at the development of this sad fate, deeply moved. He has borne his share of pains; chide him not, therefore, that he calls upon his friends for sympathy. Since so much which is sad dies, unmourned, the death of oblivion, the poet has here proposed to himself, in this one-fabled lot, as in a funeral urn, to collect the tears for much that has been neglected." But not all human experiences can properly be portrayed in a novel. I am inclined to think, however, that in these times, when the bond of marriage is lightly assumed and lightly broken, and the passion of love is the

284

together conclusive of its impurity. The work itself

[1] Hegel's Philosophy of Art, Bryant, p. 136 *et seq.*

sport of children, a novel treating this collision ethically is timely and desirable.

A second question is, Does Goethe portray the collision from a true ethical standpoint? The answers of different commentators to this question have differed *toto cælo*. Goethe says, "Not many pleasant remarks were vouchsafed me about that novel." The Encyclopædia Britannica says, "In 1809 he finished the 'Elective Affinities,' a story which is always cited to prove the immoral tendency of his works." Bettine vehemently upbraids Goethe for not having done precisely what the accusers of the novel say that he has done; namely, for not having made love the conqueror. In this country it has been considered sufficient to prove the immoral tendency of the "Elective Affinities," that a person prominently connected with social movements, accounted disreputable, should have been invited to write the Introduction to one of its editions. It has been taken for granted, that, if it could serve any purpose of such persons, it must necessarily be bad; but the Introduction candidly admits that the work will furnish cold comfort for such as find the restraints of permanent marriage irksome, and that to such its conservatism will prove an unwelcome surprise. When one remembers that the advocates of slavery, polygamy, and drunkenness have long been accustomed to draw their strongest arguments from the Bible, the fact that persons alleged to be impure have commended the "Elective Affinities" is not al-

285

furnishes no warrant whatever for such conclusion. Much of the unintelligent, hostile criticism of the novel is really based on the assumption that Goethe's own life indicated a loose view of marriage, and that therefore the immoral construction of his work is the true one. But Goethe says, and with direct reference to this novel, "The late Reinhard of Dresden said he often wondered that I had such severe principles with respect to marriage, while I was so tolerant in everything else." Those who have studied the novel intelligently and deeply,—e. g. Solger, Rosenkranz, Düntzer, Herman Grimm, and Mrs. C. K. Sherman,—all these thorough students of the work find in it a

profoundly moral content. Lewes, with a dispassionate and unpartisan liberality, agrees neither with those who find the novel moral, nor with those who find it immoral. He thinks all depends upon how you take it; and this is superficially true. One may say that the final catastrophe results from the failure of the personages to respect the validity of love (Charlotte takes this view of the death of the child); or one may say that the error of falling in love with a person already married can only be atoned by death.

The ethical content of the work is, in my view, this: the necessary subordination, in the sphere of real life, of subjective passion, even though pure and true, to the objective institution, even though not ideally perfect. Ottilie's love is innocent; it had its beginning long before the interference of other claims; it is as deep and true and perfect as the artist could

286

make it; and in itself considered, it is entitled to realization in marriage; for

"Love, in human wise to bless us,
In a noble *pair* must be;
But divinely to possess us,
It must form a precious *Three*."

But, unfortunately for Ottilie, Edward's obstinacy has erected an impassable barrier here. If her love is valid against a marriage of friendship, his is not. He has no right to marry and unmarry at will. The interests of society, and therefore the true interests of the individual, demand permanence for the family. The fact that Charlotte does not love Edward, and that she would be willing to have the marriage dissolved, is not sufficient. It is not a question of subjective inclination.

It being settled, then, that the existing marriage must not be violated, the effect upon the individuals concerned will depend upon their respective characters. The Captain and Charlotte easily restrain and renounce their passion. They are not made for love. Ottilie endeavors to renounce, sincerely and religiously strives to overcome, and perhaps would have succeeded so far as to live on heart-broken, but tranquil, if she could have had help, or even no

hindrance, from Edward; for though her whole being has gone into her love, she has strength of character and patience enough to wait,—for after all it is but waiting. Goethe says, "What a happy moment that will be when one day they wake again together!"

287

Death cancelled the marriage bond. It is in the sphere of real life, here in this world, that their love must be subordinated. External marriage, without true spiritual union, is only "till death do us part,"—so that Ottilie could look to the future with happy expectation. But how could she ever be happy with Edward? He is so obstinate, yet so weak,—so selfish, yet without self-control; but love is self-denying, not self-seeking, and perhaps Ottilie can make a true lover even of Edward.

Rosenkranz thinks that the Fate element in this novel is of principal importance. He says, "The 'Elective Affinities' represent to us a tragic fate." This statement is misleading, if understood to mean that the triumph of Fate over man is the main content of the work. Such interpretation would be correct, if this narrow span were all; but to one who measures justly the capacity and endurance of the human spirit, Fate is a subordinate factor. It is evident from expressions in "Meister," that Goethe views the complications of Fate merely as obstacles which the true spirit must overcome. The Stranger says to Wilhelm: "The fabric of our life is formed of necessity and chance. The reason of man takes its station between them, and may rule them both; it treats the necessary as the groundwork of its being; the accidental it can direct, and guide, and employ for its own purposes; and only while this principle of reason stands firm and inexpugnable does man deserve to be named the god of this lower

288

world. But woe to him who, from his youth, has used himself to search in necessity for something of arbitrary will,—to ascribe to chance a sort of reason, which it is a matter of religion to obey! Is conduct like this aught else than to renounce one's understanding, and give unrestricted scope to one's inclina-

"tions?" It seems as if Goethe might have had this passage in mind when he created the character of Goe-Edward, and the circumstances with which he has surrounded him. Whether we consider the outer fate of external events, or the inner fate of tempera-ment and natural disposition, both of which aspects of fate have full play in this novel, yet it is equally true of both that it is the business of the human spirit to overcome fate, and free itself from all deter-mination save the highest self-determination.

The supposition that the influence of external fate is the principal content of the "Elective Affinities" contradicts Goethe's conception of the true method of a novel; he makes Serlo and Wilhelm agree, "that in the novel some degree of scope may be allowed to Chance, but that it must always be led and guided by the sentiments of the personages; on the other hand, that Fate, which by means of outward, uncon-nected circumstances carries forward men, without their own concurrence, to an unforeseen catastrophe, can have place only in the drama; that Chance may produce pathetic situations, but never tragic ones."

The "Elective Affinities" teaches many valuable lessons as to the conduct of life. I select these: it

289

teaches, that the elective affinity of love cannot be ignored, if one would marry happily; that one must cure his spiritual diseases by the activity of his own soul, neither accusing Fate of his misfortunes, nor seeking relief in the mediation of accident; but it teaches most explicitly of all, that man, as a rational being, may not yield, as a chemical element may, to a natural affinity, but must regard his duties and preserve inviolate the institutions of society,—dis-regarding them only at peril of his life.

290

CHILD LIFE AS PORTRAYED BY GOETHE.

BY MRS. CAROLINE K. SHERMAN.

EVERY great poem is of necessity an organic unity. Its parts, even to minute details, are dependent each on the other and subservient to the whole, as the whole in its turn is likewise subservient to each of its parts. The poet may claim to sing as the birds sing, admitting no other motive than the relief of his love-laden heart; he may be conscious of no earnest moral purpose, no avowed intention of putting in rhyme things never yet attempted in prose or verse. Yet, if he be a genuine poet, his song freely expresses the dominant impulse, which gives the key-note, and all the variations but echo and re-echo the main idea. Goethe more than any other poet has disclaimed the charge of ultimate ends and final purposes in his writings, and still students of Goethe pore over his works, bent on finding the central unifying idea, its manifold form of expression, its artistic development, as also its deep moral significance. And with right they do this; for the poet, whether working con-sciously or otherwise, in so far as he is a poet, works

291

not from any whim or caprice, but according to the divine harmony within him, bringing the chaotic dis-order of the world of fact into forms of relation and beauty, reducing the distracted many to the Complete One, and finding in that One the harmonious All, an organic whole.

Still, although recognizing, as we do, the vital unity of each of Goethe's masterpieces, the interde-pendence of all the parts, and their necessary relation to the whole, it is nevertheless altogether possible that many an episode may be thrown in, having no direct bearing on the whole; that beauty here, as elsewhere, may be "its own excuse for being"; and that one might as well ask why the blush was on the rose, or the tint on the peach, as to question the significance of the various phases of childhood por-trayed in Goethe's works. Yet as a Darwin finds utility even in the most delicate beauty,—finds that it renders an all-important service in the development of Better up to Best, so we see that Goethe quite as often passes from the *beautiful* by way of the true to the *useful*, as from the useful by way of the true to the beautiful, and that the Child Life which he de-lights to picture is no idle accessory, but has always a distinct bearing on the whole.

It was but natural that the morning-red of Goe-the's own happy childhood should lend some color to these portraits. Here, as elsewhere, Goethe looked in his own heart and wrote. His childhood was, in many respects, an ideal one,—not extraordinary in

292

any abnormal sense: on the contrary, it was normal, as following the highest type, and reaching the flower and perfection of childhood.

Beautiful in person, endowed with healthful physi-cal senses, the world of illusion was to him a veritable paradise of delights. He had a comprehensive mind, that grasped the things of sense, and easily discovered their order and relation. Prompted by that childish curiosity which later leads to rich scientific investi-gation, study was to the child Goethe but the open-ing of realm beyond realm of new discovery. On the moral side there was neither the hypersensitive conscience that belongs to the child of weak nerves, and whose fate is to die young, nor yet was there a rude indifference to the rights and privileges of others. A strongly affectionate nature and heart-felt sympathy for all about him, no doubt, had a con-trolling influence in a moral direction; while, on the religious side, as a boy Goethe was full of awe and reverence for that Unseen Power, which he recog-nized, not only as the beneficent Creator and wise Preserver, but also as the awful Thunderer, the grim Destroyer, laying waste the earth by fire and flood. This Unseen Power, even at that early age, con-founded the boy's faith. He found it hard to recon-cile divine goodness with painful facts; but here, as later in the problem of Faust, a healthful optimism prevailed, and the boy trusted, as the heart of child-hood will trust, that "somehow good will be the final goal of ill"; and then, with that "familiar grasp of

293

things divine" so becoming in the reverent child, he built an altar to his unknown God, hoping, since the great God did not deign to manifest himself in the flesh, that he might at least approach him with sacrificial offerings of beauty, and worship him by

means of symbols. Here, too, we see that the sensuous child-poet was father of the man. From first to last, Goethe could approach the Infinite with 'no cold, formal abstractions. In beautiful, sensuous forms he must meet his divinity, make his confession, and breathe his aspirations. From the beautiful to the good, from the good to the beautiful, was Goethe's impulse, or, as Plato has it, "from fair forms to those still fairer, and so on up to the highest Good." This tendency in the child Goethe from the beautiful to the good was nothing individual, peculiar to himself. It is the natural tendency of every healthful child, and when parents and teachers will understand it there will be less need of arbitrary rules and dogmatic precepts.

Goethe's surroundings as a child were favorable for a normal development. The inflexibility of the overwise father, sternly in earnest for the good of his children, was modified by the joyous sunny temperament of the mother. The father appealed to the head, the mother to the heart. If the father was sometimes over-persistent and inexorable in his demands, the little mother, as Goethe was pleased to call her, could charm away any ill effect by her glad presence. Not that the father was a hard taskmaster,

294

but he had his own views of education, which to him were ideal, and in many respects were so; only it is so hard sometimes to draw the dividing line between what is ideal and what is mere hobby. Goethe's father occasionally overstepped this boundary, which is pardonable, perhaps, when we remember how excellent his plans were in the main, and what a strong influence for good they exerted on the boy,—when we remember, too, that the ideal system of education, which Goethe unfolds in "Wilhelm Meister," existed in crude form in the brain of the elder Goethe.

How happily Goethe remembered his childhood,—his free play in the world of sense, his first hints of ethical and spiritual powers,—he has narrated in the autobiographical sketches, which he calls Truth and Poetry, and which by no means signify Truth and Fiction,

but Truth and that kind of Poetry which, as Aristotle says, comes nearer to vital truth than history. What is given in detail in these sketches is again found in lines of exquisite poetry in the Prelude to "Faust," which find an echo in every heart that yet remembers its own glad spring-time:—

"Then give me back the years again
When mine own spirit too was growing,
When my whole being was a vein
Of native songs within me flowing;
Then slept the world in misty blue,
Each bud the nascent wonder cherished,
And all for me the flowerets grew
That on each meadow richly flourished:

295

Though I naught had, I had a treasure,
The thirst for truth and in illusion pleasure.
Give me the free, unshackled pinion,
The height of joy, the depth of pain,
Strong hate, and stronger love's dominion,
O, give me back my youth again!"

The portraits of child life in Goethe's works that are most familiar are those of Felix and of Mignon in "Wilhelm Meister." This social romance, as we all know, represents the development of the individual as he passes through the various phases of social life, seeking not so much to contradict and subvert these social forms, as was the case with the aggressive Faust, but wisely to appropriate from them that which shall tend to his own advancement. Not revolution, but evolution, is Wilhelm Meister's motto. He finds no fault with the established order of things,—is no radical reformer, who sees the world out of joint, and considers it his duty to set it right. He accepts his environment as it is, with the purpose of wringing from it that which is peculiarly his own, or that which will bring him into most harmonious relations with his conditions. We know through what various degrees of culture Wilhelm Meister passed;—the beneficial influence which commercial pursuits had upon him, leading him to recognize the value of material gain only so far as it was subservient to spiritual needs, and the influence of the dramatic profession, by which he was led from that which seems to that which is.

Art showed him his own possibilities and at the same time his limitations.

296

Through religion he recognized his position and relation to the universe. We know what an important part woman plays in the history of this development. At every stage of the process her power is manifest. She may attract, she may repel; but either force, attraction or repulsion, has its weight and affects his course.

It was specially fitting that in this novel, which deals with the development of the individual as such, woman should have had so active a part; for thus far in the world's history her influence has been chiefly with man as an individual. How great that power has been, Goethe is free to admit. If he has delineated women as they are, with their weak littlenesses and frivolities, he has also shown the divine power of woman and the moral order which reigns where woman reigns. "But," says Goethe, "what in us women leave uncultivated, children cultivate when we retain them near us." Wilhelm passes through all the stages of apprenticeship; yet not until he recognizes and assumes the duties of a parent does his apprenticeship end. Now he is no longer an isolated individual, a mere learner, a passive recipient. He is bound by family ties, and is now conscious of his duties and privileges as a citizen. It is the child Felix, well named the Happy-One, who gives the finishing stroke to his apprenticeship. "Notwithstanding his experience of life, it seemed as if his observation of this child was giving him his first clear insight into human nature. Both the theatre and the

297

world appeared to him as a multitude of thrown dice, upon whose upper surface a higher or a lower number was marked, and which when added together make up a certain sum. But here in this child one single die was placed before him, upon whose several sides the value and worthlessness of human nature were plainly indicated."

Felix, as we know, was the son of Wilhelm and Mariana. He is first introduced as a child of three years, bright as the sun. "His clear eyes and open

countenance were shaded by the most beautiful golden locks, and his dark, delicate, and softly bending eyebrows adorned a forehead of glittering whiteness, while the ruddy hues of health glowed upon his cheeks." Goethe's ideal of healthy, happy childhood. At first the reader supposes him to be the child of the sickly sentimental Aurelia; but when he called her mother without any tenderness of tone, we at once suspect that this healthful child of nature is not the offspring of the super-emotional woman. Goethe understood the laws of heredity too well for that. Felix bears a close resemblance to his father, in that he is docile and tractable, passive in a receptive sense, yet, like his father, active and ready to appropriate and assimilate that which is peculiarly his own. Felix is no saint. He has the faults of a child. He persists in drinking from the decanter, instead of using the glass, and preferred eating from the dish rather than from a plate. He slams the doors, or leaves them open. In other words, he is the winsome, attractive, natural child of

298

the Kindergarten, rather than the morbidly good child of the Sunday-school book. His heart is tender and affectionate, but human rather than humane. When the cook cut up some pigeons, he struck at her; but the favorable impression which this produced on his father was soon destroyed, when he saw him mercilessly killing frogs and tearing butterflies' wings to pieces,—like the child of our acquaintance, who thought it cruelly wicked to kill robins, but all right to kill sparrows. Felix was also highly delighted when he could sit down in a corner with a book; saying with a serious face, "I must study this learned stuff," though he was ignorant of his letters, and refused to learn them.

Wisely directed, he will become the well-balanced man. The father sees this, and now the chief anxiety of the man, who had hitherto lived only for self-development, is the education of his boy,—his other Ego; and yet almost the first observation which the father makes, an observation common to all parents, is that the child is educating him rather than he educating the child. For the child's sake he values prop-

erty, studies social politics and the various forms of public life. So completely now is his life controlled by the interests of the child, and pedagogics form so important a part of the Journeymanship, that it would seem almost as if the child's development, and not that of the father, were the central idea,—calling to mind the old insolvable problem, "Does the tree exist for the blossom, or the blossom for the tree?"

299

The harmonious culture of all the faculties is the father's aim for the child. To this end he follows as well as bends the natural inclination. Before giving instruction he waits for the child to ask, "What is it?" or, as Jean Paul says, is cautious not to give the draught before the child has the thirst.

With an enthusiasm worthy of Frederick Fröbel he enters into the child's interests and sympathies, valuing symbolic culture and industrial training. So far as is possible, he places him in the midst of glad surroundings, well knowing that a happy environment is to a child what sunshine is to a plant. Those good people whom he would have the child imitate must also be glad and happy, since children usually copy those individuals who seem to live most happily. He will have the child educated to live in the *Now*, and find its happiness in the way of culture rather than at some distant end. The happiness, however, which Goethe seeks for children, is not simply glad, sensuous animal existence. The child has within him the possibilities of rational and spiritual being. He can attain complete development, actual happiness, only in the realization of these. Happiness for child or man is found only in moral freedom. Selfishness is the fate and fetter of the child, as well as of the adult. Each in his own way must work out the difficult problem from fate to freedom. At every step, the child, as well as the father, is called upon to renounce. Never for the sake of self-renunciation, however. It must be the denial of self only for the higher profession of self.

300

In the harmonious culture of all the varied powers of the child, Goethe emphasizes with special stress

that which no one brings into the world, and yet that upon which depends everything through which a man becomes a man on every side,—Veneration. The child must reverence that which is *above* him, which is reflected and revealed at first in his parents, teachers, and superiors. He must reverence what is *beneath* him,—that which humbly ministers to his happiness and well-being, as also that which hurts or harms him; for even this he must recognize as a force, which it well behooves him to treat with respect, and to which he must on many an occasion make terms of peace, and perhaps sacrificial offerings. He must also respect himself, not with vain pride and isolated egotism, but remembering that he too is one of many,—he, too, is a central point from which good can and ought to emanate.

These three forms of reverence are one, and the one is three. There cannot be reverence for what is above us without lifting ourselves toward it and so increasing our self-respect; and the humblest is so allied to the highest that in respecting the lowest one does reverence to the highest. Goethe had need to lay emphasis on this one point of veneration, without which there can be no true culture. Without reverence for what is above him, the child may have self-assertion, but never self-respect. Without due regard for that which is beneath him, he will be at the tender mercies of Fate, and never arrive at the only true manhood, which is self-possession, ethical freedom.

301

Wilhelm Meister finds for Felix a school in which reverence holds as important a place as mathematics,—a school in which all formal outward signs of courtesy and respect rest on deep moral and religious foundations. Men are wont to call this ideal school of Goethe Utopian and visionary, but the dream of one age becomes the possibility of the next. Our children's children *may* attend common schools where ethics, and even religion emancipated from dogmatism, will find place in the curriculum.

While Felix is the glad, happy child, everywhere at home where there is earth, air, and sunshine, Mignon seems no child of earth, but a waif from that Paradiso

which is all love, light, and harmony. Felix has native strength. He can make his way from fate to freedom, wrestling, conquering, or renouncing. This world is his, element, and as child or man he will wring from it that which is best for him. But Mignon is nowhere at home. A yearning, an irresistible longing, fills her heart. Her kingdom is not of this world. Hunt for it as much as she may, the home she seeks is laid down on no map. Goethe portrays her as a child of sunny Italy, the offspring of a most unfortunate union, which a pitiless Fate cruelly brought about in the tenderest guise. Her father was a religious enthusiast, given over to emotions half spiritual, half physical, which for a time exalted him to the seventh heaven and then cast him into an abyss of dejection and misery. Rescued from this unnatural condition by the power of love, he learns when it is

302

too late that the object of his love is his own sister. With all the reckless frenzy incident to such a nature, he will hear nothing of renunciation. He looks upon social law as a violence to nature. In the madness of despair he demands that the heart should follow the cold impulse of unconscious nature rather than the cold formal rules of reason. He refuses to see that he is not living in the free world of his own thoughts, but in a state where laws and regulations are as unchanged as the principles of nature, because they are based upon nature.

So we see that, while the religious element is the leading trait in his character, it is the *form* of religion for which he cares, and not its moral content. He will have the emotional part of religion, its ecstasies, its soul intoxications and sweet deliriums, but not its self-abnegations, and triumphs that come only of painful conquests. Fate overtakes him, since he follows inclination rather than duty. He becomes a wretched wanderer, finding consolation for the gloomy vagaries of his brain only in his harp. The mother too was of a religious disposition. She never knew the character of her offence. By a pious fraud she was led to believe that she had sinned against her spiritual nature in engaging herself to a priest. Her misery and re-

pentance over this unwilling sin is greater even than her love for her child. Religious madness and enthusiasm happily cheer her soul, and death brings a speedy release.

These were the parents of Mignon. Deprived of

303

their care, she lived with a worthy family near the sea. "Soon she evinced the greatest fancy for climbing, and to imitate the difficult feats of the rope-dancer seemed to be a mere impulse of her nature. To do this more easily, she changed clothes with the boys who were her companions, and, although such conduct was considered unbecoming, it was permitted. Her love of wandering often led her far from home, and, though she often went astray and for long periods, she never failed eventually to return. She would then take her seat beneath the pillars of a portico before a large country mansion in the neighborhood, where she was allowed to remain as long as she pleased. She would rest upon the steps, or at times, running through the spacious hall, would linger among the statues." One day she continued absent. She was stolen by a band of strolling players, who knew her value as a rope-dancer. Rescued by Wilheim Meister from their brutal treatment, he became her protector. Her singular nature as well as her origin is a mystery. She frequently remained quite silent for an entire day. Sometimes, however, she answered more readily, but in so strange a way that it left doubtful whether her peculiarity arose from shrewdness or ignorance of the language, as she generally expressed herself in broken German mingled with French and Italian, and yet in no language could she express herself with facility; and the difficulty seemed to arise from her mode of thought rather than from any defect of speech. Notwithstanding her great wish to learn, her progress

304

was slow and laborious. It was the same with her writing, —a task at which she toiled. It was only when she sang and touched the guitar that she appeared to have an organ which opened and displayed the emotion of her soul.

It may be noted, in passing, that Goethe takes a generous pity on those quiet reticent natures who have little gift of language. He is sure to find for them some form of expression that will be a relief to the overburdened heart, and by means of which we may know the rich fulness of their nature. Ottilie, in the "Elective Affinities," is better understood through her diary, and Mignon, who lacks even the ordinary gift of language, finds free expression only in music. Goethe recognized the value of his own ready power of expression, and the words which he puts in the mouth of Tasso were no doubt his own sentiment:

"Though in their mortal anguish men are dumb,
To me a God hath given to tell my grief."

"The force of Mignon's ripening nature often rendered Wilhelm anxious and fearful. The warmth of her disposition toward him seemed to increase daily, and her whole being seemed agitated with a silent restlessness." That love which can brook no rival becomes with her an all-absorbing, though only half-conscious passion. This ungratified love preys on her frail body, and finally destroys it; but not until Mignon has learned the one lesson which this greatest of novels teaches, — self-renunciation, which is no stoical abnegation, but the surrendering of the

305

demonic, as Emerson calls it, for a celestial love. She becomes

"Faithful, but not fond,
Bound for the just, but not beyond."

Like Ottilie, she finds sweet consolation in useful activity and willing service. An unerring instinct leads her to comfort the old harper, whom she little dreams to be her own father. She teaches Felix to read, and whenever her heart feels any want she resolves that Felix shall fill the void. More and more she seems to lose her hold upon earth. Dressed in long white attire, and sitting with Felix in her lap, she resembled a departed spirit, while the boy was life itself. It seemed as if heaven and earth were in one embrace. The death which soon follows is hardly death, but rather a glad transition, as if the yearning spirit had now found its native home.

Goethe has thrown an indescribable charm about this mysterious child, whose deep and impenetrable nature scarcely allows us to conjecture its emotions. Nothing therein is plain and evident save her grateful love to her benefactor, and the vague weird notes of her music, which hint far more than they express. "Know'st thou the land?" is the continuous refrain which she echoes and re-echoes. Her home-sick soul longs for its far-off home, and utters that cry which is the cry of every human soul far off from God, who is our home.

As in the old Greek tragedies the chorus always gives the word of explanation, so in the chorus which

306

celebrates the obsequies of Mignon we have the significance of this mysterious child, whose being was love and harmony, but who could find no rest or satisfaction in the discordant world of sense. "Look forward with the eyes of the spirit," says the chorus. "Let imagination awake, which bears Life, the fairest and highest, to a habitation beyond the stars." And again, "Children, hasten into life! In the pure robe of beauty, may Love meet you with heavenly countenance and the garland of immortality." Wilhelm Meister is brought to realize that he is not only a social and moral being, and capable of development as such, but that he is also a religious being. In his own soul a voice echoes again and again, "Know'st thou the land?" He may not be able to answer the question, satisfactorily. He certainly knows that he will find no answer in the world of sense, for it is laid down on no maps. He may try to avoid the question, but it will force itself upon him whether he will or not. It will appeal to him in Nature and in all the varied forms of Art, but most of all in music. For there is no speech or language which appeals so directly to the human soul as music.

Music, when sensuous and coming of a lower strain, appeals to the lower nature with seductive power. It is all absorbing and sense-intoxicating. The victim knows the raptures of ecstasy and the madness of despair. But when music appeals, not from sense to sense, but from soul to soul, it creates an unrest, a

dissatisfaction with the things of sense, and leads the soul beyond these and beyond the limits of formal reason into the higher realms of insight and faith,— a faith that is beyond reason, not below it.

Mignon had no language but music, and indeed needed none. Renouncing the mysterious seductions of sense, she rises

307

"Higher far,
Upward into the pure realm
Where all form
In one only form dissolves," —

"The angel choir
Seek not to know of youth or maid!" —

where there is no thought of sex,

where there is no seal of silence, and soul answers to soul in its own language.

In the drama "Götz with the Iron Hand," we have a picture of Karl, the only child of the great hero. This play is rather a series of pictures than a genuine drama. There is no central point about which the entire interest revolves, and the characters are interesting simply as portraits taken in various positions and placed in contrast with each other as light and shade. Götz, the hero of the play, is a man and a hero after one's own heart. His very presence is a mighty force. He creates about him that enthusiasm of humanity which compels his adherents to follow him to death. Like many of the true knights of old, he goes about *right-ing* the wrong wherever he finds it. As an individual he is without fear or reproach. Like the other knights

308

of the fifteenth century, he asserts his liberty and independence, and this liberty, so far as it pertains to himself and his followers, is no selfish, licentious liberty. It is liberty to correct the wrong and enforce the right according to his own ideas,—the liberty of asserting his moral self. He has learned the meaning of *I* in its most exalted sense, but he has not learned the meaning of *You*. A new era has dawned. Fraternity is now the word, as well as Liberty. The new era is irresistible, and Götz tenaciously clinging

to the relics of the past, obstinately resisting the progress of events, is overtaken by his fate; for Nature punishes ignorance and narrow-mindedness as she punishes crimes.

The calm, quiet picture of the meek little Karl might seem to have no connection with the bold egoism of Götz, or with the leading idea that men cannot successfully wage war against the World-Historical Spirit. We see Karl first as begging his aunt for the story of the *Good* Child. That he should ask for a story of a good child rather than of a bad one, is indicative of Karl's quiet, effeminate nature; for most children prefer the story of the bad child, not because they themselves are bad, but because they like the tragic, and are sure that dramatic collision will happen when the bad antagonizes the good. The aunt requires the boy to tell her the familiar story, and he is taught to repeat it with such literal exactness that the spirit is entirely lost in the verbiage. Later the father comes, and the joy and interest of the boy

309

are manifested by going to the provision cellar with his aunt, rather than to the stable with the hostler.

"He never will be his father," said the hostler, "else he would have gone with me to the stables."

When he greets his father, he does not look upon him with proud admiration as a hero. He simply asks, "Have you brought me anything?" Then he tells his father, "I have learned a great deal."

"What may that be?" asks the father.

"Jaxthausen is a village and a castle on the Jaxt, which has appertained in property and heritage for two hundred years to the lords of Berlichingen."

"Do you know the lords of Berlichingen?" asks the father, who sees with contempt that the boy's learning is so abstruse that he does not know his own father. "To whom does Jaxthausen belong?"

"Jaxthausen is a village and a castle upon the Jaxt—"

"I did not ask that," returned the father. "I knew every path, pass, and ford about this place before ever I knew the *name* of the village, castle, or river. Is your mother in the kitchen?"

"Yes, papa, they are cooking a lamb and turnips."

"Do you know that too, Jack Turnspit?"

"And my aunt is roasting an apple for me."

"Can't you eat it raw?"

"It tastes better roasted."

And when he is introduced to Weislingen, the child says, "Be merry, dinner will soon be ready." "Happy boy!" says Weislingen, "that knowest no worse evil than the delay of dinner."

310

This picture of the placid, meek boy heightens by contrast the heroic valor of his father. We have said that this play is rather a series of contrasting pictures than a genuine drama. Yet the little scene of Karl with his father has a closer bearing on the leading idea of the play than at first appears. As the father will not come into harmony with the spirit of the times, but clings persistently to a past that is dying or dead, so the son is carelessly indifferent to things and facts about him, and clings to far-off, meaningless words. The son ignores the *Here*, as the father ignores the *Now*.

Goethe's greatest drama offers little scope to children; for, with the first kiss of Faust, Margaret is no longer a child, and Euphorion, the offspring of Faust and Helen, is more of an allegorical character than living flesh and blood. Yet in connection with the child Euphorion occurs a passage which without question emphasizes the high estimate that Goethe eventually placed upon the family relation,—

"Love in human wise to bless us
In a noble pair must be,
But divinely to possess us,
It must form a precious three,"—

311

and the child of this ideal union is significantly named Euphorion, "Bringer of Good."

It is worthy of notice, that, when Goethe wishes to make a woman specially attractive, he surrounds her with beautiful children. "Nothing," said Goethe, "is more charming than to see a mother with a child upon her arm." "Nothing is more revered than a mother among many children." Ottilie is never so beautiful as when holding Edward's child. Charlotte in the midst of her younger brothers and sisters is the finest of the many fine pictures in "Werther." Goethe is said to have borrowed this scene from Rousseau. He borrowed not so much from Rousseau as directly from nature. Because Rousseau had given an equally beautiful picture was no reason why Goethe should not repeat it. As Chaucer was accustomed to say that he took possession of whatever he found directed to G. Chaucer, so no great poet need hesitate over any material at hand, provided he is sure the divine spark is his own.

Goethe not only develops the characters of his heroines by their contact with children, but he finds their relation to children the readiest way of describing them. With a single stroke of his pen he draws the distinction between Theresa and Natalie when he says, "Theresa trains children, Natalie instructs them." While Goethe ornaments Ottilie, Charlotte, Natalie, and Mignon with children, his weak characters, like the frivolous Philina and the super-sentimental Aurelia, have no power to attract them,—indeed, children are repelled from them,—but eventually, when Philina develops into a useful woman, worthy of the name, children are drawn to her.

Goethe has clearly shown that, where women are denied the marriage which the heart prompts, their resort is not, as has been hinted, in marriage with

312

another. According to Goethe, their happiness is then found in useful service, especially to children. This is manifestly the case with Ottilie and with Mignon. Not to be crushed with the agony of disappointment, and not to realize the full measure of desolation, they spend themselves in useful activity, the noblest form of which is the care and instruction of children; and it may safely be said that nowhere has the realistic Goethe followed nature more closely than when he makes the instruction of children the happy alternative for those who are denied the perfect expression of love.

Although the children portrayed by Goethe occupy, of necessity, a subordinate position, they fill, as we have seen, no insignificant parts. As an artist Goethe might have introduced them simply as ornaments, for Beauty's sake alone; but although Goethe is preeminently an artist, he is none the less a rigid moralist and utilitarian of the strictest order. Everywhere in his works children serve a wise economy and earnest moral purpose,—developing the individual, as in "Meister," to a closer sympathy with humanity; or compelling the individual for their sake to a more refined degree of Morality, as in the "Elective Affinities"; or demanding of society as well as the individual that renunciation which recognizes the claims of children as paramount to all other considerations,—a renunciation which, in its turn, leads to the higher advancement of society, as well as of the individual.

313

XI.

HISTORY OF THE FAUST POEM.

By DENTON J. SNIDER.

THE connection between the composition of "Faust" and Goethe's own life has always been felt to be very intimate; the two run parallel. "Faust" ushers in the spiritual life of the poet, and closes with his bodily life; the work, quiescent for long periods, always starts afresh, gathering and preserving the bloom of many rich poetical epochs. Every true reader wishes to see the poem unfolding out of the life of the poet, and also to behold each portion developing out of the preceding portion, naturally and in due order. A history of the Faust poem, then, is the requirement; which will be, not a mere record of external incidents and facts, but an inner, genetic history of the work in its double relation to the poet and itself.

Critical opinion is divided concerning the point of time when Goethe first conceived and began to work upon his "Faust." The prevailing view has been that the beginning was made about the year 1772 or 1773, when the poet was twenty-three years old. Says Loeper (*Einleitung*, p. 5): "The day and hour

cannot be exactly fixed when Goethe, in that most fruitful period of his life as regards dramatic conceptions, 1772–76, laid hold of the Faust fable. But Schröer, in the Introduction to his excellent commentary on the poem, has given good reasons for referring its beginning at least as far back as 1769. This is also the date assigned by Eckermann and Riemer, who are supposed to have had documents for making out the chronology of the poet's works now inaccessible. Two citations from Goethe's letters bearing on this point are worth translating. "It is no trifling matter to represent outside of one's self, in the eighty-second year, what one has conceived in his twentieth." (Letter to Zelter, June 1, 1831.) Goethe was twenty years old in 1769. Again, in a letter to Wilhelm von Humboldt, March 17, 1832, written five days before his death, he says: "It is *over* sixty years since the conception of 'Faust' lay before me clear, but the succession of its parts less complete."

The answer to these and similar passages is, that the old Goethe was inaccurate in his memory of the events of his youth. In a general way, however, it may be said that the conception of "Faust" goes back nearly forty years before the complete edition of the First Part, in 1808, and fully sixty years before the completion of the Second Part. Such is the first grand fact of the poem, a fact unique in literature; in one long human life the work blossoms, unfolds, matures; this life of the Poet is but his outer setting

315

in Time, yet it deeply suggests the life of the legend developing through the centuries.

In the history of the Faust legend we see how the fable of Faust has unfolded with the unfolding of the race, and bears in it the image of the ages. The true mythus is a growth, a never-ceasing development of an original germ, in which the people have put their own idea, and in this idea the spiritual march of the world mirrors itself; the legend grows with the growth of man, out of the same seedling, to the same altitude. Now Goethe the individual

has to go through the same process to be the true singer; the Faust legend in its primitive germ will sprout within him in early youth, will grow through life, and bear its last fruits in extreme old age. The poet truly lives the life of the legend which he embodies in writ; and under its form he has to pass through what his race has passed through. Before he can sing his task to completeness, he must live, in those sixty years of his, ideally sixty centuries of his people at least. In him the Faust legend is no artificial thing, picked up from the outside to make verses about, but it is the germinal dot of his being, which blooms afresh in one individual life, the life of the legend and the race.

It is then, a matter of importance to trace back to Goethe's childhood the first faint impress of the legend stamped upon his susceptible soul. He had seen a puppet-play on the subject of Faust in Frankfort when a boy,— probably had seen it often; then,

316

we may suppose, the first vague possibility was planted in him. The puppet-play which he saw is not known, but it was probably derived from Marlowe's "Doctor Faustus," which, though its original source was the old Frankfort Faust-book of Spiess, had been brought back to Germany by strolling bands of English players, and had shaped the dramatic form of the Faust legend. Thus the great Elizabethan era of dramatic creation throws out a line of descent to the German poem of Goethe. Shakespeare, as we see from several allusions, was also aware of the Faust legend, which, however, had not yet been ripened for him by time; hence, with true instinct, he chose, as his grand embodiment of the Teutonic mythus, the story of Hamlet the Dane, who is a first-cousin to German Faust, physically and spiritually, and, like Faust, was educated at the Protestant school of Wittenberg.

Perhaps we can point out the very egg that Marlowe's drama laid in Goethe's poem, which will hatch it out to a bird of such wonderful plumage and pinion. In the soliloquy that begins his play, Marlowe introduces Faust as disgusted with all knowledge, and

giving himself up to magic. This is the primitive germ of denial, not by any means carried out to its full development by Marlowe; but Goethe will pick up the same germ in the first soliloquy of Faust, the form and substance of which are given by Marlowe, and let it unfold under the storm and sunshine of his whole life. The Faust of Marlowe is a Protes-

317

tant Faust, tragic, the Devil gets him; through the puppet-play the germinal negation of that Protestant Faust, protesting in it against all science and truth, drops into the youthful soul of Goethe, most fertile of all spiritual soils. Goethe himself has, perhaps unconsciously, told his own tale; he has in his "Wilhelm Meister" unfolded the history of a germ laid in a child's soul by seeing a puppet-play; thence the child gets a tendency or impulse which unfolds into its life, whose record is that novel.

But a far mightier element was at work in the period, struggling, fermenting with some new change. There was a Faust spirit in the air of Germany, of all Europe, during Goethe's youth, and it was giving premonitions of the great impending Revolution, social and political. A time kindred in many respects to the Reformation awoke the sleeping Faust legend out of its peaceful century's slumber, and made it spring up with fresh life in all susceptible German hearts, particularly in those of the young poets. Several of Goethe's immediate circle of friends, Müller, Klinger, Lenz, tried their hand at writing Fausts. The great literary protagonist of new Germany, Lessing, had planned and partly written a Faust drama; moreover, he had distinctly declared that the Faust legend offered a true theme for a great national poem.

The restless spirit of the time, struggling, protesting, was loudly calling for its poet, when the young Goethe stepped forth from the nameless ranks of men

318

with a response forever memorable. That first response was "Götz" and "Werther," in which productions the literary period of Germany known as "Storm and Stress" culminated in a vast tumultuous overflow

of emotion, eternally self-generating and eternally self-destroying. The poet finished them in his Titanic vein; they had of course to be tragic, indeed self-annihilating; their end must be in the final conclusive protest against the world called death. Other poems, like "Prometheus" and "The Wandering Jew," conceived in the same spirit, he could not finish; in them the half-conscious thought seems to rise out of chaos and say: "Dear Poet, the problem in this world is not to die, but to live; to master fate, not to yield thereto; and it is thy function to reveal such mastery to mortal men."

In the same Titanic vein he conceived his Faust, whose disgust at knowledge he had himself experienced, chiefly in his student life at the University of Leipzig, whereby he had learned, as he declares, the vanity of all human science, at the early age of eighteen. He wrote much upon his "Faust" at this stormy period, almost finished it as is supposed, yet did not. Why? He could not; he had run against a wall which barred all progress, and which rose higher with advancing years. He first felt the vague instinct, then came to the clear insight, that Faust must be redeemed, must pass out of his Titanic protest into reconciliation. This is the wall which stopped him

319

so many, many years, but which he will at last climb over, when he will reveal the Paradise within. Of "Werther" he says, that he freed himself, by writing it, of his own tragic sentimentality; he slaughtered the sentimental hero of his romance, and thereby saved himself; through such vicarious offering of his shadow, he escaped the ghost-world. Clearly it will be his duty next time to save his hero as well as himself.

No sooner had he looked into the depths of the Faust legend, and had struggled to embody it, than he discovered his inability. It was the truest instinct which led him to lay it aside, and to wait for the experience of life. He must grow into the legend as the legend itself grew. This became the method of his life,—to unfold into completeness; it also became the method of his poem; his own life gave the

literary procedure. "Faust" unfolds, step by step, not simply in the mind of its author, but also in its outer artistic form. Goethe had in his soul a vast germ, which could bloom and be fruitful only with time; the poem, imaging the poet's process, starts with a vast germ laid in Faust's soul; this germ is what develops through its own law into the existent work, a self-unfolding whole.

In this sense of mirroring the poet's innermost spiritual development, the poem is a biography; hardly in any other sense. It does not give the events of Goethe's life, it does not give the rise of its own poetical parts in chronological order; "Faust" was written backwards, forwards, and in between, at

320

various times of life. It might be called an ideal biography recording in the highest form of art the supreme moments of the supreme man of the age, which moments appear in the poem in succession, but really are the products of years of waiting and preparation. The mountain peaks, sunlit in the distance, we from the plain see in continuous line; but there are valleys deep and broad between them. Still the method of the poem is that of a growth, as Goethe's life was a growth. Here the poem and the life fall together, in this deepest fact of spiritual unfolding.

Not alone in life and art, but also in nature, Goethe saw the same essential fact. Nature is a self-unfolding too; from a primitive form she develops into a variety of forms; the leaf in the vegetable kingdom is to become flower, fruit, and even tree. "The Metamorphosis of Plants," a treatise by the poet on botany, is a beautiful image of the Faust method, a very Faust drama of plant life, and indeed the process of Goethe's own development. The poem grew as the flower; life, with its rain and sunshine, fostered it. Yet we must not think that, because it is life, it is not an idea; the idea is the very essence of life.

In the history of the composition of the First Part of Faust, there are two distinct periods, which are marked by definite dates: these are the first period, ending with the edition of 1790, and the second pe-

riod, ending with the edition of 1808. These two periods are the clear landmarks, most important for

321

understanding the growth of the book, as well as the drift of the discussion upon it; we shall try to state what was contributed to the work by each of these periods, shunning as far as possible the vast fog-world of conjecture which environs the poem to infinity.

In 1790 Goethe gathered his Faust efforts of more than twenty years, and printed what he called "Faust, a Fragment," containing a little less than one half of the present First Part. In it, beside lesser omissions, were two great gaps, the first of which began with the second soliloquy of Faust, and extended to Mephisto's interview with the student, thus constituting the intellectual kernel of the poem,—altogether about 1,165 lines in the original. Doubtless some portions of this large deficit had been already sketched,—as, for instance, the scene of the Easter festival; but the whole was too fragmentary to be published even in this Fragment. It will be observed that the omitted section is in the main the unfolding of Mephisto. This deepest transformation of time and human experience the young poet could not manage: it was the first wall that he ran against. Still he saw that the thing had to be managed; the grand difficulty was, How? Wait, patient man! till the germ blossom and ripen; wait, and the secret will be told thee in full. Hardly less significant is the second great gap, containing those last scenes in which Mephisto is subjected to Faust, and is made an instrument for the attempted rescue of Margaret, who, nigh to death, is lying in the triple prison of the law, of insanity,

322

and of her own conscience. The poet probably knew, in a vague way, that all this had to be done too; but he could not get clear about the manner of doing it. With time, however, and valiant struggle, this last dark gap will be overarched with a perfect rainbow of poetry.

Such were the two grand omissions, highly significant of the poet and his development. But that which was announced in the Fragment of 1790, and

announced for all time, was the primitive denial of Faust and the fall of Margaret. These two phases, in their very statement, we feel to be connected by some secret thread; to raise this secret thread into clear daylight is the great poetic problem. The first soliloquy, which was then printed, gives the germ of the whole poem, the original dual forces from which it springs: negation on the one hand, aspiration on the other. Then takes place that prodigious leap to the scenes in which Mephisto appears a full-fledged active person in the world. What connection between that first denial and this sudden fiend, with final outcome of his work in the fate of Margaret? Such is the chasm over which the bridge is to be built, and the poet must live it into being. From that primal negation as the germ, Mephisto will unfold; and Faust, from the dry student and professor, will be transformed into the youthful, passionate lover.

In this Fragment we can observe two chief experiences, that of the university with its unsatisfactory

323

knowledge, and that of a great breach in the Family; both lay in the life of the young Goethe. But to show, step by step, how the Family is destroyed by that first negation, is the work of a far longer and deeper experience, which speaks of dire encounters with the Devil himself, whose genesis in this part is the supreme intellectual feat of the book. In the Fragment of 1790 we also find the "Witches' Kitchen," written at Rome in 1787. This scene, in connection with "Auerbach's Cellar," introduces us to the Perverted World, the true realm of Mephisto, and furnishes the immediate motive for Margaret's fall. But this phase of the poem is not complete in the Fragment; the Perverted World is still to receive an addition in "Walpurgis Night."

The reception given by the public to the Fragment of 1790 was by no means favorable; it was not at all to be compared to the mighty outburst of enthusiasm that hailed the appearance of "Werther." Goethe himself, in a half-humorous, half-complaining way, hints the lack of appreciation in the "Prologue

on the Stage," prefixed first to the edition of 1808. Olympian Goethe, then, does want some recognition from mortals for his world-compelling work. A slight undertone of disappointment one may hear from him at this time, as he sadly strings his lyre; but cheer up, mighty heart! for no man knows better than thou, "What glitters is born for the moment, what is genuine endures for all time." If the general public was cold toward the work, the criti-

324

cism of the time was hardly better, and showed no appreciation of the significance of the poem. Indeed, when did it, or how can it? Loeper has dug out for us some hints of its tendency which are interesting. It laid hold savagely of small external details; it declared the language to be "dark, unintelligible," the usual charge of the ready critic against everything which he does not take in with his newspaper glance. It declared also, that the great master of German speech wrote bad German. Give us, O critic! some of your good German. And the style was not elegant, being written "in the tone of a street ballad-singer"; many of its incidents and expressions were "such as only the lowest populace could take delight in." So it is. What of it? Imagine a "Faust," or a "Hamlet," appearing to-day; then imagine what the Press and Magazine would make of it. Such a lack of recognition is not a matter evitable in the present state of the human mind,—nay, not a matter regretable, when truly looked into; it is the fiery discipline which tests the permanent value of the great book, as well as the literary grit of the author. The diurnal writ cannot possibly measure the eternal writ, which is incommensurable,—cannot have any sympathy with it or knowledge of it,—hence can only light the fires of depreciation.

But under this ephemeral judgment another judgment, that of the eternal kind, was forming slowly but surely. Not till the great book takes possession of great souls, and grows to be a living fibre of their spiritual being, has it reached the tribunal

325

which is to adjudicate its rights; then it will enter upon its true inheritance, and commence receiving even its canonization. After many years the mightiest thinkers of philosophic Germany, Schelling and Hegel, begin to utter the ultimate decision upon this Fragment. The first German critical minds, the two Schlegels, also contribute their part in the mean time; their school, the modern Romantic, gives continuous help for its appreciation. The most sympathetic and deepest-seeing of all these early views is that of Schelling, which deserves special emphasis at this point. Schelling could have known only the first Fragment when he delivered his lectures on the "Method of Academic Study" at Jena and Würzburg, 1802-5; yet he seems to divine, not merely the completed First Part, but the completed Second Part, in the final redemption and completion of the hero. The great philosopher turns a rapt seer in speaking of the poem, "which as yet must be grasped by anticipation rather than by knowledge," and he at once proclaims it to be "an original work in every respect, only to be compared with itself, and resting on itself." He sees far in advance that "the conflict must be solved in a higher way," and that Faust, "elevated to higher spheres, will be completed,"—the very vision of the end of the Second Part. It looks almost as if the poet had followed the prophecy of the philosopher, or that the latter somehow had got-

326

ten a peep into the workshop of the poet. Moreover, Schelling feels the great scientific value of the book, "sufficient to rejuvenate science in this age"; he seems to feel that the development of the poem rests upon the same foundation as science itself, and advises its study to all "who wish to penetrate into the true sanctuary of Nature." Yet this does not hinder it from being philosophic in the profoundest sense, and he declares that, "if any poem can be called philosophic, this predicate must be applied to Goethe's 'Faust' *alone.*" Thus the two extreme poles of the great poem are indicated: it has the true development of Nature, and the true idea of Philosophy, in harmony; moreover, it is poetic in

the best sense, yet is philosophic also, revealing "a new kind of Fate," the Fate not merely of the Deed, but also of Knowledge. Thus the mighty twins, Poetry and Philosophy, eternally fighting and clawing one another in the brains of lesser critics and poets, unite in one grand symphonious strain before the mind of Schelling, as he casts his look upon Goethe's poetic creation. Such is the broad view of the German philosopher,—quite the universal view, spoken in a few far-glancing prophetic words toward the close of his lectures. Nothing better has been said or can be said upon the poem, and the interpreter has but to fill out in detail the vast outlines of Schelling's hints, avoiding the merely poetic, or merely philosophic, or merely scientific, or any other merely one-sided method of exposition.

327

Hegel's profound appreciation of Faust is well known to his readers, but it has to be sought chiefly from books of his which were published after the completed Faust of 1808, and hence need not be cited in this connection. Still, in one of his early works, "The Phenomenology of Spirit," finished to the thunder of the cannon at the battle of Jena, he gives a subtle interpretation of the Earth-Spirit in the Hegelian manner, showing that the fragment had produced so strong an impression upon his thought, that he assigned it a place among the historic phases of consciousness.

Many years have passed since the appearance of the Fragment in 1790; but clearly it is creating its world, and rearing its own readers. It has gone deeply into the great spirits of the time and found lodgment there; assuredly they will take care of it, they will impart to it a share of their own immortality. That which makes the great book immortal is that it lives in the highest souls, those truly immortal. With time it will be preserved against the millions and the ravages of time. In this matter one feels always like speaking to the poet face to face, and addressing him out of the future centuries, not for his sake, as he hears it not, but for the sake of all toilsome unknown workers:—"Take heart, O much-tried scribe of the ages! be not cast down because the phantom of the populace buzzes neglectfully past thee; it will long be dead when thou art living, nay, it will be chiefly known hereafter for not having

328

known thee. Gird up thy loins anew; a yet greater task is before thee, nothing less than to generate out of the soul of thy time the Devil lurking therein, and to reveal him in body to the sons of men. The greatest task laid upon human scribe is thine; up, and be a-doing, courageous heart! thou alone of the milliards of these later centuries canst perform it."

Thus we may pass from the first period, embracing the Fragment of 1790; we now come to the second period of composition, which lies between the Fragment of 1790 and the completed First Part of 1808. In this period the two capital additions are the genesis of Mephisto, as Evil Principle, out of Faust's denial, and the beginning of his subjection to Faust in the attempted rescue of Margaret. The two great gaps which we noted in the Fragment are thus filled, and the poem in its First Part attains completeness after almost forty years of effort. These are doubtless the gaps of which Goethe repeatedly speaks in his correspondence with Schiller, and whose problem, though quiescent for long periods, never fully left him. The genetic hint, scarcely observable in the Fragment, has now unfolded into a conscious purpose, and the idea of final purification and restoration, vague and unclear in the Fragment, breaks forth into the full clearness of knowledge.

The Perverted World, or Mephisto's realm, also receives its completion in the two scenes of "Walpurgis Night." We saw in the Fragment the beginning and wild progress of this Perverted World in

329

two other scenes, "Auerbach's Cellar" and "Witches' Kitchen"; now it is unfolded into correspondence with a total plan. To this period belong the two Prologues, in which the poet indicates a clear consciousness of the nature of his theme and of his work. Moreover, in the "Prologue in Heaven," the Lord definitely promises that he will lead the struggling Faust through to light, in which promise we have a glimpse beyond the First Part of "Faust" into the Second Part.

The reception of the completed First Part was far more favorable than the reception of the Fragment had been. On all sides, there seems to have been a pretty general agreement as to the prodigious significance of the book. But the way had been prepared. The Fragment during eighteen years had been absorbed into many appreciative spirits, who were not only ready for, but had vaguely anticipated, the completed work. Moreover the scope of Goethe's other activities,—scientific, poetic, literary,—as well as the unity of his genius in all these activities, had begun to dawn generally upon his countrymen. Still there seems to have been nothing like an adequate exposition of it till ten years had passed, when Schubarth's book on "Faust" (1818) opens the long and ever-increasing list of commentaries, a list manifestly not to be closed by the present book. The criticism of "Faust" in Germany has been a prolific plant in fruitful soil, with many local turns and variations which no foreigner cares to follow. It has fluctuated

330

with the spiritual tendencies of the German people, indicating plainly that the great poem always mirrors itself differently at different periods, and must have with the new epoch a new interpretation. The older phase of Faust criticism seems to occupy itself more with the thought or idea of the poem, though not neglecting philological, mythological, and other aids. This phase is properly the philosophic, receiving its light from the unparalleled sunburst of German Philosophy during the first quarter of the present century. The later phase of Faust criticism seems to concern itself more about the external unity, or rather the want of unity, in the poem; its method is the historic, and shows the reaction against philosophy. Both these phases have their strong and weak sides, both supplement pretty well each other's defects. Let not the true-hearted student yield to the cry, that he should throw away the old, and take the new criticism, which is seriously inferior to the old, or philosophic, in depth

of insight, while both need much correction in regard to sobriety of judgment.

The recent criticism of the First Part of "Faust" turns chiefly upon the manner in which the two editions of 1790 and of 1808 are to be viewed. The one set of critics sees in the completed First Part a double and inconsistent plan, two contradictory ideas, held together only by the art of the bookbinder, and not by that of the poet. The additions made in 1808 to the Fragment are, it is declared, really a different, nay, an antagonistic poem. Kuno Fischer, who may

331

be taken as a representative man of this party, says that the two sections of the poem, that of 1790 and that of 1808, "proceed from tendencies fundamentally diverse; they are in character wholly heterogeneous, and they are so to the extent of complete opposition." Thus our First Part, over whose completion we shouted such a hallelujah of rejoicing, has by the completion really been made incomplete, and old Goethe has been caught playing on the public another of his tricks of mystification. Fischer goes on to state that there is a fundamental difference between the two editions in the conception of both Mephisto and Faust. In the Fragment of 1790 Mephisto is declared not to be the Devil, such as he is in the later work, but a mischievous imp, "an elementary ghost," in the service of the Earth-Spirit. In reply to this view, Oettingen (*Vorlesungen über Faust,* Vol I p. 10) points out numerous passages in the Fragment which directly contravene Fischer's assumption, showing that Mephisto is regarded in them as the genuine Devil. Still, it cannot be denied that the Devil in lighter moods is fond of his impish joke, harmless enough; witness the scene in "Auerbach's Cellar." But this milder phase may well consist with his deepest deviltry. Still further, Fischer states that there is a contradiction in the character of Faust: in the original conception he was a sort of Prometheus in conflict with the established rule of the Gods, a genuine world-stormer, and hence tragic; but in the later, added part, the idea of purification

332

through struggle and suffering was introduced, with final reconciliation of the hero purged of Titanic denial. Again the answer has been made to this argument, that it really proves no inherent contradiction, but rather the contrary; Faust does begin as a world-storming Titan, but the whole course of the poem shows him cleansed of his Titanism, and coming into harmony with the world-order. Still it continues to be stubbornly maintained that the Fragment has the unity, and the total work has the split from top to bottom.

It is perhaps characteristic of the intellectual German of to-day, that this theory of Faust — shaded, to be sure, in manifold colors, from hazy gray to jet-black — is held by the most considerable German critics of the present time, Julian Schmidt, Friedrich Vischer, Karl Biedermann, etc. It finds its first germ in C. H. Weisse's book (1837), one of the earlier interpretations of "Faust," but the theory there is not at all drawn out to its later consequences. A kind of cult of the fragment of 1790 seems to have arisen in Germany, intimated in the words of Gutzkow: "'Faust' as Fragment is much dearer to all of us, than the completed 'Faust.'" Who are *all of us?* Certainly not the whole adoring the Whole, but some fragment worshipping the Fragment. The true and final conclusion of the theory is boldly drawn by Gwinner and others, who maintain that the sole unity is the Fragment, and that the real fragment is the completed Part, while the completed two parts

333

of "Faust" are but the fragment of a fragment. The course of the poem runs thus: it begins perfect, grows to imperfection, and ends in a kind of self-annihilation, doubly discordant and dissevered. The poet, too, in the utter perversity of his nature, calls his complete work a fragment, and his fragment a complete Part, and his two fragments, doubly scattered, his complete work. Truly the saying of ancient Hesiod, that the half is more than the entire thing, has now become a reality, nay, a twofold reality, for the fragment is the whole, and the whole is the fragment.

In such manner certain sets of German critics seem to have turned the Faust poem upside down, and are attempting to read the book that way; while Father Goethe himself is set on his head, and is asked to walk somehow with feet in the air. They call it the layer theory, inasmuch as "Faust" is not taken as a grand architectural work, but a series of stratified scenes, piled like stones one on top of another, which the critical mattock can pry apart and scale off into pieces large and small. Of course the divisive process need not and will not stop at any given point short of infinity: if we can split the completed work into two or four portions, why not into a dozen, and so on, according to the endless divisibility of matter? Schröer has taken hold of the Margaret episode, the most closely connected part of all "Faust," in this spirit, and has divided it into two distinct portions, with still further subdivision into

334

separate pictures, moving one after another in a sort of panoramic fashion. Upon which procedure one observation may be made: anatomy is absolutely necessary for all true critical, as well as physiological science; but the whole purpose and end of it is, not to leave the scattered parts lying about at random, but to recombine them into the one complete living conception of the bodily or poetic organism.

It is curious to observe that the discussion on "Faust" seems to be running parallel to that on another great poetical book, the first Literary Bible, old Homer. The unity of both is torn to shreds; the notion of unity seems the reddest of red rags to the present infuriated critical bull, wildly laying about itself in Germany. It is bent desperately on fighting the fact, on proving by a violent toss of the horns that the fact is not the fact, but some other ghost. The unity of the Iliad was the prime fact of it, with few slight protests, ancient and modern, up to the time of Wolf, — the fact which gave it quite its chief worth, and which preserved it through so many centuries. Yet we have lived to see a German critic arrange the Iliad anew into a number of disparate songs, according to the principle of discord, and not of unity; as if

the supreme object of criticism were to turn all the harmonies of the earth back into chaos and old night. The next thing will be an edition of "Faust," not in the well-ordered unity in which the poet left it, but dislocated by the lever of the critic, and stratified anew according to his method of its origin. Tear down the

335

grand Gothic cathedral, pile up the stones in layers; then we have the thing as it was originally, in the womb of Mother Earth, and our brilliant critical sagacity finds its true outcome in the realm of primeval disorder.

Thus, however, has the critic furnished in himself the best commentary on the poem; by his denial he has come to exemplify in his own person the denial of Faust; he is transformed to a Faust denying Faust, through the very excess of study and shrewdness. It is indeed strange. One asks, What can the sceptical understanding not do? The world turns to haze, without solidity; the last book of the ages is getting to be as mythically uncertain as the first; and Goethe, scarce fifty years in his grave, whom many hundreds of people now living have seen and remember, is beginning to be a fable, and to share already the fate of his eldest brother, the Chian bard.

Such is the one line of Faust criticism, much maintained in Germany; yet even there it has valiant opponents, who meet the enemy at every point with huge stones and sharp javelins. This new school may be regarded as a necessary reaction against the excesses of the philosophical school, which was too often inclined to build an air-palace of its own, with little foundation in the poem. It is, however, itself committing excesses which foretell its doom; Germany will weary of it, as she wearied of the earlier criticism, and will return to seek for the rational idea of the work, the idea which generates it, and is not foisted

336

upon it. The facts which the great industry and microscopic acuteness of the new criticism have brought to light will not be lost, but will be united in a new and deeper synthesis with the thought of the poem. The only sound method is to accept the facts fully and sincerely, then to see them in their completeness, which brings them into a connected, indeed creative whole. And the prime fact is, Goethe has left this "Faust" as a unity, arranged according to an idea, not by chance, or by mere chronological sequence. This guiding idea which orders the poem must always be the main thing for the one who wishes to comprehend, and not merely enjoy, the work.

Still, as Nature often reveals her secret in her monstrosities, it is worth while to see the ground of this new layer theory. There is a difference between the part of "Faust" which appeared in 1790, and the added part which appeared in 1808. The difference exists, but the deeper fact is the unity which locks together these different parts. In the Fragment the problem is stated; in the completed Faust it is solved. But many cannot see the solution; many, too, believe that there is no solution; these must prefer the Fragment. Such minds will always divide the First Part of "Faust" into two parts, and select their favorite: individual character and insight at last determine the choice. But the poet had certainly a different view, and if we wish to work in his spirit, we must follow the way he points, and grapple with the work till it yield its secret solvent thought.

337

If the new criticism must prove unsatisfactory, nay, in its extreme tendency, repugnant, to those who wish to see the poem as Goethe saw it and left it, that same criticism has been very beneficial in turning a strong light upon the essential and most difficult fact in the work, namely, the genesis of Mephisto. It has compelled those of us who believe in the Faust poem rather than in the Faust fragment to look into the great book anew, under a keener light, and to find the unity in a deeper sense than it has yet been found. I believe that the poem comes out of these critical fires more fully appreciated, seen in clearer, greater, truer outlines, than was possible without such discipline.

The genesis of Mephisto, which lies between the first denial and the final compact, may be well called the grand central fact of the poem; it was, however, the grand obstacle to the poet, — was that which he had to wait for nearly forty years, from youth to the beginning of old age. What was his own development during that time in its cardinal points? If we can bring them together in our glance, perhaps we may be able to see the spiritual history of the genesis aforesaid, or some suggestion thereof. Out of what and into what did the poet have to pass, before he could write that wonderful evolution of the modern Devil? As early as 1769, possibly earlier, he had in him the Denial of Faust seen in the first soliloquy; then or not long afterward he had the full-formed Mephisto in activity with the Student and with Margaret; what

338

connection between the Denial and the Devil? The young poet feels that the one is the source of the other, that the one must be generated out of the other; but he possessed no literary form adequate for such a task, nor could he get it from any quarter, — with good reason, for the literature of the world as yet contained no such literary form. Genetic hints do indeed occur in Shakespeare, even in old Homer; but they are sudden flashes, prophecies of the coming form, by no means developed into an explicit procedure. Goethe then not merely must have the new thought, but must find the new form; he has to live it into being along with his life. This creation of a new literary form is what makes "Faust" an original poem, and its appearance an epoch in the world's literature.

Such was the difficulty which rose up against the continuation of Faust; yet the same difficulty lies in the entire period of Goethe's early poetic activity, that period usually called his Titanism. He began a "Prometheus," the world's accepted type of Titanic struggle, but he never could finish it; he ran against the obstacle which stopped his "Faust." Two other works, "Mahomet" and "The Wandering Jew," conceived in the same spirit, had to remain fragments for the same reason. He began a novel, "Wilhelm Meister"; but, with all the external incitement of friends, he could not bring it to an end, because the end lay not in him. He broke with his Titanism, saw that it would bring nothing to a close but itself;

still, like the huge boulders of some mighty primitive energy, the fragments of these early efforts lie scattered through several portions of his works. The fine poem called "Ilmenau" (1783) indicates the transition; it shows the break with the past, with the period of "Storm and Stress," and also hints the unsettled state of the future.

339

Still the poet was growing, growing into this very genetic method. He had begun to study science in his way, to take long deep glances into Nature, the first and last of his teachers. He discovered the intermaxillary bone in man, not by scientific induction so much as by poetic intuition, — that vision which beholds, not the particular thing or fact in isolation, but the total creative process, of which this is but a link. The glance which sees in the particular thing or fact the entire cycle of Nature — sees in the single bone the whole skeleton of the one animal and of all animals — is Goethe's glance, penetrating the genetic procedure of the physical world, and hinting from afar a kindred literary procedure.

But this last stage has not yet arrived, — indeed, cannot yet arrive; he makes the transition into Art by a new mighty experience. This is the journey to Italy, the most important epoch of his life, falling almost midway between his birth and death, when he was old enough to understand fully the lesson of the past world, young enough still to be moulded by that lesson. At once the fermentation began to settle, the soul to purify itself, and he reached a new harmonious insight into the world-order, and into the

340

expression thereof; he became a new man, looking upon a new world; all that had been impeded and was incomplete in his life and works now began to move toward freedom and completeness. The influence was a new birth of the whole man: Nature, Life, Art, Poetry, all felt the fresh creative breath of that Italian spring.

First, the vegetable world revealed itself to him in Italy, he says, in a garden at Palermo, where he fully saw that wonderful metamorphosis in which the leaf generates itself, and in that genetic process purifies itself more and more into higher forms, till at last it completes itself in the total plant. That little book, called "The Metamorphosis of Plants," written after his return from Italy, showing all the stages of the genesis of the plant from the leaf, is still Nature's grand suggestion of the genesis of Mephisto, and remains to this day the best guide to a true insight into the genesis of "Faust," — the book itself being a poem, a genetic drama of the plant. In like manner he showed the metamorphosis of the vertebral into the cranial bones, and carried the genesis of forms through the animal world. A great, many-sided activity he unfolded, yet with one thought at bottom; that thought was genesis, which became his conscious principle; he saw it everywhere in Nature, looked for it in Art, and in the history of Art, and intended to apply it universally in his great work on Man and Nature, of which, however, but a few outlines remain.

341

Already in Italy this spiritual metamorphosis began to pass into the literary works which he took with him to that country. "Iphigenie" from a prose drama was transformed into an ideal example of classic beauty, — a veritable symbol of Goethe's own transformation under Italian skies. "Tasso" was also transformed and rewritten in the same classic spirit and measure. A new world had indeed dawned upon him; or it was rather the transfiguration of the old world into a new existence.

Of necessity he began to employ his new insight in a higher realm, that of spiritual production, of which the first great literary fruit after his return was the completion of "Meister's Apprenticeship." We have seen how that work lay unfinished before the Italian journey; no completeness was possible in it then, as there was no completeness in the author. But now he sees the way, he will remodel the whole work, and bring it to an end; Meister too is to reveal the genetic hint, and carry it over into the novel, and therewith into the spiritual world, out of Nature, even into education. It is, indeed, the principle of human life and character; the erring man is to be seen going through his process of self-purification, of self-correction of errors, the grand human discipline in the mastery of fate. "In every endowment lies the force to bring it to perfection," says the Abbé, who is the almost invisible Jupiter Olympius, hovering over this truly modern epic. The nature of Meister unfolds through manifold errors into its true being; in him we watch

342

the genesis of a human soul out of its primordial germ into reality.

With the completion of the apprenticeship of Meister, the grand obstacle which stopped Goethe so many years was broken down; he had entered the paradise of supreme poetic creation. The great literary deed was done, yet not completely done; a literary expression had been found for one phase of the new idea applied to life; but there was still another phase, stronger, deeper, more universal. In Meister the function of error in the grand human discipline is told, turned over and over, and emphasized in a thousand varied forms; but now error is to deepen into denial, the unconscious mistake is to become conscious negation, — in fine, is to become the Devil Therewith rises the new task, vaster, more desperate, more soul-cleaving; a gigantic task, which the poor mortal may well shun, — to call up and put into body the "spirit that denies," the modern Destroyer. The negation of Truth, the intensified embodiment of all error, wandering, waywardness, the conscious Denial burning with a sulphurous torch, indeed, the very Devil, is now to unfold before our eyes into a reality, and to accompany the man through his long earthly career, till he work himself free of his diabolic counterpart, purify himself, and ascend to heaven.

The task has to be done: there is no escape of the true poet from his call. Scarcely had he finished "Meister," when the mightier problem seized hold of him, the final ground and mystery of all creation, the

343

genesis of evil. Yet this problem, so new, was nevertheless his oldest poetic task, had indeed lurked underneath all his activity since his twentieth year, had

sent him to Nature for lessons, had driven him to Italy for expression and clarification, had made him write "Meister" for training; this Faust question is really the spiritual substrate of Goethe's entire productivity, the mother soil out of which shoot up all his works and his life. In 1797–98 the Prologues were written, in which we see him deep in his work; and we catch, from his correspondence with Schiller, faint indications that the embryonic Mephisto was lustily struggling within him.

But it is not a matter which can be despatched with a few rapid pen-strokes. Still a ten years' struggle, O valiant man! awaits thee; untold birth-throes will wrench thy being till thou be delivered of Satan, who will himself, "the old hell-lynx," be made to sweat roundly in the process (*ihr habt mich weidlich schwitzen machen*). Let no lack of man's recognition put down the God who now commands the work; rouse thyself anew; the years of long preparation are past; the hair on thy temples has turned gray since the first early conception of thy task, but it lives in thee still; thou hast travelled all the realms of Nature, Life, Art, in thy toilsome apprenticeship, and written its record; but now it is done. Thy supreme effort must be made, thy genius is invoking thee to exercise the Devil out of thy "Faust," and out of thyself into the world, and by thy magic speech to ban him into writ,

345

there to stay forever. Then thou art free, but not till more than eighty years have passed over thy head, and the last line be set down; then thou mayst dismiss thyself from thy terrestrial task, and say to thine Ariel, "Now to the elements."

XII.

GOETHE'S WOMEN.

By Mrs. JULIA WARD HOWE.

THE topic here set down to my name was assigned me months ago, and appeared at the time one most congenial to my wishes. Goethe's women! how charming to renew my acquaintance with them! What a lovely literary pleasure to take up the varied narratives in which they play their part! Vain thought! I had my Goethe-time long ago, when as a girl I read "Faust," "Götz von Berlichingen," and others of the plays, and when, a young mother, I quieted a baby with one hand, while the other turned over the pages of "Wilhelm Meister," and so my Goethe Gallery is seen through a long vista of years. I, too, who once adored the Teuton rule, do so no longer. Heaven forbid that my grandchildren should be fed upon the tonic of "blood and iron"! Give me American rule, American training, with its lapses even and its faults. For, though Germany did wonderfully take the lead in critical thought during the first half of this century, when the moment came for

346

liberal action, she shrank away, and lost the world's leadership, and will never regain it. And how did her Nemesis, Bismarck, obtain the mastery over her daring thought and unrepentant speculation? Let me grimly parody, in reply, a line of Robert Browning:—

"Just for a handful of silver he had us;
Just for a ribbon to stick on our coat."

Having said thus much, and refusing to bow to a cocked hat, even if worn by a German Prince and set up by a German Emperor, I will look back at the social and literary glories which once illuminated two hemispheres from the narrow heaven of a small German principality.

Coming, at so late a date, into this Goethe symposium, I must fear more than ever to touch upon ground already occupied by those who have preceded me. One who speaks of Goethe's Women must needs speak of the man Goethe, of "Faust," of "Wilhelm Meister," and of much besides. And I avail myself of the title of the theme given me to speak, not only of the women whom Goethe has brought into the world of literature, but also of those who were known and prized by him. From the living gallery of his friends to the marble gallery of his fancies, we may step in true progress. Or might I rather say, that we may find the beautiful forms of his imagination to be as like to those cherished in his affections, as the trees on the bank are to the trees in the river,—only that, like the clear stream.

347

the master's mind adds to their beauties a glory of its own?

The real women in the first place, and the Mother first of all,—characterized by that substantial value which belongs to a class that neither cringes nor aspires. We must thank the Germans for many words; and may go into their language to help our own, just as a child may go into its grandmother's store-closet to commit a theft which his mother would not leave unpunished. The word I have in mind at this time is *bürgerlich*, which, taken strictly, corresponds to *bourgeois* in French, and to "upper-middle-class" in English. The German term, however, seems to make a stand for itself. The French *bourgeois* has a little sarcastic tang, which Molière gave it. "Upper-middle-class" is rather hopelessly suggestive of caste and confusion. But *bürgerlich*, *bürgerlikke*, brings to our mind those substantial mediævals who were rich enough to afford a velvet doublet and a gold chain,—who could lend the Court money, but who would not borrow manners from it. So Goethe's mother was *bürgerliche*, although beloved of princes, not only for her son's, but for her own sake; with great manners and her gold snuff-box for great days, but with a simple and genuine love of life, its real duties and real values. How naïve and kindly is her anxiety that the cakes to be served at her funeral shall be rich and good enough for the occasion! She does not appreciate the Frau von Staël, and Goethe did not either. Yet

348

she is a woman poetical in sentiment and rich in feeling.

The sister, Cornelia, the dear companion of Goethe's youth, the confidante of his first literary schemes and aspirations, was a young girl whose plainness of per-

son made her self-distrustful, but whose character, to those capable of divining it, revealed an inner beauty to which the outer charm would have seemed superfluous.

The lady-loves, so numerous,—often succeeding each other without an interval between the old love and the new,—how worthy do they for the most part appear in what is known of them! Each has her individual charm. The first, Frederika Brion, is a blooming rustic. The second, Lotte, is a girl in higher position, gay and sedate by turns, the betrothed of Goethe's friend, who bitterly resents the portraiture of both given to the world in "Werther." The third, fourth, and fifth, Anna, Sibylla, and Maximiliane, are less known to us. The sixth, Lili, is a city belle, the daughter of a wealthy banker, and something of a coquette. She was the inspirer of some of the poet's best-known lyrics, such as,

> "Heart, my heart, what is this feeling
> That doth weigh on me so sore?"

349

Of her inspiring, too, was the poem entitled "Lili's Menagerie," in which, says Lewes, "he expresses his surly disgust at the familiar faces which surround her,"—the Bear of the menagerie being a portrait of himself. Goethe follows her about to scenes of uncongenial gayety, in braided coat, gazing at her "amid the glare of chandeliers." In his conversations with Eckermann, he calls her his first, last, and only love, all others in comparison deserving only to be classed as inclinations. When he says of this affection, "It has influenced my style," he pays her the utmost tribute that a literary man can offer to a woman. He loves, but marries not. The first attractions find him precocious in feeling, and mature enough in judgment to distrust himself. It costs him bitter tears to forsake his sweethearts. We can imagine that the tears shed by them must have been more bitter, and cannot put out of sight the disadvantage suffered by these young girls, when, after every appearance of serious intention, the brilliant youth flits from them, and leaves them in (to say the least) awkward isola-

tion. The fact that he did so leave them reminds me of a humorous device in Offenbach's "Orphée aux Enfers." Jupiter, wishing to make love to Pluto's fair bride, descends in the form of a monstrous butterfly, and presently hands forward his card, saying, "Je suis le Baron de Jupiter." The great Goethe, on the contrary, comes like a lord and departs like a butterfly.

In the judgments which this unedifying course has drawn upon him, Goethe is often blamed as though he had been throughout a free and voluntary agent. This is not a fair reading of the matter. Goethe in his youth was subject to all the complications which

350

result from the conflict between temperament and those "circumstances over which we have no control," that would seem to be a convenient invention of modern times. The wishes of his parents—strong and determined people—would naturally be present to his mind in anything of so much moment as a matrimonial alliance. From Frederika he seems to have been parted by a sense of the unfitness of the relation,—responding to the remonstrances of his friend Merck. With Lili he exchanged the kiss of betrothal, and soon after, at the instance especially of his sister, thought better of it, and never saw her more until the heads of both were gray. But now he goes to Court, and beholds the great ladies of the day. One of these, the Frau von Stein, becomes his Muse, and for ten years holds him in her vassalage. The relation between them, though an intimate one, seems to have escaped scandal; Frau von Stein having held a position of much respect in the society of the day, and having no doubt preserved through all excitements the strictest sense of the *convenances*, and of the penalty of their violation. The Frau von Stein is known to have been intellectual in her tastes and elegant in her accomplishments. For the length of time already mentioned she remained a guiding luminary in Goethe's heaven, the confidante of his thoughts, his sentiments, and his literary projects.

In his fortieth year, he met the woman who was destined to be the mother of his only child, and the companion of his later years. This was Christiane

351

Vulpius, a woman of poor descent, inheriting from an unworthy father only the curse of a morbid appetite for intoxicating liquors. Lewes, in his Life of Goethe, finds much to say in explanation of a course of conduct which cost the great Master much of his social prestige, and robbed him forever of the friendship of Frau von Stein. "Christiane had," says Lewes, "quick mother-wit, a lively spirit, a loving heart, and great aptitude for domestic duties." Madame Schopenhauer describes her as endowed with "golden brown locks, laughing eyes, kiss-provoking lips, a small and gracefully rounded figure," and likens her in appearance to a youthful Bacchus. The "Roman Elegies" record Goethe's feeling for her, while the fact that he partly wrote for her his invaluable "Metamorphoses of Plants" shows her to have been possessed of an education sufficient to enable her to share some of his studies. The *liaison*, which must have begun soon after their first acquaintance, in 1788, led, eighteen years later, to a marriage, at which their son, already eighteen years of age, was present. To this son, born in 1789, the Duke August had stood as godfather,—an act which shows that, although disapproved, the connection with Christiane was not ruinous to Goethe's court favor.

352

Bettine von Arnim we may mention as a gracious episode of Goethe's later life,—an evening star on the edge of his sunset glory. Like the evening star, she shows herself, and presently "fades in the light that she loves." Of great romantic interest in the social history of the time, Bettine does not much avail us in the present connection, for it does not appear that she exerted any influence over Goethe's literary life. One other woman we may name, Fräulein von Levezow, whose beauty, spiritual or personal, smote the ancient heart even in extreme old age, and provoking to no unseemly act of folly, called forth the "Elegie aus Marienbad."

I have called to mind very briefly some of the women who are known to have had an influence upon Goethe's life, because they are sure to have had some share in the parentage of that ideal family from which his fame in great measure derives. I am not able, however, to trace out the traits and features which might make this relationship evident. His biographers have already done this,—none better, perhaps, than Lewes.

If we compare Goethe's method with those most in favor with us to-day, we shall be impressed above all with its generosity. In the line of this comparison, I first think of the great English masters, Dickens and Thackeray. From them my mind turns to the works of two of my own countrymen, Messrs. Howells and James. All of these writers have satirized women. In all of them, to my mind, though not in all to the same extent, the points remarked upon are petty, and the inferred damage to character, to say the least, disproportionate. Literary women

353

sometimes show the same, or even a greater, uncharity toward their own sex. An especial example of this I find in the volume called "Modern Women," of which the authorship is attributed to a lady well known in both hemispheres as a writer of fiction. Shall we say that these are truths which wound in the telling, but which should nevertheless be told? Methinks it is the low interpretation of character and of life that wounds. Good surgery works for mitigation, not for mutilation. Cynical writers take from us our left arm of faith and our right arm of courage. They take from us the swift feet of sympathy, which would serve humanity, were not humanity represented as not worth serving nor caring for.

Goethe has shown us in his writings some very poorly behaved women, and has shown them without a word of reprobation. Marianne and Philine, in "Wilhelm Meister," are of this class,—characters which no one would dare to present in English literature so baldly as Goethe has presented them in

the phraseology of his mother tongue. Martha, in "Faust," is vile, and Gretchen trebly criminal. Where is generosity shown in these very literal renderings of women whose life and standard are low? I find that in these, as in his higher creations, Goethe does not lose sight of the ideal value of human life and character. Philine is redeemed through maternity. We see her at last presented to a noble lady, to whom she avows the commonplace level of her intel-

354

lectual aspirations, but says, on the other hand, "I love my husband and my children," and so passes unreproved. Marianne is a sketch left much in shadow; yet she wins our human sympathy when we dimly see her dying of grief for a lover whom she deserved to lose, but whose loss left her inconsolable.

But all these melancholy pictures fade before the piteous pathos of Gretchen,—Gretchen, the simple peasant maiden, who knows no harm, and means no harm to any one. On her way from church, to which she went "full of innocence," the Devil sets his snare for her. The handsome gallant, urged forward by the fiend, touches her imagination. "Wer mag der Herr seyn?" A great gentleman to her,—ay, and in himself a deeply philosophic man, with an exquisite sense even of the beauty of the innocence against which he sins. Goethe does not spare one horror from the tale of what befalls her. The low, stupid misery in which she cowers in the straw, her dim reason presenting the past to her in an intangible shape,—nothing real to her but her helpless loneliness, her forsaken condition, and the hangman and gallows waiting for her. This agonizing story is portrayed with the greatest mastership. The guileless soul of the girl who relates to Faust how she brought up her baby sister, how the little cradle stood ever by her bed, how many a weary hour the little nursling cost her:

"Doch schmeckt dafür das Essen, schmeckt die Ruh."

355

How touching her catechism of Heinrich, as Faust has taught her to call him!

GRETCHEN.

Now say how does it stand with thy religion?
Thou art indeed a heartily good man,
Only of that, I fear me, thou art careless.

FAUST.

Let that alone, my child; thou know'st I love thee,
And for my loves will give my life and blood,—
Would steal from none his altar and his creed.

GRETCHEN.

That's not the right thing yet, one must believe.

FAUST.

Must one?

GRETCHEN.

Thou honorest not the holy sacrament.
Dost thou believe in God?

FAUST.

Sweet, who dares say,
"I believe in God"? Ask thou the priest, the sage,
Their answer seems to mock the questioner.

And the tragedy of her swoon in the cathedral, and of the bitter thoughts which precede it:—

"How different, Gretchen, was 't with thee
When blameless thou this altar didst approach,
From the clasped missal lisping prayers,
Half childish play, half God in thy young heart!
How swims thy head! what misdeeds in thy thought!"

In nothing has Goethe shown more power than in this unique portraiture. A peasant girl, as he must

356

have known them, led away, destroyed, ruined, as he must have seen them, alas! too often,—the moral of this story needs no pointing. Even Hood's "Think of it, dissolute man," would be an impertinence. To womankind it almost seems to say: "If God so clothe with womanhood the very grass of the field, what should you women be who grow up in honor, safety, and knowledge?"

But why should we linger with this poor child in her dismal prison, when we can climb with the master to such heights of noble imagination? Let us admire, first of all, the breadth of view which includes so simple and forlorn a creature, and her very opposite, the woman who sits in her bower to trace

out the silver embroidery of the heavens, Macaria the blessed! We may say that this revelation did not come to the great master all at once. Already in "Götz," his earliest work, the later performance is foreshadowed. Adelheid, the beautiful, corrupt woman, Elizabeth, the strong and simple one, are drawn with mastery, albeit they are only touched in. But the Goethe series would properly begin with Charlotte, a conventional type, if a charming one. She is *bürgerliche, bourgeoise*, of that sort which is as good as anything. No trace in her of the defrauded duchess, of the woman who condescends to live her life, holding her merits and pretensions far above her sphere. She takes her fate as she finds it, is conscientious in the cutting of bread and butter, intends to make a good wife to her prosaic husband, and,

357

though unavoidably touched by Werther's devotion to her, and for a moment stirred by it from her mental equilibrium, is sure to regain her peace of mind, and to end her days worthily and happily, as is best. In George Sand's handling, the *dénouement* might have been far different. "Werther," like Rousseau's "Heloise," gives one cause to reflect upon the changes which make the great romance of one period appear tame and dull in another.

In Goethe's greatest drama, "Faust," and in his greatest romance, "Wilhelm Meister," the artist cuts deep down into the quick of simple, natural passion, always with a high handling and intent. He gives us, too, the conventional glimpses of character which society affords, — the actress, who vainly loves Wilhelm's caustic friend, Jarno; the lady sketched in as stopping at the inn, and reaching home late on her birthday; the little family celebration of it, spoiled by the delay, but still more by the jealous anger which steals her soul away; her faithless lover being present to her mind, while her unloved husband moves before her eyes, scarcely noticed. But before we pass so far, Mignon stays our way, pathetic, like Gretchen, an estray, orphaned by the unspeakable crime of her parents, but with the instincts of a higher race, aspiring heavenward in her loneliness

and desolation, her melancholy a sweet, angelic minor, that ends with a rising cadence. The song, "Kennst du das Land?" is like some magical crystal ball, held in the hand, but in which one sees

358

visions of things far distant. Mignon gives us all Italy in that one beautiful crystallization, — the blooming thickets, the gleaming fruit, the soft air, the mountain passes, the ancestral halls rich in sculptures. Who can show us so much in so little? Only a magician, — and he puts his wonder-ball in the hand of a child.

"Die Schöne Seele," the fair soul, is a Protestant saint of a type not unfamiliar in Goethe's time, — not often seen nor much favored in our own day. The absorbing power of religious enthusiasm, divorcing youth and beauty from the gay and busy world, and turning the sweet, pure eyes all to the contemplation of things transcending human sense, — this portraiture is a very strong and perfect one. But religion in our day is not interpreted after this ascetic fashion. Nature and she embrace with one hand, and aspire with the other. I need not here enlarge upon this fortunate change. The reaction from mediaeval forms of devotion is too well known to need illustration at my hand. Let us, however, think of this, — that Goethe thought this now obsolete type worth preserving in his glorious work. And let us question whether we cannot have the singleness of heart, the unquestioning conscience, of his Schöne Seele, without that technical sundering from social ties and interests which she received as the commandment of Heaven, but against which we of to-day must rebel. Piety of this sort is to-day called Pietism, and stands upon a level with other *isms*.

359

Casting about in my mind for a *schöne Seele* of our own time, I see before me the thoughtful eyes and spirit-pure face of Elizabeth Stuart Phelps. Single and devout is she, and somewhat withdrawn from the world, and yet such a Nature-friend that the heaven which she loves to picture is full of human delights, translated out of excess, out of selfishness,

out of danger. In it the good are holy, harmless, and heavenly forever, but are human withal, as Christ was human.

Macaria, darling of the gods, to whom are whispered the secrets of the universe, sees in the starry heavens the path and power of each distant luminary, and builds sublimely in her own brain the plan of the Master Architect through whom it all came to be. Having had acquaintance once with an eminent astronomer, and knowing, as every one knows, that the study of astronomy involves much laborious calculation, as well as the keenest observation, I asked him what Goethe could have meant by drawing the portrait of a woman who knew all these wonders by intuition. He replied, "There is no understanding what a man like Goethe meant by much that he wrote, and this with the rest." But I find something intelligible even in this mystic description. Goethe's feeling of the intuitive power of women was a very strong one. He may have added to it a moment's trifling with the somnambulic phenomena which Swedenborg and other mystics had already introduced to the world. The intuitive power of woman is indeed

360

precious to society; and one of the great fears which accompany the advance of the sex in rationalistic and purely intellectual discipline, is the dread lest in the drill of their new acquisitions they should lose this distinctive and invaluable trait. I need not here take up this matter either, but I will say, as I said before, "Goethe thought this work suggestive." We therefore may ponder upon it.

Two poems of Goethe's, "Der Gott und die Bajadin," and "Die Braut von Corinth," breathe the fulness of youthful passion, unrestrained by the critical after-thought which makes the great poet appear even greater in the anatomy of human feeling than in its expression. In both of these poems we feel the reaction against the pietistic and exclusive ethic which must often have appeared to Goethe in the light of a Pharisaic tyranny not to be endured.

Mahadöh, lord of earth, visits the Dancing-girl, who greets him as a stranger with smiling hospi-

tality. Of the god the poet says:

"If he judge or if he share,
Manlike he with man must fare."

And so the divine visitor sees beneath the painted cheek a gentle nature, and smiles to find,

"In deepest perdition, a womanly heart."

He becomes her guest, her master, her spouse. Waking from her dream of wedded bliss, she finds him dead. Those who bear him to his funeral pyre deny her the widow's precious right, to be burned

361

with her husband; but she, leaping into the flames, is caught in his embrace, and carried to the region of the Immortals. This story illustrates the passive religion of the Hindoo woman.

In early Christendom, a youth betrothed to a young girl in Corinth journeys thither from his distant home and claims the hospitality of the house to which he stands thus related. Here, in the deep of night, he is visited by a vampire, the ghost of his betrothed, who has met death in a convent to which her mother's vows had consigned her on recovery from a dangerous illness. Surprised by the mother, the fatal, horrible visitor touches us by this piteous appeal:

"Hearken, mother, now my latest prayer,
And a sexton send who shall be my friend,
And my narrow, wretched home unclose.
Bring in flames the loving to repose!
When the spark shall show,
When the ashes glow,
To the old-time deities we'll go."

"The Erl King" is the only poem of Goethe's which offers itself to my mind as having the same terrific suggestion and horror as are found in this composition. Its horror, however, is mystical and pathetic, condensed from the shadows and chills of evening deepening into night, while the Bride is seen by flashes of vivid lightning whose accompanying thunder shakes, with the primeval forces of Nature, the foundations of the new, aspiring Faith.

The climax of Goethe's gyneology — you will allow me this word — is reached in the concluding sentence

362

of "Faust," — "Das Ewig-Weibliche zieht uns hinan," "The Eternal Womanly attracts us, draws us on." The gravity of the nominative here seems to ask a grave interpretation of the verb. *Anziehen* literally means "to draw on," metaphorically means "to attract." Let us give it the weight of both meanings, and interpret it as expressing the attraction which indeed draws or leads us on. This wonderful phrase has been often quoted, and much dwelt upon. As the last word of a mighty life-drama, — a drama whose intense interest holds the world wherever presented to-day, — we are glad to find in it a deep meaning. After the chorus of the angels, and the visitation of the Demon, after daring speculation and more daring sin, after the vanity of imagination, after the substantiality of possession, comes the final voice, "Das Ewig-Weibliche."

It might seem strange if people of our dimensions should feel it incumbent upon them to apologize for anything that a mighty man like Goethe did or said. Still is it one of the meekening reflections belonging to our race, that the greatest of men (could we give one that rank) cannot be rightly judged without the tenderness of human charity. Goethe's unjustifiable treatment of his early loves, his unjustifiable relation with the mother of his boy, — these are matters that call for charitable judgment. And I find the world more bound to charity to-day than heretofore, on account of the improved methods of analysis which belong to our later thought and culture. Phrenology

363

and the study of heredity enable the analyst of human nature in our time to trace the effects of leading characteristics more fully and subtly than was possible in earlier times, in which divisions were more crude and absolute.

The power of Goethe's imagination in matters personal to himself is shown in the circumstance that the mere anticipation of a first meeting with Frau von Stein cost him three sleepless nights. What impossible perfections he expected to find in her, we can hardly conjecture, — prosaic creatures that we are, who would not lie awake one night for any pre-

sentation that can be imagined! This vivid imagination, we must think, would have been apt to lend its brilliant coloring to the encounters of a first acquaintance. Its ecstasy, though supreme, would necessarily be short-lived. Onward, onward, would this flying steed bear its rider, who is not always its master. So the enchantment of one personage would vanish with the enchantment of the surrounding scene. The scene, the personage, remain : the flying one, whose nature it is to fly, has gone.

Of his strangely delayed marriage we may conjecture that the scandal occasioned by the relation preceding it was much less than would have been, at the time, that of a marriage so unequal and unsuitable. Goethe, the world-man, had, no doubt, respect to this consideration. Years pass on, — years of faithful affection and service on the part of his companion. The power of the hearth and home has grown

364

supreme with him. Troubles gather around him, — troubles in which Christiane's better qualities have afforded him real comfort and support. He determines to give the dignity of wifehood to the woman around whom have centred the tender and intimate associations of nearly twenty years. Even with these grave reasons behind it, the marriage causes loud and instant blame. Goethe's friends, however, were glad of it, and Christiane's conduct, we are told, confirmed their approbation of the step.

The modern theory of imagination is that all quick and fine perception is in a great degree dependent upon it. We must think Goethe in this respect most exceptionally gifted. In the wide range of female character which his works unfold to us, this perception of the beautiful impresses me as the trait most characteristic of him. The exquisite tenderness and simplicity of his Gretchen, so unstrained, so true to nature, shows the wonderful sense with which he looked upon the lowliest creatures. Egmont's Clärchen has the same pathos, though not the same character. Gretchen's sweet soul makes itself felt through the poverty of her speech, which is narrow and all peasant-like. Clärchen is city-bred, and has

the gift of expression:—

"Freudvoll und leidvoll,
Gedankenvoll seyn;
Himmel hoch jauchzend,
Zum Tode betrübt;
Glücklich allein
Ist die Seele, die liebt."

365

Of this simple womanhood he has also given us a charming picture in that dialogue which brings before us a man of high culture, who, among the ruins of some ancient fane or city, encounters a mother with her infant child. He muses of the past, and of all the great "may have beens." The woman can tell him nothing of all this, has no talisman with which to call up visions of centuries long vanished. But her baby wakes, and she speaks to him the language of all time:—

"Hat es geschlafen, liebes Herz!"

And this brings a ray of purest light serene into the sombre picture.

Equally at home is he with high dames,—with Leonora of Este, Tasso's beloved.—with the calm, sweet daughter of Agamemnon.

This sense of beauty, then, clothes the Goethean world with varied glories. It is universal, in shadow as in light. It lifts the depths of human nature into the daylight of God's providence. To its fine interpretation, nothing is absolutely common, nothing is hopelessly unclean. Nor is this a mere worship of what may delight the outer senses. The value of the beautiful, in form, in character, and in life,—this deep and steadfast persuasion goes with our poet from his first work to his last. Deeply Christian is this trait, for it is the combination of the three foremost graces of Christianity, Faith, Hope, and Charity.

366

An intense sense of the pleasurable accompanied this keen perception of all beauties. The expression of this, here and there, has led many to think of Goethe as an Epicurean, in the least worthy interpretation of the term. He belongs, on the contrary,

of the world.

if to the sect at all, to its high philosophic order. This view will, in all probability, have been sufficiently presented and considered in this philosophic company. I need not dwell upon the love of scientific observation and research which eminently placed him with the great dignitaries of the sect. But of his *eudaimonistic* temperament itself I have a word to say.

Pleasure-lovers are of two sorts, the self-engrossed and the benevolent. It is a narrow interpretation, even of enjoyment, which can regard it as a solitary good, in which the welfare of others has properly no part. I cannot for one moment think of Goethe as imprisoned in the fetters of this selfish greed, which grasps what others offer, snatches what they refuse, and exults in what it gathers, while it gives nothing. No, that serene nature must have been a light-diffusing one. Where he came, things took on at once a brighter aspect. The dull and trivial small change of society was redeemed in his hands to a genuine currency; the icicles of form and custom became living gems in his sunshine. He was a great *present* help and power, and his literary legacies, precious as they are, are poor in comparison with what it would have been to see him, to hear him, to feel his wonderful

367

magnetism for one half-hour. This great soul carried its great life with it, and made a paltry Ducal residence the literary centre of Continental Europe. Kings and conquerors did him homage. He, rendering respect and courtesy where they were due, paid homage only to truth.

The last scene comes. Is it still the Eternal Womanly? Not to laurel and crown does it call thee, Goethe! not to the princely court, the gay dames, the admiring world. All this thou hast had, as was thy right. Thou hast wrought in thy morning, and noontide, and evening. Night comes now, and brings thee rest. Like a little child on its mother's breast the great man sinks back on the bosom of the infinite love. The Eternal Womanly, the eternally loving, folds him to a slumber which, as we think of it, seems to still for a moment the heart

368

XIII.

GOETHE'S FAUST.

By W. T. HARRIS.

We have often heard that Shakespeare is to be regarded as the greatest of the world's literary men. Especially since the analyses of the great literary critics and philosophers of Germany, this verdict has been gaining universal acceptance among English-speaking nations. The significance of this estimate of Shakespeare is not so easy to discover. Let any young person try to state wherein the great world-poets are so eminent above their fellows, and he may be led to change his opinion many times before he satisfies himself or us with the standard of criticism that he adopts. Is it the music of Shakespeare's verse, or the charm of his metaphor, or the interest of his situations, or the ideal suggestions of his words, or the conformity of his dramatic solutions to the desires and aspirations of the heart? No, it is not any one nor all of these things that would or could deserve the honor that is paid to Shakespeare, or Dante, or even Homer.

369

It is doubtless a great thing—far greater than the items mentioned—to have the poetical insight that can see the spiritual significance of things, and express this by metaphor and personification. In proportion to the insight of the poet, he sees the correspondence between the visible and invisible, and invents new modes of expression for truth discerned internally. The great world-poets have this faculty in an eminent degree, but they share it with other great poets. Their place apart from and above the circle of great poets is due to something else than this eminent degree of insight into the spiritual correspondences in nature. To this insight they add what may be called an ethical insight, which may be more fully described as an intuitive knowledge

of human life in its individual and social aspects. Shakespeare and Homer see in every deed its consequences to society, and the retroactive consequences upon the doer. We call such insight a knowledge of human nature, — a knowledge of life.

Given a human action, certain effects will follow. But this action has also presuppositions, and these the great poet sees as well as the consequences. He not only sees them, but presents them in their completeness. Shakespeare probed human experience to the bottom, and discovered one by one all of its presuppositions, and collected them and exhibited them to the spectator. Inasmuch as there is no isolated man, but each one is a member of society it is requisite to portray the status of society, in order to explain the particular deed of the individual A common man acts in accordance with use and

370

wont, and follows without deviation the beaten track marked out for him by his fellows, — his immediate kinsmen and neighbors. The heroic character, with an eccentric orbit, collides with society and makes a theme for tragedy. In the portrayal of such collisions the ethical might of society and the dæmonic power of the individual come into clear relief, and furnish us opportunity to study social and ethical laws. For it is only when we feel the universality and necessity of a determination or characteristic that we truly know it.

While it satisfies the ordinary story-teller to relate the direct particulars of the collision of his hero, and these only, nothing will content Shakespeare but a complete presentation of all the accessories. His drama will so expound the action that we may see the antecedents which have furnished occasion, as well as all the concomitant reactions which accompany and follow it. A very small item being given, — by some Geoffrey of Monmouth, Holinshed, or Saxo Grammaticus, — Shakespeare proceeds to discover the world of presuppositions necessary to make that isolated item a piece of living reality. Given the small arc, and he computes the total circle; given the deed of Hamlet, or Cymbeline, or Macbeth, and

forthwith he conjures up all the concrete relations, the Family, Society, and State, — the moral status of the individual, and his ethical interaction with the social condition in which he lives, and the subtle casuistry by which the hero directs his course.

371

An insight into the correspondence between nature and mind is the first requisite of a great poet; but an equal insight into the ethical relation of the individual to the social whole is the additional requisite. Without this second insight into human life, the poet cannot belong to the select circle of world-poets. He may "write poetry for poets," —as it is called, — with the former species of insight; but he cannot be a people's poet unless he sees the mediation of the individual with the institutions of the race. For while the individual acts in his own person, the social whole acts through institutions and through individuals set apart and endowed with representative might. No deed is isolated, all deeds are interdependent; only the totality of conditions enables us to comprehend the puniest act. See the part in the whole, and then you are able to see the reflection of the whole in the part.

This is not a doctrine of necessity and fatalism, as it might at first seem, but the true doctrine of freedom and moral responsibility. Freedom demands self-determination, — that the deed shall return upon its author, so that he shall receive its consequences. Now, human society, looked at closely, is an organism for this very purpose. The individual reflects society and is reflected by society. What he deals out to his neighbors comes back to him, in circles of greater or less circumference, according to the degree of generality in which he works. Through society in its industrial, domestic, and social aspects, this

372

reflection of his deed upon the doer is of an implicit character; in the State it is explicit; the State letting him go free when his deed does not infringe on the rights of society, but otherwise reflecting back his deed upon him in the inconvenient form of prison bars and hempen cords.

The deed must be shown in its relations in order to exhibit this reflection ; the fewer relations, the less reflection and the less truth. Shakespeare excels all poets in the portrayal of this reflection of the deed upon the doer. It is not to be expected of a poet that he shall be conscious of his method, or of the logical process involved in the dramatic relations which he places before us. No artist should divide his attention between the abstract and the concrete in this manner. His best work he will accomplish from the instinct of his art. Shakespeare instinctively adopted his method of exhaustively reflecting and presenting the elements of a situation, and we doubt not he felt rather than thought that this and that accessory must be uttered and expressed, because it stood out in his creative imagination as essentially belonging to the representation of the deed.

The correspondence between spiritual being and nature renders possible the expression of what is seen as inward fact. All language has arisen through this first insight of the poet. The second insight of the poet has given us the ethical sentiments, the feeling of the solidarity of the individual with the social

373

whole. Slightly paraphrasing Shakespeare's language in "Troilus and Cressida": "Man, however richly he may be endowed, [" how dearly ever parted,"] however much he may possess in world's goods or intellectual acquirements, cannot make boast to have that which he hath, nor feels what he possesses but by reflection from the recognition of his fellow men ; as when his virtues shining upon others heat them, and they retort that heat again to the first giver." This thought becomes the possession of mankind in an emotional form through the works of the world-poets.

As Orpheus is fabled to have built Thebes with the sound of his lyre, so each people has its Orpheus who has made a spiritual city for it. Although the great artist does not first think out his subject in a logical or philosophical form, and then proceed to clothe it in marble, in tones, or in rhymes and metre,

yet his creative imagination seizes and fixes the shapes and forms which hover before it as typical expressions of his problem of life. For each person finds himself here involved in a "problem of life." Nevertheless, a work of art is not an allegory. It is rather, as Carlyle says, a phantasmagory embodying a many-sided meaning. When we analyze it, we may find logic and dialectic in it as well as in other objects,—or just as we find laws in unconscious nature.

Homer, the first great people's poet of the Western or European world, taught man to recognize in na-

374

ture the presence of the human spirit. The motions, sounds, and apparitions of the beings of nature express some desire or meaning of the invisible conscious beings who form the sphere of reality behind the visible world. But Homer reveals likewise human nature, both as heroic individual and also as representative of institutions,—the State and the Family. The glorious Achilles, the type of beautiful and powerful individuality, has to be subordinated to legally constituted authority,—to Agamemnon, who is endowed with the power of the nation: hence the song of Troy. The Family too is sacred as an institution, and the attack upon it by the hero Paris is the occasion of the war. Thus, by presenting to the Greeks the picture of their twofold nature, realized in beautiful individuality and in ethical might, Homer made his people conscious of themselves.

Dante, another great world-poet, has revealed human nature in its twofold aspect of religious life with individual life in conflict with it. The highest institution, the Church, when not corrupted by individuals who represent it temporarily, is the Celestial Paradise. From this highest institution descends to the institutions of the State and the Family a dispensation of authority which gives them religious superiority over the individual. By disregarding these institutions and finding his motives of action in his selfish passions, the individual falls into one or more of the seven mortal sins and finds the Inferno in the fulness of selfish gratification. Dante as a poet does

375

not so much make the revelation of the beautiful—Homer's function—as of the holy. He does not indicate the correspondences of nature which reveal the soul as finding free expression in matter, but, rather, the correspondences that emblem the struggle of the soul against its material environment, and its victory or defeat. Homer shows us the incarnation of the soul, while Dante shows us its resurrection. Shakespeare is the poet of society, not so much in its national aspect or religious aspect as in its free civil aspect.[1]

It is left to the individual in civil society to take the initiative; he makes such combinations as he chooses, in view of his own welfare and the conditions about him. Acting in this unrestrained manner, the individual may come into collision with either institution,—the State, Church, or Family; or he may collide simply with the normal conditions of free civil activity. These conditions or laws of free civil combination, which rule the sphere of human activity in which the individual procures his food, clothing, shelter, amusement, and culture, are the written and unwritten laws of thrift, economics, morality, and courtesy, which in the aggregate make up social policy and insure success to the individual as his meed. That mankind form a solid unit socially is the presupposition of Shakespeare, and it has become still more a conscious presupposition in an epoch of

376

telegraphs, daily newspapers, and society novels. In Shakespeare there are no mere lay figures, but each one has a will of his own and a personal interest commensurate with his individuality. The world of Shakespeare, compared with that of Homer or Dante, is one of infinite details. But a unity is found for these details in the principle of reflection. The central event of the drama is reflected in each single movement or phase of movement in the drama. The great impending world-tragedy of the senate-house in Rome is reflected in the fantasy of plebeians, and

their rumor reaches Cæsar on the fatal morning:

"Most horrid sights seen by the watch. . . .
Graves have yawned, and yielded up their dead; . . .
Fierce fiery warriors fought upon the clouds, . . .
Which drizzled blood upon the Capitol."

The very elements reflect the premonitions in the minds of the people. So, too, around the castle at Inverness on the night of Duncan's murder:

"The heavens, as troubled with man's act,
Threaten his bloody stage. . . . On Tuesday last,

A falcon, towering in her pride of place,
Was by a mousing owl hawked at and killed.
And Duncan's horses, . . .
Turned wild in nature, broke their stalls, flung out. . . .
. . . . 'Tis said they ate each other."

When seemingly detached and indifferent details reflect the central action of the work of art, its unity is intensified to the highest degree. In Shakespeare we learn that the slightest word or deed of the man is

377

reflected back by the social environment, even when the organized institutions, the State, the Church, the Family, do not take cognizance of it.

In this line of world-poets comes Goethe as the fourth. His central thought is that of the mediation of the individual for himself. In his writings the great institutions appear in the background of the scene in their substantial might; but what especially interests Goethe is not the primary and immediate effect of the deeds of the individual, nor yet their secondary effect, the reaction of the institutions against those deeds, but the third phase, that of the formation of character in the individual, through his readjustment of his aims and purposes in view of the effect of his deeds. The growth of character through experience is not the direct and conscious theme of poetry before Goethe. Homer shows us the change of purpose in Achilles by reason of the reaction of his deeds upon himself. Dante shows how the reaction of deeds upon the personality forms an environment which may be of the Inferno, the Purgatory, or the Paradiso. The Purgatory shows growth of character through persistent will-power,

[1] "Homer is the poet of the nation; Shakespeare, the poet of society; Goethe, the poet of the individual." H. C. Brockmeyer.

but it does not descend from the type and symbol to the concrete every-day life. It constructs an artificial world beyond life, and concentrates the vices and virtues into single types. Shakespeare, on the other hand, deals with the very concrete itself, and furthermore does not exhibit the purgatorial stage, in which character is formed by persistent endeavor.

378

He shows the Inferno in its concretest form, — rarely the Paradiso. But while he is farther off than Dante from Goethe, in this matter of the omission of purgatory he is nearer in the fact that he approaches the problem of the individual in some of his tragedies, and especially in his "Hamlet." In a certain sense "Hamlet" is the prototype of the literature of the present. The problem of the individual is how to adjust himself to his time, or how "to set it right," if he is in advance of his time in any respect. But Shakespeare only states the problem, he does not solve it. He lets accident, weakness, or surplus of will-power and strong passions, lead to error, and then shows how error reacts to deepen temporary aberration into permanent character. The tragic characters tend to insanity through the fixing of their ideas in one channel. That which in their nature was a mere proclivity, easily held in abeyance by the will-power, now becomes an irresistible passion, forced onward by its own results, and they find it easier to go onward than to return.

Goethe has treated the problem of the individual in two great works of art, — the "Faust" and the "Wilhelm Meister." In "Faust" the individual has measurably attained his culture, but finds himself in collision with the world through the fact that he has arrived at agnosticism. The "Meister" traces for us the career of a youth, from the beginning at the bottom of the ladder, up to a point where he becomes clear in regard to his relations to the world.

379

Faust is relatively mature as regards his education or culture. Meister is immature in regard to everything.

Inasmuch as the problem of the individual is not that of the production of the universal, — not that of the founding of a state, or a church, or any great institution, but rather the adjustment of himself as an individual to the institutions already existing, — it follows that the first occupation to which he is called is that of education, — education, however, in the broadest sense of the word. To adapt the individual to life, to solve his problem, is to educate him into such habits of living that he may contribute his mite to society and receive in return the help of his fellow-men. The individual in each epoch of civilization has his revolt against the subjugation of his independence. He does not wish to be subordinated, without his consent, to an alien might. The process of education reconciles him to the institutions, by convincing him that they are necessary for the realization of his rational self. If they had not been made by others, and handed down from the immemorial past, he would set about making them now. As it is, he builds them anew by giving them his hearty support. Progress of the individual on this line is a continued participation in the civilization of one's age, — a thoroughly positive citizenship.

380

But, over against this, there is possible another career of education or culture. Supposing that there is a very deep spirit of independence in the individual, he finds a difficulty in the bridge that leads from his own opinions and conceits to the adoption of the conviction of society. He rebels against the required subordination to public opinion, and will not bow to its behests, either as fashion of the community, social usage, law of the state, or mandate of religion. He stands at the threshold, and demands of each that it shall demonstrate to him its necessity as a rational thing before he shall adopt it. He will yield to it if it proves its rational character, but if it is only a conventional affair, a mere fashion, he will have none of it. Now the cases of strong individuality may become so frequent as to be the rule, instead of the exception. Then an age of revolution ensues, and the education of the age lays stress on the self-activity of the individual, and inveighs against authority. The centrifugal power of individuality is increased, and the centripetal power of obedience to established order becomes weakened, until it loses its constraining power. The French Revolution ensues. Individuality alone is held sacred, and all external authority accursed. Sansculottism is the result. Under the banner of Liberty, Equality, and Fraternity for all, there is a swift descent to absolute personal tyranny. Each one finds a limit to his liberty in the liberty of his fellow, and through the collision arises universal distrust. The guillotine is the only remedy. Only dead enemies are safe enemies to have. Disciplined by this reign of terror, authority is again restored. Rational authority, it

381

has been found, must assert itself first as a mere external constraint against the individual, and initiate a process of enlightenment in him. He may learn why he obeys law and duty and fashion, and change his blind obedience into a rational obedience, which is freedom. But at all events he must obey.

In Goethe's life, extending from 1749 to 1832, the one great event in world history is the French Revolution. Indeed, our American Revolution, with its Declaration of Independence and its "All men are born free and equal," is in a certain sense a reflection of the European movement. Not only France, but all Europe, had been set aflame in Goethe's youth by Rousseau's work on the Inequality among Men. Their thoughts had been turned in the direction of democracy by his "Contrat Social" and his "Émile." The conservers of institutions knew no means of checking the revolution in the popular consciousness. No intellectual bridge could be furnished, over which it could go from pure individualism to an insight into the necessity of institutions for the realization of freedom. Hence, all things were readjusted by revolution. In the end, a necessity, which all could see, reestablished institutional authority in France. Meanwhile the rest of Europe looked on and pondered the problem. The German mind had set itself about the task of discovering a theoretical necessity for the institutions of civilization. Immanuel Kant, starting

from the theoretical foundation of Hume,—which might be regarded as the basis also of Rousseauism,—

382

had reduced the problem to its lowest terms, and finally demonstrated the necessity of the postulates of authority, moral and otherwise, for the conduct of human life. Eight years before the destruction of the Bastile, Kant published his theoretical philosophy, "A Critique of Pure Reason," showing the limits of the speculative faculty to grasp the problems of the world. The year before the French Revolution began, he published the "Critique of the Practical Reason," completing his demonstration of the necessity in human nature for the sacrifice of the individual to his higher self, as defined in the moral law and organized into institutions in the form of civilization. Thus, while the historical process went on in France, as an external phenomenon with deafening explosions, in the still world of German thought there went on a corresponding theoretical process, which more swiftly reached the positive solution. But there was another solution in progress. In the world of literature a new world-poet had been born, who was to devote his entire life to the same problem, and to leave its solution in great works of art.

It must not be understood that any of the solutions of this problem of individualism are merely negative. As suggested by Hume, stated by the Encyclopaedists, put into universal literary form by Rousseau, occasion was given for a threefold answer. There was the practical answer, realistic to the last degree,—the answer beginning with the destruction of the Bastile, passing through the Reign of Terror into its logical

383

consequence, Napoleonism, and closing at Waterloo. There was the theoretic, speculative solution in the Kantian Critiques of the Reason, and besides this the solution of the world-literary man, Goethe. The political answer was not a mere negative one, for it refused to return to its beginning. All Europe read the verdict: No more abstract tyranny for the people. Authority, it is true, there must be; yes, but an authority that expresses the welfare of the social

whole, and is reflected in the rational conviction of each individual. Not only France came to this basis, but all Europe was led to adopt it. The Kantian solution in its first aspect is negative: "Man cannot know truth theoretically," — the conclusion of the Critique of the Pure Reason. But in the Critique of the Practical Reason the solution is positive. Man in order to be a social being, or even a rational being, must set up above himself the moral law as absolute authority. In this moral authority root the institutions of civilization: they are its instruments of realization. The literary solution of Goethe is likewise thoroughly affirmative. Rousseau had given literary form to the problem. In his wonderful prose, the question went home to the consciousness of Europe and Europeans, wherever they were. Goethe put into literary form the answer to this problem, and his answer is reaching the consciousness of the world, by progressive degrees, throughout this century and the centuries to follow.

The individual, as we have seen, if he is endowed

384

with a strong feeling of independence, may at any time stand on his threshold and challenge the approach of authority. As a mere individual affair, it is not of much significance. But it is possible also to find an entire historical epoch, as we have seen, given to this assertion of the individual against external authority. This genesis of individual protest against all authority justifies its treatment by a world-poet as a world-problem. Or, it might be said, the universal nature of the problem avails to give a universal significance to its literary solution and to elevate Goethe into the rank of world-poet.

We learn that Goethe, at the early age of twenty years, discovered in the popular legend of Faust the vehicle for the literary statement of the problem and its solution. He saw, in short, the problem of the reconciliation of man as individual with man as social whole, and divined the affirmative answer. He tells us himself,[1] in his letter to Wilhelm von Hum-

boldt, in 1832, that his youthful conception of Faust had been before him for more than sixty years, "the whole series having been from the first clear to me, though not in all their details." "I have always," he writes, "quietly kept my original plan in view, and have worked out singly those scenes which happened to interest me most; so that there remained gaps in the Second Part, only to be bridged over by investing them with an interest proportioned to the rest."

385

Faust as a mythological character embodies the conception of an individual who obtains the service of the intellect for his selfish ends, and sacrifices his future good for present enjoyment. In its different elaborations it had come to express nearly every one of the phases that Goethe afterwards united in his work, with the essential exception that there was no other than a tragic dénouement for its hero. Using this legend for a vehicle, Goethe, after his manner, connected and subordinated the details into one whole which animated the parts. Every circumstance had its motive furnished for it. That which lay in it as enigmatic or unconscious, Goethe brought up to light and expressed with fulness. Why should Faust sell his soul to the Evil One? Evidently, thought Goethe, the all-sufficient motive for this is despair of attaining the blessedness of divine life. What does such despair presuppose? Unsatisfied aspiration, was the reply. The condition of this, again, perennially arose through a species of philosophic speculation, which arrived at the conviction that the Universal Power of Nature is not a personal one like man, but something formless and negative to the persistence of all forms.

386

In the eighth book of his Autobiography, he tells us of his studies of the alchemists and Hermetic writers. He carried these on in his twentieth year, assisted by his friend, the Fräulein von Klettenberg. They read the works of Welling, Paracelsus, Basil Valentine, Van Helmont, and Starkey. He traced

all these writings to their source in the Neo-Platonic school of philosophers. Here was a fountain of

[1] Quoted by Hermann Grimm, "Life and Times of Goethe." See English Translation by Sarah Holland Adams, p. 502.

theosophy. Those thinkers busied themselves with the problem of Nature and the Absolute. The History of the Church and of the Heretics, by Arnold, gave him the necessary clue to the relation which these Neo-Platonic speculations held to the accepted Christian doctrines, and at this early age Goethe had grappled seriously with the profoundest questions that can occupy the mind of man. Nowhere as in the history of heresy do we discover the genuine speculative basis of the Christian dogmas. The heresies arose through an effort on the part of individuals to find the necessary truth of the doctrines of the Church. The real speculative basis of these doctrines was developed by the Church fathers in their controversial treatises directed against those heresies. One familiar with those theological discussions, and especially with the Neo-Platonic and Gnostic speculations, will not be surprised to read, in the eighth book of the "Wahrheit und Dichtung," the statement of the view which Goethe himself had formed.[1] Attention is called particularly to his view of the possible annihilation of the wicked by continued concentration upon themselves, and of the prevention of this by an act of grace.

The speculations of Gnosticism and Neo-Platonism were little known during the Middle Ages. The contact with the Arabian learning in the tenth and

387

succeeding centuries, and finally the westward migration of learned Greeks after the fall of Constantinople, gave a great impulse to the study of mysticism in the fifteenth and sixteenth centuries. A mixture of physical, metaphysical, and theological doctrines, expressed in a technique derived from all three sources, constituted this mysticism, often called "Theosophy." The chemical knowledge involved originated, of course, with the Arabians, and it is important to note that the metaphysics and theology were influenced in their doctrines by the alchemy connected with it. For chemistry reveals to us the mutability of material forms. In the retort, a substance can be compelled to change from one form to

[1] Page 300 of Bohn's Translation.

---

another.

The tendency of the mind is to generalize the facts before it. Hence the alchemist swiftly concluded: there is no form that abides, not even the form of consciousness whose shape is to be subject and object of itself. The substance, or true being, is formless. It is an energy, but an energy that acts only in two ways, to produce form or to destroy form. In itself it is in no wise any form whatever. Form belongs only to product or result,—it is *natura naturata*, and not *natura naturans*. What follows from this is evidently the doctrine of Pantheism: God is pure negative Might, and all that has form is finite and perishable. Man, too, is perishable. Moreover, by reason of the fact that consciousness is a form, it cannot appertain to the Absolute. Hence, too, the

388

Absolute cannot be known by human reason, because there can be nothing distinguished except by its form, and hence a formless absolute is a pure nothing to the mind. That the legend of Faust is the reflection in the popular mind of this study of alchemy, there is no doubt. Goethe takes this for granted, and accordingly places his Faust in a lofty arched Gothic chamber, surrounded by the appliances of alchemy, a library, and "ancestral lumber." In the very first scene Goethe proceeds to express in the mouth of Faust the agnostic standpoint of Pantheism: "I have been through all human learning, and know that nothing can be known."[1] He summons up spirits, the moving principle of nature, or the Macrocosm which shows all things in the world connected by interdependence.

We cannot know one thing except through the rest on which it depends. That which possesses form is dependent on the formless. We can pursue the hidden substance from one form to another, but never overtake it in its pure essence. Hence Faust, who aspires to know truth, is in despair. Recourse

[1] "In the first sentence of the poem, the theme, or the 'argument,' is stated in its naked abstractness, just as Achilles' wrath is the first sentence of the Iliad." Brockmeyer, Letters on Faust, III.

---

to magic only serves to convince him of the hopelessness of knowing the Absolute. For by magic he has summoned the spirit of the Macrocosm and the Earth Spirit. The former symbolizes his study of

389

the infinite network of relations which constitutes nature. He cannot press through these relations to reach the Absolute; or if he does, he encounters pure negation of all form. All form is show alone,—a mere shadowy manifestation of the Absolute. Nor is it any better with the Earth Spirit which rules a part of the Macrocosm, the earth-sphere. The celestial and the supercelestial worlds are beyond the sphere of the Earth Spirit. But Faust cannot comprehend even the earth process. It is too general, too vast, for him. The spirit that lives in "Being's floods and Action's storm" is so general and so formless that he is both birth and grave of all form. Man cannot hope to know him nor participate in his eternity. Hence aspiration for knowledge is spurned by the Absolute, and there remains only despair.

Here, therefore, is the matter for the tragedy.[1] It lies so deep that it may be regarded as including all

[1] "The denial of the possibility of the manifestation of self-conscious intelligence in the individual [i. e. the denial that man can know truth] is the denial of the possibility of its realization in the family, society, and the State [i. e. secular institutions], as well as the denial of the actualization of that intelligence in the forms of Art, Religion, and Philosophy. [For there can be no Art or manifestation of the infinite in the finite, if there is no possibility of recognizing it by conscious intelligence. So, too, religion and philosophy would be impossible.] Now if this denial of the possibility of knowing truth assume the form of a conviction in the consciousness of an individual, a nation, an age, then there results a contradiction which involves in the sweep of its universality the entire spiritual world of man. For it is the self-consciousness of that individual, nation, or age in direct conflict with itself,—not with this or that particularity of itself, but with its entire content *in the sphere of manifestation*, [i. e., as Mr. Brockmeyer has explained the technical use of "manifestation," it includes only the sphere of the individual man, and not the sphere of institutions,] with the receptivity for, the production of, and the aspiration after the Beautiful, the Good, the True, within the individual himself; *in the sphere of realization* with the family, with society, and with the State; and finally *in the sphere of actuality* with art, religion, and philosophy. Now this contradiction is precisely what is presented in the proposition, 'Man cannot know truth.' This was in the history of modern thought

390

other collisions within it. Most works of art specialize the collision and treat of an attack on the Family, or the State, or some one institution; but the Faust collision strikes at the very nature of institutions, and hence includes all the collisions treated in Art.[1]

Hence the collision is so general that it demands two very different dramas for its full treatment. The ordinary drama must deal with individuals, and show them to us in their actions and sufferings. But the individual cannot embody all institutions. Only one of these, the Family, can be presented in its complete circle of individuals. The State and the Church

391

cannot be presented except typically, by representative individuals and by allegorical masquerades. Thus we have a First Part of "Faust," in which the individual is shown to us directly as unscrupulous pleasure-seeker, who destroys the Family through the consequences of his deeds, by destroying, one after another, all the individuals of it. Then follows a Second Part, in which the practical conclusion of "Faust" as it is embodied in the fiend Mephistopheles makes its appearance in the State; then shows itself in Art and Religion, and is overcome in all these realms. The poet does not state for us the argument in logical terms, but he pictures for us the genesis of Faust's convictions, and their consequences when carried out.

The work commences with the beautiful Dedication, which expresses Goethe's objective attitude towards the great poem on the occasion of his return to

the result of Kant's philosophy, which was the philosophy of Germany at the time of the conception of Goethe's Faust." Letters on Faust, III.

[1] "This theme, then, is nothing more nor less than the self-consciousness in contradiction with itself, in conflict with its own content. Hence, if the poem is to portray this theme, this content in its totality, it must represent it in three spheres: first, *manifestation*, — Faust in conflict with himself; second, *realization*, — Faust in conflict with the family, society, and the State; thirdly, *actualization*, — Faust in conflict with art, religion, and philosophy." Letters on Faust, III.

it in 1797, after a lapse of twenty-three years. The Prelude on the Stage describes the three attitudes possible towards a work of art. Art may exist solely for amusement, in which case the Merry Andrew would be its culminating achievement. To the manager, Art is merely a vocation by which he gets his living, and hence he looks beyond the content to its effect in "drawing a full house." Finally, Art to the poet means the utterance of the highest inspirations, and the picturing of human nature in all its tragic greatness to the astonished spectator. The poet's idea includes amusement and terror,

392

pleasure and pain, — and, above all, wisdom, derived from the spectacle of human nature in its entirety. For this includes "the whole circle of creation, and a progress from heaven through the world to hell," and also a counter movement in the opposite direction.

The Prologue in Heaven gives us, in the style of the old miracle play, a hint of the vast design of "Faust." It takes advantage of this crude form to give us, in the way of an outline, a glimpse of the spiritual geography within which we may locate Faust. How the problem of evil arises in creation, through the very nature itself of the creative process, is suggested. Creation should reflect God, but the reflection should take place in imperfect creatures, and hence be an imperfect reflection. The finite individual, to reflect God, must be first endowed with self-activity or free will; but he may use this selfishly as well as piously. Hence the possibility of temptation by Mephistopheles, — the spirit of negation, exclusion, limitation, finitude, or selfishness. God has placed in the finite being a hunger for infinitude, — in short, what is called aspiration. Hence there is progressive development possible. This problem of evil is inherent in any theory of creation. For the finite must by self-activity come into the Divine Image. But the possession of freedom to act for itself involves the possibility of selfish actions which mar the Divine Image. The Prologue shows us the comprehensiveness of the problem of "Faust." Endowed

393

with infinite aspiration, ("the glimmering of heaven's light that he calls reason,") but with finite capacity of intellect and will, man cannot choose but err. He "uses his light to be most brutal of brutes," says Mephistopheles. But the Lord says, in substance: "Man is prone to error because he is struggling to satisfy this aspiration; in his ignorance and restlessness he tries one thing after another, but will never be content with any solution that does not satisfy this divine aspiration. Hence it is permitted to the spirit of selfishness to hold out temptations to the individual, offering satisfaction to him in the form of delights of the flesh or gratification of selfish ambition for power." Mephistopheles thinks that he can satisfy this divinely created soul with dust of the earth, and so gain permanent acquisition of it. The Lord knows that, though the soul can be diverted from the true way, it never can remain satisfied with the wages of sin. It will grow more and more discontented and restless with its lot. The possession of the glimmering of heaven's light in the shape of reason will forever prevent any finite pleasure from sating the soul of Faust, and will make it impossible for Mephistopheles to win his wager.

We start, in the first scene, with the feeling of despair at the agnosticism which Faust has fallen into. The origin of this (in his studies into alchemy) is shown. He comes upon the idea of a universal principle of relativity in nature, and concludes, like Herbert Spencer in recent times, that he pursues

394

absolute truth in vain.[1] He leaves the problem of nature in general, and confines his attention to the earth, and even here is rudely repulsed.[2]

"What am I then capable of comprehending, if I cannot comprehend my earthly environment?" "You may know only your trade." Infinite subdivision of

[1] "The conviction that human intelligence is incapable of absolute knowledge is one that has been slowly gaining ground as civilization has advanced." Spencer's First Principles, p. 68.

[2] "Receptivity for and production of the truth are negated by the conviction that man cannot know truth, but on the wings of aspiration he sallies forth into the realm of magic, of mysticism, of sub-

labor is necessary in order that man, the individual, may find what he can master. The same subdivision of science is necessary in order to get a sufficiently small field of view to enable the individual to behold it. How absurd then to call man a Microcosm, and boast of his power to know the truth of the universe![1]

395

The pain of this discovery is brought before us by the ensuing dialogue between Faust the aspiring seer and Faust in his vocation of professor; for Wagner the "famulus" is the type of the latter. Faust storms bitterly against the limitations. He knows the difference between hearsay and direct insight. Wagner is seeking the satisfaction of his soul in mere erudition, that collects but does not comprehend; that declaims the eloquence of others; that delights in poring over parchments; that digs in shallow trash, and rejoices to find an earth-worm. Faust has been through that stage of culture, and knows that erudition alone can never satisfy. The teaching of what he does not thoroughly comprehend, or grasp together as a whole, is odious to him.[2] He

396

perceives on his shelf a vial of poison and takes it down. If the Earth-Spirit scorns him, he in his turn can show his power to rend asunder his body, — the earthly concretion which holds him, or perhaps constitutes him. He can negate life, if he cannot comprehend it: "Now is the time to prove by deeds that human dignity quails not before the heights of the gods." He too can by his own act destroy his own form, like the pantheistic God that is above all form.

But during his bitter meditations the night has passed and morning has come. Of all the mornings of the year this is Easter morning, the day of the festival celebrating the rising of the Son of Man from the dead. Such a festival celebrates, therefore, the conviction that man survives his finite individuality and is immortal. If that religious belief is true doctrine, it is evident that the negative doctrine — of the Earth-Spirit and the Absolute Relativity of the Macrocosm — cannot be true. The Absolute cannot be a formless abstract power that makes and breaks forms like bubbles, but it must be an absolute Person, — yes, a divine-human Being, — who draws up beings out of the dust into his image, and preserves their individuality beyond the grave.

397

Faust listens to this announcement of the New Covenant. After the Chorus of Angels announcing the risen Christ, comes the Chorus of Women singing of the tender offices performed on pure finitude, — on a dead body, — and closing with the lament at the removal of the physical remains of the dear one. To this the angels respond with the comforting assurance of the resurrection of the individual loving and loved one. Then the disciples lament their separation from the risen one, and the angels exhort them to bring into reality his presence, by living his life of love and self-sacrifice for others. This is a complete statement of Christian doctrine: (1.) God is divine-human, who sacrifices himself for men; (2.) Let man, filled with His spirit, live for others, thus making the divine spirit the real spirit of humanity, and thus forming the highest of institutions, the Church; (3.) Man is immortal as an individual, but by renunciation of his selfish individuality he must be born again as a new and free individuality.

Faust hears these "heavenly tones," this comforting hymn, which once in other days he had heard with childish faith. Life had then seemed worth living. How does it happen that this religious doctrine makes life worth living, while the scientific truth has just now led him to suicide? He will defer suicide until he can examine once again the validity of religion. And so he goes out on Easter morning to see what it is that makes life worth living to his fellow men.

398

In the scene before the Gate, he stops to listen to the voices that declare the various objects in which the people can find happiness: the hunter's lodge, the mill, the river tavern, the crowd, pretty girls, strong beer, a pipe of stinging tobacco, jolly rows and squabbles, etc. Faust takes note of these objects silently, and listens further to the citizens who discuss town politics, and congratulate themselves on being out of harm's way while their fellow men in Turkey are not; soldiers, whose trade is destruction of life and property, singing of the conquest of lofty castles and proud women, in the same beautiful metre that the angels had sung at daybreak. Faust advances toward the crowd gathered under the lime trees, and remarks in a learned way on the influence of advancing spring in thawing the rivers and reviving the herbage in the fields. So this day draws out the people from the vocations in which they are buried as in narrow tombs, and they come out and

---

[1] jectivity. For if reason with its mediation is impotent to create an object for this aspiration, let us see what emotion and imagination without mediation can do for subjective satisfaction. And here all is glory, all is freedom. The imagination seizes the totality of the universe, and revels in ecstatic vision. What a spectacle! But, alas, a spectacle only! How am I to know, to comprehend, the fountain of life, the centre of which articulates this totality? See here another generalization: the practical world as a whole [typified in the Erd-Geist]. Ah! that is my sphere; here I have a firm footing; here I am master; here I command spirits. Approach and obey your master! 'Yes, I'm he; am Faust thy peer.' 'Peer of the spirit thou comprehendest, — not of me.' No, indeed, Mr. Faust, thou dost not include within thyself the totality of the practical world, but only that part thereof which thou dost comprehend, — only thy vocation; and hark! 'it knocks!' O death! I see 't is my vocation indeed. 'It is my famulus!'" Letters on Faust, IV.

[2] "And this too is merely a delusion; the great mystery of the practical world shrinks to this dimension, — a bread-professorship!' It would seem so; for no theory of the practical world is possible without the ability to know truth. As individual you may imitate the individual, as the brute his kind, and thus transmit a craft; but you cannot seize the practical world in transparent forms and present it as an harmonious totality to your fellow man, for that would require that these transparent intellectual forms should possess objective validity, — and this they have not, according to your conviction." Letters on Faust, IV.

add color to the landscape. It is a sort of sun-myth, apparently, to Faust. He is glad, however, to think of a resurrection from the narrowness of one's vocation, on which the speech of the Earth-Spirit had led him to reflect so bitterly. As he approaches, all crowd around him, to show him the greatest honor as the wise physician who has saved their lives from the pestilence. Wagner by his side congratulates him on his reception, and envies his happiness at being so reverenced. The Wagner element in Faust must have been greatly delighted; but the doubting spirit of culture in him at once reacts. He sees the other side:

399

"My father and I raged through these vales and mountains worse than any pestilence with our empirical remedies; the patients died, and no one asked who got well; and now I must live to hear the reckless murderers praised!"

Although he finds no happiness in the recognition of his power over his fellow men, he finds in it a suggestion. If I, Faust, cannot know truth, I can see at least what an opportunity for selfish gratification it affords me. If the Earth-Spirit scorns me and sends me back to my vocation, I can certainly use my vocation as the means of procuring physical pleasure. To be sure, such a life for the mere sake of living is a dog's life. For if a man uses his highest spiritual powers merely for "getting a living," (meaning by that expression procuring his food, drink, clothing, and shelter by it,) he does not live for the highest ends, but makes the highest ends quite subordinate to lower aims. Wagner's view of the object of life seems to be a dog's view, or rather he seems to make his vocation into a dog which he keeps for his service and comfort. He accordingly takes home with him to his study the thought of the dog view of life.[1] With the

400

poodle he returns to the study pondering the view of life that proposes to live for the sake of living. He now proceeds to take up the question which had occurred to him on hearing the bells on Easter morning: Is a divine revelation possible to a being who cannot know the truth?

The verse of St. John's Gospel that reveals the nature of God as divine-human from all eternity is, of course, the special passage to examine. In that

401

verse it is revealed that God becomes a creature, and manifests himself to creatures. The revelation is made in the Greek language with the word *Logos*. One might say that this word must have meant something to the Greek mind, or else it would not have revealed the Christian idea expressed by it. But, at all events, no one can translate it into his own language unless he understands it. The dictionary meaning of *Logos* is "word," "reason," etc. Faust tries "word," but at once reflects that a word cannot be a word before it has a meaning, and hence

cannot have been "in the beginning." *Logos* must therefore be translated "meaning," or "sense." But a meaning is not a power, and hence cannot originate anything; if the meaning were the first, nothing would have followed. An energy is required; hence *Logos* must be translated "Power." Further reflection discovers that nothing begins until a power acts; hence for "power" must be substituted "deed." There is a real beginning only in a *deed*. But, alas! Faust sees that he has been enabled to find the right word solely by his intellect. If he cannot understand the sense of the original by rethinking it, he cannot find words into which to translate it. Therefore, if he cannot know truth, he cannot understand a revelation of it, and hence there can be no revelation of it to him.[1]

402

The poodle idea gets restless during this examination. It has become a serious matter. If I cannot know truth, I can by my power of intellect use my fellow men for my pleasure. I can take the world

---

[1] To Wagner it is immaterial whether he knows what he needs, provided he sees the day when the man who has been worse to the people than the very pestilence itself receives public honors; but to Faust, to the man really in earnest, who is not satisfied when he has squared life with life, and obtained zero for a result, or who does not merely live to make a living, but demands a rational end for life, and, in default of that rational end, spurns life itself, — to such a man this whole scene possesses little significance indeed. It possesses, however, some significance, even for him! For if it is indeed true that man cannot know truth, — that the high aspiration of his soul has no object, — then this scene demonstrates, at least, that Faust possesses power over the practical world. If he cannot know this world, he can at least swallow a considerable portion of it, and this scene demonstrates that he can exercise a great deal of choice as to the parts selected: do you see this conviction?

"Do you see this conviction? Do you see this dog? Consider it well: what is it, think you? Do you perceive how it encircles us nearer and nearer, — becomes more and more certain, and, if I mistake not, a luminous emanation of gold, of honor, of power, follows its wake? It seems to me as if it drew soft magic rings, as future fetters, round our feet! See, the circles become smaller and smaller, — 'tis already near: come, come home with us! The temptation here spread before us by the poet, to consider the dog 'well,' is almost irresistible; but all we can say in this place is, that if one will look upon what is properly called a vocation in civil society, eliminate from it all higher ends and motives other than the simple one of making a living, — no matter with what pomp and circumstance, — no doubt he will readily recognize the poodle. But we must hasten to the studio to watch further developments, for the conflict is not as yet decided. We are still to examine the possibility of a divine revelation to man, who cannot know truth." Letters on Faust, V.

[1] "And for this purpose, — our newly acquired conviction that we possess power over the practical world, although not as yet in a perfectly clear form before us, comfortably lodged behind the stove, where it properly belongs, — we take down the original text of the New Testament in order to realize its meanng in our own loved mother tongue. It stands written, 'In the beginning was the Word.' Word? Word? Never! *Meaning* it ought to be! Meaning what? Meaning? No, it is *Power!* No, *Deed!* Word, meaning, power, deed, — which is it? Alas! how am I to know, unless I can know truth? 'Tis even so, our youthful recollections dissolve in mist, into thin air, and nothing is left us but our newly acquired conviction, the restlessness of which during this examination has undoubtedly not escaped your attention. 'Be quiet, there, behind the stove.' 'See here, poodle, one of us two has to leave this room.' What, then, is the whole content of this conviction, which, so long as there was the hope of a possibility of a worthy object for our aspirations, seemed so despicable? What is it that governs the practical world of finite motives, the power that adapts means to ends, regardless of a final, of an infinite end? Is it not the Understanding? and although Reason — in its search after the final end, with its perfect system of absolute means, of infinite motives and interests — begets subjective chimeras, is it not demonstrated that the understanding possesses objective validity? Nay, look upon this dog well · does it not swell into colossal proportions? — is no dog at all, in fact, but the very power that holds absolute sway over the finite and negative, — the understanding itself, — Mephistopheles in proper form." Letters on Faust, V.

for my oyster. Unscrupulous self-gratification at the expense of my fellow men is fiendish. While to ply one's vocation merely for the sake of making a living is only the idea of a dog, or any other animal, to live and enjoy myself at the expense of the injury of my fellow beings is demonic. Here is the transmutation of the

403

dog into a devil. Out of the poodle comes Mephistopheles, and Faust forswears all aspirations for divine things, making a compact to renounce them, provided he can be sated with earthly pleasure.

The exorcism of the demon uses the magic formulæ, but with a subtle reference to an underlying kernel of meaning. The spirit is not one of earth (*Incubus* or *Kobold*), air (*Sylph*), fire (*Salamander*), or water (*Undine*); it does not belong to nature at all, in fact, but to spirit. It is the intellect used simply for itself and against all else, and is therefore "the spirit that vilely transpierced" One,—the Divine Being who took upon himself the sins and punishment of others, and gave the infinite exemplar of unselfishness. This renunciation for the sake of others is the test that reveals the character of any form of sinful nature. Mephistopheles believes that all that is ought to be destroyed. In this respect he partakes of the nature of the formless god of Pantheism. All forms arise out of Substance by negation, and all return into the formless substance by means of a second negation.

All form is *Maya*, or illusion, says the Hindoo. But Mephistopheles is not generally so abstract in his views as he expresses himself on his first appearance to Faust. He usually "opposes his cold devil's fist, clenched in impotent malice against the beneficent creating power," as Faust is made to suggest. While the Creative Word delights in nursing into being the

404

myriad forms of nature, and in drawing them up by evolution into human beings, His image, with whom to share his blessedness, Mephistopheles, on the contrary, inspired by a spirit of envy which is the antithesis of this divine altruism, wishes to beat back

into chaos all that has come into being. He wishes to share with no one else, and hence realizes the ideal of pure selfishness.

In the compact made with Mephistopheles in the following scene, the stipulations are such that Faust is certain to escape, if he retains any aspiration. If the delights of the senses can please him to satiety, of course he has lost his soul to the Evil One. "If ever I stretch myself in quiet on a bed of ease, if thou canst cheat me with enjoyment, be that day my last. . . . If ever I say to the passing moment, 'Stay, for thou art fair,' then mayest thou cast me into chains." But in his quest of happiness that does not turn into pain, he will pass entirely out of the realm of pleasures of appetite and passion, and come to those of ambition and power; these he will pass by to the pleasures of culture in art and literature, which he will desert for the final happiness of laboring for the good of his fellow men. Arrived at altruism, he has arrived at what is diametrically opposed to the nature of the demon with whom he has made a compact. Mephistopheles must satisfy him, then, by giving him such happiness as heaven affords,—that is to say, the happiness reached through unselfish devotion to others. This fiend must serve him, therefore,

405

and assist him in his benevolent undertakings, until he wellnigh destroys his own diabolic character.

The compact signed, the next question is how to enjoy himself. Faust's good impulses would lead him to share the pain and pleasure of humanity, and thus widen his own life by adding to it the life of the race. But his selfishness, incarnated in Mephistopheles, at once rebukes him, and exhorts him to the use of all as a means of his pleasure.[1] He despises all theories, all reflections on the regulative principles of human conduct, and wishes Faust to give them up. The gibes of Mephistopheles against philosophy and school learning are taken in good faith as Goethe's best wisdom by many readers. This adoption of the code of

1 "'Away with this striving after the impossible ! What though your body is your own, is that which I enjoy less mine ? If I can pay for six brave steeds, are they not mine, with all their power?

the Evil One is itself quite as comical as anything in the wit of Mephistopheles. Goethe of course recognized this in its fulness; for he makes Mephistopheles soliloquize after the departure of Faust: "Only let him despise reason and science, the highest strength that man possesses, and even if he had not contracted himself to the Devil he would notwithstanding go to destruction." 406

The scene with the Student emphasizes the Mephistophelian view of school education. It satirizes logic and grammar, chemistry and anatomy, philosophy and jurisprudence, theology and medicine, suggesting sensuality as the proper substitute for earnest pursuit of art and science. That Goethe himself passed through all these stages of Mephistophelic opinion there can be no doubt. He was a Titan when at college in Leipzig. He attacked institutions again and again in his early life. But he outgrew this spirit of revolt by degrees. The French Revolution is the great outward event that had its reflection in the souls of the brilliant youth of that epoch. Goethe records his final verdict on that frame of mind by putting its favorite expressions into the mouth of Mephistopheles. In the passage of his Autobiography above referred to, (Book VIII. p. 300, Bohn's Translation,) we can see how he had surmounted his own speculative doubts of the warranty of civilization by the study of Neo-Platonism and Mysticism, very soon after his return from Leipzig and before he conceived his Faust. It must be supposed, however, that the very general and

I run as if on four and twenty legs, and am held to be of some consequence. Away, therefore : leave off your cogitating,—away into the world ! I tell you, a man who speculates is like a brute led by evil genii in circles round and round upon a withered heath, while close at hand smile beauteous pastures green. Just look at this place. Call you this living,—to plague yourself and the poor boys to death with ennui ? Leave that to your good neighbor, the worthy Mr. Bookworm. Why should you worry yourself threshing such straw ?' The extraordinary good sense of this advice is so apparent, that it cannot be without some immediate effect, which we perceive in the scene where the different studies are reviewed by the aid of its radiance concentrated into

'All theory, my friend, is gray,
But green the golden tree of life,'

as the focal point. With this final adieu to the past, we congratulate ourselves upon the 'new career'!" Letters on Faust, VI.

407

abstract character of his conviction rendered necessary a long time to leaven the concrete details of his view of life. In the course of his great literary work of art, we are given to understand his final classification or all mental attitudes towards the world.

All being ready, Faust's companion spreads the mantle[1] with proper care, and they are off on their journey.

Now the question arises, What shall be the content of the first scene in which this new conviction of Faust is to be realized? Obvious enough, — the Easter morning, with its crowds of people going gayly forth to enjoy their holiday, will suggest idleness, and "loafing," as it is called, which, however, cannot be endured in solitude. There must be idle company to make idleness palatable. But an idle company are not able to enjoy their leisure purely for itself; they must forget themselves by telling amusing stories. But really artistic talent cannot be displayed without labor; the easiest wit is that lowest species which deals in profanity and obscenity. Hence we have scurrilous songs full of scandal. The choicest morsel for the idler is scandal relating to the established order of things, — the government, the Church, the industries of the community, the morals of those in

408

power. But this does not suffice to dissipate the ennui of such a company. There is no recourse but to benumb consciousness by strong drink; this alone is effective, for it loosens the hold of the senses on reality, and substitutes a world of illusion: "False form and word! change sense and place! be here, be there!" Each one sees a beautiful country, with vineyards and grapes close at hand, and when error looses the bandage from their eyes they find themselves in the attitude of deadly quarrel, with knives drawn. This is truly "a devil's mode of jesting," and

1 "'What about the immediate start, conveyance, etc.?' Well, I suppose Faust is not the only one that has travelled on the quality of his cloth! 'To fly through the air on Mephisto's cloak,' sounds very poetic, but to pass in society upon the strength of appearance is such an every-day occurrence that it is quite prosaic." Letters on Faust, VI.

it does not seem to possess any attractions for Faust.[1]

The next scene brings Faust to the Witches' Kitchen, whose contents are represented symboli-

409

cally, as being too gross, or else too complex and prosy, for literal description. It would seem that the next experiment after the idler's holiday would be the attempt to find happiness in fashionable society. Isolate this phase of life, and make it the supreme object for man, and is it any more than a witches' kitchen? Its ball-rooms, late suppers, empty talk, and the catering for it with food and drink less adapted to satisfy hunger than to inflame passion, the clothing that does not clothe, the cosmetics and other means to manufacture forms of youth and beauty out of ugliness, — all these seem to be typified. But there is also gaming with dice, lotteries, fortune-telling, and the getting of riches by chance, — which also very accurately characterizes the frame of mind which lives for the world of mere fashion and appearance. The same principle carried into literature is satirized by putting it into the mouths of the apes: "We speak and we see; we hear and we rhyme; and if we are lucky, and if things fit, 't is thoughts, and we're thinking." Close in sequence, after games of chance and lotteries, follow peculation and forgeries by aid of the witches' multiplication-table, which can, when necessary,

1 "We witness a peculiar social phenomenon in Auerbach's Cellar, where we have arrived in time to find our hero joining in the chorus

'We are as happy as cannibals,
Nay, as five hundred hogs,' —

or, if not our hero, Mephisto for him, — for you will notice that Faust says only, 'Good evening, gentlemen,' and 'I should like to leave now,' during the whole scene, — the very leader of the crowd in wit, song, and wine. Nay, as to the latter, he cannot refrain from giving them a little touch of his chemical science, which can dispense with the old grape-wine process, and still give perfect satisfaction to his customers, — a fact of some importance, one would suppose, to the landlord. And thus it would appear that our hero is not left to trust entirely to the quality of his cloth for the practical wherewithal. But the little 'Feuer-luft,' which one would at first have been inclined to interpret Fame, resolves itself into 'fire-water,' or rather the art to make this, to work the miracle of natural science. The whole wedding feast at Galilee on the principles of natural science." Letters on Faust, VII.

"Of one make ten,
And two let be,
And three make even, — then art thou rich."

"The high power of science hidden from all comes to him who thinks not," says the witch who presides over the kitchen. Here too Faust sees in the magic mirror of fashion beautiful forms; but if he approaches

410

too near, he perceives that they are manufactured (by the milliner?). The potation brewed in this kitchen seems to be a species of philter, a sort of "beggars' broth," which inflames the sensual passions.

All this pleases Faust no better than the wine cellar. He thinks the fashionable apes and their conversation "the most disgusting I ever saw," and "thoroughly abominates the absurd apparatus, these frantic gestures, and repulsive cheats," and his head splits at the nonsense as of a "hundred idiots declaiming in full chorus."[1]

Now commences the Margaret episode. From the

411

drinking saloon and the life of fashion, the drama proceeds to the institution of the family, realized in the persons of Margaret, her mother, and her brother. Hitherto we have had no tragedy, but only a strug-

1 The "Letters on Faust" present a different interpretation of this scene; but I prefer to follow an interpretation given by their author in an earlier course of lectures. The following remarks also, from Letter VIII., contain hints that point in the direction I have followed: "Owing to the age of the man, and the practical inconvenience he may experience therefrom in his new career,

'For idle dalliance too old,
Too young to be without desire,'

he would find it, no doubt, convenient to decrease the one and increase the other. For in this new career, the strength and number of his desires are an essential element, especially when there is every prospect of ample means for their gratification. As regards external appearance, that can readily be managed by a judicious use of cosmetics, the tailor's art, and kindred appliances. But the physical desires, the sexual passions, for example, require youth to yield full fruition. Proper culture, however, not to mention aphrodisiacs, will do much, even in this direction." Other commentators seem to prefer the interpretation given in the "Letters on Faust." A. Wyssard (London, 1883, The Intellectual and Moral Problem of Goethe's Faust), for example, says: "Mephisto takes him to the Witches' Kitchen, that is to say, to those places of vulgar sin where the mystery of love is prostituted to the service of degrading voluptuousness," etc.

gle within the mind of Faust. His conviction has taken the shape embodied by Mephistopheles, and in a few short, swift scenes we are plunged into a terrible collision with the external world. First in order are the scenes which show us the meeting of Margaret just coming from the cathedral; then her room and the casket; the promenade, and Faust in love; the neighbor's house and the craft of Mephistopheles; the street scene and the resolution taken; the garden scene and the garden arbor. Then comes the scene called "Forest and Cavern," wherein Goethe has painted a powerful reaction in the soul of Faust. His emotional nature revolts against the evil influence that drags him onwards, and he tries by absence to subdue his lawless passion. Under the temporary influence of a pure love, he finds himself likewise in harmony with creation once more, and he recognizes his "brothers in the still wood, the air, the water."

But Mephistopheles finally overcomes his virtuous scruples by suggesting the picture of Margaret pining away with longing for him, — a picture realized in the next scene, in Margaret's room, where we hear her sing, "My peace is gone," — expressing the fatal attraction which draws her like a night-moth into the flame.

412

In Martha's garden we see them after Faust's return. Margaret is anxious in regard to his religion. Faust parries her questions with a series of answers drawn from his pantheistical system of thought. M. "Do you believe in God?" F. "Who would dare to answer yes or no to such a question? The world exists, and the heavens; a vast correlated system of energies is alike revealed and hidden by these phenomena, which we see and which we are. For we are products of nature and moved irresistibly by its ultimate force. Call this immediate feeling of love, which moves thee and me, God, love, heart, or bliss, — it is all one. I have no name for it. It is the all-embracing and sustaining unity of the universe which takes on these myriad forms, but is above and beyond them all. Feeling is all in all. Hence let us yield to it." Poor Margaret is confused by the technical expressions of philosophy, to which she is not accustomed. She admits that it is all fine and good, like the words of the priest, but for all that there is something wrong about it, for it lacks Christianity. She means to express by this her knowledge that the Church condemns it all. She has seen that Faust does not honor the holy sacraments, or at least does not desire any participation in them. Faust thinks himself an "advanced liberal" who is willing that each should have his own belief. The spirit of the Macrocosm is void of all form, and hence is neither personalty nor any physical force, but indifferent to all existing things, and also indifferent to all moral

413

distinctions and religious ordinances. It is in complete harmony with the collision which produces the entire movement of the drama that Faust shall put forward these agnostic arguments to overcome the religious scruples of Margaret. A God so transcendent as to be indifferent to all distinctions cannot be known as to his will and purposes; but through our feeling we may know Him in the form of immediate impulse. "Obey impulse and leave the talk about divine commandments to dishonest priests." The conclusion is forthcoming: "You see this vial? only three drops in your mother's drink will envelop her in a deep but pleasant sleep."

In view of this obvious interpretation of the scene, we are filled with amazement at the opinion of Mr. Lewes, that "grander, deeper, holier thoughts are not to be found in poetry"! But what shall we say to those who insist that this passage expresses "Goethe's creed"? When Goethe called himself a polytheist as poet and artist, a pantheist as a student of nature, and a theist in his moral and spiritual nature, it is easy to understand how these seemingly contradictory predicates are harmonized. As a poet, all nature is personified, and is full of correspondences to the soul. The poet animates and personifies objects direct, and is essentially on the standpoint of Homer and the ancient polytheism. Again, in natural science relativity becomes the chief category, and every object is traced out into some previous condition by its relations and processes. This interrelation points towards an

414

ultimate unity of all, indifferent to particular forms, but itself a persistent energy. Here is a pantheistic standpoint. But the necessity of self-activity in the ultimate energy brings before us the duplicate unity which we have in self-conscious being, and so we return from Pantheism to Theism even in the science of nature. Therefore Goethe in his letter to Jacobi admits that he "needs a personal God for his personal nature as a moral and spiritual man." But if any evidence is sought for Goethe's ripest convictions, it must be found in his greatest and maturest work, the "Faust." This scene should convince us that Goethe did not esteem highly any religion founded on the indifferent supreme being of Pantheism.[1]

415

The scene at the Fountain reflects in a "severely realistic" form the popular ethical sense before which Margaret's conscience now condemns her. The scenes increase in tragic earnestness. At the shrine of the Mater Dolorosa she appeals for rescue from shame and death. In the night scene we see the reflection of the deed of Faust in the consciousness of the

[1] I give in this view substantially Mr. Brockmeyer's interpretation of the significance of Faust's creed, as I remember it in his lectures; it is not given in his "Letters." The following quotations from the latter are in place here.

"This young woman, clad in purity and faith, is met at the temple of the living God, at once the primary source and the still existing refuge of the sacredness of the family relation. The severely realistic character of Gretchen, therefore, is determined by the theme; and the scene where she relates her daily occupations of cooking, washing, sweeping, etc., besides the exquisite motive which the poet employs to transfigure its prosaic commonplace, ought not to be wanting." Letters on Faust, IX.

"That the family relation is impossible under the conviction of Faust, or that an existing family should be destroyed (the mother poisoned, the child drowned, the brother slain, and the sister stand before the judgment-seat of God as the self-acknowledged author, cause, or whatever name you may give to the connection which she had with these effects), by a man's giving practical effect to the convictions of Faust, is acknowledged and realized by the general consciousness of the age, as is abundantly proved by the effect which the part of the work under consideration has produced." Letters on Faust, IX.

brother of Margaret. Valentine attacks the serenaders and is slain. Faust and Mephistopheles flee from the country, and we may suppose they go to scenes of dissipation in the great city where we meet them on Walpurgis Night. The Cathedral scene follows. Is Margaret at the funeral of her murdered brother, or rather, perhaps, of her mother? The critics find difficulties in either case. Valentine in his soliloquy made no allusion to his mother. The fact that the accusing spirit asks, "Pray'st thou for thy mother's soul?" seems to intimate that it is her funeral. The *Dies Irae* is sung as the "Sequence for the Dead" in the Catholic burial service. This fact makes one of the two contingencies probable. But it was more poetical to leave this matter a mere suggestion. It increases our horror to remember that, when we saw Margaret coming from the cathedral on a former occasion, she was "so innocent that she had nothing to confess." The evil spirit (*Böser Geist*), or the *accusing* spirit, personifying Conscience, suggests the contrast to Margaret: "How

416

different was it with thee," etc. When the organ peals and the Chorus sings, the accusing spirit continues to comment on the verses of the judgment hymn. The first, sixth, and seventh verses are given in the text. The spirit, however, translates the substance of the second ("Horror seizes thee!"), third ("The trumpet sounds! the graves tremble!"), and fourth ("Thy heart from its ashes flames up again in torment"). The fifth verse has the same content as the sixth, and the accuser echoes the sense of both: "Hide thyself! Sin and shame never remain concealed. Air? Light? Woe to thee!" Then at the seventh verse, which brings to a climax the helplessness of the sinner, the spirit reminds her that she can claim no advocate on that day when the just are scarcely sure of their defence: "The glorified turn their faces from thee; the pure ones shudder to offer thee their hands. Woe!" The situation represented here is sublime and terrible beyond all others in this drama.[1]

[1] Mr. Brockmeyer pronounces it the most tragic scene in all literature, for the reasons stated

Here is the finite before the infinite, the innocent led astray into crime and sin, and brought before the last tribunal. A full consciousness of this judgment takes possession of Margaret while her reason is yet unshaken, though her soul has been tried by successive shocks. The pathos of the scene reaches its highest point through the fact that the trial and condemnation are wholly unseen by the world. An ex-

417

ternal trial before her fellow men could not be so terrible as this judgment by her accusing conscience while the holy Chorus announces the eternal edicts. The spectator would cry out at once against any external court that condemned so dreadfully the victim of fiendish conspiracy. It is she alone who can imagine that the spirits of light avert their faces and refuse their helping hands. The closing scene of the Second Part of Faust shows us the counterpart to this scene in the cathedral.

From this scene before the heavenly judgment we descend in the following to the region of hell. Faust and Mephistopheles have fled from justice, and we are to seek them,—perhaps in Paris at some Jardin Mabille,—certainly this is the type described in the Walpurgis Night. In the celebration on the Brocken are to be found all manner of correspondences with what is infernal in human character. Spiritual jays, owls, mice, fireflies, will-o'-the-wisps, vermin, all assemble with the witches on the wild desert at the top of the Brocken. It is a realm beyond the border, hence the place of outlaws, the criminal realm. Human savagery celebrates its Witches' Sabbath on this mountain top, lighted up, as is well known, by Mammon. For Mammon is wealth used in sensuality and other selfish pleasure. A spiritual storm rages there, the elements all in collision.

Sitting around dying embers at the outskirts of the crowd, Mephistopheles comes up with the sore-heads. These are they who have lived for selfish pleasure,

418

and now retain their passions and ambition, but have worn out their capacity for enjoyment. They con-

sider themselves most unjustly treated by the world. A general thinks his nation ungrateful for his services; a minister thinks that all things go badly since he left the cabinet; an unsuccessful author complains that people do not read sensible works any longer. Mephistopheles mocks them all: "Since my own cask has run down to the lees, I feel that the world also is near its end." Then Lilith and the obscene witches. But in the midst of dissipation Faust thinks of Margaret, and is haunted by the sight of a "pale, fair girl, standing alone and far off." "She drags herself but slowly from the place, and seems to move with fettered feet. I must own she seems to me to resemble poor Margaret. . . . How strangely does a single red line, no thicker than a knife, adorn that lovely neck!" Faust does not wait for the Intermezzo,—a "new performance" that is given on the Brocken. It is the counterpart of the Prelude on the stage, and shows us the Walpurgis Night in literature. The spirit of Mephistopheles is portrayed in its various literary incarnations. The plot is the quarrel between the two ideals in art typified by Oberon and Titania. Art is either for the revelation of the divine, or for amusement and to make a living.

Faust learns the fate of Margaret, "long wretchedly astray on the face of the earth, and now imprisoned and under sentence of death." A reaction sets in, which Mephistopheles is not able to meet, as

419

before, on the scene of the "Dreary Day." The indignant reply of Faust to Mephistopheles's "She is not the first," is annihilating in its force. They pass through the "open field," where the gibbet stands, to the dungeon. Margaret is discovered insane. In her ravings she lives over again the tragic moments of her history, and anticipates in her fantasy the scene of the execution, which forms the climax. But even in the presence of the scaffold she repels all offers of succor from the conspirator against her peace. She exclaims on seeing Mephistopheles: "What rises up from the threshold there? He! He! Send him away! What does he want in this holy place? He seeks me." She appeals to the judgment of God

against the fiend. To be saved from the gallows and from God's judgment by the interposition of the Evil One is to be lost forever. She prefers the solemn human ceremony that deprives her of life, to the life of an outcast. Goethe expresses this sense of the substantial nature of social life in institutions, as contrasted with mere individual life, in Margaret's reply to Faust's "Only consent! the door lies open": "What avails it flying? They will waylay me! It is so miserable to be obliged to beg one's living, and with a bad conscience too. How wretched to wander in a foreign land, and after all be rearrested!" The very thought drives her into her ravings again.

At her refusal to be rescued, Mephistopheles pronounces the words, "She is judged," meaning that she has preferred to accept the fate decreed by the court.

420

But a voice from above says, "She is saved." As Faust hastens out of the dungeon, he hears the voice of Margaret calling his name. The voice comes fainter and fainter to his ears as his distance increases. He joins Mephistopheles and "disappears."

The First Part of Faust thus ends negatively. It is deeply tragic, but not in the usual manner. It is not the hero's death that we see. He does not collide with institutions and go down. His innocent victim is the one who suffers, and the guilty one escapes. In this defect we see the necessity for a Second Part. The old miracle play, like the Don Juan epos, makes the hero meet his doom in hell flames. But Goethe preserves Faust in order to treat the theme exhaustively, and finally solve it affirmatively. Thus far we have had a subjective conflict within Faust's mind, and an objective conflict with a single institution, the family. Faust's practical resolution to make the world his oyster has not resulted in happiness. On the contrary, when Margaret paints the last scene at the block, Faust says, "Oh that I had never been born!" His emotional nature, the very part of him that hungers for the pleasure of gratification, evidently is not constituted so as to adapt itself to the theory of Mephistopheles. He cannot be made happy by unscrupulous selfishness that heeds not another's

pain.[1]

421

Many persons affect to admire the first part of Faust who do not find any necessity for the second part. They do not duly consider that the first part by itself is a monstrosity, judged by the standard of works of art. What drama or what novel would allow its hero to destroy an entire family of innocent people, and yet escape due punishment at the hand of his fellow men? Even the puppet play was careful to punish Faust in the fires of hell; but Goethe's Faust, in its first part, does not show us the hand of society avenging itself on the true criminal, nor does it, on the other hand, show the conditions of the compact with Mephistopheles fulfilled, so that the soul of Faust is in danger of forfeiture.

With all these crimes, Faust has not found his moment of happiness which he can bid "Stay, for thou art fair." Mephistopheles cannot claim him, for he has not gratified him with sensual delight, according to the terms of the bond. Faust's soul has not become wholly devilish, because he has wished to save Margaret from her fate, and, failing in that, is plunged in deep remorse. Remorse, it is true, is not the punishment required by a work of art. The punishment should come from the hand of society to satisfy the conditions of a drama. But remorse is sufficient in this play to cheat Mephistopheles of his due. Hence,

422

both the external and internal conditions of the play demand the continuation of the drama into another part.[1]

When setting out on the journey Mephistopheles

[1] "As the result of the subjective collision, we had the conclusion, that, if man cannot know truth, he can enjoy sensual pleasure. Taking this for the principle of our action, we entered the world of reality, and lo! it crumbles under our feet. Not life, not perpetuity of the race, but death, — blank nothingness ; the conclusion reads, 'If man cannot know truth, then he cannot exist.'" Letters on Faust, IX.

[1] "The destruction of the family and the preservation of the destroyer will hardly pass for a satisfactory solution, either logical or artistic. To regard the poem, however, in this light, would be our

names the destination: "The little world and the great world we will see." The little world contains what may be represented directly in its proper persons. All the members of the family may be brought before us in the drama ; but we cannot see in like manner all the members of a state or of civil society ;

423

nor can art and religion be presented except in a typical manner to us. Two different modes of art, therefore, prevail in the Faust. Objects of universal scope and significance, like nature and humanity as a whole, or like the process of empirical science, the realm of philosophical ideas, or the history of the Christian religion, are represented in types or mythological figures, such as Dante has used in the Terrestrial Paradise, where the elements of the Church and their history are emblematically bodied forth. Thus we have such forms as the Erdgeist, the Macrocosm, the dog, the Homunculus, the Mothers, and the closing scene in Heaven, all adumbrating what cannot be presented to us immediately, like the family, whose members we may see and hear.[1]

Mephistopheles is the mythological impersonation

own act, and the consequent difficulty one of our own creation. For this world be an attempt to make rather than to read the poem. And whatever merit or demerit might attend the undertaking, it would hardly be fair to attribute either the one or the other to the author of Faust. For in this poem we have for our theme, 'the self-conscious intelligence in conflict with itself, — with its entire content.' Not the content with itself, but the self-conscious intelligence on the one side, and its content on the other. Included within this content [as a single phase of it], we have the institution of the family. Hence, the collision presented is one not inherent in this institution, for that involves as its presupposition the valid existence thereof, [i.e. a collision in the family presupposes the family,] but between the family and its negation. It is, therefore, not an independent, but a subordinate collision. . . . Since the family is only a part of this content, the conflict is not exhausted by the destruction of the family, any more than it was exhausted at the end of the rational subjective collision which resulted in the destruction of the rational vocation of Faust, and delivered him over to the guidance of the understanding with its finite aims, — sensual indulgence. Hence, no solution is presented [in this First Part], or is possible as yet." Letters on Faust, IX.

[1] This is an epitome of Brockmeyer's view, given at length in his lectures (unpublished). He holds that presentative art is used chiefly in the First Part, but representative art in the Second Part.

of unscrupulous selfishness, which sacrifices others for its own greed. It is the human subjective counter-part of the Earth-Spirit, who is conceived to create a world of human beings, and endow them with aspira-tions for infinite truth, but who withholds from them all possibility of attainment,—who is, in short, a birth and a grave for all individuals. If man wor-ship such a god, and take him as a model on which to mould his own character, he will of course become a "spirit that denies." He will not feel himself bound to respect any finite particular beings like men, nor

424

any being subordinate to him, because such are not respected by the Absolute. He will respect only the great negative powers of nature, over which he can exercise no control, and which therefore resemble in this regard the Absolute. Mephistopheles justifies himself, accordingly, by saying that all things called forth into being out of the void are destined for de-struction again by the same pantheistic energy that created them, and therefore "it were better had they never been created." Like the Earth-Spirit, too, he has reserved the flame for his element. Hence, one might trace out the logical connection between the Earth-Spirit and Mephistopheles,—the former con-ceived as the objective universal process of the world, and the latter as a human character formed in imita-tion of that type as an ideal.

Goethe believed in typical facts (*Urphänomene*) in science, as he tells us himself. The Second Part of Faust deals in artistical devices equivalent to those types in nature. In consequence of this form of rep-resentation, the entire work is an enigma to most readers. Portions of the Margaret episode are vividly clear to all,—as if written with lightning flashes on a thunder-cloud. But it is of far more importance to the literary student to master Goethe's typical forms. They constitute a system of mythology, under which the modern world masquerades, just as truly as the Greek world did under Homer's system of Olympian deities. A long life of keenest observation and re-flection, reinforced by poetic inspiration, is summed

425

up in these new symbols. It is the highest object of intellectual culture to comprehend those vast general processes of the social world which generate these problems of life, of which all art worthy of the name treats. Such phenomena as the French Revolution and the Napoleonic wars, the American Republic, productive industry, the revival of art, modern liter-ature, the scientific spirit,—all these and their like are intimately concerned with Mephistopheles and the victory over him.

He who aspires to find in literature something higher than mere idle amusement, therefore, will study Faust, and especially its Second Part. Ear-nest study will discover the significance of the vast shadowy forms, and the student will by degrees learn to use those mythologic types, and think out by their aid solutions to the problems of the world. Classic literature has furnished us with mythologic person-ages and events as means of expression for life; but for life as it was in the classic epoch, and for life in all ages only in so far as it is identical with it. The poetical insight discovers the essentials of human life, and expresses them in any age or in any nation. But the temporary environment of those essentials, and the consciousness that characterizes the epoch, require special treatment. Hence, it is necessary for a new world-poet to appear in each epoch, if its prosy elements are to be made poetical, and the age is to have a spectacle of itself in its recognizable features.

The Second Part of Faust moves in an atmosphere entirely different from that of the First Part. It is serene and full of light,—a truly Celestial Paradise compared with the Inferno of the First Part. The "little world," where the individual can make or mar, is behind us in the journey, and we are arrived at the "great world" of institutions which transcend the individual might and are the joint product of the social whole.

The first and opening scene portrays for us the in-fluences of nature and the lapse of time, which heal spiritual as well as physical wounds. In the case of

426

spiritual injuries, there must be repentance and re-nunciation, a removal of the cause, just as in the case of physical wounds there must be a removal of the producing causes before the healing process can set in. Tepid winds, the fragrance of flowers, shadow and twilight, night's repose,—these are the elves that draw out the barbs that remorse fixes in the soul These fiery bitter arrows of self-reproach (*des Vorwurfs glühend bittre Pfeile*) allude to his genuine repentance for the evil he has done. Mephistopheles repents of nothing, and suffers no grief in his mind. But Faust has a human heart besides his evil principles, and suffers for his sins.

A new day awakes after the beautiful Chorus of the Elves recording the march of the Hours. Ariel an-nounces the approach of the sun, a symbol of the Absolute, and we have an allusion to the baffled pur-suit of pure truth. The full light of the sun cannot

be borne, but one may gaze refreshed upon its re-fracted image in the rainbow. So, instead of pure truth, let us look upon its refracted image in the institution of the State, which we shall see in its visible representative.

In the second scene we behold this Emperor and his court. It is not *a* State, but *the* State,—the Holy Roman Empire, which in the time of Charle-magne included all Western and Central Europe, and under his successors in the Middle Ages included Italy and Germany, but finally was confined to the latter country. It is the true "Monarchy" of Dante, whose universal power shall bring unity of law, and consequently peace, to all the world. It is borne in mind that the coronation of the Emperor took place in Goethe's city, Frankfort, and in his youth he had seen the great festival accompanying it.

In the Emperor, Goethe has given us a Faust of the type we have seen in the First Part. He wishes to be amused and is not scrupulous as to the means. He is a selfish pleasure-seeker, who has virtually signed a compact with Mephistopheles. Faust has passed beyond this phase of immediate sensuality by the purgatorial influences of sin and remorse, and now

427

has ambition for power, and will soon develop a passion for art. The description of the condition of the Empire, on the verge of ruin, is given through the mouths of the Chancellor, Commander-in-chief, Treasurer, and Lord High Steward. Unscrupulous devices of Mephistopheles at once provide means for cele-

428

brating the Carnival. This is prepared under the direction of Faust, who embodies in the masquerade a political phantasmagoria showing the genesis and destruction of the State. In like manner, the classical Walpurgis Night gives the genesis of Greek art out of Egyptian and Syrian art,—a sort of symbolic-classic phantasmagoria, as the "Helena" is called a "Classico-Romantic Phantasmagoria" by Goethe himself; the latter shows the genesis of modern or romantic art through the study of the classic art.

Amusement and play have this significance: man loves to see himself as a social whole. In play the individual enjoys the sense of his potential greatness without the real labor and suffering necessary to produce it. The species, the race, is a giant; the individual, by contrast, a puny dwarf. The Carnival as an annual festival has this significance: man delights to see the image of society, and to feign that he as individual is free to assume any station or vocation for himself. The beggar may masquerade as king, the slave as master, the male as female, the high as low, celebrating in this way the fact that each man is in substance all men. It was not a wide departure from the original and traditional purport of the carnival, therefore, for Goethe to employ it, as he does, to adumbrate the genesis and destruction of the highest political institution, and show us civil society, with its many vocations, grounded on the power of civil government.

In the Carnival scene we see peace and plenty under

429

the masks of the olive branch and the wheat sheaf, beauty and refinement typified by the fancy nosegay and the budding roses. Then the gardeners, the mother and daughter, and the dumb show following it, illustrate the social instinct to veil the natural under the form of the ideal. The drunken man is the consequence of the gratification of mere natural appetite: intoxication may realize the carnival at any season of the year. But the natural appetites must be restrained if society is to be, and for this purpose the Graces enter on the scene. These insist on seeing the ideal, in place of the real. They restore freedom and charm to society. The Fates, who follow next, state the limits, laws, and measures that result from the application of the ideal to the real, and hence they are kindred of the Graces. They set up a standard, or norm. But the Graces have counterparts, the Furies. Reject the Graces, who treat each one as if he embodied all human perfection,—and this is the essence of courtesy,—and take note only of human limitations and imperfections of individuality, and you will invoke the Furies. Hatred and jealousy, calumny and slander, destroy the social bond, and lead on to violence: Tisiphone mixes poison, and sharpens daggers, and sets in motion the infinite progress of the feud and blood revenge.

Authority is shown to be necessary as the foundation of society, and to control the Furies. Its mask now enters as a Colossus, an elephant guided by Prudence sitting on his neck, with two chained fig-

430

ures walking on either side, in whom we are to recognize Fear and Hope, the former signifying mistrust, which suspects evil in one's neighbor, and thus lacks confidence sufficient to combine with its fellow men; the latter, Hope, in the sense of green trustfulness, which goes to the other extreme, and places all its fortune in the hands of other individuals, and thus reaches the same result, the destruction of society. High aloft rides Victory, dazzling the sight. Zoilo-Thersites, the partisan defamer who works to undermine civil authority, is chastised by the herald.

Under the sway of civil order, property becomes secure, and wealth may be accumulated. The car of Plutus (the god of wealth) accordingly enters now, guided by a boy charioteer dressed in the robes of Apollo as leader of the Muses, who tells us that he is Poesy. While Poesy guides the car of Plutus, a taste for the beautiful converts wealth into a blessing for all people. The poet uses wealth in the service of art; he gilds all prose reality with the gold of his own imagination, so that no one looks upon it any more as a plain ugly fact, but sees it shining with the ideal. Just in this way Walter Scott has gilded the lakes and moorlands of Scotland, or Longfellow and Whittier and Hawthorne have gilded places and scenes in New England. After the boy-Apollo has snapped his fingers, gold and pearls and costliest jewels abound. He uses wealth for pictures, statues, stately temples, scientific museums, parks for healthful amusement. We learn to see the prose fact trans-

431

figured by associations with human interests, and crowned with an aureola of historic importance.

The chariot of wealth is drawn by dragons or watchful guardians of property,—the police, the civil and criminal judiciary, and the men of the law. In contrast to the right user of wealth comes the starveling, Mephistopheles masquerading as Avarice, sitting on a chest of gold behind Poesy. He uses wealth to corrupt the morals of the people, and, for effeminate luxury or for selfish hoarding purposes, keeps property out of channels of greatest usefulness.

Poesy now takes leave of Plutus, and extravagance under the influence of Mephistopheles, dissipates the wealth in the form of molten gold, which the crowd struggle to obtain. Wild riot ensues.

The Emperor comes in under the mask of Pan, as a selfish tyrant, with rough satyrs, gnomes, fauns, giants, and nymphs, typifying selfish courtiers and the hangers-on at the licentious court circle that surrounded the central power in the Holy Roman Empire, and especially the French king just previous to the Revolution. Waste of property on the part of men in power demoralizes the industries of the people. The destruction of the civil authority takes place through the evil influence of the parasites that infest the highest political power. The whole fabric of the State flames up in one disastrous revolution, in which the Emperor Pan ("L'état c'est moi") is consumed in flames,—or appears to be in the representation. The herald laments,

and Plutus (the mask of Faust) announces the Carnival closed.

432

The following scene shows a pleasure garden, in which the Emperor thanks Faust for the amusement he has received from the masquerade. To his great surprise, the ministers enter and report all their former difficulties overcome by the new invention,— the Mephistophelian principle has invented for the use of the State an inconvertible paper money!¹

Goethe had studied the phenomenon of the French "assignats," and seen their wonderful inflation and disastrous collapse. All becomes prosperous at once: commerce being stimulated to the highest degree, agriculture and manufactures flourish. With plenty of money we must have amusement. The beautiful must be presented by Faust in its highest form,— Greek art. Helen must be brought back and "materialized." Mephistopheles cannot create the beautiful, for he engages only to adapt finite means to finite ends; the beautiful is produced by putting the finite under the form of the infinite, i. e. by making it appear as expressing personal freedom. But Mephistopheles, as principle of negation, can show how to think abstractly, so he gives a "little key" (*Nein,* = not, i. e. the negative typifies all abstraction), to Faust,

433

and advises him to seek the "Mothers." He cautions him to hold the key off from his body; and with good reason, for if one is to understand the mode of thinking of another people far separated by time, he must free himself from his subjective personal likes and dislikes, and get an objective criterion. The operation of the key he describes: "Sink, then! I might say also, rise! it is the same thing: fly that which has come into being, in the unbound spaces of forms."

¹ "Paper money is the money of the understanding ; gold, the money of the reason." Brockmeyer's Lectures on Faust (unpublished).

This wonderful commentator has not carried out his interpretation beyond the First Part of Faust, except so far as to lay the basis for, and show the necessity of, the two parts, and indicate the two styles of treatment and the two different spheres of life to be treated

This seems a poetic way of describing philosophic reflection, which abstracts from the conditions of existence in order to reach pure ideas. The "Mothers" are enthroned goddesses, spaceless and timeless like Plato's archetypal ideas. Mephistopheles describes these with much particularity. They are seen by the light of a glowing tripod engaged in creating and transforming finite things,— "the eternal amusement of the eternal intelligence." The patterns of all creatures hover round them. Plutarch describes the Platonic ideas as "the causes, forms, and original images of all things which have been and which shall be." Commentators find passages in Plutarch's Morals which may have furnished Goethe the poetic images here used, but it is clear enough that the idea is Platonic, and traces to Plato's Pythagoreanism. While it is interesting to examine minutely the details of this remarkable device by which Faust brings up Helen from the underworld, it is not necessary for the general purposes of comprehending Faust. Goethe wishes to embody in a type the method of the

434

a priori road to the principles of the Beautiful. No modern can understand the spirit of Greek art without such a journey to the "Mothers." The Mephistophelian "spirit that denies" cannot accompany Faust on his journey thither, although it has to furnish a necessary key, abstraction from one's own environment. Greek art has an environment peculiar to it, and it is necessary to comprehend that in order to see its genesis.

Faust brings up Paris and Helen to the stage, and exhibits them to the mighty Emperor,— much as Racine and Corneille produced for the court of Louis XIV. their French-Greek plays. But here we are to learn that the *a priori* method, although sufficient to accomplish such wonders as these, does not suffice for the soul that falls in love with art. Faust touches Paris with his key, and an explosion follows. The "materialized" spirits vanish, and Faust lies senseless on the ground. The danger of this method of producing art is, that, when the artist comes to the

concrete, he supplies modern details and environment, and not the antique. He falls out of his part. The Greek art exists for the Greek type of culture, Helen for Paris, and Paris for Helen. If Faust wishes Helen for himself, he must create in himself the Greek type of culture by the slow process of studying its genesis step by step. His *a priori* method may bring him to the spectacle of the beautiful, but it does not give him creative possession of it. French-Greek art is after all not Greek in spirit, although it has

435

some external resemblance to it. Racine and Corneille both touched the resuscitated Greek with their magic key. Like Faust, they insisted in putting themselves into the play, or, what is the same thing, making the Greek form of the drama hold modern personages and ways of life.

Faust became unconscious of the modern environment in his absorption with the classic, and took no more interest in the affairs of the Emperor's court. Mephistopheles must seek out a means for the nearest approach to the antique beautiful, and accordingly returns to Wagner, the spirit of analytical investigation and prose erudition. For the substantial restoration of the Greek spirit, and the contemplation of Greek art in that spirit, in our age, we must have something besides the *a priori* production of it. There must be excavations, and the collection of fragments, which are to be studied piece by piece, in the manner that erudition and archaeology have undertaken.

The Homunculus represents this spirit of specialization: it is confined in a bottle, and typifies the German archaeologist realized in Winckelmann and his followers, and, less directly, the entire modern spirit of inductive science.

If sufficiently limited, a field of investigation mapped out may be exhausted by the individual specialist: when he knows it exhaustively, he learns to see the relativity of all its details. Each detail is dependent upon and suggests all the others. It thus

436

becomes alive, for the definition of a living organism is this: each part is both means and end to all the other parts. Sufficiently specialized and narrowed down, the province may be so exhaustively investigated that the living bond of connection may be found, and a living being is produced, — an Homunculus in a bottle. Wagner is the sort of scholar who learns to "confine his attention to the dative case," in order that he may not simply rehash erudition already existent, but himself make new contributions to it. We think of Winckelmann patiently measuring the contour of the several features of the face, as he found them in antique statues, and recording the angle which the open eyelids made as a canon by which to identify Venus, Juno, and Diana by this feature alone. The history of modern science abounds in Homunculi. Cuvier specializes comparative anatomy, and can see the whole animal in a newly discovered fossil bone from the Eocene strata; Lyell can read its history in a pebble; Niebuhr can see the actual history adumbrated in a Roman myth, and, like Lyell, interpret it as a sort of drift boulder of humanity, broken off from its connecting strata, and ground into its shape under the glaciers of revolution; Agassiz could reconstruct the whole fish from one of its scales.

With Homunculus to light the way, Faust may find Helen, of a surety. The classical Walpurgis Night shows the process by which Greek art itself was found. It began with traditions from Egypt and Syria, and developed out of their art-forms, half ani-

437

mal, half human, such as the sphinxes, griffins, sirens, centaurs, pygmies, and dactyls. Progressive metamorphoses separated the human from the animal, and finally reached the sea-nymph, Galatea, as the perfect human form. The artists of Rhodes claim to be the first to represent the high gods in human forms. The Cabiri (or "mighty ones") of the Phœnicians and Egyptians, sons of Phtha (the Egyptian Vulcan), the divine metal-worker, indicate the bronze statues of the gods produced by Phtha (hence called his sons), and mark an important transition towards Greek art. The studies into the origin of the earth, rather poetic

conjectures than scientific conclusions, divide between a water principle and a fire principle. Thales and Anaxagoras represent these tendencies, and find place in Goethe's poem because they mark the undercurrent of reflection that guides unseen the development of Greek art in its selection of a worthy representation of the divine form. The fire, symbol of spirit, with water, symbol of organic matter, are united in Greek art so that neither preponderates. Homunculus aspires to free himself from the confinement of his bottle, — empiricism strives to return to a vision of the totality. On the appearance of Galatea, shining with the radiance of perfect beauty, he breaks his glass against her chariot, and becomes Eros, or poetic inspiration, which sees the whole in each part.

In the study of art Faust arrives at the insight into the formative principle in the divine. Instead of being negative to form, as Pantheism supposes, it is

438

rather the formative energy that Polytheism presupposes. Proteus, who is indifferent to all forms and yet ceaselessly incarnating himself, teaches Homunculus how to escape from his bottle, proving himself to be the principle that initiates forms, and breaks forms only to grow by transformation into higher ones. The poet learns to recognize in all things the one spiritual principle; and this is the reason that he speaks in the language of metaphor and personification, having learned that all things are means of spiritual expression.

The *a priori* mode of reaching Greek art gave place to the other method of specialization, which sufficed to bring Greece before us in its actual genesis. But the result of the specialized inquiry conducts us back to the standpoint of immediate insight, typified by Eros, i.e. poetic or artistic insight, which sees all nature a revelation of the spiritual totality, just as a single bone revealed the living animal to Cuvier.

The "Helena" has the advantage of the wonderful commentary of Thomas Carlyle. Faust finds Helen; Euphorion is born, adumbrating modern art and literature arising from the union of the Greek and Teutonic principles. The Greek sought the representation

of free individuality; the Teutonic seeks the realization of freedom in actual life: the union of the two is Romantic art, — the art whose principle is infinite aspiration. But Faust does not find his problem solved by art, — Classic or Romantic. One great thing he has learned from it, as we have seen, — the Divine

439

reveals itself in forms, and above all in the human form. This points towards a divine-human nature. The Absolute is at least a form-giving principle, and loves to initiate forms and to perfect them. The real essence of the human form, it is true, is not the body, but the soul, — an energy whose characteristic is to be subject and its own object. This principle of form as the essential form therefore transcends physical form, although it finds expression in the latter. Faust leaves art, and struggles up to a more adequate communion with the essential truth, that he has now seen a glimpse of. There is a more intimate acquaintance possible than through art. He can recognize the Divine in his fellow man, and feels the Absolute to be the Spirit of the invisible Church of humanity.

In the fourth act we see Faust aspiring to become a useful citizen in the secular world. He desires to see the people multiply and be well fed, and, what is more important, "taught and well bred," and above all active in helping each other.

The Mephistophelian Emperor has lived for a while in luxury by means of his paper money, but the deluge came at last in the shape of revolution. Faust is,

440

however, no longer in the negative mood, but wishes to build up rather than tear down. He assists the Emperor to quell the insurrection. He does not ask in return the gift of a principality, but only the shore of the sea, with the privilege of reclaiming the land covered by the ocean wastes. It is a place for labor rather than a finished product that he wants. He does

440

not conceive the Absolute to be a fixed result, like a work of art, nor a mere negative process, like the formless Absolute of Pantheism. He is an Energy that delights to make that which is bad good, and that which is good better, in the interest of human

beings.

The fifth act shows us Faust engaged in this labor of building dikes and canals, and a busy people settling on the newly recovered land, and an ocean commerce thriving.

Here at last Faust has found the moment which seems "fair," and he could live in the thought of it forever without tedium. This, then, is the goal and object of human nature, that condition for which it was intended. To be the builder of a great public benefit gives him a consciousness that is ever gratifying. In the service of his fellow men he sees that he can always be happy. He overcomes finally his worst enemy, impatience (he had cursed patience deeper than all on occasion of his compact with Mephistopheles) and now renounces magic. He sees in magic the unscrupulous might that looks only to the end desired, and is not duly considerate of the welfare of the human interests which furnish the means. The burning of the cottage of Baucis and Philemon by his agents, under the guidance of Mephistopheles, is represented as teaching him this last lesson. He refuses now to recognize his nearly helpless condition, worn out and blind with age and life's cares. He finds refuge from all grief in absorption in his great

441

work. He will set at once about draining a pestilential marsh that still remains by the neighboring hill. Space will be furnished for many millions of human beings, — not to dwell in repose, but daily earning their freedom, and in the constant feeling of their mutual dependence. With this thought, which can bring happiness to him even in the physical pain of death, he dies. Mephistopheles has brought him to say to the passing moment, "Stay, for thou art fair," and technically in one sense won his wager; but in reality he has lost his wager, for he has not found any sensual delights nor selfish delights of any kind that could satisfy Faust. He has found that, not selfishness, but altruism alone, can satisfy human nature. The angels, therefore, win Faust's soul. They appear in the clouds and drive away the demons with a shower of roses (symbols of love). The good

does not fight with weapons of hate; but to the demonic nothing is so repulsive as love and self-sacrifice for others.

The closing scene is the noblest culmination of this wonderful drama. It shows us the four great leading ideas of Christianity which have characterized the four epochs of its history.

Pater Ecstaticus is the type that prevailed in the first epoch. Then the individual had to renounce not only his animal nature, but also the heathen civilization, and flee to the desert, seeking as a hermit to purify himself within. He sought later, under the lead of St. Benedict, to create artificial desert caves

442

by building monasteries with high walls, which shut out civilization, although in the midst of it. The monastery improved on the solitary hermit life by forming a Christian community, a Church. Pater Ecstaticus is eager for martyrdom, to purge away the earthly dross that dims his purity.

Next came, in the thirteenth century, two wonderful men, St. Dominic and St. Francis. Both issued forth from the monastery to conquer the world outside of its walls. It was not sufficient to shut out the world; sin must be shut out from the world. St. Dominic's movement is typified by Pater Profundus. The Dominicans revived learning, and mastered the literatures and philosophies of ancient times, and built up the vast structure of Christian theology. They recognized God, not as hostile to nature and science and literature, but as the Creator of them. Hence, Pater Profundus recognizes "messengers of God's love" in the lightnings and torrents that had been thought the work of the Devil

Pater Seraphicus, typifying the movement of St. Francis, who went out to the lowliest people, and repeated Christ's mission to the beggars and outcasts, expresses his tender love for that which is most in need. "Boys with a soul and sense half shut," having died before they saw the light of this life, are for the angel souls the sweetest gain. They have been deprived of the experience of the earth-life, but the angels will see to it that it is all made up to them

by imparting to them their experience. "Use my

443

eyes," says the holy father, and "gaze upon the world of human experience." This is the finest touch in Faust. Instead of the cold haughtiness of the Earth-Spirit, who repels human finitude, Goethe has found that God's love is so tender toward individuality that it nurses into being and fulness even the embryonic forms that fail to mature in the earth-life. The spirit of Faust is placed in charge of these embryonic souls, who receive him in his "chrysalis state," and proceed to loosen the flakes of earthly nature that encompass him.

Doctor Marianus (named from Maria, because he proclaims the Virgin) is the complement of Pater Seraphicus in that he utters the doctrine that the highest principle in the universe is God's grace, symbolized under the form of the Holy Virgin, who appears as Mater Gloriosa, surrounded by penitent women, among whom we recognize Margaret.

It has been suggested, however, by Rosenkranz and others, that Doctor Marianus represents the soul of Faust after it has grown "fair and great by holy living," as the chorus of blessed boys pronounces him after the earthly flakes are removed. Pater Ecstaticus is represented as "hovering up and down"; Pater Profundus as in the "lower region"; Pater Seraphicus as in the "middle region"; Doctor Marianus as "in the highest, purest cell." It would seem from this that Doctor Marianus is intended as a fourth in the list of historical types. Düntzer informs us that "Doctor" was substituted for "Pater," as first written. The "blessed

444

boys" who welcomed Faust hover about him, and announce that Faust is outgrowing them with mighty limbs, and that he will return them a rich reward for their assistance; he will share with them his rich earthly experience. Doctor Marianus exhorts the penitents to look up to the tender glance of the Madonna, who has been drawn near to the earth to assist them. This, coming directly after the Mater Gloriosa has assigned Faust for instruction as an immature spirit ("Still blindeth him the new glare of day") to Mar-

Goethe's Portrait — a Lithograph by Delacroix
Frontispiece of French Translation of Faust, *Paris 1828*

garet, in reply to her petition, proves that Goethe could not have intended to represent him under the title Doctor Marianus.

Margaret's prayer to the Mater Gloriosa intentionally recalls her prayer to the Mater Dolorosa in the First Part.

A Chorus Mysticus closes the drama, uniting in one statement the doctrines of the Holy Fathers and of the Doctor, and announces the doctrine of divine grace as the supreme principle: " All that is perishable is but a symbol; the inadequate grows here to complete reality; the indescribable here is accomplished; the Eternal-Womanly draweth us on."

The womanly element in the Divine Being describes especially the tenderness and graciousness that nurture what is feeble and impotent, and lacking character, into strength and maturity. The infant lacks responsibility, and cannot be treated from the standpoint of justice without destroying him. His deed of caprice must not be returned upon him as on a

445

mature person. His freaks and irrationality are borne patiently by the mother, and his individuality gradually drawn out and developed. Hence, the feminine element in the Divine Nature has especial reference to God's grace, which, according to Goethe, deals with a world of imperfect creatures, and leads them towards their own good through their freedom.

In the eighth book of the Autobiography, already referred to, Goethe indicates such a view of theology at the age of twenty years as corresponds with the conclusion of this Second Part of Faust. When man had fallen, instead of permitting him to lapse into annihilation, the Elohim chose to initiate a movement of restoration, and to save by an act of divine condescension what was otherwise lost through perversion of its own freedom.

It is, if I am not mistaken, the most interesting event in literary history, that Goethe should conduct his hero from pantheistic agnosticism to Christian theism.

INDEX.

THE MANCHESTER QUARTERLY. No. I.—JANUARY, 1882. pp. 1-13.

A SUMMER DAY AT CONCORD, MASSACHUSETTS.

BY THE REV. STUART J. REID.

THE circumstances under which I visited Concord were somewhat exceptional, and therefore allow me, by way of preface, to begin this short paper of gossip with a snatch from a conversation, the scene of which was London, and the time April in the present year. "If you go to America, you must by all means get a glimpse of Concord, the dear old home of my childhood!" said Julian Hawthorne to me, as I told him, over his own fire, of my intention to visit the Dominion of Canada in the course of the then approaching summer. "What—go to America, and not see Concord?" exclaimed my friend, dwelling with loving frequency upon the very word, as if the name awoke old music in him; "Whatever else you miss, Concord you must see. You must go to the 'Old Manse,' and climb up the steep stair at the 'Wayside' to my father's study in the tower-room. I will give you letters of introduction to my relatives and friends, and they will gladly show you all that there is to be seen there now; and—but let us change the subject; it makes me feel quite home-sick here, in London, to-night, to talk of Concord and my father!" I, of course, thanked Mr. Hawthorne warmly for his kindness; but, at the same time, I felt compelled to tell him frankly that I unfortunately saw but little prospect of visiting that shrine of many pilgrim feet of which he spoke so enthusiastically, and around which, naturally, and yet in a special sense, some of his own most sacred memories and hallowed associations clustered. My work—a literary engagement—took me to Quebec; and I expressed to him a fear, which happily was not realized, that it would chain me there, or at least to Canada, during the whole of my sadly too brief sojourn in Transatlantic regions. "But you must never dream of going to America without visiting New York and Boston; and, when you are in Boston, you are almost within a stone's throw of Concord. Now, go, and I will introduce you to my friends." So I went and duly saw Concord for the first, and, probably, for the last time, on a beautiful blue day—Tuesday, August 2nd; nor when I reached the spot did I miss the welcome which I had been led, in London, to expect. I can scarcely believe that it is still less than five months ago since I found myself wandering down the shady lane which leads from the railway station towards the sweet New England village, which, in two or three words, I shall now attempt to depict. By a curious, but most happy coincidence, I passed almost immediately from Saratoga to Concord, and to me, with perhaps rather antiquated ways and notions, the relief of such a change of scene and society was singularly grateful. Saratoga reminded me of Bunyan's account of Vanity Fair; Concord suggested Goldsmith's picture of "Sweet Auburn." Excitement, frivolity, vulgarity, and display marked the full swing of the season in America's world-renowned pleasure city, but Concord was worthy of its harmonious name; it appeared completely shut off from the restless, feverish spirit of the age; there was an old-fashioned charm of aspect about its sleepy streets—an old-world air of repose seemed to rest upon the houses, and scholarly contentment reigned supreme. I could not help thinking, as I rambled about the quiet and restful place, as if the Puritans had somehow managed to carry intact a quaint English village of the time of the Commonwealth across the stormy Atlantic, and as if their descendants, conscious that they possessed an unusual treasure, had guarded the spot with religious care. To find a spot like Concord on American soil fills an Englishman with as much delight as an Italian sky may be supposed to feel when his eyes are gladdened in our wintry climate by the brilliant colours of some choice exotic which suggest instantly the sunny skies which arch his distant home. Concord did not gain its pleasant name

by chance. It keeps green the memory of the honourable and peaceful purchase of the place from the Indians by a little group of English Puritans, who in the year that John Hampden refused to pay the ship-money (1637) resolved there to seek "quiet from the fear of evil." In early and Concord days—days around which tradition and romance have woven an almost idyllic charm—the saintly Eliot, the "Apostle of the Indians," often made the little village the centre of his operations, and fanned his own spiritual enthusiasm at its Puritan firesides. Through Eliot's holy life and patient work the condition and character of the wandering tribes of Massachusetts was much uplifted. The Indian name of the settlement was Muskèt-a-Quid, or the "Grass-grown River;" and the broad meadows which stretch widely in gentle undulations for many miles on either side of the lovely stream which steals slowly and softly past the back of the town, were greatly esteemed by the original sons of the soil as prolific hunting grounds. Concord River, with its radiant maples, its swaying willows, its graceful vines, its floating lilies, and the old romance and the new which broods like an atmosphere around its shady banks, possesses a subtle fascination, for all who can think and feel, which is equally welcome and strong. Here, during dim and shadowy centuries—in which truant fancy can play without knocking her head against hard facts—the Indians were accustomed to glide along in their frail but beautiful boats on their way to the tangled recesses of the far-famed Walden Woods. By the winding banks of this "grass-grown river," poets, and scholars, and lovers, from the neighbouring town, have sought and found the sweet seclusion which they coveted. Here, once, beneath these very trees, swinging his stick with careless air, wandered, the summer through, with bent head and leisurely steps, the quiet, agile figure of Nathaniel Hawthorne, lost in mental search for the solution of the complicated plot of one of his weird and imaginative romances. It is Sunday, August 21st, 1842, and Hawthorne is going through the woods to call at Emerson's, to return a book which Margaret Fuller—who is on a visit there—has lent him. As he rambles through the leafy solitude, the spirit of the woods enters into his own, and he breaks forth into a tender lament over the already waning glories of the year:—"Alas for the summer! The grass is still verdant on the hills and in the valleys; the foliage of the trees is as dense as ever, and as green; the flowers are abundant all along the margin of the river, and in the hedge-rows, and deep among the woods; the days, too, are as fervid as they were a month ago, and yet in every breath of wind and in every beam of sunshine there is an autumnal influence. I know not how to describe it. Methinks there is a sort of coolness amid all the heat, and a mildness in the brightest of the sunshine. A breeze cannot stir without thrilling me with the breath of autumn, and I behold its pensive glory in the far golden gleams among the long shadows of the trees. The flowers, even the brightest of them, the golden-rod and the gorgeous cardi-

nals—the most glorious flowers of the year—have this gentle sadness amid their pomp. Pensive autumn is exposed in the glow of every one of them. I have felt this influence earlier in some years than in others. Sometimes autumn may be perceived even in the early days of July. There is no other feeling like that caused by this faint, doubtful, yet real perception—a rather prophecy of the year's decay, so deliciously sweet and sad at the same time"—(American Note Book, vol. ii. p. 112). Hard by, in Walden Woods, when Hawthorne wrote those words, his friend Thoreau was dreaming the best years of his romantic life away in undimmed communion with the trees and flowers and birds, which he loved so well. And here, to-day, beneath life's sunset sky, still walks to "meet the night that soon shall shape and shadow overflow," though now, alas! with feeble step and slow, the stately and venerable figure of Ralph Waldo Emerson, one of that elect company of great teachers whose words the world will not willingly let die. Concord river is the supposed scene of the following lines, which I copy from *Poems of Places* :—

"The boat is as full as a boat should be,
Just nobody in it but you and me."
As brown as the leaves are her beautiful eyes,
And as graceful her hand on the water lies,
As she catches the leaves which languid float
On the lazy current along the boat.
Now she asks its name as she tears one apart—
"Fair lady, that is a 'floating heart.'"

Sad wrecks of years have drifted down
In the dreamless ocean to sink and drown,
Since the beautiful eyes saw that lovely night,
And haloed the river with visions bright,
But the "floating heart" that was caught that day
Has never been able to get away!

The scene around Concord cannot be described as having any very marked characteristics, but there is nevertheless an aspect of friendly security and tranquil peace about it, which is not merely in itself inviting, but which seems also to afford a perfect setting for the little town which nestles beneath the abundant foliage of its ancient elms. And when at last I gained the quiet village green, and looked down the sunny, straggling, and deserted street, and glanced upward at the solemn trees which seemed to be stretching out their old arms, not merely in blessings on the place, but as if to ward off the invasion of change, I felt that Concord was worthy of its name, and worthy also to be the home of the great men who have there been wisely content to spend serene and simple lives, marked by "plain living and high thinking"—and to pursue the even tenor of their way—unvexed by avarice or ambition. For I venture to think that the broad provinces of America, with their many wonderful and suggestive scenes, have, after all, nothing to show the stranger which in its way is more truly attractive than Concord with its famous battle-field of 1775, its quaint old meeting-houses still redolent with noble Puritan traditions, its historic homes, its winding river, its shady lanes, its romantic woods, and, above all, its

sweet God's acre, "Sleepy Hollow," with its pine-fringed heights and flower-clad dells, where rest the world-worn and the weary whose souls have reached "the fadeless green and holy peace of Paradise."

But Concord is not willing to rest upon its past reputation, or even to base its claims to distinction to-day upon the lingering presence on its village street of even the wise and gracious Ralph Waldo Emerson himself. Most of us are probably aware that Concord now possesses a summer School of Philosophy, which meets annually for a term of some five weeks in the playtime of the year—the vacation months of July and August—and which attracts an audience "fit but few" of students and scholars drawn by a common instinct from all parts of America. Even in the United States the precise object of the Concord School of Philosophy is not generally too well understood, and therefore a few words perhaps of explanation in regard to it can here be scarcely out of place. I am indebted for some of the facts which I am now about to state to the *Critic*, a New York journal of literature and art. The founder of the Concord School of Philosophy was not Mr. Emerson, but his old neighbour and friend, Mr. Bronson Alcott, the well-known transcendentalist, in his way a sort of New England Samuel Taylor Coleridge, and the father of the now famous novelist—Louisa May Alcott, authoress of *Little Men*, *Little Women*, and other kindred stories of a distinctly feminine type. The Concord School of Philosophy, which assembles in a rustic-looking building called the Hillside Chapel, which stands amongst the trees in Mr. Alcott's garden, and within a stone's throw of Hawthorne's house, has a history which, though short, is significant and interesting. The men and women who sat in this New England school of philosophy day after day last summer, discussing high, and often obscure, themes of religion and philosophy, have not inaptly been termed the spiritual descendants of the Transcendentalists of 1840. Mr. Alcott, who is now a hale old man, of florid aspect, approaching eighty, in full possession of every faculty, and with unabated zest of inquiry, has happily lived to accomplish a long-cherished dream of his youth. So far back as 1842, Mr. Alcott had already begun to collect books for the library of a school of philosophy, which even then he was anxious to establish in some part of New England ; and in that very year he felt himself committed to his scheme, as a wealthy English friend of his bequeathed to him, in trust, a collection of curious and valuable books, which Mr. Alcott brought over from London, and deposited, temporarily, on his own shelves, at the Orchard House, Concord. These books, with many that have since been gathered or given, now form the nucleus of the library of the Concord School. In 1849, Mr. Alcott issued a circular containing the names of a number of distinguished men, who were described as "deserving of better acquaintance, and as disposed for closer fellowship of thought and endeavour." The names attached to that circular are remarkable, and are naturally, in many cases, more remarkable now, after a lapse of a

generation, than when first written down. Amongst them I find the names of Dr. Howe, Dr. Hedge, James Freeman Clarke, Thos. Starr King, E. P. Whipple, T. Wentworth Higginson, Lloyd Garrison, Russell Lowell, Wendell Phillips, Thoreau, Theodore Parker, Ellery Channing, and Waldo Emerson. These gentlemen were requested to "discuss the advantage of organizing a club or college for the study and diffusion of the ideas and tendencies proper to the nineteenth century." Nothing, however, came of this delightfully vague and ambitious proposal beyond the establishment of what was called the "Town and Country Club," a literary assembly, which blazed through a brief existence, and then suddenly flickered out. "All things come round, however, to one who will but wait ;" and Mr. Alcott retired with philosophic composure to his scholarly seclusion at Concord, strong in the persuasion that his scheme for a Transcendental School was not dead, but sleeping. Multitudes thought, as time moved on, that there was no life in it, whatever Mr. Alcott imagined ; and certainly, when forty years had passed away without the slightest movement or sign of one, such a verdict could scarcely be considered rash. But, to quote the title of one of Kingsley's books, "At Last," Mr. Alcott, regarding the year 1878 as the fulness of the times, took steps, in conjunction with his disciples, Dr. Harris and Mr. Sanborn, to

organize a School of Philosophy at Concord ; and accordingly, on July 15th, 1879, the first session was publicly inaugurated, when Mr. Alcott, as Dean of the Faculty, delivered an introductory address, in which he welcomed the students, and explained the object of the school. If the subjects were frequently profound, the plan adopted was always simplicity itself. It was merely a combination of formal lectures and free conversations, and the meetings were conducted very much after the manner of the Social Science Association, or, for the matter of that, this august assemblage. For the first two years Emerson, who has all along shown a warm interest in the movement, took an active part in the proceedings, and delivered to a reverent group of sympathetic listeners—with all the early charm and grace of expression—the matured thoughts of a singularly beautiful old age. Emerson is not now, alas! so frequent a visitor to any of the haunts around Concord which once he knew so well, but every second day or so found him this summer seated in his high-backed chair in a place of honour in the little School of Philosophy at Concord.

I shall never forget Concord, with its village green, its quaint and ancient houses, and its old-times ways. I shall always recall with vivid pleasure my visit to its famous battle-field hard by the "old manse," whose very "mosses" Hawthorne has taught us all to love, and I shall never fail to recall the thrill of delight I felt as I read on the simple monument which marks the spot the words which Emerson wrote regarding it :—

By the rude bridge that arched the flood,
Their flag to April's breeze unfurled,

Here once the embattled farmers stood
And fired the shot heard round the world !

I shall cherish the memory of my visit to the old **Manse,** and of my pilgrimage to the study at the Wayside—a small, plain tower room, with a tall desk between the window and the fire, at which Hawthorne used to stand to write. From the Wayside I went to "Sleepy Hollow," where Hawthorne sleeps well, and as I approached his grave beneath the swaying pines—a plain white stone, which bears the solitary but sufficient word "Hawthorne"—I found by a happy coincidence that the old gardener—a man who helped in 1864 to bury the author of the *Scarlet Letter*—there was planting that honoured grave that very day with fresh laurels.

But beyond all else, in that Summer Day at Concord, was the visit which I paid to the School of Philosophy. It was refreshing to one's mind and spirit to sit through a golden August morning in the garden house, with the flowers around, and the song of birds filling the quiet air, and to listen to a grave group of scholars as they discussed the influence of Kant on the moral elevation of the world. Some sixty or seventy people were assembled, and these quite filled the little meeting house. On one wall hung a portrait of Thoreau, framed appropriately enough with evergreens, and the walls were adorned with brackets on which stood busts of Homer, Plato, and Emerson. A bowl of Concord water lilies stood upon the table, and sent their fragrance through the place ; and at one side of the table, in a place of honour, sat Emerson, leaning eagerly forward, with the gracious bearing, and wise smile, and stately, polite manner which the social demands of two generations have neither "dimmed nor fatigued into impatience." There were not a few notable men in that small assembly, but to me, and perhaps to most, the centre of attraction was the greatest of them all—the venerable philosopher of Concord, of whom I have just spoken. Dr. Hedge, one of the professors at Harvard University, was reading a paper that morning, a paper on Kant, with whom in his youth he had come into contact; and Emerson, in the loving charge of his daughter, had walked down through the freshness of the summer day from his historic home to listen to the words of an old and valued friend. There was a look of serene and absolute peace on Emerson's gentle face, and the whole expression and attitude of the man, as he sat in his high-backed chair intently listening with the utmost respect to every word that was said, suggested to me the kindred ideas of meekness and might. Time has dealt very tenderly with the face and form of the great thinker, and he stands to-day, under the weight of fourscore years, erect and active. I had several opportunities of learning how deeply the people for miles around the sweet old Puritan settlement revere and admire the illustrious thinker who has never been too busy to enter into the common cares and joys of those about him, and who has spent amongst his own people a life that has fully redeemed, in all directions, even its own high promise. In the afternoon of that Summer Day at Concord, I had the honour of an inter-

view with Emerson, in the seclusion of his own little study, and I shall always cherish with reverent gratitude the memory of his kindness to me that day. Whilst casting about, to discover how best to give you my general impressions of that visit, my eye fell upon a passage of Emerson's own, in which he describes a visit which, in 1833, he paid to Coleridge at Highgate, and the words he applies to Coleridge express exactly my recollections of himself :—
" I was in his company for about an hour, but find it impossible to recall the largest part of his discourse, which was often like so many printed paragraphs in his book, and as I might have foreseen, the visit was rather a spectacle than a conversation, for he was old and pre-occupied." The only sign of age, however, which Emerson displayed was a failure of memory and an almost utter inability to recall names. His pre-occupation vanished completely away when he found that I could tell him about the son of his old friend, the " little Julian, whom I taught to climb the apple-trees in this garden." It was delightful to listen, as the old man eloquent related one incident after another of far-off Concord days, when Hawthorne and Thoreau were his daily companions and friends by river and through wood. Of Thomas Carlyle Emerson spoke with much feeling and respect, and said—"From my point of view, at least, you have had no greater man in England than Thomas Carlyle, within the range of my lifetime." "My study is only a little room, sir," said the old philosopher as he walked rapidly up and down its narrow bounds, rubbing his hands together with a quick, nervous movement; "it is only a little room, sir !" "Yes, sir," I felt bound to reply, " it *is* only a little room; but it is not the size of the room, but what comes out of it." " When do you leave Concord?" said he, turning abruptly upon me. " To-night, sir." " And when do you leave Boston?" "On Thursday: I must sail for England on Saturday." " Will you come and see me to-morrow ?" I thanked him, but felt, though sorely tempted, that it would scarcely have been fair to take him at his word, and so most respectfully informed him that I feared it was impossible. I left his presence as the sinking sun was flooding the quiet room with mellow splendour, which threw into bold relief the faded backs of long rows of well-used books, and, in that golden light, I took my last glance of one who is both great and good. I know no words which will more perfectly apply to Emerson, or express my own impressions of him as I bade farewell to him on that summer day, than those which he himself has put into my lips :—

Spring still makes spring in the mind
When sixty years are told ;
Love wakes anew this throbbing heart,
And we are never old.
Over the winter glaciers
I see the summer glow,
And through the wild-piled snowdrift
The warm rosebuds below.

Emerson's own life, in all its length and breadth, is itself a splendid witness to the truth of his words—" The essence of greatness is the perception that virtue is enough."

LIST OF THOSE ATTENDING THE FIRST SESSION OF THE CONCORD SCHOOL OF
PHILOSOPHY (JULY—AUGUST, 1879)

[Copied without altering the imperfect alphabetizing from
a typescript among the newspaper clippings preserved in
the Concord Free Public Library, Concord, Massachusetts.]

Alcott, A. Bronson   Concord, Mass.
Andrews, Prof. E. B. Newton Centre,
    Mass.
Ames, C. H.   Boston, Mass.
Ames, Miss Lucia   Boston, Mass.
Alexander, Rev. W. S.   New Orleans, La.
Ames, Mrs. John W.   Concord, Mass.
Andrews, Mrs. P. D.   New York City
    (Prin. Pub. Sch. no. 10, Jersey
    City Heights)
Arnett, Miss Aroline   Tidioute, War-
    ren Co., Pa. (In school at War-
    saw, N.Y.)
Albee, John   New Castle, N.H.
Allen, Miss Sarah   Jacksonville, Ill.
Alcott, Miss Louisa   Concord, Mass.
Abbott, E. P.   Newport, N.H.
Ansley, Mrs. Sarah   Concord, Mass.
Adams, Miss A. D.   Waltham, Mass.
Allen, Lawson   Amherst (Woburn), Mass.
Adams, Miss Adeline L.   Auburndale,
    Mass.

Blake, H. G. O.   Worcester, Mass.
Block, L. J.   Jacksonville, Ill.
Beers, Prof. H. A.   New Haven, Conn.
Bell, Miss Clara   Springfield, Mass.
Brown, Miss Laura A.   Acton, Mass.
Bartol, Rev. C. A.   Boston, Mass.
Bryan, Judge C.   Akron, Ohio
Beeson, Miss Sue V.   St. Louis, Mo.
Bacon, Miss Fannie M.   St. Louis, Mo.
Blanchard, Mrs. W. P.   Concord, Mass.
Beach, Miss Ellen F.   211 W. Newton
    St., Boston, Mass.
Brewster, Mrs. Caroline F.   Cambridge,
    Mass.
Bolton, Mrs. Sarah K.   Boston, Mass.
Bradford, George   Concord, Mass.
Bubin, Miss Josy A.   Lynn, Mass.
Butterick, Miss Kate P.   Concord, Mass.
Barrett, Mrs. J. F.   Concord, Mass.
Bridgeman, R. L.   Advertiser Reporter,
    Boston, Mass.
Barrett, Miss Jennie   Concord, Mass.
Brewster, William   Cambridge, Mass.
Bean, Miss Lizzie   Concord, Mass.
Beach, Miss E. F.   Normal School,
    Boston, Mass.
Bartlett, Miss Martha   Concord, Mass.
Briggs, Miss M. B.   Norton, Mass.
Brown, Herbert   Concord, Mass.
Boutwell, Hon. Geo. S.   Groton, Mass.
Boutwell, Miss Georgiana   Groton, Mass.
Bibb, Miss Grace C.   Columbia, Mo.
Brooks, Miss C. L.   Cambridgeport, Mass.
Barrett, Mrs. E. M.   Lexington, Mass.

Bissell, Arthur D.   Ahmednagar, In-
    dia   Amherst, Mass.
Blaisdell, Miss Anne   Concord, Mass.
Bates, Mrs. Chas. H.   Salem, Mass.
Betters, Edward D.   New York City
Bartlett, George   Concord, Mass.
Bigelow, Miss Jennie S.   Jamaica
    Plain, Mass.
Blackley, Mrs. Agnes   Concord, Mass.
Blair, A. L.   Troy Daily Times,
    Troy, N.Y.
Baker, John   Springfield, Mass.

Cheney, Mrs. E. D.   Jamaica Plain,
    Boston, Mass.
Cropsey, Miss N.   Indianapolis, Ind.
Campbell, W. R.   Mendon, Ill. An-
    dover, Mass.
Carlton, Miss Grace   Concord, Mass.
Cook, George   Keene, N. H.
Curtis, William   Westboro, Mass.
Chase, Miss Lucy   Worcester, Mass.
Chase, Miss Sarah   Worcester, Mass.
Cheney, Miss C. F.   Concord, Mass.
Cheney, Mrs. L. P.   Concord, Mass.
Cutter, Miss Rose M.   Boston, Mass.
Chase, Miss C. L.   Concord, Mass.
Chapman, Mrs. John   Concord, Mass.
Claflin, Mrs. William   Boston, Mass.
Carpenter, Miss Florence   Charles-
    town, Mass.
Chase, Henry   Concord, Mass.
Chase, Mrs. Henry   Concord, Mass.
"Carswell, Marie"   Correspondent of
    N.Y. Commercial Advertiser
    Cincinnati   (with a friend)
Crosby, Mrs. W. O.   Jamaica Plain,
    Mass.
Croly, Miss Abbie   Syracuse, N.Y.
Constantini, Miss Frederika   New
    York City
Constantini, Miss Helen   New York City

Davidson, Thomas   Boston, Mass.
Denman, Mrs. M. B.   Quincy, Ill.
Davenport, Miss Mary   Care of Mrs.
    William Claflin, Boston, Mass.
Durp, Mrs. Kate   New York City

Emery, S. H., Jr.   Concord, Mass.
Emerson, R. W.   Concord, Mass.
Emery, Mrs. Mary M.   Concord, Mass.
Emery, Miss Constance   Concord, Mass.
Emerson, Miss Ellen   Concord, Mass.
Elwell, Frank   Concord, Mass.
Emerson, Dr. E. W.   Concord, Mass.
Emerson, Miss Annie   Exeter Normal,

550

Dorchester, Mass.
Emerson, Miss Frances B.   Dorchester,
    Mass.
Ellison, Miss Sarah L.   Waltham, Mass.
Emerson, Mrs. E. W.   Concord, Mass.

Farquhar, Henry   U. S. Coast Survey,
    Cambridge, Mass.
Forgeaud, Miss May L.   San Francisco,
    Cal.
French, Mrs. H. F.   Concord, Mass.
Freeland, Mrs. A. C.   Pearl St., Wor-
    cester, Mass.
Forgeaud, Mrs. E. W.   San Francisco,
    Cal.
French, Daniel   Concord, Mass.

Goddard, Mrs. M. L.   Boston, Mass.
Gordon, Miss Anna   Auburndale, Mass.
Grout, Rev. H. M.   Concord, Mass.
Grout, Mrs. H. M.   Concord, Mass.
Grout, Miss Alice M.   Concord, Mass.
Gilman, Miss Julia M.   Clifton Springs,
    N.Y.
Gardner, Miss L. L.   Winchester, Mass.

Harris, Prof. W. T.   St. Louis, Mo.
Haskell, Miss Ellen M.   17 Angell St.,
    Providence, R.I.   Norton, Mass.
Hammond, George W.   Boston, Mass.
Hammond, Mrs. George W.   Boston, Mass.
Higginson, T. W.   Cambridge, Mass.
Hoar, Mrs. Edward   Concord, Mass.
Howard, Miss C. L.   Springfield, Mass.
Hatfield, J. B. T.   New York City
Hosmer, Miss Jane   Concord, Mass.
Hosmer, Miss C. E.   Concord, Mass.
Hoar, Miss Elizabeth   Concord, Mass.
Hoar, Miss Clara D.   Concord, Mass.
Hampton, Miss Lillie   Bedford, Mass.
Hosmer, Miss Mary L.   Concord, Mass.
Hosmer, Miss Abbie P.   Concord, Mass.
Hoar, Miss Carrie   Concord, Mass.
Hoar, Miss Florence   Concord, Mass.
Hosmer, Rev. Dr.   Formerly Pres.
    Antioch College, Newton, Mass.
Hosmer, Prof. James K. St. Louis, Mo.
Hallowell, Richard P.   West Medford,
    Mass.
Holland, Miss Emma   Sister of Mr.
    H. of Concord   Cambridge, Mass.
Haskins, Rev. S. M.   Brooklyn, N.Y.
Hathaway, Miss Harriet E.   Brooklyn,
    N.Y.
Howe, Rev. E. Franklin   Newtonville,
    Mass.
Hazard, Rowland G.   Peacedale, R.I.
Howard, Miss Emily W.   Boston, Rox-
    bury
Hill, J. B.   Emerson's friend
    Mason, N.Y.
Hoar, Mrs. George F.   Worcester, Mass.
Hoar, Hon. George F.   Worcester, Mass.
Harrison, Miss Corinne   Newburn, N.C.
Harding, Rev. J. W.   Springfield Re-

publican, Springfield, Mass.
Harlow, Mrs. Andrew J.   Concord, Mass.
Hobart, Arthur   266 Devonshire St.,
    Boston, Mass.
Hosmer, Mrs. H. J.   Concord, Mass.
Howard, Miss Sophia W.   Springfield,
    Mass.
Hobson, Miss Anne   Concord, Mass.
Hosmer, Mrs. F. C.   Wilkesbarre, Pa.
Hyde, Miss E. M.   Hartford, Conn.
Hunt, Mrs. William   Concord, Mass.
Hoar, Hon. E. R.   Concord, Mass.
Hildreth, Mrs. Charles K.   New York
    City
Howe, Mrs. George   Concord, Mass.
Houghton, Miss Augusta   Somerville,
    Mass.
Houghton, Miss Belle   Somerville, Mass.

Jones, Dr. H. K.   Jacksonville, Ill.
James, E. J.   Evanston, Ill.
Johnson, O. S.   Fairhaven, Vt.
Jones, Mrs. H. K.   Jacksonville, Ill.
Jacobs, Miss Lilla M.   Concord, Mass.

Kidney, Rev. Dr. J. S.   Faribault,
    Minn.
Kenyon, Miss Elvira E.   Plainfield, N.J.
Keyes, Miss Alicia   Concord, Mass.
Kettell, Mrs. Edward   Concord, Mass.
King, Mrs. George A.   Concord, Mass.
Keyes, Mrs. Joseph B.   Concord, Mass.
Kettell, Mrs. John B.   Boston, Mass.
Keyes, Mrs. John   Concord, Mass.
King, Miss Minnie   Concord, Mass.
King, George A.   Concord, Mass.

Lockwood, C. B.   Cleveland, Ohio
Leavitt, Miss J.   Concord, Mass.
Lathrop, G. P.   Concord, Mass.
Lathrop, Mrs. G. P.   Concord, Mass.
Lunt, Mrs.   Bedford, Mass.
Lazarus, Miss Emma   New York City
Lowe, Mrs. Charles   and three
    children.   Somerville, Mass.
Lawrence, Mrs.   Lynn, Mass.
Lowell, Mrs. Charles R.   Care of
    Francis C. Shaw, Staten Island, N.Y.
Lewis, Mrs. Elizabeth   Chicago, Ill.
Leavitt, Miss Charlotte   Providence,
    R.I.
Leache, Miss Irene K.   Norfolk, Va.

Mitchell, Mrs. E. M.   Denver, Colo.
    St. Louis, Mo.
Mann, Miss P.   133 W. 41st St., New
    York City
McClure, E. W.   Concord, Mass.
Minot, George L.   420 Washington St.,
    Boston, Mass.
Mann, Dr. J. P.   133 W. 41st St.,
    New York City
Morris, Prof. George S.   Ann Arbor,
    Mich.
McClure, Miss A. E.   Concord, Mass.

Mann, Mrs. J. P.   New York City
Morrison, Miss Mary   Milton Boston,
    Mass.
Mitchell, Miss Maria   Poughkeepsie, N.Y.
Mason, Miss Eleanor   E. Plainfield,
    N.J.
Minns, George   Concord, Mass.
Morrison, Mrs. Isaac L.   Jacksonville,
    Ill.
Merker, Miss M.   Louisville, Ky.
Mitchell, Miss Fannie   Lincoln, Mass.

Nicholson, Miss   Indianapolis, Ind.
Nichols, C. W.   Bridgeport, Conn.
Nesmith, Miss H. L.   Westfield, N.J.
Norcross, Miss Louisa   Concord, Mass.
Norcross, Miss Fannie   Concord, Mass.

O'Connor, Miss Jennie   St. Louis, Mo.
O'Connor, Miss Minnie   27 Somerset St.,
    St. Louis, Mo.
Orth, John   Boston, Mass.
Orne, Edward A.   10 Irving Place,
    Charlestown, Mass.

Peirce, Prof. Benjamin   Cambridge,
    Mass.
Preston, Mrs. Harriet W. Danvers, Mass.
Peabody, Miss Elizabeth   Concord, Mass.
Pritchard, Miss N. J.   Concord, Mass.
Pierson, Mrs. Margaret G. Boston, Mass.
Pierson, Miss Lulu   Boston, Mass.
Paine, Dr. H. D.   26 W. 30th St., New
    York City
Peirce, Miss Augusta   Lincoln, Mass.
Peirce, Miss Helen   Lincoln, Mass.
Powers, Rev. Dr. H. N.   Bridgeport,
    Conn.
Porter, Miss Juliette   Worcester, Mass.
Panin, Ivan   Harvard Cambridge,
    Mass.
Pratt, Fred.   Concord, Mass.

Russell, Prof. E. H.   Worcester, Mass.
Robinson, T. B.   Paris, Mo.
Rolfe, H. W.   Amherst, Ayer, Mass.
Ripley, Miss Elizabeth B. Concord, Mass.
Rudolphe, Charles   Springfield
    Amherst, Mass.
Reynolds, Rev. Grindall   Concord, Mass.
Ricketson, Daniel   New Bedford, Mass.
Russell, Mrs. E. H.   Worcester, Mass.
Rickoff, Mrs. Rebecca D.   Cleveland,
    Ohio
Rice, Miss Jessie   Watertown, Mass.
Robbins, Miss   Belmont, Mass.
Reynolds, Mrs. L. M.   Concord, Mass.
Robinson, Dr. J. A.   Jackson, Mich.
Robinson, Miss Louisa   Watertown,
    Mass.
Rockwell, Miss E.   Wilkesbarre, Penn.
Reynolds, Miss Alice   Concord, Mass.
Robinson, Mrs. W. S.   Malden, Mass.

Sanborn, F. B.   Concord, Mass.
Smith, Augustus D.   Aurora, Ill.,
    Amherst, Mass.
Shumway, Edgar S.   Belchertown,
    Amherst, Mass.
Smith, Mrs. G. H.   Lincoln, Mass.
Stebbins, Giles B.   Detroit, Mich.
Sanborn, Mrs. F. B.   Concord, Mass.
Simmons, Miss E. R.   Cambridge, Mass.
Snow, Miss L. E.   Boston, Mass.
Schrader, Miss Bertha   Concord, Mass.
Sanborn, Vic[tor]   Concord, Mass.
Stone, Miss Lucy   Dorchester, Mass.
Sweetser, Eleanor H.   Lynn, Mass.
Smith, Miss Emma F.   Concord, Mass.
Simmons, Mrs. G. F.   Cambridge, Mass.
Smith, Mrs. Julia   Concord, Mass.
Sharp, Miss E. B.   Dorchester, Mass.
Straight, Mrs. Emma D.   Normal School
    Oswego, N.Y.
Straight, Prof. H. H.   Oswego, N.Y.
Safford, Dr. Mary J.   Boston, Mass.
Shattuck, Mrs. S. D.   Malden, Mass.
Stebbins, Mrs. Giles B.,   180 Henry
    St., Detroit, Mich.
Street, Professor   Wisconsin
Street, Mrs. Professor   Wisconsin
Scripture, Mrs. Augusta   Lincoln, Mass.
Stetson, Miss Ellen   W. Lexington,
    Mass.
Sherwood, Miss Elizabeth Rome, N.Y.
Spaulding, Rev. H. G.   Cambridge, Mass.
Stoddard, Miss A. J.   Boston, Mass.
Sanderson, Miss L. J.   Winchester,
    Mass.
Stow, Mrs. J. W.   San Francisco, Cal.

Thompson, Miss Ella   Lyndonville, Vt.
Tupper, F. P.   Towanda, Penn.
Trull, Dr. W. G.   Concord, Mass.
Thayer, Adin   Worcester, Mass.
Tolman, Miss Hattie   Boston, Mass.
Thurber, Mr. S.   Worcester, Mass.
Thompson, Phillips   Boston, Mass.
Thompson, Mrs. Elizabeth   124 W. 45th
    St., New York City
Tiletson, Mrs. Mary   W. Concord, Mass.
Townsend, Miss S. T.   Boston, Mass.
Trull, Mrs. W. B.   Concord, Mass.
Talbot, Mrs. I. T.   Boston Concord,
    Mass.
Talbot, Miss Marion   Boston Concord,
    Mass.
Talbot, Miss Edith   Boston Concord,
    Mass.

Van Vorst, Miss Helen   Lincoln, Mass.

Wood, Miss Annie C.   Norfolk, Va.
Weir, Miss Jennie   Concord, Mass.
Whaley, Miss Norvell   Concord, Mass.
Warren, Miss Cornelia L. Boston, Mass.
Willman, J. W.   Malden, Mass.
Wade, Mrs. William   Chelsea, Mass.

Woodward, Mrs. S. W.   Chelsea, Mass.
Woodward, Belle M.   Chelsea, Mass.
Woodward, Frank E.   Chelsea, Mass.
Williams, Mrs. H. B.   Salem, Mass.
Wadley, Miss Mary   Concord, Mass.
Whiting, Charles G.   Republican
    Springfield, Mass.
Wilder, Dr. Alexander   Newark, N.J.
Wheildon, Miss Alice   Concord, Mass.
Wheildon, Mrs. W. W.   Concord, Mass.
Watson, C. W.   New York City
Whitney, Miss Maria   Concord, Mass.
Wolcott, Mr. E.   Jacksonville, Ill.
Wentworth, Mrs. Paul   New York City
Wasson, D. A.   Medford, Mass.
Williams, C. H. S.   Concord, Mass.
Williams, Mrs. C. H. S.   Concord, Mass.
Watson, Prof. William   107 Marlboro
    St., Boston, Mass.

Weir, Miss Elizabeth   Concord, Mass.
Ward, Rev. Julius H.   Boston, Mass.
Wentworth, Paul   New York City
Wallace, Mr. Ellerslie   Philadelphia,
    Penn.
Weston, Mr. S. B.   Shelburne Falls,
    Mass.
Watkins, Miss A. E.   Clifton Springs,
    N.Y.
Warner, Miss Ellen B.   Springfield, Mass.
Willard, Mrs. Frances E.   Chicago, Ill.
Wood, Miss Carrie P.   Concord, Mass.
Wood, Miss Emma   Staten Island, N.Y.
Wolcott, Miss Edith   Jacksonville, Ill.
Wolcott, Mrs. M. D.   Jacksonville, Ill.
Whaley, Miss Fannie   Concord, Mass.
Whiting, Miss Florence   Concord, Mass.

York, E. D.   Pottsville, Penn.

DIRECTORY OF THE PRINCIPAL NAMES IN THE CONCORD SCHOOL AND SUCCESSORS

ABBOTT, FRANCIS ELLINGWOOD

ADLER, FELIX

ALBEE, JOHN

ALCOTT, AMOS BRONSON

ALGER, WILLIAM ROUNSEVILLE

ALLEN, REV. JOSEPH HENRY

AMES, CHARLES GORDON

ANAGNOS, JULIA ROMANA (HOWE)

AZARIAS, BROTHER (See Mullaney.)

BARTLETT, GEORGE B.

BARTOL, CYRUS AUGUSTUS

BASCOM, JOHN

BENTON, JOEL

BLAKE, HARRISON GRAY OTIS

BLOCK, LOUIS [LEWIS?] J.

BROWN, FILLMORE, M.D.

BROWN, FLORENCE WHITING

BROWN, REV. OLYMPIA

BUSH, REV. JAMES S.

BUTLER, NICHOLAS MURRAY

CAMPBELL, HELEN

CHADWICK, JOHN WHITE

CHANNING, ELLERY, the Younger

CHANNING, WILLIAM HENRY

CHENEY, EDNAH DOW

CHILD, LYDIA MARIA

CHUBB, PERCIVAL

CLARK, ANNA (STEINIGER)

CLARK, FREDERIC

CLARKE, JAMES FREEMAN

COLLYER, ROBERT

CONNOR, REV. ROWLAND

COOKE, GEORGE WILLIS

CRANCH, CHRISTOPHER PEARSE

CROWTHERS, SAMUEL M.

DAVIDSON, THOMAS

DENTON, WILLIAM

DEWEY, JOHN

DICKINSON, ANNA ELIZABETH

DOLBEAR, AMOS EMERSON

DOLE, CHARLES FLETCHER

DOWDEN, EDWARD

DROPPERS, GARRITT

DWIGHT, JOHN SULLIVAN

ELIOT, CHARLES WILLIAM

ELIOT, SAMUEL ATKINS

ELLINGER, MORRIS

EMERSON, EDWARD WALDO

EMERSON, RALPH WALDO

EMERY, SAMUEL HOPKINS, JR.

ERNST, C. W.

EVERETT, CHARLES CARROLL

FERRI, PROFESSOR (University of Rome)

FISKE, JOHN

FLEISCHER, CHARLES

FRANCKE, KUNO

FROTHINGHAM, OCTAVIUS BROOKS

GALLAUDET, EDWARD MINER

GANNETT, WILLIAM CHANNING

GARDINER, H. N.   (Prof. in Smith Coll.)

GARMAN, CHARLES EDWARD

GARRISON, WILLIAM LLOYD

GREW, MARY

GUNTON, GEORGE

HALE, EDWARD EVERETT

HARRIS, WILLIAM TORREY

HASKINS, DAVID GREENE, JR.

HATHAWAY, MRS. AMALIA J.

HAWTHORNE, JULIAN

HAYNES, JOHN C.

HAZARD, ROWLAND GIBSON

HEDGE, FREDERIC HENRY

HEWETT, WATERMAN THOMAS

HIGGINSON, THOMAS WENTWORTH

HOAR, GEORGE FRISBIE

HOLBROOK, MARTIN LUTHER, M.D.

HOLLAND, ROBERT AFTON

HOVEY, RICHARD

HOWE, JULIA WARD

HOWISON, GEORGE HOLMES

HUBBARD, REV. JOHN P.

HUGHES, THOMAS

HUNT, THOMAS STERRY

HYSLOP, JAMES HERVEY

JAMES, HENRY, SR.

JAMES, WILLIAM

JANES, LEWIS GEORGE

JEFFERSON, CHARLES E.

JOHNSON, SAMUEL

JONES, HIRAM K.

JONES, REV. JESSE HENRY

KEDNEY, JOHN STEINFORT

KINNEY, MRS. ELIZABETH CLEMENTINE
    DODGE STEDMAN

LATHROP, GEORGE PARSONS

LAZARUS, EMMA

LINTON, WILLIAM JAMES

LLOYD, HENRY DEMAREST

LONGFELLOW, SAMUEL

LOWE, MARTHA ANN (PERRY)

McCOSH, JAMES

McQUAID, BP. BERNARD JOHN

MALCOLM, REV. CHARLES F.

MALLOY, CHARLES

MARVIN, JOSEPH BENSON

MEAD, EDWIN DOAK

MEARS, JOHN WILLIAM

MITCHELL, MRS. ELLEN

MONTGOMERY, EDMUND, M.D.

MOORE, FILMORE, M.D.

MORRIS, GEORGE SYLVESTER

MORSE, SIDNEY HENRY

MOTT, LUCRETIA

MOZOOMDAR, PROTAP CHUNDER

MULFORD, REV. ELISHA

MULLANEY, PATRICK FRANCIS

NEWTON, RICHARD HEBER

NORTON, CHARLES ELIOT

OWEN, ROBERT DALE

PARSONS, THOMAS

PARTON, JAMES

PARTRIDGE, WILLIAM ORDWAY

PEABODY, REV. ANDREW PRESTON

PEABODY, ELIZABETH PALMER

PEIRCE, CHARLES SANDERS

PERRIN, RAYMOND S.

PHILLIPS, WENDELL

PORTER, NOAH

POTTER, WILLIAM JAMES

POWELL, AARON MACY

POYEN BELLEISLE, RENÉ DE

PRATT, CHARLES E.

QUINCY, JOSIAH PHILLIPS

REYNOLDS, GRINDALL

RICHARDSON, CHARLES FRANCIS

RICKETSON, DANIEL

RUUTZ-REES, JANET E.

SALTER, WILLIAM MACKINTYRE

SANBORN, FRANKLIN BENJAMIN

SARGENT, JOHN TURNER

SAVAGE, MINOT JUDSON

SCHMIDT, NATHANIEL

SCHURMAN, JACOB GOULD

SEVERANCE, CAROLINE MARIA SEYMOUR

SHACKFORD, CHARLES CHAUNCY

SHERMAN, MRS. CAROLINE K.

SMITH, GERRIT

SNIDER, DENTON JAQUES

SOLDAN, FRANK LOUIS

SPENCER, ANNA GARLIN

SPOHR, WILHELM

STANTON, ELIZABETH CADY

STEINIGER-CLARK, MRS. ANNA

STOREY, MOORFIELD

THAYER, WILLIAM ROSCOE

TOWNE, EDWARD C.

TRUEBLOOD, BENJAMIN FRANKLIN

UNDERWOOD, SARA A.

UNDERWOOD, W. H.

WASSON, DAVID ATWOOD

WATSON, BENJAMIN MARSTON

WATSON, JOHN

WEISS, JOHN

WESTON, S. BURNS

WHIPPLE, CHARLES K.

WHITE, ANDREW DICKSON (of Cornell U.)

WILDER, ALEXANDER

WILLIS, OLYMPIA BROWN

WISE, ISAAC MAYER

WOODBERRY, GEORGE EDWARD

YOUMANS, EDWARD LIVINGSTON